COMMANDMENTS BY GOD IN THE QURAN

Compiled By

CH. NAZAR MOHAMMAD

P.O. Box 194
LAHORE–54662 (PAKISTAN)

The Message Publications
New York

1st North American Edition: March 1991

Published by:
The Message Publications
166-26 89th Ave.
Jamaica, N.Y. 11432
Tel: (718) 658-5163
Fax: (718) 658-1255

Can be purchased from:

I.C.N.A. Book Service, U.S.A.
166-26 89th Ave.
Jamaica, N.Y. 11432
Tel: (718) 657-4090
Fax: (718) 658-1255

I.C.N.A. Book Service, Canada
100 Mclevin Ave. Unit 3A
Scarborough, Ontario
Canada M1B2Y5
Tel: (416) 609-2452
Fax: (416) 292-3437

Printed by:
Al-Huda Publishers
2510 Electronic Ln., Ste 907
Dallas, Texas 75220
Tel: (214) 902-0297
Fax: (214) 902-0051

Commandments by God in the Quran

The Message Publications
New York

Translation of certain Arabic words into English

The late Dr. Ismail Raji al-Faruqi in his book "Towards Islamic English" write

> "Many Arabic words are simply not translatable into English.
> Many are rendered into English with difficulty."

Some of such words are:

As-Salah often translated as "prayer." Prayer actually more closely co responds to "Dua." Salah is the act of worship performed five time daily according to prescribed ways.

Ibadah often translated as "worship" actually means to worship Allah an out of love for Him to obey Him in what He has ordered and to fo low the example of His Prophet Muhammad (peace be upon him

Iman often translated as "faith" etc. actually means the conviction or ce tainty that Allah is indeed the One and Only God and that Muhan mad is His last prophet and commitment to obey their command

Zakah often translated as "Alms", "charity" etc. when directed to Muslim actually means obligatory sharing of wealth with the poor and th community in order to purify the rest. This is to say the right of Alla in the fortune of His servants, which right is assigned to speci categories of the needy.

Sabr often translated as "patience" etc. actually means to remain firm an steadfast against ordeals and calamities.

Qadar often translated as "fate" actually means Allah's assignment of enc to all process of life and existence.

Shirk often translated as "association of some being with Allah" actua includes all means, things and concepts, etc.

Kafir often translated as "disbeliever" etc. actually means one wh solemnly says that Allah is not God or is not the subject of His a tributes. It also means that who disavows the bounties of God, th ungrateful.

Zulm often translated as "transgression" etc. actually means the act c action of committing injustice.

Fitnah often translated as "mischief" or "tumult" etc. actually means mis guidance, dissuasion etc. from the path laid by Allah.

Fasad often translated as "dispute" etc. actually means all of the followin disruption — imbalance — disharmony — corruption — danger - drought.

Ihsan often translated as "doing a favor" etc. actually means the perfe fulfillment of the commandments of Allah in whatever one is doin in relation to others or to himself.

Jihad often translated as "holy war" etc. actually means self exertion i the cause of Allah including against baser self or against aggre sion or oppression using peaceful and violent means.

COMMANDMENTS BY GOD IN THE QURAN

A Present to You!

The purpose of this present is to acquaint readers with the edicts contained in the Qur'an regarding the various aspects of everyday life. Their study will show that in matters of *Bilmaroof* (doing good deeds) these are no different from those required by Law or the society in the U.S. This has contributed to its greatness. In the matter of *Almunker* (forbidding) there are many differences and the present problems arising in the U.S. are the result of those transgressions of these edicts.

However, there is one major difference. A Muslim is required to observe these commandments as an act of worship, namely in obedience to and to seek the pleasure of Allah. Consequently he does not seek ways to get around these. For him these commandments are eternal and no society or authority can make changes in these.

Amplification of the Qur'anic edicts is to be found in the study of the sayings of the Prophet Muhammad (peace be upon him) — *Ahadith*.

His life history *Seerah* exemplifies how these are to be applied in everyday life.

The world would be a much better place to live in with peace of mind, tranquillity and contentment if the people practiced and lived according to these Qur'anic edicts.

Presented by A. Jalil, Chairman
Post Box 962
Elberton, Georgia 30635

On behalf of Al-Huda Islamic Center Inc.
2808 South Milledge Avenue
Athens, Georgia 30605

LIST OF TOPICS

14. QUALITIES OF THE PIOUS

15. WORLDLY WEALTH AND ITS REALITY

16. ECONOMY

In the name of Allah, The Compassionate, The Merciful

FOREWORD

The present conditions of a human being on the earth are very paradoxical. There are very rich nations like Japan and America where the quantity of millionaires cannot be counted. On the other hand, there are countries where human beings are so deprived that in countries like Ethiopia, people die of hunger because they lack food and shelter.

There are countries which have become so powerful that they cannot tolerate any independent but inimical ruler and they invade those countries to arrest the ruler as well as subjugate them, and that Government should be in accordance with their liking. There are some countries which have been under the rule of neighbouring countries for the last 70 years. There are other countries which have literacy of more than 90% and others having as little literacy as 15%.

The age of the present civilisation is about 7,000 years. The efforts of the human being to improve the quality of his life is well-known to the present generation. There are physical comforts of all types to make life as easy as possible. Communication has reached a stage that on Fax, the contents of any document are transmitted instantly to any part of the world. Instant payment from the bank counter is available 24 hours. Posh cars are there for inland traffic. Jumbo jets can take you to the farthest part of the world in a few hours. Cooking, cleaning, washing, household chores are being done by automatic devices. Production per 8 hours has reached a stage which was unthinkable. Democracy is accepted as a way of life practically all over the world.

Man has also endeavoured to exalt his status in the Universe of which his earth is only a tiny speck. Having already stepped on the Moon, he is planning to conquer Mars. His potentialities appear to be limitless.

But in spite of all these achievements no one, rich or poor, employer or employee, landlord or peasant, ruler or a man in the street, resident of a developed country or of the poorest country, feels happy or contented. There is no Peace of Mind.

Naturally, the poor, in whatever country they may be, are dissatisfied because of lack of means to meet their daily necessities of food, clothing, shelter and medical care. On the other hand, billionaires, whether in America or Japan or West Germany or in any other country, are leading miserable lives due to their self-created problems.

SOCIAL SIDE

In advanced countries parents think that they are absolved of all responsibilities for their sons and daughters when they reach the age of 18 years or even earlier. Sons and daughters do not care for their parents. It has become an individualistic society. Due to the so-called liberalisation of society, sex has become almost free from any restraint. Marriage is going by the board, and the phenomena of "The girl and boy living together" seem to have become the norm. The rate of divorce has reached unmanageable proportions. There are lots of children living with single parents. In such cases, the future of the children has become bleak with resultant misery of the parents and the society in general.

ECONOMY

The rich have become oblivious of the needs of the poorer society. The percentage of have-nots is on the increase. In the United States, Mr. Reagan the former President, had openly declared that the Federal Government could no longer fund the needs of poorer society. He left them to be looked after by the State Governments who had got limited funds. The aid to poorer families is becoming less and less every day. The situation in America is being repeated in almost all other developed countries. The other day, there was a news item that in London alone, one million people had no shelter over their heads and were living on streets.

The rich passers-by see the misery around them, but the demands of their artificial needs are so exorbitant and pressing, that they do not find any spare funds to relieve the unfortunate situation of the have-nots.

Sweden is a highly developed country, with 95% or more of its population doing extremely well in the so-called amenities of the modern world. And yet, surprisingly, all their luxury is fake. It fails to give these people true happiness. They seem to feel that they lack something of such a paramount

importance that, without it, life is meaningless and futile. No wonder that the rate of suicide in Sweden surpasses all other countries.

On the International level, sharp division has occurred in the so-called North and South countries. The sympathy that leaders of North express for the poor South is merely lip service. Although it is appreciated that there cannot be any lasting peace unless living standard of the South is raised, yet the developed countries have no funds either to write off the existing debts of the developing countries or to give them further loans for Development. The Loans to the poor nations had been mostly in the form of Armaments which were priced very high with interest rates unpayable by the recipients of these loans. It will be well nigh impossible for them to pay the same. The developing countries have to pay a sum of 1,500 billion Dollars. The amount being loaned to them these days is hardly sufficient for paying back the instalment of the loans as well as interest. If the debtor countries adhere to payment on schedule, they have got hardly any funds for development of their economy and necessary social uplift of their people. The crisis might develop so that existing Governments are overthrown and there is a general chaos. One can imagine the hazards to be faced by developing countries as well as developed countries.

The Aid that had been granted to the poor countries was actually a loan with heavy interest rates. As they could not repay the same, the sum total that they owed to Lenders had become so heavy that there was almost a refusal to pay back. The negotiations are being held to make repayments according to revised schedules. But there are very few Lenders who would forego the repayments.

Same is the case with individuals. The condition of the debtor is rarely taken into view in a compassionate way. Everyone looks to his own Rights, but nobody considers his obligations to help the poor in the real sense of the term.

The economy as a whole has become unmanageable. If any intelligent being from outer space were to see what the humans on this globe were doing to one another, he would hardly believe his eyes!

In 1960's or early 1970's, the University students in America and younger generation adopted hippyism. It meant that hippies disdained the present system of accumulating wealth. They had decried the life of those who from morn till evening were busy accumulating what they considered as wealth.

A scion of Kennedy tribe committed suicide about 5 years back. It was said to be an over-dose of some drug. The question that arises is why should

such a wealthy young man start taking drugs. The answer, perhaps, is that his own wealth and the wealth of his family did not prevent him from taking to drugs so that he could become oblivious of the ills of society.

IN SHORT THERE IS NO PEACE OF MIND TO BE FOUND ANYWHERE IN THIS WORLD. Industrial development is no answer.

POLITICS

The United Nations have failed to maintain peace in the world. Capitalism, Communism do not give the necessary answer to the problems faced by an individual or a society, regardless of the country to which he belongs. The proper way of living has yet to be defined.

GUIDANCE

The question arises whether God created this world and human beings on this earth without giving necessary guidance to Man as to how he should conduct his life so as to be at peace with his fellow human beings and with Nature.

We know that for this purpose, God sent his Apostles from time to time to give necessary guidance to men. These Apostles lived their lives amongst their fellow-men and delivered the necessary Message received by them from God. As society developed, further guidance was given by sending revised instructions through other Apostles to suit the development of Knowledge and mind of human beings.

The last Apostle was Muhammad of Arabia (May peace be upon him) whose message in verbatim exists today in the Quran. It claims that guidance from God is given in detail for all eventualities. It claims that if a person leads his life in accordance with the Commandments given by God, he would achieve Peace of Mind. The principles enunciated therein are so vast and comprehensive that if human beings of all times to come would lead their lives in accordance with the said principles laid down therein, Justice would prevail amongst the various nations as well as in the lives of human beings.

TEXT OF QURAN

Quran was revealed in Arabic. The revelation was completed on different occasions in 23 years. It is, therefore, not in the same form of a book as usually one comes across. If a Reader goes through Quran from the beginning to the end, he comprehends very little. The contents contain history of

by-gone people; the existence of one God illustrated by giving different examples and besides other things, there are numerous Injunctions as to how a human being should lead his life. All these contents are intermingled in various Suras and Ayats.

In this volume, I have endeavoured to compile all the Commandments given in the Quran under different headings, for different subjects. The Holy Book covers the entire panorama of man's life on earth. It defines virtue and vice, the good and the evil, the spiritual and the mundane. It lays down man's duties of his fellow-men, his children, his neighbours, the poor, the down-trodden, even the animals. It also defines the individual's role towards society, and the state. It also tells how to prepare for defence, and how to wage war when forced to do so, where to draw the line of battling with the enemy, and how to treat the prisoners, the aged, the women, and the children during war. It tells what kind of earning is allowed, and what is disallowed, how to earn your wealth rightly, and how to spend it rightly. It also tells how to rule, and when to obey. It prepares you for life in this world and the next.

If these Commandments are followed, man should be able to find Peace of Mind – the elixir which all humanity yearns for, and which in the modern age, seems to elude everyone.

It may be noted that Christians and Jews of the time in the life of Muhammad (Peace be upon him) and his followers were at war and therefore, many Ayats in Chapter 9, Sub-chapter:

1. **Attitude towards the Christians**
2. **Attitude towards the Jews**

codified the treatment for Tribes at war and had particular reference to those times. Normal behaviour is dealt with in other Ayats of the Chapters.

In many Ayats more than one subject has been mentioned and only that portion relevant to the theme has been included. It will be obvious that the Ayats have been taken out of context, but as the Commandments are universal and for all time to come. The same have been stated as they appear in Quran.

As already stated, Quran is in Arabic. The Commandments given in this book are the English version and the same have the inevitable shortcomings of translation in an alien language. Full references have been given, and further research, if necessary, can be made by referring to the original book and the numerous interpretations published by scholars of different languages, religions, and nationalities, during the last 1,400 years since the Quran was revealed.

There are some words in the beginning of a Sura which are unintelligible like 'Alif lam meem'; 'Ta sin', etc. Same have been put as in the original book. It would be futile to place any meaning on the same.

It is necessary that when we pronounce the Apostle's name: Muhammad, we should pray for him. In the contents, this has been noted as 'PBUH' (Peace be upon him).

I consider it my duty to draw the readers' attention to the Divine answer which was revealed for all our problems of today and tomorrow. I am sure that life led in accordance with these Commandments would bring Peace to the minds of the devout followers as well as others.

No effort has been spared to try and have this volume without errors and if any reader comes across any, please inform the Publisher so that they may be corrected in the next edition.

I made use of translations of Quran by Allam Yusuf Ali, Mahmud Y. Zayid and Muhammad Asad. I am indebted to the Islamic Culture Centre, London and specially to Mr. Youssef Omar and Sh. Zahran Ibraim for necessary help in translation. I am grateful to my late colleague Mr. S. M. Nawaz for translating the Headings of different Chapters from my Book in Urdu (a local language). I am also grateful to Mr. Qamar-ud-Din Butt, my Office Assistant and Mr. Zaheer Salam of Ferozesons (Pvtr) Limited, Lahore for their help in printing the book. May God compensate all of them.

I am very grateful to my co-workers and especially to Mr. Mohammad Husain for allowing me to devote the necessary time and make use of the facilities of the Company in which I work. May Allah compensate all of them.

In the end, I request those who follow these Commandments to pray for my deliverance on the Day of Judgement.

Lahore-Pakistan

NAZAR MOHAMMAD

THE HOLY QURAN AND CONTEMPLATION OF THE UNIVERSE

(1)

In the name of Allah, The Compassionate, The Merciful

ATTRIBUTES OF THE HOLY QURAN

This Book is not to be doubted. It is a guide for the righteous, who have faith in the unseen and are steadfast in prayers; who spend out of what we have given them; who believe in that which has been revealed to you and to others before you, and firmly believe in the life to come.

Sura: 2, Ayat: 2–4.

If you are in doubt of what We have revealed to Our Servant, produce one chapter comparable to it. Call upon your helpers besides God to assist you, if what you say be true. But if you fail, as you are sure to fail, then guard yourselves against the fire whose fuel is men and stones, prepared for the unbelievers.

Sura: 2, Ayat: 23-24.

We have sent down to you clear revelations: none will deny them except the evildoers.

Sura: 2, Ayat: 99.

If We abrogate any verse or cause it to be forgotten, We will replace it by a better one or one similar. Do you not know that Allah has power over all things.

Sura: 2, Ayat: 106.

Such are those that buy error with guidance, and torture with forgiveness. How steadfastly they seek the fire! That is because Allah has revealed the Book with the truth; those that disagree about it are in extreme schism.

Sura: 2, Ayat: 175-176.

The month of Ramadhan is the month in which the Quran was revealed, a book of guidance with proofs of guidance distinguishing right from wrong.

Sura: 2, Ayat: 185.

He has revealed to you the Book with the truth, confirming what preceded

it; and He has already revealed the Torah and the Gospel for the guidance of men, and the distinction between right and wrong.

Those that deny Allah's revelations shall be sternly punished; Allah is Mightly and capable of punishment.

Sura: 3, Ayat: 3-4.

It is He Who has revealed to you the Book. Some of its verses are precise in meaning — they are the foundation of the Book — and others allegorical. Those whose hearts are infected with disbelief follow the allegorical part, so as to create dissension and to interpret it. But no one knows its interpretation except Allah. Those who are well-grounded in knowledge say: 'We believe in it: it is all from our Lord. But only the wise take heed. Lord, do not cause our hearts to go astray after You have guided us. Grant us Your own mercy; You are the munificent Giver.

Sura: 3, Ayat: 7-8.

Such are the revelations of Allah; We recite them to you in all truth. Allah desires no injustice to His creatures.

Sura: 3, Ayat: 108.

You to whom the Book was given! Believe in that which We have revealed, confirming that which you have, before We obliterate faces and turn them backward, or lay Our curse on you as We laid it on the Sabbath-breakers. What Allah ordains shall be accomplished.

Sura: 4, Ayat: 47.

Will they not ponder on the Quran? If it had not come from Allah, they could have surely found in it many contradictions.

Sura: 4, Ayat: 82.

We have revealed to you the Book with the truth, so that you may arbitrate among men by that which Allah has shown you. You shall not plead for traitors. Implore Allah's Forgiveness: He is Forgiving, Merciful.

Sura: 4, Ayat: 105-106.

Allah has revealed to you the Book and wisdom and taught you what you did not know before. Allah's goodness to you has been great indeed.

Sura: 4, Ayat: 113.

O believers, have faith in Allah and His Apostle, in the Book He has revealed to His Apostle, and in the Book He formerly revealed. He that denies Allah, His angels, His scriptures, His apostles, and the Last Day, has strayed far from the truth.

Sura: 4, Ayat: 136.

Allah Himself bears witness by that which He has revealed to you that it has been revealed with His knowledge; and so do the angels. There is no better witness than Allah.

Sura: 4, Ayat: 166.

Those that disbelieve and debar others from the path of Allah have strayed far from the truth.

Sura: 4, Ayat: 167.

Men, you have received clear proof from your Lord. We have sent forth to you a glorious light.

Sura: 4, Ayat: 174.

People of the Book! Our Apostle has come to reveal to you much of what you have hidden of the Book, and to forgive you much. A light has come to you from Allah and a glorious Book, with which He will guide to the paths of peace those that seek to please Him; He will lead them by His will from darkness to the light; He will guide them to a straight path.

Sura: 5, Ayat: 15-16.

And to you We have revealed the Book with the truth confirming what was revealed before it in the other Books, and standing as a guardian over it. Therefore give judgement among them in accordance with Allah's revelations and do not yield to their fancies (swerving) from the truth that has been made known to you.

We have ordained a law and a path for each of you. Had Allah pleased, He could have made you one nation: but that He might prove you by that which He has bestowed upon you. Vie with one another in good works, for to Allah you shall all return and He will declare to you what you have disagreed about.

Sura: 5, Ayat: 48.

That which Allah has revealed to you will surely increase the wickedness and unbelief of many of them. We have stirred among them enmity and hatred, which will endure till the Day of Resurrection. Whenever they kindle the fire of war, Allah puts it out. They spread evil in the land, and Allah does not love the evildoers.

Sura: 5, Ayat: 64.

Say: 'What thing counts most in testimony?'

Say: 'Let Allah be a witness between me and you.

This Quran has been revealed to me that I may thereby warn you and all whom it may reach....

Sura: 6, Ayat: 19.

And this is a blessed Book which We have revealed, confirming what came before it, that you may warn the Mother City* and those that dwell around her. Those who have faith in the life to come will believe in it and be steadfast in their prayers.

Sura: 6, Ayat: 92.

Thus We make plain Our revelations, so that they may say: 'You have studied well,' and that this may become clear to men of understanding.

Sura: 6, Ayat: 105.

Should I seek a judge other than Allah when it is He Who has revealed the Quran for you fully explained? Those to whom We have given the Book know that it is the truth revealed by your Lord. Therefore have no doubts.

Perfected are the words of your Lord in truth and justice. None can change them. He is the Hearing, the Knowing.

Sura: 6, Ayat: 114-115.

And now We have revealed this Book with Our blessings. Observe it and keep from evil, so that you may find mercy and not say: 'The Book was revealed only to two sects before us; we have no knowledge of what they read'; or: 'Had the Book been revealed to us, we would have been better guided than they.'

A clear sign has now come to you from your Lord: a guidance and a blessing. And who is more wicked than the man who denies the revelation of Allah and turns away from them? Those that turn away from Our revelations shall be sternly punished for their indifferences.

Sura: 6, Ayat: 155–157.

Alif lam mim sad. (This) Book is revealed to you; let your heart not be troubled about it. It is revealed to you that you may thereby warn the unbelievers and admonish the faithful.

Sura: 7, Ayat: 1-2.

We have bestowed on them a Book which We have made plain with knowledge, a guidance and a blessing to true believers.

Sura: 7, Ayat: 52.

And if you do not recite to them a revelation, they say: 'Have you not yet invented one?' Say: 'I follow only what is revealed to me by my Lord. This Book is a veritable proof from your Lord, a guide and a blessing to true believers.'

Sura: 7, Ayat: 203.

***Makkah**

When the Quran is recited, listen to it in silence so that Allah may show you mercy.

Sura: 7, Ayat: 204.

Alif lam ra. These are the verses of the sound Book. Does it seem strange to mankind that We should have revealed Our will to a mortal from among themselves, saying: 'Give warning to mankind, and bear the good tidings to those who believe that they have a reward with their Lord?'

Sura: 10, Ayat: 1-2.

This Quran could not have been composed by any but Allah. It confirms what was revealed before it and fully explains the Scriptures. There is no doubt about it, from the Lord of the Creation.

Sura: 10, Ayat: 37.

If they say: 'It is his own invention, say: 'Compose one Sura like it. Call on whom you may besides Allah to help you, if what you say be true!'

Sura: 10, Ayat: 38.

Men, an admonition has come to you from your Lord, a healing for what is in the hearts, a guide and a blessing to true believers.

Say: 'In Allah's grace and mercy let them rejoice, for these are better than that which they amass.'

Sura: 10, Ayat: 57-58.

If you are in doubt of what We have revealed to you, ask those who have read the Book before you. The truth has come to you from your Lord: therefore do not be one of the doubters. Nor shall you deny the revelations of Allah, for then you shall be lost.

Sura: 10, Ayat: 94-95.

Say: 'Men! The truth has come to you from your Lord. He that follows the right path follows it to his own advantage, and he that goes astray does so at his own peril. I am not your keeper.'

Sura: 10, Ayat: 108.

Observe what is revealed to you, and have patience till Allah makes known His judgement. He is the best of judges.

Sura: 10, Ayat: 109.

Alif lam ra. (This is) a Book with verses most perfected, then made plain from the Wise, the Aware. That you should serve none but Allah. I am (sent) to you by Him to warn you and to give you good news.

And seek forgiveness of your Lord and turn to Him in repentance. He will

make a good provision for you till an appointed day and will bestow His grace upon those that have merit. But if you turn away, then beware of the torment of a fateful day. To Allah you shall all return. He has power over all things.

Sura: 11, Ayat: 1–4.

Or, if they say: 'He has invented it* himself,' say to them: Produce ten invented chapters like it. Call on whom you will of those besides Him, if what you say be true. But if they fail you, know that it is revealed with Allah's knowledge, and that there is no god but Him. Will you then accept Islam?'

Sura: 11, Ayat: 13-14.

Alif lam ra. These are the verses of the Book which clearly indicates (right and wrong). We have revealed it in the Arabic tongue so that you may understand.

We will narrate to you the best of narratives by revealing this Quran, though before We revealed it you were unaware.

Sura: 12, Ayat: 1–3.

....In their histories is a lesson to men of understanding. This is no invented tale, but a confirmation of previous (scriptures), an explanation of all things a guidance and a blessing to true believers.

Sura: 12, Ayat: 110-111.

Alif lam mim ra. These are the verses of the Book. That which is revealed to you from your Lord is the truth, yet most men have no faith.

Sura: 13, Ayat: 1-2.

Those to whom We have given the Book rejoice in what is revealed to you, while some factions deny a part of it. Say: 'I am commanded to serve Allah and to associate none with Him. To Him I pray, and to Him I shall return.'

And thus We have revealed it, a (code of) judgements in the Arabic tongue. If you succumb to their desires after the knowledge you have been given, none shall save or protect you from Allah.

We have sent forth other apostles before you and given them wives and children. Yet none of them could work miracles except by Allah's leave. Every term has its Book. Allah confirms or abolishes what He pleases. With Him is the Mother Book.

Sura: 13, Ayat: 36–39.

Alif lam ra. We have revealed to you this book so that, by the will of their Lord, you may lead men from darkness to light; to the path of the Mighty, Glorious One: the path of Allah; Allah to whom belongs all that is in the

---

***The Quran**

heavens and the earth.

Sura: 14, Ayat: 1-2.

This is a clear message to mankind. Let them heed thereby, and know that Allah is One God. Let the wise bear this in mind.

Sura: 14, Ayat: 52.

Alif lam ra. These are the verses of the Book which clearly indicates (right and wrong).

Sura: 15, Ayat: 1-2.

It was We who revealed the Quran, and We will certainly preserve it.

Sura: 15, Ayat: 9.

We have given you the seven oft-repeated verses and the glorious Quran.

Sura: 15, Ayat: 87.

As we sent down (punishment) upon the dividers who broke up the Quran into parts (believing in some and denying others), so by the Lord, We will question them all about that they did.

Sura: 15, Ayat: 90—93.

(When) it is said to those who guard against evil: 'What has your Lord revealed?' they will reply: 'That which is best.' Good is the reward of those that do good works in this present life: but far better is the reward of the life to come.

Sura: 16, Ayat: 30.

(We sent) them with clear proofs and Books. And We revealed to you the Reminder (Quran) so that you may make clear to men what has been revealed to them, and that they may give thought.

Sura: 16, Ayat: 44.

We have not revealed to you the Book except that you may declare to them the truth concerning which they are disputing. It is a guide and a blessing to those who believe.

Sura: 16, Ayat: 64.

And on the day when We shall raise up in every nation a witness against them from among themselves. We (shall) bring you to testify against your people: to you We have revealed the Book which manifests the truth about all things, a guide, a blessing, and good news to those who submit to Allah.

Sura: 16, Ayat: 89.

When you recite the Quran, seek refuge in Allah from the accursed devil:
Sura: 16, Ayat: 98.

When We change one verse for another — Allah knows best what He reveals — they say: 'You* are an imposter.' Indeed, most of them know not.
Say: 'The Holy Spirit brought it down from your Lord in truth to reassure the faithful, and to give guidance and good news to those that surrender themselves to Allah.'
Sura: 16, Ayat: 101-102.

We do know that they say: 'A mortal taught him.' But he to whom they allude speaks a foreign tongue, while this is eloquent Arabic speech.
Sura: 16, Ayat: 103.

This Quran will guide to that which is most upright. It promises the believers who do good works a rich reward, and threatens those who deny the life to come with a grievous scourge.
Sura: 17, Ayat: 9-10.

We have made plain (Our revelations) in this Quran so that (the unbelievers) may take warning. Yet it has only added to their unbelief.
Sura: 17, Ayat: 41.

When you recite the Quran, We place between you and those who deny the life to come a hidden barrier. We cast a veil upon their hearts and deafness in their ears, lest they understand it. (That is why) when you mention your Lord alone in the Quran, they turn their backs in flight.
Sura: 17, Ayat: 45-46.

We reveal of the Quran that which is a healing and mercy to true believers, though it adds nothing but ruin the evildoers.
Sura: 17, Ayat: 82.

If We pleased We could take away that which We have revealed to you: then you should find none to plead with Us on your behalf, except for mercy from your Lord: for His bounty to you is great indeed.
Sura: 17, Ayat: 86-87.

Say: 'If men and jinn combined to write the like of this Quran, they would surely fail to compose one like it, though they helped one another.'
Sura: 17, Ayat: 88.

And We have set forth in this Quran every kind of parable, yet the greater

---

***Muhammad**

part of men refuse (to respond) except with ingratitude.

Sura: 17, Ayat: 89.

We have sent down (the Quran) in truth, and in truth it has come down. We have sent you forth only to proclaim good news and to give warning.

Sura: 17, Ayat: 105.

(It is) a Quran which We have divided into sections so that you may recite it to the people with deliberation. We have imparted it by gradual revelation.

Sura: 17, Ayat: 106.

Say: 'It is up to you to believe or not to believe in it. Those to whom knowledge was given before its revelation prostrate themselves upon their faces when it is recited to them and say: "Glorious is our Lord. His promise has been fulfilled." They fall down upon their faces, weeping; and as they listen, their humility increases.'

Sura: 17, Ayat: 107—109.

Praise be to Allah Who has revealed the Book to His servant shorn of crookedness and unswerving from the truth, so that he may give warning of a dire scourge from Him, proclaim to the faithful who do good works that a rich and everlasting reward awaits them, and admonish those who say that Allah has begotten a son. Surely of this they could have no knowledge, neither they nor their fathers: a monstrous blasphemy is that which they utter. They preach nothing but falsehood.

Sura: 18, Ayat: 1—5.

Recite what is revealed to you in the Book of your Lord. None can change His words. You shall find no refuge other than Him.

Sura: 18, Ayat: 27.

In this Quran, We have set forth for men all manner of parables. But man is in most things contentious.

Sura: 18, Ayat: 54.

We have revealed to you (the Quran) in your own tongue that you may thereby proclaim good tidings to the upright and give warning to contentious people.

Sura: 19, Ayat: 97.

Taha. It was not to distress you that We revealed the Quran, but to admonish the God-fearing. It is a revelation from Him who has created the earth and the lofty heavens.

Sura: 20, Ayat: 1—4.

Thus We recount to you the history of past events.
A Message of Our own We have given you: those that reject it shall bear a heavy burden on the Day of Resurrection. They shall bear it for ever: an evil burden for them on the Day of Resurrection.

Sura: 20, Ayat: 99–101.

Thus We sent it down, an Arabic Quran, and explained in it warnings and threats so that they may guard themselves against evil and so that it may be a reminder for them.

Sura: 20, Ayat: 113.

We have revealed a Book for your admonition. Will you not understand?

Sura: 21, Ayat: 10.

If anyone thinks that Allah will not give victory (to His Apostle) in this world and in the world to come, let him tie a rope to the ceiling of his house and cut (himself) off. Then let him see if his wiles have done away with that which has enraged him.
We have sent it in clear verses. Allah gives guidance to whom He will.

Sura: 22, Ayat: 15-16.

This is a sura (chapter) which We have revealed and sanctioned, proclaiming in it clear revelations, so that you may take heed.

Sura: 24, Ayat: 1.

We have sent down revelations showing you the right path, and a story about those who have gone before you and an admonition to righteous men.

Sura: 24, Ayat: 34.

We have sent down revelations showing clearly (the truth). Allah guides whom He will to a straight path.

Sura: 24, Ayat: 46.

Blessed be He who has revealed Al-Furqan (the Criterion) to His servant, that he may be a warner to all mankind.

Sura: 25, Ayat: 1.

The unbelievers say: 'This is but a forgery of his own invention, in which others have helped him.'
Unjust is what they say and false.
And they say: 'Fables of the ancients he has written: they are dictated to him morning and evening.'
Say: 'It was sent down by Him Who knows the secrets of heaven and earth. He is Forgiving, Merciful.'

Sura: 25, Ayat: 4–6.

The Apostle says: 'Lord, my people have treated this Quran as a forsaken thing.'

Sura: 25, Ayat: 30.

The unbelievers ask: 'Why was the Quran not revealed to him all at once? (We have revealed it) thus so that We may strengthen your faith. We have imparted it to you by gradual revelation. No sooner will they come to you with an argument than We shall reveal to you the truth and properly explain it.

Sura: 25, Ayat: 32-33.

Had it been Our will, We could have raised a warner in every town. Do not yield to the unbelievers, but fight them strenuously with it (the Quran).

Sura: 25, Ayat: 51-52.

Ta sin mim. These are the verses of the Book which clearly indicates (right and wrong).

Sura: 26, Ayat: 1-2.

Verily this is revealed by the Lord of the Creation. The Faithful Spirit brought it down into your heart, that you might warn mankind in plain Arabic speech. It was (foretold) in the scriptures of the ancients.

Sura: 26, Ayat: 192—196.

Is it not sufficient proof for them that the learned of the Children of Israel know it? If We had revealed it to a non-Arab, and he had recited it to them, they still would not have believed. We thus put it in the hearts of the evildoers: they shall not believe in it until they see the woeful scourge which in their heedlessness will suddenly smite them. And then they will say: 'Shall we be reprieved?'

Sura: 26, Ayat: 197—203.

It was not the devils who brought down this revelation: it is neither in their interest nor in their power. Indeed, they are too far away to overhear it.

Sura: 26, Ayat: 210—212.

Ta sin. These are the verses of the Quran, the Book which indicates (right and wrong); a guidance and joyful news to true believers, who attend to their prayers and pay the alms-tax and firmly believe in the life to come.

Sura: 27, Ayat: 1—3.

You have received the Quran from Him Who is Wise and All-Knowing.

Sura: 27, Ayat: 6.

This Quran declares to the Children of Israel most of that concerning which they disagree. It is a guidance and blessing to true believers.

Sura: 27, Ayat: 76-77.

(Say): 'I am bidden to serve the Lord of this City, which He has made sacred. All things are His.'

'I am commanded to surrender to Him, and to recite the Quran. He that takes the right path shall himself have much to gain.'

To him who goes astray, say: 'I am only a warner.'

Sura: 27, Ayat: 91-92.

Ta sin mim. These are the verses of the Book which makes plain (right and wrong). We shall recount to you some of the story of Musa and Pharaoh in truth for people who believe.

Sura: 28, Ayat: 1—3.

Say: 'Bring down from Allah a scripture that is a better guidance than these and I will follow it, if what you say be true!'

If they do not answer you, know that they are the slaves of their desires. And who is in greater error than the man who is led by his desires without guidance from Allah? Allah does not guide the evildoers.

Sura: 28, Ayat: 49-50.

We have caused Our Word to reach them so that they may give thought.

Sura: 28, Ayat: 51.

He who has ordained the Quran to you will surely bring you back (to Makkah). Say: 'My Lord best knows him who brings guidance, and him who is in gross error.'

You never hoped that this Book would be sent to you except as mercy from your Lord. Therefore give no help to the unbelievers.

Sura: 28, Ayat: 85-86.

Proclaim the portions of the Book that are revealed to you and be steadfast in prayer. Prayer fends away indecency and evil. But the greatest thing is to remember Allah. Allah has knowledge of all your actions.

Sura: 29, Ayat: 45.

Likewise We revealed the Book to you. Those to whom We gave the Scriptures believe in it, and so do some of these (pagan Arabs). Only the unbelievers deny Our revelations.

Sura: 29, Ayat: 47.

Is it not enough for them that We have revealed to you the Book which is

recited to them? Surely in this there is a blessing and admonition to true believers.

Sura: 29, Ayat: 51.

In this Quran We have set forth for men all manner of examples. Yet if you recite to them a single verse, the unbelievers will surely say: 'You are preaching lies.'

Sura: 30, Ayat: 58.

Alif lam mim. These are the revelations of the Wise Book, a guidance and a blessing to the righteous, who attend to their prayers, pay the alms-tax, and firmly believe in the life to come. These are rightly guided by their Lord and will surely prosper.

Sura: 31, Ayat: 1—5.

Alif lam mim. The revelation of the Book in which there is no doubt is from the Lord of the Creation.

Or do they say: 'He* has invented it himself?'

It is the truth from your Lord so that you may forewarn a nation, whom none has warned before you, and that they may be rightly guided.

Sura: 32, Ayat: 1—3.

Those to whom knowledge has been given can see that what is revealed to you from your Lord is the truth, leading to the path of the Almighty, the Glorious One.

Sura: 34, Ayat: 6.

Those who recite the Book of Allah and attend to their prayers and give alms in private and in public may hope for imperishable gain. Allah will give them their rewards and enrich them from His own abundance. He is Forgiving and Rewarding.

Sura: 35, Ayat: 29-30.

What We have revealed to you in the Book is the truth confirming what was before it. Allah knows and observes His servants.

Then We gave the Book as inheritance to those of Our servants whom We have chosen. Some of them wrong their souls, some follow a middle course, and some, by Allah's leave, vie with each other in charitable works: this is the supreme virtue.

Sura: 35, Ayat: 31-32.

This is a revelation of the Mighty One, the Merciful, so that you may warn

---

***Muhammad**

a people whose fathers were not warned, and, therefore, they are heedless.

Sura: 36, Ayat: 5-6.

We have taught Muhammad no poetry, nor does it become him (to be a poet). This is but a reminder and an eloquent Quran to admonish the living and to pass judgement on the unbelievers.

Sura: 36, Ayat: 69-70.

Sad. By the Quran, full of admonition. Verily the unbelievers are (steeped) in false pride and opposition.

Sura: 38, Ayat: 1-2.

It is a Book that We have revealed with Our blessings, so that the wise might ponder its revelations and take warning.

Sura: 38, Ayat: 29.

The revelation of the Book is from Allah, the Mighty, the Wise One. We have revealed to you the Book in truth: therefore serve Allah offering sincere devotion.

Sura: 39, Ayat: 1-2.

Allah has now revealed the best of scriptures, a Book uniform and (yet) repeating pairs (of promises and threats and the like). The skins of those who fear their Lord tremble (for fear) of it; but then their skins and hearts soften to remembrance. Such is Allah's guidance: He bestows it on whom He will. But he whom Allah leaves in error shall have none to guide him.

Sura: 39, Ayat: 23.

We have given mankind in this Quran every kind of parable, so that they may take heed. It is an Arabic Quran free from all crookedness, that they may guard themselves against evil.

Sura: 39, Ayat: 27-28.

We have revealed to you the Book in truth (for the instruction) of mankind. He that follows the right path shall follow it to his own advantage; and he that goes astray shall do so at his own peril. You are not their keeper.

Sura: 39, Ayat: 41.

Ha mim. The revelation of this Book is from Allah, the Mighty One, the All-Knowing, Who forgives sin and accepts repentance. His punishment is stern, and He is Bountiful.

There is no god but Him. To Him is the final return.

Sura: 40, Ayat: 1–3.

None but the unbelievers dispute the revelations of Allah....

Sura: 40, Ayat: 4.

Ha mim. This is a revelation from the Compassionate, the Merciful: A Book the verses of which are well expounded, an Arabic Quran for men of understanding. It is a good news and a warning.

Sura: 41, Ayat: 1–4.

Those who deny Our word when it is preached to them (shall be sternly punished). This is a mighty Book. Falsehood cannot get at it from before or behind. It is a revelation from a Wise and Glorious God.

Sura: 41, Ayat: 41-42.

Had We revealed the Quran in a foreign tongue they would have said: 'If only its verses were expounded! Why in a foreign tongue, (when) the Prophet is Arabian?'

Say: 'To the true believers it is a guide and a healing balm. But those who believe not, there is deafness in their ears and blindness in their eyes. They are like men called from afar.'

Sura: 41, Ayat: 44.

Say: 'Think: if this (Quran) is indeed from Allah and you deny it, who can err more than he who openly defies Him?'

Sura: 41, Ayat: 52.

Thus We have revealed to you an Arabic Quran, that you may warn the Mother City* and all around it; that you may forewarn them of the Day of Gathering which is sure to come: when some will be in Paradise, and some in Hell.

Sura: 42, Ayat: 7.

It is Allah Who has sent down the Book in truth, and the Balance. And how can you tell? The Hour of Doom may be fast approaching.

Sura: 42, Ayat: 17.

Ha mim. By the Book which makes plain (right and wrong), We have revealed the Quran in the Arabic tongue that you may understand. It is in the Mother Book with Us, sublime and full of wisdom.

Sura: 43, Ayat: 1–4.

They also say: 'Why was this Quran not revealed to some great man from

---

***Makkah**

the two towns* ?' Is it they who apportion your Lord's blessings?

Sura: 43, Ayat: 31-32.

Therefore hold fast to that which is revealed to you: you are on the right path.

Sura: 43, Ayat: 43.

It is an admonition to you and to your people. You shall be questioned all.

Sura: 43, Ayat: 44.

Ha mim: We swear by the Book which makes plain (right and wrong) that We sent it down during a blessed night. We revealed it to warn mankind, on a night when every precept was made plain as a commandment from Ourself.

Sura: 44, Ayat: 1–5.

We have revealed this to you in your own tongue so that they may take heed. Wait then; they (too) are waiting.

Sura: 44, Ayat: 58-59.

Ha mim. The revelation of the Book is from Allah, the Mighty One, the All-Knowing.

Sura: 45, Ayat: 1-2.

Such are the revelations of Allah. We recite them to you in all truth. But in what revelation will they believe, after (they deny) Allah Himself (and all His signs)?

Sura: 45, Ayat: 6.

Such is (Our) guidance. Those who deny the revelations of their Lord shall suffer the torment of a hideous scourge.

Sura: 45, Ayat: 11.

These are clear proofs to men and a guidance and mercy for those who truly believe.

Sura: 45, Ayat: 20.

Ha mim. The revelation of the Book is from Allah, the Mighty One, the Wise One.

Sura: 46, Ayat: 1-2.

Say: 'Think if this Quran is indeed from Allah and you reject it, and if a witness from the Children of Israel has vouched for the like and accepted Islam, while you yourselves deny it with scorn (how unjust you are), Truly,

---

***Makkah and Medina**

Allah does not guide the wrongdoers.'

Sura: 46, Ayat: 10.

The unbelievers say of the faithful: 'Had it been any good they would not have believed in it before us.' And since they reject its guidance they say: 'This is an ancient falsehood.'

Yet before it there was the Book of Musa, a guide and a blessing to all men. This Book confirms it. It is revealed in the Arabic tongue to forewarn the wrongdoers and to give good news to the righteous.

Sura: 46, Ayat: 11-12.

(Tell) how We sent to you a band of jinn who, when they came and listened to the Quran, said to each other: 'Hush!' 'Hush!' As soon as it was ended they betook themselves to their people and gave them warning. 'Our people,' they said, "We have just been listening to a Book revealed since the time of Musa, confirming what came before it and directing to the truth and to a straight path.

Sura: 46, Ayat: 29-30.

Will they not ponder on the Quran? Are there locks upon their hearts?

Sura: 47, Ayat: 24.

We well know what they say. You shall not use force with them. Admonish with this Quran whoever fears My warning.

Sura: 50, Ayat: 45.

Do they say: 'He has invented it* himself'? Indeed, they have no faith. Let them produce a scripture like it, if what they say be true!

Sura: 52, Ayat: 33-34.

We have made the Quran easy to remember: but will any take heed?

Sura: 54, Ayat: 17.

We have made the Quran easy to remember: but will any take heed?

Sura: 54, Ayat: 22.

We have made the Quran easy to remember: but will any take heed?

Sura: 54, Ayat: 32.

We have made the Quran easy to remember: but will any take heed?

Sura: 54, Ayat: 40.

***The Quran.**

(God) Most Gracious! He has taught the Quran.

Sura: 55, Ayat: 1-2.

I swear by the shelters of the star — a mighty oath, if you but knew it that this is a glorious Quran, (inscribed) in a hidden book which none may touch except the purified; a revelation from the Lord of all creatures.

It is this scripture that you scorn? And have you made its denial your means of livelihood?

Sura: 56, Ayat: 75—82.

Had we brought down this Quran upon a mountain, you would have seen it humble itself and crack for fear of Allah.

Such are the parables We set forth to men, so that they may give thought.

Sura: 59, Ayat: 21.

It is He Who has sent forth among the unlettered an apostle of their own to recite to them His revelations, to purify them and to instruct them in the Scriptures and wisdom, though they have hitherto been in gross error, together with others of their own kin who have not yet joined them. He is the Mighty, the Wise One.

Such is the grace of Allah: He bestows it on whom He will. His grace is infinite.

Sura: 62, Ayat: 2—4.

When they hear Our revelations, the unbelievers almost devour you with their eyes. 'He is surely possessed,' they say.

But it is nothing less than a warning to all men.

Sura: 68, Ayat: 51-52.

I swear by all that you can see, and all that is hidden from your view, that this is the utterance of a noble messenger. It is not poet's speech: scant is your faith! It is no sooth-sayer's divination: how little you reflect! It is a revelation from the Lord of all creatures.

Sura: 69, Ayat: 38—43.

Had he invented lies concerning Us, We would have seized him by the right hand and cut off his heart's vein: not one of you could have protected him.

It is but an admonition to righteous men. We know that there are some among you who will deny it.

It is the despair of the unbelievers. It is the indubitable truth. Praise, then, the name of your Lord, the Almighty.

Sura: 69, Ayat: 44—52.

Say: 'It is revealed to me that a party of jinn listened to (Allah's revelations) and said: "We have heard a wondrous Quran giving guidance to the right path. We believed in it and shall henceforth serve none besides Our Lord.

Sura: 72 Ayat: 1–2

.... And with measured tone recite the Quran. We are about to address to you words of great gravity.

Sura: 73, Ayat: 4-5.

Do not move your tongue (with the revelation) so that you may hasten (committing) it (to memory). We Ourself shall see to its collection and recital. When We read it, follow its words attentively; We shall Ourself explain its meaning.

Sura: 75, Ayat: 16—19.

We have revealed to you the Quran by gradual revelation, therefore await with patience the judgement of your Lord and do not yield to the sinner and the unbelieving.

Sura: 76, Ayat: 23-24.

Nay, this is an admonition; let him who will, bear it in mind. It is set down on honoured pages, purified and exalted, by the hands of devout and gracious scribes. Honourable and Pious and Just.

Sura: 80, Ayat: 11—16.

Surely this is the word of a noble messenger having power, with the Lord of the Throne secure, obeyed, moreover trustworthy.

Sura: 81, Ayat: 19—21

This is naught but an admonition to all men: to those among you that have the will to be upright. Yet you cannot will, except by the will of Allah, Lord of the Creation.

Sura: 81, Ayat: 27—29.

Why then do they not have faith, or kneel in prayer when the Quran is read to them?

Sura: 84, Ayat: 20-21.

Indeed this is a glorious Quran, in a guarded tablet.

Sura: 85, Ayat: 21-22.

We revealed this (Quran) on the Night of Qadr.

Sura: 97, Ayat: 1.

In the name of Allah, The Compassionate, The Merciful

VENERATION OF THE HOLY QURAN

Allah has instructed you in the Book that when you hear His revelations being denied or ridiculed, you must not sit and listen to them unless they engage in other talk, or else you shall yourselves become like them.

Sura: 4, Ayat: 140.

When you see those that scoff at Our revelations, withdraw from them till they engage in some other talk. If the devil causes you to forget, leave the wrongdoers as soon as you remember.

Sura: 6, Ayat: 68.

When the Quran is recited, listen to it in silence so that Allah may show you mercy.

Sura: 7, Ayat: 204.

The true believers are those whose hearts are filled with awe at the mention of Allah, and whose faith grows stronger as they listen to His revelations. They are those who put their trust in their Lord, pray steadfastly, and spend of that which We have given them.

Sura: 8, Ayat: 2-3.

When you recite the Quran, seek refuge in Allah from the accursed devil: no power has he over believers who put their trust in their Lord. He only has power over those who befriend him, and those who serve other gods besides Allah.

Sura: 16, Ayat: 98—100.

Keep up your prayer at the decline of the sun till the darkness of the night and (keep) the recital of the Quran at dawn. Surely the recital of the Quran at dawn is witnessed.

Sura: 17, Ayat: 78.

Proclaim the portions of the Book that are revealed to you and be steadfast

in prayer. Prayer fends away indecency and evil. But the greatest thing is to remember Allah. Allah has knowledge of all your actions.

Sura: 29, Ayat: 45.

Those who recite the Book of Allah and attend to their prayers and give alms in private and in public may hope for imperishable gain. Allah will give them their rewards and enrich them from His own abundance. He is Forgiving and Rewarding.

Sura: 35, Ayat: 29-30.

The unbelievers say: 'Give no heed to this Quran. Interrupt its reading with booing and laughter, so that you may gain the upper hand.'

We will sternly punish the unbelievers and pay them back for the worst of their deeds.

Sura: 41, Ayat: 26-27.

Say: 'Think: if this (Quran) is indeed from Allah and you deny it, who can err more than he who openly defies Him?'

Sura: 41, Ayat: 52.

And when he comes to know ought of our revelations he takes it scoffingly. For such there is a shameful doom.

Sura: 45, Ayat: 9.

That this is a glorious Quran, (inscribed) in a hidden book which none may touch except the purified; a revelation from the Lord of all creatures.

Is it this scripture that you scorn? And have you made its denial your means of livelihood?

Sura: 56, Ayat: 77—82.

And with measured tone recite the Quran.

Sura: 73, Ayat: 4.

Verily the rising by night is (the time) when impression is strongest and speech more certain. You have by day prolonged occupations (with work).

Sura: 73, Ayat: 6-7.

Why then do they not have faith, or kneel in prayer when the Quran is read to them?

Sura: 84, Ayat: 20-21.

In the name of Allah, The Compassionate, The Merciful

OBSERVATION OF NATURE, AND CALL TO MEDITATE THEREON

Your God is One God. There is no god but Him. He is the Compassionate, the Merciful.

In the creation of the heavens and the earth; in the alternation of night and day; in the ships that sail the ocean with what is beneficial to man; in the water which Allah sends down from the sky and with which He revives the earth after its death, dispersing over it all manner of beasts; in the movements of the winds, and in the clouds that are driven between earth and sky: surely in these there are signs for people who understand.

Sura: 2, Ayat: 163-164.

This is a declaration to mankind: a guide and an admonition to the righteous.

Sura: 3, Ayat: 138.

There have been examples before you. Roam the world and see what was the fate of those who disbelieved (their apostles).

Sura: 3, Ayat: 137.

In the creation of the heavens and the earth, and in the alternation of night and day, there are signs for men of sense; those that remember Allah when standing, sitting, and lying down, and reflect on the creation of the heavens and the earth (saying): 'Lord, You have not created these in vain. Glory be to You! Save us from the torment of Fire, Lord.

Sura: 3, Ayat: 190-191.

Praise is due to Allah, Who has created the heavens and the earth and created darkness and light. Yet the unbelievers set up other gods as equals with their Lord.

It is He Who has created you from clay. He has decreed a term for you (in this world) and another one set with Him (in the next). Yet you are still in

doubt.

Sura: 6, Ayat: 1-2.

Say: 'Tell me: If Allah took away your hearing and your sight and set a seal upon your hearts, could any god but Allah restore them to you?

See how We make plain to them Our revelations. And yet they turn away.

Sura: 6, Ayat: 46.

It is Allah Who splits the seed and the fruit – stone. He brings forth the living from the dead, and the dead from the living. Such is Allah. How then can you turn away from Him?

He kindles the light of dawn. He has ordained the night for rest and the sun and the moon for reckoning.

Such is the ordinance of Allah, the Mighty, the Knowing.

It is He that has created for you the stars, so that they may guide you in the darkness of land and sea. We have made plain Our revelations to men who understand.

It was He that created you from one being and furnished you with a dwelling and a resting-place. We have made plain (Our) revelations to men of understanding.

He sends down water from the sky, and with it brings forth the buds of every plant. From these We bring forth green foliage and close-growing grain, palm-trees laden with clusters of dates within reach, vineyards and olive groves and pomegranates (which are) alike and different. Behold their fruits when they bear fruit and ripen. Surely in these there are signs for true believers.

Sura: 6, Ayat: 95–99.

He sends forth the winds as carriers of the good news of His mercy, and when they have carried up a heavy cloud, He drives it on to some dead land and lets water fall upon it, bringing forth all manner of fruit. Thus He will raise the dead to life. Perchance you will take heed.

Good soil yields fruit by Allah's leave. But poor and scant are the fruits which spring from barren soil. Thus We make plain Our revelations to those who render thanks.

Sura: 7, Ayat: 57-58.

Were the people of those towns secure from being overtaken by Our punishment in the night whilst they were sleeping?

Were they secure from being overtaken by Our wrath in the morning while at their play?

Did they feel themselves secure from Allah's scheming? None feels secure from it except those who shall be lost.

Sura: 7, Ayat: 97–99.

Is it not plain to those who inherit the earth after its people (had gone) that if We pleased We could punish them for their sins and set a seal upon their hearts, leaving them bereft of hearing?

Sura: 7, Ayat: 100.

It was He that made the sun brightness and the moon light, ordaining the latter's phases that you may learn the number of years and the reckoning. He created them only to manifest the truth. He makes plain His revelations to men of understanding.

In the alternation of night and day, and in all that Allah has created in the heavens and the earth, there are signs for righteous men.

Sura: 10, Ayat: 5-6.

This present life is only like water which We send down from the clouds so that the luxuriant herbage sustaining man and beast may grow; until when the earth puts on its lovely garment and becomes adorned, and its people think that they are its masters, down comes Our scourge upon it, by night or in broad day, laying it waste, as though it has not blossomed yesterday. Thus We make plain Our revelations to thoughtful men.

Allah invites you to the Home of Peace. He guides whom He will to a straight path.

Sura: 10, Ayat: 24-25.

Say: 'Who provides for you from heaven and earth? Who has endowed you with sight and hearing? Who brings forth the living from the dead, and the dead from the living? Who ordains all things?'

They will reply: 'Allah.'

Say: 'Will you not take heed, then? Such is Allah, your true Lord. That which is not true must needs be false. How then can you turn away from Him?'

Thus the word of your Lord is made good; the evildoers have no faith.

Sura: 10, Ayat: 31-33.

Say: 'Behold what the heavens and the earth contain!' But neither signs nor warnings will avail the unbelievers.

Sura: 10, Ayat: 101.

Many are the marvels of the heavens and the earth; yet they pass them by and pay no heed to them. The greater part of them believe in Allah only if they associated others with Him.

Sura: 12, Ayat: 105-106.

Have they not travelled in the land and seen what was the end of those before them? Better is the world to come for those that keep from evil. Can you

not understand?

Sura: 12, Ayat: 109.

It was Allah Who raised the heavens without visible pillars. He then ascended His throne and forced the sun and the moon into His service, each pursuing an appointed course. He ordains all things. He makes plain His revelations so that you may firmly believe in meeting your Lord.

It was He who spread out the earth and placed upon it firm mountains and rivers. And of all fruits, He has put in it couples (male and female) and drew the veil of night over the day. Surely in these there are signs for thinking men.

Sura: 13, Ayat: 2-3.

And in the land, there are adjoining plots: gardens of vines and corn and palm-trees, the single and the clustered. They are watered with one water. Yet we make some excel others in taste. Surely in this there are signs for men of understanding.

Sura: 13, Ayat: 4.

Say: 'Who is the Lord of the heavens and earth?'

Say: 'Allah.'

Say: 'Why then have you chosen protectors besides Him, who, even to themselves, can do neither harm nor good?'

Say: 'Are the blind and the seeing alike? Does darkness resemble the light?'

Have those they associate with Allah brought into being a creation like His, so that both creations appear to them alike?

Say: 'Allah is the Creator of all things. He is the One, the Conqueror.'

Sura: 13, Ayat: 16.

Do you not see that Allah has created the heavens and the earth with truth? He can destroy you if He wills and bring into being a new creation: that is no difficult thing for Him.

Sura: 14, Ayat: 19-20.

It is Allah who made the heavens and the earth, and sends down water from the sky with which He brings forth fruits for your sustenance. He drives the ships which, by His leave, sail the ocean in your service. He has created rivers for your benefit, and the sun and the moon, which steadfastly pursue their courses. And He has subdued to you the night and the day. He grants you all that you ask Him. If you reckoned up Allah's favours, you could not count them. Truly, man is wicked and thankless.

Sura: 14, Ayat: 32–34.

We have spread out the earth and set upon it immovable mountains. We

have caused to grow in it from every ordained thing; and we have made in it means of subsistence for you and for him for whom you do not provide.

Sura: 15, Ayat: 19-20.

And there is not a thing but with Us are the storehouses of it; and We do not send it down except in a known measure. We send the fertility winds and send water from the sky from which We make you drink and which you cannot store.

Sura: 15, Ayat: 21-22.

And surely it is We who give life and death. We are the Inheritor.

We know those who have gone before, and those who will come. Your Lord will gather them all before Him. He is Wise, Knowing.

Sura: 15, Ayat: 23—25.

He created man from a little germ: yet he is a professed disputer. And the cattle He created for you. In them, you have warm clothing and (other) benefits. And of them you eat. And in them there is beauty for you when you bring them home and when you lead them to pasture.

They carry your burdens to a land, which you could not otherwise reach except with painful toil. Your Lord is Compassionate, Merciful.

(He has given you) horses, mules, and donkeys, which you may ride or use as ornaments; and He creates what you do not know.

It rests with Allah to show the right path. Some turn aside from it, but had He pleased, He would have guided you all aright.

Sura: 16, Ayat: 4—9.

It is He who sends down water from the sky, which provides drink for you and brings froth the trees on which your cattle feed. And thereby He brings up corn and olives, dates and grapes and all the fruits. Surely, in this there is a sign for thinking men.

Sura: 16, Ayat: 10-11.

He has made the night and the day, and the sun and the moon, subservient to you: the stars also serve you by His leave. Surely in this there are signs for men of understanding.

And what He created for you in the earth is of various hues: surely in this there is a sign for thoughtful men.

Sura: 16, Ayat: 12-13.

It is He who has subjected to you the ocean, so that you may eat of its fresh fish and bring up from it ornaments with which to adorn your persons. And you see the ships ploughing their course through it. (All this He has created)

that you may seek His bounty and render thanks to Him.

Sura: 16, Ayat: 14.

He set firm mountains upon the earth lest it should move away with you; and rivers, and roads, so that you may be rightly guided. By the stars, too, are men directed.

Sura: 16, Ayat: 15-16.

Is He, then, who has wrought the creation, like him who has created nothing? Will you not take heed?

Sura: 16, Ayat: 17.

(We sent) them with clear proofs and Books. And We revealed to you the Reminder (Quran) so that you may make clear to men what has been revealed to them, and that they may give thought.

Sura: 16, Ayat: 44.

Are those who plot evil confident that Allah will not cave in the earth beneath them, or that His scourge will not fall upon them whence they do not know? Or that He will not smite them in the course of their journeys when they cannot escape, or that He will not give them over to slow destruction? Yet your Lord is Compassionate and Merciful.

Sura: 16, Ayat: 45—47.

Allah sends down water from the sky with which He quickens the earth after its death. Surely in this there is a sign for men who listen.

Sura: 16, Ayat: 65.

In cattle too you have a worthy lesson. We give you to drink of that which is in their bellies, between the bowels and the blood-streams: pure milk, a pleasant (beverage) for those who drink it.

Sura: 16, Ayat: 66.

And (you have) the fruits of the palm and of the vine, from which you derive intoxicants and wholesome food.

Surely in this there is a sign for men of understanding.

Sura: 16, Ayat: 67.

Your Lord revealed to the bee, (saying): 'Build your homes in the mountains, in the trees, and in the hives which men shall make for you. Feed on every kind of fruit, and follow the trodden paths of your Lord.'

From its belly comes forth a fluid of many hues, a healing (drink) for men. Surely in this there is a sign for those who would give thought.

Sura: 16, Ayat: 68-69.

Allah created you, and He will cause you to die. Some of you shall have their lives prolonged to abject old age, when all that they once knew they shall know no more. Allah is Knowing, Mighty.

Sura: 16, Ayat: 70.

Allah has caused some of you to excel others in worldly possessions. Those who have been favoured do not give their wealth to those whom their right hands possess so as to be equal in that respect. Would they deny Allah's goodness?

Sura: 16, Ayat: 71.

Allah has given you wives from among yourselves, and through them He has granted you sons and grandsons. He has provided you with good things: will they then believe in falsehood and deny His favours?

Sura: 16, Ayat: 72.

Allah brought you out of your mothers' wombs devoid of all knowledge, and gave you ears and eyes and hearts, so that you may give thanks.

Sura: 16, Ayat: 78.

Do they not see the birds that wing their flight in heaven's vault? None sustains them but Allah. Surely in this there are signs for true believers.

Sura: 16, Ayat: 79.

Allah has given you houses to dwell in, and the skins of beasts for shelter, so that you may find them light on the day of wandering and on the day of halting; while from their wool, fur, and hair He has given you comfort and domestic goods for a time.

Sura: 16, Ayat: 80.

Allah has given you of what He has created shelter. And He has given you refuge in the mountains. He has furnished you with garments to protect you from the heat and with coats of armour to shield you in your wars. Thus He perfects His favours to you, so that you may submit to Him.

But if they turn away, your mission is only to give plain warning.

Sura: 16, Ayat: 81-82.

We made the night and the day two signs. And We blot out the sign of the night and make the sign of day shine forth so that you may seek the bounty of your Lord and learn the number of years and reckoning. We have made all things manifestly plain to you.

Sura: 17, Ayat: 12.

It is your Lord who drives ships at sea so that you may seek His bounty. He

is indeed Merciful towards you.

When at sea a misfortune befalls you, all but He of those to whom you pray forsake you; yet when He brings you safe to dry land, you turn your backs upon Him, Truly, man is ever thankless.

Are you confident that He will not cave in the earth beneath you, or let loose a deadly sand-storm upon you? Then you shall find none to protect you.

Or are you confident that He will not take you back into it, and smite you with a violent tempest and drown you for your thanklessness? Then you shall find none to help you against Us.

Sura: 17, Ayat: 66—69.

We have bestowed blessings on Adam's children and carried them by land and sea. We have provided them with good things and exalted them above many of Our creatures.

Sura: 17, Ayat: 70.

Nothing prevents men from having faith when guidance is revealed to them but the excuse: 'Could Allah have sent a human being as an apostle?'

Say: 'Had the earth been a safe place for angels to dwell in, We would have sent forth to them an angel from heaven as an apostle.'

Sura: 17, Ayat: 94-95.

Coin for them a simile about his life. It is like vegetation of the earth that flourishes when watered by the rain, soon turning into stubble which the wind scatters abroad. Allah has power over all things.

Wealth and children are the ornament of this life. But deeds of lasting merit are better with your Lord in reward and hope.

And (remember) the day when We shall blot out the mountains and you will see the earth a levelled plain; when We shall gather all mankind together, leaving not a soul behind.

They shall be ranged before your Lord, who will say to them: 'You have returned to Us as We created you at first. Yet you thought Our promise to you was not to be fulfilled.'

The book will be set down (before them), and you shall see the sinners dismayed at that which is inscribed in it. They shall say: 'Woe to us! What can this book mean? It omits nothing small or great: all are noted down! and they shall find their deeds recorded there. Your Lord will wrong no one.

Sura: 18, Ayat: 45—49.

Do not the disbelievers see that the heavens and the earth were one solid mass which we tore asunder, and that We made every living thing of water? Will they not have faith?

Sura: 21, Ayat: 30.

We set firm mountains upon the earth lest it should move away with them, and hewed out highways (in the rock) so that they might be rightly guided.

We made the heaven like a canopy and provided it with strong support: yet from its signs they turn away.

Sura: 21, Ayat: 31-32.

It was He who created the night and the day, and the sun and the moon; each floats in an orbit of its own.

Sura: 21, Ayat: 33.

Men, if you are in doubt about the Resurrection, remember that We first created you from dust, then from a life-germ, then from a clot, and then from a lump of flesh partly formed and partly unformed, so that We might manifest to you (Our power).

We cause to remain in the Wombs whatever We please for an appointed term, and then We bring you forth as infants, that you may grow up and reach your prime. Some of you die (young), and some live on to abject old age when all that they once knew they shall know no more.

And you see the earth dry and barren: but no sooner do We send down rain upon it than it begins to stir and swell, putting forth every kind of radiant bloom. That is because Allah is the Truth: He gives life to the dead and has power over all things.

And the Hour of Doom is sure to come — in this there is no doubt. And Allah will raise up those in the graves.

Sura: 22, Ayat: 5—7.

How many a town have We destroyed while it was sinful, so that it lies in ruins, and how many a deserted well and lofty palace!

Have they never journeyed through the land so that they may have hearts to reason with, or ears to hear with? It is not the eyes, but the hearts in the breasts, that are blind.

Sura: 22, Ayat: 45-46.

Allah is Truth, and Falsehood is all that they invoke besides Him. He is the Most High, the Supreme One.

Do you not see that Allah sends down water from the sky and forthwith the earth becomes green? Allah is Gracious, Knowing.

His is all that the heavens and the earth contain. He is the Self-sufficient, the Glorious One.

Sura: 22, Ayat: 62—64.

Do you not see that He has subdued to you all that is on the earth? He has also given you ships which sail the sea at His bidding. He holds the sky from falling down: (This it shall not do) except by His own will. Compassionate is

Allah, and Merciful to men.

Sura: 22, Ayat: 65.

It is He who has given you life, and He who will cause you to die and make you live again. Surely man is ungrateful.

Sura: 22, Ayat: 66.

O men, this is a parable. Listen to it. Those whom you invoke besides Allah could never create a single fly, though they combined to do this. And if a fly carried anything from them, they could never retrieve it. Powerless is the invoker and the invoked.

They do not have a right estimate of God's power. For Allah is powerful and Mighty.

Sura: 22, Ayat: 73-74.

We did create man from an essence of clay: then placed him, a life-germ, in a safe enclosure. The germ We made a clot of blood, and the clot a lump of flesh. This We fashioned into bones, then clothed the bones with flesh, and then produced it as another creation. Blessed be Allah, the noblest of creators!

You shall surely die hereafter, and be restored to life on the Day of Resurrection. We have created seven ways above you; of Our creation, We are never heedless.

We sent down water from the sky in due measure, and lodged it into the earth. But if We please, We can take it all away.

With it, We caused vineyards and palm-groves to spring up, yielding abundant fruit for your sustenance. Also a tree which grows on Mount Sinai and gives oil and relish for the eaters.

In the cattle, too, you have an example of Our power. You drink of that which is in their bellies, you eat their flesh, and gain other benefits from them besides. By them, as by ships that sail the sea, you are carried.

Sura: 23, Ayat: 12—22.

Should they not heed the Word of Allah?

Or was anything revealed to them that had not been revealed to their forefathers?

Or is it because they do not know their Apostle that they deny him?

Do they say he is possessed?

He has proclaimed to them the truth. But most of them abhor the truth.

Sura: 23, Ayat: 68—70.

It was He who gave you ears, eyes, and hearts: yet you are seldom thankful.

It was He who placed you on the earth, and before Him you shall be assembled.

It is He who gives life and death, and His is the alteration of the night and the day. Can you not understand?

Sura: 23, Ayat: 78—80.

Say: 'Whose is the earth and all that it contains? (Tell me) if you know the truth.'

'Allah's,' they will reply.

Say: 'Then will you not take heed?'

Say: 'Who is the Lord of the seven heavens, and of the Glorious Throne?'

'Allah,' they will reply.

Say: 'Will you keep from evil, then?'

Say: 'In whose hands is the sovereignty of all things, protecting all, while against Him there is no protection? Tell me, if you know the truth.'

'In Allah's,' they will reply.

Say: 'How then can you be so bewitched?'

Sura: 23, Ayat: 84—89.

Allah makes the night and the day succeed one another: surely in this there is lesson for clear-sighted men.

Allah created every animal from water. Some creep upon their bellies, others walk on two legs, and others on four. Allah creates what He pleases. He has power over all things.

Sura: 24, Ayat: 43—45.

It is He who drives the winds as harbingers of His mercy, and sends down pure water from the sky, so that He may give life to dead lands and provide drink for cattle and many people that We have created.

We have made plain to them Our revelations so that they may take heed. Yet most men decline to render thanks.

Sura: 25, Ayat: 48—50.

It was He who sent the two seas rolling, the one sweet and fresh, the other salt and bitter, and set a barrier between them, and an insurmountable obstruction.

It was He who created man from water and gave him kindred of blood and of marriage. Your Lord is All-Powerful.

Yet the unbelievers worship that which can neither help nor harm them. Surely the unbeliever is a helper (of evil) against his Lord.

Sura: 25, Ayat: 53—55.

Do they not see the earth, how We have brought forth in it all kinds of beneficial plants? Surely in this there is a sign; yet most of them do not believe.

Your Lord is the Mighty One, the Merciful.

Sura: 26, Ayat: 7—9.

Do they wish to hasten Our punishment? (Think!) If We let them live in ease for many years, and then the scourge with which they are threatened falls upon them, of what avail will their past enjoyments be to them?

Sura: 26, Ayat: 204—207

(Surely worthier is He) who made the heavens and the earth. He sends down water from the sky, bringing forth gardens of delight. Try as you may, you cannot cause such trees to grow.' Another god besides Allah? Yet they set up equals with Him.

(And surely worthier is He) who has established the earth and watered it with running rivers; who has set mountains upon it and placed a barrier between the Two seas. Another god besides Allah? Indeed most of them are ignorant men.

(Surely worthier is He) who answers the oppressed when they cry out to Him and relieves affliction, and makes you inheritors of the earth. Another god besides Allah? How little you reflect!

(Surely wortheir is He) who guides you in the darkness of land and sea and sends the winds as harbingers of His mercy. Another god besides Allah? Exalted be He above their idols!

(Surely worthier is He) who originates the creation and then reproduces it; who gives you sustenance from earth and sky. Another god besides Allah? Say: 'Show us your proof, if what you say be true!'

Sura: 27, Ayat: 60—64.

Do they not see how We have made the night for them to rest in and the day to give them light? Surely there are signs in this for true believers.

Sura: 27, Ayat: 86.

How many a nation have We destroyed that once flourished in wanton ease! Its dwellings are but rarely inhabited; We were its only heirs.

Sura: 28, Ayat: 58.

Say: 'Think! If Allah should enshroud you in perpetual night till the Day of Resurrection, what other god could give you light! Will you not hear?'

Say: 'Think! If Allah should give you perpetual day until the Resurrection, what other god could bring you the night to sleep in? Will you not see?'

In His mercy He has given you the night that you may rest in it, and the day that you may seek His bounty and render thanks.

Sura: 28, Ayat: 71—73.

Do they not see how Allah initiates the Creation, and then reproduces it? That is easy enough for Allah.

Sura: 29, Ayat: 19.

Say: 'Roam the earth and see how Allah initiated the Creation'. Then Allah will create a later Creation. Allah has power over all things.

Sura: 29, Ayat: 20.

We coin these similes for the instruction of men; but none will grasp their meaning except the wise.

Allah has created the heavens and the earth in truth. Surely in this there is a sign for true believers.

Sura: 29, Ayat: 43-44.

If you ask them who it is who has created the heavens and the earth and subjected the sun and the moon, they will say: 'Allah.' How then can they turn away from Him?

Sura: 29, Ayat: 61.

If you ask them who it is that sends down water from the sky and thereby quickens the earth after its death, they will reply: 'Allah.' Say: 'Praise, then, be to Allah!' But most of them do not understand.

Sura: 29, Ayat: 63.

The life of this world is but a sport and a pastime. It is the abode in the Hereafter that (is the true) life: if they but knew it.

Sura: 29, Ayat: 64.

Do they not see how We have made a safe sanctuary while all around them men are carried off by force? Would they believe in falsehood and deny Allah's goodness?

Sura: 29, Ayat: 67.

They know some outward show of this life, but of the life to come they are heedless. Have they not considered that Allah did not create the heavens and the earth and all that lies between them except in truth, and for an appointed term? Yet most men deny that they will ever meet their Lord.

Have they never journeyed through the land and seen what was the fate of their forebears? Far mightier were they; they tilled the land and built upon it more than these have built. And to them, too, their apostles came with undoubted signs. Allah did not wrong them, but they wronged themselves.

Sura: 30, Ayat: 7—9.

He brings forth the living from the dead, and the dead from the living, and revives the earth after its death. Likewise you shall be brought forth.

And of His signs is that He created you from dust and behold: you became men and multiplied throughout the earth. And of His signs is that He gave you wives from among yourselves, that you might live in tranquillity with them,

and put love and kindness in your hearts. Surely, there are signs in this for thinking men.

Sura: 30, Ayat: 19—21.

And of His signs are the creation of heaven and earth and the diversity of your tongues and colours. Surely there are signs in this for all mankind.

And of His signs is that you sleep at night and seek by day His bounty. Surely there are signs in this for those who hear.

And of His signs is that He shows you the lightning (to inspire) fear and hope. He sends down water from the sky, and with it, He quickens the earth after its death. Surely in this there are signs for men of understanding.

And of His signs is that the heaven and earth firm at His bidding. And when with one shout He will summon you out of the earth, you shall go out to Him.

Sura: 30, Ayat: 22—25.

When evil befalls men they turn in prayer to their Lord. But no sooner does He make them taste His mercy than some of them become polytheists, showing no gratitude for what We gave them. Enjoy yourselves (awhile), but (in the end) you shall know (your error),

Or have We revealed to them a sanction which enjoins that which they associate with Him?

When We give men a taste of mercy, they rejoice in it, but when evil befalls them through their own fault they grow despondent. Do they not see that Allah gives abundantly to whom He will and sparingly to whom He pleases? Surely there are signs in this for true believers.

Sura: 30, Ayat: 33—37.

It is Allah who has created you and given you your sustenance. He will cause you to die hereafter and will then bring you back to life. Can any of your partners do the least of these?

Sura: 30, Ayat: 40.

Say: 'Roam the earth and see what was the end of those who flourished before you. Most of them worshipped others besides Allah.'

Sura: 30, Ayat: 42.

Behold then the tokens of Allah's mercy; how He gives fresh life to the earth after its death. He it is who brings back the dead to life. He has power over all things.

Sura: 30, Ayat: 50.

He created the heavens without visible pillars and set immovable mountains on the earth lest it should shake with you. He dispersed upon it all manner of beasts, and sent down water from the sky with which He caused all

kinds of goodly plants to grow.

Such is Allah's creation: now show me what the other besides Him created. Truly, the unbelievers are in the grossest error.

Sura: 31, Ayat: 10-11.

Do you not see how Allah has subjected to you all that the heavens and the earth contain and lavished on you both His visible and unseen favours? Yet some would argue about Allah without knowledge or guidance or illuminating scriptures.

Sura: 31, Ayat: 20-21.

Do you not see how Allah causes the night to pass into the day and the day into the night and has forced the sun and the moon (into His service), each running for an appointed term? Allah is cognizant of all your actions. Verily He is the Truth, while that which they invoke besides Him is false. Allah is the Most High, the Supreme One.

Do you not see how the ships speed upon the ocean by Allah's grace, so that He may reveal to you His wonders? Surely there are signs in this for every steadfast, thankful man.

When the waves, like giant shadows envelop them, they pray to Allah with all devotion. But no sooner does He bring them safe to land than some of them falter (between faith and unbelief). Truly, only the treacherous and the ungrateful deny Our revelations.

Sura: 31, Ayat: 29—32.

Who created all things in the best way. He first created man from clay, then bred his offspring from a drop of paltry fluid. He then moulded him and breathed into him of His spirit. He gave you eyes and ears and hearts: yet you are seldom thankful.

Sura: 32, Ayat: 7—9.

Do they not know how many generations We have destroyed before them amid whose dwellings they walk. Surely in this there are clear signs. Will they not then heed?

Do they not see how We drive the rain to the parched lands and bring forth therewith crops of which they and their cattle eat? Have they no eyes to see with?

Sura: 32, Ayat: 26-27.

Men, bear in mind Allah's goodness towards you. Is there any other creator who provides you from heaven and earth? There is no god but Him. How then can you turn away?

Sura: 35, Ayat: 3.

Allah created you from dust, then from a life-germ. Then he made you pairs (males and females). No female conceives or is delivered without His knowledge. No man grows old or has his life cut short but in accordance with His decree. All this is easy for Allah.

The two seas are not alike. The one is fresh, sweet and pleasant to drink from, while the other is salt and bitter. From each you eat fresh fish and bring up ornaments to wear. And you see the ships plough their course through them so that you may seek His bounty and give thanks.

He causes the night to pass into the day and the day into the night. He has forced the sun and the moon into His service, each running for an appointed term. Such is Allah, your Lord. His is the sovereignty. Those whom you invoke besides Him have power over nothing. If you pray to them they cannot hear you, and even if they hear you they cannot answer you. On the day of Resurrection they will reject your associating others with Allah. None can tell you (the truth) like the One who is All-Knowing.

Sura: 35, Ayat: 11–14.

Did you not see how Allah sent down water from the sky and brought forth fruits of different hues? In the mountains there are streaks of various shades of red and white, and jet-black rocks. Men, beasts, and cattle have their different colours, too.

From among His servants, it is the learned who fear Allah. Allah is Mighty and Forgiving.

Sura: 35, Ayat: 27-28.

Have they not journeyed through the land and seen the fate of those who went before them, nations far mightier than they?

There is nothing in heaven or earth beyond the power of Allah. All-Knowing is He and Mighty.

Sura: 35, Ayat: 44.

Let the once-dead earth be a sign to them. We gave it life, and from it produced grain for their sustenance. We provided it with the palm and the vine and watered it with gushing springs, so that they might feed on its fruit. It was not their hands that made all this. Should they not give thanks?

Glory be to Him who created pairs of all the things which the earth grows and of their own kind and that of which they have no knowledge.

A sign for them is the night. From it We draw out the day – and they are plunged in darkness.

The sun hastens to its resting-place: that is the decree of the Mighty One, the All-Knowing.

And for the moon, We have ordained mansions till it becomes again as an old dry palm-branch.

The sun is not allowed to overtake the moon, nor does the night outpace the

day. Each in its own orbit runs.

Sura: 36, Ayat: 33–40.

Do they not see how among the things Our hands have made We have created for them the cattle of which they are masters? We have subjected these to them, that they may ride on some and eat the flesh of others; and they draw other benefits and (diverse) drinks from them. Will they not give thanks?

Sura: 36, Ayat: 71–73.

Is man not aware that We created him from a little life-germ?

Yet he is an open opponent. He makes comparisons for us, and forgets his own creation. He asks: 'Who will give life to rotten bones?'

Say: 'He will give them life again We created them at first: He has knowledge of every (kind of) creation; He who gives you from the green tree a fire with which you light your fuel.'

Has He who created the heavens and the earth no power to create their like? That He surely has. He is the All-Knowing Creator. When He decrees a thing He need only say: 'Be.' and it is.

Glory be to Him who has control of all things, and to Him you will all be brought back.

Sura: 36, Ayat: 77–83.

He created the heavens and the earth in truth. He causes the night to overlap the day and the day to overlap the night. He made the sun and the moon obedient to Him, each running for an appointed term. He is the Mighty, the Forgiving One.

He created you from a single being, then from that being He created its mate. He has given you eight of the cattle in pairs. He creates you in your mothers' wombs by stages in threefold darkness.

Such is Allah, your Lord. His is the Sovereignty. There is no god but Him. How, then, can you turn away from Him?

Sura: 39, Ayat: 5-6.

Do you not see how Allah sends down water from the sky which penetrates the earth and gathers in springs beneath? He brings forth plants of various colours. They wither, they turn yellow, and then He turns them to chaff. Surely in this there is an admonition for men of understanding.

Is he whose heart Allah has opened to Islam, thus receiving light from his Lord, (like him who disbelieves)? But woe to those whose hearts are hardened against the remembrance of Allah! Truly, they are in the grossest error.

Sura: 39, Ayat: 21-22.

It is He who reveals to you His signs and sends down for you sustenance

from the sky. Yet none takes heed except he who turns to Him.

Sura: 40, Ayat: 13.

It was Allah who made for you the night to rest in and the day to (give you) light. Allah is bountiful to men, yet most men do not give thanks.

Such is Allah your Lord, the Creator of all things. There is no god but Him. How then can you turn away from Him?

Sura: 40, Ayat: 61-62.

It is Allah who has given you the earth for a dwelling-place and the sky for a canopy. He has moulded your bodies and given you a comely shape and provided you with good things.

Such is Allah, your Lord. Blessed be Allah, Lord of the Creation.

Sura: 40, Ayat: 64.

It was He who created you from dust, then from a life-germ, and then a clot of blood. He then brings you forth as a child, then (lets you) reach manhood, and then grow into old age — though some of you die young — so that you may reach an appointed term, and understand.

Sura: 40, Ayat: 67.

It is He who ordains life and death. If He decrees a thing, He need only say: 'Be,' and it is.

Sura: 40, Ayat: 68.

It is Allah who has provided you with cattle, that you may ride on some and eat of the flesh of others — many benefits you have from them — and that you may satisfy through them a desire in your hearts. On them and on ships you are carried.

He reveals to you His signs. Which of Allah's signs do you deny?

Sura: 40, Ayat: 79—81.

Have they never journeyed through the land and seen what was the end of those who have gone before them? More numerous were they and far greater in prowess and in monuments (left behind); yet all their labours were of no use to them.

Sura: 40, Ayat: 82.

Say: 'Do you indeed disbelieve in Him who created the earth in two days? And do you set up equals with Him? He is the Lord of the Worlds.'

He set upon the earth firm mountains towering high above it. He pro-

nounced His blessing upon it and in four days measured therein sustenance alike for those who ask. Then He turned to the sky, which was smoke, and to it and to the earth He said: 'Come both of you willingly, or unwillingly.'

'We do come willingly, they answered.

Sura: 41, Ayat: 9–11.

And among His signs is that you see the earth dry and barren: but when He sends down rain upon it, it stirs and swells. He who gives it life will restore the dead to life. Allah has power over all things.

Sura: 41, Ayat: 39.

Say: 'Think: if this (Quran) is indeed from Allah and you deny it, who can err more than he who openly defies Him?'

Sura: 41, Ayat: 52.

Creator of the heavens and the earth, He has given you wives from among yourselves and cattle, male and female. By this means He multiplies you. Nothing can be compared with Him. He alone hears all and sees all.

His are the keys of the heavens and the earth. He gives abundantly to whom He will and sparingly to whom He pleases. He has knowledge of all things.

Sura: 42, Ayat: 11-12.

Among His signs is the creation of the heavens and the earth and the living things which He has dispersed over them. If He will, He can gather them all together.

Sura: 42, Ayat: 29.

Yet, if you ask them* who created the heavens and the earth, they will surely answer: 'The Almighty, the All-Knowing, created them.'

(It is He) who has made the earth a resting-place for you and made in it routes for you that you may find your way; who sends down water from the sky in due measure and thereby quickens the dead land — even thus you shall be restored to life; who has created all living things in pairs and made for you the ships and beasts on which you ride, so that you mount upon their backs, and as you sit firm on them you may recall the goodness of your Lord and say: "Glory to Him who has subjected these to us. But for Him we could never have accomplished this. To our Lord we shall all return."

Would Allah choose daughters from those He has created for Himself and choose sons for you?

Yet when the birth of one of those (daughters) they attribute to the Merciful is announced to one of them, his face darkens and he is filled with gloom. Would they ascribe to Allah females who adorn themselves with trinkets and are powerless in disputation?

***The Makkans**

They regard as females the angels who are Allah's servants. Did they witness their creation? Their claims shall be noted down and they shall be closely questioned.

Sura: 43, Ayat: 9–19.

They also say: 'Why was this Quran not revealed to some great man from the two towns?' *

Is it they who apportion your Lord's blessings? it is We who apportion to them their livelihoods in this world, exalting some in rank above others, so that the one may take the other into his service. Better is your Lord's mercy than all their hoarded treasures.

Sura: 43, Ayat: 31-32.

In your own creation, and in the beasts that are scattered far and near, are signs for true believers; in the alternation of night and day, in the sustenance Allah sends down from heaven with which He revives the earth after its death, and in the marshalling of the winds, are signs for men of understanding.

Such are the revelations of Allah. We recite them to you in all truth. But in what revelation will they believe after (they deny) Allah Himself (and all His signs)?

Sura: 45, Ayat: 3–6.

It is Allah who has subdued to you the ocean so that ships may sail upon it at His bidding; so that you may seek His bounty and render thanks to Him.

He has subjected to you what the heavens and the earth contain; all is from Him. Surely there are signs in this for thinking men.

Sura: 45, Ayat: 12-13.

Say: 'Think if this Quran is indeed from Allah and you reject it, and if a witness from the Children of Israel has vouched for the like and accepted Islam, while you yourselves deny it with scorn (how unjust you are). Truly, Allah does not guide the wrongdoers.'

Sura: 46, Ayat: 10.

Do they not see that Allah who created the heavens and the earth and was not wearied by their creation can restore the dead to life? Yes, He has power over all things.

Sura: 46, Ayat: 33.

How many a city mightier than your own city, which has cast you out, have We destroyed and there was none to help them.**

---

* Makkah and Madina **Muhammad

Can he who follows the guidance of his Lord be compared to him whose misdeeds are made to seem fair to him, and to those who follow their desires?

Sura: 47, Ayat: 13-14.

Have they never observed the sky above them (and marked) how We built it up and furnished it with ornaments, leaving no crack (in its expanse)?

We spread out the earth and set upon it immovable mountains. We brought forth in it all kinds of delectable plants — a lesson and an admonition to every penitent servant.

We sent down blessed water from the sky with which We brought forth gardens and the harvest grain, and tall palm — trees laden with clusters of dates, a sustenance for men; thereby giving new life to some dead land. Such shall be the Resurrection.

Sura: 50, Ayat: 6—11.

How many generations, far greater in prowess, have We destroyed before them! They searched the entire land: but could they find a refuge? Surely in this there is a lesson for every man who has a heart or gives an ear and is aware.

Sura: 50, Ayat: 36-37

On earth there are signs for firm believers; and also in yourselves. Can you not see?

Sura: 51, Ayat: 20-21.

We built the heaven with Our might, giving it a vast expanse, and stretched the earth beneath it. Gracious is He who spread it out. And all things We made in pairs, so that you may give thought.

Sura: 51, Ayat: 47—49.

Were they created out of the void? Or were they their own creators?
Did they create the heavens and the earth? Surely they have no faith!

Sura: 52, Ayat: 35-36.

That all things shall in the end return to Allah; that it is Allah who moves to weeping and laughter and ordains life and death; that Allah created the sexes, the male and the female, from a drop of ejected semen, and will create all things anew; that it is He who gives wealth and contentment; that He is the Lord of Sirius;* that it was He who destroyed ancient Aad and Thamud, sparing no one, and before them the people of Nuh who were more unjust and more tyrannical. The Mu'tafikah He also ruined, so that there fell on them what fell on those.**

---

* The Dog-star, worshipped by the pagan Arabs. **The ruined cities where Lut's people lived.

Which then of your Lord's blessings would you deny?

Sura: 53, Ayat: 42—55.

And in the past We destroyed your fellows. Will you not take warning?

Sura: 54, Ayat: 51.

He created man and taught him articulate speech.

The sun and the moon pursue their ordered course. The plants and the trees bow down in adoration.

He raised the heaven on high and set the balance, that you might not transgress the balance.

Sura: 55, Ayat: 3—8.

He laid the earth for His creations. Therein are fruits and blossom — bearing palm, chaff — covered grains and scented herbs. Which of your Lord's blessings would you deny?

Sura: 55, Ayat: 10—13.

He has let loose the two seas: they meet one another. Between them stands a barrier which they cannot overrun. Which of your Lord's blessings would you deny?

Pearls and corals come from both. Which of your Lord's blessings would you deny?

His are the ships that sail like mountains upon the ocean. Which of your Lord's blessings would you deny?

All who live on earth are doomed to die. And the face of your Lord will abide for ever, in all its majesty and glory. Which of your Lord's blessings would you deny?

All those in heaven and earth beseech Him. Everyday He exercises His power. Which of your Lord's blessings would you deny?

Sura: 55, Ayat: 19—30.

Consider the seeds you grow. Is it you that give them growth or We? If We pleased We could turn your harvest into chaff, so that, filled with wonderment, (you would exclaim): 'We are laden with debts! Surely we are deprived.'

Consider the water which you drink. Was it you that brought it down from the cloud or We? If We pleased, We could make it salty. Why then do you not give thanks?

Observe the fire which you light. Is it you that create its wood, or We? We have made it a reminder for man, and a comfort for the wayfarer of the desert.

Sura: 56, Ayat: 63—73.

Know that Allah restores the earth to life after its death. We have made plain to you Our revelations that you may grow in wisdom.

Sura: 57, Ayat: 17.

Do you see any fault in the work of the Merciful? Turn up your eyes: can you detect any rift?

Then look once more and yet again: your eyes will in the end grow dim and weary.

Sura: 67, Ayat: 3-4.

Whether you speak in secret or aloud, He knows what is in your hearts. Shall He who has created all things not know? He is Gracious and All-Knowing.

It is He who has subdued the earth to you. Walk about its regions and eat of His provisions. To Him all shall return (at the Resurrection).

Sura: 67, Ayat: 13—15.

Are you confident that He who is in heaven will not cause the earth to cave in beneath you and (cause you) to be swallowed by it as it shakes?

Are you confident that He who is in heaven will not let loose on you a sandy whirlwind? You shall before long know how (terrible) was My warning.

Those who have gone before you also denied their apostles: but how terrible was My rejection!

Sura: 67, Ayat: 16—18.

Do they not see the birds above their heads, spreading their wings and closing them? None save the Merciful sustains them. He observes all things.

Who is it that will defend you like an entire army, if not the Merciful? Truly, the unbelievers are in error.

Sura: 67, Ayat: 19-20.

Who will provide for you if He withholds His sustenance? Yet they persist in arrogance and in rebellion.

Who is more rightly guided, he that goes grovelling on his face, or he that walks upright upon a straight path?

Sura: 67, Ayat: 21-22.

Say: 'It is He who has created you and given you ears and eyes and hearts. Yet you are seldom thankful.'

Sura: 67, Ayat: 23.

Say: 'Think: if all the water that you have were to sink down into the earth, who would give you running water in its place?

Sura: 67, Ayat: 30.

We sent forth Nuh to his people, saying: 'Give warning to your people before a woeful scourge overtakes them.'

He said: 'My people I come to warn you plainly. Serve Allah and fear Him, and obey me. He will forgive you your sins and respite you till an appointed time. When Allah's time arrives, none shall put it back. Would that you understood this!'

'Lord.' said Nuh, 'day and night I have called my people, but my call has only added to their aversion. Each time I call on them to seek Your pardon, they thrust their fingers in their ears and draw their cloaks over their heads, persisting in sin and bearing themselves with insolent pride. I called out loud to them, and appealed to them in public and in private. "Seek forgiveness of your Lord," I said. "He is ever ready to forgive you. He sends down for you abundant water from the sky and bestows upon you wealth and children. He provides you with gardens and rivers. Why do you deny the greatness of Allah when He has made you in stages? Can you not see how He created the seven heavens one above the other, placing in them the moon as a light and the sun as a lantern? Allah has brought you forth from the earth like a plant, and to the earth He will restore you. Then He will bring you back afresh. He has made the earth a vast expanse for you, so that you may walk in its spacious paths." '

Nuh said: 'Lord, my people have disobeyed me and followed those whose wealth and offspring only hastened their perdition. They have devised an outrageous plot, and said: "Do not renounce your gods. Do not forsake Wadd or Sowa or Yaghuth or Ya'uq or Nasr." They have led numerous men astray. You surely drive the wrongdoers to further error.

And because of their sins they were overwhelmed by the Flood and cast into the Fire. They found none to help them besides Allah.

Sura: 71, Ayat: 1—25.

Does man think We shall never put his bones together again? Indeed, We can remould his very fingers!....

Sura: 75, Ayat: 3—5.

Does man think that he will be left aimless? Was he not a drop of ejected semen? Then he became a clot of blood; then Allah created and moulded him and made of him the pair of male and female. Is He then not able to raise the dead to life?

Sura: 75, Ayat: 36—40.

Surely there came over man a period of time when he was nothing that mattered. We have created man from sperm mixed (with ovum) to put him to proof. So we have endowed him with sight and hearing. We have shown him the right path, whether he be grateful or ungrateful.

Sura: 76, Ayat: 1—3.

Did We not spread the earth like a bed and raise the mountains like pegs?

And (have We not) created you in pairs and gave you rest in sleep? We made the night a mantle, and ordained the day for work. We built above you seven mighty heavens and placed in them a shining lamp. We sent down abundant water from the clouds, bringing forth grain and varied plants, and gardens thick with foliage.

Sura: 78, Ayat: 6—16.

Are you harder to create than the heaven which He has built? He raised it high and fashioned it, giving darkness to its night and brought out its light.

And the earth He extended after that; and then drew from it water and pastures. And the mountains He fixed — a provision for you and your cattle.

Sura: 79, Ayat: 27—33.

Confound man! How ungrateful he is.

From what did Allah create him? From a little life-germ He created him and proportioned him. He makes his path smooth, then causes him to die and stows him in a grave. He will surely bring him back to life if He pleases. Yet he declines to do His bidding.

Let man reflect on the food he eats: how We pour down the rain in torrents and cleave the earth asunder; how We bring forth the corn, the grapes, and the fresh vegetation; the olive and the palm, the thickets, the fruit-trees and green pasture, for you and for your cattle to delight in.

Sura: 80, Ayat: 17—32.

O man! What evil has enticed you away from your gracious Lord who created you, gave you an upright form, and well-proportioned you? In whatever shape He willed He could have surely moulded you.

No, you deny the Last Judgement. Yet there are guardians watching over you, noble recorders who know of all what you do.

Sura: 82, Ayat: 6—12.

Do they not think that they will be raised to life upon a fateful day, the day when all mankind will stand before the Lord of the Worlds?

Sura: 83, Ayat: 4—6.

Why then do they not have faith, or kneel in prayer when the Quran is read to them?

The unbelievers deny it; but Allah knows best the falsehood they believe in. Therefore proclaim to all a woeful doom.

Sura: 84, Ayat: 20—24.

For every soul there is a guardian watching over it. Let man reflect from what he is created. He is created from ejected fluid that issues from between

the loins and the ribs.

Surely He has power to bring him back to life.

Sura: 86, Ayat: 4–8.

Praise the Name of your Lord, the Most High, who has created all things and well proportioned them; who has ordained (their) destinies and guided (them); who brings forth green pasture, then turns it to withered grass.

Sura: 87, Ayat: 1–5.

Do they not reflect on the camels, how they were created? The heaven, how it was raised up? The mountains, how they were set down? The earth, how it was levelled flat?

Sura: 88, Ayat: 17–20.

We created man into toil and strife.

Does he think that none has power over him? He will (boastfully) say: 'I have wasted vast wealth.' Does he think that none observes him?

Have We not given him two eyes, a tongue, and two lips, and shown him the two highways (of good and evil)? Yet he would not scale the height.

Sura: 90, Ayat: 4–11.

What, then, can after this make you deny the Last Judgement?

Is Allah not the best of judges?

Sura: 95, Ayat: 7-8.

Is he not aware that when those in the graves are raised and what is in the breasts is laid open, their Lord on that day will be knowing?

Sura: 100, Ayat: 9–11.

Have you not considered how Allah dealt with the Masters of the Elephant?*

Did He not foil their strategem and send against them flocks of birds which pelted them with claystones, so that they became like plants cropped by cattle?

Sura: 105, Ayat: 1–5.

---

*The allusion is to the expeditions of Abraha against Makkah.
It took place in the year in which Muhammad was born.

In the name of Allah, The Compassionate, The Merciful

UNITY OF GOD

Say: 'Men.! If you are in doubt concerning my religion, (know that) I worship none of those you serve besides Allah, but I serve Allah who will cause you to die for I am commanded to be one of the faithful, and (I was bidden): "Set your face uprightly towards religion, and do not be a polytheist. Do not pray besides God to anything which can neither help nor harm you, for if you do you will become a wrongdoer.

Sura: 10, Ayat: 104–106.

I have left the faith of those that disbelieve in Allah and deny the life to come. I follow the faith of my fathers, Ibrahim, Ishaq, and Yaqub. We must never serve any besides Allah. Such is the gift which Allah has bestowed upon us and all mankind. Yet most men do not give thanks.

My two fellow-prisoners! Are sundry gods better than Allah, the One, the Conqueror? Those whom you serve besides Him are nothing but names which you and your fathers have invented and for which Allah has revealed no sanction. Judgement rests with Allah only. He has commanded you to worship none but Him. That is the true faith: yet most men do not know.

Sura: 12, Ayat: 37–40.

Say: 'Praise be to Allah who has never begotten a son; who has no partner in His Sovereignty; who needs none to defend Him from humiliation.' Proclaim His greatness.

Sura: 17, Ayat: 111.

In the name of Allah, The Compassionate, The Merciful

THE GLORIOUS NAMES OF ALLAH

Allah has the Most Excellent Names. Call on Him by His names and keep away from those that pervert them. They shall be punished for their misdeeds.

Sura: 7, Ayat: 180.

Compare none with Allah: He has knowledge, but you have not.

Sura: 16, Ayat: 74.

Say: 'Call on Allah or on Al-Rahman. By whatever name you call (is well). His are the Most Beautiful Names.

Pray neither with a loud voice nor with a low one, but seek between these extremes a middle course.

Sura: 17, Ayat: 110.

He is Allah. There is no god but Him. His are the Most Beautiful Names.

Sura: 20, Ayat: 8.

He is Allah, the Creator, the Originator, the Modeller. His are the Most Gracious Names. All that is in heaven and earth glorifies Him. He is the Mighty, the Wise One.

Sura: 59, Ayat: 24.

MAN'S BIRTH
AND
DEATH

(2)

In the name of Allah, The Compassionate, The Merciful

THE STORY OF THE BIRTH OF MAN

Men, have fear of your Lord, Who created you from a single soul. From that soul He created its mate, and through them He bestrewed the earth with countless men and women.

Fear Allah, in Whose name you plead with one another, and honour the mothers who bore you. Allah is everwatching over you.

Sura: 4, Ayat: 1.

Your Lord said to the angels: 'I am creating man from dry clay, from black moulded loam. When I have fashioned him and breathed of My spirit into him, kneel down and prostrate yourselves before him.'

Sura: 15, Ayat: 28-29.

(Satan) said: 'Since You have left me in error, I will seduce mankind on earth: I will seduce them all, except those that faithfully serve you.'

He replied: 'This the right course for Me. You shall have no power over My servants, except the sinners who follow you. They are all destined for Hell.'

Sura: 15, Ayat: 39—43.

He created man from a little germ: yet he is a professed disputer.

Sura: 16, Ayat: 4.

And when We said to the angels: 'Prostrate yourselves before Adam,' they all prostrated themselves except Satan, who refused.

'Adam,' We said, 'This is your enemy and your wife's. Let him not turn you out of Paradise and plunge you into affliction. Here you shall not hunger or be naked; you shall not thirst, or feel the scorching heat.'

But Satan whispered to him, saying: 'Shall I show you the Tree of Immortality and a kingdom which never decays?

They both ate of its fruit, so that they beheld their nakedness and began to cover themselves with leaves. Thus Adam disobeyed his Lord and went astray.

Then his Lord had mercy on him; He relented towards him and rightly guided him.

Sura: 20, Ayat: 116−122.

Allah brings His creatures into being and then He reproduces them. To Him He will recall you all.

Sura: 30, Ayat: 11.

In the name of Allah, The Compassionate, The Merciful

SOUL

Your Lord said to the angels: 'I am creating man from dry clay, from black moulded loam. When I have fashioned him and breathed of My spirit into him, kneel down and prostrate yourselves before him.'

Sura: 15, Ayat: 28-29.

They put questions to you about the Spirit. Say: 'The Spirit is by my Lord's command. Little indeed is the knowledge vouchsafed to you.'

Sura: 17, Ayat: 85.

In the name of Allah, The Compassionate, The Merciful

DEATH

No one dies unless Allah permits. The term of every life is fixed. And he that desires the reward of this world, We shall give him of it; and he that desires the reward of the life to come, We shall give him of it. And We will reward the thankful.

Sura: 3, Ayat: 145.

O believers, do not follow the example of the infidels, who say of their brothers when they meet death abroad or in battle: 'Had they stayed with us, they would not have died, nor would they have been killed.' Allah will make that a regret in their hearts. It is Allah Who ordains life and death. He has knowledge of all your actions.

Sura: 3, Ayat: 156.

If you should die or be slain in the cause of Allah, His forgiveness and His mercy would surely be better than all the riches they amass. If you should die or be slain, before Him you shall all be gathered.

Sura: 3, Ayat: 157-158.

Every soul shall taste death. You shall receive your rewards only on the Day of Resurrection. Whoever is spared Hell and is admitted to Paradise shall surely gain (his end); for the life of this world is nothing but a fleeting vanity.

Sura: 3, Ayat: 185.

Wherever you be, death will overtake you: though you put yourselves in lofty towers.'

When they are blessed with good fortune, they say: 'This is from Allah.' But when evil befalls them, they say: 'The fault was yours.'

Say to them: 'All is from Allah!'

What has come over these men that they should show such lack of understanding?

Sura: 4, Ayat: 78.

It is He Who has created you from clay. He has decreed a term for you (in this world) and another one set with Him (in the next). Yet you are still in doubt.

Sura: 6, Ayat: 2.

'He reigns supreme over His servants. He sends forth guardians who watch over you and carry away your souls without fail when death overtakes you.

Sura: 6, Ayat: 61.

Could you but see the wrongdoers when death overwhelms them! With hands outstretched, the angels (will say): 'Yield up your souls. You shall be rewarded with a shameful punishment this day, for you have said of Allah what is untrue and scorned His revelations. And now you have returned to Us, alone, as We created you at first, leaving behind all that We have bestowed on you. Nor do We see with you your intercessors, those whom you claimed to be the partners (of Allah). Broken are the ties which bound you, and that which you presumed has failed you.'

Sura: 6, Ayat: 93-94.

Now surely to Allah belongs all that the heavens and the earth contain. The Promise of Allah is true, though most of them may not know. It is He Who ordains life and death, and to Him you shall all return.

Sura: 10, Ayat: 55.

Every soul shall taste death. We will prove you all with good and evil by way of trial. To Us you shall be recalled.

Sura: 21, Ayat: 35.

He that hopes to meet his Lord (must know) that Allah's appointed hour is sure to come. He alone hears all and knows all.

Sura: 29, Ayat: 5.

Every soul shall taste death, and in the end you shall return to Us.

Sura: 29, Ayat: 57.

It is Allah Who has created you and given you your sustenance. He will cause you to die hereafter and will then bring you back to life.

Sura: 30, Ayat: 40.

Say: 'The angel of death, who has been given charge of you, will carry off your souls. Then to your Lord you shall all return.'

Sura: 32, Ayat: 11.

Say: 'Nothing will your flight avail you. If you escaped from death or

slaughter, you would enjoy this world only for a little while.'

Sura: 33, Ayat: 16.

Allah takes away men's souls upon their death, and those that do not die during their sleep. Those who are doomed He keeps with Him, and restores the others for a time ordained. Surely there are signs in this for thinking men.

Sura: 39, Ayat: 42.

And when the agony of death justly overtakes him, they will say: 'This is the fate you have striven to avoid.'

Sura: 50, Ayat: 19.

It was We that ordained death among you. Nothing can hinder Us from replacing you by others like yourselves or transforming you into beings you know nothing of.

Sura: 56, Ayat: 60-61.

Say: 'The death from which you shrink is sure to overtake you. Then you shall be sent back to Him Who knows the visible and the unseen, and He will declare to you all that you have done.'

Sura: 62, Ayat: 8.

But Allah reprieves no soul when its term expires. Allah has knowledge of all your actions.

Sura: 63, Ayat: 11.

Blessed be He in Whose hands is all sovereignty: He has power over all things.

He created life and death that He might put you to the test and find out which of you acquitted himself best. He is the Mighty, the Forgiving one.

Sura: 67, Ayat: 1-2.

But when (man's soul) reaches the throat and it is said: 'Is there a magician to save him?'; and when he knows it is the final parting and the pangs of death assail him — on that day to your Lord he shall be driven.

Sura: 75, Ayat: 26—30.

In the name of Allah, The Compassionate, The Merciful

LIFE AFTER DEATH

Say: 'My Lord enjoins justice. Turn to Him wherever you kneel in prayer and call on Him with true devotion. You shall return to Him as He created you.'

Sura: 7, Ayat: 29.

'Vain are the deeds of those who disbelieve in Our signs and in the life to come.

Sura: 7, Ayat: 147.

And (remember) the day when We shall blot out the mountains and you will see the earth a levelled plain; when We shall gather all mankind together, leaving not a soul behind.

Sura: 18, Ayat: 47.

They say: 'There is this life and no other. We live and die; nothing but Time destroys us.' Surely of this they have no knowledge. They are merely guessing.

Sura: 45, Ayat: 24.

In the name of Allah, The Compassionate, The Merciful

INTERVAL BETWEEN DEATH & RESURRECTION

Until when death comes to a wrongdoer, he will say: 'Lord, let me go back, that I may do good works in the world I have left behind.'

Never! It is only a word which he will speak. Behind them there shall stand a barrier till the Day of Resurrection.

Sura: 23, Ayat: 99-100.

In the name of Allah, The Compassionate, The Merciful

DOOMSDAY

The day will surely come when each soul will be confronted with whatever good it has done. As for its evil deeds, it will wish they were a long way off. Allah admonishes you to fear Him. He is compassionate towards His servants.

Sura: 3, Ayat: 30.

Do not follow the example of those who became divided and opposed to one another after clear proofs had been given them. These shall be sternly punished on the day when some faces will be bright (with joy) and others blackened (with grief). To the black-faced sinners it will be said: 'Did you disbelieve after embracing the true faith? Taste then our scourge, for you were unbelievers! As for those whose faces will be bright, they shall abide forever in Allah's mercy.

Sura: 3, Ayat: 105–107.

Every soul shall taste death. You shall receive your rewards only on the Day of Resurrection. Whoever is spared Hell and is admitted to Paradise shall surely gain (his end); for the life of this world is nothing but a fleeting vanity.

Sura: 3, Ayat: 185.

If you avoid the grave sins you are forbidden, We shall pardon your evil deeds and admit you to an honourable place (Paradise).

Sura: 4, Ayat: 31.

Not by the smallest ant's weight will Allah wrong (any man). He that does a good deed shall be repaid twofold. Allah will bestow on him a rich recompense.

Sura: 4, Ayat: 40.

Allah: there is no god but Him. He will gather you all together on the Day of Resurrection: that day is sure to come. And whose is a truer word than Allah's?

Sura: 4, Ayat: 87.

Allah will say: 'This is the day when their truthfulness will benefit the truthful. They shall for ever dwell in gardens watered by running streams. Allah is pleased with them and they with Him. That is the supreme triumph.'

Sura: 5, Ayat: 119.

Say: 'To whom belongs all that the heavens and the earth contain?' Say: 'To Allah. He has decreed mercy for Himself, and will gather you all on the Day of Resurrection: that day is sure to come. Those who have forfeited their own souls will never have faith.'

Sura: 6, Ayat: 12.

Say: 'I will never disobey my Lord, for I fear the torment of a fateful day.'
He who is delivered (from the torment) of that day shall have received Allah's mercy. That is the glorious triumph.

Sura: 6, Ayat: 15-16.

On the day when We gather them all together We shall say to the polytheists: 'Where are your partners now, those whom you claimed (to be your gods)?' They will not argue, but will say: 'By Allah, our Lord, we have never been polytheists.'

Sura: 6, Ayat: 22-23.

If you could see them when they are set before their Lord! He will say: 'Is this not the truth?' 'Yes, by our Lord,' they will reply, and He will say: 'Taste then Our scourge, the reward of your unbelief!'

Sura: 6, Ayat: 30.

They are lost indeed, those who deny that they will ever meet Allah. When the Hour of Doom overtakes them unawares, they will exclaim: 'Alas, we have neglected much in our lifetime!' And they shall bear their burdens on their backs. Evil are the burdens they shall bear.

Sura: 6, Ayat: 31.

And warn with it those who dread to be brought before their Lord that they have no guardian or intercessor besides Allah, so that they may guard themselves against evil.

Sura: 6, Ayat: 51

It was He Who created the heavens and the earth in all truth. On the day when He says: 'Be,' it shall be. His word is the truth. His shall be the sovereignty on the day when the trumpet is sounded. He has knowledge of the visible and the unseen. He alone is the Wise, the Knowing.

Sura: 6, Ayat: 73.

And now you have returned to Us, alone, as We created you at first, leaving behind all that We have bestowed on you. Nor do We see with you your intercessors, those whom you claimed to be the partners (of Allah). Broken are the ties which bound you, and that which you presumed has failed you.'

Sura: 6, Ayat: 94.

Say: 'Should I seek any but Allah fcr my God, when He is the Lord of all things? Each man shall reap the fruits of his own deeds: no soul shall bear another's burden. In the end you shall all return to your Lord, and He will inform you about that in which you differed.'

Sura: 6, Ayat: 164.

On that day, (their deeds) shall be weighed with justice. Those whose scales are heavy shall triumph; but those whose scales are light shall lose their souls, because they have denied Our revelations.

Sura: 7, Ayat: 8-9.

They ask you about the Hour (of Doom) and when it is to come, Say: 'None knows except my Lord. He alone will reveal it at the appointed time. A fateful hour it shall be, both in the heavens and on earth. It will come suddenly.

They will put questions to you, as though you had full knowledge of it. Say: 'None knows about it save Allah, though most men are unaware of this.'

Sura: 7, Ayat: 187.

And on the day when We assemble them all together, We shall say to the polytheists: 'Keep to your places, you and your partners!' We will separate them one from another, and then their partners will say to them: 'It was not us that you worshipped. Allah is our all-sufficient witness: we were unaware of your worship.

Thereupon, each soul will know what it has done. They shall be sent back to Allah, their true Lord, and that which they invented will escape them.'

Sura: 10, Ayat: 28—30.

The day (will come) when He will gather them again, as though they had stayed (in this world) but an hour of the day. They will recognize one another. Lost are those that disbelieve in meeting their Lord and do not follow the right path.

Sura: 10, Ayat: 45.

Whether We let you witness some of that with which we threaten them, or cause you to die (before it falls upon them), to Us they shall return. Allah is watching over what they do.

Sura: 10, Ayat: 46.

Such was the scourge which your Lord has visited upon the sinful towns. His punishment is stern and harrowing.

Surely in this there is a sign for him that dreads the terrors of the life to come. That is a day on which all men shall be assembled. That shall be a witnessed day.

We shall not defer it except until an appointed term. On that day no man shall speak but by His leave. Some shall be damned, and others blessed. The damned shall be cast into the Fire where, groaning and wailing, they shall abide as long as the heavens and the earth endure, unless your Lord ordains otherwise; your Lord accomplishes what He will. As for the blessed, they shall dwell in paradise as long as the heavens and the earth endure, unless your Lord ordains otherwise. (Theirs) shall be an unfailing gift.

Sura: 11, Ayat: 102—108.

All shall appear before Allah. The weak will say to those who were haughty: 'We were your followers. Can you protect us from Allah's chastisement?'

They will say: 'Had Allah guided us we would have guided you. It is now the same whether we panic or bear patiently. There is no way out for us.'

Sura: 14, Ayat: 21.

On the day when the earth is changed into a different earth and the heavens (into new heavens), mankind shall stand before Allah, the One, the Conqueror. On that day, you shall see the guilty bound together with chains; their garments shall be of pitch, and their faces (shall be) covered with flames.

Allah will reward each soul according to its deeds. Swift is Allah's reckoning.

Sura: 14, Ayat: 48—51.

We did not create the heavens and the earth and what is between them except in truth. The Hour of Doom is sure to come.

Sura: 15, Ayat: 85.

They solemnly swear by Allah that He will never raise the dead to life. But surely Allah's promise is binding on Him, though most men may not know it. This is in order that He might show them that in which they differ, and in order that those who disbelieve might know that they were lying. When We decree a thing, We need only say: 'Be,' and it is.

Sura: 16, Ayat: 38—40.

To Allah belongs the unseen of the heavens and the earth. The business of the Final Hour shall be accomplished in the twinkling of an eye, or even less. Allah has power over all things.

Sura: 16, Ayat: 77.

On the day We will call a witness from every nation, then ermission will not be given to the unbelievers, nor shall they be allowed to ke amends.

Sur 16, Ayat: 84.

And on the day when We shall raise up in every nation a ness against them from among themselves, We (shall) bring you to testi gainst your people: to you We have revealed the Book which manifests the h about all things, a guide, a blessing, and good news to those who submi Allah.

Sura: 16, Ayat: 89.

On the day when every man will come pleading for himself and when every soul will be requited for its deed, they will not be dealt with unjustly.

Sura: 16, Ayat: 111.

The works of each man We have bound about his neck. On the Day of Resurrection, We shall confront him with a book spread wide open (saying): 'Read your book. Enough for you this day that your own soul should call you to account.'

Sura: 17, Ayat: 13-14.

'What!' they also say. 'When we are turned to bones and dust, shall we be restored as a new creation?'

Say: 'You shall, whether you turn to stone or iron, or any other substance which you may think unlikely to be given life.'

They will ask: 'Who will restore us?'

Say: 'He that created you at first.'

They will shake their heads and ask: 'When will this be?'

Say: 'It may be near at hand. On that day, He will summon you all, and you shall answer Him with praise. You shall think that you have stayed away but for a little while.'

Sura: 17, Ayat: 49—52.

There is no town but shall be destroyed or sternly punished by Us before the Day of Resurrection. That is written in the Book.

Sura; 17, Ayat: 58.

The day will surely come when We shall summon every nation with its Imam. Those who are given their books in their right hands will read their recorded doings, and shall not in the least be wronged. But those who have been blind in this life, shall be blind in the life to come and go farther astray.

Sura: 17, Ayat: 71-72.

And (remember) the day when We shall blot out the mountains and you will see the earth a levelled plain; when We shall gather all mankind together,

leaving not a soul behind.

They shall be ranged before your Lord, who will say to them: 'You have returned to Us as We created you at first. Yet you thought Our promise to you was not to be fulfilled.'

The book will be set down (before them), and you shall see the sinners dismayed at that which is inscribed in it. They shall say: 'Woe to us! What can this book mean? It omits nothing small or great: all are noted down!' and they shall find their deeds recorded there. Your Lord will wrong no one.

Sura: 18, Ayat: 47—49.

The day will surely come when We will gather the righteous in multitudes before the Lord of Mercy, and drive the sinful (like thirsty cattle) into Hell.

Sura: 19, Ayat: 85-86.

There is none in the heavens or on earth but shall return to Him in utter submission. He has kept strict count of all (His creatures) and numbered them; and one by one they shall approach Him on the Day of Resurrection.

Sura: 19, Ayat: 93—95.

The Hour of Doom is sure to come. But I choose to keep it hidden, so that every soul may be rewarded for its labours. Let those who disbelieve in it and yield to their desires not turn your thoughts from it, lest you perish.

Sura: 20, Ayat: 15-16.

From the earth We have created you, and to the earth We will restore you; and from it We will bring you back (to life).

Sura: 20, Ayat: 55.

....an evil burden for them on the Day of Resurrection, the day when the Trumpet shall be sounded.

On that day, We shall assemble all the sinners. Their eyes will become dim (with terror), and they shall murmur among themselves: 'You have stayed away but ten (days).'

We know full well what they will say. The most upright among them will declare: 'You have stayed away but one day.'

They ask you about the mountains. Say: 'My Lord will crush them to fine dust and leave them a desolate waste, with no hollows nor jutting mounds to be seen therein.'

On that day, men will have no choice but to follow their truthful summoner, their voices hushed before the Lord of Mercy; and you shall hear no sound except the faint sound (of marching feet). On that day none shall have power to intercede for them except him that has received the sanction of the Merciful and whose word is acceptable to Him.

Sura: 20, Ayat: 100—109.

(All) faces shall be humbled before the Living One, the Eternal. Those who are burdened with sin shall come to grief, but those who have believed and done good works shall fear neither inequity nor injustice.

Sura: 20, Ayat: 111-112.

But who gives no heed to My warning shall live in distress and come before Us blind on the 'Day of Resurrection.' 'Lord,' he will say, 'why have You brought me blind before You while (in my life-time) I had sight?'

He will answer: 'Thus Our revelations were declared to you and you forgot them. So this day you are yourself forgotten.'

Sura: 20, Ayat: 124—126.

The Day of Reckoning for mankind is drawing near, yet the people heedlessly turn away.

Sura: 21, Ayat: 1.

They say: 'When will this promise be fulfilled, if what you say be true?'

If only the unbelievers knew the day when they shall be powerless to shield their faces and their backs from the fire of Hell; the day when none shall help them! It will overtake them unawares and stupefy them. They shall have no power to ward it off, nor shall they be reprieved.

Other apostles have been mocked before you; but those who scoffed at them were smitten by the very thing they mocked.

Sura: 21, Ayat: 38—41.

We shall set up just scales on the Day of Resurrection, so that no man shall in the least be wronged. Actions as small as a grain of mustard seed We will bring (to be weighed out). And sufficient are We as reckoners.

We showed Musa and Harun the criterion (to distinguish between right and wrong), and gave them light and a message for the righteous: those who fear their Lord in secret and dread the terrors of Judgement-day.

And this is a blessed Message which We have revealed. Will you then reject it?

Sura: 21, Ayat: 47—50.

(It is ordained that) no nation We have destroyed shall ever rise again. But when Gog and Magog are let loose and rush headlong down every hill; when the true promise nears its fulfilment; the eyes of the unbelievers will fixedly stare (and they will say): 'Woe to us! Of this we have been heedless. We have done wrong.'

Sura; 21, Ayat: 95—97.

On that day, We shall roll up the heaven like a scroll of writings. As we produced the first creation, so will We reproduce it. This is a promise We shall as-

suredly fulfil.

Sura: 21, Ayat: 104.

Men, have fear of your Lord. The catastrophe of the Hour of Doom shall be terrible indeed. When that day comes, every suckling mother shall forsake her infant, every pregnant female shall deliver her burden, and you shall see mankind reeling like drunkards although not drunk: but dreadful will be Allah's chastisement.

Sura: 22, Ayat: 1-2.

That is because Allah is the Truth: He gives life to the dead and has power over all things.

And the Hour of Doom is sure to come - in this there is no doubt. And Allah will raise up those in the graves.

Sura: 22, Ayat: 6-7.

Those who believe, the Jews, the Sabaeans, the Christians, the Magians, and the Polytheists, Allah will judge them on the Day of Resurrection. He bears witness to all things.

Sura: 22, Ayat: 17.

On that day Allah will reign supreme. He will judge them all. Those that have embraced the true faith and done good works shall enter the Gardens of Delight, but the unbelievers who have denied Our revelations shall receive an ignominious punishment.

Sura: 22, Ayat: 56-57.

Those who defame honourable but unaware believing women shall be cursed in this world and in the next. Theirs shall be a woeful punishment on the day when their own tongues, hands, and feet will testify to what they did. On that day, Allah will justly requite them. They shall know that Allah is the glorious Truth.

Sura: 24, Ayat: 23—25.

To Allah belongs what the heavens and the earth contain. He has knowledge of what you are about. On the day when they return to Him. He will declare to them all that they have done. He has knowledge of all things.

Sura: 24, Ayat: 64.

They deny the Hour of Doom. For those who deny that hour, We have prepared a blazing fire.

Sura: 25, Ayat: 11.

And they ask: !When will this promise be fulfilled, if what you say be true?!

Say: !A part of what you hasten may well be near to you.!

Sura: 27, Ayat: 71–72.

On that day We shall gather from every nation a multitude of those who disbelieved Our revelations. They shall be led in separate bands. And when they come, He will say (to them): !You denied My revelations although you knew nothing of them. What was it you were doing?! Our judgement will smite them for their sins, and they shall be dumbfounded.

Do they not see how We have made the night for them to rest in and the day to give them light? Surely there are signs in this for true believers.

On that day the Trumpet shall be sounded and all who dwell in heaven and earth be seized with fear, except those whom Allah will be pleased (to exempt). All shall come to Him abased.

The mountains which you take to be firm will pass away like clouds. Such is the might of Allah, who has rightly perfected all things. He has knowledge of all your actions.

Those that have done good shall be rewarded with what is better, and shall be secure from the terrors of that day.

But those that have done evil shall be hurled headlong into the Fire. Shall you not be rewarded according to your deeds?

Sura: 27, Ayat: 83–90.

On that day (Allah) will call to them saying: 'What answer did you give Our apostles?' And on that day such will their confusion be that they will ask no questions.

Sura: 28, Ayat: 65-66.

On the day when the Hour of Doom strikes, the wrongdoers will be speechless with despair. None of their partners (Associate gods) will intercede for them; indeed, they shall deny their partners (Associate gods).

On the day when the Hour of Doom strikes, mankind will be separated one from the other. Those who have believed and done good works shall rejoice in a fair garden, but those who have disbelieved and denied Our revelations and the meeting of the life to come, shall be delivered up for punishment.

Sura: 30, Ayat: 12–16.

When the Hour of Doom strikes, the wrongdoers will swear that they had stayed but one hour. Thus they are ever deceived.

But those to whom knowledge and faith have been given will say: 'You have stayed in Allah's book till the Day of Resurrection. This is the Day of Resurrection: yet you did not know it.'

On that day, their pleas shall not avail the wrongdoers, nor shall they be asked to make amends.

Sura: 30, Ayat: 55–57.

Men, fear your Lord, and fear the day when no parent shall avail his child nor any child his parent. Allah's promise is surely true. Let the life of this world not deceive you, nor let the Dissembler trick you concerning Allah.
Sura: 31, Ayat: 33.

People ask you about the Hour of Doom. Say: 'The knowledge of it is with God alone. Who knows? It may well be that it is near at hand.'
Sura: 33, Ayat: 63.

He will surely reward those who have faith and do good works; they shall be forgiven and a generous provision shall be made for them. But those who strive to belittle Our revelations shall suffer the torment of a harrowing scourge.
Sura: 34, Ayat: 4-5.

They ask: 'When will this promise be fulfilled, if what you say be true?'
Say: 'Your day is already appointed. Not for one hour can you hold it back, nor can you hasten it.'
Sura: 34, Ayat: 29-30.

Allah sends forth the winds which set the clouds in motion. We drive them on to some dead land and revive the soil after its death. Such is the Resurrection.
Sura: 35, Ayat: 9.

They also say: 'When will this promise be fulfilled, if what you say be true?'
They await but one blast, which will overtake them whilst they are disputing. They will make no will, nor shall they return (to their kinsfolk).
And the Trumpet is blown, and behold, from the graves they rush forth to their Lord. 'Woe to us!' They will say. 'Who has roused us from our resting-place? This is what the Lord of Mercy promised: the apostles have spoken the truth!' And it is but one shout and they are all gathered before Us.
Sura: 36, Ayat: 48–53.

It will be one cry and they shall see. They will say: 'Woe to us. This is the Day of Judgement.' (The angels then will say): 'This is the Day of Separation which you denied?'
Sura: 37, Ayat: 19–21.

Say: 'I fear, if I disobey my Lord, the torment of a fateful day.'
Sura: 39, Ayat: 13.

You shall die. And they shall die. Then, on the Day of Resurrection, you

shall dispute in your Lord's presence with one another.

Sura: 39, Ayat: 30-31.

Say: 'Lord, Creator of the heavens and the earth, who has knowledge of the visible and the invisible, You alone can judge the disputes of Your servants.'

If the wrongdoers had all the treasures of the earth and as much besides, they would gladly offer it on the Day of Resurrection to redeem themselves from the torment of the scourge. For Allah will show them that with which they have never reckoned. The evils of their deeds will become manifest to them, and what they scoffed at will encompass them.

Sura: 39, Ayat: 46–48.

On the Day of Resurrection, you shall see those who uttered falsehoods about Allah with faces blackened. Is there not in Hell a home for the arrogant?

Sura: 39, Ayat: 60.

The Trumpet shall be sounded and all who are in heaven and earth shall fall down fainting, except those that shall be spared by Allah. Then the Trumpet will sound again and they shall rise and gaze around them. The earth will shine with the light of its Lord, and the Book will be laid open. The prophets and witnesses shall be brought in and all shall be judged with fairness: none shall be wronged. Every soul shall be paid back according to its deeds, for Allah knows of all their actions.

Sura: 39, Ayat: 68–70.

They shall say: 'Lord, twice You have made us die, and twice You have given us life. We now confess our sins. Is there no way out of this?'

(They shall be answered): 'You have incurred this fate because when Allah was invoked alone, you disbelieved; but when you were bidden to serve other gods besides Him you believed in them. (Today) judgement rests with Allah, the Most High, the Supreme One.'

Sura: 40, Ayat: 11-12.

....the day when they shall rise up (from their graves) with nothing hidden from Allah. And to whom is the sovereignty on that day? To Allah, the One, the Mighty.

On that day every soul shall be paid back what it has earned. On that day none shall be wronged. Swift is Allah's reckoning.

Sura: 40, Ayat: 16-17.

Forewarn them of the approaching day, when men's hearts will leap up to their throats and choke them; when the wrongdoers will have no friend, no in-

tercessor who will be heard. Allah knows the furtive looks of the eyes and what the hearts conceal. He will judge men with fairness, but those whom they invoke besides Him can judge nothing at all. Allah hears and observes all men.

Sura: 40, Ayat: 18–20.

The Hour of Doom is sure to come: yet most men do not believe.

Sura: 40, Ayat: 59.

It is Allah who has sent down the Book in truth, and the Balance. And how can you tell? The Hour of Doom may be fast approaching.

Those who deny it seek to hurry it on; but the true believers dread its coming and know it is the truth. Indeed, those who doubt the Hour are far astray.

Sura: 42, Ayat: 17.

Are they waiting for the Hour of Doom to overtake them unawares, without warning? On that day friends shall become enemies one to another, except the God-fearing.

Sura: 43, Ayat: 66-67.

Wait for the day when the sky will pour down visible smoke, enveloping all men: this will be a dreadful scourge.

Sura: 44, Ayat: 10-11.

Yet the unbelievers say: 'We shall die but one death, nor shall we ever be restored to life. Bring back to us our fathers, if what you say be true.'

Who are better they or the people of Tubba* and those who came before them? We destroyed them all, for they too were wicked men.

It was not in sport that We created the heavens and the earth and all that lies between them. We only created them in truth. But of this most men have no knowledge.

The Day of Judgement is the appointed time for all. On that day no man shall help his friend; none shall be helped save those on whom Allah will have mercy. He is the Mighty One, the Merciful.

Sura: 44, Ayat: 35–42.

And when Our clear revelations are recited to them, their only argument is: 'Bring back to us our fathers, if what you say be true!'

Say: 'It is Allah who gives you life and later causes you to die. It is He Who will gather you all on the Day of Resurrection. Of this there is no doubt; yet most men do not know it.'

***The people of Himyar in South Arabia.**

Allah's is the sovereignty in the heavens and the earth. On the day when the Hour of Doom arrives, those who have denied His revelations will assuredly be lost.

Sura: 45, Ayat: 25—27.

You shall see all the nations on their knees. Each nation shall be summoned to its book (and a voice will say to them): 'You shall this day be rewarded for your deeds. This Record of Ours speaks with truth against you. We have recorded all your actions.'

As for those who have faith and do good works, their Lord will admit them into His mercy. That shall be a glorious triumph.

To the unbelievers (a voice will say): 'Were My revelations not recited to you? Did you not scorn them and commit evil? When it was said to you: 'Allah's promise is true: the Hour of Doom is sure to come.' You replied: 'We know nothing of the Hour of Doom. It is but a vain conjecture, nor are we convinced.'

The evil of their deeds will manifest itself to them, and the scourge at which they scoffed will encompass them.

Sura: 45, Ayat: 28—33.

On the day when the unbelievers are brought before the fire of Hell (We shall say to them): 'You squandered away your precious things in your earthly life and took your fill of pleasure. An ignominious punishment shall be yours this day, because you behaved with pride and without just cause on earth and committed evil'.

Sura: 46, Ayat: 20.

On the day when th unbelievers are brought before the fire of Hell they shall be asked: 'Is this not real?' 'Yes, by the Lord.' they will answer. 'Then taste Our punishment' (He will reply), 'for you were unbelievers.'

Sura: 46, Ayat: 34.

Bear up then with patience, as did the steadfast apostles before you, and do not seek to hurry on (their doom). On the day when they behold the scourge with which they are threatened, their life on earth will seem to them no longer than an hour.

That is a warning. Shall any perish except the evildoers?

Sura: 46, Ayat: 35.

Were we worn out by the first creation? Yet they are in doubt about a new creation.

Sura: 50, Ayat: 15.

And when the agony of death justly overtakes him, they will say: 'This is

the fate you have striven to avoid.' And the Trumpet shall be sounded. Such is the threatened day.

Each soul shall come attended by one (angel) to drive, and another to bear witness. (One of them will say): 'Of this you have been heedless. But now we have removed your veil. Today your sight is keen.

Sura: 50, Ayat: 19—22.

....the day when men will hear the Cry in truth. On that day they will rise up from their graves.

It is We Who ordain life and death. To Us all shall return.

On that day the earth will be rent asunder over them (and they shall rush forth) in haste. That is the Gathering, which is easy for Us to do.

Sura: 50, Ayat: 41—44.

By those (winds) that scatter (dust), and those bearing the load (of rain); and those (ships) gliding with ease; and by (the angels) who deal out blessings to all men; that which you are promised is true, and the Last Judgement shall surely come to pass!

Sura: 51, Ayat: 1—6.

Woe to the liars who dwell in darkness and are heedless of the life to come.

'When will the Day of Judgement be?' they ask. On that day they shall be tried in the Fire, (and a voice will say to them): 'Taste your trial. This is what you have sought to hasten!'

Sura: 51, Ayat: 10—14.

This is a warner like the warners of old. The coming (judgement) is near at hand; none but Allah can disclose its hour.

Do you marvel then at this revelation and laugh (lightheartedly) instead of weeping. Rather prostrate yourselves before Allah and worship Him.

Sura: 53, Ayat: 56—62.

The Hour (of Judgement) is drawing near, and the moon is cleft in two. Yet when they see a sign (the unbelievers) turn their backs and say: 'Strong magic!'

They deny the truth and follow their own fancies. But every matter will be settled.

Sura: 54, Ayat: 1—3.

On the day when the Crier summons them to a hard task, with downcast eyes they shall come out from their graves as if they were scattered locusts. The unbelievers will cry: 'This is indeed a hard day!'

Sura: 54, Ayat: 6—8.

Their army shall be routed and put to flight.

The Hour of Doom is their appointed time. And that Hour will be most grevious and bitter.

Sura: 54, Ayat: 45-46.

We shall surely find the time to judge you, O two armies. Which of your Lord's blessings would you deny?

Mankind and jinn, if you have power to penetrate the confines of heaven and earth, then penetrate them! But this you shall not do except with Our own authority. Which of your Lord's blessings would you deny?

Flames of fire shall be lashed at you, and brass. There shall be none to help you. Which of your Lord's blessings would you deny?

When the sky splits asunder and reddens like a rose or stained leather, which of your Lord's blessings would you deny? On that day neither man nor jinnee shall be asked about his sins. Which of your Lord's blessings would you deny?

The wrongdoers shall be known by their marks; they shall be seized by their forelocks and their feet. Which of your Lord's blessings would you deny?

Sura: 55, Ayat: 31—42.

When the Event comes-and no soul shall then deny its coming-some shall be abased and others exalted.

When the earth is shaken with a (violent) shock and the mountains crumble away and scatter abroad into fine dust, you shall be divided into three multitudes: those on the right—(happy) shall be those to the right; those on the left—(wretched) shall be those on the left and those to the fore shall be foremost. Such are they that shall be brought near to their Lord in the gardens of delight:

Sura: 56, Ayat: 1—12.

Say: 'Those of old and those of later times shall be brought together on an appointed day.

Sura: 56, Ayat: 49-50.

Who will give a generous loan to Allah? He will pay him back twofold and he shall receive a rich reward.

The day will surely come when you shall see the true believers, men and women, with their light shining before them and in their right hands (and a voice saying to them): 'Rejoice this day. You shall enter gardens watered by running streams in which you shall abide forever.' That is the supreme triumph.

On that day the hypocrites, both men and women, will say to the true believers: 'Wait for us that we may borrow some of your light.' But they will

answer: 'Go back and seek some other light!'

A wall with a gate shall be set before them. Inside there shall be mercy, and out, to the fore, the scourge (of Hell).

Sura: 57, Ayat: 11—13.

On the day when Allah restores them all to life He will inform them of their actions. Allah has recorded it, although they have forgotten it. Allah is witness to all things.

Sura: 58, Ayat: 6.

On the Day of Resurrection neither your kinsfolk nor your children shall avail you. Allah will judge between you. He is cognizant of all your actions.

Sura: 60, Ayat: 3.

The unbelievers think that they will not be raised from the dead. Say: 'By the Lord, you shall assuredly be raised to life! Then you shall be told of all that you have done. That is easy enough for Allah.'

Sura: 64, Ayat: 7.

Believe then in Allah and His Apostle and in the light which We have revealed. Allah has knowledge of all your action.

The day on which He will assemble you, the day on which you shall be gathered—that shall be a day of mutual loss and gain. Those who believe in Allah and do what is right shall be forgiven their sins and admitted to gardens watered by running streams, where they shall dwell for ever. That is the supreme triumph.

Sura: 64, Ayat: 8-9.

They ask: 'When will this promise be (fulfilled), if what you say be true?'

Say: 'Allah alone has knowledge of that. My mission is but to warn you plainly.'

But when they see it drawing near, the faces of the unbelievers will turn black with gloom and a voice will say: 'This is the doom which you have challenged.'

Sura: 67, Ayat: 25—27.

On the day when the dread event takes place and they are bidden to prostrate themselves, they will not be able. They shall have their eyes cast down and shall be utterly humbled; for they were already bidden to prostrate themselves when they were safe.

Sura: 68, Ayat: 42-43.

When the Trumpet sounds a single blast; when the earth with all its mountains is lifted up and with one mighty crash is shattered into dust-on that day

the Dread Event will come to pass.

The sky will be rent asunder; so that day it will be frail. The angels will stand on all its sides. And eight (of them) will carry the throne of your Lord above them. On that day you shall be displayed before Him, and no secret of yours will remain hidden.

Sura: 69, Ayat: 13—18.

A questioner called for chastisement to befall the unbelievers.

None can ward it off. (A chastisement) from the Lord of the Ways of Ascent, To Him the angels and the Spirit ascend in one day, the measure of which is fifty thousand years.

Sura: 70, Ayat: 1—4.

They think (the Day of Judgement) is far off; but We see it near at hand.

On that day the heavens shall become like molten brass, and the mountains like wool. No friend will ask a friend (a question) though they are put in sight of each other. To redeem himself from the torment of that day the sinner will gladly sacrifice his children, his wife, his brother, the kinsfolk who gave him shelter, and all the people of the earth, if then this might deliver him.

By no means. It is a flaming Fire. It drags (them) down by (their) scalps; and it shall call him who turned his back (on the true faith) and amassed riches and covetously hoarded them.

Sura: 70, Ayat: 6—18.

If they* follow the right path We shall vouchsafe them abundant rain, and thereby put them to the proof. He who gives no heed to his Lord's warning shall be sternly punished.

Sura: 72, Ayat: 16-17.

Say: 'I cannot tell whether the scourge with which you are threatened is imminent, or whether my Lord will set for it a far-off day. He alone has knowledge of what is hidden: His secrets He reveals to none, except to the apostles whom He elects. He sends down guardians who walk before them and behind them.

Sura: 72, Ayat: 25—27.

Leave to Me those that deny the truth, those that enjoy the comforts of this life; bear with them yet a little while. We have (in store for them) heavy fetters and a blazing fire, choking food and harrowing torment. (This shall be their lot) on the day when the earth shakes with all its mountains, and the mountains crumble into heaps of shifting sand.

Sura: 73, Ayat: 11—14.

***The Makkans**

If you disbelieve, how will you escape the day that will make your children grey-haired (the day) on which the heaven will split apart? Allah's promise shall be fulfilled.

Sura: 73, Ayat: 17-18.

When the Trumpet sounds, that shall be a day of distress and far from easy for the unbelievers.

Sura: 74, Ayat: 8—10.

But when the sight of mortals is confounded and the moon eclipsed; when sun and moon are brought together — on that day man will ask: 'Whither shall I flee?'

No, there shall be no place of refuge. For on that day all shall return to your Lord.

On that day man shall be informed of all that he has done first and last. He shall be a witness against himself, even though he were to offer excuses.

Sura: 75, Ayat: 7—15.

We fear from our Lord a day grim and distressful.

Sura: 76, Ayat: 10.

These love this fleeting life and leave (unheeded and unattended to) in front of them a heavy day.

Sura: 76, Ayat: 27.

By the gales, sent forth in swift succession; by the raging tempests and the rain-spreading winds; by your Lord's revelations, discerning good from evil and admonishing by plea or warning: that which you have been promised (of threats) shall befall.

Sura: 77, Ayat: 1—7.

When the stars are blotted out; and when the sky is rent asunder and the mountains crumble into dust; when Allah's apostles are brought together on the appointed day-when will all this be? Upon the Day of Judgement!

Would that you knew what the Day of Judgement is! Woe on that day to the disbelievers!

Sura: 77, Ayat: 8—15.

....On that day they shall not speak, nor shall it be open to them to make pleas.

Woe on that day to the disbelievers! Such is the Day of Judgement. We shall assemble you all, together with past generation. if then you are cunning, try your spite against Me!

Woe on that day to the disbelievers!

Sura: 77, Ayat: 34—40.

Fixed is the Day of Judgement. On that day the Trumpet shall be sounded and you shall come in multitudes. The gates of heaven shall swing open and the mountains shall pass away and become like vapour.

Sura: 78, Ayat: 17—20.

They did not fear Our reckoning and roundly denied Our revelations. But We have recorded all their doings in a book. We shall say: 'Taste this: you shall have nothing but mounting torment!'

Sura: 78, Ayat: 27—30.

On that day, when the Spirit and the angels stand up in their ranks, they shall not speak; except him who shall receive the sanction of the Merciful and declare what is right.

That day is sure to come. Let him who will, seek a way back to his Lord.

Sura: 78, Ayat: 38-39.

We have forewarned you of an imminent scourge: the day when man will look upon his works and the unbeliever will cry: 'Would that I were dust?'

Sura: 78, Ayat: 40.

On the day when the Trumpet sounds its first blast followed by the second, men's hearts that day shall tremble with their eyes downcast.

Sura: 79, Ayat: 6—9.

They say: 'Shall we indeed be restored to (our) first state even after we are rotten bones?'

They say: 'That would then be a vain return.' But with one single cry, they shall be awakened.

Sura: 79, Ayat: 10—14.

But when the great disaster comes — the day when man will call to mind his labours and when Hell is brought in sight (of all) — those who transgressed and chose this present life will find themselves in Hell.

Sura: 79, Ayat: 34—39.

They question you about the Hour of Doom: 'When shall it be?' How are you concerned with its declaration? Your Lord alone knows when it will come.

You are but a warner for those who fear it.

On the day when they behold it, it will be as if they had tarried only a single

evening or the morning following it.

Sura: 79, Ayat: 42–46.

But when the deafening cry comes, on that day each man will forsake his brother, his mother and his father, his wife and his children: for each one of them will on that day have enough concern of his own.

On that day there shall be beaming faces, smiling and joyful. And on that day there shall be faces covered with dust and veiled with darkness. These shall (be the faces of) the wicked and the unbelieving.

Sura: 80, Ayat: 33–42.

When the sun is folded up; when the stars fall down and the mountains are blown away; when camels big with their young are left untended and the wild beasts are brought together; when the seas are burning and men's souls are reunited (with their bodies); when the infant girl,* buried alive, is asked for what crime she was slain; when the records of men's deeds are laid open and heaven is stripped bare; when Hell burns fiercely and Paradise is brought near: then each soul shall know what it has done.

Sura: 81, Ayat: 1–14.

When the sky is cleft asunder; when the stars are scattered, and the oceans are rolled together; when the graves are overturned; each soul shall know what it has done and what it has failed to do.

Sura: 82, Ayat: 1–5.

Would that you knew what the Day of Judgement is! Oh, would that you knew what the Day of Judgement is! It is the day when every soul can do nothing for another and Allah will then reign supreme.

Sura: 82, Ayat: 17–19.

Do they not think that they will be raised to life upon a fateful day, the day when all mankind will stand before the Lord of the Worlds?

Sura: 83, Ayat: 4–6.

Truly, the record of the sinners is in Sijjin. Would that you know what Sijjin is! It is a sealed book.

Woe on that day to the disbelievers who deny the Last Judgement! None denies it except every aggressive sinner.

Sura: 83, Ayat: 7–12.

When the sky is rent asunder, obeying its Lord as it must do; when the earth is expanded and casts out all that is within it and becomes empty, obey-

---

***A reference to the practice of burying infant girls alive in Pre-Islamic Arabia.**

ing its Lord as it must do; (then) O man, strive hard towards your Lord until you meet Him.

He that is given his book in his right hand shall have a lenient reckoning and go back rejoicing to his people. But he that is given his book from behind his back shall call down destruction on himself and burn in the fire of Hell.

Sura: 84, Ayat: 1—12.

....on the day when men's consciences are searched. Helpless he shall be, with no supporter.

Sura: 86, Ayat: 8—10.

Have you heard of the overwhelming Event?

On that day there shall be downcast faces, broken and worn out, burnt by a scorching fire, drinking from a seething fountain. Their only food shall be bitter thorns, which will neither sustain nor satisfy hunger.

On that day (there shall be) radiant faces, of men well-pleased with their labours, in a lofty garden. There they shall hear no idle talk. A gushing fountain shall be there, and raised soft couches with goblets; silken cushions ranged in order and rich carpets spread out.

Sura: 88, Ayat: 1—16.

To Us they shall return, and We will bring them to account.

Sura: 88, Ayat: 25-26.

No! But when the earth is crushed to fine dust, and your Lord comes down with the angels, in their ranks, and Hell is brought near—on that day man will remember his deeds. But what will memory avail him?

He will say: 'Would that I had done good works in my lifetime!' But on that day none will punish as He will punish, nor will any bind with chains like His.

Sura: 89, Ayat: 21—26.

When the earth is shaken in her last convulsion; when the earth brings forth its burdens and man asks 'What may this mean?'—on that day it will proclaim its tidings, for your Lord will have inspired it.

On that day mankind will come in broken bands to be shown their labours. Whoever does an atom's weight of good shall see it, and whoever does an atom's weight of evil shall see it also.

Sura: 99, Ayat: 1—8.

Is he not aware that when those in the graves are raised and what is in the breasts is laid open, their Lord on that day will be knowing?

Sura: 100, Ayat: 9—11.

The Disaster! What is the Disaster?

Would that you knew what the Disaster is!

On that day men shall become like scattered moths and the mountains like tufts of carded wool.

Then he whose scales are heavy shall dwell in bliss; but he whose scales are light, the Abyss shall be his home.

If only you knew what this is like!

It is a scorching fire.

Sura: 101, Ayat: 1–11.

ELEMENTS OF FAITH

(3)

In the name of Allah, The Compassionate, The Merciful

ELEMENTS OF FAITH

The Apostle believes in what has been revealed to him by his Lord, and so do the faithful. They all believe in Allah and His Angels, His books, and His apostles. We discriminate against none of His Apostles. They say: 'We hear and obey. Grant us your forgiveness, Lord; to You we shall all return.

Sura: 2, Ayat: 285.

O believers, have faith in Allah and His Apostle, in the Book He has revealed to His Apostle, and in the Book He formerly revealed. He that denies Allah, His angels, His scriptures, His apostles, and the Last Day, has strayed far from the truth.

Sura: 4, Ayat: 136.

In the name of Allah, The Compassionate, The Merciful

FAITH IN GOD AND THE DAY OF JUDGEMENT

Believers, Jews, Sabaeans, and Christians-whoever believes in Allah and the Last Day and does what is right-shall have nothing to fear or to regret.

Sura: 5, Ayat: 69.

Those that have faith and do not taint their faith with wrongdoing shall surely have security, and follow the right path.

Sura: 6, Ayat: 82.

Nor yield to the wishes of those that deny Our revelations, disbelieve in the life to come, and set up (other gods) as equals with their Lord.

Sura: 6, Ayat: 150.

'Vain are the deeds of those who disbelieve in Our signs and in the life to come. Shall they not be rewarded according to their deeds?'

Sura: 7, Ayat: 147.

If anything could make you marvel, then you should surely marvel at those who say: 'When we are dust, shall we be raised to life again?'

Such are those who deny their Lord. Their necks shall be bound with chains. They are the people of the Fire. In it they shall abide for ever.

Sura: 13, Ayat: 5.

....Who join together what He has bidden to be united; who fear their Lord and dread the terrors of Reckoning-day.

Sura: 13, Ayat: 20-21.

Your God is one God. Those that deny the life to come have faithless hearts and are puffed up with pride.

Sura: 16, Ayat: 22.

How ill they judge!

Evil is the similitude of those who deny the life to come. But most sublime is

the similitude of Allah. He is the Mighty, the Wise One.

Sura: 16, Ayat: 59-60.

Allah has caused some of you to excel others in worldly possessions. Those who have been favoured do not give their wealth to those whom their right hands possess so as to be equal in that respect. Would they deny Allah's goodness?

Sura: 16, Ayat: 71.

Men, if you are in doubt about the Resurrection, remember that We first created you from dust, then from a life-germ, then from a clot, and then from a lump of flesh partly formed and partly unformed, so that We might manifest to you (Our power).

We cause to remain in the wombs whatever We please for an appointed term, and then We bring you forth as infants, that you may grow up and reach your prime. Some of you die (young), and some live on to abject old age when all that they once knew they shall know no more.

And you see the earth dry and barren: but no sooner do We send down rain upon it than it begins to stir and swell, putting forth every kind of radiant bloom.

Sura: 22, Ayat: 5.

Are you seeking a reward of them? Your Lord's recompense is better. He is the most munificent Giver.

You are calling them to a straight path, but those who deny the life to come will ever stray from the right path.

Sura: 23, Ayat: 72—74.

They deny the Hour of Doom. For those who deny that hour, We have prepared a blazing fire. When it sees them from a far-off place, they shall hear it raging and roaring.

Sura: 25, Ayat: 11-12.

Put your trust in the Mighty One, the Merciful, who observes you when you stand upright and (sees) your movements among those who prostrate themselves. He hears all and knows all.

Sura: 26, Ayat: 217—220.

Ta sin. These are the verses of the Quran, the Book which indicates (right and wrong); a guidance and joyful news to true believers, who attend to their prayers and pay the alms-tax and firmly believe in the life to come.

As for those who deny the life to come, We make their foul deeds seem fair to them so that they blunder about in their folly. Such as those who will be st-

ernly punished and in the Hereafter have much to lose.

Sura: 27, Ayat: 1–4.

They have got no knowledge of the life Hereafter. Surely they are in doubt about it and their eyes are sealed.

The unbelievers say: 'When we and our fathers are turned to dust, shall we be raised to life? We were promised this once before, and so were our fathers. It is but a fable of the ancients.'

Sura: 27, Ayat: 66–68.

But those who have disbelieved and denied Our revelations and the meeting of the life to come, shall be delivered up for punishment.

Sura: 30, Ayat: 16.

These are the revelations of the Wise Book, a guidance and a blessing to the righteous, who attend to their prayers, pay the alms-tax, and firmly believe in the life to come. These are rightly guided by their Lord and will surely prosper.

Sura: 31, Ayat: 2–5.

(We shall say to them): 'Taste Our punishment for you forgot this day. We, too, will forget you. Taste Our eternal scourge, which you have earned by your misdeeds.'

Sura: 32, Ayat: 14.

The unbelievers say: 'Shall we show you a man* who claims that when you have been mangled into bits you will be raised to life again? Has he invented a lie about Allah, or is he mad?' Truly, those who deny the life to come are in torment and in farthest error.

Sura: 34, Ayat: 7-8.

Yet Satan had no power over them except that We would know who believed in the life to come from him who is in doubt about it. Your Lord watches over all things.

Sura: 34, Ayat: 21.

Musa said: 'I take refuge in my Lord and in your Lord from every proud man who denies the Day of Reckoning.'

Sura: 40, Ayat: 27.

Say: 'I am no more than a man like yourselves. It is revealed to me that your God is one God. Therefore take the right path to Him and implore Him

---

***Muhammad**

to forgive you. Woe to those who associate others with Him, who give no alms and disbelieve in the life to come. For those who believe and do good works, is an enduring reward.'

Sura: 41, Ayat: 6—8.

Yet they still doubt that they will ever meet their Lord. Surely Allah encompasses all things.

Sura: 41, Ayat: 54.

It is Allah who has sent down the Book in truth, and the Balance. And how can you tell? The Hour of Doom may be fast approaching.

Those who deny it seek to hurry it on; but the true believers dread its coming and know it is the truth. Indeed, those who doubt the Hour are far astray.

Sura: 42, Ayat: 17-18.

Those who say: 'Our God is Allah,' and follow the straight path shall have nothing to fear or to regret. They shall for ever dwell in Paradise as a reward for what they did.

Sura: 46, Ayat: 13-14.

So that you may have faith in Allah and His apostle and that you may assist Him, honour Him, and praise Him, morning and evening.

Sura: 48, Ayat: 9.

He is Allah, besides whom there is no other god. He knows the visible and the unseen. He is the Compassionate, the Merciful.

Sura: 59, Ayat: 22.

He is Allah, besides whom there is no other god. He is the Sovereign Lord, the Holy One, the Giver of Peace, the Keeper of Faith; the Guardian, the Mighty One, the All-Powerful, the Most High! Exalted be He above the partners they ascribe to Him.

Sura: 59, Ayat: 23.

He is Allah, the Creator, the Originator, the Modeller. His are the most gracious names. All that is in heaven and earth glorifies Him. He is the Mighty, the Wise One.

Sura: 59, Ayat: 24.

All that is in heaven and earth glorifies Allah. He is the Mighty, the Wise One.

Sura: 61, Ayat: 1.

O believers, be Allah's helpers. When Isa the son of Mariam said to the dis-

ciples: 'Who will come with me to the help of Allah?' they replied: 'We are Allah's helpers'.

Sura: 61, Ayat: 14.

He who believes in Allah and does good works shall be admitted to gardens watered by running streams.

Sura: 65, Ayat: 11.

Say: 'It is He who has created you and given you ears and eyes and hearts. Yet you are seldom thankful.

Say: 'It was He who multiplies you on the earth, and before Him you shall be assembled.'

Sura: 67, Ayat: 23-24.

(We shall say): 'Lay hold of him and bind him. Burn him in the blazing Fire, then fasten him with a chain seventy cubits long. For he did not believe in Allah, the Most High, nor did he urge the feeding of the poor.

Sura: 69, Ayat: 30—34.

Indeed, man was created impatient. When evil befalls him he is despondent; but blessed with good fortune he grows niggardly.

Not so the worshippers who are steadfast in prayer; . . . who truly believe in the Day of Reckoning.

Sura: 70, Ayat: 19–23 . . . 26

Each soul is held in pledge for what it earns, except those of the right hand. These will in their gardens ask the sinners: 'What has brought you into Hell?' They will reply: 'We never prayed or fed the hungry. We engaged in vain disputes and denied the Day of Reckoning till the inevitable (death) overtook us.'

Sura: 74, Ayat: 38—47.

No, verily they have no fear of the Hereafter.

Sura: 74, Ayat: 53.

I swear by the Day of Resurrection, and by the self-reproaching soul!

Does man think We shall never put his bones together again? Indeed, We can remould his very fingers!

Yet man desires to go on sinning.

Sura: 75, Ayat: 1—5.

They who keep their vows and dread the far-spread terrors of the Day (of Judgement), who though they hold it dear, give sustenance to the poor man,

the orphan, and the captive, (saying): 'We feed you for Allah's sake only; we seek of you neither recompense nor thanks: for we fear from Him a day of anguish and of woe.

So Allah will deliver them from the evil of that day and make their faces shine with joy.

Sura: 76, Ayat: 7—11.

These love this fleeting life and leave (unheeded and unattended to) in front of them a heavy day.

Sura: 76, Ayat: 27.

Did We not destroy the men of old and cause others to follow them? Thus shall We deal with the guilty.

Woe on that day to the disbelievers! Did We not create you from an unworthy fluid, which We kept in a safe receptacle for an appointed time? All this We did; how excellent is Our work!

Woe on that day to the disbelievers! Have We not made the earth draw together the living and dead? have We not placed high mountains upon it and given you fresh water for your drink?

Woe on that day to the disbelievers!

Sura: 77, Ayat: 16—28.

They say: 'Shall we indeed be restored to (our) first state even after we are rotten bones?'

They say: 'That would then be a vain return.'

Sura: 79, Ayat: 10—12.

O man! What evil has enticed you away from your gracious Lord who created you, gave you an upright form, and well-proportioned you? In whatever shape He willed he could have surely moulded you.

No, you deny the Last Judgement. Yet there are guardians watching over you, noble recorders who know of all what you do.

Sura: 82, Ayat: 6—12.

Woe on that day to the disbelievers who deny the Last Judgement! None denies it except every aggressive sinner.

Sura: 83, Ayat: 11-12.

Have you thought of him that denies the Last Judgement? It is he who turns away the orphan and does not urge others to feed the poor.

Sura: 107, Ayat: 1—3.

In the name of Allah, The Compassionate, The Merciful

BELIEF IN ANGELS

Whoever is an enemy of Allah, His angels, or His apostles, or of Gabriel or Michael, (will surely find that) Allah is the enemy of the unbelievers.

Sura: 2, Ayat: 98.

Righteousness does not consist in whether you face towards the east or the west. The righteous man is he who believes in Allah and the Last Day, in the angels and the Book and the prophets; who for the love of Allah gives his wealth to his kinsfolk, to the orphans, to the needy, to the wayfarers and to the beggars, and for the redemption of captives; who attends to his prayers and pays the alms-tax; who is true to his promises and steadfast in trial and adversity and in times of war. Such are the true believers; such are the God-fearing.

Sura: 2, Ayat: 177.

The Apostle believes in what has been revealed to him by his Lord, and so do the faithful. They all believe in Allah and His angels, His books and His apostles. We discriminate against none of His apostles. They say: 'We hear and obey. Grant us your forgiveness, Lord; to You we shall all return.

Sura: 2, Ayat: 285.

O believers, have faith in Allah and His Apostle, in the Book He has revealed to His Apostle, and in the Book He formerly revealed. He that denies Allah, His angels, His Scriptures, His apostles, and the Last Day, has strayed far from the truth.

Sura: 4, Ayat: 136.

In the name of Allah, The Compassionate, The Merciful

FAITH IN THE DIVINE BOOKS

The Apostle believes in what has been revealed to him by his Lord, and so do the faithful. They all believe in Allah and His Angels, His books, and His apostles...We discriminate against none of His apostles. They say: 'We hear and obey. Grant us your forgiveness, Lord; to You we shall all return.

Sura: 2, Ayat: 285.

In the name of Allah, The Compassionate, The Merciful

REWARD AND PUNISHMENT

Allah does not charge a soul with more than it can bear. It shall be requited for whatever good and whatever evil it has done.

Sura: 2, Ayat: 286.

As for those who disbelieved, they shall be sternly punished in this world and in the world to come: there shall be none to help them.

Sura: 3, Ayat: 56.

As for those that have faith and do good works, they shall be given their reward in full. Allah does not love the evil-doers.'

Sura: 3, Ayat: 57.

No one dies unless Allah permits. The term of every life is fixed. And he that desires the reward of this world, We shall give him of it; and he that desires the reward of the life to come, We shall give him of it. And We will reward the thankful.

Sura: 3, Ayat: 145.

Every soul shall taste death. You shall receive your rewards only on the Day of Resurrection. Whoever is spared Hell and is admitted to Paradise shall surely gain (his end); for the life of this world is nothing but a fleeting vanity.

Sura: 3, Ayat: 185.

You shall not kill one another. Allah is Merciful, but he that does that through wickedness and injustice shall be burned in fire. That is an easy thing for Allah.

Sura: 4, Ayat: 30.

Not by the smallest ant's weight will Allah wrong (any man). He that does a good deed shall be repaid twofold. Allah will bestow on him a rich recompense.

Sura: 4, Ayat: 40.

It shall not be in accordance with your wishes, nor shall it be in accordance with the wishes of the people of the Book. He that does evil shall be requited with it: there shall be none to protect or help him.

Sura: 4, Ayat: 123.

But the believers who do good works, whether men or women, shall enter Paradise. They shall not suffer the least injustice.

Sura: 4, Ayat: 124.

Let the man who seeks the reward of this life know that Allah holds the rewards of this life and of the next. He is Hearing, Seeing.

Sura: 4, Ayat: 134.

And why should Allah punish you if you render thanks to Him and truly believe in Him? Allah is Rewarding, Knowing.

Sura: 4, Ayat: 147.

Allah will reward those that have faith and do good works; He will enrich them from His own abundance. As for those who are scornful and proud, He will sternly punish them, and they shall find none besides Allah to protect or help them.

Sura: 4, Ayat: 173.

Allah has promised those that have faith and do good works forgiveness and a rich reward.

Sura: 5, Ayat: 9.

Know that Allah is stern in retribution, and that He is Forgiving and Merciful.

Sura: 5, Ayat: 98.

Those that have faith and do not taint their faith with wrongdoing shall surely have security, and follow the right path.'

Sura: 6, Ayat: 82.

Sin neither openly nor in secret. Those that commit sin shall be punished for their sins.

Sura: 6, Ayat: 120.

They all get degrees (of reward) according to their deeds. Your Lord is watching over all their actions.

Sura: 6, Ayat: 132.

Say: 'Do all that is in your power, my people, and I will do what is in mine.

You shall before long know to whom will be the good end of the abode. The wrongdoers shall not triumph.'

Sura: 6, Ayat: 135.

He that does a good deed shall be repaid tenfold; but he that commits a sin shall be punished only for it. None shall be wronged.

Sura: 6, Ayat: 160.

Say: 'Should I seek any but Allah for my God, when He is the Lord of all things? Each man shall reap the fruits of his own deeds: no soul shall bear another's burden. In the end you shall all return to your Lord, and He will inform you about that in which you differed.'

Sura: 6, Ayat: 164.

As for those that have faith and do good works — We never charge a soul with more than it can bear — they are the people of Paradise, and there they shall abide for ever.

Sura: 7, Ayat: 42.

Say: 'Do as you will, Allah will behold your works and so will His Apostle and the faithful; then you shall return to Him who knows alike the unseen and the visible, and He will declare to you all that you have done.

Sura: 9, Ayat: 105.

Each sum they give, be it small or large, and each journey they undertake, shall be noted down, so that Allah may reward them for their noblest deeds.

Sura: 9, Ayat: 121.

To Him is the return of you all: Allah's promise shall be fulfilled. He gives being to His creatures, and in the end He will bring them back to life, so that He may justly reward those who have believed and done good works. As for the unbelievers, they shall drink boiling water and be sternly punished for their unbelief.

Sura: 10, Ayat: 4.

For those that do good is a reward and more. Neither blackness nor misery shall cover their faces. They are the people of Paradise: in it they shall abide for ever.

As for those that have earned evil, evil shall be rewarded with like evil. Misery will cover them — they shall have none to defend them from Allah — as though their faces were veiled with the night's black patches. They are the people of Hell: in it they shall abide for ever.

Sura: 10, Ayat: 26-27.

If they disbelieve you, say: 'My deeds are mine and your deeds are yours. You are not accountable for my actions, nor am I for yours.'

Sura: 10, Ayat: 41.

You shall be engaged in no affair, neither shall you recite on it any portion of the Quran, nor shall you do any action, but We will be witnesses over you. Not an atom's weight in earth or heaven escapes your Lord, nor is there any object smaller or greater, but is recorded in a glorious book.

Now surely the servants of Allah have nothing to fear or to regret. Those that have faith and keep from evil,

Sura: 10, Ayat: 61—63.

If they say: 'He has invented it himself,' say: 'If I have indeed invented it, then on me be my guilt. I am innocent of your crimes.'

Sura: 11, Ayat: 35.

Thus We established Yusuf in the land to dwell wherever he liked. We bestow Our mercy on whom We will, and never deny the righteous their reward. Better is the reward of the life to come for those who believe in Allah and keep from evil.

Sura: 12, Ayat: 56-57.

This is the Paradise which the righteous have been promised: it is watered by running streams: eternal are its fruits and eternal are its shades. Such is the reward of the righteous. But the reward of the unbelievers is the Fire.

Sura: 13, Ayat: 35.

Allah will strengthen the faithful with (His) steadfast Word, both in this life and the Hereafter. He leaves the wrongdoers in error. Allah accomplishes what He pleases.

Sura: 14, Ayat: 27.

Be they men or women, those that embrace the faith and do what is right We will surely grant a happy life; We shall reward them according to their noblest actions.

Sura: 16, Ayat: 97.

If you do good, it shall be to your own advantage; but if you do evil, you shall sin against yourselves.'

Sura: 17, Ayat: 7.

He that seeks guidance shall be guided to his own advantage, but he that errs shall err at his own peril. No soul shall bear another's burden. Nor do We

punish until we have sent forth an apostle.

Sura: 17, Ayat: 15.

He that desires this fleeting life We hasten to him in it whatever We will: (We hasten that) to whom We please. Then We have prepared Hell for him; he will burn in it despised and helpless.

As for him that desires the life to come and strives for it as he ought to, being also a believer — those are they whose striving is amply rewarded by Allah.

On all — on these and those — We bestow the bounty of your Lord, and the bounty of your Lord was never withheld (from any one).

Sura: 17, Ayat: 18—20.

He that does good works in the fullness of his faith, his endeavours shall not be lost: We record them all.

Sura: 21, Ayat: 94.

Those who believe, the Jews, the Sabaeans, the Christians, the Magians, and the polytheists, Allah will judge them on the Day of Resurrection. He bears witness to all things.

Sura: 22, Ayat: 17.

We charge no soul with more than it can bear. We have a Book which speaks the truth: none shall be wronged.

Sura: 23, Ayat: 62.

Those that have done good shall be rewarded with what is better, and shall be secure from the terrors of that day.

But those that have done evil shall be hurled headlong into the Fire. Shall you not be rewarded according to your deeds?

Sura: 27, Ayat: 89-90.

He that does good shall be rewarded with what is better. But he that does evil, the evildoers will be requited only for what they do.

Sura: 28, Ayat: 84.

Do men think that once they say: 'We are believers,' they will be left alone and not be tried?

We tested those who have gone before them. Allah knows those who are truthful and those who are lying.

Or do the evildoers think that they will escape (Our punishment)? How ill they judge!

Sura: 29, Ayat: 2—4.

As for those who have faith and do good works, We shall cleanse them of their sins and reward them according to their noblest deeds.

Sura: 29, Ayat: 7.

The unbelievers say to the faithful: 'Follow us, and we will bear the burden of your sins.' But they will bear none of their sins. They are surely lying.

They shall bear their own burdens, and other burdens besides. On the Day of Resurrection, they shall be questioned about their falsehoods.

Sura: 29, Ayat: 12-13.

Those who disbelieve will answer for their unbelief, while the righteous will make ready their blissful home: for then Allah will in His bounty reward those who have embraced the faith and done good works. Allah does not love the unbelievers.

Sura: 30, Ayat: 44.

But We will inflict on them the lighter punishment (of this world) before the supreme punishment (of the world to come), so that they may return (to the right path).

Sura: 32, Ayat: 21.

We offered the trust to the heavens, to the earth, and to the mountains, but they refused to bear it, and were afraid of it. Man undertook to bear it, but he has proved unjust and foolish.

Allah will surely punish the hypocrites, men and women, and the unbelievers, both men and women; but Allah pardons believing men and believing women. Allah is Forgiving and Merciful.

Sura: 33, Ayat: 72-73.

Say: 'Who provides for you from heaven and earth?'

Say: 'Allah. It is certain that we or you are rightly guided or are in evident error.'

Say: 'You are not accountable for our sins, nor are we accountable for your actions.'

Say: 'Our Lord will bring us all together, then He will rightly judge between us. He is the All-Knowing Judge.'

Sura: 34, Ayat: 24—26.

The unbelievers shall be sternly punished, but those that accept the true faith and do good works shall be forgiven and richly rewarded.

Sura: 35, Ayat: 7.

No (soul) shall bear another's burden. If a laden (soul) cries out for help, nothing of (its burden) will be carried even by a relative.

You shall admonish none but those who fear their Lord though they cannot see Him, and are steadfast in prayer. He that purifies himself has much to gain. To Allah shall all things return.

Sura: 35, Ayat: 18.

This is but an admonition. The righteous shall return to a blessed retreat — the Gardens of Eden whose gates shall be open to them....

But doleful shall be the return of the transgressors. They shall burn in the fire of Hell, a dismal resting-place.

Sura: 38, Ayat: 49-50, 55-56

If you render Him no thanks, know that Allah does not need you. Yet the ingratitude of His servants does not please Him. If you are thankful, your thanks will please Him.

No soul shall bear another's burden. To Allah you shall all return and He will declare to you what you have done. He knows your inmost thoughts.

Sura: 39, Ayat: 7.

Say: 'My servants who believe, fear your Lord. Those who do good works in this life shall receive a good reward. Allah's earth is vast. Those that endure with fortitude shall be requited without measure.'

Sura: 39, Ayat: 10.

Say: 'I fear, if I disobey my Lord, the torment of a fateful day.'

Sura: 39, Ayat: 13.

Say: 'My people, do as best you can and so will I. You shall before long know who will receive a punishment of shame, and who will be overtaken by an everlasting punishment.'

Sura: 39, Ayat: 39-40.

He who was a true believer said: 'Follow me, my people, that I may rightly guide you. O my people, the life of this world is nothing but a (passing) comfort, but the life to come is an everlasting mansion. Those that do evil shall be rewarded with like evil; but those that have faith and do good works, both men and women, shall enter the Gardens of Paradise and receive blessings without number.

Sura: 40, Ayat: 38—40.

He that does good does it for his own soul; and he that commits evil does so at his own peril. Your Lord is never unjust to His servants.

Sura: 41, Ayat: 46.

We shall tell the unbelievers what they did and visit upon them a stern

chastisement.

Sura: 41, Ayat: 50.

You shall see the wrongdoers aghast at what they have earned, and it shall befall them.

Sura: 42, Ayat: 22.

Say: 'For this I demand of you no recompense except love of relatives. He that does a good deed We add to its goodness for him. Allah is Forgiving and Bountiful in His rewards.'

Sura: 42, Ayat: 23.

If a misfortune befalls you, it is the fruit of your own labours. He forgives much.

Sura: 42, Ayat: 30.

Tell the believers to pardon those who do not look forward to the days of Allah, so that He may reward men according to their deeds. He that does what is right does it to his own advantage; and he that commits evil does so at his own peril. To your Lord you shall all return.

Sura: 45, Ayat: 14-15.

Do the evildoers think that they are equal in Our sight to the believers who do good works, so that in life and death shall be alike? How ill they judge!

Sura: 45, Ayat: 21.

There are degrees for all, according to their deeds, so that Allah may duly requite them for their works. They shall not be wronged.

Sura: 46, Ayat: 19.

As for the faithful who do good works and believe in what is revealed to Muhammad — which is the truth from their Lord — He will forgive them their sins and improve their state.

Sura: 47, Ayat: 2.

This is because the unbelievers follow falsehood, while the faithful follow the truth from their Lord. Thus Allah sets forth for mankind their examples.

Sura: 47, Ayat: 3.

Allah destroyed them utterly. A similar fate awaits the unbelievers, because Allah is the protector of the faithful, and because the unbelievers have no protector.

Allah will admit those who believe and do good works to gardens watered by running streams. The unbelievers take their fill of pleasure and eat as the

cattle eat: but Hell shall be their home.

Sura: 47, Ayat: 10—12.

The life of this world is but a sport and a pastime. if you believe in Him and guard yourselves against evil, He will reward you, and will not ask for all your wealth.

Sura: 47, Ayat: 36.

Burn in its flames. It is alike whether you are patient or impatient. You shall be rewarded according to your deeds.'

Sura: 52, Ayat: 16 .

Give no heed, then, to those who ignore Our warning and seek only the life of this world. This is the sum of their knowledge. Your Lord knows best who has strayed from His path, and who is rightly guided.

To God is what the heavens and the earth contain. He will requite the evil-doers according to their deeds, and bestow a good reward on those who do good works.

(To) those who avoid the grossest sins and indecencies and commit only small offences, Allah is of vast forgiveness.

Sura: 53, Ayat: 29—32.

Thus We reward the thankful.

Sura: 54, Ayat: 35.

Shall the reward of goodness be anything but good? Which of your Lord's blessings would you deny?

Sura: 55, Ayat: 60-61

Believe then in Allah and His Apostle and in the light which We have revealed. Allah has knowledge of all your actions.

The day on which He will assemble you, the day on which you shall all be gathered — that shall be a day of mutual loss and gain. Those who believe in Allah and do what is right shall be forgiven their sins and admitted to gardens watered by running streams, where they shall dwell for ever. That is the supreme triumph.

Sura: 64, Ayat: 8-9.

O believers, guard yourselves and guard your kindred against the Fire which has fuel of men and stones, whose keepers are fierce and mighty angels who never disobey Allah's command and promptly do His bidding. They will say to the unbelievers: 'Make no excuses for yourselves this day. You shall be rewarded according to your deeds.'

Sura: 66, Ayat: 6-7.

Surely the righteous have gardens of bliss with their Lord. Are We to deal with the true believers as We deal with the wrongdoers? What has come over you? How do you judge?

Sura: 68, Ayat: 34—36.

Each soul is held in pledge for what it earns, except those of the right hand. These will in their gardens ask the sinners: 'What has brought you into Hell?' They will reply: 'We never prayed or fed the hungry. We engaged in vain disputes and denied the Day of Reckoning till the inevitable (death) overtook us.'

Sura: 74, Ayat: 38—47.

The righteous surely shall dwell in bliss. But the wicked surely shall burn in Hell.

Sura: 82, Ayat: 13-14.

But the record of righteous shall be in Illiyin. Would that you know what Illiyin is! It is a sealed book, seen only by those who are closest to Allah.

The righteous shall surely dwell in bliss. Reclining upon soft couches they will look around them: and in their faces you shall mark the glow of joy. They shall be given to drink of a pure wine, securely sealed, whose very dregs are musk; for this let all men emulously strive; a wine tempered with Tasnim, a spring at which the favoured will refresh themselves.

The evildoers used to scoff at the faithful and wink at one another as they pass by them. When they return to their own folk they speak of them with jests and when they see them they say: 'These are erring men!' Yet they were not sent to be their guardians.

But on that day the faithful will mock the unbelievers as they recline upon their couches and gaze around them.

Shall (not) the unbelievers be rewarded according to their deeds?

Sura: 83, Ayat: 18—36.

Save those who embrace the true faith and do good works; for theirs is an unfailing recompense.

Sura: 84, Ayat: 25.

What, then, can after this make you deny the Last Judgement? Is Allah not the best of judges?

Sura: 95, Ayat: 7-8.

When the earth is shaken in her last convulsion; when the earth brings forth its burdens and man asks 'What may this mean?' — on that day it will proclaim its tidings, for your Lord will have inspired it.

On that day mankind will come in broken bands to be shown their labours. Whoever does an atom's weight of good shall see it, and whoever does an

atom's weight of evil shall see it also.

Sura: 99, Ayat: 1–8.

You are distracted by worldly gain until you visit the graves.

But no, you shall know. Again no, you shall know.

Indeed, if you knew the truth with certainty, you would see the fire of Hell: you would see it with your very eyes.

On that day, you shall be questioned about the pleasures (you indulged in).

Sura: 102, Ayat: 1–8.

In the name of Allah, The Compassionate, The Merciful

THE STRAIGHT PATH

You alone we worship, and to You alone we look for help. Guide us to the straight path, The Path of those upon whom You bestowed favours, not those who have invited Your wrath, nor those who have gone astray.

Sura: 1, Ayat: 4—7.

Allah guided by His will those who believed in the truth which had been disputed. Allah guides whom He will to the right path.

Sura: 2, Ayat: 213.

Allah is my God and your God: therefore, serve Him. That is the straight path.

Sura: 3, Ayat: 51.

But how can you disbelieve when Allah's revelations are recited to you and His own Apostle is in your midst! He that holds fast to Allah shall be guided to the right path.

Sura: 3, Ayat: 101.

Say: 'Come, I will tell you what your Lord has made binding on you: that you shall serve no other gods besides Him; that you shall show kindness to your parents; that you shall not kill your children because you cannot support them; We provide for you and for them; that you shall not commit foul sins, whether openly or in secret, and that you shall not kill — for that is forbidden by Allah — except for a just cause. Thus Allah exhorts you, that you may discern.

Do not touch the property of orphans, but strive to improve their lot until they reach maturity. Give just weight and full measure; We never charge a soul with more than it can bear. Speak for justice, even if it affects your own kinsmen. Be true to the covenant of Allah. Thus He exhorts you, so that you

may take heed.

This path of Mine is straight. Follow it and do not follow other paths, for they will lead you away from Him. Thus Allah commands you, so that you may guard yourselves against evil.

Sura: 6, Ayat: 151–153.

Ya sin. I swear by the Wise Quran that you are one of those sent upon a straight path.

Sura: 36, Ayat: 1–4.

Did I not enjoin you, Sons of Adam, not to serve Satan who is your acknowledged enemy, and that you should worship Me? Surely that was the right path. Yet he has led many of you astray. Had you no sense?

Sura: 36, Ayat: 60–62.

And thus We have inspired you with a spirit of Our will when you knew nothing of faith or scripture, and made it a light whereby We guide those of Our servants whom We please. You shall surely guide them to the right path of Allah.

Sura: 42, Ayat: 52.

In the name of Allah, The Compassionate, The Merciful

THE BENEFITS OF FAITH

As for the faithful who do good works and believe in what is revealed to Muhammad (P.B.U.H.) – which is the truth from their Lord – He will forgive them their sins and improve their state.

Sura: 47, Ayat: 2

In the name of Allah, The Compassionate, The Merciful

PEACE OF MIND

Say: 'Allah leaves in error whom He will, and guides those who repent and have faith and whose hearts find comfort in the remembrance of Allah. Surely in the remembrance of Allah all hearts are comforted.

Sura: 13, Ayat: 27-28

THE PURPOSE OF HUMAN LIFE

(4)

In the name of Allah, The Compassionate, The Merciful

THE AIM OF LIFE

Say: 'My prayers and my devotions, my life and my death, are all for Allah. Lord of the Creation: He has no partner. Thus I am commanded, being the first of the Muslims.'

Sura: 6, Ayat: 162-163.

He it is Who made the heavens and the earth in six days — And His throne was on water — that he might try you and see who of you excels in works.

If you* say: 'After death you shall be raised to life,' the unbelievers declare: 'This is nothing but plain magic.'

Sura: 11, Ayat: 7

Had your Lord pleased, He would have made mankind a single nation. Yet they cease not differing, save those whom the Lord has shown mercy. For this end He has created them. The word of your Lord shall be fulfilled: 'I will fill Hell with Jinn and men, all together.'

Sura: 11, Ayat: 118-119.

We have made that which is on earth an ornament for it, so that We may test them as to which of them do best.

We will surely reduce all that is on it to barren dust.

Sura: 18, Ayat: 7-8.

It was not in sport that We created the heavens and the earth and all that lies between them. Had it been Our will to find a pastime, We could have found one near at hand if We were to do it.

We will hurl Truth at Falsehood, until Truth shall triumph and Falsehood be no more. Woe shall befall you, for all the (falsehoods) you have uttered.

Sura: 21, Ayat: 16—18.

Every soul shall taste death. We will try you in good and evil ordeals.

---

*Muhammad (P.B.U.H)

To Us you shall be recalled.

Sura: 21, Ayat: 35.

Allah created the heavens and the earth with (the aim of manifesting) the truth and to reward each soul according to its deeds. And they shall not be wronged.

Sura: 45, Ayat: 22.

I only created mankind and the jinn that they might worship Me.

Sura: 51, Ayat: 56.

Blessed be He in Whose hands is all sovereignty: He has power over all things.

He created life and death that He might put you to the test and find out which of you acquitted himself best. He is the Mighty, the Forgiving One.

Sura: 67, Ayat: 1-2.

We have created man from sperm mixed (with ovum) to put him to proof. So we have endowed him with sight and hearing. We have shown him the right path, whether he be grateful or ungrateful.

Sura: 76, Ayat: 2-3.

We created man into toil and strife.

Sura: 90, Ayat: 4.

In the name of Allah, The Compassionate, The Merciful

THE REALITY OF THE WORLD

There are some who say: 'Lord, give us good in this world.' These shall have no share in the Hereafter. But there are others who say: 'Lord, give us what is good both in this world and in the next and keep us from the fire of Hell. These shall have a share of what they have earned. Swift is the reckoning of Allah.

Sura: 2, Ayat: 200—202.

For the unbelievers, the life of this world is decked with all manner of temptations. They scoff at the faithful, but those that fear Allah shall be above them on the Day of Resurrection. Allah gives without measure to whom He will.

Sura: 2, Ayat: 212.

Those who disbelieve, neither their riches nor their children shall in the least save them from Allah. They shall become the fuel of Fire.

Sura: 3, Ayat: 10.

Men are tempted by the lure of women and offspring, of hoarded treasures of gold and silver, of splendid horses, cattle, and plantations. These are the comforts of this life, but far better is the return to Allah.

Say: 'Shall I tell of better things than these, with which the righteous shall be rewarded by their Lord? Theirs shall be gardens watered by running streams, where they shall dwell forever: wives freed from impurity, and grace from Allah.' Allah is watching over His servants:

Sura: 3, Ayat: 14-15.

Every soul shall taste death. You shall receive your rewards only on the Day of Resurrection. Whoever is spared Hell and is admitted to Paradise shall surely gain (his end); for the life of this world is nothing but a fleeting vanity.

Sura: 3, Ayat: 185.

Do not be deceived by the activities of the unbelievers in this land. Their

prosperity is brief. Hell shall be their home, a dismal resting-place.

Sura: 3, Ayat: 196-197.

The life of this world is but a sport and a pastime. Surely better is the life to come for those who are righteous. Will you not understand?

Sura: 6, Ayat: 32.

Avoid those that treat faith as a sport and a pastime and are seduced by the life of this world. Admonish them hereby lest a soul be damned by its own sins. It has no guardian or intercessor besides Allah: and though it offers every ransom, it shall not be accepted from it. Such are those that are damned by their deeds. They shall drink boiling water and be sternly punished for their unbelief.

Sura: 6, Ayat: 70.

(Then He will say): 'Jinn and men! Did there not come to you apostles of your own who proclaimed to you My revelations and warned you of this day?'

They will reply: 'We bear witness against our own souls.' Indeed, the life of this world beguiled them. They will testify to their own faithlessness.

Sura: 6, Ayat: 130.

The people of the Fire will cry out to the people of Paradise: 'Give us some water, or some of that which Allah has given you." But the blessed shall reply: 'Allah has forbidden both to the unbelievers, who made their religion a pastime and an idle sport, and who were beguiled by their earthly life.'

On this day We will forget them as they forgot the meeting of that day: for they denied Our revelations.

Sura: 7, Ayat: 50-51.

We dispersed them through the earth in multitudes — some were righteous men, others were not — and tested them with blessings and misfortunes so that they might desist (from sin). Then others succeeded them who inherited the Book and availed themselves of the vanities of this life, saying: 'We shall be forgiven our sins.' But if similar vanities came their way, they would again seize them.

Are they not committed to the covenant of the Book, which they have studied well, to tell nothing of Allah but what is true? Surely the world to come is a better prize for those that guard themselves against evil. Have you no sense?

Sura: 7, Ayat: 168-169.

Believers, why is it that when it is said to you: 'March in the cause of Allah.' You linger slothfully in the land? Are you content with this life in preference to the life to come? Few indeed are the blessings of this life, compared to those

of the life to come.

Sura: 9, Ayat: 38.

Let neither their riches nor their children rouse your envy. Through these Allah seeks to punish them in this life, so that they shall die unbelievers.

Sura: 9, Ayat: 85.

Those who deny do not expect meeting Us, delighting in the life of this world and contenting themselves with it, and those who give no heed to Our revelations, their abode is the Fire on account of what they earned (of misdeeds).

Sura: 10, Ayat: 7-8.

This present life is only like water which we send down from the clouds so that the luxuriant herbage sustaining man and beast may grow; until when the earth puts on its lovely garment and becomes adorned, and its people think that they are its masters, down comes Our scourge upon it, by night or in broad day, laying it waste, as though it has not blossomed yesterday. Thus We make plain Our revelations to thoughtful men.

Allah invites you to the Home of Peace. He guides whom He will to a straight path.

Sura: 10, Ayat: 24-25.

The day (will come) when He will gather them again, as though they had stayed (in this world) but an hour of the day. They will recognize one another. Lost are those that disbelieve in meeting their Lord and do not follow the right path.

Sura: 10, Ayat: 45.

Say: 'Those that invent falsehoods about Allah shall not prosper. (They may take their) ease in this life, but to Us they shall (in the end) return, and We will sternly punish them for their unbelief.'

Sura: 10, Ayat: 69-70.

Those that desire the life of this world with all its frippery shall be rewarded for their deeds in their own lifetime: they will not suffer any loss. These are the men who in the world to come will have nothing but the Fire. Vain is what they did in it and fruitless are their works.

Sura: 11, Ayat: 15-16.

Allah gives abundantly and sparingly to whom He pleases. Those who disbelieve rejoice in this life: but brief indeed is the comfort of this life compared to the life to come.

Sura: 13, Ayat: 26.

That which you have is transitory, but that which Allah has is enduring. We shall reward the steadfast according to their noblest deeds.

Sura: 16, Ayat: 96.

Those who disbelieve in Allah after their belief — not he who recants while his heart remains loyal to the faith, but he who opens his breast for disbelief — shall incur the wrath of Allah and be sternly punished. For such men love the life of this world more than the life to come. Allah gives no guidance to the unbelievers.

Sura: 16, Ayat: 106-107.

He that desires this fleeting life We hasten to him in it whatever We will: (We hasten that) to whom we please. Then We have prepared Hell for him; he will burn in it despised and helpless.

As for him that desires the life to come and strives for it as he ought to, being also a believer — those are they whose striving is amply rewarded by Allah.

On all — on these and those — We bestow the bounty of your Lord, and the bounty of your Lord was never withheld (from any one).

See how We have exalted some above others. Yet the life to come is greater by degrees and is more exalted.

Sura: 17, Ayat: 18—21.

We have made that which is on earth an ornament for it, so that We may test them as to which of them do best.

Sura: 18, Ayat: 7.

Coin for them a simile about this life. It is like vegetation of the earth that flourishes when watered by the rain, soon turning into stubble which the wind scatters abroad. Allah has power over all things.

Wealth and children are the ornament of this life. But deeds of lasting merit are better with your Lord in reward and hope.

Sura: 18, Ayat: 45-46.

Do not strain your eyes toward the worldly benefits we have bestowed on some of them, for with these We seek only to try them. Your Lord's provision is better and more lasting.

Sura: 20, Ayat: 131.

And He will ask: 'How many years did you live on earth?'

They will reply: 'A day or possibly less. Ask those who have kept count.'

He will say: 'Brief indeed was your sojourn, if you but knew it! Did you think that We had created you in vain and that you would never be recalled to

Us?'

Sura: 23, Ayat: 112—115.

The life of this world is but a sport and a pastime. It is the abode in the Hereafter that (is the true) life: if they but knew it.

Sura: 29, Ayat: 64.

Men, fear your Lord, and fear the day when no parent shall avail his child nor any child his parent. Allah's promise is surely true. Let the life of this world not deceive you, nor let the Dissembler trick you concerning Allah.

Sura: 31, Ayat: 33.

Men, the promise of Allah is true. Let the life of this world not deceive you, nor let the Dissembler trick you about Allah. Satan is your enemy: therefore treat him as an enemy. He tempts his followers so that they may become the people of the Fire.

Sura: 35, Ayat: 5-6.

It was not in vain that We created the heavens and the earth and all that lies between them. That is the fancy of the unbelievers. But woe to the unbelievers because of the fire of Hell!

Sura: 38, Ayat: 27.

He who was a true believer said: 'Follow me, my people, that I may rightly guide you. O my people, the life of this world is nothing but a (passing) comfort, but the life to come is an everlasting mansion.

Sura: 40, Ayat: 38-39.

Whoever seeks the tilth of the world to come, We will increase his tilth; and whoever desires the tilth of this world, We give him some of it: but in the Hereafter he shall have no share at all.

Sura: 42, Ayat: 20.

That which you have been given is but the fleeting comfort of this life. Better and more enduring is that which Allah has for those who believe and put their trust in Him; who avoid gross sins and indecencies and, when angered, are willing to forgive; who obey their Lord, attend to their prayers, and conduct their affairs by mutual consent; who bestow in alms a part of that which We have given them and, when oppressed, seek to redress their wrongs.

Sura: 42, Ayat: 36—39.

Is it they who apportion your Lord's blessings? It is We who apportion to them their livelihoods in this world, exalting some in rank above others, so that the one may take the other into his service. Better is your Lord's mercy

than all their hoarded treasures.

But for the fear that all mankind might have become one community (of unbelievers), We would have given those who deny the Lord of Mercy dwellings with silver roofs, and (silver) stairs on which to go up, and (silver) doors and couches to recline upon; and also ornaments of gold: for all these are but the fleeting comforts of this life. The life to come with your Lord is for the righteous.

Sura: 43, Ayat: 32—35.

They say: 'There is this life and no other. We live and die; nothing but Time destroys us.' Surely of this they have no knowledge. They are merely guessing.

Sura: 45, Ayat: 24.

That is because you scoffed at Allah's revelations and were deceived by your earthly life.'

On that day there shall be no way out for them, nor shall they be asked to make amends.

Sura: 45, Ayat: 35.

Allah will admit those who believe and do good works to gardens watered by running streams. The unbelievers take their fill of pleasure and eat as the cattle eat: but Hell shall be their home.

Sura: 47, Ayat: 12.

The life of this world is but a sport and a pastime. If you believe in Him and guard yourselves against evil, He will reward you, and will not ask for all your wealth.

Sura: 47, Ayat: 37.

Give no heed, then, to those who ignore Our warning and seek only the life of this world. This is the sum of their knowledge. Your Lord knows best who has strayed from His path, and who is rightly guided.

Sura: 53, Ayat: 29-30.

Know that the life of this world is but a sport and a pastime, a show and an empty vaunt among you, a quest for greater riches and more children. It is like rain (which causes a plant to grow). The tillers rejoice in it, but then it withers and turns yellow soon becoming worthless stubble. In the life to come is a woeful punishment and also forgiveness from Allah and His pleasure. The life of this world is but a vain provision.

Sura: 57, Ayat: 20.

Believers, let neither your riches nor your children beguile you of Allah's

remembrance. Those that do this shall have much to lose.

Sura: 63, Ayat: 9.

Believers, you have an enemy in your wives and children: beware of them. But if you overlook their offences and forgive and pardon them, then know that Allah is Forgiving and Merciful.

Your wealth and children are but a temptation. Allah's reward is great. Therefore fear Him with all your hearts, and be attentive, obedient and charitable. Give in charity for the benefit of your soul.

Those who are saved from their own greed will surely prosper.

Sura: 64, Ayat: 14—16.

Blessed be He in Whose hands is all sovereignty: He has power over all things.

He created life and death that He might put you to the test and find out which of you acquitted himself best. He is the Mighty, the Forgiving One.

Sura: 67, Ayat: 1-2.

Yet you (men) love this fleeting life and are heedless of the life to come.

Sura: 75, Ayat: 20-21.

These love this fleeting life and leave (unheeded and unattended to) in front of them a heavy day.

Sura: 76, Ayat: 27.

Those who transgressed and chose this present life will find themselves in Hell;

Sura: 79, Ayat: 37—39.

Yet you prefer this life, although the life to come is better and more lasting.

Sura: 87, Ayat: 16-17.

In the name of Allah, The Compassionate, The Merciful

THE DIVINE WILL

Creator of the heavens and the earth! When he decrees a thing, He need only say 'Be,' and it is.

Sura: 2, Ayat: 117.

Allah gives without measure to whom He will.

Sura: 2, Ayat: 212.

Allah gives His sovereignty to whom He will. He is Munificent and All-Knowing.'

Sura: 2, Ayat: 247.

By Allah's will, they routed them. Dawud slew Goliath, and Allah bestowed on him sovereignty and wisdom and taught him what He pleased. Had Allah not defeated some by the might of others, the earth would have been utterly corrupted. But Allah is bountiful to His creatures.

Sura: 2, Ayat: 251.

Had Allah pleased, those who succeeded them would not have fought against one another after the clear signs had been given them. But they disagreed among themselves; some had faith, and others had none. Yet had Allah pleased, they would not have fought against one another. Allah does what He will.

Sura: 2, Ayat: 253.

You cause the night to pass into the day, and the day into the night; You bring forth the living from the dead and the dead from the living. You give without stint to whom You will.'

Sura: 3, Ayat: 27.

Say: 'Grace is in the hands of Allah: He bestows it on whom He will. He is Munificent and All-Knowing.

Sura: 3, Ayat: 73.

Allah was not to leave the faithful in your condition, but only to separate the evil from the good. Nor was He to reveal to you what is hidden. But He chooses those of His apostles whom He will. Therefore have faith in Allah and His Apostle; for if you have faith and guard yourselves against evil, your reward shall be rich indeed.

Sura: 3, Ayat: 179.

Allah wishes to make this known to you and to guide you along the paths of those who have gone before you, and to turn to you in mercy. He is Wise, Knowing.

Sura: 4, Ayat: 26.

Allah would lighten your burdens, and man was created weak.

Sura: 4, Ayat: 28.

Had Allah pleased, they would not have associated others with Him. We have not made you their keeper, nor are you their guardian.

Sura: 6, Ayat: 107.

If We sent down the angels to them and cause the dead to speak with them and ranged all things before them, they would still not believe, unless Allah willed it. But most of them are ignorant men.

Thus We have assigned for every prophet an enemy: the devils among men and jinn, who inspire one another with vain and varnished falsehoods. But had your Lord pleased, they would not have done so. Therefore leave them to their own inventions, so that the hearts of those who have no faith in the life to come may be inclined to it and, being pleased, persist in their sinful ways.

Sura: 6, Ayat: 111—113.

Such is the path of your Lord, a straight path. We have made plain Our revelations to thinking men.

Sura: 6, Ayat: 126.

We strongly established you on earth and provided you with a livelihood: yet you are seldom thankful.

Sura: 7, Ayat: 10.

Nor will Allah leave men in error after He has given them guidance, until He has made plain to them all that they should avoid. Allah has knowledge of all things.

Sura: 9, Ayat: 115.

Had Allah hastened the punishment of men as they would (like Him to) hasten their reward, their fate would have certainly been decreed. Therefore We

let those who deny the Last Judgement blunder about in sin.

Sura: 10, Ayat: 11.

Say: 'Had Allah pleased, I would never have recited it to you, nor would He have given you any knowledge of it. A long time I dwelt amongst you before it was revealed. Will you not understand?

Sura: 10, Ayat: 16.

Allah invites you to the Home of Peace. He guides whom He will to a straight path.

Sura: 10, Ayat: 25.

Allah does not bless the work of the evildoers. By His words He vindicates the truth, much as the guilty may dislike it.'

Sura: 10, Ayat: 81-82.

Had your Lord pleased, all the people of the earth would have believed in Him. Would you then force men to be believers?

Sura: 10, Ayat: 99.

No soul can have faith except by the will of Allah. He will visit His scourge upon the senseless.

Sura: 10, Ayat: 100.

Then we shall save Our apostles and the true believers. It is but just that We should save the faithful.

Sura: 10, Ayat: 103.

If Allah afflicts you with a misfortune none can remove it but He; and if He wills good for you, none can withhold His bounty. He is bountiful to whom He will. He is the Forgiving, the Merciful.

Sura: 10, Ayat: 107.

Those that desire the life of this world with all its frippery shall be rewarded for their deeds in their own lifetime: they will not suffer any loss. These are the men who in the world to come will have nothing but the Fire. Vain is what they did in it and fruitless are their works.

Sura: 11, Ayat: 15-16.

Such was the scourge which your Lord has visited upon the sinful towns. His punishment is stern and harrowing.

Sura: 11, Ayat: 102.

Had your Lord pleased, He would have made mankind a single nation. Yet

they cease not differing, save those whom the Lord has shown mercy. For this end He has created them. The word of your Lord shall be fulfilled: "I will fill Hell with jinn and men, all together.'

Sura: 11, Ayat: 118-119.

They bid you hasten the evil before the good. Yet many were the punishments before them. Your Lord is Merciful to men, despite their wrongdoing; yet stern is He in retribution.

Sura: 13, Ayat: 6.

Allah does not change a people's lot unless they change what is in their hearts. If He seeks to afflict them with a misfortune, none can ward it off. Besides Him, they have no protector.

Sura: 13, Ayat: 11.

We have sent no apostle but in the language of his own people, so that he might make plain to them (his message). But Allah leaves in error whom He will and guides whom He pleases. He is the Mighty, the Wise One.

Sura: 14, Ayat: 4.

Had Allah pleased, He would have united you into one nation. But He leaves in error whom He will and gives guidance to whom He pleases. You shall be questioned about what you did.

Sura: 16, Ayat: 93.

He that seeks guidance shall be guided to his own advantage, but he that errs shall err at this own peril. No soul shall bear another's burden. Nor do We punish until we have sent forth an apostle.

Sura: 17, Ayat: 15.

When We resolve to annhilate a town, We first command those that live in luxury (to obey Us). But they transgress therein. Thus the sentence is justly pronounced against it and We utterly destroy it.

How many generations have We destroyed since Nuh's time! It is sufficient that your Lord knows and sees His servants' sins.

Sura: 17, Ayat: 16-17.

On all — on these and those — We bestowed the bounty of your Lord, and the bounty of your Lord was never withheld (from any one).

Sura: 17, Ayat: 20.

There is no town but shall be destroyed or sternly punished by Us before the Day of Resurrection. That is written in the Book.

Sura: 17, Ayat: 58.

We have bestowed blessings on Adam's children and carried them by land and sea. We have provided them with good things and exalted them above many of Our creatures.

Sura: 17, Ayat: 70.

Nothing prevents men from having faith when guidance is revealed to them but the excuse: 'Could Allah have sent a human being as an apostle?'

Say: 'Had the earth been a safe place for angels to dwell in, We would have sent forth to them an angel from heaven as an apostle.'

Sura: 17, Ayat: 94-95.

That was one of Allah's signs. He whom Allah guides is rightly guided; but he whom He leaves in error shall find no friend to guide him.

Sura: 18, Ayat: 17.

There protection comes only from Allah, the true God. He is the best to reward and the best in requitting.

Sura: 18, Ayat: 44.

Who is more wicked than the man who, when reminded of his Lord's revelations, turns away from them and forgets what his hands have done? We have cast veils over their hearts, lest they should understand Our words, and made them hard of hearing. Call them as you may to the right path, they shall never be guided.

Sura: 18, Ayat: 57.

You (have no need) to speak aloud; for He has knowledge of all that is secret and all that is yet more hidden.

Sura: 20, Ayat: 7.

Every soul shall taste death. We will prove you all with good and evil by way of trial. To Us you shall be recalled.

Sura: 21, Ayat: 35.

(It is ordained that) no nation We have destroyed shall ever rise again.

Sura: 21, Ayat: 95.

Do you not see that to God bow all things in the heavens and on earth: the sun and the moon and the stars, the mountains and the trees, the beasts and many men? Yet many have deserved His scourge. He who is humbled by Allah has none to honour him. God does what He pleases.

Sura: 22, Ayat: 18.

Allah will defend the true believers (against evil). Verily God does not love

the treacherous and the thankless.

Sura: 22, Ayat: 38.

Had Allah not repelled some men by the might of others, the monasteries and churches, the synagogues and mosques in which Allah's name is frequently remembered, would have been utterly destroyed. But whoever, helps Allah shall be helped by Him. Allah is truly Powerful and Mighty.

Sura: 22, Ayat: 40.

They bid you hasten the punishment. God will not break His promise. Each day with your Lord is like a thousand years in your reckoning.

Sura: 22, Ayat: 47.

And how many a town which was sinful have We given respite! Then I seized it. To Me shall all things return.

Sura: 22, Ayat: 48.

He chooses His messengers from the angels and from men. He hears all and observes all. He knows what is before them and behind them. To Him shall all things return.

Sura: 22, Ayat: 75-76.

After them We raised other generations — no people can delay their doom or go before it and sent forth Our apostles in succession. Yet time after time they disbelieved their apostles, so that We made them follow one another and made them a byword (for iniquity). Gone are the unbelievers.

Sura: 23, Ayat: 42.

We charge no soul with more than it can bear. We have a Book which speaks the truth: none shall be wronged.

Sura: 23, Ayat: 62.

Allah is the light of the heavens and the earth. His light may be compared to a niche that enshrines a lamp, the lamp within a glass which (looks) as if it were a brilliant star. (It is) lit from a blessed olive tree, neither eastern nor western. Its very oil would almost shine forth, though no fire touched it. Light upon light; Allah guides to His light whom He will.

Sura: 24, Ayat: 35.

You will perhaps fret yourself to death on account of their unbelief. If We will, We can reveal to them a sign from heaven before which they will bow their heads in utter humility.

They deny and turn their backs on each fresh warning they receive from the Merciful: they have indeed denied, but the truth of that which they have

laughed to scorn will before long dawn upon them.

Sura: 26, Ayat: 3–6.

Never have We destroyed a town which We did not warn and admonish beforehand. We are never unjust.

Sura: 26, Ayat: 208-209.

Nor did your Lord destroy the nations until He had sent apostles to their capital cities proclaiming to them Our revelations. We do not destroy towns except when their populations sin.

Sura: 28, Ayat: 59.

Your Lord creates what He will and chooses freely, but they have no power to choose. Glorified and exalted be He above all that they associate with Him.

Sura: 28, Ayat: 68.

In His mercy He has given you the night that you may rest in it, and the day that you may seek His bounty and render thanks.

Sura: 28, Ayat: 73.

Do they not see how Allah initiates the Creation, and then reproduces it? That is easy enough for Allah. Say: 'Roam the earth and see how Allah initiated the Creation. Then Allah will create a later Creation. Allah has power over all things; He punishes whom He will and shows mercy to whom He pleases. To Him you shall be turned.'

Neither on earth nor in heaven shall you be beyond reach: nor have you any guardian or helper besides Allah.

Sura: 29, Ayat: 20–22.

Countless are the beasts that do not bear their provisions. Allah provides for them, as He provides for you. He alone hears all and knows all.

Sura: 29, Ayat: 60.

He gives victory to whom He will. He is the Mighty One, the Merciful.

That is Allah's promise; to His promise He will never be untrue. Yet most men do not know it.

Sura: 30, Ayat: 5-6.

And of His signs is that He sends the winds as bearers of good tidings, so that you may taste of His mercy and ships may sail at His bidding; so that you may seek His bounty and render thanks to Him.

We sent before you other apostles to their peoples and they showed them clear signs. We punished the guilty, and rightly succoured the true believers.

It is Allah who drives the winds that raise the clouds. He spreads them as he

will in sky and breaks them up, so that you can see the rain falling from their midst. When He sends it down upon His servants, they are filled with joy, though before its coming they may have lost all hope.

Behold then the tokens of Allah's mercy; how He gives fresh life to the earth after its death. He it is who brings back the dead men to life. He has power over all things.

Sura: 30, Ayat: 46—50.

Allah creates you weak: after weakness He gives you strength, and after strength infirmity and grey hairs. He creates whatever he will. He is the All-Knowing, the Almighty.

Sura: 30, Ayat: 54.

We suffer them to take their ease awhile, and then will drive them to stern punishment.

Sura: 31, Ayat: 24.

Allah alone has knowledge of the Hour of Doom. He sends down the rain and knows what is in the wombs. No mortal knows what he will earn tomorrow; no mortal knows in what land he will die. Surely Allah is Knowing, Aware.

Sura: 31, Ayat: 34.

Would that you could see the wrongdoers when they hang their heads before their Lord! They will say: 'Lord, we now see and hear. Send us back and we will never do wrong again. We are firm believers.

Had it been Our Will, We could have guided every soul. But My word shall be fulfilled: 'I will fill the pit of Hell with jinn and men all together.'

Sura: 32, Ayat: 12-13.

The blessings Allah bestows on man none can withhold; and what He withholds none can bestow apart from Him. He is the Mighty, the Wise One.

Sura: 35, Ayat: 2.

The blind and the seeing are not alike, nor are the darkness and the light. The shade and the heat are not alike, nor are the living and the dead. Allah can cause whom He will to hear Him, but you cannot make those who are in their graves hear you.

Sura: 35, Ayat: 19—22.

If it was Allah's will to punish men for their misdeeds, not one creature would be left alive on the earth's surface. But He respites them till an appointed time. And when their hour comes, they shall know that Allah has

been watching over all His servants.

Sura: 35, Ayat: 45.

It is We who will bring back the dead to life and record the deeds of men and the marks they leave behind: We note all things in a clear book.

Sura: 36, Ayat: 12.

He whom We bring to old age, we reverse his growth. Can they not understand?

Sura: 36, Ayat: 68.

Are We to treat alike those that have faith and do good works, and those that corrupt the earth with wickedness? Are We to treat the righteous as We treat the wicked?

Sura: 38, Ayat: 28.

We shall help Our apostles and the true believers both in this world and on the day when the witnesses rise to testify. On that day no excuse will help the evildoers. Our curse, and an evil home, await them.

Sura: 40, Ayat: 51-52.

The blind and the seeing are not alike, nor are those that have faith and do good works and the sinner. Yet you seldom think.

Sura: 40, Ayat: 58.

Yet they became divided only after knowledge had reached them, out of envy among themselves. And had it not been for a word that had already gone forth from your Lord, reprieving them till an appointed term they would surely have been punished (in this life). Those who inherited the Book after them have their grave doubts too.

Sura: 42, Ayat: 14.

Do they say: 'He has framed a falsehood about Allah.' But if Allah pleased He could seal your heart. He will reduce falsehood to nothing and vindicate the truth by His words. He knows the secret thoughts of men.

He accepts the repentance of His servants and pardons their sins. He has knowledge of all your actions.

He hears the prayers of those who have faith and do good works, and gives them more of His bounty. But a woeful punishment awaits the unbelievers.

Sura: 42, Ayat: 24—26.

If they turn away, know that We have not sent you to be their keeper. Your only duty is to warn them.

Sura: 42, Ayat: 48.

To Allah belongs the sovereignty in the heavens and the earth. He creates what He will. He gives daughters to whom He will and sons to whom He pleases. To some He gives both sons and daughters, and to others he gives none at all. Mighty is Allah and All-knowing.

Sura: 42, Ayat: 49-50.

(Remember) Ibrahim, who said to his father and to his people: 'I am innocent of what you worship. (I worship) only Him who created me, for He will rightly guide me.' He made this an abiding precept among his descendants, so that they might turn (to none but Allah).

Yes, I allowed these men and their fathers to live in comfort until there came to them the truth and an apostle making (things) clear. But now that the truth has come to them, they say: 'It is witchcraft. We do reject it.'

Sura: 43, Ayat: 26—30.

Do the evildoers think that they are equal in Our sight to the believers who do good works, so that in life and death they shall be alike? How ill they judge!

Sura: 45, Ayat: 21.

Allah created the heavens and the earth with (the aim of manifesting) the truth and to reward each soul according to its deeds. And they shall not be wronged.

Sura: 45, Ayat: 22.

It was in truth that We created the heavens and the earth and all that lies between them; (We created them to last) for an appointed term. Yet the unbelievers give no heed to Our warning.

Sura: 46, Ayat: 3.

We shall put you to the proof until We know those who strive and the resolute among you and test all that is said about you.

Sura: 47, Ayat: 31.

If the unbelievers fought you, they would have been put to flight, and would have found none to protect or help them.

Such was the way of Allah in days gone by: and you shall find no change in Allah's way.

Sura: 48, Ayat: 22-23.

We created man. We know the promptings of his soul, and are closer to him than (his) jugular vein.

When the two Keepers receive (him), the one seated on his right, the other on his left, each word he utters shall be noted down by a vigilant guardian.

And when the agony of death justly overtakes him, they will say: 'This is

the fate you have striven to avoid.

Sura: 50, Ayat: 16—19.

We have created all things according to a measure. We command but once: (Our will is done) in the twinkling of an eye.

And in the past We destroyed your fellows. Will you not take warning?

All their deeds are in their books: every action, small or great is noted down.

Sura: 54, Ayat: 49—53.

It is He who brings down clear revelations to His servant, so that He may lead you out of darkness into the light. Allah is Compassionate and Merciful to you.

Sura: 57, Ayat: 9.

It was He who created you. And some of you are unbelievers, while others have faith. He is cognizant of all your actions.

He created the heavens and the earth in truth and He shaped you and gave you good shapes. To Him you shall all return.

He knows what the heavens and the earth contain, and knows all that you hide and all that you reveal. He knows what is in your hearts.

Sura: 64, Ayat: 2—4.

The unbelievers think that they will not be raised from the dead. Say: 'By the Lord, you shall assuredly be raised to life! Then you shall be told of all that you have done. That is easy enough for Allah.'

Sura: 64, Ayat: 7.

Blessed be He in Whose hands is all sovereignty:
He has power over all things.

He created life and death that He might put you to the test and find out which of you acquitted himself best. He is the Mighty, the Forgiving One.

Sura: 67, Ayat: 1-2.

Whether you speak in secret or aloud, He knows what is in your hearts, Shall He who has created all things not know? He is gracious and All-knowing.

Sura: 67, Ayat: 13-14.

If they* follow the right path We shall vouchsafe them abundant rain, and thereby put them to the proof. He who gives no heed to his Lord's warning

***The Makkans**

shall be sternly punished.

Sura: 72, Ayat: 16-17.

We have appointed none but angels to guard the Fire, and made their number a subject for dispute among the unbelievers, so that those to whom the Scriptures were given may be convinced and the true believers strengthened in their faith; that those to whom the Scriptures were given, and the true believers, may have no doubts; and that those in whose hearts there is disease, together with the disbelievers, may say: 'What could Allah mean by this?' Thus Allah leaves in error whom He will and guides whom He pleases. None knows the warriors of your Lord but Himself. This is no more than an admonition to mankind.

Nay, by the moon! By the receding night and the forthcoming dawn, it is one of the greatest misfortunes, a warning to all men; alike to those of you that would like to march on and those that would like to remain behind.

Sura: 74, Ayat: 31—37.

This is indeed an admonition. Let him that will, take the right path to his Lord. Yet you cannot will, except by the will of Allah. Allah is Wise and All-knowing.

Sura: 76, Ayat: 29-30.

I swear by this city, and you are free from obligation in it; And (I swear) by the begetter, and all whom he begot: We created man into toil and strife.

Sura: 90, Ayat: 1—4.

It is for Us to give guidance. Ours is the life of this world and the life to come. I warn you, then, of the blazing fire.

Sura: 92, Ayat: 12—14.

Every hardship is followed by ease. Every hardship is followed by ease.

Sura: 94, Ayat: 5-6.

We created man with the most noble image and in the end We shall reduce him to the lowest of the low: except the believers who do good works, for theirs shall be a recompense never to be cut off.

Sura: 95, Ayat: 4—6.

The unbelievers among the People of the Book and the pagans would not desist (from unbelief) until the Clear Proof was given them: an apostle from Allah reading purified pages containing correct decrees.

Sura: 98, Ayat: 1—3.

Indeed, if you knew the truth with certainty, you would see the fire of Hell:

you would see it with your very eyes.

On that day, you shall be questioned about the pleasures (you indulged in).

Sura: 102, Ayat: 5–8.

In the name of Allah, The Compassionate, The Merciful

HUMAN NATURE

Allah wishes to forgive you, but those who follow their own appetites wish to see you far astray. Allah would lighten your burdens, and man was created weak.

Sura: 4, Ayat: 27-28.

When misfortune befalls man, he prays to Us lying on his side, sitting or standing. But as soon as We relieve his affliction, he pursues his former ways, as though he never prayed for Our help. Thus their foul deeds seem fair to the transgressors.

Sura: 10, Ayat: 12.

And if We show mercy to a people after some misfortune has afflicted them, then they begin to scheme against Our revelations. Say: 'More swift is Allah's scheming. Our messengers are recording what you scheme.'

Sura: 10, Ayat: 21.

It is He who enables you to traverse through land and sea until when you are in the ships, and they sail carrying them in a pleasant wind, a violent wind overtakes them, and billows surge upon them from every side and they fear that they are encompassed. Then they pray to Allah with all fervour, saying: 'Deliver us from this peril and and we will be truly thankful.'

Yet when He has delivered them, they commit evil in the land and act unjustly.

O men, it is your own souls that you are corrupting by your enjoyment in this life: to Us you shall in the end return, and We will declare to you all that you have been doing.

Sura: 10, Ayat: 22-23.

If We show man Our mercy and then withhold it from him, he yields to despair and becomes ungrateful. And if after adversity We bestow favours upon him, he says: 'Gone are my sorrows from me,' and grows jubilant and boastful.

Except those who are steadfast and do good works, they shall have forgiveness and a rich reward.

Sura: 11, Ayat: 9—11.

If you reckoned up Allah's favours, you could not count them. Truly, man is wicked and thankless.

Sura: 14, Ayat: 34.

He created man from a little germ: yet he is a professed disputer.

Sura: 16, Ayat: 4.

Whatever good you have is from Allah, and to Him you turn for help when misfortune befalls you. Yet no sooner does He remove your ills than some of you set up other gods besides Him giving no thanks for what we grant them. Take your pleasure, then, (in this life); you shall before long know.

Sura: 16, Ayat: 53—55.

Yet man prays for evil as fervently as he prays for good. Truly, man is ever hasty.

Sura: 17, Ayat: 11.

When at sea a misfortune befalls you, all but He of those to whom you pray forsake you; yet when He brings you safe to dry land, you turn your backs upon Him. Truly, man is ever thankless.

Sura: 17, Ayat: 67.

Yet when We bestow favours on man, he turns his back and holds aloof. But when evil befalls him, he grows despondent.

Sura: 17, Ayat: 83.

In this Quran, We have set forth for men all manner of parables. But man is in most things contentious.

Nothing can prevent men from having faith and seeking forgiveness of their Lord, now that guidance has been revealed to them: unless they are waiting for the fate of the ancients to overtake them or to see Our scourge with their own eyes.

Sura: 18, Ayat: 54-55.

Impatience is the stuff man is made of. You shall before long see My signs: do not ask Me to hasten them.

Sura: 21, Ayat: 37.

It is He who has given you life, and He who will cause you to die and make

you live again. Surely man is ungrateful.

Sura: 22, Ayat: 66.

If We showed them mercy and relieved their misfortunes, they would still blunder about in their transgression. We punished them, but they neither humbled themselves to their Lord nor did they submissively invoke Him. And when We opened on them a gate of severe chastisement, they plunged into utter despair.

Sura: 23, Ayat: 75—77.

When evil befalls men they turn in prayer to their Lord. But no sooner does He make them taste His mercy than some of them become polytheists, showing no gratitude for what We gave them.

Sura: 30, Ayat: 33-34.

When We give men a taste of mercy, they rejoice in it, but when evil befalls them through their own fault they grow despondent.

Sura: 30, Ayat: 36.

Evil appears on land and sea as a result of the (evil) which men's hands have done. (Allah has ordained it thus for men) so that they may taste the fruit of their own works and mend their ways.

Sura: 30, Ayat: 41.

Yet if We let loose on them a wind which makes (their plants) seem yellow, they would still continue to be ungrateful.

Sura: 30, Ayat: 51.

We offered the trust to the heavens, to the earth and to the mountains, but they refused to bear it, and were afraid of it. Man undertook to bear it, but he has proved unjust and foolish.

Allah will surely punish the hypocrites, men and women, and the unbelievers, both men and women; but Allah pardons believing men and believing women. Allah is Forgiving and Merciful.

Sura: 33, Ayat: 72-73.

Never did we send a warner to a town but the wealthy in it said: 'We do not believe in that with which you have been sent.' And they said: 'We have been given more wealth and children (than the faithful). Surely we shall never be punished'.

Sura: 34, Ayat: 34-35.

Is man not aware that We created him from a little life-germ? Yet he is an

open opponent.

Sura: 36, Ayat: 77.

When harm is done to man, he prays to his Lord and turns to Him in repentance; yet no sooner does He bestow on him His favour than he forgets that for which he had prayed before and sets up equals to him, in order to lead men away from His path.

Say: 'Enjoy your unbelief awhile; you shall surely be consigned to Hell.'

Sura: 39, Ayat: 8.

When harm befalls man he calls upon Us; but when We vouchsafe him Our favour, he says: 'I have been given it merely because of his own knowledge.' By no means! It is but a test: yet most men do not know it.

Sura: 39, Ayat: 49.

Man never wearies of praying for good things. But when evil befalls him he loses hope and grows despondent. And if We give him a taste of some mercy from Us after affliction, he is sure to say: "This is my own. I do not think the Hour of Doom will ever come. And even if I return to my Lord, He will surely reward me well.' We shall tell the unbelievers what they did and visit upon them a stern chastisement.

Sura: 41, Ayat: 49-50.

When We show favour to man, he turns away and holds aloof; but when evil befalls him he is loud in prayer.

Sura: 41, Ayat: 51.

When We give a man a taste of (Our) mercy, he rejoices in it; but when through his own fault evil befalls him he is ungrateful.

Sura: 42, Ayat: 48.

Yet they attribute to some of His Servants a share with Him (In His godhead)! Surely man is monstrously ungrateful.

Sura: 43, Ayat: 15.

When an undoubted prophet had come to them and they turned away from him, saying: 'A madman, taught (by others)!'

Yet if We slightly relieve their affliction they will return (to unbelief).

Sura: 44, Ayat: 13–15.

Indeed, man was created impatient. When evil befalls him he is despondent; but blessed with good fortune he grows niggardly.

Not so the worshippers who are steadfast in prayer; who set aside a due portion of their goods for the needy and the dispossessed; who truly believe in

the Day of Reckoning and dread the punishment of their Lord; who restrain their carnal desire save for their wives and slave-girls, for these are lawful to them: he who lusts after other than these is a transgressor, who keep their trusts and promises and bear true witness; and who attend to their prayers with promptitude. These shall be laden with honours and shall dwell in fair gardens.

Sura: 70, Ayat: 19–35.

Does man think that We cannot assemble his bones? Nay, We are able to put together in perfect order the very tips of his fingers. But man wishes to do wrong (even) in the time in front of him. He questions: 'When is the Day of Resurrection?'

Sura: 75, Ayat: 3–6.

Those love this fleeting life and leave (unheeded and unattended to) in front of them a heavy day.

Sura: 76, Ayat: 27.

Confound man! How ungrateful he is.

Sura: 80, Ayat: 17.

As for man, when his Lord tests him by exalting him and bestowing favours on him, he says: 'My Lord is bountiful to me.' But when He tests him by restricting his subsistence, he says: 'My Lord humiliates me.'

No! But you show no kindness to the orphan, nor do you urge one another to feed the poor. Greedily you lay your hands on the inheritance of the weak and you love riches with all your hearts.

Sura: 89, Ayat: 15–20.

I swear by this city, and you are free from obligation in it; And (I swear) by the begetter and all whom he begot: (We created man into toil and strife).

Sura: 90, Ayat: 1–4.

By the Fig, and by the Olive!

By Mount Sinai, and this inviolate city.*

We created man with the most noble image and in the end We shall reduce him to the lowest of the low: except the believers who do good works, for theirs shall be a recompense never to be cut off.

Sura: 95, Ayat: 1–6.

Indeed, man transgresses in thinking himself self-sufficient. Verily to your Lord is the return.

Sura: 96, Ayat: 6–8.

***Makkah**

Surely man is ungrateful to his Lord. To this he himself shall bear witness. And truly on account of his love of wealth he is niggardly.

Sura: 100, Ayat: 6–8.

You are distracted by worldly gain until you visit the graves.

Sura: 102, Ayat: 1-2.

By time, man is in loss, except those who believe and do good works and exhort one another to truth and to patience.

Sura: 103, Ayat: 1–3.

PROPHETHOOD

(5)

In the name of Allah, The Compassionate, The Merciful

A PROPHET FOR EACH COMMUNITY

To every nation is (sent) an apostle. When their apostle comes, justice is done among them; they are not wronged.

Sura: 10, Ayat: 47.

The unbelievers say: 'Why has no sign been given him by his Lord?' But your mission is only to give warning. Every nation has its guide.

Sura: 13, Ayat: 7.

We raised an apostle in every nation, saying: 'Serve Allah and avoid the idols.'

Sura: 16, Ayat: 36.

For every nation We have ordained a ritual which they observe. Let them not dispute with you concerning this. Call them to the path of your Lord: surely you are rightly guided.

Sura: 22, Ayat: 67.

In the name of Allah, The Compassionate, The Merciful

DIFFERENCES IN THE RANKS OF PROPHETS

Of these messengers, We have exalted some above others. To some Allah spoke directly; others He raised to a lofty status. We gave Isa, the son of Mariam, clear signs and strengthened him with the Holy spirit.

Sura: 2, Ayat: 253.

The Apostle believes in what has been revealed to him by his Lord, and so do the faithful. They all believe in Allah and His angels, His books, and His apostles. We discriminate against none of His apostles. They say: 'We hear and obey. Grant us your forgiveness, Lord; to You we shall all return.

Sura: 2, Ayat: 285.

Those that deny Allah and His apostles, and those that draw a line between Allah and His apostles, saying: 'We believe in some, but deny others', — thus seeking a middle way — these indeed are the unbelievers. For the unbelievers We have prepared a shameful punishment.

Sura: 4, Ayat: 150-151.

As for those that believe in Allah and His apostles and discriminate against none of them, they shall be rewarded by Allah. He is Forgiving, Merciful.

Sura: 4, Ayat: 152.

Your Lord is best aware of all who dwell in heaven and earth.

We have exalted some prophets above others. To Dawud, We gave the Zabur.

Sura: 17, Ayat: 55.

In the name of Allah, The Compassionate, The Merciful

PURPOSE OF STORIES REGARDING PROPHETS

And all we relate to you of the account of the messengers is (meant) to put courage into your heart, and through this the truth is revealed to you, with precepts and admonitions for true believers.

Sura: 11, Ayat: 120.

In their histories is a lesson to men of understanding.

This is no invented tale, but a confirmation of previous (scriptures), an explanation of all things, a guidance and a blessing to true believers.

Sura: 12, Ayat: 111.

We formerly sent forth Musa with Our signs (saying): 'Lead your people out of the darkness into the light, and remind them of the annals of Allah.' Surely in this there are signs for every steadfast, thankful man.

Sura: 14, Ayat: 5.

In the name of Allah, The Compassionate, The Merciful

ONE CODE OF LIFE AND ONE PLAN OF ACTION

Say: 'We believe in Allah and that which is revealed to us, and in what was revealed to Ibrahim, Ismail, Ishaq, Yaqub, and the tribes; to Musa and Isa and the other prophets from their Lord. We make no distinction between any of them, and to Allah we have surrendered ourselves.'

Sura: 2, Ayat: 136.

And thus We have made you a just nation, so that you may testify against mankind and that your own Apostle may testify against you.

Sura: 2, Ayat: 143.

Say: 'Allah has declared the truth. Follow the faith of Ibrahim. He was an upright man, no polytheist.

Sura: 3, Ayat: 95.

And to you We have revealed the Book with the truth confirming what was revealed before it in the other Books, and standing as a guardian over it. Therefore give judgement among them in accordance with Allah's revelations and do not yield to their fancies (swerving) from the truth that has been made known to you.

We have ordained a law and a path for each of you. Had Allah pleased, He could have made you one nation: but that He might prove you by that which He has bestowed upon you. Vie with one another in good works, for to Allah you shall all return and He will declare to you what you have disagreed about.

Sura: 5, Ayat: 48.

Say: 'My Lord has guided me to a straight path, to an upright religion, to the faith of the upright Ibrahim, who was no polytheist.'

Sura: 6, Ayat: 161.

Fight for the cause of Allah with the devotion due to Him. He has chosen you and laid on you no burdens in the observance of your faith, the faith of Ibrahim your father. He has given you the name of Muslims before and in this

so that His Apostle may be a witness for you, and that you yourselves may be witnesses for your fellow-men.

Therefore attend to your prayers and pay the alms-tax and hold fast to Allah, for He is your Guardian. A gracious Guardian and a gracious Helper!

Sura: 22, Ayat: 78.

As for those who argue about Allah after obedience has been rendered to Him, their arguments will have no weight with their Lord, and His wrath will fall upon them. They shall be sternly punished.

Sura: 42, Ayat: 16.

And now, We have set you on the right path. Follow it and do not yield to the desires of ignorant men.

Sura: 45, Ayat: 18.

In the name of Allah, The Compassionate, The Merciful

THE DISTINCTIVE QUALITIES OF THE PROPHET OF ISLAM

Indeed We have sent forth to you an apostle of your own people who will recite to you Our revelations and purify you of sin, who will instruct you in the Book and in wisdom and teach you that of which you have no knowledge.

Sura: 2, Ayat: 151.

Muhammad is no more than an apostle: other apostles have passed away before him. If he die or be slain, will you recant? He that recants will do no harm to Allah. But Allah will reward the thankful.

Sura: 3, Ayat: 144.

It was thanks to Allah's mercy that you dealt so leniently with them. Had you been cruel and hard-hearted, they would have surely deserted you. Therefore, pardon them and implore Allah to forgive them. Take counsel with them in the conduct of affairs; and when you are resolved, put your trust in Allah. Allah loves those that trust (in Him).

Sura: 3, Ayat: 159.

Allah has surely been gracious to the faithful in sending them an apostle from among themselves to declare to them His revelations, to purify them, and to instruct them in the Book and in wisdom; for before that they were in monstrous error.

Sura: 3, Ayat: 164.

We have sent you forth as an apostle to mankind. Allah is (your) all-sufficient witness.

He that obeys the Apostle obeys Allah Himself. As for those that pay no heed to you, know then that We have not sent you to be their keeper.

Sura: 4, Ayat: 79-80.

People of the Book! Our Apostle has come to reveal to you much of what you have hidden of the Book, and to forgive you much. A light has come to you

from Allah and a glorious Book, with which He will guide to the paths of peace those that seek to please Him; He will lead them by His will from darkness to the light; He will guide them to a straight path.

Sura: 5, Ayat: 15-16.

People of the Book! Our Apostle has come to reveal to you Our will after an interval during which there were no apostles, lest you should say: 'No one has come to give us good news or to warn us.' Now a prophet has come to give you good news and to warn you. Allah has power over all things.

Sura: 5, Ayat: 19.

Apostle, proclaim what is revealed to you from your Lord: If you do not, you will not have conveyed His message. Allah will protect you from all men. He does not guide the unbelievers.

Sura: 5, Ayat: 67.

The duty of the Apostle is only to give warning. Allah knows all that you hide and all that you reveal.

Sura: 5, Ayat: 99.

Say: 'I do not tell you that I possess the treasures of Allah or know what is hidden, nor do I claim to be an angel. I follow only that which is revealed to me.'

Sura: 6, Ayat: 50.

Say: 'My Lord has guided me to a straight path, to an upright religion, to the faith of the upright Ibrahim, who was no polytheist.'

Say: 'My prayers and my devotions, my life and my death, are all for Allah, Lord of the Creation: He has no partner. Thus I am commanded, being the first of the Muslims.'

Sura: 6, Ayat: 161–163.

I will show mercy to those that keep from evil, give the alms-tax, and believe in Our signs; and to those that shall follow the Apostle – the unlettered Prophet – whom they shall find mentioned in the Torah and the Gospel. He will enjoin righteousness upon them and forbid them to do evil. He will make good things lawful to them and prohibit all that is foul. He will relieve them of their burdens and of the shackles that weigh upon them. Those that believe in him and honour him, those that aid him and follow the light sent forth with him, shall surely succeed.

Sura: 7, Ayat: 157.

Say: 'People, I am sent forth to you all by Allah. His is the sovereignty in the heavens and the earth. There is no god but Him. He ordains life and death.

Therefore, have faith in Allah and His Apostle, the Unlettered Prophet, who believes in Allah and His Word. Follow him so that you may be rightly guided.'

Sura: 7, Ayat: 158.

Say: 'I have not the power to acquire benefits or to avert evil from myself, except by the will of Allah. Had I possessed knowledge of what is hidden, I would have availed myself of much that is good, and no harm would have touched me. But I am no more than one who gives warning and good news to true believers.'

Sura: 7, Ayat: 188.

And if you do not recite to them a revelation, they say: 'Have you not yet invented one?' Say: 'I follow only what is revealed to me by my Lord. This Book is a veritable proof from your Lord, a guide and a blessing to true believers.'

Sura: 7, Ayat: 203.

It is He Who has sent forth His Apostle with guidance and the true faith to make it triumphant over all religions, however much the polytheists may dislike it.

Sura: 9, Ayat: 33.

And there are others among them who molest the Prophet, saying: "He believes everything he hears." Say: 'He hears only what is good for you. He believes in Allah and puts his trust in the faithful. He is a blessing to the true believers among you. Those that wrong the Apostle of Allah shall be sternly punished.'

Sura: 9, Ayat: 61.

There has now come to you an apostle of your own, one who grieves at your sinfulness and is solicitous over you; one who is compassionate and merciful to true believers.

Sura: 9, Ayat: 128.

Alif lam ra. These are the verses of the sound Book. Does it seem strange to mankind that We should have revealed Our will to a mortal from among themselves, saying: 'Give warning to mankind, and bear the good tidings to those who believe that they have a reward with their Lord?'

Sura: 10, Ayat: 1-2.

When Our clear revelations are recited to them, those who do not hope to meet Us say to you: 'Bring us a Quran other than this, or make changes in it.'

Say: 'It is not for me to make a change in it by myself. I follow only what is

revealed to me. I cannot disobey my Lord, for I fear the punishment of a fateful day.'

Sura: 10, Ayat: 15.

Alif lam ra. (This is) a Book with verses most perfected, then made plain from the Wise, the Aware. That you should serve none but Allah. I am (sent) to you by Him to warn you and to give you good news.

And seek forgiveness of your Lord and turn to Him in repentance. He will make a good provision for you till an appointed day and will bestow His grace upon those that have merit. But if you turn away, then beware of the torment of a fateful day.

Sura: 11, Ayat: 1—3.

Say: 'This is my path. With sure knowledge, I call on you to have faith in Allah, I and all my followers. Glory be to Him! I am not one of the polytheists.'

Sura: 12, Ayat: 108.

The unbelievers say: 'Why has no sign been given him by his Lord?' But your mission is only to give warning. Every nation has its guide.

Sura: 13, Ayat: 7.

Thus We have sent you forth to a nation before whom others have passed away, that you may recite to them Our revelations. Yet they deny the Lord of Mercy. Say: 'He is my Lord. There is no god but Him. In Him I have put my trust, and to Him I shall return.'

Sura: 13, Ayat: 30.

We have sent forth other apostles before you and given them wives and children. Yet none of them could work miracles except by Allah's leave. Every term has its Book. Allah confirms or abolishes what He pleases. With Him is the Mother Book.

Sura: 13, Ayat: 38-39.

We have sent no apostle but in the language of his own people, so that he might make plain to them (his message). But Allah leaves in error whom He will and guides whom He pleases. He is the Mighty, the Wise One.

Sura: 14, Ayat: 4.

(We sent) them with clear proofs and Books. And we revealed to you the Reminder (Quran) so that you may make clear to men what has been revealed to them, and that they may give thought.

Sura: 16, Ayat: 44.

But if they turn away, your mission is only to give plain warning.

Sura: 16, Ayat: 82.

And on the day when We shall raise up in every nation a witness against them from among themselves, We (shall) bring you to testify against your people: to you We have revealed the Book which manifests the truth about all things, a guide, a blessing, and good news to those who submit to Allah.

Sura: 16, Ayat: 89.

We do know that they say: 'A mortal taught him.' But he to whom they allude speaks a foreign tongue, while this is eloquent Arabic speech.

Sura: 16, Ayat: 103.

Glory be to Him who made His servant go by night from the sacred Mosque to the farthest Mosque whose precincts We have blessed, that We might show him (some) of Our signs. He is the Hearer, the Seer.

Sura: 17, Ayat: 1.

Nothing prevents men from having faith when guidance is revealed to them but the excuse: 'Could Allah have sent a human being as an apostle?'

Sura: 17, Ayat: 94.

We have sent down (the Quran) in truth, and in truth it has come down. We have sent you forth only to proclaim good news and to give warning.

Sura: 17, Ayat: 105.

Say: 'I am but a mortal like yourselves. It is revealed to me that your God is one God. Let him that hopes to meet his Lord do what is right and worship none besides Him.'

Sura: 18, Ayat: 110.

We have revealed to you (the Quran) in your own tongue that you may thereby proclaim good tidings to the upright and give warning to contentious people.

Sura: 19, Ayat: 97.

We have not sent you forth but as a mercy to mankind.

Sura: 21, Ayat: 107.

Say: 'O men, I have been sent to warn you plainly. Those that accept the true faith and do good works shall be forgiven and richly rewarded; but those who seek to confute Our revelations shall be the people of Hell.'

Sura: 22, Ayat: 49–51.

Say: 'Obey Allah and obey His Apostle. If you turn away, he is still bound to fulfil his duty, and you yourselves are bound to fulfil yours. If you obey him, you shall be guided. The duty of an apostle is only to give a plain message.'

Sura: 24, Ayat: 54.

They also say: 'How is it that this Apostle eats and walks about the market-places? Why has no angel been sent down with him to warn us? Or (why) has no treasure been given him, no garden to provide his sustenance?'

And the wrongdoers say: 'The man you follow is surely bewitched.'

See what they compare you with? Surely they have gone astray and cannot return to the true path.

Blessed be He who, if He wills, can give you better things than these: gardens watered by running streams and palaces.

Sura: 25, Ayat: 7—10.

We have sent no apostles before you who did not eat or walk about in the market-place. We test you by means of one another. Will you not have patience? Your Lord observes all.

Sura: 25, Ayat: 20.

....No sooner will they come to you with an argument than We shall reveal to you the truth and properly explain it. Those who will be dragged headlong into Hell shall have an evil plight and shall go farther away from the (right) path.

Sura: 25, Ayat: 32—34.

Say: "I am bidden to serve the Lord of this City, which He has made sacred. All things are His."

'I am commanded to surrender to Him, and to recite the Quran. He that takes the right path shall himself have much to gain.'

To him who goes astray, say: 'I am only a warner.'

Sura: 27, Ayat: 91-92.

You were not present on the mountain-side when We called (out to Musa). Yet (We have sent you forth) as a blessing from your Lord to forewarn a people to whom no warner has been sent before, so that they may take heed and may not say, when evil befalls them on account of their misdeeds: 'Lord, had You sent us an apostle, we would have obeyed Your revelations and believed in them.'

Sura: 28, Ayat: 46-47.

You never hoped that this Book would be sent to you except as mercy from your Lord. Therefore give no help to the unbelievers.

Sura: 28, Ayat: 86.

'If you deny me, likewise other nations before you denied their apostles. An apostle's duty is but to give plain warning.'

Sura: 29, Ayat: 18.

Never have you* read a book before this, nor have you ever transcribed one with your right hand. Had you done either of these, the unbelievers might have doubted. But in the hearts of those who are endowed with knowledge it is clear revelations. Only the wrongdoers deny Our signs.

Sura: 29, Ayat: 48-49.

They ask: 'Why has no sign been given him by his Lord?' Say: 'Signs are in the hands of Allah. My mission is only to give plain warning.'

Sura: 29, Ayat: 50.

You have a good example in Allah's Apostle for anyone who looks to Allah and the Last Day and remembers Allah always.

Sura: 33, Ayat: 21.

No blame shall be attached to the Prophet for doing what is sanctioned for him by Allah. Such was the way of Allah with the prophets who passed away before him — Allah's decrees are pre-ordained — who fulfilled the mission with which Allah had charged them, fearing Allah and fearing none besides Him. Sufficient is Allah's reckoning.

Sura: 33, Ayat: 38-39.

Muhammad is the father of no man among you. He is the Apostle of Allah and the last of the Prophets. Allah has knowledge of all things.

Sura: 33, Ayat: 40.

Prophet, We have sent you forth as a witness, a bearer of good news, and a warner; one who shall call men to Allah by His leave and guide them like a shining light.

Sura: 33, Ayat: 45-46.

Prophet, We have made lawful to you the wives to whom you have granted dowries and those whom your right hand possesses and whom Allah has given you as booty; the daughters of your paternal and maternal uncles and of your paternal and maternal aunts who migrated with you; and any other believing woman who gives herself to you and whom you wished to take in marriage. This is only for you and not any other believer.

We well know the duties We have imposed on the faithful concerning their wives and those whom your right hand possesses, so that there should be no

---

***Muhammad**

difficulty for you. Allah is Forgiving and Merciful.

You may defer any of your wives you please and invite any of your wives you please. Nor is it unlawful for you to receive any of those whom you have temporarily set aside. That is more proper, so that they may be contented and not vexed, and may all be pleased with what you give them.

Allah knows what is in your hearts. He is All-Knowing and Benignant.

No (other) women shall henceforth be lawful to you — nor are you (allowed) to supplant (any of) them by other wives, even though their beauty should please you greatly—: (none shall) be lawful to you) beyond those whom you (already) has come to possess. And God keeps watch over everything.

Sura: 33, Ayat: 50—52.

We have sent you forth to all mankind, so that you may give them good news and warn them. But most men have no knowledge.

Sura: 34, Ayat: 28.

Say: 'I exhort you to one thing: stand up before Allah in pairs or singly and ponder whether your compatriot* is truly mad. He is sent forth to warn you against a dreadful scourge.'

Say: 'I demand no recompense of you: keep it for yourselves. My reward is only with Allah. He is a witness to all things.'

Say: 'My Lord hurls the truth. He has knowledge of all that is hidden.'

Say: 'Truth has come. Falsehood has vanished and shall return no more.'

Say: 'If I am in error, the loss is surely mine; but if I am in the right, it is because of that which my Lord has revealed to me. He hears all and is near at hand.'

Sura: 34, Ayat: 46—50.

You are but a warner. We have sent you with the truth as bearer of good news and as a warner.

Sura: 35, Ayat: 23-24.

I swear by the Wise Quran that you are one of those sent upon a straight path.

Sura: 36, Ayat: 2—4.

Say: 'Truly I am a warner. There is no god but Allah, the One, the Almighty. He is the Lord of the heavens and the earth and all that lies between them: the Illustrious, the Benignant One.'

Sura: 38, Ayat: 65-66.

***Muhammad**

I had no knowledge of the exalted Chiefs when they dispute among themselves. It was revealed to me, only that I might warn you plainly.

Sura: 38, Ayat: 69-70.

Say: 'For this I demand of you no recompense. Nor do I pretend to be what I am not. This is an admonition to mankind; you shall before long know its truth.'

Sura: 38, Ayat: 86—88.

You shall die. And they shall die. Then, on the Day of Resurrection, you shall dispute in your Lord's presence with one another.

Sura: 39, Ayat: 30-31.

Say: 'I am forbidden to serve those whom you invoke besides Allah, now that clear proofs have been given me from my Lord. I am commanded to surrender myself to the Lord of the Worlds.'

Sura: 40, Ayat: 66.

Say: 'I am no more than a man like yourselves. It is revealed to me that your God is one God. Therefore take the right path to Him and implore Him to forgive you. Woe to those who associate others with Him, who give no alms and disbelieve in the life to come. For those who believe and do good works, is an enduring reward.'

Sura: 41, Ayat: 6—8.

Say: 'For this I demand of you no recompense except love of relatives.

Sura: 42, Ayat: 23.

If they turn away, know that We have not sent you to be their keeper. Your only duty is to warn them.

Sura: 42, Ayat: 48.

As a command from us we are sending an apostle — a mercy from the Lord. He is the Hearer, the Knower.

Sura: 44, Ayat: 5-6.

And now, We have set you on the right path. Follow it and do not yield to the desires of ignorant men.

Sura: 45, Ayat: 18.

Say: 'I am no prodigy among the apostles; nor do I know what will be done with me or you. I follow only what is revealed to me, and my only duty is to give plain warning.'

Sura: 46, Ayat: 9.

We have sent you* forth as a witness and as a bearer of good news and warnings, so that you may have faith in Allah and His apostle and that you may assist Him, honour Him, and praise Him, morning and evening.

Sura: 48, Ayat: 8-9.

It is He that has sent forth His Apostle with guidance and the true faith, so that He may exalt it above all religions. Allah is the All-sufficient Witness.

Sura: 48, Ayat: 28.

By the star when it sets, your companion* is neither in error, nor is he deceived!

He does not speak out of his own fancy. This is no other than an inspired revelation. He is taught by one who is mighty in power, and vigorous.**

He stood on the uppermost horizon; then drawing near, he came down within two bows' length or even closer, and revealed to His servant that which he revealed .

His heart did not lie what he saw. How can you,* then, question what he sees?**

He beheld him once again at the farthest lote-tree. Near it is the Garden of Abode.

When that tree was covered with what covered it, his eyes did not wander, nor did they turn aside: for he saw some of his Lord's greatest signs.

Sura: 53, Ayat: 1—18.

It is He who has sent forth among the unlettered an apostle of their own to recite to them His revelations, to purify them, and to instruct them in the Scriptures and wisdom, though they have hitherto been in gross error, together with others of their own kin who have not yet joined them. He is the Mighty, the Wise One.

Such is the grace of Allah: He bestows it on whom He will. His grace is infinite.

Sura: 62, Ayat: 2—4.

Obey Allah and obey the Apostle. If you give no heed to him, know that Our Apostle's duty is no more than to make plain his message.

Sura: 64, Ayat: 12.

Have fear of Allah, you men of understanding, who have believed.

---

*Muhammad **Gabriel ***The unbelievers

Allah has now sent down to you a Reminder; an apostle proclaiming to you the revelations of Allah in all plainness so that he may lead the faithful who do good works from darkness to the light. He who believes in Allah and does good works shall be admitted to gardens watered by running streams where he shall dwell for ever. Allah has made for him a generous provision.

Sura: 65, Ayat: 10-11.

When the Prophet confided a secret to one of his wives; and when she disclosed it and Allah informed him of this, he made known one part of it and said nothing about the other. And when he had acquainted her with it, she said: 'Who told you this?' He replied: 'The Wise One, the All-Knowing, told me.'

Sura: 66, Ayat: 3.

NUN. By the Pen and what they write. By the grace of your Lord, you are not mad. An unfailing recompense awaits you. Surely you have a Sublime Character.

Sura: 68, Ayat: 1—4.

Say: 'I will pray to my Lord and associate none with Him.'

Sura: 72, Ayat: 20.

Say: 'I have no control over any good or evil that befalls you.'

Say: 'None can protect me from Allah, nor can I find any refuge besides Him. (My mission is) only to make known His messages; those that disobey Allah and His Apostle shall abide forever in the fire of Hell.'

Sura: 72, Ayat: 21—23.

Say: 'I cannot tell whether the scourge with which you are threatened is imminent, or whether my Lord will set for it a far-off day. He alone has knowledge of what is hidden. His secrets He reveals to none, except to the apostles whom He chooses. He sends down guardians who walk before them and behind them.

Sura: 72, Ayat: 25—27.

You are but a warner for those who fear it.

Sura: 79, Ayat: 45.

Surely this is the word of a gracious and mighty messenger, held in honour by the Lord of the Throne, obeyed and faithful.

No, your companion is not mad. He saw him on the clear horizon. He does not withhold the unseen.

Sura: 81, Ayat: 19—24.

We shall make you recite (Our revelations), so that you shall not forget any of them, except what Allah pleases. He has knowledge of all that is manifest, and all that is hidden.

Sura: 87, Ayat: 6-7.

By the light of day, and by the night when it falls, your Lord has not forsaken you, nor does He abhor you.

The life to come holds a richer prize for you than this present life. Surely your Lord will give you what will please you.

Did He not find you an orphan and give you shelter?

Did He not find you wandering and guide you?

Did He not find you poor and enrich you?

Therefore do not oppress the orphan, nor drive away the beggar. But proclaim the bounty of your Lord.

Sura: 93, Ayat: 1—11.

Have We not opened forth your heart and relieved you of the burden which weighed down your back?

Have We not given you high renown? Every hardship is followed by ease. Every hardship is followed by ease.

When you have finished resume your toil, and seek your Lord with all fervour.

Sura: 94, Ayat: 1—8.

We have given you* abundance. Pray to your Lord and sacrifice to Him. He that hates you shall remain childless.

Sura: 108, Ayat: 1—3.

***Muhammad**

In the name of Allah, The Compassionate, The Merciful

REVERENCE FOR THE PROPHET

Believers, do not say (to Our Apostle) Ra'ina, but say Undhurna*. Take heed; the unbelievers shall be sternly punished.

Sura: 2, Ayat: 104.

O Believers, obey Allah and His Apostle, and do not turn away from him when you hear him (speak). Do not be like those who say: 'We hear,' but give no heed to what they hear.

Sura: 8, Ayat: 20-21.

O believers, obey Allah and the Apostle when he calls you to that which gives you life. Know that Allah stands between man and his heart, and that in His presence you shall all be gathered.

Sura: 8, Ayat: 24.

The believers are only those who have faith in Allah and His Apostle, and who, when they are with him on some affair collecting people together, do not depart till they have begged his leave. The men who ask your leave are those who truly believe in Allah and His Apostle. When they ask your leave to go away on some business of their own, grant it to whomever you please and implore Allah to forgive them; Allah is Forgiving, Merciful.

Sura: 24, Ayat: 62.

Do not make the calling of the Apostle among yourselves like your calling one another. Allah knows those of you who steal away, concealing themselves. Let those who disobey his orders beware, lest some affliction befall them or some woeful scourge be visited upon them.

Sura: 24, Ayat: 63.

The Prophet is closer to the Believers than their own selves, and his wives

---

***These words mean 'Listen to us' and 'Look upon us' respectively; but in Hebrew the sound of the first conveys the sense, 'Our evil one'. The Jews used the expression as a derisive pun.**

are their mothers....

Sura: 33, Ayat: 6.

You have a good example in Allah's Apostle for anyone who looks to Allah and the Last Day and remembers Allah always.

Sura: 33, Ayat: 21.

O you who have attained to faith! Do not enter the Prophet's dwellings unless you are given leave; (and when invited) to a meal, do not come (so early as) to wait for it to be readied: but whenever you are invited, enter (at the proper time); and when you have partaken of the meal, disperse without lingering for the sake of mere talk: that, behold, might give offence to the Prophet, and yet he might feel shy of (asking) you (to leave): but God is not shy of (teaching you) what is right....

Sura: 33, Ayat: 53.

God and His Angels send blessings on the Prophet: O believers! send your blessings on him, and salute him with all respect.

Sura: 33, Ayat: 56.

Believers, do not behave like those who slandered Musa. Allah cleared him of their calumny and he was exalted in Allah's sight.

Sura: 33, Ayat: 69.

Believers do not be forward in the presence of Allah and His Apostle. Have fear of Allah: He hears all and knows all.

Sura: 49, Ayat: 1.

Believers, do not raise your voices above the voice of the Prophet, nor speak aloud when speaking to him as you do to one another, lest your labours should come to nothing, without your knowledge.

Sura: 49, Ayat: 2.

Those who speak softly in the presence of Allah's Apostle are the men whose hearts Allah has tested for piety. They shall receive forgiveness and a rich reward.

Sura: 49, Ayat: 3.

Those who shout at you whilst you are in your chambers, most of them lack understanding. If they had waited until you went out to them, it would have been better for them. But Allah is Forgiving and Merciful.

Sura: 49, Ayat: 4-5.

Believers, if an evildoer brings you a piece of news, inquire first into its

truth, lest you should wrong others unwittingly and repent of what you have done.

Know that Allah's apostle is among you. If he were to obey you in many matters, you would surely fall into distress. But Allah has endeared the Faith to you and beautified it in your hearts, making unbelief, wrongdoing, and disobedience abhorrent to you. Such are those who are rightly guided — a grace and favour from Allah, Allah is Wise and All-Knowing.

Sura:49, Ayat: 6—8.

Believers, when you consult the Apostle, give alms before such consultation. That is best and purest for you. But if you lack the means, know that Allah is Forgiving and Merciful.

Sura: 58, Ayat: 12.

Do you hesitate to offer alms before your consultations with him? If you do not — and Allah will pardon your offence — then recite your prayers and pay the alms — tax and show obedience to Allah and His Apostle. Allah is cognizant of all your actions.

Sura: 58, Ayat: 13.

In the name of Allah, The Compassionate, The Merciful

DAROOD – A TRIBUTE TO THE PROPHET

God and His Angels send blessings on the Prophet: O believers! send your blessings on him, and salute him with all respect.

Sura: 33, Ayat: 56.

In the name of Allah, The Compassionate, The Merciful

FINALITY OF PROPHETHOOD

This day I have perfected your religion for you and completed My favour to you. I have chosen Islam to be your faith......

Sura: 5, Ayat: 3.

Muhammad is the father of no man among you. He is the Apostle of Allah and the last of the Prophets. Allah has knowledge of all things.

Sura: 33, Ayat: 40.

We have sent you forth to all mankind, so that you may give them good news and warn them. But most men have no knowledge.

Sura: 34, Ayat: 28.

In the name of Allah, The Compassionate, The Merciful

THE PROPHET AS THE IDEAL MAN

You have a good example in Allah's Apostle for anyone who looks to Allah and the Last Day and remembers Allah always.

Sura: 33, Ayat: 21.

In the name of Allah, The Compassionate, The Merciful

PRAISE FOR THE PROPHET'S COMPANIONS

You are the best nation that has ever been raised up for mankind. You enjoin justice and forbid evil. You believe in Allah.

Had the people of the Book believed, it would have surely been better for them. Some of them are true believers, and most of them are evildoers.

Sura: 3, Ayat: 110.

Yet there are other desert Arabs who believe in Allah and the Last Day, and regard what they spend as a means of bringing them close to Allah and to the prayers of the Apostle. Indeed, closer they shall be brought; Allah will admit them to His mercy. He is Forgiving, Merciful.

As for those who led the way, the first of the muhajirs* and the ansar, and those who nobly followed them, Allah is pleased with them and they with Him. He has prepared for them gardens watered by running streams, where they shall dwell for ever. That is the supreme triumph.**

Sura: 9, Ayat: 99-100.

Allah turned in mercy to the Prophet, the muhajirs and the ansar, who stood by him in the hour of adversity, when some of them were on the point of losing heart. He turned to them in mercy. Surely to them He is Compassionate, Merciful.

And (He was also merciful) to the three who had been left behind. So that as the earth, for all its vastness, and their own souls, seemed to close in upon them, they knew there was no refuge from Allah except in Him. Then He turned to them in mercy so that they might repent. Allah is the Forgiving One, the Merciful.

Sura: 9, Ayat: 117–119.

You have a good example in Allah's Apostle for anyone who looks to Allah

---

*Muhammad's early followers who emigrated with him to Madinah

**Muhammad's supporters in Madinah

and the Last Day and remembers Allah always.

When the true believers saw the Confederates they said: 'This is what Allah and His Apostle have promised us; surely their promise has come true.' And this only increased their faith and submission.

Among the believers there are men who have been true to their covenant with God. Some of them have paid their vow by death and others await their end.

Sura: 33, Ayat: 21—23.

Allah was well pleased with the faithful when they swore allegiance to you under the tree. He knew what was in their hearts. Therefore He sent down tranquillity upon them and rewarded them with a speedy victory and with the many spoils which they have taken.

Sura: 48, Ayat: 18-19.

Muhammad is Allah's Apostle. Those who are with him are hard on the unbelievers but merciful to one another. You see them bow and prostrate themselves, seeking the grace of Allah and His good will. Their marks are on their faces, the traces of their prostrations. Thus they are described in the Torah and in the Gospel: (they are) like the seed which puts forth its shoot and strengthens it, so that it rises stout and firm upon its stalk, delighting the sowers. Through them Allah seeks to enrage the unbelievers. God has promised those of them who will believe and do good works forgiveness and a rich reward.

Sura: 48, Ayat: 29.

Know that Allah's apostle is among you. If he were to obey you in many matters, you would surely fall into distress. But Allah has endeared the Faith to you and beautified it in your hearts, making unbelief, wrongdoing, and disobedience abhorrent to you. Such are those who are rightly guided — a grace and favour from Allah. Allah is Wise and All-Knowing.

Sura: 49, Ayat: 7-8.

(A share of the spoils shall also fall) to the poor muhajirs* who have been driven from their homes and possessions; who seek Allah's grace and bounty and support Allah and His Apostle. These are the true believers.

Those, before them, who had homes in the City and embraced the Faith before them love those who have sought refuge with them; they entertain no desire in their hearts for what they are given, but rather prefer them above**

---

*Those who emigrated with Muhammad to Madinah

**Madinah

themselves, though they are in want. Those that preserve themselves from their own greed shall surely prosper.

Those that came after them say: 'Forgive us, our Lord, and forgive our brothers who embraced the Faith before us. Do not put in our hearts any malice towards the faithful. Lord, You are Compassionate and Merciful.'

Sura: 59, Ayat: 8–10.

FOUNTAIN HEAD OF GUIDANCE

(6)

In the name of Allah, The Compassionate, The Merciful

PERFECTION OF RELIGION

This day I have perfected your religion for you and completed My favour to you. I have chosen Islam to be your faith.

Sura: 5, Ayat: 3.

In the name of Allah, The Compassionate, The Merciful

PROCLAMATIONS OF THE END OF FALSEHOOD

Do not confound truth with falsehood, nor knowingly hide the truth.
Sura: 2, Ayat: 42.

Say: 'Truth has come and falsehood has been overthrown. Falsehood was bound to be discomfited.'
Sura: 17, Ayat: 81.

It was not in sport that We created the heavens and the earth and all that lies between them. Had it been Our will to find a pastime, We could have found one near at hand if We were to do it.

We will hurl Truth at Falsehood, until Truth shall triumph and Falsehood be no more. Woe shall befall you, for all (the falsehoods) you have uttered.
Sura: 21, Ayat: 16—18.

Say: 'My Lord hurls the truth. He has knowledge of all that is hidden'.

Say: 'Truth has come. Falsehood has vanished and shall return no more.'
Sura: 34, Ayat: 48-49.

We have given you a glorious victory,* so that Allah may forgive your past and future sins, and perfect His favour to you; that He may guide you to the right path and bestow on you His mighty help.

It was He who sent down tranquillity into the hearts of the faithful so that their faith might grow stronger. His are the forces of the heavens and the earth. Allah is Wise and All-Knowing.

(He has done this) so that He may also bring the believers, both men and women, into gardens watered by running streams, there to abide for ever; that He may forgive them their sins, which is in Allah's sight a great triumph.
Sura: 48, Ayat: 1—5.

***Refers to the victories of Islam**

When Allah's help and victory come, and you see men embrace His religion in multitudes, celebrate the praise of your Lord and seek His pardon. He is ever disposed to mercy.

Sura: 110, Ayat: 1–3.

In the name of Allah, The Compassionate, The Merciful

EXPANSION OF ISLAM

They seek to extinguish the light of Allah with their mouths; but Allah will perfect His light, much as the unbelievers may dislike it.

Sura: 61, Ayat: 8.

In the name of Allah, The Compassionate, The Merciful

DIVINE INJUNCTIONS – A TRUST

We offered the trust to the heavens, to the earth, and to the mountains, but they refused to bear it, and were afraid of it. Man undertook to bear it, but he has proved unjust and foolish.

Allah will surely punish the hypocrites, men and women, and the unbelievers, both men and women; but Allah pardons believing men and believing women. Allah is Forgiving and Merciful.

Sura: 33, Ayat: 72-73.

In the name of Allah, The Compassionate, The Merciful

GUIDANCE DEPENDS ON THE WILL OF GOD

That was one of Allah's signs. He whom Allah guides is rightly guided; but he whom He leaves in error shall find no friend to guide him.

Sura: 18, Ayat: 17.

In the name of Allah, The Compassionate, The Merciful

ALLAH – THE SOURCE OF ALL GUIDANCE

Allah guides to His light whom He will.
Allah sets forth parables for men. He has knowledge of all things.

Sura: 24, Ayat: 35.

We have sent down revelations showing clearly (the truth). Allah guides whom He will to a straight path.

Sura: 24, Ayat: 46.

In the name of Allah, The Compassionate, The Merciful

MAN HIMSELF RESPONSIBLE FOR HIS HERESY

And when Our judgement has been passed, the devil will say to them: 'True was the promise which Allah made you. I too made you a promise, but did not keep it. Yet I had no power over you except that I called you, and you answered me. Do not now blame me, but blame yourselves. I cannot help you, nor can you help me. I deny your associating me formerly with Allah.'

The wrongdoers shall be sternly punished.

Sura: 14, Ayat: 22.

ROMOTION OF RELIGION

(7)

In the name of Allah, The Compassionate, The Merciful

THE CALL TO SPREAD FAITH

Let there become of you a nation that shall call for righteousness, enjoin justice, and forbid evil. Such men shall surely triumph.

Sura: 3 Ayat: 104.

You are the best nation that has ever been raised up for mankind. You enjoin justice and forbid evil. You believe in Allah.

Sura: 3, Ayat: 110.

But Allah knows what is in their hearts. Let them be. Admonish them and sternly rebuke them.

Sura: 4, Ayat: 63.

Why are you thus divided concerning the hypocrites, when Allah Himself has cast them off on account of their misdeeds? Would you guide those whom Allah has caused to err? He whom Allah has led astray cannot be guided.

Sura: 4, Ayat: 88.

....They committed evil and never restrained one another from wrong-doing. Evil is what they were doing.

Sura: 5, Ayat: 79.

And warn with it those who dread to be brought before their Lord that they have no guardian or intercessor besides Allah, so that they may guard themselves against evil. Do not drive away those that call on their Lord morning and evening, seeking only to gain His favour. You are not by any means accountable for them, nor are they accountable for you. If you drive them away, you shall yourself become an evildoer.

Sura: 6, Ayat: 51-52.

Those that fear Allah are not by any means accountable for them. "They should admonish only" so that they may guard themselves against evil.

Sura: 6, Ayat: 69.

Avoid those that treat faith as a sport and a pastime and are seduced by the life of this world. Admonish them hereby lest a soul be damned by its own sins. It has no guardian or intercessor besides Allah: and though it offers every ransom, it shall not be accepted from it. Such are those that are damned by their deeds. They shall drink boiling water and be sternly punished for their unbelief.

Sura: 6, Ayat: 70.

And when some asked: 'Why do you admonish men whom Allah will destroy or sternly punish?' they replied: 'We admonish them so that we may be free from blame in the sight of your Lord, and that they may guard themselves against evil.'

Sura: 7, Ayat: 164.

Therefore, when they forgot the warning they had been given, We delivered those who had warned them against evil, and sternly punished the wrongdoers for their misdeeds.

Sura: 7, Ayat: 165.

Among those whom We created there are some who give true guidance and act justly.

Sura: 7, Ayat: 181.

Show forgiveness, enjoin justice, and avoid the ignorant. If you are afflicted by the devil's temptation, seek refuge in Allah; He hears all and knows all.

If those that guard themselves against evil are touched by a temptation from the devil, they have but to recall Allah's precepts and they shall see the light.

Sura: 7, Ayat: 199–201.

The true believers, both men and women, are friends to each other. They enjoin what is just and forbid what is evil; they attend to their prayers and pay the alms-tax and obey Allah and His Apostle. On these Allah will have mercy. He is Mighty, Wise.

Sura: 9, Ayat: 71.

Others there are who have confessed their sins; their good works had been intermixed with evil. Perchance Allah will turn to them in mercy. He is Forgiving, Merciful. Take alms from their wealth, so that they may thereby be cleansed and purified, and pray for them: for your prayers will give them comfort. Allah is Hearing, Knowing.

Sura: 9, Ayat: 102–104.

It is not right that all the faithful should go (to war) at once. Some of them

only should, and some should stay behind to instruct themselves in religion and admonish the others when they return, so that they may take heed.

Sura: 9, Ayat: 122.

Say: 'Men! The truth has come to you from your Lord. He that follows the right path follows it to his own advantage, and he that goes astray does so at his own peril. I am not your keeper.'

Observe what is revealed to you, and have patience till Allah makes known his judgement. He is the best of judges.

Sura: 10, Ayat: 108—109.

Were there among the generations that have gone before you any upright men who preached against corruption in the land, except the few whom We delivered from among them? The wrongdoers pursued their worldly pleasures and thus became guilty.

Sura: 11, Ayat: 116.

Yet, though you desire it, most men will not believe.

You shall demand of them no recompense for this. It is a reminder to all mankind.

Sura: 12, Ayat: 103-104.

Proclaim, then, what you are bidden and avoid the polytheists. We will Ourself sustain you against those that mock you — those who serve other gods besides Allah. They shall before long know.

Sura: 15, Ayat: 94—96.

He sends down the angels with the Spirit by His will to those of His servants whom He chooses, (bidding them proclaim); 'There is no god but Me: therefore, fear Me.'

Sura: 16, Ayat: 2.

(We sent) them with clear proofs and Books. And We revealed to you the Reminder (Quran) so that you may make clear to men what has been revealed to them, and that they may give thought.

Sura: 16, Ayat: 44.

Call men to the path of your Lord with wisdom and mild exhortation. Reason with them in the most courteous manner. Your Lord best knows those who stray from His Path and best knows those who are rightly guided.

Sura: 16, Ayat: 125.

Be patient (then); and your patience is (possible) only by Allah's (help). Do not grieve for the unbelievers, nor distress yourself at their intrigues.

Sura: 16, Ayat: 127.

Recite what is revealed to you in the Book of your Lord. None can change His words. You shall find no refuge other than Him.

Sura: 18, Ayat: 27.

....and at length came here as I ordained. I have chosen you for Myself. Go, you and your brother, with My signs, and do not cease to remember Me. Go both of you to Pharaoh, for he has transgressed all bounds. Speak to him with gentle words; he may yet heed and fear (God).'

Sura: 20, Ayat: 40−44.

Say: 'It is revealed to me that your God is one God. Will you submit to Him?'

If they turn back, say: 'I have warned you all alike, though I cannot tell whether what you are promised is imminent or far off. Allah knows your spoken words and what you hide. And I know not if this may be a trial for you and a provision for a time.'

Sura: 21, Ayat: 108−111.

(He will assuredly help) those who, once made masters in the lands, will attend to their prayers and pay the alms-tax, enjoin justice and forbid evil. Allah controls the destiny of all things.

Sura: 22, Ayat: 41.

For every nation We have ordained a ritual which they observe. Let them not dispute with you concerning this. Call them to the path of your Lord: surely you are rightly guided.

Sura: 22, Ayat: 67.

Had it been Our will, We could have raised a warner in every town. Do not yield to the unbelievers, but fight them strenuously with it (the Quran).

Sura: 25, Ayat: 51-52.

We have sent you only to proclaim good news and to give warning. Say: 'I demand of you no recompense for this except that he who will may take (the right) path to his Lord.'

Sura: 25, Ayat: 56-57.

Admonish your nearest kinsfolk and show kindness to the believers who follow you. If they disobey you, say: 'I am not accountable for what you do.'

Sura: 26, Ayat: 214−216.

(Say): 'I am bidden to serve the Lord of this City, which He has made sacred. All things are His.

'I am commanded to surrender to Him, and to recite the Quran. He that

takes the right path shall himself have much to gain.'

To him who goes astray, say: 'I am only a warner.'

Sura: 27, Ayat: 91-92.

Let no one turn you away from Allah's revelations, now that they have been revealed to you. Call men to your Lord, and serve none besides Him.

Invoke no other god with Allah. There is no god but Him.

Sura: 28, Ayat: 87-88.

And do not argue with the People of the Book except in the best way, unless it be with those among them who do evil. Say: 'We believe in that which is revealed to us and which was revealed to you. Our God and your God is one. To Him we surrender ourselves.'

Likewise We revealed the Book to you. Those to whom We gave the Scriptures believe in it, and so do some of these (pagan Arabs). Only the unbelievers deny Our revelations.

Sura: 29, Ayat: 46-47.

You cannot make the dead hear you, nor can you make the deaf hear your call if they turn their backs and give no heed; nor can you guide the blind out of their error. None shall give ear to you save those who believe in Our revelations, and are submissive to Our will.

Sura: 30, Ayat: 52-53.

(Luqman said) My son, be steadfast in prayer, enjoin justice, and forbid evil. Endure with fortitude whatever befalls you. That is a duty incumbent on all.

Do not turn away from men with scorn, nor walk proudly on the earth: Allah does not love the arrogant and the vain-glorious. Rather let your gait be modest and your voice low: the harshest of voices is the braying of the asses.'

Sura: 31, Ayat: 17—19.

Say: 'This is a fateful message: Yet you give no heed to it.

Sura: 38, Ayat: 67-68.

....Say: 'For this I demand of you no recompense. Nor do I pretend to be what I am not. This is an admonition to mankind; you shall before long know its truth.'

Sura: 38, Ayat: 86—88.

And who speaks better than he who calls others to the service of Allah, does what is right, and says: 'I am one of the Muslims.'

Sura: 41, Ayat: 33.

Thus We have revealed to you an Arabic Quran, that you may warn the Mother City* and all around it; that you may forewarn them of the Day of Gathering which is sure to come: when some will be in Paradise, and some in Hell.

Sura: 42, Ayat: 7.

Therefore call (men to the true faith), and follow the straight path as you are bidden. Do not follow their desires, but say: 'I believe in all the scriptures that Allah has revealed. I am commanded to exercise justice among you. Allah is our Lord and your Lord. We have our own works and you have yours; let there be no argument between us. Allah will bring us all together, for to Him we shall return.'

Sura: 42, Ayat: 15.

And when Isa came with clear signs, he said: 'I have come to you with wisdom and to make plain to you some of the things about which you differ. Fear Allah and follow me. Allah is my Lord and your Lord: therefore serve Him. That is the right path.'

Yet the factions disagreed among themselves. But woe to those who did wrong from the chastisement of a grievous Day.

Sura: 43, Ayat: 63—65.

We will know what they say. You shall not use force with them. Admonish with this Quran whoever fears My warning.

Sura: 50, Ayat: 45.

Thus whenever an apostle came to those that flourished before them they cried: 'Sorcerer!' or 'Madman!' Have they handed down this (cry) from one generation to the next? Surely they are transgressors all.

Give no heed to them; you shall incur no blame.

Sura: 51, Ayat: 52—55.

Therefore, give warning. By the grace of Allah, you are neither a soothsayer nor a madman.

Sura: 52, Ayat: 29.

O believers, be Allah's helpers. When Isa the son of Mariam said to the disciples: 'Who will come with me to the help of Allah? they replied: 'We are Allah's helpers.'

Some of the Children of Israel believed in him while others did not. We aided the believers against their enemies and they triumphed over them.

Sura: 61, Ayat: 14.

---

*Makkah

You* who are wrapped up in your vestment, arise and give warning.
Magnify your Lord, cleanse your garments, and keep away from all pollution.
Bestow no favours expecting gain. Be patient for your Lord's sake.
Sura: 74, Ayat: 1–7.

He* frowned and turned away when the blind man came towards him.
How can you* tell? He might purify himself. He might be mindful and the Reminder might profit him.
But to him who is wealthy you do attend: although the fault would not be yours if he remained uncleansed. Yet to him who came to you with zeal and awe, you gave no heed.
Nay, this is an admonition; let him who will, bear it in mind.
Sura: 80, Ayat: 1–12.

We shall guide you to the smoothest path. Therefore give warning, if warning will avail them. He that fears Allah will heed it, but the wicked sinner will avoid it. He shall be cast into the great Fire where he shall neither die nor live.
Sura: 87, Ayat: 8–13.

Therefore give warning. Your duty is only to warn them: you are not their keeper. As for those that turn their backs and disbelieve, Allah will inflict on them the supreme chastisement.
Sura: 88, Ayat: 21–24.

Have We not given him two eyes, a tongue, and two lips, and shown him the two highways (of good and evil)? Yet he would not scale the height.
Would that you knew what the Height is! It is the freeing of a bondsman; the feeding, in the day of famine, of an orphaned relation or a needy man in distress; to be one of those who believe, enjoin patience and enjoin mercy.
Sura: 90, Ayat: 8–17.

Man is in loss, except those who believe and do good works and exhort one another to truth and to patience.
Sura: 103, Ayat: 2-3.

***Muhammad**

In the name of Allah, The Compassionate, The Merciful

RESPONSIBILITY OF THE HEAD OF FAMILY

O believers, guard yourselves and guard your kindred against the Fire which has fuel of men and stones, whose keepers are fierce and mighty angels who never disobey Allah's command and promptly do His bidding. They will say to the unbelievers: 'Make no excuses for yourselves this day. You shall be rewarded according to your deeds.'

Sura: 66, Ayat: 6-7.

In the name of Allah, The Compassionate, The Merciful

AN INSTRUCTIVE LESSON

We have sent down to you revelations showing you the right path, and a story about those who have gone before you and an admonition to righteous men.

Sura: 24, Ayat: 34.

In the name of Allah, The Compassionate, The Merciful

PROPAGATION OF EVIL

Those that disbelieve and debar others from the path of Allah have strayed far from the truth. Allah will not forgive those who disbelieve and act unjustly; nor will He guide them to any path other than that of Hell; in it they shall remain for ever. That is no difficult thing for Allah.

Sura: 4, Ayat: 167–169.

Many are those that are misled through ignorance by their fancies: but your Lord best knows the transgressors.

Sura: 6 Ayat: 119

Then the people of Paradise will cry out to the people of the Fire: 'What our Lord promised we have found to be true. Have you, too, found the promise of your Lord to be true?'

'Yes,' they shall answer, and a herald will cry out among them: 'Cursed are the evildoers who have debarred others from the path of Allah and sought to make it crooked, and who had no faith in the life to come.

Sura: 7, Ayat: 44-45.

Do not corrupt the land after it has been purged of evil. That is best for you, if you are true believers.

'Do not sit in every road, threatening believers and debarring them from the path of Allah, nor seek to make that path crooked.

Remember how He multiplied you when you were few in number. Consider the fate of the evildoers.

Sura: 7, Ayat: 85-86.

Be they men or women, the hypocrites are all alike. They enjoin what is evil, forbid what is just, and tighten their purse strings. They forsook Allah, so Allah forsook them. Surely the hypocrites are evildoers.

Sura: 9, Ayat: 67.

As for those who break Allah's covenant after accepting it, who part what

He has bidden to be united and commit evil in the land, a curse shall be laid on them, and they shall have an evil abode (in Hell).

Sura: 13, Ayat: 25.

Woe to the unbelievers, because of stern punishment. Those who love this life more than the life to come, debar others from the path of Allah and seek to make it crooked are far astray.

Sura: 14, Ayat: 2-3.

(As for) those that disbelieve and debar others from the path of Allah, We shall add to their chastisement for their misdeeds.

Sura: 16, Ayat: 88.

Some wrangle about Allah, though they have neither knowledge nor guidance nor an illuminating Book. He, who bends his side in scorn to lead others astray from Allah's path, for him is disgrace in this life and shall taste the torment of Hell on the Day of Resurrection. 'This,' We shall say, 'is the reward of your misdeeds. Allah is not unjust to His servants.'

Sura: 22, Ayat: 8—10.

Those who delight in spreading slanders against the faithful shall be sternly punished in this life and in the next. Allah knows, but you do not.

Sura: 24, Ayat: 19.

Some there are who would gladly pay for a frivolous tale, so that in their ignorance they may mislead others from the path of Allah and make fun of it. For these We have prepared a shameful punishment.

When Our revelations are recited to him, he turns his back in scorn, as though he never heard them: as though his ears were sealed. To him proclaim a woeful scourge.

Sura: 31, Ayat: 6-7.

Allah will bring to nothing the deeds of those who disbelieve and debar others from His path.

Sura: 47, Ayat: 1.

Those who disbelieve and debar others from Allah's path and in the end die unbelievers shall not be shown forgiveness by Allah.

Sura: 47, Ayat: 34.

Have you seen the man who forbids a servant when he prays. Have you seen if he follows the right guidance or enjoins piety?

Think: if he denies the truth and gives no heed, does he not know that Allah observes all things?

Sura: 96, Ayat: 9—14.

In the name of Allah, The Compassionate, The Merciful

CONCEALING THE TRUTH

Those that hide the clear proofs and the guidance We have revealed after We have proclaimed them in the Book, shall be cursed by Allah and shall be cursed by the cursors; except those that repent and mend their ways and make known the truth. Towards them I shall relent. I am, the Relenting One, the Merciful.

Sura: 2, Ayat: 159-160.

Those that suppress any part of the Book Allah has revealed in order to gain a small price shall swallow nothing but fire into their bellies. On the Day of Resurrection, Allah will neither speak to them nor purify them. Theirs shall be a woeful punishment.

Sura: 2, Ayat: 174.

In the name of Allah, The Compassionate, The Merciful

BARTERING OF FAITH FOR WORLDLY GAINS

Woe to those that write the Scriptures with their own hands and then declare: 'This is from Allah,' in order to gain a small (worldly) price for it. So woe to them because of what their hands have written, because of that which they gain.

Sura: 2, Ayat: 79.

Those that suppress any part of the Book Allah has revealed in order to gain a small price shall swallow nothing but fire into their bellies. On the Day of Resurrection, Allah will neither speak to them nor purify them. Theirs shall be a woeful punishment.

Such are those that buy error with guidance, and torture with forgiveness. How steadfastly they seek the Fire.

Sura: 2, Ayat: 174-175.

Those that sell the covenant of Allah and their own oaths for a paltry price shall have no share in the world to come. Allah will neither speak to them, nor look at them, nor purify them on the Day of Resurrection. Theirs shall be a woeful punishment.

Sura: 3, Ayat: 77.

When Allah made a covenant with those to whom the Book was given, He said: 'Proclaim these to mankind and do not suppress them.' But they cast the Scriptures behind their backs and sold them for a paltry price. Evil was their bargain.

Sura: 3, Ayat: 187.

In the name of Allah, The Compassionate, The Merciful

CONCENTRATE ON SELF REFORM

Would you enjoin righteousness on others and forget it yourselves? Yet you read the Scriptures. Have you no sense?

Sura: 2, Ayat: 44.

Believers, you are accountable for yourselves; he that goes astray cannot harm you if you are on the right path. You shall all return to Allah, and He will inform you of what you have done.

Sura: 5, Ayat: 105.

In the name of Allah, The Compassionate, The Merciful

DISPARITY BETWEEN WORD AND THE DEED

Would you enjoin righteousness on others and forget it yourselves? Yet you read the Scriptures. Have you no sense?

Sura: 2, Ayat: 44.

And there are those who built a mosque to cause harm and to spread unbelief and disunite the faithful, and to provide refuge for him* who had made war on Allah and His Apostle before. They swear that their intentions were good, but Allah bears witness that they are lying. You shall not set foot in it. It is more fitting that you should pray in a mosque founded on piety from the very first. There you shall find men who would keep pure. Allah loves those that purify themselves.

Who is a better man, he who founds his house on the fear of Allah and His good pleasure, or he who builds on the brink of a crumbling precipice, so that it will fall with him into the fire of Hell? Allah does not guide the wrongdoers.

Sura: 9, Ayat: 107—109.

Believers, why do you say what you never do? It is most odious in Allah's sight that you should say that which you do not do.

Sura: 61, Ayat: 2-3.

Those to whom the burden of the Torah was entrusted and yet refused to bear it are like a donkey laden with books. Wretched is the example of those who deny Allah's revelations. Allah does not guide the wrongdoers.

Sura: 62, Ayat: 5.

---

*Abu Amir

In the name of Allah, The Compassionate, The Merciful

WHAT THE POETS SAY

Poets are followed by erring men. Behold how aimlessly they rove in every valley, preaching what they never practise. Not so are the true believers who do good works and remember Allah and defend themselves only after they had been wronged.

Sura: 26, Ayat: 224–227.

In the name of Allah, The Compassionate, The Merciful

PRINCIPLES OF DISCUSSION

Call men to the path of your Lord with wisdom and mild exhortation. Reason with them in the most courteous manner. Your Lord best knows those who stray from His path and best knows those who are rightly guided.

Sura: 16, Ayat: 125.

And do not argue with the People of the Book except in the best way, unless it be with those among them who do evil. Say: 'We believe in that which is revealed to us and which was revealed to you. Our God and your God is one. To Him we surrender ourselves.'

Sura: 29, Ayat: 46.

In the name of Allah, The Compassionate, The Merciful

INVOKING DIVINE DISPLEASURE ON FALSEHOOD

To those that dispute with you concerning Isa after the knowledge you have received, say: 'Come, let us gather our sons and your sons, our wives and your wives, our people and your people. We will pray together and call down the curse of Allah on every liar.'

Sura: 3, Ayat: 61.

In the name of Allah, The Compassionate, The Merciful

NO COMPULSION IN RELIGION

There shall be no compulsion in religion. True guidance is now distinct from error. He that renounces the idols and puts his faith in Allah shall grasp the firmest handle that will never break. Allah is Hearing, Knowing.

Sura: 2, Ayat: 256.

Had your lord pleased, all the people of the earth would have believed in Him. Would you then force men to be believers?

Sura: 10, Ayat: 99

....nor obey him whose heart We have made heedless of Our remembrance; who follows his desires and whose case exceeds due bounds.

Say: This is the truth from your Lord. Let him who will, believe in it, and him who will, deny it.

Sura: 18, Ayat: 28-29.

In the name of Allah, The Compassionate, The Merciful

A GOOD WORD

Do you not see how Allah sets forth a parable that the good works is like a good tree whose root is firm and its branches are in the sky, yielding its fruit every season by Allah's leave? Allah gives parables to men so that they become mindful.

Sura: 14, Ayat: 24-25.

Tell My servants to be courteous in their speech. The devil would sow discord among them; he is the sworn enemy of man.

Sura: 17, Ayat: 53.

In the name of Allah, The Compassionate, The Merciful

AN EVIL WORD

And the parable of an evil word is like an evil tree torn out of the earth and has no stability.

Sura: 14, Ayat: 26.

In the name of Allah, The Compassionate, The Merciful

ABUSING FALSE DEITIES

Do not revile (the idols) which they invoke besides Allah, lest in their ignorance they should spitefully revile Allah.

Sura: 6, Ayat: 108.

In the name of Allah, The Compassionate, The Merciful

THE END OF ALL HERESY

Behold him who rejects Our signs and yet says: 'I shall surely be given wealth and children'!

Has he gained knowledge of the unseen? Or has the Merciful made him such a promise?

By no means! We will record his words and make his punishment long and terrible. We shall inherit what he speaks of (wealth and children) and he will come before Us all alone.

Sura: 19, Ayat: 77–80.

STRIVING FOR TRUTH

(8)

In the name of Allah, The Compassionate, The Merciful

RESOLVE IS THE REAL THING

And there are those who built a mosque to cause harm and to spread unbelief and disunite the faithful, and to provide refuge for him* who had made war on Allah and His Apostle before. They swear that their intentions were good, but Allah bears witness that they are lying. You shall not set foot in it. It is more fitting that you should pray in a mosque founded on piety from the very first. There you shall find men who would keep pure. Allah loves those that purify themselves.

Who is a better man, he who found his house on the fear of Allah and His good pleasure, or he who builds on the brink of a crumbling precipice, so that it will fall with him into the fire of Hell? Allah does not guide the wrongdoers.

Sura: 9, Ayat: 107—109.

***Abu Amir**

In the name of Allah, The Compassionate, The Merciful

ENDEAVOUR ESSENTIAL TO SUPPLEMENT RESOLVE

As for him that desires the life to come and strives for it as he ought to, being also a believer—those are they whose striving is amply rewarded by Allah.

Sura: 17, Ayat: 19.

In the name of Allah, The Compassionate, The Merciful

PERMANENCE OF TRUTH

Thus Allah depicts truth and falsehood. The scum is cast away, but that which is of use to man remains behind. Thus Allah coins His parables.

Sura: 13, Ayat: 17.

In the name of Allah, The Compassionate, The Merciful

SERVICING THE TRUTH

O believers, be patient and let your patience never be exhausted. Stand firm in your faith and fear Allah, so that you may triumph.

Sura: 3, Ayat: 200.

In the name of Allah, The Compassionate, The Merciful

AFFIRMATION OF TRUTH

Allah will say: 'This is the day when their truthfulness will benefit the truthful. They shall for ever dwell in gardens watered by running streams. Allah is pleased with them and they with Him. That is the supreme triumph.'

Sura: 5, Ayat: 119.

O believers, have fear of Allah and stand with the truthful.

Sura: 9, Ayat: 119.

Say: 'This is my path. With sure knowledge, I call on you to have faith in Allah, I and all my followers. Glory be to Him! I am not one of the polytheists.'

Sura: 12, Ayat: 108.

Say: 'This is the truth from your Lord. Let him who will, believe in it, and him who will, deny it.'

For the wrongdoers, We have prepared a fire which will encompass them like the walls of a pavilion.

Sura: 18, Ayat: 29.

As for those that have faith and do good works, We waste not the reward of him who does good work.

Sura: 18, Ayat: 30.

Among the believers there are men who have been true to their covenant with God. Some have died, and others await their end, yielding to no change, so that Allah may reward the truthful for their truthfulness and sternly punish the hypocrites - or show them mercy if He will: Allah is Forgiving and Merciful.

Sura: 33, Ayat: 23-24.

For Muslim men and women, for believing men and women; for devout men and women; for men and women who are patient; for men and women

who humble themselves; for men and women who give charity; for men and women who fast; for men and women who guard their chastity; and for men and women who remember Allah much—for them all has God prepared forgiveness and a great reward.

Sura: 33, Ayat: 35.

Believers, fear Allah and speak the truth. He will bless your works and forgive you your sins. He who obeys Allah and His Apostle shall win a great victory.

Sura: 33, Ayat: 70-71.

And he who brings the truth, and he who believes in it—they surely are the God-fearing. Their Lord will give them all that they desire. Thus shall the righteous be rewarded.

Thus Allah will do away with their foulest deeds and reward them according to their noblest actions.

Sura: 39, Ayat: 33—35.

In the name of Allah, The Compassionate, The Merciful

PERSEVERANCE

Follow then the right path as you are bidden, together with those who have repented with you, and do not transgress. He is aware of what you do.

Sura: 11, Ayat: 112.

In the name of Allah, The Compassionate, The Merciful

TO EXCEL IN DOING GOOD DEEDS

Each one has a goal towards which he turns. So emulate one another in good works. And wherever you be, Allah will bring you all before Him. He has power over all things.

Sura: 2, Ayat: 148.

We have ordained a law and a path for each of you. Had Allah pleased, He could have made you one nation; but that He might prove you by that which He has bestowed upon you. Vie with one another in good works, for to Allah you shall all return and He will declare to you what you have disagreed about.

Sura: 5, Ayat: 48

Do they think that in giving them wealth and children We are hastening to do them good? By no means! They do not understand.

Those who live in fear of their Lord; who believe in the revelations of their Lord; who worship none besides their Lord; who give what they give with their hearts filled with awe, (knowing) that they will return to their Lord:

Sura: 23, Ayat: 55—61

Therefore vie (with one another) for the pardon of your Lord, and for a Paradise as vast as heaven and earth, prepared for those who believe in Allah and His Apostles. Such is the grace of Allah: He bestows it on whom He will. His grace is infinite.

Sura: 57, Ayat: 21.

They shall be given to drink of a pure wine, securely sealed, whose very dregs are musk; for this let all men emulously strive;

Sura: 83, Ayat: 25-26.

In the name of Allah, The Compassionate, The Merciful

STRUGGLE AND STRIFE

Are they seeking a religion other than Allah's, when every soul in heaven and earth has submitted to Him, willingly or by compulsion? To Him they shall all return.

Sura: 3, Ayat: 83.

And who has a nobler religion than the man who surrenders himself to Allah, does what is right, and follows the faith of Ibrahim the upright, whom Allah Himself chose to be His friend?

Sura: 4, Ayat: 125.

Believers, have fear of Allah and seek the means by which you get His favour. Fight valiantly for His cause, so that you may triumph.

Sura: 5, Ayat: 35.

Believers, if any of you renounce the faith, Allah will replace them by others who love Him and are loved by Him, humble towards the faithful and stern towards the unbelievers, striving for Allah's cause and fearless of man's censure. Such is the grace of Allah: He bestows it on whom He will. He is Munificent Knowing.

Sura: 5, Ayat 54.

Tell the unbelievers that if they mend their ways, their past shall be forgiven; but if they persist in sin, let them reflect upon the fate of their forefathers.

Make war on them until persecution is no more and Allah's religion reigns supreme. If they desist, Allah is congnizant of all their actions; but if they give no heed, know then that Allah will protect you. He is the noblest helper and protector.

Sura: 8, Ayat: 38-39.

If they repent and take to prayer and pay the alms-tax, they shall become your brothers in the faith. Thus We make plain Our revelations for men of

understanding.

But if, after coming to terms with you, they break their oaths and revile your faith, make war on the leaders of unbelief—for no oaths are binding with them—so that they may desist.

Sura: 9, Ayat: 11-12.

It is He who has sent forth His Apostle with guidance and the true faith to make it triumphant over all religions, however, much the polytheists may dislike it.

Sura: 9, Ayat: 33.

It is not right that all the faithful should go (to war) at once. Some of them only should, and some should stay behind to instruct themselves in religion and admonish the others when they return, so that they may take heed.

Sura: 9, Ayat: 122.

Say: 'Men! If you are in doubt concerning my religion, (know that) I worship none of those you serve besides Allah, but I serve Allah who will cause you to die for I am commanded to be one of the faithful, and (I was bidden): 'Set your face uprightly towards religion, and do not be a polytheist.

Sura: 10, Ayat: 104-105.

Fight for the cause of Allah with the devotion due to Him. He has chosen you and laid on you no burdens in the observance of your faith, the faith of Ibrahim your father. He has given you the name of Muslims before and in this so that His Apostle may be a witness for you, and that you yourselves may be witnesses for your fellow-men.

Therefore attend to your prayers and pay the alms-tax and hold fast to Allah, for He is your Guardian. A gracious Guardian and a gracious Helper!

Sura: 22, Ayat: 78.

He that hopes to meet his Lord (must know) that Allah's appointed hour is sure to come. He alone hears all and knows all.

He who strives, strives for himself. Allah does not need His creatures' help.

Sura: 29, Ayat: 5-6.

Those who fight for Our cause, We will surely guide to Our own paths. Allah is with the righteous.

Sura: 29, Ayat: 69.

Therefore set your face in devotion to the true faith, the upright nature with which Allah has endowed man. Allah's creation cannot be changed. This is surely the true religion, although most men do not know it.

Turn to Allah and fear Him. Be steadfast in prayers and be not of those

who associate others with Allah, those who split up their religion into sects, each exulting in its own beliefs.

Sura: 30, Ayat: 30–32.

He has ordained for you the faith which He enjoined on Nuh and which we have revealed to you, and which We enjoined on Ibrahim, Musa and Isa (saying): 'Observe this Faith and be not divided therein.' Hard for the polytheists is that to which you call them. Allah chooses to Himself whom He will, and guides to Himself those that repent.

Sura: 42, Ayat: 13.

That man can have nothing but what he strives for; that (the fruit of) his striving will soon come in sight; then will he be rewarded with a reward complete.

Sura: 53, Ayat: 39–41.

In the name of Allah, The Compassionate, The Merciful

TO SERVE MANKIND REGARDLESS OF COLOUR AND CREED

And they feed, for the love of God, the indigent, the orphan, and the captive, (Saying): 'We feed you for the sake of God alone: No reward do we desire from you, nor thanks. We only fear a Day of distressful Wrath from the side of our Lord.'

Sura: 76, Ayat: 8—10.

In the name of Allah, The Compassionate, The Merciful

SOURCE OF GOOD AND EVIL

Wherever you be, death will overtake you: 'though you put yourselves in lofty towers.'

When they are blessed with good fortune, they say: 'This is from Allah'. But when evil befalls them, they say: 'The fault was yours'.

Say to them: 'All is from Allah!'

What has come over these men that they should show such lack of understanding?

Sura: 4, Ayat: 78.

Whatever good befalls you (man), it is from Allah: and whatever ill, from yourself.

We have sent you forth as an apostle to mankind. Allah is (your) all-sufficient witness.

Sura: 4, Ayat: 79.

If Allah afflicts you with evil, none can remove it but He; and if He blesses you with good fortune, know that He has power over all things.

Sura: 6, Ayat: 17.

Say: 'Nothing will befall us except what Allah has ordained. He is our Guardian. In Allah, let the faithful put their trust.'

Sura: 9, Ayat: 51.

If Allah afflicts you with a misfortune none can remove it but He; and if He wills good for you, none can withhold His bounty. He is bountiful to whom He will. He is the Forgiving, the Merciful.'

Sura: 10, Ayat: 107.

It rests with Allah to show the right path. Some turn aside from it, but had He pleased, He would have guided you all alright.

Sura: 16, Ayat: 9.

Those who associate other gods with Allah say: 'Had Allah pleased, neither we nor our fathers would have served other gods besides Him; nor would we have forbidden anything without His sanction.' Thus also did those before them. Yet what should apostles do but give plain warning.?

Sura: 16, Ayat: 35.

Whatever good you have is from Allah, and to Him you turn for help when misfortune befalls you. Yet no sooner does He remove your ills that some of you set up other gods besides Him giving no thanks for what We grant them. Take your pleasure, then, (in this life); you shall before long know.

Sura: 16, Ayat: 53–55.

No misfortune can befall the earth, or your own persons, but is recorded in a book before We bring it into being. That is easy for Allah; so that you may not grieve for the good things you miss or be overjoyed at what you gain. Allah does not love the haughty, the vain-glorious.

Sura: 57, Ayat: 22-23.

In the name of Allah, The Compassionate, The Merciful

BAD COMPANY

Allah has instructed you in the Book that when you hear His revelations being denied or ridiculed, you must not sit and listen to them unless they engage in other talk, or else you shall yourselves become like them. Allah will surely gather in Hell the hyprocrites and the unbelievers.

Sura: 4, Ayat: 140.

O believers, do not choose the infidels rather than the faithful for your friends. Would you give Allah a clear proof against yourselves?

Sura: 4, Ayat: 144.

When you see those that scoff at Our revelations, withdraw from them till they engage in some other talk. If the devil causes you to forget, leave the wrongdoers as soon as you remember.

Sura: 6, Ayat: 68.

....and because they pay no heed to vain talk, but say: 'We have our actions and you have yours. Peace be upon you. We do not seek (the company of) ignorant men.'

Sura: 28, Ayat: 54-55.

....therefore await with patience the judgement of your Lord and do not yield to the sinner and the unbelieving.

Sura: 76, Ayat: 23-24.

In the name of Allah, The Compassionate, The Merciful

REFUSAL TO ACCEPT WHAT IS WRONG

You will please neither the Christians nor the Jews unless you follow their faith. Say: 'The guidance of Allah is the only guidance.' And if after all the knowledge you have been given you yield to their desires, there shall be none to help or protect you from the wrath of Allah.

Sura: 2, Ayat: 120.

You that are true believers, do not walk in the footsteps of Satan. He that walks in Satan's footsteps is incited by him to indecency and evil. But for Allah's grace and mercy, none of you would have been cleansed of sin. Allah purifies whom He will; He hears all and knows all.

Sura: 24, Ayat: 21.

And now We have set you on the right path. Follow it and do not yield to the desires of ignorant men;

Sura: 45, Ayat: 18.

Your Lord knows best those who stray from His path, and those who are rightly guided. Give no heed to the disbelievers: they wish you were pliant, so that they would be pliant. Nor yield to the wretch of many oaths the mischief-making slanderer, the opponent of good, the wicked transgressor, the bully who is besides this of doubtful birth. Though he has wealth and children, when Our revelations are recited to him, he says: 'They are but fables of the ancients.'

Sura: 68, Ayat: 7—15.

We have revealed to you the Quran by gradual revelation, therefore, await with patience the judgement of your Lord and do not yield to the sinner and the unbelieving.

Sura: 76, Ayat: 23-24.

Have you seen the man who forbids a servant when he prays.

Sura: 96, Ayat: 9-10.

No, never obey him! Prostrate yourself and come nearer.

Sura: 96, Ayat: 19.

In the name of Allah, The Compassionate, The Merciful

OPPOSING THE EVIL PERSON

Nor yield to the wretch of many oaths, the mischief—making slanderer, the opponent of good, the wicked transgressor, the bully who is besides this of doubtful birth. Though he has wealth and children, when Our revelations are recited to him, he says: 'They are but fables of the ancients.' On the nose We will brand him!

Sura: 68, Ayat: 10—16.

In the name of Allah, The Compassionate, The Merciful

BLIND ADOPTION OF ANCESTRAL CREEDS

When it is said to them: 'Come to that which Allah has revealed, and to the Apostle,' they reply: 'Sufficient for us is the faith we have inherited from our fathers,' even though their fathers knew nothing and were not rightly guided.

Sura: 5, Ayat: 104.

When they commit an indecent act, they say: 'This is what our fathers used to do before us. Allah Himself enjoined it.'

Say: 'Allah does not enjoin what is indecent. Would you tell of Allah what you do not know?'

Sura: 7, Ayat: 28.

In the name of Allah, The Compassionate, The Merciful

HELPING THOSE WHO DO GOOD DEEDS, AND NON-CO-OPERATION WITH THE EVILDOERS

....You shall not plead for traitors. Implore Allah's forgiveness: He is Forgiving, Merciful. Nor shall you plead for those who betray themselves; Allah does not love the treacherous or the sinful.

They seek to hide themselves from men but they cannot hide themselves from Allah. He is with them when they utter in secret what does not please Him: He has knowledge of what they do.

Yes, you may plead for them in this life, but who will plead for them with Allah on the Day of Resurrection? Who will be their defender?

Sura: 4, Ayat: 105–109.

Do not allow your hatred for those who would debar you from the Holy Mosque to lead you into sin. Help one another in what is good and pious, not in what is wicked and sinful. Have fear of Allah, for He is stern in retribution.

Sura: 5, Ayat: 2.

O believers, have fear of Allah and stand with the truthful.

Sura: 9, Ayat: 119.

Your Lord knows best those who stray from His path, and those who are rightly guided. Give no heed to the disbelievers: they wish you were pliant, so that they would be pliant. Nor yield to the wretch of many oaths, the mischief-making slanderer, the opponent of good, the wicked transgressor, the bully who is besides this of doubtful birth. Though he has wealth and children, when Our revelations are recited to him, he says: 'They are but fables of the ancients.'

Sura: 68, Ayat: 7–15.

ASSOCIATING FALSE DEITIES WITH GOD

(9)

In the name of Allah, The Compassionate, The Merciful

THE CORRECT RELIGION

The unbelievers have this day despaired of (vanquishing) your religion. Have no fear of them: fear Me.

This day I have perfected your religion for you and completed My favour to you. I have chosen Islam to be your faith.

He that is constrained by hunger to eat of what is forbidden, not intending to commit sin, then surely Allah is Forgiving, Merciful.

Sura: 5, Ayat: 3.

Follow then the right path as you are bidden, together with those who have repented with you, and do not transgress. He is aware of what you do.

And put no trust in the wrongdoers, lest you get touched by the Fire. You have no protectors besides Allah. Then you will not be helped.

Sura: 11, Ayat: 112-113.

Therefore set your face in devotion to the true faith, the upright nature with which Allah has endowed man. Allah's creation cannot be changed. This is surely the true religion, although most men do not know it.

Turn to Allah and fear Him. Be steadfast in prayer and be not of those who associate others with Allah, those who split up their religion into sects, each exulting in its own beliefs.

Sura: 30, Ayat: 30—32.

He has ordained for you the faith which He enjoined on Nuh and which We have revealed to you, and which We enjoined on Ibrahim, Musa and Isa (saying): 'Observe this Faith and be not divided therein.' Hard for the polytheists is that to which you call them. Allah chooses to Himself whom He will, and guides to Himself those that repent.

Sura: 42, Ayat: 13.

Yet they were enjoined to serve Allah offering him sincere devotion, to attend to their prayers and to pay the alms-tax. That, surely, is the true faith.

Sura: 98, Ayat: 5.

Say: 'Unbelievers, I do not worship what you worship, nor do you worship what I worship. I shall never worship what you worship, nor will you ever worship what I worship. You have your own religion, and I have mine.'

Sura: 109, Ayat: 1–6.

In the name of Allah, The Compassionate, The Merciful

HEATHENISM

O believers, submit all of you to Allah and do not walk in Satan's footsteps; he is your sworn enemy.

Sura: 2, Ayat: 208.

If you lapse back after the clear signs that have been shown to you, know that Allah is Mighty and Wise.

Sura: 2, Ayat: 209.

For the unbelievers, the life of this world is decked with all manner of temptations. They scoff at the faithful, but those that fear Allah shall be above them on the Day of Resurrection. Allah gives without measure to whom He will.

Sura: 2, Ayat: 212.

They ask you about the sacred month. Say: 'To fight in this month is a grave offence; but to debar others from the path of Allah, to deny Him, and to expel His worshippers from the Holy Mosque, is far more grave in His sight. Idolatry is worse than carnage.'

They will not cease to fight against you until they force you to renounce your faith — if they are able. But whoever of you recants and dies an unbeliever, his works shall come to nothing in this world and in the world to come. Such men shall be the people of Hell, and there they shall abide forever.

Sura: 2, Ayat: 217.

Those who disbelieve, neither their riches nor their children shall in the least save them from Allah. They shall become the fuel of Fire.

Sura: 3, Ayat: 10.

As for those who disbelieved, they shall be sternly punished in this world and in the world to come: There shall be none to help them.

Sura: 3, Ayat: 56.

How will Allah guide those who lapse into unbelief after embracing the faith and acknowledging the Apostle as true, and after receiving clear proofs? Allah does not guide the evil-doers.

Sura: 3, Ayat: 86.

Their reward shall be the curse of Allah, the angels, and all men: under it they shall abide forever. Their punishment shall not be lightened, nor shall they be reprieved; except those who afterwards repent and mend their ways, for Allah is Forgiving and Merciful.

Sura: 3, Ayat: 87—89.

As for those that disbelieve and die unbelievers, no ransom shall be accepted from them: although it be as much gold as would fill the entire earth. They shall be sternly punished, and none shall help them.

Sura: 3, Ayat: 91.

Do not follow the example of those who became divided and opposed to one another after clear proofs had been given them. These shall be sternly punished on the day.

Sura: 3, Ayat: 105.

When some faces will be bright (with joy) and others blackened (with grief). To the black-faced sinners it will be said: 'Did you disbelieve after embracing the true faith? Taste then our scourge, for you were unbelievers.

Sura: 3, Ayat: 106.

Guard yourself against the Fire prepared for unbelievers.

Sura: 3, Ayat: 131.

There have been examples before you. Roam the world and see what was the fate of those who disbelieved (their apostles).

Sura: 3, Ayat: 137.

Those who accept the faith and then renounce it, who again embrace it and again deny it and grow in unbelief — Allah will neither forgive them nor rightly guide them.

Sura: 4, Ayat: 137.

Those that deny Allah and His apostles, and those that draw a line between Allah and His apostles, saying: 'We believe in some, but deny others,' — thus seeking a middle way — these indeed are the unbelievers. For the unbelievers We have prepared a shameful punishment.

Sura: 4, Ayat: 150-151.

Those that disbelieve and debar others from the path of Allah have strayed far from the truth. Allah will not forgive those who disbelieve and act unjustly; nor will He guide them to any path other than that of Hell; in it they shall remain for ever. That is no difficult thing for Allah.

Sura: 4, Ayat: 167–169.

As for those who disbelieve and deny Our revelations, they shall become the people of Hell.

Sura: 5, Ayat: 11.

As for the unbelievers, if they possessed all that the earth contains and as much besides to redeem themselves from the torment of the Day of Resurrection, it shall not be accepted from them. Theirs shall be a woeful punishment.

Sura: 5, Ayat: 36.

....As for those who disbelieve, because of what they do, disaster will not cease to afflict them, or crouch at their very doorstep until Allah's promise is fulfilled. Allah will not break His promise.

Sura: 13, Ayat: 31.

Those who disbelieve in their Lord, their works are like ashes which the wind scatters on a stormy day: they shall not be able to gain anything from what they earn; that is straying far away (from the truth).

Sura: 14, Ayat: 18.

Those who disbelieve in Allah after their belief — not he who recants while his heart remains loyal to the faith, but he who opens his breast for disbelief — shall incur the wrath of Allah and be sternly punished. For such men love the life of this word more than the life to come. Allah gives no guidance to the unbelievers.

Sura: 16, Ayat: 106-107.

Never think that the unbelievers will be beyond (God's) reach in this world. Hell shall be their home, and it is indeed an evil refuge!

Sura: 24, Ayat: 57.

....Those who believe in falsehood and deny Allah shall surely be lost.'

Sura: 29, Ayat: 52.

But those who have disbelieved and denied Our revelations and the meeting of the life to come, shall be delivered up for punishment.

Sura: 30, Ayat: 16.

....He that gives thanks to Him has much to gain, but if any one is ungrate-

ful, Allah is Self-Sufficient and Glorious.'

Sura: 31, Ayat: 12.

When it is said to them: 'Follow what Allah has revealed,' they reply: 'We will follow nothing but what we found our fathers following.' Yes, even though Satan is inviting them to the scourge of Hell.

Sura: 31, Ayat: 21.

As for those that disbelieve, let their unbelief not vex you. To Allah they shall return and He will declare to them all that they have done. Allah has knowledge of what is in hearts.

We suffer them to take their ease awhile, and then will drive them to stern punishment.

Sura: 31, Ayat: 23-24.

Allah has laid His curse upon the unbelievers and prepared for them a blazing Fire. Abiding there for ever they shall find none to protect or help them.

Sura: 33, Ayat: 64-65.

The unbelievers shall be sternly punished, but those that accept the true faith and do good works shall be forgiven and richly rewarded.

Sura: 35, Ayat: 7.

It is He who made you inheritors of the earth. He who denies Him shall bear the burden of his unbelief. In denying Him the unbelievers increase nothing for themselves except odium in the sight of Allah; and their unbelief increases nothing but their perdition.

Sura: 35, Ayat: 39.

But to the unbelievers a voice will cry: 'Allah's abhorrence of you is greater than your hatred of yourselves. You were called to the Faith, but denied it.'

Sura: 40, Ayat: 10.

Allah will bring to nothing the deeds of those who disbelieve and debar others from His path.

Sura: 47, Ayat: 1.

But the unbelievers shall be consigned to perdition. He will bring their deeds to nothing. That is because they have opposed His revelations. So He will frustrate their works.

Sura: 47, Ayat: 8-9.

Allah will admit those who believe and do good works to gardens watered

by running streams. The unbelievers take their fill of pleasure and eat as the cattle eat: but Hell shall be their home.

Sura: 47, Ayat: 12.

Those who disbelieve and debar others from the path of Allah and oppose the Apostle after guidance has been shown to them shall in no way harm Allah. He will bring their works to nothing.

Sura: 47, Ayat: 32.

(Then a voice will cry): 'Cast into Hell every hardened unbeliever, every opponent of good works, and every doubting transgressor who has set up another god besides Allah. Hurl him into the terrible doom.'

Sura: 50, Ayat: 24—26.

Those who believe in Allah and His apostles are the truthful men who shall testify in their Lord's presence. They shall have their reward and their light. But those that disbelieve Our revelations and deny them are the heirs of Hell.

Sura: 57, Ayat: 19.

Have you not heard of those who disbelieved before you? They tasted the fruit of their unbelief, and a grievous punishment is yet in store for them. That is because, when their apostles brought them clear signs, they said: 'Shall men be our guides?' They denied the truth and gave no heed.

Sura: 64, Ayat: 5-6.

But those who disbelieve Our revelations and deny them shall be the people of the Fire and shall abide therein for ever. Evil shall be their fate.

Sura: 64, Ayat: 10.

For those who reject their Lord (and Cherisher) is the Penalty of Hell: and evil is (such) destination.

Sura: 67, Ayat: 6.

We know that there are some among you who will deny it.

It is the despair of the unbelievers. It is the indubitable truth. Praise, then, the name of your Lord, the Almighty.

Sura: 69, Ayat: 49—52.

The unbelievers among the People of the Book and the pagans shall burn for ever in the fire of Hell. They are the vilest of all creatures.

Sura: 98, Ayat: 6.

Say: 'Unbelievers, I do not worship what you worship, nor do you worship what I worship. I shall never worship what you worship, nor will you ever worship what I worship. You have your own religion, and I have mine.'

Sura: 109, Ayat: 1—6.

In the name of Allah, The Compassionate, The Merciful

ASSOCIATING OTHER DEITIES WITH GOD

Yet there are some who worship other objects besides Allah, bestowing on them the adoration due to Allah, and the love of Allah is stronger in the faithful. But if they face their punishment, the wrongdoers will know that might is His alone and that Allah is stern in retribution.

Sura: 2, Ayat: 165.

Allah will not forgive those who associate other gods with Him; but He will forgive whom He will for other sins. He that associates other gods with Him is guilty of a heinous sin.

Sura: 4, Ayat: 48.

Allah will not forgive setting up partners with Him. He will forgive whom He will all other sins. He that sets up partners with Allah has strayed far from the truth.

Sura: 4, Ayat: 116.

....He that worships other gods besides Allah shall be forbidden Paradise by Allah, and his abode shall be in the Fire. The evildoers shall have no helpers.

Sura: 5, Ayat: 72.

Say: 'Will you serve instead of Allah that which can neither harm nor help you? Allah is Hearing, Knowing.'

Sura: 5, Ayat: 76.

Say: 'What thing counts most in testimony?'

Say: 'Let Allah be a witness between me and you. This Quran has been revealed to me that I may thereby warn you and all whom it may reach. Will you really witness that there are other gods besides Allah?'

Say: 'I will witness (to no such a thing)!'

Say: 'He is but one God. I deny the gods you serve besides Him.'

Sura: 6, Ayat: 19.

And how should I fear what you set up with Him when you yourselves are not afraid of setting up with Him what He has not sanctioned. Which of the two parties is more deserving of safety? (Tell me), if you know the truth.

Sura: 6, Ayat: 81.

Those that have faith and do not taint their faith with wrongdoing shall surely have security, and follow the right path.'

Sura: 6, Ayat: 82.

....Nor yield to the wishes of those that deny Our revelations, disbelieve in the life to come, and set up (other gods) as equals with their Lord.

Sura: 6, Ayat: 150.

Say: 'Come, I will rehearse what God has (really) prohibited you from': join not anything as equal with Him. ....

Sura: 6, Ayat: 151.

Say: 'My prayers and my devotions, my life and my death, are all for Allah, Lord of the Creation: He has no partner. Thus I am commanded, being the first of the Muslims.'

Say: 'Should I seek any but Allah for my God, when He is the Lord of all things?....

Sura: 6, Ayat: 162—164.

Say: 'My Lord has forbidden all indecent acts, whether overt or disguised, sin and wrongful oppression; He has forbidden you to associate with Him that which is not sanctioned by Him, or to tell of Allah what you do not know.'

Sura: 7, Ayat: 33.

Those whom you invoke besides Allah are, like yourselves, His servants. Call on them, and let them answer you, if what you say be true!

Sura: 7, Ayat: 194.

O believers, know that the idolators are unclean. Let them not approach the Sacred Mosque after this year is ended. If you fear poverty, Allah, if He pleases, will enrich you through His bounty. He is Knowing, Wise.

Sura: 9, Ayat: 28.

....For I am commanded to be one of the faithful, and (I was bidden): "Set your face uprightly towards religion, and do not be a polytheist.

Sura: 10, Ayat: 105.

His is the true prayer. Those to which they pray besides Allah give them no answer. They are like a man who stretches out his hands to the water and bids

it rise to his mouth: it cannot reach it! Vain are the prayers of the unbelievers.

Sura: 13, Ayat: 14.

Have you not seen those who change thanks to Allah's grace into disbelief and drive their people into the House of Perdition? They shall burn in Hell; evil shall be their fate.

They set up equals with Allah to lead others astray. Say to them: 'Take your pleasure: You are surely destined for Hell.'

Sura: 14, Ayat: 28—30.

Allah has said: 'You shall not serve two gods, for He is but one God. Revere none but Me.'

His is what the heavens and the earth contain. To Him, obedience is due always. Would you then fear any but Allah?

Sura: 16, Ayat: 51-52.

They set aside to what they do not know a portion of what We have given them. By Allah, you shall be questioned about your false inventions!

Sura: 16, Ayat: 56.

....Will they then believe in falsehood and deny His favours?

They worship besides Allah that which can confer on them no benefits from heaven or earth. Nor have they any power.

Sura: 16, Ayat: 72-73.

Serve no other gods besides Allah, lest you be despised, forsaken. Your Lord has enjoined you to worship none but Him....

Sura: 17, Ayat: 22-23.

These injunctions are but a part of the wisdom which your Lord has revealed to you. Take no other god besides Allah, lest you should be cast into Hell, despised and helpless.

Sura: 17, Ayat: 39.

Do the unbelievers think that they can make My servants patrons besides Me? We have prepared Hell to be their dwelling-place.

Sura: 18, Ayat: 102.

Say: 'I am but a mortal like yourselves. It is revealed to me that your God is one God. Let him that hopes to meet his Lord do what is right and worship none besides Him.'

Sura: 18, Ayat: 110.

There are some who serve Allah and (yet stand) on the very fringe (of the

true faith). When blessed with good fortune they are content, but when an ordeal befalls them they turn around, forfeiting this life and the Hereafter. That way true perdition lies.

He calls on, besides Allah, that which can neither harm nor help him. That is the supreme folly.

He calls on that which would sooner harm than help him: an evil master and an evil friend.

As for those who have faith and do good works, Allah will admit them to gardens watered by running streams. Allah indeed does what He pleases.

Sura: 22, Ayat: 11—14.

Such (is Allah's commandment). He that reveres the sacred rites of Allah shall fare better in the sight of his Lord.

The flesh of cattle is lawful to you, except that which you are told (to avoid). Guard yourselves against the filth of idols and avoid all falsehood. (Be) true (in faith) to Allah, associating none with Him. He who associates others with Allah is like him who falls from heaven and is snatched away by the birds or carried by the wind to some far-off region.

Sura: 22, Ayat: 30-31.

Yet they worship besides Allah that for which no sanction is revealed and of which they know nothing. Truly, the wrongdoers shall have none to help them.

Sura: 22, Ayat: 71.

He that invokes another god besides Allah — a god of whose divinity he has no proof — his reckoning will be only with his Lord. The unbelievers shall never prosper.

Sura: 23, Ayat: 117.

Yet (the unbelievers) serve, besides Him, other gods which can create nothing and were themselves created: (gods) which can neither help nor harm themselves, and which have no power over life or death, or the raising of the dead.

Sura: 25, Ayat: 3.

Those who invoke no other god besides Allah and do not kill the soul which God has forbidden except for a just cause; who do not commit adultery. For he that does this shall meet with evil: his punishment shall be doubled on the Day of Resurrection, and he shall abide therein for ever in disgrace, unless he repents and believes and does good works, for then Allah will change his sins to good actions: Allah is ever Forgiving and Merciful.

Sura: 25, Ayat: 68—70.

Call on no other god besides Allah, lest you incur His punishment.

Sura: 26, Ayat: 213.

Let no one turn you away from Allah's revelations, now that they have been revealed to you. Call men to your Lord, and serve none besides Him.

Invoke no other god with Allah. There is no god but Him....

Sura: 28, Ayat: 87-88.

And (tell of) Ibrahim. He said to his people: 'Serve Allah and fear him. That would be best for you, if you but knew it. You worship idols besides Allah and invent falsehoods. Those whom you serve besides Him can give you no provision. Therefore seek the bounty of Allah, and worship Him. Give thanks to Him, for to Him you shall return.

Sura: 29, Ayat: 16-17.

Those whom they took besides Allah may be compared to the spider's cobweb. Surely the spider's is the frailest of all dwellings, if they but knew it.

Sura: 29, Ayat: 41.

....Those who believe in falsehood and deny Allah shall surely be lost.'

Sura: 29, Ayat: 52.

Or have We revealed to them a sanction which enjoins that which they associate with Him?

Sura: 30, Ayat: 35.

....He that gives thanks to Him has much to gain, but if any one is ungrateful, Allah is Self-Sufficient and Glorious.

Sura: 31, Ayat: 12.

....Luqman said to his son when admonishing him: 'My son, associate none with Allah, for to associate others with Him is a tremendous wrong.'

Sura: 31, Ayat: 13.

We have revealed to you the Book in truth: therefore serve Allah offering sincere devotion.

To Allah alone is true worship due. As for those who choose other guardians besides Him (saying): 'We serve them only that they may bring us nearer to Allah. Allah Himself will judge between them concerning their differences. He does not guide the untruthful disbelievers.

Sura: 39, Ayat: 2-3.

Say: 'It is Allah I serve in sincere devotion. As for yourselves, serve what you will besides Him.'

Say: 'They shall lose much, those who will forfeit their souls and all their kinsfolk on the Day of Resurrection. That will be the great loss indeed'.

Sura: 39, Ayat: 14-15.

Allah set forth this parable. There are two men: the one has many partners (as master) who are ever at odds among themselves; the other has one master. Are these two to be held alike?

Sura: 39, Ayat: 29.

Is Allah not all-sufficient for His servant? Yet they threaten you with those (gods) besides Him. Truly, he whom Allah leaves in error has none to guide him. But he whom Allah guides, none can lead astray. Is not Allah Mighty, capable of retribution?

Sura: 39, Ayat: 36-37.

Say: 'Would you bid me serve a god other than Allah, O ignorant men?'

It has already been revealed to you and those who have gone before you, that if you worshipped other gods besides Allah, your works would come to nothing and you would be among the losers.

Sura: 39, Ayat: 64-65.

Say: 'I am forbidden to serve those whom you invoke besides Allah, now that clear proofs have been given me from my Lord. I am commanded to surrender myself to the Lord of the Worlds.'

Sura: 40, Ayat: 66.

It will then be said to them: 'Where are those whom you set up besides Allah?'

They reply: 'They have failed us. Indeed what we used to invoke before is nothing.' Thus God leaves the unbelievers in error (And it will be said):

'That is because you rejoiced on earth in things other than the truth, and led a wanton life. Enter the gates of Hell and stay therein for ever. Evil is the home of the arrogant.'

Sura: 40, Ayat: 73—76.

Among His signs are the night and the day, and the sun and the moon. But do not prostrate yourselves before the sun or the moon; rather prostrate yourselves before Allah, who created them both, if you would truly serve Him.

Sura: 41, Ayat: 37.

As for those who take other protectors besides Him, Allah Himself is watching over them. You are not a guardian over them.

Sura: 42, Ayat: 6.

Had it been Allah's will, He could have made them all one nation. But Allah brings whom He will into His mercy; the wrongdoers have no friend and no helper.

Or have they set up other guardians besides Him? Surely Allah alone is the Guardian. He brings back the dead to life and has power over all things.

Sura: 42, Ayat: 8-9.

Have they partners who have made lawful to them in religion what Allah has not allowed? Had the decisive word not been pronounced already, their fate would surely have been settled in this life. The wrongdoers shall endure a harrowing torment.

Sura: 42, Ayat: 21-22.

Say: 'Do you see those whom you invoke besides Allah? Show me what part of the earth they have created! Have they a share in the heavens? Bring me a scripture revealed before this or some other vestige of knowledge, if what you say be true.'

Who is in greater error than he who invokes besides Allah those who will never hear him till the Day of Resurrection — who are, indeed, unconscious of his prayers?

Sura: 46, Ayat: 4-5.

Set up no other gods besides Allah. I am a warner to you from Him.

Sura: 51, Ayat: 51

They are but names which you invented, you and your fathers: Allah has sent down no authority for them. They follow vain conjectures and the whims of their own souls, although the guidance of their Lord has come to them.

Is man to attain all that he desires? For to Allah belongs the Hereafter and the present life.

Sura: 53, Ayat: 23—25.

Say: 'I will pray to my Lord and associate none with Him.'

Sura: 72, Ayat: 20.

Say: 'Unbelievers, I do not worship what you worship, nor do you worship what I worship. I shall never worship what you worship, nor will you ever worship what I worship. You have your own religion, and I have mine.'

Sura: 109, Ayat: 1—6.

In the name of Allah, The Compassionate, The Merciful

ATTRIBUTING UNTRUTHS TO GOD

They say: 'These cattle, and these crops are forbidden. None may eat of them save those whom we permit.' So they assert. And there are other cattle whose backs are forbidden, and others over which they do not pronounce the name of Allah, thus committing a sin against Him. Allah will punish them for their invented lies.

They also say: "What is in the wombs of these cattle is lawful to our males but not to our wives." But if it is still-born, they all partake of it. He will punish them for that which they attribute to Him. He is Wise, Knowing.

Sura: 6, Ayat: 138-139.

Say: 'My Lord has forbidden all indecent acts, whether overt or disguised, sin and wrongful oppression; He has forbidden you to associate with Him that which is not sanctioned by Him, or to tell of Allah what you do not know.'

Sura: 7, Ayat: 33.

Who is more wicked than the man who invents a falsehood about Allah or denies His revelations? Such men shall have their share of (punishment prescribed in) the Book, and when Our messengers (angels) come to carry off their souls they shall say to them: 'Where now are those whom you invoked besides Allah?' 'They have forsaken us,' they will answer, and will admit that they were unbelievers.

Sura: 7, Ayat: 37.

Who is more wicked than the man who invents a falsehood about Allah or denies His revelations? Truly, the evildoers shall not prosper.

Sura: 10, Ayat: 17.

Say: 'Tell me, have you considered the things that Allah has given you and made lawful and unlawful? Has Allah given you His leave, or do you invent falsehoods in His name?'

What will those who invent falsehoods about Allah think on the Day of Resurrection? Allah is Bountiful to men: yet most of them do not give thanks.

Sura: 10, Ayat: 59-60.

Say: 'Those that invent falsehoods about Allah shall not prosper. (They may take their) ease in this life, but to Us they shall (in the end) return, and We will sternly punish them for their unbelief.'

Sura: 10, Ayat: 69-70.

And who is more wicked than the man who invents a falsehood about Allah? Such men shall be brought before their Lord, and witnesses will say: 'These are they who lied about Allah.'

Allah's curse is on the wrongdoers, who debar others from His path and seek to make it crooked, and who deny the life to come.

Sura: 11, Ayat: 18-19.

And when you speak falsely do not utter: 'This is lawful, and this is forbidden,' in order to invent a falsehood about Allah. Those who invent falsehoods about Allah shall never prosper. Brief is their enjoyment (of this life), and grievous the punishment that awaits them.

Sura: 16, Ayat: 116-117.

And who is more wicked than the man who invents a falsehood about Allah and denies the truth when it is declared to him? Is there not a home in Hell for the unbelievers?

Sura: 29, Ayat: 68.

Who is more wicked than the man who invents a falsehood about Allah and denies the truth when it is declared to him? Is there not a home in Hell for the unbelievers?

Sura: 39, Ayat: 32.

On the Day of Resurrection, you shall see those who uttered falsehoods about Allah with faces blackened. Is there not in Hell a home for the arrogant?

But Allah will deliver those who fear Him, for they have earned salvation. No harm shall touch them, nor shall they ever grieve.

Sura: 39, Ayat: 60-61.

And who is more wicked than the man who invents a falsehood about Allah when called to Islam?....

Sura: 61, Ayat: 7.

In the name of Allah, The Compassionate, The Merciful

DENYING DIVINE REVELATIONS

Have faith in My revelations, which confirm your Scriptures, and do not be the first to deny them. Do not sell My revelations for a paltry price and guard yourself from Me.

Sura: 2, Ayat: 41.

As for those who disbelieve and deny Our revelations, they shall become the people of Hell.

Sura: 5, Ayat: 10.

But those that disbelieve and deny Our revelations shall be the people of Hell.

Sura: 5, Ayat: 86.

Those that deny Our revelations are deaf and dumb (and) in darkness. Allah leaves in error whom He will, and guides to the right path whom He pleases.

Sura: 6, Ayat: 39.

....Nor yield to the wishes of those that deny Our revelations, disbelieve in the life to come and set up (other gods) as equals with their Lord.

Sura: 6, Ayat: 150.

So that you may find mercy and not say: 'The Book was revealed only to two sects before us: we have no knowledge of what they read'; or: 'Had the Book been revealed to us, we would have been better guided than they.'

A clear sign has now come to you from your Lord: a guidance and a blessing. And who is more wicked than the man who denies the revelations of Allah and turns away from them? Those that turn away from Our revelations shall be sternly punished for their indifference.

Sura: 6, Ayat: 156-157.

Children of Adam, when apostles of your own come to proclaim to you My

revelations, those that take warning and mend their ways will have nothing to fear or to regret; but those that deny and scorn Our revelations shall be the people of the Fire, and there they shall remain for ever.

Sura: 7, Ayat: 35-36.

The gates of heaven shall not be opened for those that have denied and scorned Our revelations; nor shall they enter Paradise until a camel shall pass through the eye of a needle. Thus shall the guilty be rewarded.

Sura: 7, Ayat: 40.

'Vain are the deeds of those who disbelieve in Our signs and in the life to come. Shall they not be rewarded according to their deeds?'

Sura: 7, Ayat: 147.

Dismal is the example of those that denied Our revelations; they were unjust to themselves.

Sura: 7, Ayat: 177.

Among those whom We created there are some who give true guidance and act justly. As for those that deny Our revelations, We will lead them step by step to ruin, whence they cannot tell; for though I bear with them, My strategem is sure.

Sura: 7, Ayat: 181–183.

They sell Allah's revelations for a small price and debar others from His path. Evil is what they do.

Sura: 9, Ayat: 9.

Who is more wicked than the man who invents a falsehood about Allah or denies His revelations? Truly, the evildoers shall not prosper.

Sura: 10, Ayat: 17.

If you are in doubt of what We have revealed to you, ask those who have read the Book before you. The truth has come to you from your Lord: therefore do not be one of the doubters. Nor shall you deny the revelations of Allah, for then you shall be lost.

Sura: 10, Ayat: 94-95.

Those who disbelieve in Allah's revelations, Allah does not guide them. A grievous punishment awaits them.

None invents falsehoods save those who disbelieve the revelations of Allah: they alone are the liars.

Sura: 16, Ayat: 104-105.

Those whom Allah guides are rightly guided; but those whom He leaves in error shall find no friend besides Him. We shall gather them all on the Day of Resurrection, prostrate upon their faces, deaf, dumb, and blind. Hell shall be their abode: whenever its flames die down, We will rekindle them into a greater fire.

Thus shall they be rewarded: because they disbelieved Our revelations and said: 'When we are turned to bones and dust, shall we be raised up as a new creation?'

Do they not see that Allah, Who has created the heavens and the earth, has power to create their like? Their fate is pre-ordained beyond all doubt. Yet the wrongdoers respond only with ingratitude.

Sura: 17, Ayat: 97—99.

Say: 'Shall we tell you who will lose most through their labours? Those whose endeavours in this world are misguided and who yet think that what they do is right; who disbelieve the revelations of their Lord and deny that they will ever meet Him.' Vain are their works. On the Day of Resurrection, We shall not give any weight to them.

Sura: 18, Ayat: 103—105.

Hell is their reward; because they had no faith and scoffed at My revelations and My apostles.

Sura: 18, Ayat: 106.

Behold him who rejects Our signs and yet says: 'I shall surely be given wealth and children!'

Has he gained knowledge of the unseen? Or has the Merciful made him such a promise?

By no means! We will record his words and make his punishment long and terrible. To Us shall return all what he speaks of and he will come before Us all alone.

Sura: 19, Ayat: 77—80.

'Lord,' he will say, 'why have You brought me blind before You while (in my lifetime) I had sight?'

He will answer: 'Thus Our revelations were declared to you and you forgot them. So this day you are yourself forgotten.'

Sura: 20, Ayat: 125-126.

Say: 'O men, I have been sent to warn you plainly. Those that accept the true faith and do good works shall be forgiven and richly rewarded; but those who seek to confute Our revelations shall be the people of Hell.'

Sura: 22, Ayat: 49—51.

When Our clear revelations are recited to them, you will notice denial in the faces of the unbelievers. They can barely restrain themselves from assaulting those who recite Our revelations to them.

Say: 'Shall I tell you what is worse than that? The Fire which Allah has promised those who deny Him. An evil fate.'

Sura: 22, Ayat: 72.

Do not howl this day, for from Us you shall receive no help. My revelations were recited to you many a time, but you turned your backs in scorn, talking nonsense about them by night.'

Sura: 23, Ayat: 65—67.

On that day We shall gather from every nation a multitude of those who disbelieved Our revelations. They shall be led in separate bands. And when they come, He will say (to them): 'You denied My revelations although you knew nothing of them. What was it you were doing? Our judgement will smite them for their sins, and they shall be dumbfounded.

Sura: 27, Ayat: 83—85.

Those that disbelieve His revelations and deny that they will ever meet Him shall despair of My mercy. Theirs shall be a woeful punishment.

Sura: 29, Ayat: 23.

Likewise We revealed the Book to you. Those to whom We gave the Scriptures believe in it, and so do some of these (pagan Arabs). Only the unbelievers deny Our revelations.

Sura: 29, Ayat: 47.

Never have you* read a book before this, nor have you ever transcribed one with your right hand. Had you done either of these, the unbelievers might have doubted. But in the hearts of those who are endowed with knowledge it is clear revelations. Only the wrongdoers deny Our signs.

Sura: 29, Ayat: 48-49.

Evil was the end of the evildoers, because they had denied the revelations of Allah and scoffed at them.

Sura: 30, Ayat: 10.

But those who have disbelieved and denied Our revelations and the meeting of the life to come, shall be delivered up for punishment.

Sura: 30, Ayat: 16.

***Muhammad**

And who is more wicked than the man who gives no heed to the revelations of his Lord when he is reminded of them? We shall punish the guilty.

Sura: 32, Ayat: 22.

Or, when it sees the punishment should say: 'Could I but live again, I would lead a righteous life.' For Allah will say: 'My revelations had come to you, but you denied them. You were arrogant and one of the unbelievers.'

Sura: 39, Ayat: 58-59.

Allah is the Creator of all things, and of all things He is the Guardian. His are the keys of the heavens and the earth. Those that deny His revelations shall assuredly be lost.

Sura: 39, Ayat: 62-63.

None but the unbelievers dispute the revelations of Allah. Do not be deceived by their fortunes in the land.

Sura: 40, Ayat: 4.

Those who dispute the revelations of Allah without authority given to them, there is nothing in their hearts but ambitions which they shall never attain. Therefore seek refuge in Allah.....

Sura: 40, Ayat: 56.

Yet even thus the men who deny His revelations turn away from Him.

Sura: 40, Ayat: 63.

Do you not see how those who dispute the revelations of Allah turn away (from the right path)? Those who have denied the Book and the message with which We have sent Our apostles shall know: when with chains and shackles round their necks they shall be dragged through boiling water and burnt in the Fire.

Sura: 40, Ayat: 69—72.

That is the reward of Allah's enemies — the Fire. Therein is their immortal abode, because they have denied Our revelations.

Sura: 41, Ayat: 28.

Those who deny Our revelations are not hidden from Our view. Is he who is cast in the Fire better than the one who emerges safe on the Day of Resurrection? Do as you will, Allah is watching over all your actions.

Those who deny Our word when it is preached to them (shall be sternly punished). This is a mighty Book. Falsehood cannot get at it from before or behind. It is a revelation from a Wise and Glorious God.

Sura: 41, Ayat: 40—42.

Woe to the lying sinner! He hears the revelations of Allah recited to him and then, as though he never heard them, persists in scorn. Forewarn him of a woeful scourge. For those that deride our revelations when they have scarcely heard them is a shameful punishment.

Hell is behind them. Their gains shall not avail them, nor shall those protectors they take besides Allah. A dreadful punishment awaits them.

Sura: 45, Ayat: 7–10.

Such is (Our) guidance. Those who deny the revelations of their Lord shall suffer the torment of a hideous scourge.

Sura: 45, Ayat: 11.

That is because you scoffed at Allah's revelations and were deceived by your earthly life.

On that day there shall be no way out for them; nor shall they be asked to make amends.

Sura: 45, Ayat: 35.

When Our clear revelations are recited to them, the unbelievers say of the truth: 'This is plain magic.'

Do they say: 'He invented it himself?'

Say: 'If I have indeed invented it*, then there is nothing that you can do to protect me from (the wrath) of Allah. He well knows what you say about it. He is all-sufficient witness between me and you. He is the Benignant One, the Merciful.'

Sura: 46, Ayat: 7-8.

The unbelievers say of the faithful: 'Had it been any good they would not have believed in it before us.

Sura: 46, Ayat: 11.

We had empowered them to do what we have empowered you to do and given them ears, eyes and hearts. Yet nothing did their ears, their eyes, or their hearts avail them since they denied the revelations of Allah. The scourge at which they scoffed encompassed them.**

Sura: 46, Ayat: 26.

Those who believe in Allah and His apostles are the truthful men who shall testify in their Lord's presence. They shall have their reward and their light. But those that disbelieve Our revelations and deny them are the heirs of Hell.

Sura: 57, Ayat: 19.

---

*The Quran **The Makkans

Those to whom the burden of the Torah was entrusted and yet refused to bear it are like a donkey laden with books. Wretched is the example of those who deny Allah's revelations. Allah does not guide the wrongdoers.

Sura: 62, Ayat: 5.

They did not fear Our reckoning and roundly denied Our revelations. But We have recorded all their doings in a book. We shall say: 'Taste this: you shall have nothing but mounting torment!'

Sura: 78, Ayat: 27—30.

When Our revelations are recited to him, he says: 'Fables of the ancients!'

Sura: 83, Ayat: 13.

But those who deny Our revelations shall stand on the left, with Hell — fire close above them.

Sura: 90, Ayat: 19-20.

In the name of Allah, The Compassionate, The Merciful

DEVIATING FROM RELIGIOUS INJUNCTIONS

He has revealed to you the Book with the truth, confirming what preceded it; and He has already revealed the Torah and the Gospel for the guidance of men, and the distinction between right and wrong.

Those that deny Allah's revelations shall be sternly punished; Allah is Mighty and capable of punishmen

Sura: 2, Ayat: 3-4.

But he that disobeys Allah and His Apostle and transgresses His bounds, shall be cast into fire and shall abide in it forever. A shameful punishment awaits him.

Sura: 4, Ayat: 14.

Those who oppose Allah and His Apostle shall be brought low as have been those before them. We have sent down clear revelations. A shameful punishment awaits the unbelievers.

Sura: 58, Ayat: 5.

....Those that disobey Allah and His Apostle shall abide forever in the fire of Hell.

Sura: 72, Ayat: 22-23.

In the name of Allah, The Compassionate, The Merciful

PREVENTING PEOPLES FROM FOLLOWING THE PATH OF GOD

Those that disbelieve and debar others from the path of Allah have strayed far from the truth. Allah will not forgive those who disbelieve and act unjustly; nor will He guide them to any path other than that of Hell; in it they shall remain for ever. That is no difficult thing for Allah.

Sura: 4, Ayat: 167—169.

....A clear sign has come to you from your Lord: a guidance and a blessing. And who is more wicked than the man who denies the revelations of Allah and turns away from them? Those that turn away from Our revelations shall be sternly punished for their indifference.

Sura: 6, Ayat: 157.

Those who disbelieve spend their wealth in debarring others from the path of Allah. They will spend it; but it will become a cause of regret for them, and in the end they will be overcome. The unbelievers shall be gathered in Hell.

Thus Allah will separate the wicked from the just. He will heap the wicked one upon another and then heap them together and cast them in Hell. Such are those that shall be lost.

Sura: 8, Ayat: 36-37.

Do not be like those who left their homes elated with insolence and vainglory. They debar others from the path of Allah: but Allah has knowledge of all their actions.

Sura: 8, Ayat: 47.

....Woe to the unbelievers, because of stern punishment. Those who love this life more than the life to come, debar others from the path of Allah and seek to make it crooked are far astray.

Sura: 14, Ayat: 2-3.

(As for) those that disbelieve and debar others from the path of Allah, We

shall add to their chastisement for their misdeeds.

Sura: 16, Ayat: 88.

Those who disbelieve and debar others from Allah's path and in the end die unbelievers shall not be shown forgiveness by Allah.

Sura: 47, Ayat: 34.

They use their faith as a disguise and thus debar others from the path of Allah. A shameful scourge awaits them.

Sura: 58, Ayat: 16.

....And Allah bears witness that the hypocrites are lying!
They use their faith as a disguise and debar others from the path of Allah.

Sura: 63, Ayat: 1-2.

In the name of Allah, The Compassionate, The Merciful

OPPOSING ALLAH AND HIS APOSTLE

Those that deny Allah's revelations and slay the prophets unjustly and kill the men who preach fair dealing — warn them of a woeful scourge. Their works shall come to nothing in this world and in the next, and there shall be none to help them.

Sura: 3, Ayat: 21.

Those that make war against Allah and His Apostle and spread disorders in the land shall be put to death or crucified or have their hands and feet cut off on alternate sides, or be banished from the land. They shall be held in shame in this world and sternly punished in the next: except those that repent before you reduce them. For you must know that Allah is Forgiving, Merciful.

Sura: 5, Ayat: 33-34.

Are they not aware that the man who defies Allah and His Apostle shall abide for ever in the fire of Hell? That surely is the supreme humiliation.

Sura: 9, Ayat: 63.

(It is the same) whether or not you beg forgiveness for them. If seventy times you beg forgiveness for them Allah will not forgive them, for they have denied Allah and His Apostle. Allah does not guide the evildoers.

Sura: 9, Ayat: 80.

You shall not pray for any of their dead, nor shall you attend their burial. For they denied Allah and His Apostle and remained sinners to the last.

Let neither their riches nor their children rouse your envy. Through these Allah seeks to punish them in this life, so that they shall die unbelievers.

Whenever a Sura was revealed, saying: 'Believe in Allah and fight along with His Apostle,' the rich among them asked you to excuse them, saying: "Leave us with those who are to stay behind."

They were content to be with those who stayed behind: a seal was set upon their hearts, leaving them bereft of understanding. But the Apostle and the men who shared his faith fought with their goods and their persons. Those

shall be rewarded with good things. Those shall surely prosper. Allah has prepared for them gardens watered by running streams, in which they shall abide for ever. That is the supreme triumph.

Sura: 9, Ayat: 84–89.

Those who disbelieve in their Lord, their works are the ashes which the wind scatters on a stormy day: they shall not be able to gain anything from what they earn; that is straying far away (from the truth).

Sura: 14, Ayat: 18.

Whenever they see you, they scoff at you, (saying): 'Is this the man whom Allah has sent as (His) Apostle? He would have turned us away from our deities, if we had not adhered to them?' But when they face their punishment, they shall know who has been more grossly misled.

Sura: 25, Ayat: 41-42.

But those who strive to belittle Our revelations shall be brought for punishment.

Sura: 34, Ayat: 38.

Those who disbelieve and debar others from the path of Allah and oppose the Apostle after guidance has been shown to them shall in no way harm Allah. He will bring their works to nothing.

Sura: 47, Ayat: 32.

But if any disbelieves in Allah and His Apostle, We have prepared a blazing Fire for the disbelievers.

Sura: 48, Ayat: 13.

Thus whenever an Apostle came to those that flourished before them they cried: 'Sorcerer!' or 'Madman!' Have they handed down this (cry) from one generation to the next? Surely they are transgressors all.
Give no heed to them; you shall incur no blame.

Sura: 51, Ayat: 52–54.

Those who oppose Allah and His Apostle shall be brought low as have been those before them. We have sent down clear revelations. A shameful punishment awaits the unbelievers.

Sura: 58, Ayat: 5.

Those who oppose Allah and His Apostle shall be brought low.

Sura: 58, Ayat: 20.

Had Allah not decreed evacuation for them, He would have surely

punished them in this world. But in the world to come they shall be punished in the Fire, because they have set themselves against Allah and His Apostle; and he that sets himself against Allah should know that Allah is stern in retribution.

Sura: 59, Ayat: 3-4.

....And when they went astray Allah let their very hearts go astray. He does not guide the evildoers.

Sura: 61, Ayat: 5.

In the name of Allah, The Compassionate, The Merciful

ATTITUDE TOWARDS THE CHRISTIANS

He said: 'Isa, I am about to cause your term on earth to end and lift you up to Me. I shall take you away from those who disbelieve and exalt your followers above them till the Day of Resurrection. Then to Me you shall all return, and I shall judge your dispute.

Sura: 3, Ayat: 55.

Yet they are not all alike. There are among the People of the Book some upright men who all night long recite the revelations of Allah and pray; who believe in Allah and the Last Day; who enjoin justice and forbid evil and vie with each other in good works. These are righteous men: whatever good they do, shall not be denied them. Allah knows the righteous.

Sura: 3, Ayat: 113—115.

They declared: 'We have put to death al-Masih Isa the son of Mariam, the Apostle of Allah.' They did not kill him, nor did they crucify him, but they mistook the crucified one for him.

Those that disagreed about him were in doubt concerning him, for what they knew about it was sheer conjecture; they did not kill him for certain.

Sura: 4, Ayat: 157.

Allah lifted him up to Him; He is Mighty, Wise.

Sura: 4, Ayat: 158.

There is none among the People of the Book but will believe in Him before his death; and on the Day of Resurrection he will be a witness against them.

Sura: 4, Ayat: 159.

People of the Book, do not transgress the bounds of your religion. Speak nothing but the truth about Allah. Al-Masih, Isa the son of Mariam, was no more than Allah's Apostle and His Word which He cast to Mariam: a spirit from Him, So believe in Allah and His Apostles and do not say: "Three". Forbear, and it shall be better for you. Allah is but one God. Allah forbid that He

should have a son! His is all that the heavens and the earth contain. Allah is the All-Sufficient Protector.

Sura: 4, Ayat: 171.

Al-Masih does not disdain to be a servant of Allah, nor do the angels who are nearest to Him.

Sura: 4, Ayat: 172.

With those who said they were Christians, We made a covenant also, but they too have forgotten much of what they were enjoined. Therefore We stirred among them enmity and hatred which shall endure till the Day of Resurrection, when Allah will declare to them all that they have done.

Sura: 5, Ayat: 14.

Unbelievers are those that say: 'Allah is Al-Masih, the son of Mariam.' For al-Masih himself said: 'Children of Israel , serve Allah, my Lord and Your Lord.' He that worships other gods besides Allah shall be forbidden Paradise by Allah and his abode shall be in the Fire. The evildoers shall have no helpers.

Sura: 5, Ayat: 72.

Unbelievers are those that say: 'Allah is one of three.' There is but one God. If they do not desist from so saying, those of them that disbelieve shall be sternly punished.

Sura: 5, Ayat: 73.

Al-Masih, the son of Mariam, was no more than an Apostle: other Apostles had gone before him. His mother was a truthful woman. They both ate earthly food.

See how We make plain to them Our revelations. Then see how they ignore the truth.

Sura: 5, Ayat: 75.

Say: 'People of the Book! Do not transgress the bounds of your religion unjustly. Do not yield to the desires of those who have already erred; who have led many astray and have themselves strayed from the straight path.'

Sura: 5, Ayat: 77.

....And that the nearest in affection to them are those who say: 'We are Christians.' That is because there are priests and monks among them; and because they are free from pride.

When they listen to that which was revealed to the Apostle, you will see their eyes fill with tears as they recognize its truth. They say: 'Lord, we believe. Count us among your witnesses.'

Sura: 5, Ayat: 82-83.

And they say: 'The Lord of Mercy has begotten a son.' Surely you say a monstrous falsehood! The very heavens might crack, the earth break asunder, and the mountains crumble to dust when they ascribe a son to the Merciful. It does not become Al-Rahman to beget one!

Sura: 19, Ayat: 88–92.

Yet they assign to Him some of His servants! Surely man is monstrously ungrateful.

Sura: 43, Ayat: 15.

He was no more than a man whom We favoured and made an example to the Children of Israel.

Sura: 43, Ayat: 59.

And remember Isa, who said to the Children of Israel: "I am sent forth to you by Allah to confirm the Torah already revealed and to give news of an apostle that will come after me whose name is Ahmad."* Yet when he came to them with clear signs, they said: 'This is plain magic.'

Sura: 61, Ayat: 6.

***Muhammad**

In the name of Allah, The Compassionate, The Merciful

ATTITUDE TOWARDS THE JEWS

Among the People of the Book there are some who, if you trust them with a heap of gold, will return it to you intact; and there are others who, if you trust them with one dinar will not hand it back unless you demand it with importunity, for they say: 'We are not bound to keep faith with the non-Jewish Arabs.' Thus, they deliberately say of Allah what is untrue.

Sura: 3, Ayat: 75.

Yet they are not all alike. There are among the People of the Book some upright men who all night long recite the revelations of Allah and pray; who believe in Allah and the Last Day; who enjoin justice and forbid evil and vie with each other in good works. These are righteous men: whatever good they do, shall not be denied them. Allah knows the righteous.

Sura: 3, Ayat: 113–115.

You to whom the Book was given! Believe in that which We have revealed, confirming that which you have, before We obliterate faces and turn them backward, or lay Our curse on you as We laid it on the Sabbath-breakers. What Allah ordains shall be accomplished.

Sura: 4, Ayat: 47.

Because of their inquity, We forbade the Jews good things which were formerly allowed them; because time after time they have debarred others from the path of Allah; because they practise usury-although they were forbidden it – and cheat others of their possessions. We have prepared a stern chastisement for those of them that disbelieve. But those of them that have deep learning and those that truly believe in what has been revealed to you and to other prophets before you; who attend to their prayers and pay the alms-tax and have faith in Allah and the Last Day – these shall be richly rewarded.

Sura: 4, Ayat: 160–162.

Allah made a covenant with the Children of Israel and raised among them twelve chieftains. He said: 'I shall be with you. If you attend to your prayers

and pay the alms-tax; if you believe in My Apostles and assist them and give Allah a generous loan, I shall forgive you your sins and admit you to gardens watered by running streams. But he that hereafter denies Me shall stray from the right path.'

But because they broke their covenant, We laid on them Our curse and hardened their hearts. They dislocate the words (of the Scriptures) from their places and have forgotten a portion of what they were enjoined. You will ever find them deceitful, except for a few of them. But pardon them and bear with them. Allah loves those who do good.

Sura: 5, Ayat: 12-13.

People of the Book! Our Apostle has come to reveal to you much of what you have hidden of the Book, and to forgive you much. A light has come to you from Allah and a glorious Book, with which He will guide to the paths of peace those that seek to please Him; He will lead them by His will from darkness to the light; He will guide them to a straight path.

Sura: 5, Ayat: 15-16.

The Jews and the Christians say: 'We are the children of Allah and His loved ones.' Say: 'Why then does He punish you for your sins? Surely you are mortals of His own creation. He forgives whom He will, and punishes whom He pleases. He has control over the heavens and the earth and all that lies between them. All shall return to Him.'

Sura: 5, Ayat: 18.

That was why We laid down for the Children of Israel that whoever killed a human being, except as a punishment for murder or for sedition in the earth, should be looked upon as though he had killed all mankind; and that whoever saved a human life should be regarded as though he had saved all mankind.

Our Apostles brought them veritable proofs; yet it was not long before many of them committed great evils in the land.

Sura: 5, Ayat: 32.

Say: 'People of the Book! Do not transgress the bounds of your religion unjustly. Do not yield to the desires of those who have already erred; who have led many astray and have themselves strayed from the straight path.

Sura: 5, Ayat: 77.

You will find that the most implacable of men in their enmity to the faithful are the Jews and the pagans....

Sura: 5, Ayat: 82.

Fight against such of those to whom the Book was given as believe neither

in Allah nor the Last Day, who do not forbid what Allah and His Apostle have forbidden, and do not embrace the true faith, until they pay tribute out of hand and are utterly subdued.

Sura: 9, Ayat: 29.

The Jews say Uzayr is the son of Allah, while the Christians say al-Masih is the son of Allah. Such are their assertions, by which they imitate those who disbelieved before. Allah's curse be on them! How they are turned away (from the truth)!

Sura: 9, Ayat: 30.

Believers, many are the rabbis and the monks who defraud men of their possessions and debar people from the path of Allah. Those that hoard up gold and silver and do not spend it in Allah's cause — proclaim to them a woeful punishment. On (that) day their treasures will be heated in the fire of Hell, and their foreheads, sides, and backs branded with them. They will be told: 'These are the riches which you hoarded. Taste then that which you were hoarding.'

Sura: 9, Ayat: 34-35.

We showed Musa and Harun the criterion (to distinguish between right and wrong), and gave them a light and a message for the righteous: those who fear their Lord in secret and dread the terrors of Judgement-Day.

And this is a blessed Message which We have revealed. Will you then reject it?

Sura: 21, Ayat: 48—50.

We gave the Children of Israel the Book, wisdom and prophethood. We provided them with good things and exalted them above the nations. We gave them plain commandments: yet it was not till knowledge had been vouchsafed them that they disagreed among themselves from evil motives. On the Day of Resurrection your Lord Himself will judge their differences.

Sura: 45, Ayat: 16-17.

Say: 'O you who are Jews, if you claim that of all men you alone are Allah's friends, then invoke death if you are truthful!'

Sura: 62, Ayat: 6.

In the name of Allah, The Compassionate, The Merciful

SECTARIANISM IN RELIGION

Do not follow the example of those who became divided and opposed to one another after clear proofs had been given them. These shall be sternly punished on the day when some faces will be bright (with joy) and others blackened (with grief). To the black faced sinners it will be said: 'Did you disbelieve after embracing the true faith?....

Sura: 3, Ayat: 105-106.

Have nothing to do with those who have split up their religion into sects. Allah will call them to account and declare to them what they have done.

Sura: 6, Ayat: 159.

....Each man shall reap the fruits of his own deeds: no soul shall bear another's burden. In the end you shall all return to your Lord, and He will inform you about that in which you differed.'

Sura: 6, Ayat: 164.

There was a time when men were one nation. Then they disagreed among themselves: and had Allah not ordained before (the deferring of their punishment), their differences would have long been settled.

Sura: 10, Ayat: 19.

Had your Lord pleased, all the people of the earth would have believed in Him. Would you then force men to be believers?

Sura: 10, Ayat: 99.

Had your Lord pleased, He would have made mankind a single nation. But only those whom He has shown mercy will cease to differ (in religion). For this end He has created them. The word of your Lord shall be fulfilled: 'I will fill Hell with jinn and men, all together.'

Sura: 11, Ayat: 118-119.

Verily, this brotherhood of yours is one brotherhood, and I am Your only

Lord. Therefore serve Me. Men have divided themselves (into schisms), but to Us they shall all return. He that does good works in the fullness of his faith, his endeavours shall not be lost: We record them all.

Sura: 21, Ayat: 92—94.

Your brotherhood is but one brotherhood, and I am your only Lord: therefore fear Me.

Yet men have divided themselves into different sects, each rejoicing in what it had.

Sura: 23, Ayat: 52-53.

Turn to Allah and fear Him. Be steadfast in prayer and be not of those who associate others with Allah, those who split up their religion into sects, each exulting in its own beliefs.

Sura: 30, Ayat: 31-32.

Yet they became divided only after knowledge had reached them, out of envy among themselves. And had it not been for a word that had already gone forth from your Lord, reprieving them till an appointed term they would surely have been punished (in this life). Those who inherited the Book after them have their grave doubts too.

Sura: 42, Ayat: 14.

As for those who argue about Allah after obedience has been rendered to Him, their arguments will have no weight with their Lord, and His wrath will fall upon them. They shall be sternly punished.

Sura: 42, Ayat: 16.

Nor did the People of the Book disagree among themselves until the Clear Proof was given them.

Sura: 98, Ayat: 4.

In the name of Allah, The Compassionate, The Merciful

APOSTACY

....But whoever of you recants and dies an unbeliever, his works shall come to nothing in this world and in the world to come. Such men shall be the people of Hell, and there they shall abide forever.

Sura: 2, Ayat: 217.

Those who accept the faith and then renounce it, who again embrace it and again deny it and grow in unbelief—Allah will neither forgive them nor rightly guide them.

Sura: 4, Ayat: 137.

Believers, if any of you renounce the faith, Allah will replace them by others who love Him and are loved by Him, humble towards the faithful and stern towards the unbelievers, striving for Allah's cause and fearless of man's censure. Such is the grace of Allah: He bestows it on whom He will. He is Munificent, Knowing.

Sura: 5, Ayat: 54.

Those who turn back after Allah's guidance has been revealed to them, it is Satan who seduces and inspires them. That is because they say to those who abhor the word of Allah: 'We shall obey you in some matters.' Allah knows their secret talk.

How (will it be) when the angels carry away their souls and strike them on their heads and backs?

That is because they follow what has incurred the wrath of Allah and abhor what please Him. So he made their deeds of no effect.

Sura: 47, Ayat: 25—28.

In the name of Allah, The Compassionate, The Merciful

PUNISHMENT OF POLYTHEISM

Allah will not forgive setting up partners with Him. He will forgive, whom He will, all other sins. He that sets up partners with Allah has strayed far from the truth.

Sura: 4, Ayat: 116.

....He that worships other gods besides Allah shall be forbidden Paradise by Allah, and his abode shall be in the Fire. The evildoers shall have no helpers.

Sura: 5, Ayat: 72.

A proclamation to the people by Allah and His Apostle on the day of the great pilgrimage:

Allah and His Apostle are free from obligation to the idolaters. If you repent, it will be well with you; but if you give no heed, know that you shall not escape His judgement.

Proclaim a woeful punishment to the unbelievers, except those idolaters who have fully honoured their treaties with you and aided none against you. With these keep faith, until their treaties have run their term. Allah loves the righteous.

Sura: 9, Ayat: 3-4.

When the sacred months are over, slay the idolaters wherever you find them. Arrest them, besiege them, and lie in ambush everywhere for them. If they repent and take to prayer and pay the alms-tax, let them go their way. Allah is Forgiving and Merciful.

Sura: 9, Ayat: 5.

If an idolater seeks asylum with you, give him protection so that he may hear the Word of Allah, and then convey him to safety. For they are ignorant men.

Sura: 9, Ayat: 6.

They honour with the believers neither treaties nor ties of kindred. Such are the transgressors.

If they repent and take to prayer and pay the alms-tax, they shall become your brothers in the faith. Thus We make plain Our revelations for men of understanding.

But if, after coming to terms with you, they break their oaths and revile your faith, make war on the leaders of unbelief—for no oaths are binding with them — so that they may desist.

Sura: 9, Ayat: 10—12.

Fight against such of those to whom the Book was given as believe neither in Allah nor the Last Day, who do not forbid what Allah and His Apostle have forbidden, and do not embrace the true faith, until they pay tribute out of hand and are utterly subdued.

Sura: 9, Ayat: 29.

It is not for the Prophet or the believers to beg forgiveness for polytheists, even though they be near of kin, after it has become manifest that they are the people of the Fire.

Sura: 9, Ayat: 113.

MORAL DISEASES

(10)

In the name of Allah, The Compassionate, The Merciful

FALSEHOOD

'Woe to you!' said Musa. 'Invent no falsehoods against Allah, or he will destroy you with His scourge. Liars will surely fail.'

Sura: 20, Ayat: 61.

....The flesh of cattle is lawful to you, except that which you are told (to avoid). Guard yourselves against the filth of idols and avoid all falsehood. (Be) true (in faith) to Allah, associating none with Him.

Sura: 22, Ayat: 30.

(And the true servants are those) who do not bear false witness and do not lose their dignity when listening to profane chatter;

Sura: 25, Ayat: 72.

Allah Himself will judge between them concerning their differences. He does not guide the untruthful disbeliever.

Sura: 39, Ayat: 3.

But one of Pharaoh's kinsmen, who in secret was a true believer, said: 'Would you kill a man merely because he says: 'My Lord is Allah?' He has brought you clear signs from your Lord. If he is lying, may his lie be on his head; but if he is speaking the truth, a part at least of what he threatens will smite you. Allah does not guide the lying transgressor.

Sura: 40, Ayat: 28.

Your Lord knows best those who stray from His path, and those who are rightly guided. Give no heed to the disbelievers:

Sura: 68, Ayat: 7–8.

In the name of Allah, The Compassionate, The Merciful

ARROGANCE

Do not think that those who rejoice in what they have done and wish to be praised for what they have not done — do not think they will escape from torture. A woeful punishment awaits them.

Sura: 3, Ayat: 188.

....Allah does not love arrogant and boastful men.

Sura: 4, Ayat: 36.

....Those who through arrogance disdain His service shall all be brought before Him.

Sura: 4, Ayat: 172.

Allah will reward those that have faith and do good works; He will enrich them from His own abundance. As for those who are scornful and proud, He will sternly punish them, and they shall find none besides Allah to protect or help them.

Sura: 4, Ayat: 173.

Do not be like those who left their homes elated with insolence and vainglory. They debar others from the path of Allah: but Allah has knowledge of all their actions.

Sura: 8, Ayat: 47.

Enter the gates of Hell to be in it for ever. Dismal is the abode of the proud.

Sura: 16, Ayat: 29.

Do not walk proudly in the earth. You cannot cleave the earth, nor can you rival the mountains in stature.

The evil of all this is odious in the sight of your Lord.

Sura: 17, Ayat: 37-38.

The true servants of the Merciful are those who walk humbly on the earth,

and when the ignorant address them they say: 'Peace!';

Sura: 25, Ayat: 63.

Pharaoh and his warriors conducted themselves in the land with pride and injustice, and thought they would never be recalled to Us. But We seized them and We cast them into the sea. Consider the fate of the evildoers.

Sura: 28, Ayat: 39.

....His people said to him: 'Do not exult (in your riches); Allah does not love the exultant. But seek, by means of that which Allah has given you, to attain the abode of the Hereafter. Do not forget your share in this world. Be good to others as Allah has been good to you, and do not strive for evil in the land, for Allah does not love the evildoers.

But he replied: 'These riches were given me on account of the knowledge I possess.'

Did he not know that Allah had destroyed before him from the generations men who were mightier and greater money-collectors than he? The wrongdoers may not be questioned about their sins.

And when he went out in all his finery among his people, those who loved this life said: 'Would that we had the like of Qarun's fortune! He is indeed a lucky man.'

But those to whom knowledge had been given said: 'Alas for you! Better is the reward of Allah for him who has faith and does good works; but none shall attain it save the patient.'

We caused the earth to swallow him, together with his dwelling, so that he found none to protect him from Allah; nor was he one of those who defended themselves. And those who on the day before had coveted his lot began to say: 'Behold! Allah gives abundantly to whom He will and sparingly to whom He pleases. Had he not shown us favour, He could have caused the earth to swallow us. Behold! The ungrateful shall never prosper.'

As for the abode of the Hereafter, we shall assign it to those who seek neither glory in this world nor evil. The blessed end is for the righteous.

Sura: 28, Ayat: 76—83.

Do not turn away from men with scorn, nor walk proudly on the earth: Allah does not love the arrogant and the vain-glorious. Rather let your gait be modest and your voice low: the harshest of voices is the braying of the asses.'

Sura: 31, Ayat: 18-19.

None believes in Our revelations save those who, when reminded of them, prostrate themselves in adoration and give glory to their Lord in all humility; who forsake their beds to pray to their Lord in fear and hope; who give in charity of that which We have bestowed on them.

Sura: 32, Ayat: 15-16.

Lest any soul should say: 'Alas! I have disobeyed Allah and scoffed at His revelations.' Or 'If Allah had guided me I would have been one of the righteous.' Or, when it sees the punishment should say: 'Could I but live again, I would lead a righteous life.'

Sura: 39, Ayat: 56–58

Your God is one God. Those that deny the life to come have faithless hearts and are puffed up with pride. Allah surely knows what they hide and what they reveal. He does not love the proud.

Sura: 40, Ayat: 22-23.

Those who dispute the revelations of Allah without authority given to them, there is nothing in their hearts but ambitions which they shall never attain. Therefore seek refuge in Allah; He hears all and sees all.

Sura: 40, Ayat: 56.

Your Lord has said: 'Call on Me and I will hear you. Those that disdain My service shall enter Hell disgraced.'

Sura: 40, Ayat: 60.

....(And it will be said): 'That is because you rejoiced on earth in things other than the truth, and led a wanton life. Enter the gates of Hell and stay therein for ever. Evil is the home of the arrogant.'

Sura: 40, Ayat: 74−76.

If they are arrogant, let them remember that those who are in Allah's presence glorify him day and night and are never wearied.

Sura: 41, Ayat: 38.

On the day when the unbelievers are brought before the fire of Hell, (We shall say to them): 'You squandered away your precious things in your earthly life and took your fill of pleasure. An ignominious punishment shall be yours this day, because you behaved with pride and without just cause on earth and committed evil.'

Sura: 46, Ayat: 20.

So that you may not grieve for the good things you miss or be overjoyed at what you gain. Allah does not love the haughty, the vainglorious; nor those who, being niggardly themselves, enjoin others to be niggardly also. He that gives no heed (should know) that Allah is Self-Sufficient and Worthy of praise.

Sura: 57, Ayat: 23-24.

In the name of Allah, The Compassionate, The Merciful

HYPOCRISY

O believers, do not mar your almsgiving with taunts and mischief-making, like him who spends his wealth for the sake of ostentation and believes neither in Allah nor in the Last Day. Such a man is like a smooth rock covered with earth: a shower falls upon it and leaves it hard and bare. They shall gain nothing from their works. Allah does not guide the unbelievers.

Sura: 2, Ayat: 264.

Do not think that those who rejoice in what they have done and wish to be praised for what they have not done — do not think they will escape from torture. A woeful punishment awaits them.

Sura: 3, Ayat: 188.

The hypocrites seek to deceive Allah, but it is Allah who deceives them. When they rise to pray, they stand up sluggishly: they pray for the sake of ostentation and remember Allah but little, wavering between this and that and belonging neither to these nor those. You cannot guide the man whom Allah has left in error.

Sura: 4, Ayat: 142—143.

Woe to those who pray but are unmindful of their prayer; who make a show (of piety) and refuse (to supply) (even) neighbourly needs.

Sura: 107, Ayat: 4—7.

In the name of Allah, The Compassionate, The Merciful

DECEPTION

And thus we have placed in every town its arch-transgressors to scheme there. But they scheme only against themselves, though they may not perceive it. When a sign is revealed to them they say: 'We will not believe in it unless we are given that which Allah's apostles have been given.' But Allah knows best whom to entrust with his message.

Allah will humiliate the transgressors and mete out to them a grievous punishment for their scheming.

Sura: 6, Ayat: 123-124.

Shall I tell you on whom the devils descend? They descend on every lying sinner. They pour hearsay vanities into their ears but most of them are liars.

Sura: 26, Ayat: 221—223.

He who seeks glory and power, — to Allah belong all glory and power. To Him ascend good words; and He exalts righteous deeds. But those who plot evil shall be sternly punished. And the plotting of those will come to nothing.

Sura: 35, Ayat: 10.

They solemnly swore by Allah that if a warner should come to them they would accept his guidance more readily than did other nations. Yet when a warner came to them, his coming only increased their repugnance, behaving arrogantly in the land and plotting evil. But evil shall recoil on those that plot evil.

Do they expect to be treated except like the ancients? No change will you find in Allah's way; nor will it be altered.

Sura: 35, Ayat: 41-42.

In the name of Allah, The Compassionate, The Merciful

TYRANNY

Allah enjoins justice, kindness and charity to one's kindred, and forbids indecency, wickedness and oppression. He admonishes you so that you may take heed.

Sura: 16, Ayat: 90.

Those who annoy Allah and His Apostle shall be cursed by Allah in this life and in the life to come. He has prepared for them a shameful punishment.

Those who annoy believing men and believing women undeservedly shall bear the guilt of slander and a gross sin.

Sura: 33, Ayat: 57-58.

Those who persecuted the believing men and women and never repented shall suffer the scourge of Hell and the torture of burning.

Sura: 85, Ayat: 10.

In the name of Allah, The Compassionate, The Merciful

TRANSGRESSION

Fight for the sake of Allah those that fight against you, but do not be aggressive. Allah does not love the aggressors.

Sura: 2, Ayat: 190.

A sacred month for a sacred month: sacred things too are subject to retaliation. If any one attacks you, attack him as he attacked you. Have fear of Allah, and know that Allah is with the righteous.

Sura: 2, Ayat: 194.

Those who annoy believing men and believing women undeservedly shall bear the guilt of slander and a gross sin.

Sura: 33, Ayat: 58.

Dawud replied: 'He has certainly wronged you in seeking to add your ewe to his flock. Many partners are unjust to one another:....

Sura: 38, Ayat: 24.

If two parties of believers take up arms against each other, make peace between them. If either of them commits aggression against the other, fight against the aggressors till they submit to Allah's judgement. When they submit, make peace between them in equity and justice; Allah loves the equitable.

Sura: 49, Ayat: 9.

In the name of Allah, The Compassionate, The Merciful

TALKING ILL

Allah does not like foul words in public, except by a man who is truly wronged. He is Hearing, Knowing, Whether you do good openly or in private, whether you forgive those that wrong you — Allah is Pardoning, Mighty.

Sura: 4, Ayat: 149.

....That you shall not commit foul sins, whether openly or in secret....

Sura: 6, Ayat: 151.

And the parable of an evil word is like an evil tree torn out of the earth and has no stability.

Sura: 14, Ayat: 26.

Successful indeed are the believers, who are humble in their prayers; who turn away from vain talk.

Sura: 23, Ayat: 1—3.

The true servants of the Merciful are those who walk humbly on the earth, and when the ignorant address them they say: 'Peace!'

Sura: 25, Ayat: 63.

(And the true servants are those) who witness no falsehood, and if they pass by futility, they pass by it with honourable (avoidance).

Sura: 25, Ayat: 72.

And when they hear vain talk, they turn away therefrom and say: 'To us our deeds, and to you yours; Peace be to you: we seek not the ignorant.'

Sura: 28, Ayat: 55.

Therefore do not oppress the orphan, nor drive away the beggar. But proclaim the bounty of your Lord.

Sura: 93, Ayat: 9—11.

In the name of Allah, The Compassionate, The Merciful

RIDICULING

Mocked were (many) Apostles before you. But those that scoffed at them were overtaken by the very scourge they had derided.

Sura: 6, Ayat: 10.

As for those that taunt the believers who give freely, and scoff at those who give according to their means, may Allah scoff at them. Theirs shall be a woeful punishment:

(It is the same) whether or not you beg forgiveness for them. If seventy times you beg forgiveness for them Allah will not forgive them, for they have denied Allah and His Apostle. Allah does not guide the evildoers.

Sura: 9, Ayat: 79-80.

Believers, let no man mock another man, who may perhaps be better than himself. Let no woman mock another woman, who may perhaps be better than herself. Do not defame one another, nor call one another by nicknames. It is an evil thing to be called by a bad name after embracing the true faith. Those that do not repent are wrongdoers.

Sura: 49, Ayat: 11.

The evildoers used to scoff at the faithful and wink at one another as they pass by them. When they return to their own folk they speak of them with jests and when they see them they say: 'These are erring men!' Yet they were not sent to be their guardians.

Sura: 83, Ayat: 29—32.

In the name of Allah, The Compassionate, The Merciful

MOCKING AT RELIGION

If you question them, they will say: 'We were only jesting and making merry. Say: 'Would you mock at Allah, His revelations, and His Apostle? Make no excuses. You disbelieved after your belief. If we forgive some of you, We will punish others, for they are guilty men.'

Sura: 9, Ayat: 65-66.

In the name of Allah, The Compassionate, The Merciful

SENSELESS QUESTIONS

O believers, do not ask questions about things which, if made known to you, would only hurt you; but if you ask them when the Quran is being revealed, they shall be made plain to you. Allah will pardon you for this; He is Forgiving, Merciful.

Sura: 5, Ayat: 101.

In the name of Allah, The Compassionate, The Merciful

MAGIC AND ITS REALITY

They accept what the devils tell of Sulayman's Kingdom. Not that Sulayman disbelieved: it is the devils who disbelieved. They teach men witchcraft and that which was revealed to the angels Harut and Marut in Babylon. Yet they never instruct any man without saying to him beforehand: 'We have been sent to tempt you; do not disbelieve.' From these two, they learn that by which they can create discord between husband and wife, although they can harm none with what they learn except by Allah's leave. They learn, indeed, what harms them and does not profit them; yet they know full well that anyone who chose it would have no share in the life to come. Vile is that for which they have sold their souls, if they but knew it!

Sura: 2, Ayat: 102.

When the truth came to them from Us they said: 'This is plain magic.' Musa said: 'Is this what you say of the truth when it has come to you? Is this magic? Magicians never prosper!'

Sura: 10, Ayat: 76-77.

In the name of Allah, The Compassionate, The Merciful

A MAGICIAN CAN NEVER SUCCEED

"Throw that which is in the right hand: Quickly will it swallow up that which they have faked what they have faked is but a magician's trick: And the magician thrives not, (no matter) where he goes."

Sura: 20, Ayat: 69.

In the name of Allah, The Compassionate, The Merciful

OMENS

....(You are forbidden) to seek division by the Arrows. That is a vicious practice.

Sura: 5, Ayat: 3.

Believers, wine and games of chance, idols and divining arrows, are abominations devised by the devil. Avoid them, so that you may prosper.

Sura: 5, Ayat: 90.

In the name of Allah, The Compassionate, The Merciful

IDOLATROUS PRACTICES

Believers, wine and games of chance, idols and divining arrows, are abominations devised by the devil. Avoid them, so that you may prosper.

Sura: 5, Ayat: 90.

Allah demands neither a bahira, nor a saibah, nor a wasilah, nor a hami.* But those who disbelieve invent lies against Allah. Most of them are lacking in judgement.

Sura: 5, Ayat: 103.

They say: 'These cattle, and these crops are forbidden. None may eat of them save those whom we permit.' So they assert. And there are other cattle whose backs are forbidden, and others over which they do not pronounce the name of Allah, thus committing a sin against Him. Allah will punish them for their invented lies.

They also say: 'What is in the wombs of these cattle is lawful to our males but not to our wives.' But if it is still-born, they all partake of it. He will punish them for that which they attribute to Him. He is Wise, Knowing.

Sura: 6, Ayat: 138-139.

***Bahira, saibah, wasilah and hami are names of animals which the pre-Islamic Arabs offered at the Ka'ba**

In the name of Allah, The Compassionate, The Merciful

MERRYMAKING

Yet when they see some merchandise or merriment, they flock to it eagerly, leaving you standing all alone.

Say: 'That which Allah has in store is far better than any merchandise or merriment. Allah is the Most Munificent Giver.'

Sura: 62, Ayat: 11.

In the name of Allah, The Compassionate, The Merciful

GAMBLING

They ask you concerning wine and gambling. Say: 'In them is great sin, and some profit, for men; but the sin is greater than the profit.'....

Sura: 2, Ayat: 219.

Believers, wine and games of chance, idols and divining arrows, are abominations devised by the devil. Avoid them, so that you may prosper.

Sura: 5, Ayat: 90.

The devil seeks to stir up enmity and hatred among you by means of wine and gambling, and to keep you from the remembrance of Allah and from your prayers. Will you not abstain from them?

Sura: 5, Ayat: 91.

In the name of Allah, The Compassionate, The Merciful

LIQOUR

They ask you concerning wine and gambling. Say: "In them is great sin, and some profit, for men; but the sin is greater than the profit."....

Sura: 2, Ayat: 219.

Believers, wine and games of chance, idols and divining arrows, are abominations devised by the devil. Avoid them, so that you may prosper.

Sura: 5, Ayat: 90.

The devil seeks to stir up enmity and hatred among you by means of wine and gambling, and to keep you from the remembrance of Allah and from your prayers. Will you not abstain from them?

Sura: 5, Ayat: 91.

In the name of Allah, The Compassionate, The Merciful

EVIL DEEDS OF THE BIG PEOPLE

Can the dead man whom We have raised to life and given a light with which he may be guided among men, be compared to him who blunders about in darkness from which he will never emerge? Thus their foul acts seem fair to the unbelievers.

And thus we have placed in every town its arch-transgressors to scheme there. But they scheme only against themselves, though they may not perceive it.

Sura: 6, Ayat: 122-123.

Never did we send a warner to a town but the wealthy in it said: 'We do not believe in that with which you have been sent.' And they said: 'We have been given more wealth and children (than the faithful). Surely we shall never be punished.'

Sura: 34, Ayat: 34-35.

In the name of Allah, The Compassionate, The Merciful

THE UNFORTUNATE ONES

Those that deny Allah's revelations and slay the prophets unjusty and kill the men who preach fair dealing — warn them of a woeful scourge. Their works shall come to nothing in this world and in the next, and there shall be none to help them.

Sura: 3, Ayat: 21-22.

Because of their iniquity, We forbade the Jews good things which were formerly allowed them; because time after time they have debarred others from the path of Allah; because they practise usury-although they were forbidden it — and cheat others of their possessions. We have prepared a stern chastisement for those of them that disbelieve.

Sura: 4, Ayat: 160-161.

O Apostle, do not grieve for those who plunge headlong into unbelief; the men who say with their tongues: 'We believe,' but have no faith in their hearts, and the Jews who listen to lies and listen for the sake of others who have not come to you. They dislocate the words (of the scriptures) from their places and say: 'If this be given you, accept it; if not, then beware!'

If Allah wishes to leave a person in error you cannot help him against Allah. For those whose hearts He does not please to purify shall be disgraced in this world and a grievous punishment in the next.

They are listeners to falsehoods and devourers of the unlawful. If they come to you, judge between them or turn away from them. If you avoid them they cannot harm you at all, but if you act as judge, judge between them with fairness. Allah, loves those that deal justly.

Sura: 5, Ayat: 41-42.

When you call to prayer, they treat it as a jest and a pastime. They do this because they are devoid of understanding.

Sura: 5, Ayat: 58.

And you will see many of them striving with one another to hasten in sin

and exceeding the limits, and their eating of what is unlawfully acquired; certainly evil is that which they do.

Why do not the learned men and the doctors of law prohibit them from their speaking of what is sinful and their eating of what is unlawfully acquired? Certainly evil is that which they work.

Sura: 5, Ayat: 62-63.

Avoid those that treat faith as a sport and a pastime and are seduced by the life of this world. Admonish them hereby lest a soul be damned by its own sins. It has no guardian or intercessor besides Allah: and though it offers every ransom, it shall not be accepted from it. Such are those that are damned by their deeds. They shall drink boiling water and be sternly punished for their unbelief.

Sura: 6, Ayat: 70.

Some He has guided, and some He has justly left in error; for they had chosen the devils for supporters instead of Allah and deemed themselves on the right path.

Sura: 7, Ayat: 30.

The people of the Fire will cry out to the people of Paradise: 'Give us some water, or some of that which Allah has given you.' But the blessed shall reply: 'Allah has forbidden both to the unbelievers, who made their religion a pastime and an idle sport, and who were beguiled by their earthly life.'

On this Day We will forget them as they forgot the meeting of that day: for they denied Our revelations.

Sura: 7, Ayat: 50-51.

We dispersed them through the earth in multitudes-some were righteous men, others were not — and tested them with blessings and misfortunes so that they might desist (from sin). Then others succeeded them who inherited the Book and availed themselves of the vanities of this life, saying: 'We shall be forgiven our sins.' But if similar vanities came their way, they would again seize them.

Are they not committed to the covenant of the Book, which they have studied well, to tell nothing of Allah but what is true? Surely the world to come is a better prize for those that guard themselves against evil. Have you no sense?

Sura: 7, Ayat: 168-169.

He whom Allah guides is rightly guided, but he whom Allah leaves in error shall surely be lost.

We have predestined for Hell many jinn and many men. They have hearts, yet they cannot understand; eyes, yet they do not see; and ears, yet they do not

hear. They are like cattle — indeed, they are the more misguided. Such are the heedless.

Sura: 7, Ayat: 178-179.

The meanest beasts in Allah's sight are those that are deaf, dumb, and devoid of reason.

Sura: 8, Ayat: 22.

Those who disbelieve spend their wealth in debarring others from the path of Allah. They will spend it; but it will become a cause of regret for them, and in the end they will be overcome. The unbelievers shall be gathered in Hell.

Thus Allah will separate the wicked from the just. He will heap the wicked one upon another and then heap them together and cast them in Hell. Such are those that shall be lost.

Sura: 8, Ayat: 36-37.

The basest creatures in the sight of Allah are the faithless who will not believe; those who, time after time, violate their treaties with you and have no fear of Allah. If you meet them in battle, deal with them so as to strike fear in those that follow them, perchance those followers will take warning.

If you fear treachery from any of your allies, you may throw back to them (their treaty) fairly. Allah does not love the treacherous.

Sura: 8, Ayat: 55—58.

When misfortune befalls man, he prays to Us lying on his side, sitting or standing. But as soon as We relieve his affliction, he pursues his former ways, as though he never prayed for Our help. Thus their foul deeds seem fair to the transgressors.

Sura: 10, Ayat: 12.

When Our clear revelations are recited to them, those who do not hope to meet Us say to you: 'Bring us a Quran other than this, or make changes in it.'

Say: "It is not for me to make a change in it by myself. I follow only what is revealed to me. I cannot disobey my Lord, for I fear the punishment of a fateful day."

Sura: 10, Ayat: 15.

As for those that have earned evil, evil shall be rewarded with like evil. Misery will cover them — they shall have none to defend them from Allah — as though their faces were veiled with the night's black patches. They are the people of Hell: in it they shall abide for ever.

Sura: 10, Ayat: 27.

If We show man Our mercy and then withhold it from him, he yields to

despair and becomes ungrateful. And if after adversity We bestow favours upon him, he says: 'Gone are my sorrows from me,' and grows jubilant and boastful.

Not so those who are steadfast and do good works. They shall have forgiveness and a rich reward.

Sura: 11, Ayat: 9—11.

If anything could make you marvel, then you should surely marvel at those who say: 'When we are dust, shall we be raised to life again?'

Such are those who deny their Lord. Their necks shall be bound with chains. They are the people of the Fire. In it they shall abide for ever.

Sura: 13, Ayat: 5.

For those that obey, Allah is good. But those that disobey Him — if they possessed all that the earth contains, and as much besides, they would gladly offer it for their ransom. Theirs shall be an evil reckoning. Hell shall be their home, a dismal resting — place.

Sura: 13, Ayat: 18.

As for those who break Allah's covenant after accepting it, who part what He has bidden to be united and commit evil in the land, a curse shall be laid on them, and they shall have an evil abode (in Hell).

Sura: 13, Ayat: 25.

And those who disbelieve say: 'Why has no sign been given him by his Lord?'

Say: 'Allah leaves in error whom He will and guides those who repent.'

Sura: 13, Ayat: 27.

Indeed, their foul devices seem fair to the unbelievers, for they are debarred from the right path. None can guide those whom Allah has left in error. They shall be punished in this life: but more painful is the punishment of the life to come. None shall protect them from Allah.

Sura: 13, Ayat: 33-34.

Woe to the unbelievers, because of stern punishment. Those who love this life more than the life to come, debar others from the path of Allah and seek to make it crooked they are far astray.

Sura: 14, Ayat: 2-3.

Have you not seen those who change, thanks to Allah's grace, into disbelief and drive their people into the House of Perdition?

Sura: 14, Ayat: 28.

The day will surely come when those who disbelieve will wish that they

were Muslims. Let them feast and make merry; and let their hopes beguile them. They shall know.

Sura: 15, Ayat: 2-3.

And if they are asked: 'What has your Lord revealed?' they say: 'Old fictitious tales!' They shall bear the full brunt of their burdens on the Day of Resurrection together with the burdens of those who in their ignorance were misled by them. Alas, how grievous the burdens they will bear!

Sura: 16, Ayat: 24-25.

They recognize the favours of Allah, then they deny them, and most of them are ungrateful.

Sura: 16, Ayat: 83.

....Allah gives no guidance to the unbelievers. They are those whose hearts and ears and eyes are sealed by Allah; they are the heedless. In the life to come, they shall assuredly be lost.

Sura: 16, Ayat: 107—109.

Allah has made an example of the city which was once safe and peaceful. Its provisions used to come in abundance from every quarter: but its people denied the favours of Allah. Therefore, He afflicted them with famine and fear as a punishment for what they did.

An apostle of their own was sent to them, but they disbelieved him. Therefore, Our scourge smote them in their sinfulness.

Sura: 16, Ayat: 112-113.

When you recite the Quran, We place between you and those who deny the life to come a hidden barrier. We cast a veil upon their hearts and deafness in their ears, lest they understand it. (That is why) when you mention your Lord alone in the Quran, they turn their backs in flight.

We well know (what they wish to) hear when they listen to you, and (what they say) when they converse in private; when the wrongdoers declare: 'You follow only a bewitched person.'

Behold what they compared you to. They have surely gone astray and cannot find the (right) path.

Sura: 17, Ayat: 45—48.

Nothing prevents men from having faith when guidance is revealed to them but the excuse: 'Could Allah have sent a human being as an apostle?'

Say: 'Had the earth been a safe place for angels to dwell in, We would have sent forth to them an angel from heaven as an apostle.'

Sura: 17, Ayat: 94-95.

Who is more wicked than the man who, when reminded of his Lord's revelations, turns away from them and forgets what his hands have done? We have cast veils over their hearts, lest they should understand Our words, and made them hard of hearing. Call them as you may to the right path, they shall never be guided.

Sura: 18, Ayat: 57.

Say: 'Shall we tell you who will lose most through their labours? Those whose endeavours in this world are misguided and who yet think that what they do is right: who disbelieve the revelations of their Lord and deny that they will ever meet Him.' Vain are their works. On the Day of Resurrection, We shall not give any weight to them.

Hell is their reward: because they had no faith and scoffed at My revelations and My apostles.

Sura: 18, Ayat: 103—106.

But the generations who succeeded them neglected their prayers and followed lusts. These shall assuredly be lost.

Sura: 19, Ayat: 59.

No fresh warning comes to them from their Lord, but they flippantly listen to it: their hearts are set on pleasure.

In private the unbelievers say to each other: 'Is this man not a mortal like you? Do you go to witchcraft even while your eyes are open?'

Sura: 21, Ayat: 2-3.

There are some who serve Allah and (yet stand) on the very fringe (of the true faith). When blessed with good fortune they are content, but when an ordeal befalls them they turn around, forefeiting this life and the Hereafter. That way true perdition lies.

He calls on, besides Allah, that which can neither harm nor help him. That is the supreme folly.

He calls on that which would sooner harm than help him: an evil master and an evil friend.

Sura: 22, Ayat: 11-12.

If they deny you, (remember that) before them the people of Nuh, Ibrahim and Lut, the tribes of Thamoud and Aad, and the dwellers of Madian had denied (their apostles). Musa was also rejected. I bore long with the unbelievers and in the end My scourge overtook them. And how terrible My utter rejection was!

Sura: 22, Ayat: 42—44.

(This He permits) so that He may make Satan's interjections a temptation

for those whose hearts are diseased or hardened — and the wrongdoers are in wide schism.

Sura: 22, Ayat: 53.

The unbelievers will never cease to doubt it until the Hour of Doom overtakes them unawares or the scourge of the Woeful Day descends upon them.

Sura: 22, Ayat: 55.

Those who delight in spreading slanders against the faithful shall be sternly punished in this life and in the next. Allah knows, but you do not.

Sura: 24, Ayat: 19.

As for the unbelievers, their works are like a mirage in a desert. The thirsty traveller thinks it is water, but when he comes near he finds that it is nothing. He finds Allah with him, who pays him back in full. Swift is Allah's reckoning.

Or like darkness on a bottomless ocean covered with clashing billows and overcast with clouds: darkness upon darkness. If he stretches out his hand, he can scarcely see it. Indeed the man from whom Allah withholds His light shall find no light at all.

Sura: 24, Ayat: 39-40.

On the day when He assembles them with all that they worship besides Allah, He will say: 'Was it you who misled My servants, or did they themselves go astray?'

They will answer: 'Glory be to You. We should not have taken other guardians besides You. But You gave them and their fathers the good things of life, so that they forgot Your warning and thus became lost people.'

(Then Allah will say): 'Now they deny what you say. You cannot avert (your doom) nor (get) help. Those of you who have done wrong, We shall sternly punish.'

Sura: 25, Ayat: 17—19.

Those who do not hope to meet Us ask: 'Why have no angels been sent to us? Why can we not see our Lord?' How arrogant they are, and how great their transgression!

On the day when they behold the angels, there will be no joy for the sinners. The angels will say: 'A barrier (for you) which cannot be crossed.' Then We shall turn to that which they have done and render it as scattered dust.

Sura: 25, Ayat: 21—23.

On that day the Merciful will truly reign supreme. A day of woe it shall be to the unbelievers.

On the day, when the wrongdoer will bite his hands, he will say: 'Would that I had taken a (straight) path with the Apostle! Woe is me! Would that I

had never chosen so-and-so for my companion! He led me astray from the Reminder after it had reached me. Satan is ever treacherous to man.'

Sura: 25, Ayat: 26–29.

If We had revealed it to a non-Arab, and he had recited it to them, they still would not have believed. We thus put it in the hearts of the evildoers: they shall not believe in it until they see the woeful scourge which in thier heedlessness will suddenly smite them. And then they will say: 'Shall we be reprieved?'

Sura: 26, Ayat: 198–202.

Shall I tell you on whom the devils descend? They descend on every lying sinner. They pour hearsay vanities into their ears but most of them are liars.

Sura: 26, Ayat: 221–223.

They say: 'If we accept the guidance with you, we shall be driven from our land.

Sura: 28, Ayat: 57.

How many a nation have We destroyed that once flourished in wanton ease! Its dwellings are but rarely inhabited; We were its only heirs.

Sura: 28, Ayat: 58.

Or do the evildoers think that they will escape (Our punishment)? How ill they judge!'

Sura: 29, Ayat: 4.

Evil was the end of the evildoers, because they had denied the revelations of Allah and scoffed at them.

Sura: 30, Ayat: 10.

In this Quran We have set forth for men all manner of examples. Yet if you recite to them a single verse, the unbelievers will surely say: 'You are preaching lies.' Thus Allah seals the hearts of ignorant men.

Sura: 30, Ayat: 58-59.

When it is said to them: 'Follow what Allah has revealed,' they reply: 'We will follow nothing but what we found our fathers following.' Yes, even though Satan is inviting them to the scourge of Hell.

Sura: 31, Ayat: 21.

When the waves, like giant shadows, envelop them, they pray to Allah with all devotion. But no sooner does He bring them safe to land then some of them falter (between faith and unbelief). Truly, only the treacherous and the ungrateful deny Our revelations.

Sura: 31, Ayat: 32.

Those that have faith and do good works shall be received in Gardens of Refuge, as a reward for that which they have done. But those who do evil shall be cast into the Fire. Whenever they try to get out of Hell they shall be driven back, and a voice will say to them: 'Taste the torment of Hell-fire, which you have persistently denied.'

Sura: 32, Ayat: 19-20.

Is he, the evil of whose deeds is made fair-seeming to him, so that he sees it good (like the man who is rightly guided)? Allah leaves in error whom He will and guides whom He pleases. Do not let your soul* expire in grief for them: Allah has knowledge of all their actions.

Sura: 35, Ayat: 8.

As for the unbelievers, theirs is the fire of Hell. They shall not die and thus be relieved, nor shall its torments be ever lightened for them. Thus, shall every thankless one be rewarded.

There they will cry out: 'Lord, remove us hence! We will then do good and not as we have done.' (But He will answer); 'Did We not make your lives long enough for any one who would be warned to take warning? Besides, the warner did come to you; taste then the torment of Hell. None shall help the wrongdoers.'

Sura: 35, Ayat: 36-37.

They solemnly swore by Allah that if a warner should come to them they would accept his guidance more readily than did other nations. Yet when a warner came to them, his coming only increased their repugnance behaving arrogantly in the land and plotting evil. But evil shall recoil on those that plot evil.

Do they expect to be treated except like the ancients? No change will you find in Allah's way; nor will it be altered.

Sura: 35, Ayat: 42-43.

The Word is proved true against the greater part of them: For they do not believe.

We have put yokes round their necks right up to their chins, so that their heads are forced up (and they cannot see).

And We have put a bar in front of them and a bar behind them, and further, We have covered them up; so that they cannot see.

The same is it to them whether you admonish them or you do not admonish them; they will not believe.

Sura: 36, Ayat: 7—10.

***Muhammad**

And when it is said to them: 'Give alms of that which Allah has given you,' the unbelievers say to the faithful: 'Are we to feed those whom Allah can feed if He chooses? Surely you are in undoubted error.'

They also say: 'When will this promise be fulfilled, if what you say be true?'

Sura: 36, Ayat: 47-48.

Then ask them if they are a difficult creation than those whom We have created. We have created them of sticky clay.

You marvel, while they scoff. When they are admonished they pay no heed. When they are shown a sign they mock at it and say: 'This is plain magic. What! When we are dead and turned to dust and bones, shall we be raised to life, we and our forefathers?'

Say: 'Yes. And you shall be held to shame.'

Sura: 37, Ayat: 11—18.

Sad. By the Quran, full of admonition. Verily the unbelievers are (steeped) in false pride and opposition.

Sura: 38, Ayat: 1-2.

Surely they are in doubt about My warning. (And) certainly they have not yet tasted My punishment.

Or have they the treasures of the mercy of your Lord, the Mighty, the Munificent One? Is theirs the sovereignty of the heavens and the earth and all that lies between them? Then let them climb up to the sky by ropes!

Sura: 38, Ayat: 8—10.

Those who have gone before them also denied their apostles, so that Our scourge overtook them unawares. Allah disgraced them in this life, but the punishment of the life to come shall be more terrible, if they but knew (it).

Sura: 39, Ayat: 25-26.

When their apostles brought them clear signs they exulted in such knowledge as they had; but (soon) the scourge at which they scoffed encompassed them.

Sura: 40, Ayat: 83.

It is good news and a warning yet most of them turn away and give no heed. They say: 'Our hearts are shielded against that to which you call us. And in our ears there is deafness. And between us and you is a veil. Do (as you please) and so we will.'

Sura: 41, Ayat: 4-5.

When their apostles came to them from before them and behind them,

(saying): "Serve none but Allah," they answered: "Had it been Allah's will, He would have sent down angels. We reject your message."'

Sura: 41, Ayat: 14.

You did not seek to hide yourselves, so that your eyes and ears and skins could not bear witness against you. Yet you thought that Allah did not know much of what you did. It is this illusion concerning your Lord that has ruined you, so that you are now among the lost.'

Sura: 41, Ayat: 22-23.

He whom Allah leaves in error has none to protect him.

You will see the wrongdoers as they face the punishment, say: 'Is there no way back?'

Sura: 42, Ayat: 44.

If they turn away, know that We have not sent you to their keeper. Your only duty is to warn them.

When We give a man a taste of (Our) mercy, he rejoices in it; but when through his own fault evil befalls him he is ungrateful.

Sura: 42, Ayat: 48.

How many a prophet did We send forth to the ancients: no prophet came to them but they scoffed at him.

Sura: 43, Ayat: 6-7.

They say: 'Had it been the will of the Merciful, we should never have worshipped them.' Surely of this they have no knowledge: they are lying.

Or have We given them a scripture before this, so that they should hold fast to it?

They say: 'We have found our fathers following a certain religion. And we are merely walking in their footsteps.'

Thus, We never sent an apostle before you to warn a nation, but its wealthy said: 'We have found our fathers following a certain religion; we are merely walking in their footsteps.'

Each (apostle) said: 'What if I bring you a better guidance than that which you found your fathers following?' But they replied: 'We deny the message you have brought.' So We punished them. Consider the fate of those who disbelieved (Our warning).

Sura: 43, Ayat: 20—25.

He that does not heed the warning of the Merciful shall have a devil for his companion. Devils turn men away from the right path, though they may think themselves rightly guided. And when finally he comes before Us, he shall say: 'Would that we were as far apart as the east is from the west.' Truly, evil is the

companion.

But because you have done wrong, that others will share your punishment will not avail you on that day.

Sura: 43, Ayat: 36–39.

But (you find one) who says to his parents. 'Fie on you! Do you threaten me with a resurrection when entire generations have passed away before me?' But they pray for Allah's help and say: 'Woe to you! Have faith. The promise of Allah is true. He replies: 'This is but a fable of the ancients. He shall justly deserve the fate of bygone nations of men and jinn: he shall assuredly be lost.

Sura: 46, Ayat: 17-18.

If you* turn away (from the faith) you would surely do evil in the land and violate the ties of kinship. Such are those on whom Allah has laid His curse, leaving them bereft of sight and hearing.

Will they not ponder on the Quran? Are there locks upon their hearts?

Sura: 47, Ayat: 22–24.

Those who turn back after Allah's guidance has been revealed to them, it is Satan who seduces and inspires them. That is because they say to those who abhor the word of Allah: 'We shall obey you in some matters.' Allah knows their secret talk.

Sura: 47, Ayat: 25-26.

That is because they follow what has incurred the wrath of Allah and abhor what pleases Him. He will surely bring their works to nothing.

Sura: 47, Ayat: 28.

(Then a voice will cry): 'Cast into Hell every hardened unbeliever, every opponent of good works and every doubting transgressor who has set up another god besides Allah. Hurl him into the terrible doom.'

Sura: 50, Ayat: 24–26.

Burn in its flames. It is alike whether you are patient or impatient. You shall be rewarded according to your deeds.'

Sura: 52, Ayat: 16.

If they saw a part of heaven falling down, they would still say: 'It is but a mass of clouds!'

Let them be, until they face the day when they shall stand dumbfounded; the day when their wiles will avail them nothing and none will help them.

And besides this a punishment awaits the wrongdoers, though most of

---

***Muhammad**

them do not know it.

Sura: 52, Ayat: 44—47.

Give no heed, then, to those who ignore Our warning and seek only the life of this world. This is the sum of their knowledge. Your Lord knows best who has strayed from His path, and who is rightly guided.

To God is what the heavens and the earth contain. He will requite the evil-doers according to their deeds, and bestow a good reward on those who do good works.

(To) those who avoid the grossest sins and indecencies and commit only small offences, Allah is of vast forgiveness.

Sura: 53, Ayat: 29—32.

Have you considered him who turns his back upon the faith, giving little at first then nothing at all? Has he knowledge of the unseen, and therefore can see?

Sura: 53, Ayat: 33—35.

Do not act like those who have forgotten Allah so that He has caused them to forget themselves. Such men are evildoers.

Sura: 59, Ayat: 19.

'Yes,' they will reply, 'but we rejected him and said: 'Allah has revealed nothing: you are in grave error.' And they will say: 'If only we listened and understood, we should not now be among the people of Hell.'

Thus they shall confess their sin. Far from Allah's mercy are the people of Hell.

Sura: 67, Ayat: 9—11.

Your Lord knows best those who stray from His path, and those who are rightly guided. Give no heed to the disbelievers: they wish you were pliant, so that they would be pliant. Nor yield to the wretch of many oaths, the mischief-making slanderer, the opponent of good, the wicked transgressor, the bully who is besides this of doubtful birth.

Though he has wealth and children, when Our revelations are recited to him, he says: 'They are but fables of the ancients.'

Sura: 68, Ayat: 7—15.

We have tried them as We tried the owners of the orchard who had sworn that they would pluck its fruit next morning without adding any reservations (such as: if it be God's will). A visitant from Allah came down upon it while they slept, and in the morning it was as black as midnight.

At daybreak they called out to one another, saying: 'Hurry to your orchard, if you would pick its fruit.' And off they went, whispering to one another: 'No

beggar shall set foot in it today.'

Thus they went out, fixed in their resolve. But when they saw it they cried: 'We have been wrong. We are utterly ruined.'

Sura: 68, Ayat: 17—27.

Therefore leave to Me those that deny this revelation. We will lead them step by step (to their ruin) in ways beyond their knowledge. I shall bear long with them: My stratagem is sure.

Sura: 68, Ayat: 44-45.

When they hear Our revelations, the unbelievers almost devour you with their eyes. 'He is surely possessed,' they say:

But it is nothing less than a warning to all men.

Sura: 68, Ayat: 51-52.

(We shall say): 'Lay hold of him and bind him. Burn him in the blazing Fire, then fasten him with a chain seventy cubits long. For he did not believe in Allah, the Most High, nor did he urge the feeding of the poor.

Sura: 69, Ayat: 30—34.

By no means. It is a flaming Fire. It drags (them) down by (their) scalps; and it shall call him who turned his back (on the true faith) and amassed riches and covetously hoarded them.

Indeed, man was created impatient. When evil befalls him he is despondent; but blessed with good fortune he grows niggardly.

Sura: 70, Ayat: 15—21.

Leave Me alone with him whom I created and endowed with vast riches and thriving children. I have made his progress smooth and easy: yet he hopes that I give him more. By no means! Surely he has been inimical to Our revelations. I will lay on him a mounting torment.

Sura: 74, Ayat: 11—17.

He pondered, and he schemed. Confound him, how he schemed! Confound him, how he schemed!

Then he looked around him, frowning and leering; then he turned away in scornful pride and said: 'This is no more than borrowed magic. It is nothing but the word of a mortal.'

I will surely cast him into the fire of Hell.

Sura: 74, Ayat: 18—26.

Each soul is held in pledge for what it earns, except those of the right hand. These will in their gardens ask the sinners: 'What has brought you into Hell?' They will reply: 'We never prayed or fed the hungry. We engaged in vain dis-

putes and denied the Day of Reckoning till the inevitable (death) overtook us.'

Sura: 74, Ayat: 38—47.

(In this life) he neither believed nor prayed; he denied the truth and turned away; and he went to his kinsfolk elated with pride.

Well have you deserved (this doom); well have you deserved it. Well have you deserved it: too well have you deserved it!

Sura: 75, Ayat: 31—35.

Surely these love the transitory and neglect a grievous day before him. We created them, and endowed their limbs and joints with strength; but if we please We can replace them by others.

Sura: 76, Ayat: 27-28.

Eat and enjoy yourselves awhile. You are wicked men.

Sura: 77, Ayat: 46.

Woe on that day to disbelievers. When they are bidden to (before God) kneel down, they do not kneel.

Sura: 77, Ayat: 47-48.

Woe on that day to the disbelievers! In what revelations after this will they believe?

Sura: 77, Ayat: 49-50.

They did not fear Our reckoning and roundly denied Our revelations. But We have recorded all their doings in a book. We shall say: "So taste you (the fruits of your deeds); for no increase shall We grant you, except in Punishment."

Sura: 78, Ayat: 27—30.

But when the great disaster comes—the day when man will call to mind his labours and when Hell is brought in sight (of all) those who transgressed and chose this present life will find themselves in Hell.

Sura: 79, Ayat: 34—39.

No! Their own deeds have cast a veil over their hearts.

No! On that day they shall be debarred from their Lord. They shall burn in Hell, and it will be said to them: 'This is the scourge that you denied!'

Sura: 83, Ayat: 14—17.

For he lived without a care among his people and thought he would never return (to Allah). Yes he would. Verily his Lord was everwatching over him.

Sura: 84, Ayat: 13—15.

Why then do they not have faith, or kneel in prayer when the Quran is read to them?
The unbelievers deny it; but Allah knows best the falsehoods they believe in.
Therefore, proclaim to all a woeful doom.

Sura: 84, Ayat: 20—24.

Yet the unbelievers deny it.
Allah surrounds them all.

Sura: 85, Ayat: 19-20.

We shall guide you to the smoothest path. Therefore give warning, if warning will avail them. He that fears Allah will heed it, but the wicked sinner will avoid it. He shall be cast into the great Fire where he shall neither die nor live.

Sura: 87, Ayat: 8—13.

As for man, when his Lord tests him by exalting him and bestowing favours on him, he says: 'My Lord is bountiful to me.' But when He tests him by restricting his subsistence, he says: 'My Lord humiliates me.'
No! But you show no kindness to the orphan, nor do you urge one another to feed the poor. Greedily you lay your hands on the inheritance of the weak, and you love riches with all your hearts.

Sura: 89, Ayat: 15—20.

Yet he would not scale the height.
Would that you knew what the Height is! It is the freeing of a bondsman; the feeding, in the day of famine, of an orphaned relation or a needy man in distress; to be one of those who believe, enjoin patience and enjoin mercy.
Those who do this shall stand on the right hand.

Sura: 90, Ayat: 11—18.

By the heaven and Him that built it; by the earth and Him that spread it; by the soul and Him that moulded it and inspired it with (knowledge of) sin and piety: blessed shall be the man who has kept it pure, and ruined he that has corrupted it!

Sura: 91, Ayat: 5—10.

But he that neither gives nor seeks Allah's reward and disbelieves in goodness, We shall smooth the path of affliction. When he breathes his last, his riches will not avail him.

Sura: 92, Ayat: 8—11.

It is for Us to give guidance. Ours is the life of this world and the life to come. I warn you, then, of the blazing fire, in which none shall burn save the

hardened sinner, who denies the truth and gives no heed.

Sura: 92, Ayat: 12–16.

Indeed, man transgresses in thinking himself self-sufficient. Verily to your Lord is the return (of all).

Sura: 96, Ayat: 6–8.

Have you seen the man who forbids a servant when he prays. Have you seen if he follows the right guidance or enjoins piety?

Sura: 96, Ayat: 9–12.

Think: if he denies the truth and gives no heed, does he not know that Allah observes all things?

Sura: 96, Ayat: 13-14.

The unbelievers among the People of the Book and the pagans shall burn for ever in the fire of Hell. They are the vilest of all creatures.

Sura: 98, Ayat: 6.

Surely man is ungrateful to his Lord. To this he himself shall bear witness.
And truly on account of his love of wealth he is niggardly.

Sura: 100, Ayat: 6–8.

You are distracted by worldly gain until you visit the graves.

Sura: 102, Ayat: 1-2.

Woe to every backbiting slanderer who amasses wealth and counts it thinking his wealth will render him immortal!
By no means! They shall be flung to the Destroying Flame.
Would that you knew what the Destroying Flame is like!
It is Allah's own kindled fire, which will rise up to the hearts of men. It will close upon them from every side, in towering columns.

Sura: 104, Ayat: 1–7.

Have you thought of him that denies the Last Judgement? It is he who turns away the orphan and does not urge others to feed the poor.

Sura: 107, Ayat: 1–3.

Woe to those who pray but are unmindful of their prayers; who make a show (of piety) and refuse (to supply) (even) neighbourly needs.

Sura: 107, Ayat: 4–7.

Pray to your Lord and sacrifice to Him. He that hates you shall remain childless.

Sura: 108, Ayat: 2-3.

In the name of Allah, The Compassionate, The Merciful

THE HYPOCRITES

There are some who declare: 'We believe in Allah and the Last Day,' yet they are not believers. They seek to deceive Allah and those who believe in Him: but they deceive none save themselves, though they may not perceive it. There is a sickness in their hearts which Allah has increased: they shall be sternly punished because they lie.

When it is said to them: 'Do not commit evil in the land,' they reply: 'We do nothing but good.' But it is they who are the evildoers, though they may not perceive it.

And when it is said to them: 'Believe as others believe,' they reply: 'Are we to believe as fools believe?' It is they who are the fools, if only they knew it!

When they meet the faithful, they declare: 'We, too, believe.' But when they are alone with their devils, they say to them: 'We follow none but you: we were only mocking.' Allah will mock at them and keep them long in sin, blundering blindly along.

Such are those that barter away guidance for error: they profit nothing, nor are they on the right path. They are like one who kindled a fire, but as soon as it lit up all around him, Allah took away their light and left them in darkness — they could not see. Deaf, dumb, and blind they shall never return (to the right path).

Or like those who, under a cloudburst from the sky with darkness, thunder and lightning, thrust their fingers in their ears at the sound of every thunderclap for fear of death: and Allah thus encompasses the unbelievers. The lightning almost takes away their sight: whenever it flashes upon them they walk on, but as soon as it darkens they standstill. Indeed, if Allah pleased. He could take away their sight and hearing: He has power over all things.

Sura: 2, Ayat: 8—20.

There are some men whose views on this life please you: they even call on Allah to vouch for that which is in their hearts; whereas, in fact, they are the deadliest of your opponents. No sooner do they leave you than they hasten to commit evil in the land, destroying crops and cattle. Allah does not love evil.

Sura: 2, Ayat: 204-205.

When it was said to them: 'Come, fight for the cause of Allah or defend yourselves,' they replied: 'If only we could fight, we would surely come with you.'

On that day, they were nearer unbelief than faith. They said with their mouths what was not in their hearts. But Allah knew their secret thoughts.

Sura: 3, Ayat: 167.

Have you seen those who claim that they believe in what has been revealed to you and to other prophets before you? They seek the judgement of the Taghut,* although they have been bidden to deny him. The devil would lead them far astray.

Sura: 4, Ayat: 60.

They would have you disbelieve as they themselves have done, so that you may be all alike. Do not befriend them until they have fled their homes for the cause of Allah. If they desert you, seize them and put them to death wherever you find them. Look for neither friends nor helpers among them, except those who join an ally of yours, or come over to you because their hearts forbid them to fight against you or against their own people. Had Allah pleased, He would have given them power over you, so that they would have taken arms against you. Therefore, if they keep away from you and cease their hostility and offer you peace, Allah bids you not to harm them.

Others you will find who seek security from you as well as from their own people. Whenever they are called back to sedition, they plunge into it headlong. If these do not keep their distance from you, if they neither offer you peace nor cease their hostilities against you, lay hold of them and kill them wherever you find them. Over such men, We give you absolute authority.

Sura: 4, Ayat: 89—91.

Give warning to the hypocrites of a stern chastisement those who choose the unbelievers rather than the faithful for their friends. Are they seeking glory at their hands? Surely all glory belongs to Allah.

Sura: 4, Ayat: 138-139.

Allah will surely gather in Hell the hypocrites and the unbelievers.

They watch your fortunes closely. If Allah grants you a victory, they say: 'Did we not stand on your side?' And if the unbelievers are victorious, they

---

***The Taghut is the one who exceeds all bounds in causing mischief**

say to them: 'Were we not mightier than you, and did we not protect you from the faithful?'

Allah will judge between you on the Day of Resurrection. He will not let the unbelievers triumph over the faithful.

The hypocrites seek to deceive Allah, but it is Allah who deceives them. When they rise to pray, they stand up sluggishly: they pray for the sake of ostentation and remember Allah but little wavering between this and that and belonging neither to these nor those. You cannot guide the man whom Allah has left in error.

Sura: 4, Ayat: 140—143.

O believers, do not choose the infidels rather than the faithful for your friends. Would you give Allah a clear proof against yourselves?

The hypocrites shall be cast into the lowest depths of the Fire: there shall be none to help them. But those who repent and mend their ways, who hold fast to Allah and are sincere in their belief — they shall be numbered with the faithful, and the faithful shall be richly rewarded by Allah.

Sura: 4, Ayat: 144—146.

O Apostle, do not grieve for those who plunge headlong into unbelief; the men who say with their tongues: 'We believe,' but have no faith in their hearts.

Sura: 5, Ayat: 41.

You see the faint-hearted hastening to woo them. They say: 'We fear lest a change of fortune should befall us.' But when Allah grants you victory or makes known His will, they shall regret what they had hidden in their breasts. Then will the faithful say: 'Are these the men who solemnly swore by Allah that they would stand by you?' Their works will come to nothing and they shall be losers.

Sura: 5, Ayat: 52-53.

Had the gain been immediate or the journey easy, they would have followed you: but the distance seemed too far to them. Yet they will swear by Allah: 'Had we been able, we would have marched with you.' They bring ruin upon themselves. Allah knows that they are lying.

Allah forgive you! Why did you give them leave to stay behind before you knew those who spoke the truth from those who invented false excuses?

Those that believe in Allah and the Last Day will not beg you to exempt them from fighting with their wealth and their persons. Allah best knows the righteous. Only those seek exemption who disbelieve in Allah and the Last Day and whose hearts are filled with doubt. And in their doubt, they waver.

Had they intended to set forth with you, they would have prepared themselves for war. But Allah did not like their going forth and held them back,

and it was said: 'Stay back with those who stay back.'

Sura: 9, Ayat: 42–46.

Say: 'Whether you give willingly or with reluctance, your offerings shall not be accepted from you; for you are wicked men.'

Nothing prevents their offerings from being accepted except that they have denied Allah and His Apostle. They pray half-heartedly and grudge their contributions.

Let neither their riches nor their children rouse your envy. Through these Allah seeks to punish them in this life, so that they shall be unbelievers.

Sura: 9, Ayat: 53–55.

Be they men or women, the hypocrites are all alike. They enjoin what is evil, forbid what is just, and tighten their purse-strings. They forsook Allah, so Allah forsook them. Surely the hypocrites are evildoers.

Sura: 9, Ayat: 67.

As for those that taunt the believers who give freely, and scoff at those who give according to their means, may Allah scoff at them. Theirs shall be woeful punishment.

(It is the same) whether or not you beg forgiveness for them. If seventy times you beg forgiveness for them Allah will not forgive them, for they have denied Allah and His Apostle. Allah does not guide the evildoers.

Sura: 9, Ayat: 79–81.

You shall not pray for any of their dead, nor shall you attend their burial. For they denied Allah and His Apostle and remained sinners to the last.

Let neither their riches nor their children rouse your envy. Through these Allah seeks to punish them in this life, so that they shall die unbelievers.

When a Sura was revealed, saying: 'Believe in Allah and fight with His Apostle,' the rich among them asked you to excuse them, saying 'Leave us with those who are to stay behind.'

They were content to be with those who stayed behind: a seal was set upon their hearts, leaving them bereft of understanding. But the Apostle and the men who shared his faith fought with their goods and their persons. Those shall be rewarded with good things. Those shall surely prosper. Allah has prepared for them gardens watered by running streams in which they shall abide for ever. That is the supreme triumph.

Sura: 9, Ayat: 84–89.

When a Sura is revealed some of them ask: 'Which of you has it strengthened in faith?' It will surely increase the faith of the believers and give them joy. As for those whose hearts are diseased, it will add to their disbelief

so that they shall die unbelievers.

Sura: 9, Ayat: 124-125.

There are some who serve Allah and (yet stand) on the very fringe (of the true faith). When blessed with good fortune they are content, but when an ordeal befalls them they turn around, forfeiting this life and the Hereafter. That way true perdition lies.

He calls on, besides, Allah, that which can neither harm nor help him. That is the supreme folly.

He calls on that which would sooner harm than help him: an evil master and an evil friend.

As for those who have faith and do good works, Allah will admit them to gardens watered by running streams. Allah indeed does what He pleases.

Sura: 22, Ayat: 11—14.

They declare 'We believe in Allah and His Apostle and obey them both.' But a party of them turn away after this. Surely these are no believers.

Sura: 24, Ayat: 47.

They solemnly swear by Allah that if you order them, they would certainly go forth. Say: 'Do not swear: true obedience (will count). Allah is cognizant of all your actions.'

Sura: 24, Ayat: 53.

Do men think that they will be left alone on saying, "We believe and that they will not be tested?

We did test those before them, and God will certainly know those who are true from those who are false.

Sura: 29, Ayat: 2-3.

Some profess to believe in Allah, yet when they suffer in His cause they treat the persecution of man as though it were the punishment of Allah. But if your Lord gives you victory, they say: 'We were on your side.'

Does Allah not know what is in the hearts of men? Most certainly Allah knows the true believers and also the hypocrites.

Sura: 29, Ayat: 10-11.

Allah well knows those of you who hold others back; who say to their comrades: 'Join our side,' and seldom take part in the fighting, being ever reluctant to assist you. When fear overtakes them they look to you for help, their eyes rolling as though they were on the point of death. But once they are out of danger they assail you with their sharp tongues, covetously demanding part of the booty. Such men have no faith. Allah will bring their deeds to nothing. That is no difficult thing for Allah.

They think the Confederates have not withdrawn. Indeed, if the Confederates should come again they would sooner be in the desert among the wandering Arabs asking news of you; but were they with you, they would take but little part in the fighting.

Sura: 33, Ayat: 18–20.

Announce to the believers the good tidings that Allah has bounteous blessings in store for them. Do not obey the unbelievers and the hypocrites: disregard their insolence.

Put your trust in Allah; Allah is your All-Sufficient Guardian.

Sura: 33, Ayat: 47-48.

If the hypocrites and those who have disease in their hearts and the scandal-mongers of Madinah do not desist, We will rouse you against them and they will be your neighbours in it only for a while. Cursed wherever they are found, they will be seized and put to death.

Such has been the way of Allah with those who have gone before them. You shall find no change in Allah's ways.

Sura: 33, Ayat: 60–62.

Some of them indeed listen to you, but no sooner do they leave your presence than they ask those to whom knowledge has been given: 'What did he say just now?' Such are the men whose hearts are sealed by Allah and who follow their own desires.

As for those who follow the right path, Allah will increase their guidance and bestow on them their righteousness.

Sura: 47, Ayat: 16-17.

The faithful say: 'If only a Chapter were revealed!' But when a forthright Chapter is revealed and war is mentioned in it, you see the infirm of heart looking towards you as though they were fainting away for fear of death. But more fitting for them – Were it to obey and say what is just, and when a matter is resolved on, it were best for them if they were true to God.

Sura: 47, Ayat: 20-21.

If you* turn away (from the faith) you would surely do evil in the land and violate the ties of kinship. Such are those on whom Allah has laid His curse, leaving them bereft of sight and hearing.

Will they not ponder on the Quran? Are there locks upon their hearts?

Those who turn back after Allah's guidance has been revealed to them, it is Satan who seduces and inspires them. That is because they say to those who abhor the word of Allah: 'We shall obey you in some matters.' Allah knows

---

***Muhammad**

their secret talk.

Sura: 47, Ayat: 22—26.

Or do those who have disease in their hearts think that Allah will not bring forth their malice? If We pleased, We could point them out to you and you would recognize them promptly by their marks. But you will surely know them from the tenor of their words. Allah has knowledge of all your actions.

Sura: 47, Ayat: 29-30.

And that He may punish the hypocrites and the idolaters, men and women, who think evil thoughts concerning Allah. A turn of evil shall befall them, and Allah's wrath is on them. He has laid on them His curse and prepared for them the fire of Hell: an evil fate.

Sura: 48, Ayat: 6.

They call out to them, saying: 'Were we not on your side?' 'Yes,' they will reply, 'but you tempted yourselves, you wavered, you doubted and were deceived by your own wishes until Allah's will was done and the Dissembler tricked you concerning Allah. Today no ransom shall be accepted from you or from the unbelievers. Hell shall be your home: you have justly earned it, a dismal end!'

Sura: 57, Ayat: 14-15.

Do you not see those who were forbidden secret counsels, then they return to that which they are forbidden and hold secret counsels for iniquity and hostility and disobedience of the Messenger? When they come to you they salute you in words with which Allah does not greet you and ask themselves: 'Why does Allah not punish us for what we say?' Hell is scourge enough for them: they shall burn in its flames, a wretched fate.

Sura: 58, Ayat: 8.

Their dread of you is more intense in their hearts than their fear of Allah: so devoid are they of understanding.

Sura: 59, Ayat: 13.

Great is their valour among themselves; you think of them as one hand, yet their hearts are divided. That is because they are surely lacking in judgement.

Like those who were but recently punished before them, they tasted the fruit of their own deeds: a grievous scourge awaits them.

Sura: 59, Ayat: 14—15.

They (their allies) may be compared to the devil, who, when he has ordered man to disbelieve and man has done his bidding, says to him: 'I here and now

disown you. I fear Allah, the Lord of the Worlds.'

Sura: 59, Ayat: 16.

When the hypocrites come to you they say:'We bear witness that you are Allah's Apostle.' Allah knows that you are indeed His Apostle, and Allah bears witness that the hypocrites are lying!

They use their faith as a disguise and debar others from the path of Allah. Evil is what they do.

That is because they believed and then renounced their faith: their hearts are sealed, so that they are devoid of understanding.

When you see them their figures please you, and when they speak, you listen to what they say. Yet they are like propped-up beams of timber. Every shout they hear they take to be against them. They are the enemy. Guard yourself against them. Allah confound them! How perverse they are!

When it is said to them: 'Come Allah's Apostle will beg forgiveness for you,' they turn their heads and you see them go away in arrogance.

Sura: 63, Ayat: 1—5.

It is alike to them whether or not you ask forgiveness for them: Allah will not forgive them. He does not guide the evildoers.

Sura: 63, Ayat: 6.

It is they who say: 'Spend nothing on those that follow Allah's Apostle until they have deserted him.' Allah's are the treasures of heaven and earth: but this the hypocrites cannot understand.

They say: 'If we return to Madinah, the more honourable (element) will soon drive out the meaner.' But honour belongs to Allah and His Apostle and the faithful: yet the hypocrites do not know it.

Sura: 63, Ayat: 7-8.

But what has befallen the unbelievers, that they scramble before you in multitudes from left and right?

Does every one of them seek to enter a garden of delight?

By no means! For We have created them of what they know!

Sura: 70, Ayat: 36—39.

SOCIAL MALADIES

(11)

In the name of Allah, The Compassionate, The Merciful

SUSPICION AND SPECULATION

If you obeyed the greater part of mankind, they would lead you away from Allah's path. They follow nothing but idle fancies and preach nothing but falsehoods.

Sura: 6, Ayat: 116.

The polytheists will say: 'Had Allah pleased, neither we nor our fathers would have associated other partners with Him; nor would we have forbidden anything. In the same way, those who have gone before them denied the truth until they felt Our scourge.

Say: 'Have you any knowledge you can show us? You believe in nothing but conjecture and follow nothing but falsehoods.'

Sura: 6, Ayat: 148.

Most of them follow nothing but mere conjecture. But conjecture is no substitute for Truth. Allah is cognizant of what they do.

Sura: 10, Ayat: 36.

To Allah belong all (who dwell) on earth and in heaven. Those who invoke associates besides Allah follow nothing but idle fancies and preach nothing but falsehoods.

Sura: 10, Ayat: 66.

When you heard it, why did the faithful, men and women, not think well of their own people, and say: 'This is an evident falsehood.'

Sura: 24, Ayat: 12.

When you heard it, why did you not say: 'It is not right for us to speak of this. Allah forbid! This is a monstrous slander.

Allah bids you never again to repeat the like, if you are true believers. Allah makes plain to you His revelations. He is Wise, All-Knowing.

Sura: 24, Ayat: 16–18.

Long before this, Yusuf came to you with clear signs but you never ceased to doubt them; and when he died you said: 'Allah will never send another Apostle after him'. Thus Allah leaves in error the doubting transgressor. Those who dispute Allah's signs without any authority that has reached them, (their conduct) is greatly abhorred by Allah and by the faithful. Thus Allah seals up the heart of every arrogant tyrant.'

Sura: 40, Ayat: 34-35.

Believers, avoid most of suspicion, for in some cases suspicion is a crime. Do not spy (on one another), nor backbite one another. Would any of you like to eat the flesh of his dead brother? Surely, you would loathe it. Have fear of Allah. He is Forgiving and Merciful.

Sura: 49, Ayat: 12.

Woe to the liars who dwell in darkness and are heedless of the life to come.

Sura: 51, Ayat: 10-11.

In the name of Allah, The Compassionate, The Merciful

KNOWLEDGE BETTER THAN CONJECTURE

And pursue not that of which you have no knowledge; for every act of hearing, or of seeing or of (feeling in) the heart will be inquired into (on the Day of Reckoning).

Sura: 17, Ayat: 36.

Yet there are some who dispute about Allah without knowledge and follow every rebellious devil. Every such devil is doomed to lead astray him who follows it, and lead him to the scourge of the Fire.

Sura: 22, Ayat: 3-4.

Those who disbelieve in the life to come call the angels by the names of females. Yet of this they have no knowledge: they follow mere conjecture, and conjecture avails nothing against truth.

Sura: 53, Ayat: 27-28.

In the name of Allah, The Compassionate, The Merciful

RELIANCE ON MUNDANE RESOURCES

Allah has helped you on many a battlefield. In the Battle of Hunain, you set great store by your numbers, but they availed you nothing: the earth, for all its vastness, seemed to close in upon you and you turned your backs and fled. Then Allah caused His tranquillity to descend upon His Apostle and the faithful: He sent to your aid invisible warriors and sternly punished the unbelievers. Thus were the infidels rewarded.

Sura: 9, Ayat: 25-26.

In the name of Allah, The Compassionate, The Merciful

RUMOUR MONGERING

When they hear any news of security or fear, they at once make it known to all; whereas if they reported it to the Apostle and to those in authority, such of them as are engaged in obtaining intelligence would indeed know (what to do with) it....

Sura: 4, Ayat: 84.

You carried with your tongues and uttered with your mouths what you did not know. You may have thought it a trifle, but in the sight of Allah it was a grave offence.

When you heard it, why did you not say: 'It is not right for us to speak of this. Allah forbid! This is a monstrous slander?'

Allah bids you never again to repeat the like, if you are true believers. Allah makes plain to you His revelations. He is Wise, All-Knowing.

Sura: 24, Ayat: 15–18.

Shall I tell you on whom the devils descend? They descend on every lying sinner. They pour hearsay vanities into their ears, but most of them are liars.

Sura: 26, Ayat: 221–223.

If the hypocrites and those who have disease in their hearts and the scandal-mongers of Madinah do not desist, We will rouse you against them and they will be your neighbours in it only for a while. Cursed wherever they are found, they will be seized and put to death.

Such has been the way of Allah with those who have gone before them. You shall find no change in Allah's ways.

Sura: 33, Ayat: 60–62.

Believers, if an evil-doer brings you a piece of news, inquire first into its truth, lest you should wrong others unwittingly and repent of what you have done.

Know that Allah's Apostle is among you. If he were to obey you in many matters, you would surely fall into distress. But Allah has endeared the Faith

to you and has made it beautiful in your hearts, making unbelief, wrongdoing, and disobedience abhorrent to you. Such are those who are rightly guided—a grace and favour from Allah. Allah is Wise and All-Knowing.

Sura: 49, Ayat: 6—8.

In the name of Allah, The Compassionate, The Merciful

BELIEVING WITHOUT EVIDENCE IS A SIN

You carried with your tongues and uttered with your mouths what you did not know. You may have thought it a trifle, but in the sight of Allah it was a grave offence.

When you heard it, why did you not say: 'It is not right for us to speak of this. Allah forbid! This is a monstrous slander?'

Allah bids you never again to repeat the like, if you are true believers. Allah makes plain to you His revelations. He is Wise, All-Knowing.

Sura: 24, Ayat: 15–18.

In the name of Allah, The Compassionate, The Merciful

SECRET COUNSELS

In most of their secret talks there is no good: but if one exhorts to a deed of charity or justice or conciliation between men, (Secrecy is permissible): To him who does this, seeking the good pleasure of God, We shall soon give a reward of the highest (value).

Sura: 4, Ayat: 114.

Shall I tell you on whom the devils descend? They descend on every lying sinner. They pour hearsay vanities into their ears, but most of them are liars.
Sura: 26, Ayat: 221–224.

Are you not aware that Allah knows what the heavens and the earth contain? There is no secret counsel between three but He is the fourth of them; nor between five but He is the sixth of them; nor between fewer or more but He is with them wherever they are. Then, on the Day of Resurrection, He will inform them of their doings. Allah has knowledge of all things.

Do you not see those who were forbidden secret counsels, then they return to that which they are forbidden and hold secret counsels for iniquity and hostility and disobedience of the Messenger? When they come to you they salute you in words with which Allah does not greet you and they ask themselves: 'Why does Allah not punish us for what we say?' Hell is scourge enough for them: they shall burn in its flames, a wretched fate.

Sura: 58, Ayat: 7-8.

Believers, when you converse in private do not speak with wickedness and enmity and disobedience towards the Apostle, but with justice and with piety. Have fear of Allah, before whom you shall be brought together.

Sura: 58, Ayat: 9.

Secret counsels are the work of the devil, who thereby seeks to annoy the faithful. Yet he can harm them not at all, except by Allah's leave. In Allah let the faithful put their trust.

Sura: 58, Ayat: 10.

In the name of Allah, The Compassionate, The Merciful

FALSE ACCUSATION

He that commits an offence or a crime and charges an innocent man with it, shall bear the guilt of calumny and gross injustice.

Sura: 4, Ayat: 112.

In the name of Allah, The Compassionate, The Merciful

SLANDER

Believers, let no man mock another man, who may perhaps be better than himself. Let no woman mock another woman, who may perhaps be better than herself. Do not defame one another, nor call one another by nicknames. It is an evil thing to be called by a bad name after embracing the true faith. Those that do not repent are wrongdoers.

Sura: 49, Ayat: 11.

Woe to every backbiting slanderer who amasses wealth and counts it.

Sura: 104, Ayat: 1-2.

In the name of Allah, The Compassionate, The Merciful

BACKBITING

Believers, avoid most of suspicion, for in some cases suspicion is a crime. Do not spy (on one another), nor backbite one another. Would any of you like to eat the flesh of his dead brother? Surely you would loathe it. Have fear of Allah. He is Forgiving and Merciful.

Sura: 49, Ayat: 12.

Woe to every backbiting slanderer who amasses wealth and counts it.

Sura: 104, Ayat: 1-2.

In the name of Allah, The Compassionate, The Merciful

SATAN'S HABIT

They (their allies) may be compared to the devil, who, when he has ordered man to disbelieve and man has done his bidding, says to him: 'I here and now disown you. I fear Allah, the Lord of the Worlds.' They shall both end in the Fire and remain therein for ever. Thus are the wrongdoers rewarded.

Sura: 59, Ayat: 16-17.

In the name of Allah, The Compassionate, The Merciful

SATAN'S DOMINATION

When you recite the Quran, seek refuge in Allah from the accursed devil: no power has he over believers who put their trust in their Lord. He only has power over those who befriend him, and those who serve other gods besides Allah.

Sura: 16, Ayat: 98-100.

THE CHARACTER OF NON-BELIEVERS

(12)

In the name of Allah, The Compassionate, The Merciful

THE DIFFERENCE BETWEEN SUBMISSION AND FAITH

The Arabs of the desert declare: 'We believe.' Say: 'You do not.' Rather say: 'We profess Islam,' for faith has not yet found its way into your hearts. If you obey Allah and His Apostle, He will not diminish a thing from (the rewards) of your labours. Allah is Forgiving and Merciful.

The true believers are those who have faith in Allah and His Apostel and never doubt; and who fight for His cause with their wealth and persons. Such are the truthful ones.

Sura: 49, Ayat: 14-15.

In the name of Allah, The Compassionate, The Merciful

PRECEDENCE OF BELIEVER OVER NON-BELIEVER

Can the man who seeks to please Allah be compared to him who has incurred His wrath? Hell shall be his home. Evil shall be his fate!

Varied are their positions with Allah. Allah is cognizant of what they do.

Sura: 3, Ayat: 162-163.

Say: 'Good and evil are not alike, even though the abundance of evil tempts you. Have fear of Allah, you men of understanding, so that you may triumph.'

Sura: 5, Ayat: 100.

Say: 'I do not tell you that I possess the treasures of Allah or know what is hidden, nor do I claim to be an angel. I follow only that which is revealed to me.'

Say: 'Are the blind and the seeing alike? Will you not think?'

Sura: 6, Ayat: 50.

Can the dead man whom We have raised to life and given a light with which he may be guided among men, be compared to him who blunders about in darkness from which he will never emerge? Thus their foul acts seem fair to the unbelievers.

And thus we have placed in every town its arch-transgressors to scheme there. But they scheme only against themselves, though they may not perceive it.

Sura: 6, Ayat: 122.

Who is a better man, he who founds his house on the fear of Allah and His good pleasure, or he who builds on the brink of a crumbling precipice, so that it will fall with him into the fire of Hell? Allah does not guide the wrongdoers.

Sura: 9, Ayat: 109.

The similitude of the two parties is as the blind and the deaf, and the seer and hearer. Can they be equal? Will you not take heed?

Sura: 11, Ayat: 24.

Is then he who knows that what has been revealed to you by your Lord is the truth, like him who is blind?

Truly, none will take heed but the wise; those who keep faith with Allah and do not break their pledge; who join together what He has bidden to be united; who fear their Lord and dread the terrors of Reckoning-day; and those who for the sake of Allah endure with fortitude, attend to their prayers, and spend of what We have given them in private and in public; and who ward off evil with good. These shall have a blissful end.

Sura: 13, Ayat: 19—22.

Are (these two) alike? — One to whom We have made a goodly promise, and who is going to reach its (fulfilment), and one to whom We have given the good things of this life, but who, on the Day of Judgement, is to be among those brought up (for punishment)?

Sura: 28, Ayat: 61.

Can he, then, who is a true believer, be compared to him who is an evil-doer? Surely they are not alike.

Sura: 32, Ayat: 18.

The blind and the seeing are not alike, nor are the darkness and the light. The shade and the heat are not alike, nor are the living and the dead. Allah can cause whom He will to hear Him, but you cannot make those who are in their graves hear you.

You are but a warner.

Sura: 35, Ayat: 19—23.

Are We to treat alike those that have faith and do good works, and those that corrupt the earth with wickedness? Are We to treat the righteous as We treat the wicked?

Sura: 38, Ayat: 28.

Can he who passes his night in adoration, standing up or on his knees, who dreads the terrors of the life to come and hopes to earn the mercy of his Lord (be compared to the unbeliever)? Are the wise and the ignorant equal? Truly, none will take heed but men of understanding.

Sura: 39, Ayat: 9.

Allah sets forth this parable. There are two men: the one who has many partners who are ever at odds among themselves; the other has one master. Are these two to be held alike? Praise be to Allah! But most of them have no knowledge.

Sura: 39, Ayat: 29.

The blind and the seeing are not alike, nor are those that have faith and do good works and the sinner. Yet you seldom think.

Sura: 40, Ayat: 58.

Those who deny our revelations are not hidden from Our view. Is he who is cast in the Fire better than the one who emerges safe on the Day of Resurrection? Do as you will, Allah is watching over all your actions.

Sura: 41, Ayat: 40.

Do the evildoers think that they are equal in Our sight to the believers who do good works, so that in life and death shall be alike? How ill they judge!

Sura: 45, Ayat: 21.

Can he who follows the guidance of his Lord be compared to him whose misdeeds are made to seem fair to him, and to those who follow their desires?

This is a description of the Paradise which the righteous have been promised. There shall flow in it rivers of unpolluted water, and rivers of milk for ever fresh; rivers of delectable wine and rivers of clearest honey. They shall have therein of every fruit and receive forgiveness from their Lord. Is this like (the lot of those) who shall abide in Hell for ever and drink scalding water which will tear their bowels?

Sura: 47, Ayat: 14-15.

The dwellers of Paradise and the people of the Fire shall not be held alike. The dwellers of Paradise alone shall be triumphant.

Sura: 59, Ayat: 20.

Who is more rightly guided, he that goes grovelling on his face, or he that walks upright upon a straight path?

Sura: 67, Ayat: 22.

Surely the righteous have gardens of bliss with their Lord. Are We to deal with the true believers as We deal with the wrongdoers? What is the matter with you? How do you judge?

Sura: 68, Ayat: 34—36.

In the name of Allah, The Compassionate, The Merciful

DISTINCTION BETWEEN THE CONDUCT OF BELIEVER AND NON-BELIEVER

This is because the unbelievers follow falsehood, while the faithful follow the truth from their Lord. Thus Allah sets forth for mankind their examples.

Sura: 47, Ayat: 3.

In the name of Allah, The Compassionate, The Merciful

NON-BELIEVERS DO NOT LEARN HISTORY'S LESSONS

Have they never journeyed through the land so that they may have hearts to gain wisdom or ears to hear with? It is not the eyes, but the hearts in the breasts, that are blind.

Sura: 22, Ayat: 46.

In the name of Allah, The Compassionate, The Merciful

THE END OF BELIEVER AND NON-BELIEVER

....Because Allah is the protector of the faithful, and because the unbelievers have no protector.

Allah will admit those who believe and do good works to gardens watered by running streams. The unbelievers take their fill of pleasure and eat as the cattle eat: but Hell shall be their home.

Sura: 47, Ayat: 10—12.

In the name of Allah, The Compassionate, The Merciful

FORGIVENESS FOR THE BELIEVER

Believers, have fear of Allah and put your trust in His Apostles. He will grant you a double share of His mercy. He will give you a light to walk in, and will forgive you: Allah is Forgiving and Merciful.

Let the People of the Book know that they have no control over the gifts of Allah; that these gifts are in His hands alone, and that He vouchsafes them to whom He will. Allah's bounty is infinite.

Sura: 57, Ayat: 28-29.

In the name of Allah, The Compassionate, The Merciful

RELATIONSHIP WITH BELIEVER OR NON-BELIEVER ON THE DAY OF JUDGEMENT

Allah has given as example to the unbelievers the wife of Nuh and the wife of Lut. They were married to two of Our righteous servants, but they deceived them. Their husbands availed them nothing against Allah. The angels said to them: 'Enter the Fire, together with those that shall enter it.'

Sura: 66, Ayat: 10.

But to the faithful Allah has given as example Pharaoh's wife, who said: 'Lord, build me a house with You in Paradise and deliver me from Pharaoh and his misdeeds. Deliver me from a wicked nation.

Sura: 66, Ayat: 11.

In the name of Allah, The Compassionate, The Merciful

DEALINGS WITH NON-BELIEVERS

Believers, do not make friends with any men other than your own people. They will spare no pains to corrupt you. They desire nothing but your ruin. Their hatred is clear from what they say, but more violent is the hatred which their breasts conceal.

We have made plain to you Our revelations, if you only understand.

See how you love them and they do not love you. You believe in the entire Book.

When they meet you they say: 'We, too, are believers.' But when alone, they bite their finger-tips with rage. Say: 'Perish in your rage! Allah has knowledge of what is in your chests.'

Sura: 3, Ayat: 118-119.

Believers, if you yield to the infidels they will drag you back to unbelief and you will return headlong to perdition.

Sura: 3, Ayat: 149.

If they incline to peace, make peace with them, and put your trust in Allah. Surely He is the Hearing, the Knowing. Should they seek to deceive you, Allah is All-sufficient for you.

Sura: 8, Ayat: 61-62.

A declaration of immunity by Allah and His Apostle to the idolaters with whom you have made agreements:

For four months you shall go unmolested in the land. But know that you shall not escape the judgement of Allah, and that Allah will humble the unbelievers.

Sura: 9, Ayat: 1-2.

A proclamation to the people by Allah and His Apostle on the day of the great pilgrimage:

Allah and His Apostle are free from obligation to the idolaters. If you repent, it will be well with you; but if you give no heed, know that you shall not

escape His judgement.

Proclaim a woeful punishment to the unbelievers, except those idolaters who have fully honoured their treaties with you and aided none against you. With these keep faith, until their treaties have run their term. Allah loves the righteous.

Sura: 9, Ayat: 3-4.

When the sacred months are over, slay the idolaters wherever you find them. Arrest them, besiege them, and lie in ambush everywhere for them. If they repent and take to prayer and pay the alms-tax, let them go their way. Allah is Forgiving and Merciful.

If an idolater seeks asylum with you, give him protection so that he may hear the Word of Allah, and then convey him to safety. For they are ignorant men.

How can the idolaters have any treaty with Allah and His Apostle, save those with whom you have made treaties at the Sacred Mosque? So long as they keep faith with you, keep faith with them. Allah loves the righteous.

Sura: 9, Ayat: 5—7.

O believers, know that the idolaters are unclean. Let them not approach the Sacred Mosque after this year is ended. If you fear poverty, Allah, if He pleases, will enrich you through His bounty. He is Knowing, Wise.

Sura: 9, Ayat: 28.

Had the gain been immediate or the journey easy, they would have followed you: but the distance seemed too far to them. Yet they will swear by Allah: 'Had we been able, we would have marched with you.' They bring ruin upon themselves. Allah knows that they are lying.

Allah forgive you! Why did you give them leave to stay behind before you knew those who spoke the truth from those who invented false excuses?

Those that believe in Allah and the Last Day will not beg you to exempt them from fighting with their wealth and their persons. Allah best knows the righteous. Only those seek exemption who disbelieve in Allah and the Last Day and whose hearts are filled with doubt. And in their doubt, they waver.

Had they intended to set forth with you, they would have prepared themselves for war. But Allah did not like their going forth and held them back, and it was said: 'Stay back with those who stay back.'

Sura: 9, Ayat: 42—46.

You shall not pray for any of their dead, nor shall you attend their burial. For they denied Allah and His Apostle and remained sinners to the last.

Let neither their riches nor their children rouse your envy. Through these Allah seeks to punish them in this life, so that they shall die unbelievers.

Whenever a Sura was revealed, saying: 'Believe in Allah and fight with His

Apostle,' the rich among them asked you to excuse them, saying: 'Leave us with those who are to stay behind.'

They were content to be with those who stayed behind: a seal was set upon their hearts, leaving them bereft of understanding. But the Apostle and the men who shared his faith fought with their goods and their persons. Those shall be rewarded with good things. Those shall surely prosper. Allah has prepared for them gardens watered by running streams, in which they shall abide for ever. That is the supreme triumph.

Sura: 9, Ayat: 84—89.

Ibrahim prayed for his father only to fulfil a promise he had made him. But when he realized he was an enemy of Allah, he disowned him. Surely Ibrahim was a compassionate and tender-hearted man.

Sura: 9, Ayat: 114.

Nuh called out to his Lord, saying: 'Lord my son was my own flesh and blood. Your promise was surely true. You are the most Just of judges.'

He said: 'O Nuh, he was no kinsman of yours. This is not a righteous deed. Do not question Me about things you know nothing of. I admonish you lest you become an ignorant man.

He said: 'My Lord, I seek refuge with You from asking thee that of which I have no knowledge. If You do not pardon me and have mercy on me, I shall be among the losers.'

Sura: 11, Ayat: 45—47.

Follow then the right path as you are bidden, together with those who have repented with you, and do not transgress. He is aware of what you do.

And put not trust in the wrongdoers, lest you get touched by the Fire. You have no protectors besides Allah. Then you will not be helped.

Sura: 11, Ayat: 112-113.

Proclaim, then, what you are bidden and avoid the polytheists. We will Ourself sustain you against those that mock you—those who serve other gods besides Allah. They shall before long know.

Sura: 15, Ayat: 94—96.

Had it been Our will, We could have raised a warner in every town. Do not yield to the unbelievers, but fight them strenuously with it (the Quran).

Sura: 25, Ayat: 51-52.

Prophet, have fear of Allah, and do not listen to the unbelievers and the Hypocrites. Allah is Wise and All-Knowing.

Sura: 33, Ayat: 1.

Do not obey the unbelievers and the hypocrites: disregard their insolence. Put your trust in Allah; Allah is your All-sufficient Guardian.

Sura: 33, Ayat: 48.

Your Lord knows best those who stray from His path, and those who are rightly guided. Give no heed to the disbelievers: they wish you were pliant, so that they would be pliant.

Sura: 68, Ayat: 7—9.

We have revealed to you the Quran by gradual revelation, therefore await with patience the judgement of your Lord and do not yield to the sinner and the unbelieving.

Sura: 76, Ayat: 23-24.

In the name of Allah, The Compassionate, The Merciful

STANDARD OF COMPANIONSHIP

Give warning to the hypocrites of a stern chastisement those who choose the unbelievers rather than the faithful for their friends. Are they seeking glory at their hands? Surely all glory belongs to Allah.

Sura: 4, Ayat: 138-139.

O believers, do not choose the infidels rather than the faithful for your friends. Would you give Allah a clear proof against yourselves?

Sura: 4, Ayat: 144.

Your only supporters and protectors are Allah, His Apostle, and the faithful: those who attend to their prayers, pay their alms-tax, and kneel down in worship.

Sura: 5, Ayat: 55.

Those who seek the support of Allah, His Apostle, and the faithful (must know) that Allah's followers are sure to triumph.

Sura: 5, Ayat: 56.

Believers, take as supporters neither those who were given the Book before you, who have made of your religion a jest and a pastime, nor the infidels. Have fear of Allah, if you are true believers. When you call to prayer, they treat it as a jest and a pastime. They do this because they are devoid of understanding.

Sura: 5, Ayat: 57.

Do not drive away those that call on their Lord morning and evening, seeking only to gain His favour. You are not by any means accountable for them, nor are they accountable for you. If you drive them away, you shall yourself become an evildoer.

Sura: 6, Ayat: 52.

....Therefore, have fear of Allah and end your disputes. Obey Allah and

His Apostle, if you are true believers.'

Sura: 8, Ayat: 1.

....He has made you strong with His help and rallied the faithful round you, making their hearts one. If you had given away all the riches of the earth, you could not have so united them....

Sura: 8, Ayat: 62-63.

Those that have embraced the faith and migrated (from Makkah), and fought for the cause of Allah with their wealth and their persons; and those that sheltered them and helped them, shall be friends to each other....

Sura: 8, Ayat: 72.

Do you (O believers) think that you will be spared unless God takes cognizance of your having striven hard (in His cause) without seeking help from any but God and His Apostle and those who believe in Him? For, God is aware of all that you do.

Sura: 9, Ayat: 16.

Believers, do not befriend your fathers or your brothers if they choose unbelief in preference to faith. Wrongdoers are those that befriend them.

Sura: 9, Ayat: 23.

The true believers, both men and women, are friends to each other. They enjoin what is just and forbid what is evil; they attend to their prayers and pay the alms-tax and obey Allah and His Apostle. On these Allah will have mercy. He is Mighty, Wise.

Sura: 9, Ayat: 71.

O believers, have fear of Allah and stand with the truthful.

Sura: 9, Ayat: 119.

The wrongdoers are patrons to each other, but the righteous have Allah Himself for their patron.

These are clear proofs to men and a guidance and mercy for those who truly believe.

Sura: 45, Ayat: 19-20.

You shall find no believers in Allah and the Last Day on friendly terms with those who oppose Allah and His Apostle, even though they be their fathers, their sons, their brothers, or their kindred. Allah has written the faith in their very hearts and strengthened them with a spirit of His own. He will admit them to gardens watered by running streams, where they shall dwell for ever. Allah is well pleased with them and they with Him. They are the party of

Allah: and Allah's party shall surely triumph.

Sura: 58, Ayat: 22.

Believers, do not make friends with those who are enemies of Mine and yours, showing them kindness when they have denied the truth that has been revealed to you and driven the Apostle and yourselves out of your city because you believe in Allah, your Lord.

If it was indeed to fight for My cause, and out of a desire to please Me that you left your city, how can you be friendly to them in secret? I well know all that you hide and all that you reveal. Whoever of you does this will stray from the right path.

If they gain ascendency over you, they will plainly show themselves your enemies, and stretch out their hands and tongues towards you with evil. They long to see you unbelievers.

On the Day of Resurrection neither your kinsfolk nor your children shall avail you. Allah will judge between you. He is cognizant of all your actions.

You have a good example in Ibrahim and those who followed him. They said to their people: 'We are clear of you and that which you worship besides Allah. We renounce you: enmity and hate shall reign between us until you believe in Allah only—except Ibrahim's saying to his father: 'I shall implore Allah to forgive you, although I have no power to save you from His punishment.' 'Lord, in You we have put our trust; do not make us a trial for the unbelievers. Forgive us, our Lord; You are the Mighty, the Wise One.'

Sura: 60, Ayat: 1—4.

Allah does not forbid you to be kind and equitable to those who have neither made war on your religion nor driven you from your homes. Allah loves the equitable. But He forbids you to make friends with those who have fought against you on account of your religion and driven you from your homes or abetted others to do so. Those who make friends with them are wrongdoers.

Sura: 60, Ayat: 8-9.

In the name of Allah, The Compassionate, The Merciful

FRIENDSHIP WITH NON-BELIEVERS

Let not the believers take those who deny the truth for their allies in preference to the believers—since he who does this cuts himself off from God in everything—unless it be to protect yourselves against them in this way. But God warns you to beware of Him: for with God is all journey's end.

Sura: 3, Ayat: 28.

Believers, do not make friends with any men other than your own people. They will spare no pains to corrupt you. They desire nothing but your ruin. Their hatred is clear from what they say, but more violent is the hatred which their breasts conceal.

We have made plain to you Our revelations, if you only understand.

Sura: 3, Ayat: 118.

See how you love them and they do not love you. You believe in the entire Book.

When they meet you they say: 'We, too, are believers.' But when alone, they bite their finger-tips with rage. Say: 'Perish in your rage! Allah has knowledge of what is in your chests.

Sura: 3, Ayat: 119.

When you are blessed with good fortune, they grieve: but when evil befalls you, they rejoice. If you persevere and guard yourselves against evil, their machinations will never harm you. Allah has knowledge of all their actions.

Sura: 3, Ayat: 120.

They would love to see you deny the truth even as they have denied it, so that you should be like them. Do not, therefore, take them for your allies until they forsake the domain of evil for the sake of God; and if they revert to (open) enmity, seize them and slay them wherever you may find them; and do not take any of them for your ally or giver of succour.

Sura: 4, Ayat: 89.

O believers, do not choose the infidels rather than the faithful for your friends. Would you give Allah a clear proof against yourselves?

The hypocrites shall be cast into the lowest depths of the Fire: there shall be none to help them. But those who repent and mend their ways, who hold fast to Allah and are sincere in their belief—they shall be numbered with the faithful, and the faithful shall be richly rewarded by Allah.

Sura: 4, Ayat: 144—146.

Believers, take neither Jews nor Christians for your friends and protectors. They are friends and protectors of one another. Whoever of you seeks their friendship and supports them shall become one of their number. Allah does not guide the wrongdoers.

Sura: 5, Ayat: 51.

Believers, take as supporters neither those who were given the Book before you, who have made of your religion a jest and a pastime, nor the infidels. Have fear of Allah, if you are true believers.

Sura: 5, Ayat: 57.

You see many of them taking the unbelievers as supporters. Evil is that to which their souls prompt them. They have incurred the wrath of Allah and shall endure eternal torment.

Sura: 5, Ayat: 80.

Had they believed in Allah and the Prophet and that which is revealed to him, they would not have taken them as supporters. But many of them are evildoers.

Sura: 5, Ayat: 81.

And incline not to those who do wrong; or the Fire will seize you; and you have no protectors other than God, nor shall you be helped.

Sura: 11, Ayat: 113.

And now, We have set you on the right path. Follow it and do not yield to the desires of ignorant men.

Sura: 45, Ayat: 18.

Do you see those that have befriended a people* who have incurred Allah's wrath? They belong neither to you nor to them. They knowingly swear to falsehoods. Allah has prepared for them a grievous scourge. Evil indeed is that which they have done.

***The Jews**

They use their faith as a disguise and thus debar others from the path of Allah. A shameful scourge awaits them.

Neither their wealth nor their children shall in the least protect them from Allah. They are the people of the Fire, and there they shall abide for ever.

On the day when Allah restores them all to life, they will swear to Him as they now swear to you, thinking that their oaths will help them. Surely they are liars.

The Devil has gained possession of them and caused them to forget Allah's warning. They are the Devil's party; and the Devil's party shall assuredly be lost.

Sura: 58, Ayat: 14–19.

You shall find no believers in Allah and the Last Day on friendly terms with those who oppose Allah and His Apostle, even though they be their fathers, their sons, their brothers, or their kindred. Allah has written the faith in their very hearts and strengthened them with a spirit of His own. He will admit them to gardens watered by running streams, where they shall dwell for ever. Allah is well pleased with them and they with Him. They are the party of Allah: and Allah's party shall surely triumph.

Sura: 58, Ayat: 22.

Believers, do not make friends with those who are enemies of Mine and yours, showing them kindness when they have denied the truth that has been revealed to you and driven the Apostle and yourselves out of your city because you believe in Allah, your Lord.

If it was indeed to fight for My cause, and out of a desire to please Me that you left your city, how can you be friendly to them in secret? I well know all that you hide and all that you reveal. Whoever of you does this will stray from the right path.

Sura: 60, Ayat: 1.

If they gain ascendancy over you, they will plainly show themselves your enemies, and stretch out their hands and tongues towards you with evil. They long to see you unbelievers.

Sura: 60, Ayat: 2.

On the Day of Resurrection neither your kinsfolk nor your children shall avail you. Allah will judge between you. He is cognizant of all your actions.

Sura: 60, Ayat: 3.

You have a good example in Ibrahim and those who followed him. They said to their people: 'We are clear of you and that which you worship besides Allah. We renounce you: enmity and hate shall reign between us until you believe in Allah only – except Ibrahim's saying to his father: 'I shall implore

Allah to forgive you, although I have no power to save you from His punishment' Lord, in You we have put our trust; do not make us a trial for the unbelievers. Forgive us, our Lord; You are the Mighty, the Wise One.'

Sura: 60, Ayat: 4.

Truly, in those men there is a good example for you (and) for him who puts his hopes in Allah and in the Last Day. He that gives no heed to you, Allah alone is Self-sufficient and Worthy of praise.

Sura: 60, Ayat: 6.

It may well be that Allah will put good will between you and those with whom you have hitherto been at odds. Allah is Mighty. He is Forgiving and Merciful.

Sura: 60, Ayat: 7.

Allah does not forbid you to be kind and equitable to those who have neither made war on your religion nor driven you from your homes. Allah loves the equitable. But He forbids you to make friends with those who have fought against you on account of your religion and driven you from your homes or abetted others to do so. Those who make friends with them are wrongdoers.

Sura: 60, Ayat: 8-9.

O believers, do not make friends with those who have incurred the wrath of Allah. Such men despair of the life to come, just as the unbelievers despair of the buried dead.

Sura: 60, Ayat: 13.

Allah has given as example to the unbelievers the wife of Nuh and the wife of Lut. They were married to two of Our righteous servants, but they deceived them. Their husbands availed them nothing against Allah.

Sura: 66, Ayat: 10.

In the name of Allah, The Compassionate, The Merciful

FUNERAL PRAYER FOR THE HYPOCRITE AND TRANSGRESSOR

You shall not pray for any of their dead, nor shall you attend their burial. For they denied Allah and His Apostle and remained sinners to the last.

Sura: 9, Ayat: 84.

REPENTANCE

(13)

In the name of Allah, The Compassionate, The Merciful

REALITY OF BASER SELF

Not that I am free from sin: man's soul often commands evil, except him to whom Allah has shown mercy. My Lord is Forgiving, Merciful.'

Sura: 12, Ayat: 53.

In the name of Allah, The Compassionate, The Merciful

EVIL DESIRES

(We said): 'Dawud, We have made you a vicegerent in the land. Rule with justice among men and do not yield to your own lust lest it should turn you away from Allah's path. Those that stray from Allah's path shall be sternly punished, because they forget the Day of Reckoning.'

Sura: 38, Ayat: 26.

In the name of Allah, The Compassionate, The Merciful

SUCCUMBING TO TEMPTATIONS

Allah wishes to forgive you, but those who follow their own lusts wish to see you far astray.

Sura: 4, Ayat: 27.

Believers, conduct yourselves with justice and bear true witness before Allah, even though it be against yourselves, your parents, or your kinsfolk. Whether he be rich or poor, know that Allah has better right over both. So do not be led by desires lest you should swerve from the truth. If you distort your testimony or decline to give it, know that Allah is cognizant of all that you do.

Sura: 4, Ayat: 135.

Say: 'Bring those witnesses of yours who can testify that Allah has forbidden this.' If they so testify, do not testify with them, nor yield to the wishes of those that deny Our revelations, disbelieve in the life to come, and set up (other gods) as equals with their Lord.

Sura: 6, Ayat: 150.

And thus We have revealed it, a (code of) judgement in the Arabic tongue. If you succumb to their desires after the knowledge you have been given, none shall save or protect you from Allah.

Sura: 13, Ayat: 37.

....Nor obey him whose heart We have made heedless of Our remembrance; who follows his desires and whose case exceeds due bounds.

Sura: 18, Ayat: 28.

But the generations Who succeeded them neglected their prayers and followed lusts. These shall assuredly be lost.

Sura: 19, Ayat: 59.

Had the truth followed their desires, the heavens, the earth, and all who dwell in them would have surely been corrupted. We have given them their

admonition; yet from their admonition they turn away.

Sura: 23, Ayat: 71.

Have you seen him who has made gods of his own desires? Would you be held responsible over him?

Do you think that most of them can hear or understand? They are like cattle, and even more misguided.

Sura: 25, Ayat: 43-44.

Say: 'Bring down from Allah a scripture that is a better guidance than these and I will follow it, if what you say be true!'

If they do not answer you, know that they are the slaves of their desires. And who is in greater error than the man who is led by his desires without guidance from Allah? Allah does not guide the evildoers.

Sura: 28, Ayat: 49-50.

Indeed, the wrongdoers are led unwittingly by their own desires. And who can guide those whom Allah has led astray? There shall be none to help them.

Sura: 30, Ayat: 29.

And now, We have set you on the right path. Follow it and do not yield to the desires of ignorant men; for they in no way can protect you from (the wrath) of Allah. The wrongdoers are patrons to each other, but the righteous have Allah Himself for their patron.

Sura: 45, Ayat: 18-19.

Do you see the man who makes his desire his god, the man whom Allah leaves in error, setting a seal upon his ears and heart and drawing a veil over his eyes? Who then can guide him after Allah (has withdrawn guidance)? Will you not take heed?

Sura: 45, Ayat: 23.

Some of them indeed listen to you, but no sooner do they leave your presence then they ask those to whom knowledge has been given: 'What did he say just now?' Such are the men whose hearts are sealed by Allah and who follow their own desires.

Sura: 47, Ayat: 16.

They are but names which you invented, you and your fathers: Allah has sent down no authority for them. They follow vain conjectures and the whims of their own souls, although the guidance of their Lord has come to them.

Is man to attain all that he desires? For to Allah belongs the Hereafter and the present life.

Sura: 53, Ayat: 23—25.

In the name of Allah, The Compassionate, The Merciful

FORGETTING GOD WHEN AFFLUENT

On the day when He assembles them with all that they worship besides Allah, He will say: 'Was it you who misled My servants, or did they themselves go astray?

They will answer: 'Glory be to You. We should not have taken other guardians besides You. But You gave them and their fathers the good things of life, so that they forgot Your warning and thus became lost peoples.'

Sura: 25, Ayat: 17-18.

In the name of Allah, The Compassionate, The Merciful

DESPAIRING OF DIVINE MERCY

(Jacob said) O my sons!

Go and seek news of Yusuf and his brother. Do not despair of Allah's mercy; none but unbelievers despair of Allah's mercy.'

Sura: 12, Ayat: 87.

Those that disbelieve His revelations and deny that they will ever meet Allah shall despair of My mercy. Theirs shall be woeful punishment.

Sura: 29, Ayat: 23.

Say: 'O My servants, you who have sinned against your souls, do not despair of Allah's mercy, for He forgives all sins. He is the Forgiving One, the Merciful.

Sura: 39, Ayat: 53.

In the name of Allah, The Compassionate, The Merciful

REPENTANCE

Their reward shall be the curse of Allah, the angels, and all men: under it they shall abide forever. Their punishment shall not be lightened, nor shall they be reprieved; except those who afterwards repent and mend their ways, for Allah is Forgiving and Merciful.

Sura: 3, Ayat: 87—89.

And Allah loves the charitable. ...
and those who, if they commit evil or wrong their souls, remember Allah and seek forgiveness of Him—for who but Allah can forgive sin—and who do not knowingly persist in what they do. These shall be rewarded with forgiveness from their Lord and gardens watered by running streams, where they shall dwell forever. Blessed is the reward of those who do good works.

Sura: 3, Ayat: 135-136.

Allah forgives those who commit evil in ignorance and then quickly turn to Him in repentance. Allah will turn to them in His mercy: For Allah is full of knowledge and wisdom.

Sura: 4, Ayat: 17.

But Allah will not forgive those who do evil and, when death comes to them, say: 'Now we repent!' Nor will He forgive those who die unbelievers. For these We have prepared a woeful scourge.

Sura: 4, Ayat: 18.

He that does evil or wrongs his own soul and then seeks pardon of Allah, will find Allah Forgiving, Merciful.

He that commits sin commits it against his own soul. Allah is Knowing, Wise.

Sura: 4, Ayat: 110-111.

The hypocrites shall be cast into the lowest depths of the Fire: there shall be none to help them. But those who repent and mend their ways, who hold fast

to Allah and are sincere in their belief—they shall be numbered with the faithful, and the faithful shall be richly rewarded by Allah.

Sura: 4, Ayat: 145-146.

But whoever repents and mends his ways after committing evil shall be pardoned by Allah. Allah is Forgiving, Merciful.

Sura: 5, Ayat: 39.

And when those who believe in Our messages come to you, say: "Peace be upon you. Your Sustainer has willed upon Himself the law of grace and mercy — so that if any of you does a bad deed out of ignorance, and thereafter repents and lives righteously, He shall be (found) much-forgiving, a dispenser of grace."

Sura: 6, Ayat: 54.

As for those that do evil and later repent and have faith, then your Lord is Forgiving, Merciful.

Sura: 7, Ayat: 153.

But Allah was not to punish them whilst you were dwelling in their midst. Nor would He punish them if they sought forgiveness of Him.

Sura: 8, Ayat: 33.

They honour with the believers neither treaties nor ties of kindred. Such are the transgressors.

If they repent and take to prayer and pay the alms-tax, they shall become your brothers in the faith. Thus We make plain Our revelations for men of understanding.

But if, after coming to terms with you, they break their oaths and revile your faith, make war on the leaders of unbelief—for no oaths are binding with them—so that they may desist.

Sura: 9, Ayat: 10—12.

Others there are who have confessed their sins; their good works had been intermixed with evil. Perchance Allah will turn to them in mercy. He is Forgiving, Merciful. Take alms from their wealth, so that they may thereby be cleansed and purified, and pray for them: for your prayers will give them comfort. Allah is Hearing, Knowing.

Do they not know that Allah accepts the repentance of His servants and takes their gifts of charity and that Allah is the Forgiving One, the Merciful?

Sura: 9, Ayat: 102—104.

And seek forgiveness of your Lord and turn to Him in repentance. He will make a good provision for you till an appointed day and will bestow His grace

upon those that have merit. But if you turn away, then I fear for you the Penalty of a Great Day:

Sura: 11, Ayat: 3.

Seek forgiveness of your Lord and turn to Him in repentance. My Lord is Merciful, Loving.'

Sura: 11, Ayat: 90.

Your Lord would not have ruined those towns, without just cause, had their inhabitants been righteous men.

Sura: 11, Ayat: 117.

We have forbidden the Jews what We have already related to you. We never wronged them, but they wronged themselves.

Surely your Lord — to those who commit evil through ignorance and afterwards repent and mend their ways – your Lord thereafter is surely Forgiving, Merciful.

Sura: 16, Ayat: 118-119.

....If you are good, He will forgive those that turn to Him.

Sura: 17, Ayat: 25.

But the generations who succeeded them neglected their prayers and followed lusts. These shall assuredly be lost. But those that repent and embrace the Faith and do what is right shall be admitted to Paradise and shall not be wronged in any way.

Sura: 19, Ayat: 59-60.

"Partake of the good things which We have provided for you as sustenance, but do not transgress therein the bounds of equity lest My condemnation fall upon you: for, he upon whom My condemnation falls has indeed thrown himself into utter ruin!"

Yet withal, behold, I forgive all sins of any who repents and attains to faith and does righteous deeds, and thereafter keeps to the right path.

Sura: 20, Ayat: 81-82.

Say: 'Lord, forgive and have mercy. You are the best of those that show mercy.'

Sura: 23, Ayat: 118.

(The true servants of the Merciful are those): who invoke no other god besides Allah and do not kill the soul which God has forbidden except for a just cause; who do not commit adultery. For he that does this shall meet with evil: his punishment shall be doubled on the Day of Resurrection, and he shall

abide therein for ever in disgrace, unless he repents, and believes and does good works, for then Allah will change his sins to good actions: Allah is ever Forgiving and Merciful.

Sura: 25, Ayat: 68—70.

He that repents and does good works truly returns to Allah by true repentance.

Sura: 25, Ayat: 71.

....'Musa, do not be alarmed,' (Said He), 'My Apostles are never afraid in My presence. As for those who sin and then do good instead of evil, I am Forgiving and Merciful to them.

Sura: 27, Ayat: 10-11.

(Saleh said): 'My people, why do you wish to hasten evil rather than good? If only you seek forgiveness of Allah, you may yet receive His mercy.'

Sura: 27, Ayat: 46.

But those who repent and embrace the faith and do what is right may hope for salvation.

Sura: 28, Ayat: 67.

Say: 'O My servants, you who have sinned against your souls, do not despair of Allah's mercy, for He forgives all sins. He is the Forgiving One, the Merciful. Turn in repentance to your Lord and surrender yourselves to Him before His scourge overtakes you, for then you will not be helped. Follow the best of what is revealed to you from your Lord before His scourge overtakes you unawares, without warning; lest any soul should say: 'Alas! I have disobeyed Allah and scoffed at His revelations.' Or 'If Allah had guided me I would have been one of the righteous.' Or, when it sees the punishment should say: 'Could I but live again, I would lead a righteous life.' For Allah will say: 'My revelations had come to you, but you denied them. You were arrogant and one of the unbelievers.'

Sura: 39, Ayat: 53—59.

Therefore have patience; Allah's promise is true. Implore Him to forgive your sins, and celebrate His praise morning and evening.

Those who dispute the revelations of Allah without authority given to them, there is nothing in their hearts but ambitions which they shall never attain. Therefore, seek refuge in Allah; He hears all and sees all.

Sura: 40, Ayat: 55-56.

He accepts the repentance of His servants and pardons their sins. He has knowledge of all your actions.

Sura: 42, Ayat: 25

Hearken to your Lord before that day arrives which none can defer against the will of Allah. For on that day there shall be no refuge for you, nor shall you be able to deny (your sins).

Sura: 42, Ayat: 47.

O believers, turn to Allah in true repentance. Your Lord may forgive you your sins and admit you to gardens watered by running streams,....

Sura: 66, Ayat: 8.

Wait, then, for the judgement of your Lord and do not act like him who was swallowed by the whale when he called out to Allah in despair. Had his Lord not bestowed on him His grace, he would have been cast down in the open to be blamed. But his Lord chose him and made him a righteous man.

Sura: 68, Ayat: 48–50.

....Recite from it then, as much as is easy (for you). Attend to your prayers, pay the alms-tax, and give Allah a generous loan. Whatever good you do you shall surely find it with Allah, ennobled and richly rewarded by Him. Implore Allah to forgive you; He is Forgiving, Merciful.

Sura: 73, Ayat: 20.

In the name of Allah, The Compassionate, The Merciful

TO GUARD AGAINST SINS

If you avoid the heinous sins you are forbidden, We shall pardon your evil deeds and admit you to an honourable place (Paradise).

Sura: 4, Ayat: 31.

Sin neither openly nor in secret. Those that commit sin shall be punished for their sins.

Sura: 6, Ayat: 120.

Say: The things that my Lord has indeed forbidden are: Shameful deeds whether open or secret; sins and trespasses against truth or reason; assigning of partners to God, for which He has given no authority; and saying things about God of which you have no knowledge.

Sura: 7, Ayat: 33.

Allah enjoins justice, the doing of good, and liberality to kith and kin, and He forbids all shameful deeds, and injustice and rebellion: so that you may take heed.

Sura: 16, Ayat: 90.

Yet there are some who dispute about Allah without knowledge and follow every rebellious devil. Every such devil is doomed to lead astray him who follows it, and lead him to the scourge of the Fire.

Sura: 22, Ayat: 3-4.

You that are true believers, do not walk in the footsteps of Satan. He that walks in Satan's footsteps is incited by him to indecency and evil. But for Allah's grace and mercy, none of you would have been cleansed of sin. Allah purifies whom He will; He hears all and knows all.

Sura: 24, Ayat: 21.

(Luqman said): 'My son, be steadfast in prayer, enjoin justice, and forbid

evil. Endure with fortitude whatever befalls you. That is a duty incumbent on all.

'Do not turn away from men with scorn, nor walk proudly on the earth: Allah does not love the arrogant and the vain-glorious. Rather let your gait be modest and your voice low: the harshest of voices is the braying of the asses.'

Sura: 31, Ayat: 17—19.

Men, the promise of Allah is true. Let the life of this world not deceive you, nor let the Dissembler trick you about Allah. Satan is your enemy: therefore treat him as an enemy. He tempts his followers so that they may become the people of the Fire.

Sura: 35, Ayat: 5-6.

Did I not enjoin you, Sons of Adam, not to serve Satan who is your acknowledged enemy, and that you should worship Me? Surely that was the right path.

Sura: 36, Ayat: 60-61.

That which you have been given is but the fleeting comfort of this life. Better and more enduring is that which Allah has for those who believe and put their trust in Him; who avoid gross sins and shameful deeds and, when angered, are willing to forgive, who obey their Lord, attend to their prayers, and conduct their affairs by mutual consultation; who spend out of what We bestow on them for Sustenance and when oppressed, seek to redress their wrongs.

Sura: 42, Ayat: 36—39.

To God is what the heavens and the earth contain: so that He rewards those who do evil, according to their deeds, and He rewards those who do good, with what is best.

(To) those who avoid grossest sins and indecencies and commit only small offences, Allah is of vast forgiveness. He knew you well when He created you from earth and when you were embryos in your mothers' wombs. Do not pretend to purity; He knows best those who guard themselves against evil.

Sura: 53, Ayat: 31-32.

In the name of Allah, The Compassionate, The Merciful

TO HAVE FAITH BEFORE DEATH

Are they waiting for the angels or your Lord Himself to come down to them, or for a sign of His to be given them? On the day when such a sign is given them, faith shall not avail the soul which had no faith before or while believing, did no good works.

Say: 'Wait if you will, we too are waiting.'

Sura: 6, Ayat: 158.

We led the Children of Israel across the sea, and Pharaoh and his legions pursued them with wickedness and tyranny. But as he was drowning he cried: 'Now I believe that there is no god save the God in whom the Children of Israel believe. To Him I give up myself.'

(Allah said): 'Now (you believe)! But before this you disobeyed and were a wrongdoer. We shall save you in your body this day, so that you may become a sign to all posterity: for most men give no heed to Our signs.'

Sura: 10, Ayat: 90—92.

Until when death comes to a wrongdoer, he will say: 'Lord, let me go back, that I may do good works in the world I have left behind.'

Never! It is only a word which he will speak. Behind them there shall stand a barrier till the Day of Resurrection.

Sura: 23, Ayat: 99-100.

Therefore set your face in devotion to the true faith before that day arrives which none may put off against the will of Allah. On that day mankind will be sundered. Those who disbelieve will answer for their unbelief, while the righteous will make ready their blissful home:

Sura: 30, Ayat: 43-44.

They ask: 'When will this judgement come, if what you say be true?'

Say: 'On the Day of Judgement no profit will be to unbelievers if they (then) believe! nor will they be granted respite.'

Sura: 32, Ayat: 28-29.

And when they saw Our Punishment they said: 'We now believe in none but Allah. We deny those we used to associate with Him.'

But their professing the Faith when they (actually) saw Our Punishment was not going to profit them. (Such has been) God's way of dealing with His servants (From the most ancient times). And even thus did the rejecters of God perish (utterly)!

Sura: 40, Ayat: 84-85.

Hearken to your Lord before that day arrives which none can defer against the will of Allah. For on that day there shall be no refuge for you, nor shall you be able to deny (your sins).

Sura: 42, Ayat: 47.

Are they waiting but for the Hour of Doom to overtake them unawares? It' portents have already come. But how will they be warned when it overtake them?

Sura: 47, Ayat: 1

QUALITIES OF THE PIOUS

(14)

In the name of Allah, The Compassionate, The Merciful

PIETY

Righteousness does not consist in whether you face towards the east or the west. The righteous man is he who believes in Allah and the Last Day, in the angels and the book and the prophets; who for the love of Allah gives his wealth to his kinsfolk, to the orphans, to the needy, to the wayfarers and to the beggars, and for the redemption of captives; who attends to his prayers and pays the alms-tax; who is true to his promises and steadfast in trial and adversity and in time of war. Such are the true believers; such are the God-fearing.

Sura: 2, Ayat: 177.

Give for the cause of Allah and do not with your own hands cast yourselves into destruction. And persevere in doing good: For Allah loves those who do good.

Sura: 2, Ayat: 195.

But the believers who do good works, whether men or women, shall enter Paradise. They shall not suffer the least injustice.

Sura: 4, Ayat: 124.

Allah will reward those that have faith and do good works; He will enrich them from His own abundance. As for those who are scornful and proud, He will sternly punish them, and they shall find none besides Allah to protect or help them.

Sura: 4, Ayat: 173.

"What cause can we have not to believe in God and the truth which has come to us, seeing that We long for our Lord to admit us to the company of the righteous?" And for their words Allah has rewarded them with gardens watered by running streams, where they shall dwell for ever. Such is the recompense of the righteous. But those that disbelieve and deny Our revelations shall be the people of Hell.

Sura: 5, Ayat: 84–86.

Such is the path of your Lord, a straight path. We have made plain Our revelations for those people who take heed. Theirs is the abode of peace with their Lord. He will give them His protection in reward for what they do.

Sura: 6, Ayat: 126-127.

He that does a good deed shall be repaid tenfold; but he that commits a sin shall be punished only for it. None shall be wronged.

Sura: 6, Ayat: 160.

As for those that have faith and do good works—We never burden a soul with more than it can bear—they are the people of Paradise, and there they shall abide for ever.

Sura: 7, Ayat: 42.

In the name of Allah, The Compassionate, The Merciful

PIOUS PEOPLE

It is a guide for the righteous, who have faith in the unseen and are steadfast in prayer; who spend out of what We have given them; who believe in that which has been revealed to you and to others before you, and firmly believe in the life to come. These are rightly guided by their Lord; these shall surely triumph.

Sura: 2, Ayat: 2–5.

Believers, Jews, Christians, and Sabaeans—whoever believes in Allah and the Last Day and does what is right—shall have their reward with their Lord; they have nothing to fear or to regret.

Sura: 2, Ayat: 62.

But those that have faith and do good works are the people of Paradise; for ever they shall abide in it.

Sura: 2, Ayat: 82.

Indeed, those that surrender themselves to Allah and do good works shall have their reward with their Lord: they shall have nothing to fear or to regret.

Sura: 2, Ayat: 112.

Righteousness does not consist in whether you face towards the east or the west. The righteous man is he who believes in Allah and the Last Day, in the angels and the Book and the prophets; who gives his wealth – however much he may cherish it – to his kinsfolk, to the orphans, to the needy, to the wayfarers and to the beggars, and for the redemption of captives; who attends to his prayers and pays the alms-tax; who is true to his promises and steadfast in trial and adversity and in times of war. Such are the true believers; such are the God-fearing.

Sura: 2, Ayat: 177.

Those that have embraced the faith and those that have left their land and fought for the cause of Allah, may hope for Allah's mercy. Allah is Forgiving

and Merciful.

Sura: 2, Ayat: 218.

There shall be no compulsion in religion. True guidance is now distinct from error. He that renounces the idols and puts his faith in Allah has grasped the most trustworthy hand-hold, that never breaks. And God hears and knows all things.

Allah is the Supporter of the faithful. He leads them from darkness to the light. As for the unbelievers, their supporters are false gods, who lead them from light to darkness. They are the heirs of Hell and shall abide in it forever.

Sura: 2, Ayat: 256-257.

Those that have faith and do good works, attend to their prayers and pay the alms-tax, will be rewarded by their Lord and will have nothing to fear or to regret.

Sura: 2, Ayat: 277.

Those who say: 'Lord, we believe in You: forgive us our sins and keep us from the torment of Fire; who are steadfast, sincere, obedient, and charitable; and who implore forgiveness in the early hours of morning.

Sura: 3, Ayat: 16-17.

You are the best nation that has ever been raised up for mankind. You enjoin justice and forbid evil. You believe in Allah.

Had the people of the Book believed, it would have surely been better for them. Some of them are true believers, and most of them are evildoers.

Sura: 3, Ayat: 110.

Be quick in the race for forgiveness from your Lord, and for a Garden whose width is that (of the whole) of the heavens and of the earth, prepared for the righteous, — Those who spend (freely), whether in prosperity, or in adversity; who restrain anger, and pardon (all) men; — for God loves those who do good; — And those who, having done something to be ashamed of, or wronged their own souls, earnestly bring God to mind, and ask for forgiveness for their sins, — and who can forgive sins except God? — and are never obstinate in persisting knowingly in (the wrong) they have done.

Sura: 3, Ayat: 133—136.

Can the man who seeks to please Allah be compared to him who has incurred His wrath? Hell shall be his home. Evil shall be his fate!

Varied are their positions with Allah. Allah is cognizant of what they do.

Sura: 3, Ayat: 162-163.

As for those that fear their Lord, theirs shall be gardens watered by run-

ning streams in which they shall abide forever, and a goodly welcome from their Lord. Allah's reward is surely better for the righteous.

Sura: 3, Ayat: 198.

As for those that have faith and do good works, we shall admit them to gardens watered by running streams, where they shall have purified spouses, and where they shall abide forever. And We shall admit them to a cool shade ever deepening.

Sura: 4, Ayat: 57.

But those that have faith and do good works shall be admitted to gardens watered by running streams, and there they shall abide forever. Such is the true promise of Allah: and whose is a truer word than Allah's?

Sura: 4, Ayat: 122.

But the believers who do good works, whether men or women, shall enter Paradise. They shall not suffer the least injustice.

And who has a nobler religion than the man who surrenders himself to Allah, does what is right, and follows the faith of Ibrahim the upright, whom Allah Himself chose to be His friend?

To Allah belongs all that the heavens and the earth contain. He has knowledge of all things.

Sura: 4, Ayat: 124–126.

And why should Allah punish you if you render thanks to Him and truly believe in Him? Allah is Rewarding, Knowing.

Sura: 4, Ayat: 147.

As for those that believe in Allah and His apostles and discriminate against none of them, they shall be rewarded by Allah. He is Forgiving, Merciful.

Sura: 4, Ayat: 152.

Believers, if any of you renounce the faith, Allah will replace them by others who love Him and are loved by Him, humble towards the faithful and stern towards the unbelievers, striving for Allah's cause and fearless of man's censure. Such is the grace of Allah: He bestows it on whom He will. He is Munificent, Knowing.

Sura: 5, Ayat: 54.

Your only supporters and protectors are Allah, His Apostle, and the faithful: those who attend to their prayers, pay their alms-tax, and kneel down in worship. Those who seek the support of Allah, His Apostle, and the faithful (must know) that Allah's followers are sure to triumph.

Sura: 5, Ayat: 55-56.

Believers, Jews, Sabaeans, and Christians — whoever believes in Allah and the Last Day and does what is right — shall have nothing to fear or to regret.

Sura: 5, Ayat: 69.

Why should we not believe in Allah and in the truth that has come down to us? Why should we not hope for admission among the righteous? And for their words Allah has rewarded them with gardens watered by running streams, where they shall dwell for ever. Such is the recompense of the righteous.

Sura: 5, Ayat: 84-85.

When those that believe in Our revelations come to you, say: 'Peace be upon you. Your Lord has decreed mercy on Himself. If anyone of you commits evil through ignorance and then repents and mends his ways, then He is Forgiving, Merciful.'

Sura: 6, Ayat: 54.

Those that have faith and do not taint their faith with wrongdoing shall surely have security, and follow the right path.

Sura: 6, Ayat: 82.

If Allah wills to guide a man, He opens his bosom to Islam. But if He pleases to leave him in error, He makes his bosom tight and constricted as though he were climbing up to the sky. Thus Allah heaps the penalty on the unbelievers.

Such is the path of your Lord, a straight path. We have made plain Our revelations for those people who take heed. Theirs is the abode of peace with their Lord. He will give them His protection in reward for what they do.

Sura: 6, Ayat: 125—127.

Say: 'Come, I will tell you what your Lord has made binding on you: that you shall serve no other gods besides Him; that you shall show kindness to your parents; that you shall not kill your children because you cannot support them; We provide for you and for them; that you shall not commit foul sins, whether openly or in secret; and that you shall not kill — for that is forbidden by Allah — except for a just cause. Thus Allah exhorts you, that you may learn wisdom.

Do not touch the property of orphans, but strive to improve their lot until they reach maturity. Give just weight and full measure; We never charge a soul with more than it can bear. Speak for justice, even if it affects your own kinsmen. Be true to the convenant of Allah. Thus He exhorts you, so that you may take heed.

This path of Mine is straight. Follow it and do not follow other paths, for they will lead you away from Him. Thus Allah commands you, so that you may guard yourselves against evil.

Sura: 6, Ayat: 151—153.

As for those that have faith and do good works—We never charge a soul with more than it can bear — they are the people of Paradise, and there they shall abide for ever.

Sura: 7, Ayat: 42.

....God replied: I will visit My punishment to whom I please: yet My mercy encompasses all things. I will show mercy to those that keep from evil, give the alms-tax, and believe in Our signs.

Sura: 7, Ayat: 156.

As for those that strictly observe the Book and are steadfast in prayer, We do not waste the reward of the righteous.

Sura: 7, Ayat: 170.

He whom Allah guides is rightly guided, but he whom Allah leaves in error shall surely be lost.

Sura: 7, Ayat: 178.

Among those whom We created there are some who give true guidance and act justly.

Sura: 7, Ayat: 181.

The true believers are those whose hearts are filled with awe at the mention of Allah, and whose faith grows stronger as they listen to His revelations. They are those who put their trust in their Lord, pray steadfastly, and spend of that which We have given them.

Sura: 8, Ayat: 2-3.

The true believers, both men and women, are friends to each other. They enjoin what is just and forbid what is evil; they attend to their prayers and pay the alms-tax and obey Allah and His Apostle. On these Allah will have mercy. He is Mighty, Wise.

Allah has promised the men and women, who believe in Him, gardens watered by running streams, in which they shall abide for ever. He has promised them goodly mansions in the gardens of Eden. And what is more, they shall have a greater favour from Allah. That is the supreme triumph.

Sura: 9, Ayat: 71-72.

Yet there are other desert Arabs who believe in Allah and the Last Day, and regard what they spend as a means of bringing them close to Allah and to the prayers of the Apostle. Indeed, it shall bring them nearer to Allah; Allah will admit them to His mercy. He is Forgiving, Merciful.

Sura: 9, Ayat: 99.

The vanguard (of Islam) — The first of those who forsook (their homes) and of those who gave them aid, and (also) those who follow them in (all) good deeds, — well-pleased is God with them, as are they with Him: For them has He prepared Gardens under which rivers flow, to dwell therein for ever: That is the supreme Felicity.

Sura: 9, Ayat: 100.

Allah has purchased of the faithful their lives and worldly goods in return for Paradise. They will fight for His cause, slay, and be slain. Such is the true pledge which He has made them in the Torah, the Gospel and the Quran and who is more true to his promise than Allah? Rejoice then in the bargain you have made. That is the supreme triumph.

Sura: 9, Ayat: 111.

Those that turn (to God) in repentance; that serve Him, and praise Him; that wander in devotion to the cause of God; that bow down and prostrate themselves in prayer; that enjoin good and forbid evil; and observe the limits set by God; — (These do rejoice). So proclaim the glad tidings to the believers.

Sura: 9, Ayat: 112.

As for those that believe and do good works, Allah will guide them because of their faith. Rivers will run beneath them in the Gardens of Delight. Their prayer there will be: 'Glory to You, Lord!' and their greeting: 'Peace!' 'Praise be to Allah, Lord of the Creation,' will be the last of their prayers.

Sura: 10, Ayat: 9-10.

For those that do right is a goodly (reward) and more (than in measure). Neither blackness nor ignominy shall cover their faces. They are the people of Paradise: in it they shall abide for ever.

Sura: 10, Ayat: 26.

Now surely the friends of Allah have nothing to fear or to regret. Those that have faith and keep from evil shall rejoice both in this world and in the next: the word of Allah cannot be changed. That is the supreme triumph.

Sura: 10, Ayat: 62—64.

If We show man Our mercy and then withhold it from him, he yields to despair and becomes ungrateful. And if after adversity We bestow favours upon him, he says: 'Gone are my sorrows from me,' and grows jubilant and boastful.

Except those who are steadfast and do good works. They shall have forgiveness and a rich reward.

Sura: 11, Ayat: 9—11

Those that have faith and do good works and humble themselves before their Lord, they are the people of Paradise, and there they shall abide for ever.

Sura: 11, Ayat: 23.

....For I have left the faith of those that disbelieve in Allah and deny the life to come. I follow the faith of my fathers, Ibrahim, Ishaq, and Yaqub. We must never serve any besides Allah. Such is the gift which Allah has bestowed upon us and all mankind. Yet most men do not give thanks.

My two fellow-prisoners! Are sundry gods better than Allah, the One, the Conqueror? Those whom you serve besides Him are nothing but names which you and your fathers have invented and for which Allah has revealed no sanction. Judgement rests with Allah only. He has commanded you to worship none but Him. That is the true faith: yet most men do not know.

Sura: 12, Ayat: 37–40.

....We bestow Our mercy on whom We will, and never deny the righteous their reward. Better is the reward of the life to come for those who believe in Allah and keep from evil.

Sura: 12, Ayat: 56-57.

Is then he who knows that what has been revealed to you by your Lord is the truth, like him who is blind?

Truly, it is those who are endued with understanding that receive admonition; those who keep faith with Allah and do not break their pledge; who join together what He has bidden to be united; who fear their Lord and dread the terrors of Reckoning-day and those who for the sake of Allah endure with fortitude, attend to their prayers, and spend of what We have given them secretly and openly and who ward off evil with good. These shall have a blissful end. They shall enter the Gardens of Eden, together with the righteous among their fathers, their wives, and their descendants. From every gate the angels will come to them (saying): 'Peace be to you for all that you have steadfastly endured. Blessed is the final reward (of Paradise).'

Sura: 13, Ayat: 19–24.

Surely in the remembrance of Allah all hearts are comforted. Blessed are those who have faith and do good works; blissful their end.'

Sura: 13, Ayat: 28-29.

But those that have faith and do good works, they shall be admitted to gardens watered by running streams, in which, by their Lord's leave, they shall abide for ever. Their greeting shall be: 'Peace!'

Sura: 14, Ayat: 23.

God will establish in strength those who believe, with the Word that stands firm, in this world and in the Hereafter; but God will leave, to stray, those who do wrong: Allah accomplishes what He pleases.

Sura: 14, Ayat: 27.

But the righteous shall dwell amongst gardens and fountains (Their greeting will be): "Enter here in peace and security". We shall remove all hatred from their hearts, and they shall recline on couches face to face, a band of brothers. Toil shall not weary them there, nor shall they ever be removed from it.'

Sura: 15, Ayat: 45.

(When) it is said to those who guard against evil: 'What has your Lord revealed?' they will reply: 'That which is best.' Good is the reward of those that do good works in this present life: but far better is the reward of the life to come. Blessed is the dwelling place of the righteous. They shall enter the Gardens of Eden. Rivers shall roll at their feet, and they shall have there all they desire. Thus shall the righteous be rewarded.

The angels will say to those whom they cause to die in purity: 'Peace be on you. Come into Paradise for what you did.'

Sura: 16, Ayat: 30—32.

Be they men or women, those that embrace the faith and do what is right We will surely grant a good and pure life; We shall reward them according to their noblest actions.

Sura: 16, Ayat: 97.

Allah is with those who keep from evil and do good (to others).

Sura: 16, Ayat: 128.

As for those that have faith and do good works, We waste not the reward of him who does good work. They shall dwell in the Gardens of Eden, with rivers rolling at their feet. They shall be decked with bracelets of gold and adorned in green garments of silk and rich brocade, reclining therein on couches; blissful their reward and happy their resting-place!

Sura: 18, Ayat: 30-31.

As for those who have faith and do good works, they shall dwell in the gardens of Paradise. There (they shall dwell) for ever desiring not to be removed to any other place.

Sura: 18, Ayat: 107-108.

But those that repent and embrace the Faith and do what is right shall be admitted to Paradise and shall not be wronged in any way.

Sura: 19, Ayat: 60.

Allah will increase the guidance of those that have followed the right path. Deeds of lasting merit shall earn you a better reward in His sight and a more auspicious end.

Sura: 19, Ayat: 76.

On those who accepted the true faith and do righteous deeds, the Compassionate will bestow love.

Sura: 19, Ayat: 96.

He that comes before his Lord laden with sin shall be consigned to Hell, where he shall neither die nor live. But he that comes before Him with true faith and good works shall be exalted to the highest rank. He shall abide for ever in the Gardens of Eternity, in gardens watered by running streams. Such shall be the recompense of those that purify themselves.'

Sura: 20, Ayat: 74—76.

But those who have believed and done good works shall fear neither inequity nor injustice.

Sura: 20, Ayat: 112.

He said: 'Get you down, both of you,—all together, from the Garden, with enmity one to another: but if, as is sure, there comes to you Guidance from Me, whosoever follows My guidance, will not lose his way, nor fall into misery.

But whosoever turns away from My Message, verily for him is a life narrowed down, and We shall raise him up blind on the Day of Judgement.'

Sura: 20, Ayat: 123-124.

But those to whom We have already shown Our favour shall be far removed from it. They shall not hear its roar, but shall delight for ever in what their souls desire.

The Supreme Terror shall not grieve them, and the angels will receive them (saying): 'This is the day you have been promised.'

Sura: 21, Ayat: 101—103.

We wrote in the Psalms after the Message had been given: 'The righteous among My servants shall inherit the earth.' Verily in this is a message to those who serve Us.

Sura: 21, Ayat: 105-106.

As for those who have faith and do good works, Allah will admit them to gardens watered by running streams. Allah indeed does what He pleases.

Sura: 22, Ayat: 14.

God will admit those that have faith and do good works to gardens watered

by running streams. They shall be adorned therein with bracelets of gold and pearls; and their garments there will be of silk. For they have been guided (in this life) to the purest of speeches; they have been guided to the Path of Him who is Worthy of (all) Praise.

Sura: 22, Ayat: 23-24.

....He that reveres Allah's rites, surely, it is from the piety of the hearts.

Sura: 22, Ayat: 32.

....Give good news to those who humble themselves, whose hearts are filled with awe at the mention of their Lord; who endure their misfortunes with fortitudes, attend to their prayers, and bestow in charity of that which We have given them.

Sura: 22, Ayat: 34-35.

Allah will defend the true believers (against evil). Verily God does not love the treacherous and the thankless.

Sura: 22, Ayat: 38.

(They are) those, who if We establish them in the land, establish regular prayer and give regular charity, enjoin the right and forbid wrong: With God rests the end (and decision) of (all) affairs.

Sura: 22, Ayat: 41.

Say: 'O men, I have been sent to warn you plainly. Those that accept the true faith and do good works shall be forgiven and richly rewarded; but those who seek to confute Our revelations shall be the people of Hell.'

Sura: 22, Ayat: 49—51.

And so that those to whom knowledge has been given may realize that this (Quran) is the truth from your Lord and thus believe in it and that their hearts may submit to it. Verily Allah will surely guide the faithful to a straight path.

Sura: 22, Ayat: 54.

Successful indeed are the believers, who are humble in their prayers; who turn away from vain talk; who give alms; who restrain themselves from sexual desires, except with their spouses — that is, those whom they rightfully possess, for these are lawful to them. Those who go beyond that are transgressors. (Successful also are those) who are true to their trusts and pledges and those who strictly guard their prayers. These are the heirs who will inherit Paradise; they shall abide there for ever.

Sura: 23, Ayat: 1—11.

Those who live in fear of their Lord; who believe in the revelations of their

Lord; who worship none besides their Lord; who give what they give with their hearts filled with awe, (knowing) that they will return to their Lord: these hasten to good things and are the first to attain them.

Sura: 23, Ayat: 57—61.

(His light is found) in houses which Allah has sanctioned to be exalted and to have therein His name glorified. In them morning and evening His praise is sung by men whom neither trade nor sale can divert from remembering Him, from offering prayers, or from giving alms; who dread the day when men's hearts and eyes shall be troubled; (who hope) that Allah will requite them for their noblest deeds and lavish His grace upon them. Allah gives without measure to whom He will.

Sura: 24, Ayat: 36—38.

But when true believers are called to Allah and His Apostle that he may pass judgement upon them, their only reply is: 'We hear and obey.' Such men shall surely prosper.

Those who obey Allah and His Apostles, those that revere Allah and fear Him, shall surely triumph.

Sura: 24, Ayat: 51-52.

Allah has promised those of you who believe and do good works to make them masters in the land as He had made their ancestors before them, to strengthen the Faith He chose for them, and to change their fear to safety. Let them worship Me and serve no other gods besides Me. Wicked indeed are they who after this deny Me.

Sura: 24, Ayat: 55.

The believers are only those who have faith in Allah and His Apostle, and who, when gathered with him upon a matter which concerns the whole community, do not depart till they have begged his leave. The men who ask your leave are those who truly believe in Allah and His Apostle. When they ask your leave to go away on some business of their own, grant it to whomever you please and implore Allah to forgive them; Allah is Forgiving, Merciful.

Sura: 24, Ayat: 62.

Say: 'Which is better, this or the Paradise of Immortality which the righteous have been promised? It is their recompense and their resort. Abiding there for ever, they shall find in it all that they desire. That is a promise given by Allah, to be prayed for!

Sura: 25, Ayat: 15-16.

The true servants of the Merciful are those who walk humbly on the earth, and when the ignorant address them they say: 'Peace!'; who pass the night

standing and on their knees in adoration of their Lord; who say: 'Lord, ward off from us the punishment of Hell, for its punishment is everlasting: an evil dwelling and an evil resting-place'; who when they spend are neither extravagant nor niggardly, but keep the golden mean; who invoke no other god besides Allah and do not kill the soul which God has forbidden except for a just cause; who do not commit adultery. For he that does this shall meet with evil: his punishment shall be doubled on the Day of Resurrection, and he shall abide therein for ever in disgrace, unless he repent and believe and do good works, for then Allah will change his sins to good actions: Allah is ever Forgiving and Merciful. He that repents and does good works truly returns to Allah.

Sura: 25, Ayat: 63—71.

(And the true servants are those) who do not bear false witness and when they listen to profane chatter, they pass on with dignity.

Sura: 25, Ayat: 72.

Who do not turn a blind eye and a deaf ear to the revelations of their Lord when they are reminded of them.

Sura: 25, Ayat: 73.

Those who pray, 'Our Lord! Grant to us wives and offspring who will be the comfort of our eyes, and give us (the grace) to lead the righteous.'

Sura: 25, Ayat: 74.

Say: 'Praise be to Allah and peace upon His servants whom He has chosen!. ...

Sura: 27, Ayat: 59.

Those that have done good shall be rewarded with what is better, and shall be secure from the terrors of that day.

Sura: 27, Ayat: 89.

(Say): 'I am bidden to serve the Lord of this City, which He has made sacred. All things are His.

'I am commanded to surrender to Him, and to rehearse the Quran. He that takes the right path shall himself have much to gain.'

To him who goes astray, say 'I am only a warner.'

Sura: 27, Ayat: 91-92.

Those to whom We gave the Book before, are believers in it. When it is recited to them, they say: 'We believe in it because it is the truth from Our Lord. We surrendered ourselves to Him before it came.'

Twice shall their reward be given them, because they have endured, repelling evil with good and giving in alms a part of that which We bestowed on

them.

Sura: 28, Ayat: 53-54.

Because they pay no heed to vain talk, but say: 'We have our deeds and you have yours. Peace be upon you. We do not seek (the company of) ignorant men.'

Sura: 28, Ayat: 55.

You cannot guide whom you please: it is Allah who guides whom He will. He best knows those who yield to guidance.

Sura: 28, Ayat: 56.

On that day (Allah) will call to them saying: 'What answer did you give Our Apostles?' And on that day such will their confusion be that they will ask no questions. But any that (in this life) had repented, believed, and worked righteousness, will have hopes to be among those who achieve salvation.

Sura: 28, Ayat: 65—67.

As for the abode of the Hereafter, we shall assign it to those who seek neither glory in this world nor evil. The blessed end is for the righteous.

Sura: 28, Ayat: 83.

As for those who have faith and do good works, We shall cleanse them of their sins and reward them according to their noblest deeds.

Sura: 29, Ayat: 7.

Those that accept the true faith and do good works shall be included among the righteous.

Sura: 29, Ayat: 9.

Those that embrace the true faith and do good works shall be for ever lodged in the mansions of Paradise, where rivers will roll at their feet. Blessed is the reward of those who labour patiently and put their trust in Allah.

Sura: 29, Ayat: 58-59.

Those who fight for Our cause, We will surely guide to Our own paths. Allah is with the righteous.

Sura: 29, Ayat: 69.

Those who have believed and done good works shall rejoice in a fair garden.

Sura: 30, Ayat: 15.

These are the revelations of the Wise Book, a guidance and a blessing to the

righteous, who attend to their prayers, pay the alms-tax, and firmly believe in the life to come. These are rightly guided by their Lord and will surely prosper.

Sura: 31, Ayat: 2—5.

(But) those who have faith and do good works shall enter the Gardens of Delight.

Sura: 31, Ayat: 8.

Whoever submits his whole self to God, and is a doer of good, has grasped indeed the most trustworthy hand-hold: and with God rests the End and Decision of (all) affairs.

Sura: 31, Ayat: 22.

None believes in Our revelations save those who, when reminded of them, prostrate themselves in adoration and give glory to their Lord in all humility; who forsake their beds to pray to their Lord in fear and hope; who give in charity of that which We have bestowed on them.

Sura: 32, Ayat: 15-16.

Those that have faith and do good works shall be received in Gardens of hospitable Homes as a reward for that which they have done.

Sura: 32, Ayat: 19.

Among the believers there are men who have been true to their covenant with God. Some have died, and others await their end, yielding to no change (in their determination) so that Allah may reward the truthful for their truthfulness and sternly punish the hypocrites—or show them mercy if He will: Allah is Forgiving and Merciful.

Sura: 33, Ayat: 23-24.

For Muslim men and women, for believing men and women; for devout men and women; for men and women who are patient; for men and women who humble themselves; for men and women who give charity; for men and women who fast; for men and women who guard their chastity; and for men and women who remember Allah much—for them all has God prepared forgiveness and a great reward.

Sura: 33, Ayat: 35.

Announce to the believers the good tidings that Allah has bounteous blessings in store for them. Do not obey the unbelievers and the hypocrites: disregard their insolence.

Put your trust in Allah; Allah is your All-sufficient Guardian.

Sura: 33, Ayat: 47-48.

Believers, fear Allah and speak the truth. He will bless your virtues and forgive you your sins. He who obeys Allah and His Apostle shall win a great victory.

Sura: 33, Ayat: 70-71.

Neither your riches nor your children shall bring you nearer to Us. But only those that have faith and do what is right—those shall be doubly rewarded for their deeds: they shall dwell in peace in the mansions (of Paradise).

Sura: 34, Ayat: 37.

The unbelievers shall be sternly punished, but those that accept the true faith and do good works shall be forgiven and richly rewarded.

Sura: 35, Ayat: 7.

....You shall admonish none but those who fear their Lord though they cannot see Him, and are steadfast in prayer. He that purifies himself has much to gain. To Allah shall all things return.

Sura: 35, Ayat: 18.

Those who recite the Book of Allah and attend to their prayers and give alms in private and in public may hope for a commerce that will never fail. Allah will give them their rewards and enrich them from His own abundance. He is Forgiving and Rewarding.

Sura: 35, Ayat: 29-30.

Then We gave the Book as inheritance to those of our servants whom We have chosen. Some of them wrong their souls, some follow a middle course, and some, by Allah's leave, vie with each other in good works: this is the supreme virtue.

Sura: 35, Ayat: 32.

You shall admonish only him who follows the Reminder and fears the Merciful, though he cannot see Him. To him give news of pardon and a rich reward.

Sura: 36, Ayat: 11.

Say: 'My servants who believe, fear your Lord. Those who do good works in this life shall receive a good reward. Allah's earth is vast. Those that endure with fortitude shall be requited without measure.'

Sura: 39, Ayat: 10.

But let those rejoice who keep off from idol-worship and turn to Allah in repentance. Give good news to My servants, who listen to My Word and fol-

low what is best in it. These are they whom Allah has guided. These are they who are endued with understanding.

Sura: 39, Ayat: 17-18.

As for those who truly fear their Lord, they shall dwell in mansions above mansions beneath which are running streams. Such is Allah's promise: He will not fail His promise.

Sura: 39, Ayat: 20.

And he who brings the truth, and he who believes in it—they surely are the God-fearing. Their Lord will give them all that they desire. Thus shall the righteous be rewarded.

Thus Allah will do away with their foulest deeds and reward them according to their noblest actions.

Sura: 39, Ayat: 33—35.

But Allah will deliver those who fear Him, for they have earned salvation. No harm shall touch them, nor shall they ever grieve.

Sura: 39, Ayat: 61.

And those who fear their Lord shall be led in companies to Paradise. When they draw near, its gates will be opened, and its keepers will say to them: 'Peace be to you: you have been good men. Enter Paradise and dwell in it for ever.'

Sura: 39, Ayat: 73.

....but those that have faith and do good works, both men and women, shall enter the Gardens of Paradise and receive blessings without number.

Sura: 40, Ayat: 40.

Those who say: 'Our Lord is Allah,' and take the right path to Him, the angels will descend on them (saying): 'Let nothing alarm or grieve you. Rejoice in the Paradise you have been promised. We are your guardians in this world and in the next. You shall find there all that your souls desire and all that you can ask for: a rich provision from the Forgiving, the Merciful.

Sura: 41, Ayat: 30—32.

And who speaks better than he who calls others to the service of Allah, does what is right, and says: 'I am one of the Muslims.'

Sura: 41, Ayat: 33.

....But those that have faith and do good works shall dwell in the meadows of gardens and receive from their Lord all that they desire. Surely this is the

supreme boon.

Sura: 42, Ayat: 22.

He hears the prayer of those who have faith and do good works and gives them more of His bounty. ...

Sura: 42, Ayat: 26.

That which you have been given is but the fleeting comfort of this life. Better and more enduring is that which Allah has for those who believe and put their trust in Him; who avoid gross sins and indecencies and, when angered, are willing to forgive, who obey their Lord, attend to their prayers, and conduct their affairs by mutal consultation; who spend out of what We bestow on them for Sustenance, and when oppressed, seek to redress their wrongs.

Sura: 42, Ayat: 36–39.

But my servants, there is no fear for you this day, nor will you grieve – you who believed in Our signs and surrendered themselves. Enter Paradise, you and your spouses, in all delight.

Sura: 43, Ayat: 68–70.

As for the righteous, they shall be in peace together amidst gardens and fountains, dressed in fine silk and in rich brocade, they will face each other.

Sura: 44, Ayat: 51–53.

Tell the believers to pardon those who do not look forward to the days of Allah, so that He may recompense men according to their deeds. He that does what is right does it to his own advantage; and he that commits evil does so at his own peril. To your Lord you shall all return.

Sura: 45, Ayat: 14-15.

And now, We have set you on the right path. Follow it and do not yield to the desires of ignorant men.

Sura: 45, Ayat: 18.

As for those who have faith and do good works, their Lord will admit them into His mercy. That shall be a manifest triumph.

Sura: 45, Ayat: 30.

Those who say: 'Our God is Allah,' and follow the straight path shall have nothing to fear or to regret. They shall for ever dwell in Paradise as a reward for what they did.

Sura: 46, Ayat: 13-14.

We have enjoined man to show kindness to his parents. With much pain his

mother bears him, and with much pain she brings him into the world. He is born and weaned in thirty months. When he grows to manhood and attains his fortieth year, let him say: Grant me, Lord, that I may give thanks for the favours You have bestowed on me and on my parents, and to do good works that will please You. Grant me good descendants. To You I turn and to You I surrender myself.'

Such are those from whom We will accept their noblest works and whose misdeeds We shall overlook. (We shall include them) among the people of Paradise: true is the promise that has been given them.

Sura: 46, Ayat: 15-16.

As for the faithful who do good works and believe in what is revealed to Muhammad—which is the truth from their Lord—He will efface from them their (past) bad deeds and will set their hearts at rest.

Sura: 47, Ayat: 2.

Allah will admit those, who believe and do good works, to gardens watered by running streams. The unbelievers take their fill of pleasure and eat as the cattle eat: but Hell shall be their home.

Sura: 47, Ayat: 12.

As for those who follow the right path, Allah will increase their guidance and bestow on them their righteousness.

Sura: 47, Ayat: 17.

....His are the forces of the heavens and the earth. Allah is Wise and All-knowing.

(He has done this) so that He may also bring the believers, both men and women, into gardens watered by running streams, there to abide for ever; that He may forgive them their sins, which is in Allah's sight a great triumph, (for man).

Sura: 48, Ayat: 4-5.

Muhammad is Allah's Apostle. Those who are with him are strong against unbelievers but merciful to one another. You see them bow and prostrate themselves, seeking the grace of Allah and His good will. Their marks are on their faces, the traces of their prostrations. Thus they are described in the Torah and in the Gospal: (they are) like the seed which puts forth its shoot and strengthens it, so that it rises stout and firm upon its stalk, delighting the sowers. Through them Allah seeks to enrage the unbelievers. God has promised those of them who will believe and do good works forgiveness and a rich reward.

Sura: 48, Ayat: 29.

The true believers are those who have faith in Allah and His Apostle and never doubt; and who fight for His cause with their wealth and persons. Such are the truthful ones.

Sura: 49, Ayat: 15.

And Paradise, not far off, shall be brought close to the righteous. (We shall say to them): 'Here is all that you were promised. It is for every penitent and faithful man who fears the Merciful, though He is unseen, and comes before Him with a contrite heart. Enter it in peace. This is a Day of Eternal Life.'

Sura: 50, Ayat: 31—34.

As to the righteous, they will be in the midst of Gardens and Springs, taking joy in the things which their Lord gives them, because, before then, they lived a good life. They were in the habit of sleeping but little by night, and in the hours of early dawn, they (were found) praying for Forgiveness; and in their wealth and possessions (was remembered) the right of the (needy), him who asked, and him who (for some reason) was prevented (from asking).

Sura: 51, Ayat: 15—19.

Those who believe and are followed in faith by their descendants, We cause their descendants to join them. And We deprive them of nothing of their work. Every individual is pledged for what he does.

Sura: 52, Ayat: 21.

'When we were living among our kinsfolk, 'they will say, 'We were not without fear for the sake of our people. But Allah has been gracious to us and has preserved us from the Scorching Wind. Truly we have prayed to Him. He is the Beneficent One, the Merciful.'

Sura: 52, Ayat: 26—28.

The righteous are in gardens and rivers, honourably seated in the presence of a Mighty King.

Sura: 54, Ayat: 54-55.

Is it not time for true believers to submit to Allah's warning and to the truth He has revealed, so that they may not be like those who were given the Scriptures before this, whose days were prolonged and whose hearts were hardened? Many of them were evildoers.

Sura: 57, Ayat: 16.

You shall find no believers in Allah and the Last Day on friendly terms with those who oppose Allah and His Apostle, even though they be their fathers, their sons, their brothers, or their kindred. Allah has written the faith in their very hearts and strengthened them with a spirit of His own. He will admit

them to gardens watered by running streams, where they shall dwell for ever. Allah is well pleased with them and they with Him. They are the party of Allah: and Allah's party shall surely triumph.

Sura: 58, Ayat: 22.

O Prophet, if believing women come to you and pledge themselves to associate in worship nothing with Allah, to commit neither theft, nor adultery, nor child-murder, to utter no monstrous falsehoods (concerning the fatherhood of their children), and to disobey you in any just matter, accept their allegiance and implore Allah to forgive them. Allah is Forgiving and Merciful.

Sura: 60, Ayat: 12.

....That shall be a day of mutual loss and gain. Those who believe in Allah and do what is right shall be forgiven their sins and admitted to gardens watered by running streams, where they shall dwell for ever. That is the supreme triumph.

Sura: 64, Ayat: 9.

No misfortune befalls except by Allah's will. He who believes in Allah, Allah guides his heart. Allah has knowledge of all things.

Sura: 64, Ayat: 11.

....And for those who fear God, He (ever) prepares a way out.
And He provides for him from (sources) he never could imagine. And if any one puts his trust in God, sufficient is (God) for him. For God will surely accomplish His purpose: Verily, for all things has God appointed a due proportion.

Sura: 65, Ayat: 2-3.

....Allah will ease the hardship of the man who fears Him.
Such is the commandment which Allah has revealed to you. He who fears Allah shall be forgiven his sins and richly rewarded.

Sura: 65, Ayat: 4-5.

....He who believes in Allah and does good works shall be admitted to gardens watered by running streams where he shall dwell for ever. Allah has made for him a generous provision.

Sura: 65, Ayat: 11.

But to the faithful Allah has given as example Pharaoh's wife, who said: 'Lord, build me a house with You in Paradise and deliver me from Pharaoh and his misdeeds. Deliver me from a wicked nation.'

Sura: 66, Ayat: 11.

But those that fear their Lord, although they cannot see Him, shall be forgiven and richly rewarded.

Sura: 67, Ayat: 12.

He who is given his book in his right hand will say: 'Ah here! Read my record I knew that I shall meet my account.' His shall be a blissful state in a lofty garden, with clusters of fruit within reach. (We shall say to him): 'Eat and drink to your heart's content because of what you did in days gone by.'

Sura: 69, Ayat: 19—24.

Indeed, man was created impatient. When evil befalls him he is despondent; but blessed with good fortune he grows niggardly.

Not so the worshippers who are steadfast in prayer; who set aside a due portion of their goods for the needy and the dispossessed; who truly believe in the Day of Reckoning and dread the punishment of their Lord, for none is secure from the punishment of their Lord; who restrain their carnal desire save for their wives and what their right hands possess, for these are lawful to them; he who lusts after other than these is a transgressor; who keep their trusts and promises and bear true witness; and who attend to their prayers with promptitude. These shall be laden with honours and shall dwell in fair gardens.

Sura: 70, Ayat: 19—35.

No, verily they have no fear of the Hereafter.

No, this is an admonition. Let him who will, take heed. But none takes heed except by the will of Allah. He is the Lord of Goodness and Forgiveness.

Sura: 74, Ayat: 53—56.

They who keep their vows and dread the far-spread terrors of the Day (of judgement), who, (on account of their love for Him,) give sustenance to the poor man, the orphan and the captive (Saying):'We feed you for Allah's sake only; we seek of you neither recompense nor thanks: for we fear from Him a day of anguish and of woe.

So Allah will deliver them from the evil of that Day and make their faces shine with joy.

Sura: 76, Ayat: 7—11.

The righteous shall dwell amidst cool shades and fountains and feed on such fruits as they desire. (We shall say to them): 'Eat and drink, and may every joy attend you! This is the reward of your labours.' Thus We shall reward the righteous.

Woe on that day to the disbelievers!

Sura: 77, Ayat: 41—45.

Those who feared to stand before their Lord and curbed their souls' desires shall dwell in Paradise.

Sura: 79, Ayat: 40-41.

The righteous surely shall dwell in bliss.

Sura: 82, Ayat: 13.

But on that day the faithful will mock the unbelievers as they recline upon their couches and gaze around them.
Shall (not) the unbelievers be rewarded according to their deeds?

Sura: 83, Ayat: 34—36.

Those who embrace the true faith and do good works; for theirs is an unfailing recompense.

Sura: 84, Ayat: 25.

Happy shall be the man who purifies himself, who remembers the name of his Lord and prays to Him.

Sura: 87, Ayat: 14-15.

(God will say): "O you human being who have attained inner peace! Return to your Lord joyful and well-pleased in His sight. Enter Paradise with My devotees."

Sura: 89, Ayat: 27—30.

But he would not try to ascend the steep uphill road.... And what could make you conceive what it is, that steep uphill road? It is the freeing of a bondsman; the feeding, in the day of famine, of an orphaned relation or a needy man in distress; to be one of those who believe, enjoin patience and deeds of kindness and compassion. Such are the companions of the Right Hand.

Sura: 90, Ayat: 11—18.

By the Soul, and the proportion and order given to it; and its enlightenment as to its wrong and its right: Truly he succeeds that purifies it, and he fails that corrupts it!

Sura: 91, Ayat: 7—10.

Your endeavours have different ends!
For him that gives (in charity) and guards himself (by obeying Allah) and believes in goodness, We shall smooth the path of salvation.

Sura: 92, Ayat: 4—7.

It is for Us to give guidance. To Us belong (the dominion over) the life of

this world and the life to come. I warn you, then of the blazing fire, in which none shall burn save the hardened sinner, who denies the truth and turns his back. But kept away from it will be the most devoted who gives in alms but not in return for any favour done to him, and who also does good only for the sake of the reward of God, Most High. Verily, he will be content.

Sura: 92, Ayat: 12—21.

We created man with the most noble image and in the end We shall reduce him to the lowest of the low: except the believers who do good works, for theirs shall be a recompense never to be cut off.

Sura: 95, Ayat: 4—6.

Yet they were enjoined nothing but to serve Allah offering Him sincere devotion, to attend to their prayers and to pay the alms-tax. That, surely, is the true faith.

Sura: 98, Ayat: 5.

But those that embrace the faith and do good works are the noblest of all creatures. Allah will reward them with the Gardens of Eden, gardens watered by running streams, where they shall dwell for ever.

Allah is well pleased with them and they with Him. Thus shall the God-fearing be rewarded.

Sura: 98, Ayat: 7-8.

Man is in loss, except those who believe and do good works and exhort one another to truth and to patience.

Sura: 103, Ayat: 2-3.

In the name of Allah, The Compassionate, The Merciful

FEAR OF DIVINE DISPLEASURE

It is only the Evil One that instils in you the fear of his allies: But have no fear of them. Fear Me, if you are true believers.

Sura: 3, Ayat: 175.

As for those that fear their Lord, theirs shall be gardens watered by running streams in which they shall abide forever, and a goodly welcome from their Lord. Allah's reward is surely better for the righteous.

Sura: 3, Ayat: 198.

O believers, be patient and let your patience never be exhausted. Vie in such perseverance; strengthen each other and fear Allah, so that you may triumph.

Sura: 3, Ayat: 200.

Men, have fear of your Lord, who created you from a single soul. From that soul He created its mate, and through them He bestrewed the earth with countless men and women.

Fear Allah, in whose name you plead with one another, and honour the mothers who bore you. Allah is ever watching over you.

Sura: 4, Ayat: 1.

....We have enjoined those to whom the Book was given before you and (enjoin) you to fear Allah. If you deny Him, know that to Allah belongs all that the heavens and the earth contain. He is Self-sufficient and Praiseworthy.

Sura: 4, Ayat: 131.

....The unbelievers have this day despaired of (vanquishing) your religion. Have no fear of them: fear Me. ...

Sura: 5, Ayat: 3.

O believers, be dutiful to Allah and bearers of just witness. Do not allow your hatred for other men to turn you away from justice. Deal justly: justice

is nearer to true piety. Have fear of Allah; He is cognizant of what you do.
Sura: 5, Ayat: 8.

....Have fear of Allah. In Allah let the faithful put their trust.
Sura: 5, Ayat: 11.

Believers, have fear of Allah and seek the means by which you get His favour. Strive with might for His cause, so that you may triumph.
Sura: 5, Ayat: 35.

....Have no fear of people; fear Me, and do not take a small price for my revelations. Unbelievers are those who do not judge in accordance with Allah's revelations.
Sura: 5, Ayat: 44.

Say: 'I will never disobey my Lord, for I fear the torment of a fateful day.'
He who is delivered (from the torment) of that day shall have received Allah's mercy. That is the glorious triumph.
Sura: 6, Ayat: 15-16.

The true believers are those whose hearts are filled with awe at the mention of Allah, and whose faith grows stronger as they listen to His revelations. They are those who put their trust in their Lord, pray steadfastly, and spend of that which We have given them.
Sura: 8, Ayat: 2-3.

O you who believe! If you fear God, He will grant you a criterion (to judge between right and wrong), and efface from you your sins (That may afflict) you, and forgive you: For God is the Lord of grace unbounded.
Sura: 8, Ayat: 29.

O believers, have fear of Allah and stand with the truthful.
Sura: 9, Ayat: 119.

We showed Musa and Harun the criterion (to distinguish between right and wrong), and gave them a light and a message for the righteous; those who fear their Lord in secret and dread the terrors of Judgement-day.
Sura: 21, Ayat: 48-49.

For every nation We have ordained a ritual, that they may pronounce the name of Allah over the animals which He has given them (for food). Your God is one God; to Him surrender yourselves. Give good news to the humble, whose hearts are filled with awe at the mention of their Lord; who endure their misfortunes with fortitude, attend to their prayers, and bestow in

charity of that which We have given them.

Sura: 22, Ayat: 34-35.

Do not corrupt the land with evil. Fear Him who created you and those who have gone before you.

Sura: 26, Ayat: 183-184.

Men, fear your Lord, and fear the day when no parent shall avail his child nor any child his parent. Allah's promise is surely true. Let the life of this world not deceive you, nor let the Chief Deceiver deceive you about God.

Sura: 31, Ayat: 33.

O Prophet, have fear of Allah, and do not listen to the unbelievers and the hypocrites. Allah is Wise and All-Knowing.

Obey what is revealed to you from your Lord, for Allah is cognizant of all your actions.

Sura: 33, Ayat: 1-2.

Believers, fear Allah and speak the truth. He will bless your works and forgive you your sins. He who obeys Allah and His Apostle shall win a great victory.

Sura: 33, Ayat: 70-71.

Say: 'My servants who believe, fear your Lord. Those who do good works in this life shall receive a good reward. Allah's earth is vast. Those that endure with fortitude shall be requited without measure.'

Sura: 39, Ayat: 10.

Say: 'I fear, if I disobey my Lord, the torment of a fateful day.'

Sura: 39, Ayat: 13.

Turn in repentance to your Lord and surrender yourselves to Him before His scourge overtakes you, for then you will not be helped. Follow the best of what is revealed to you from your Lord before His scourge overtakes you unawares, without warning; lest any soul should say: 'Alas! I have disobeyed Allah and scoffed at His revelations.' Or 'If Allah had guided me I would have been one of the righteous.' Or, when it sees the punishment should say: 'Could I but live again, I would lead a righteous life.' For Allah will say: 'My revelations had come to you, but you denied them. You were arrogant and one of the unbelievers.'

Sura: 39, Ayat: 54—58.

Believers, have fear of Allah and put your trust in His Apostles. He will grant you a double share of His mercy. He will provide for you a Light by

which you shall walk (straight in your path) and will forgive you: Allah is Forgiving and Merciful.

Let the People of the Book know that they have no control over the gifts of Allah; that these gifts are in His hands alone, and that He vouchsafes them to whom He will. Allah's bounty is infinite.

Sura: 57, Ayat: 28-29.

Believers, have fear of Allah. Let every soul look to what he sends ahead for the morrow. Fear Allah, for He is cognizant of all your actions.

Do not act like those who have forgotten Allah so that He has caused them to forget themselves. Such men are evildoers.

Sura: 59, Ayat: 18-19.

Your wealth and children are but a temptation. Allah's reward is great. Therefore fear Him with all your hearts, and be attentive, obedient and charitable. Give in charity for the benefit of your souls.

Those who are saved from their own greed will surely prosper.

Sura: 64, Ayat: 15-16.

Thus when they fulfil their waiting term, either take them back on equitable terms or part with them on equitable terms; and take for witness two persons from among you, endued with justice, and establish the evidence (as) before God. Such is the admonition given to him who believes in God and the Last Day. And for those who fear God, He (ever) prepares a way out.

And He provides for him from (sources) he never could imagine. And if any one puts his trust in God, sufficient is (God) for him. For God will surely accomplish His purpose: Verily, for all things has God appointed a due portion.

Sura: 65, Ayat: 2-3.

Such is the commandment which Allah has revealed to you. He who fears Allah shall be forgiven his sins and richly rewarded.

Sura: 65, Ayat: 5.

....Have fear of Allah, you men of understanding, who have believed.

Allah has now sent down to you a Reminder.

Sura: 65, Ayat: 10.

But those that fear their Lord, although they cannot see Him, shall be forgiven and richly rewarded.

Sura: 67, Ayat: 12.

Who dread the punishment of their Lord, for none is secure from the punishment of their Lord.

Sura: 70, Ayat: 27-28.

'Go to Pharaoh: he has transgressed all bounds; and say: 'Will you reform youself? I will guide you to your Lord, so that you may have fear of Him.'

Sura: 79, Ayat: 17–19.

But those that embrace the faith and do good works are the noblest of all creatures. Allah will reward them with the Gardens of Eden, gardens watered by running streams, where they shall dwell for ever.

Allah is well pleased with them and they with Him. Thus shall the God-fearing be rewarded.

Sura: 98, Ayat: 7-8.

In the name of Allah, The Compassionate, The Merciful

TRUST IN GOD

Two parties of you became faint-hearted, but Allah was their protector. In Him let the faithful put their trust.

Sura: 3, Ayat: 122.

....And when you are resolved, put your trust in Allah. Allah loves those that trust (in Him).

Sura: 3, Ayat: 159.

If Allah helps you, none can overcome you. If He abandons you, who then can help you? Therefore, in Allah let the faithful put their trust.

Sura: 3, Ayat: 160.

They promise to obey you: but as soon as they leave you, a number of them plot in secret to do otherwise than what you bade them. Allah takes note of all their plots. Therefore let them be, and put your trust in Allah. He is your all-sufficient Guardian.

Sura: 4, Ayat: 81.

And when the hypocrites and the cowards said: 'Their religion has deceived them.' But he that puts his trust in Allah (shall find) Allah Mighty, Wise.

Sura: 8, Ayat: 49.

If they incline to peace, make peace with them, and put your trust in Allah. Surely He is the Hearing, the Knowing.

Sura: 8, Ayat: 61.

Say: 'Nothing will befall us except what Allah has ordained. He is our Guardian. In Allah, let the faithful put their trust.'

Sura: 9, Ayat: 51.

Musa said: 'O my people, if you believe in Allah, in Him put your trust if

you surrender yourselves (to Him).

They said: 'In Allah We have put our trust. Our Lord! make us not a trial for those who practise oppression. Deliver us, through Your mercy, from the unbelievers.'

Sura: 10, Ayat: 84—86.

Allah alone has knowledge of what is unseen in the heavens and in the earth; to Him everything shall be referred. Serve Him, and put your trust in Him. Your Lord is watching over all your actions.

Sura: 11, Ayat: 123.

And those who after they have been oppressed emigrated for the cause of Allah, We will provide them with a good (abode) in this life: but better is the reward of the life to come, if they but knew it. It is those who are steadfast and on their Lord they rely.

Sura: 16, Ayat: 41-42.

When you recite the Quran, seek refuge in Allah from the accursed devil: no power has he over believers who put their trust in their Lord. He only has power over those who befriend him, and those who serve other gods besides Allah.

Sura: 16, Ayat: 98—100.

And put your trust in Him who lives and dies not; and celebrate His praise; and enough is He to be acquainted with the faults of His servants.

Sura: 25, Ayat: 58.

Put your trust in the Mighty One, the Merciful, Who observes you when you stand upright and (sees) your movements among those who prostrate themselves. He hears all and knows all.

Sura: 26, Ayat: 217-218.

Therefore put your trust in Allah, for undoubtedly you are (on the path) of the manifest truth.

Sura: 27, Ayat: 79.

He that surrenders himself to Allah and leads a righteous life has grasped indeed the most trustworthy hand-hold; and with God rests the End and decision of (all) affairs.

Sura: 31, Ayat: 22.

Put your trust in Him: He is your All-sufficient Guardian.

Sura: 33, Ayat: 3.

Announce to the believers the good tidings that Allah has bounteous blessings in store for them. Do not obey the unbelievers and the hypocrites: disregard their insolence.

Sura: 33, Ayat: 47-48.

....Say: 'Allah is my All-sufficient Patron. In Him let the faithful put their trust.'

Sura: 39, Ayat: 38.

That which you have been given is but the fleeting comfort of this life. Better and more enduring is that which Allah has for those who believe and put their trust in Him.

Sura: 42, Ayat: 36.

Secret counsels are the work of the devil, who thereby seeks to annoy the faithful. Yet he can harm them not at all, except by Allah's leave. In Allah let the faithful put their trust.

Sura: 58, Ayat: 10.

Allah – there is no god but Him. In Allah let the faithful put their trust.

Sura: 64, Ayat: 13.

....And if any one puts his trust in God, sufficient is (God) for him. For God will surely accomplish His purpose: Verily, for all things has God appointed a due proportion.

Sura: 65, Ayat: 3.

Say: 'He is (God) most Gracious: we have believed in Him, and in Him we put our trust: So, soon will you know which (of us) it is that is in manifest error.'

Sura: 67, Ayat: 29.

In the name of Allah, The Compassionate, The Merciful

FEAR OF FELLOW-MEN

It is only the Evil One that instils in you the fear of his allies: Be you not afraid of them, but fear Me, if you have faith.

Sura: 3, Ayat: 175.

Are you not aware of those who were told to hold back their hands (from fight) but establish regular prayers and spend in regular charity? When (at length) the order for fighting was issued to them, behold! a section of them feared men as — or even more than — they should have feared God: They said: 'Our Lord! Why have you ordered us to fight? Would you not grant us respite to our (natural) term or near (enough)?' Say: 'Short is the enjoyment of this world: the Hereafter is the best for those who do right: Never will you be dealt with unjustly in the very least!

Sura: 4, Ayat: 77.

....The unbelievers have this day despaired of (vanquishing) your religion. Have no fear of them: fear Me. ...

Sura: 5, Ayat: 3.

....Have no fear of people; fear Me, and do not take a small price for my revelations. Unbelievers are those who do not judge in accordance with Allah's revelations.

Sura: 5, Ayat: 44.

In the name of Allah, The Compassionate, The Merciful

VIRTUE

Had the people of those towns believed and kept from evil, We would have showered upon them the riches of heaven and earth. But they denied, and We punished them for their misdeeds.

Sura: 7, Ayat: 96.

....He that is righteous and patient, — never will God suffer the reward to be lost, of those who do right.'

Sura: 12, Ayat: 90.

Nor were the apostles whom We sent before you other than mortals from among the townsmen, to whom We sent revelations.

Have they not travelled in the land and seen what was the end of those before them? Better is the world to come for those that keep from evil. Can you not understand?

Sura: 12, Ayat: 109.

Allah is with those who keep from evil and do good (to others).

Sura: 16, Ayat: 128.

Enjoin prayer on your people and be diligent in its observance. We ask you to provide no provision; We shall Ourself provide for you. Blessed shall be the end of the devout.

Sura: 20, Ayat: 132.

He that reveres Allah's rites, surely it is from the piety of the hearts.

Sura: 22, Ayat: 32.

Their flesh and blood does not reach Allah; it is your piety that reaches Him. Thus he has subjected them to you, so that you may glorify Him for guiding you.

And give good news to the righteous.

Sura: 22, Ayat: 37.

On the Day of Resurrection, you shall see those who uttered falsehoods about Allah with faces blackened. Is there not in Hell a home for the arrogant?

But Allah will deliver those who fear Him, for they have earned salvation. No harm shall touch them, nor shall they ever grieve.

Sura: 39, Ayat: 60-61.

No, verily they have no fear of the Hereafter.

No, this is an admonition. Let him who will, take heed. But none takes heed except by the will of Allah. He is the Lord of Goodness and Forgiveness.

Sura: 74, Ayat: 53–56.

In the name of Allah, The Compassionate, The Merciful

FORTITUDE

O believers, seek assistance in patience and prayer. Allah is with those that are patient.

Sura: 2, Ayat: 153.

Be sure we shall test you with something of fear and hunger, some loss in goods or lives or the fruits (of your toil), but give glad tidings to those who patiently persevere, — Who say, when afflicted with calamity: 'To God we belong, and to Him is our return':—They are those on whom (Descend) blessings from God, and Mercy, and they are the ones that receive guidance.

Sura: 2, Ayat: 155—157.

Those who say: 'Lord, we believe in You: forgive us our sins and keep us from the torment of Fire; who are steadfast, sincere, obedient, and charitable; and who implore forgiveness at break of day.

Sura: 3, Ayat: 16-17.

When you are blessed with good fortune, they grieve: but when evil befalls you, they rejoice. If you persevere and guard yourselves against evil, their machinations will never harm you. Allah has knowledge of all their actions.

Sura: 3, Ayat: 120.

Did you think that you would enter Heaven without God tests those of you who fought hard (in His Cause) and remained steadfast?

Sura: 3, Ayat: 142.

You shall be tried and tested in your possessions and your persons, and be subjected to the insults of those to whom the Scriptures were given before you and of the polytheists. But if you endure with fortitude and guard yourselves against evil, you shall prove your mettle.

Sura: 3, Ayat: 186.

O you who believe! Persevere in patience and constancy; vie in such perse-

verance; strengthen each other; and fear God; that you may prosper.
Sura: 3, Ayat: 200.

And if there is a party among you who believes in the Message with which I have been sent, and a party which does not believe, hold yourselves in patience until God does decide between us: for He is the best to decide.
Sura: 7, Ayat: 87.

Obey Allah and His Apostle and do not dispute with one another, lest you should lose courage and your resolve weaken. Have patience: Allah is with those that are patient.
Sura: 8, Ayat: 46.

Allah has now lightened your burden, for He knows that you are weak. If there are a hundred steadfast men among you, they shall vanquish two hundred; and if there are a thousand, they shall, by Allah's will, defeat two thousand. Allah is with those that are steadfast.
Sura: 8, Ayat: 66.

Observe what is revealed to you, and have patience till Allah makes known his judgement. He is the best of judges.
Sura: 10, Ayat: 109.

If We show man Our mercy and then withhold it from him, he yields to despair and becomes ungrateful. And if after adversity We bestow favours upon him, he says: 'Gone are my sorrows from me,' and grows jubilant and boastful.
Except those who are steadfast and do good works. They shall have forgiveness and a rich reward.
Sura: 11, Ayat: 9—11.

Therefore have patience; the righteous shall not lose their reward.
Sura: 11, Ayat: 115.

They said: 'Are you indeed Joseph?' He said: 'I am Joseph, and this is my brother: God has indeed been gracious to us (all): behold, he that is righteous and patient, — never will God suffer the reward to be lost, of those who do right.'
Sura: 12, Ayat: 90.

Those who for the sake of Allah endure with fortitude, attend to their prayers, and spend of what We have given them in private and in public; and who ward off evil with good: These shall have a blissful end. They shall enter the Gardens of Eden, together with the righteous among their fathers, their

wives, and their descendants. From every gate the angels will come to them, (saying): 'Peace be to you for all that you have steadfastly endured. Blessed is the final reward (of Paradise).'

Sura: 13, Ayat: 22—24.

Those who after they have been oppressed emigrated for the cause of Allah, We will provide them with a good (abode) in this life: but better is the reward of the life to come, if they but knew it. (It is) those who are steadfast and on their Lord they rely.

Sura: 16, Ayat: 41-42.

What is with you must vanish: What is with God will endure. And We will certainly bestow, on those who patiently persevere, their reward according to the best of their actions.

Sura: 16, Ayat: 96.

But verily your Lord, — to those who leave their homes after trials and persecutions, — and who thereafter strive and fight for the Faith and patiently persevere, — your Lord, after all this is Oft-Forgiving, Most Merciful.

Sura: 16, Ayat: 110.

If you punish, let your punishment be proportionate to the wrong that has been done you. But if you are patient, it is certainly best for the patient.

Sura: 16, Ayat: 126.

Be patient (then); and your patience is (possible) only by Allah's (help). Do not grieve for the unbelievers, nor distress yourself at their intrigues.

Allah is with those who keep from evil and do good (to others).

Sura: 16, Ayat: 127-128.

Therefore, bear with what they say. Give glory to your Lord before sunrise and before sunset. Praise Him in parts of the night and at the two ends of the day so that you may be pleased.

Sura: 20, Ayat: 130.

....Give good news to the humble, whose hearts are filled with awe at the mention of their Lord; who endure their misfortunes with fortitude, attend to their prayers, and bestow in charity of that which We have given them.

Sura: 22, Ayat: 34-35.

Among my servants there were those who said: 'Lord, we believe in You. Forgive us and have mercy on us: You are the Best of the Merciful.'

But you treated them with ridicule, so much so that (ridicule of) them made you forget My Message while you were laughing at them!.

I have rewarded them this day for their patience and constancy: they are indeed the ones that have achieved Bliss.

Sura: 23, Ayat: 109—111.

Who say: 'Lord, give us joy in our wives and children and make us examples to those who fear You'. These shall be rewarded with the highest place for their patience. There they shall find welcome and greeting.

Sura: 25, Ayat: 74-75.

And when he went out in all his finery among his people, those who loved this life said: 'Would that we had the like of Qarun's fortune! He is indeed a lucky man.'

But those to whom knowledge had been given said: 'Alas for you! Better is the reward of Allah for him who has faith and does good works; but none shall attain it save the patient.'

Sura: 28, Ayat: 79-80.

Those that embrace the true faith and do good works shall be for ever lodged in the mansions of Paradise, where rivers will roll at their feet. Blessed is the reward of those who labour patiently and put their trust in Allah.

Sura: 29, Ayat: 58-59.

Therefore, have patience. Allah's promise is true. Let not those who have no certainty of faith, make you impatient.

Sura: 30, Ayat: 60.

My son, be steadfast in prayer, enjoin justice, and forbid evil. Endure with fortitude whatever befalls you. That is a duty incumbent on all.

Sura: 31, Ayat: 17.

Have patience at what they say. ...

Sura: 38, Ayat: 17.

Say: 'My servants who believe, fear your Lord. Those who do good works in this life shall receive a good reward. Allah's earth is vast. Those that endure with fortitude shall be requited without measure.'

Sura: 39, Ayat: 10.

Therefore have patience; Allah's promise is true. Implore Him to forgive your sins, and celebrate His praise morning and evening.

Sura: 40, Ayat: 55.

Good and evil deeds are not alike. Requite evil with good, and he, between whom and you is enmity, will become your dearest friend. But none will attain

this save those who endure with fortitude and are truly fortunate.

Sura: 41, Ayat: 34-35.

Those who avenge themselves when wronged incur no guilt. But great is the guilt of those who oppress their fellowmen and conduct themselves with wickedness and injustice. These shall be sternly punished.

To endure with fortitude and to forgive is an act of great resolution.

Sura: 42, Ayat: 41−43.

Bear then with what they say. Glorify your Lord before sunrise and before sunset. Praise Him in the night, and after prostrations.

Sura: 50, Ayat: 39-40.

Therefore await with patience the judgement of your Lord: We are watching over you. Glorify your Lord when you waken; in the night-time praise Him, and at the setting of the stars.

Sura: 52, Ayat: 48-49.

Wait, then, for the judgement of your Lord and do not act like him who was swallowed by the whale when he called out to Allah in despair.

Sura: 68, Ayat: 48.

Therefore conduct yourself with becoming patience.

Sura: 70, Ayat: 5.

Bear patiently with what they* say and leave their company with dignity.

Sura: 73, Ayat: 10.

You who are wrapped up in your vestment, arise and give warning.**

Magnify your Lord, cleanse your garments, and keep away from all pollution.

Bestow no favours expecting gain. Be patient for your Lord's sake.

Sura: 74, Ayat: 1−7.

To be one of those who believe, enjoin patience and enjoin mercy.

Sura: 90, Ayat: 17.

By time, man is in loss, except those who believe and do good works and exhort one another to truth and to patience.

Sura: 103, Ayat: 1−3.

---

*The unbelievers **Muhammad

In the name of Allah, The Compassionate, The Merciful

MISFORTUNE EMANATING FROM GOD

No misfortune befalls except by Allah's will. He who believes in Allah, Allah guides his heart. Allah has knowledge of all things.

Sura: 64, Ayat: 11.

In the name of Allah, The Compassionate, The Merciful

FORGIVENESS AND COURTESY

Give for the cause of Allah and do not with your own hands cast yourselves into destruction. Be Charitable; Allah loves the charitable.

Sura: 2, Ayat: 195.

A kind word and forgiveness are better than charity followed by injury. Allah is Self-sufficient and Indulgent.

Sura: 2, Ayat: 263.

Satan threatens you with poverty and orders you to commit what is indecent. But Allah promises you His forgiveness and His bounty. Allah is Munificent and All-Knowing.

Sura: 2, Ayat 268.

Obey Allah and the Apostle that you may find mercy. And hasten to earn the forgiveness of your Lord and a Paradise as wide as heaven and earth, prepared for the righteous who spend alike in prosperity and adversity, for those who curb their anger and those who forgive their fellow-men. And Allah loves the charitable.

Sura: 3, Ayat: 132—134.

It was thanks to Allah's mercy that you dealt so leniently with them. Had you been cruel and hard-hearted, they would have surely deserted you. Therefore, pardon them and implore Allah to forgive them. Take counsel with them in the conduct of affairs; and when you are resolved, put your trust in Allah. Allah loves those that trust (in Him).

Sura: 3, Ayat: 159.

....And have forgotten a portion of what they were enjoined. You will ever find them deceitful, except for a few of them. But pardon them and bear with them. Allah loves those who do good.

Sura: 5, Ayat: 13.

Serve Allah and associate none with Him. Show kindness to your parents

and your kindred, to the orphans and to the needy, to your near and distant neighbours, to your fellow-travellers, to the wayfarers, and to the slaves whom you own. Allah does not love arrogant and boastful men, who are themselves niggardly and enjoin others to be niggardly also; who conceal that which Allah of His bounty has bestowed upon them — We have prepared a shameful punishment for the unbelievers — and who spend their wealth for the sake of ostentation, believing neither in Allah nor in the Last Day. He that chooses the devil for his friend, an evil friend has he.

Sura: 4, Ayat: 36—38.

Allah does not like foul words in public, except by a man who is truly wronged. He is Hearing, Knowing. Whether you do good openly or in private, whether you forgive those that wrong you — Allah is Pardoning, Mighty.

Sura: 4, Ayat: 148-149.

Show forgiveness, enjoin justice, and avoid the ignorant.

Sura: 7, Ayat: 199.

We did not create the heavens and the earth and what is between them except in truth. The Hour of Doom is sure to come: Therefore, forgive them nobly. Your Lord is the Creator, the Knower.

Sura: 15, Ayat: 85-86.

Allah enjoins justice, kindness and charity to one's kindred, and forbids indecency, wickedness and oppression. He admonishes you so that you may take heed.

Sura: 16, Ayat: 90.

If you punish, let your punishment be proportionate to the wrong that has been done you. But if you are patient, it is certainly best for the patient.

Sura: 16, Ayat: 126.

For every nation We have ordained a ritual, that they may pronounce the name of Allah over the animals which He has given them (for food). Your God is one God; to Him surrender yourselves.

Give good news to the humble, whose hearts are filled with awe at the mention of their Lord; who endure their misfortunes with fortitude, attend to their prayers, and bestow in charity of that which We have given them.

Sura: 22, Ayat: 34-35.

Let not the honourable and rich among you swear not to give to their kindred, the poor, and those who have emigrated for the cause of Allah. Rather, let them pardon and forgive. Do you not wish Allah to forgive you?

He is Forgiving, Merciful.

Sura: 24, Ayat: 22.

Let evil be rewarded with like evil. But he that forgives and seeks reconcilement shall be rewarded by Allah. He does not love the wrongdoers.

Sura: 42, Ayat: 40.

Those who avenge themselves when wronged incur no guilt. But great is the guilt of those who oppress their fellow men and conduct themselves with wickedness and injustice. These shall be sternly punished.

To endure with fortitude and to forgive is an act of great resolution.

Sura: 42, Ayat: 41–43.

(God also hears) his (the Prophet's) cry: 'Lord, these men are unbelievers.'

Bear with them and wish them peace. They shall (before long) know.

Sura: 43, Ayat: 88-89.

Tell the believers to pardon those who do not look forward to the days of Allah, so that He may reward men according to their deeds. He that does what is right does it to his own advantage; and he that commits evil does so at his own peril. To your Lord you shall all return.

Sura: 45, Ayat: 14-15.

Bear up then with patience, as did the steadfast apostles before you, and do not seek to hurry on (their doom). On the day when they behold the scourge with which they are threatened, their life on earth will seem to them no longer than an hour.

That is a warning. Shall any perish except the evildoers?

Sura: 46, Ayat: 35.

O you who believe! Truly, among your wives and your children are (some that are) enemies to yourselves: so beware of them! But if you forgive and overlook, and cover up (their faults), verily God is Oft-Forgiving, Most Merciful.

Sura: 64, Ayat: 14.

In the name of Allah, The Compassionate, The Merciful

VENGEANCE

The prohibited month for the prohibited month, — and so for all things prohibited, — there is the law of equality. If then any one transgresses the prohibition against you, transgress you likewise against him. But fear God, and know that God is with those who restrain themselves.

Sura: 2, Ayat: 194.

Allah does not like foul words in public, except by a man who is truly wronged. He is Hearing, Knowing. Whether you do good openly or in private, whether you forgive those that wrong you — Allah is Pardoning, Mighty.

Sura: 4, Ayat: 148-149.

If you punish, let your punishment be proportionate to the wrong that has been done you. But if you are patient, it is certainly best for the patient.

Sura: 16, Ayat: 126.

Thus shall it be. He that repays an injury in kind and then is wronged again shall be helped by Allah. Allah is Forgiving, Merciful.

Sura: 22, Ayat: 60.

Good and evil deeds are not alike. Requite evil with what is better and he, between whom and you is enmity, will become your dearest friend. But none will attain this save those who endure with fortitude and are truly fortunate.

Sura: 41, Ayat: 34-35.

That which you have been given is but the fleeting comfort of this life. Better and more enduring is that which Allah has for those who believe and put their trust in Him; who avoid gross sins and indecencies and, when angered, are willing to forgive; who obey their Lord, attend to their prayers, and conduct their affairs by mutual consent; who bestow in alms a part of that which We have given them, and when oppressed, seek to redress their wrongs.

Sura: 42, Ayat: 36—39.

Let evil be rewarded with like evil. But he that forgives and seeks reconcilement shall be rewarded by Allah. He does not love the wrongdoers.

Sura: 42, Ayat: 40.

Those who avenge themselves when wronged incur no guilt. But great is the guilt of those who oppress their fellow men and conduct themselves with wickedness and injustice. These shall be sternly punished.

To endure with fortitude and to forgive is an act of great resolution.

Sura: 42, Ayat: 41—43.

In the name of Allah, The Compassionate, The Merciful

CONTROLLING ANGER

And hasten to earn the forgiveness of your Lord and a Paradise as wide as heaven and earth, prepared for the righteous who spend alike in prosperity and in adversity, for those who curb their anger and those who forgive their fellow-men.

Sura: 3, Ayat: 133-134.

It was thanks to Allah's mercy that you dealt so leniently with them. Had you been cruel and hard-hearted, they would have surely deserted you. Therefore, pardon them and implore Allah to forgive them. Take counsel with them in the conduct of affairs; and when you are resolved, put your trust in Allah. Allah loves those that trust (in Him).

Sura: 3, Ayat: 159.

That which you have been given is but the fleeting comfort of this life. Better and more enduring is that which Allah has for those who believe and put their trust in Him; who avoid gross sins and indecencies and, when angered, are willing to forgive.

Sura: 42, Ayat: 36-37.

In the name of Allah, The Compassionate, The Merciful

VIRTUE ENDS EVIL

And establish regular prayers at the two ends of the day and at the approaches of the night: For those things that are good remove those that are evil: Be that the word of remembrance to those who remember (their Lord): Sura: 11, Ayat: 114.

In the name of Allah, The Compassionate, The Merciful

GOOD IN RETURN FOR EVIL

Allah does not like foul words in public, except by a man who is truly wronged. He is Hearing, Knowing. Whether you do good openly or in private, whether you forgive those that wrong you—Allah is Pardoning, Mighty.

Sura: 4, Ayat: 148-149.

Repel evil with that which is best: We are well acquainted with the things they say. And say 'O my Lord! I seek refuge with You from the suggestions of the Evil Ones.' 'And I seek refuge with You O my Lord! lest they should come near me.'

Sura: 23, Ayat: 96—98.

When it is recited to them, they say: 'We believe in it because it is the truth from Our Lord. We surrendered ourselves to Him before it came.'

Twice shall their reward be given them, because they have endured, repelling evil with good and giving in alms a part of that which We bestowed on them;

Sura: 28, Ayat: 53-54.

Good and evil deeds are not alike. Requite evil with good, and he, between whom and you is enmity, will become your dearest friend. But none will attain this save those who endure with fortitude and are truly fortunate.

Sura: 41, Ayat: 34-35.

In the name of Allah, The Compassionate, The Merciful

DOING GOOD TO OTHERS

But because they broke their covenent, We laid on them Our curse and hardened their hearts. They dislocate the words (of the Scriptures) from their places and have forgotten a portion of what they were enjoined. You will ever find them deceitful, except for a few of them. But pardon them and bear with them. Allah loves those who are kind.

Sura: 5, Ayat: 13.

Bestow no favours expecting gain. Be patient for your Lord's sake.

Sura: 74, Ayat: 6-7.

In the name of Allah, The Compassionate, The Merciful

TREATING THE IGNORANT

Show forgiveness, enjoin justice, and avoid the ignorant. If you are afflicted by the devil's temptation, seek refuge in Allah; He hears all and knows all.

If those that guard themselves against evil are touched by a temptation from the devil, they have but to recall Allah's precepts and they shall see the light.

Sura: 7, Ayat: 199—201.

If an idolater seeks asylum with you, give him protection so that he may hear the Word of Allah, and then convey him to safety. For they are ignorant men.

Sura: 9, Ayat: 6.

The true servants of the Merciful are those who walk humbly on the earth, and when the ignorant address them they say: 'Peace!'.

Sura: 25, Ayat: 63.

Twice shall their reward be given them, because they have endured, repelling evil with good and giving in alms a part of that which We bestowed on them; and because they pay no heed to vain talk, but say: 'We have our actions and you have yours. Peace be upon you. We do not seek (the company of) ignorant men.'

Sura: 28, Ayat: 54-55.

(God also hears) his (the Prophet's) cry: 'Lord, these men are unbelievers.' Bear with them and wish them peace. They shall (before long) know.

Sura: 43, Ayat: 88-89.

He is the Lord of the East and the West: there is no god but Him. Accept Him for your Protector.

Bear patiently with what they* say and leave their company with dignity.
Sura: 73, Ayat: 9-10.

And leave Me (alone to deal with) those in possession of the good things of life, who (yet) deny the Truth; and bear with them for a little while.
Sura: 73, Ayat: 11.

***The unbelievers**

In the name of Allah, The Compassionate, The Merciful

INGRATITUDE OF BLESSINGS

If We show man Our mercy and then withhold it from him, he yields to despair and becomes ungrateful. And if after adversity We bestow favours upon him, he says: 'Gone are my sorrows from me,' and grows jubilant and boastful.

Sura: 11, Ayat: 10.

Whatever good you have is from Allah, and to Him you turn for help when misfortune befalls you. Yet no sooner does He remove your ills than some of you set up other gods besides Him giving no thanks for what We grant them. Take your pleasure, then (in this life); you shall before long know.

Sura: 16, Ayat: 53–55.

Allah has made an example of the city which was once safe and peaceful. Its provisions used to come in abundance from every quarter: but its people were ungrateful for the favours of Allah. Therefore, He afflicted them with famine and fear as a punishment for what they did.

Sura: 16, Ayat: 112.

In the name of Allah, The Compassionate, The Merciful

THE GRATEFUL

Remember Me, then, and I will remember you. Give thanks to Me and never deny Me.

Sura: 2, Ayat: 152.

....God does not wish to place you in a difficulty, but to make you clean and to complete His favour to you, that you may be grateful.

Sura: 5, Ayat: 6.

Have you not seen those who change thanks to Allah's grace into disbelief and drive their people into the House of perdition? They shall burn in Hell; evil shall be their fate.

They set up equals with Allah to lead others astray. Say to them: 'Take your pleasure: you are surely destined to Hell.'

Sura: 14, Ayat: 28—30.

It is He Who brought you forth from the wombs of your mothers when you knew nothing; and He gave you hearing and sight and intelligence and affections: That you may give thanks (To God).

Sura: 16, Ayat: 78.

....He that gives thanks has much to gain; but he who is ungrateful truly, Allah is All-sufficient and Bountiful!'

Sura: 27, Ayat: 40.

Your Lord is bountiful to men: yet most of them do not give thanks.

Sura: 27, Ayat: 73.

In His mercy He has given you the night that you may rest in it, and the day that you may seek His bounty and render thanks.

Sura: 28, Ayat: 73.

....He that gives thanks to Him has much to gain. But if any one is ungrate-

ful, Allah is Self-sufficient and Glorious.'

Sura: 31, Ayat: 12.

....'Work you, Sons of David, with thanks! But few of My servants are grateful!"

Sura: 34, Ayat: 13.

Therefore do not oppress the orphan, nor drive away the beggar. But proclaim the bounty of your Lord.

Sura: 93, Ayat: 9–11.

Surely man is ungrateful to his Lord. To this he himself shall bear witness. For, verily, to the love of wealth is he most ardently devoted.

Sura: 100, Ayat: 6–8.

WORLDLY WEALTH AND ITS REALITY

(15)

In the name of Allah, The Compassionate, The Merciful

THE DIVINE BOUNTY

If We pleased We could take away that which We have revealed to you: then you should find none to plead with Us on your behalf, except for mercy from your Lord: for His bounty to you is great indeed.

Sura: 17, Ayat: 86-87.

Believers, have fear of Allah and put your trust in His Apostles. He will grant you a double share of His mercy. He will give you a light to walk in, and will forgive you: Allah is Forgiving and Merciful.

Let the People of the Book know that they have no control over the gifts of Allah; that these gifts are in His hands alone, and that He vouchsafes them to whom He will. Allah's bounty is infinite.

Sura: 57, Ayat: 28-29.

....And for those who fear God, He (ever) prepares a way out.

And He provided for him from (sources) he never could imagine. And if anyone puts his trust in God, sufficient is (God) for him. For God will surely accomplish His purpose. Verily, for all things has God appointed a due proportion.

Sura: 65, Ayat: 2-3.

In the name of Allah, The Compassionate, The Merciful

HONOUR

Say: 'O God Lord of Power (and Rule), You give Power to whom You please, and You take away Power from whom You please: You endue with honour whom you please and You bring low whom You please: In Your hand is all good. Verily, over all things You have power.

Sura: 3, Ayat: 26.

Give warning to the hypocrites of a stern chastisement; those who choose the unbelievers rather than the faithful for their friends. Are they seeking glory at their hands? Surely all glory belongs to Allah.

Sura: 4, Ayat: 138-139.

....He who is humbled by Allah has none to honour him. God does what He pleases.

Sura: 22, Ayat: 18.

....For Allah is Powerful and Mighty.

Sura: 22, Ayat: 74.

He who seeks glory and power (should know), to Allah belong all glory and power. To Him ascend good words, and He exalts righteous deeds. But those who plot evil shall be sternly punished. And the plotting of those will come to nothing.

Sura: 35, Ayat: 10.

Men, We have created you from a male and a female, and made you into nations and tribes that you might get to know one another. The noblest of you in Allah's sight is the most righteous of you. Allah is Wise and All-Knowing.

Sura: 49, Ayat: 13.

They say, 'If we return to Medina, surely the more honourable (element) will expel therefrom the meaner.' But honour belongs to God and His Apostle, and to the Believers; but the hypocrites know not.

Sura: 63, Ayat: 8.

In the name of Allah, The Compassionate, The Merciful

EARNING AN HONOURABLE SUSTENANCE

Say: 'O men! I am (sent) to you only to give a clear warning: 'Those who believe and work righteousness, for them is forgiveness and a sustenance most generous.

'But those who strive against Our Signs, to frustrate them, they will be companions of the Fire.'

Sura: 22, Ayat: 49–51.

In the name of Allah, The Compassionate, The Merciful

LIFE OF POVERTY

Satan threatens you with poverty and orders you to commit what is indecent. But Allah promises you His forgiveness and His bounty. Allah is Munificent and All-Knowing.

Sura: 2, Ayat: 268.

And in no wise covet those things in which God has bestowed His gifts more freely on some of you than on others: to men is allotted what they earn, and to women what they earn: But ask God of His bounty. For God has full knowledge of all things.

Sura: 4, Ayat: 32.

There are some among them who speak ill of you* concerning the distribution of alms. If a share is given them, they are contented: but if they receive nothing, they grow resentful.

Would that they were satisfied with what Allah and His Apostle have given them, and would say: 'Allah is All-sufficient for us. He will provide for us from His own abundance, and so will His Apostle. To Allah, we will return.

Sura: 9, Ayat: 58-59.

***Muhammad**

In the name of Allah, The Compassionate, The Merciful

CHANGE OF TIMES

If you have suffered from a wound, so did the enemy. We alternate these vicissitudes among mankind so that Allah may know the true believers and choose martyrs from among you — for He does not love the evildoers.

Sura: 3, Ayat: 140.

In the name of Allah, The Compassionate, The Merciful

TRIAL

Be sure We shall test you with something of fear and hunger, some loss in goods or lives or the fruits (of your toil), but give glad tidings to those who patiently persevere, —

Who say, when afflicted with calamity: 'To God we belong, and to Him is our return': —

They are those on whom (descend) blessings from God, and Mercy, and they are the ones that receive guidance.

Sura: 2, Ayat: 155—157.

Did you think that you would enter Heaven without God tests those of you who fought hard (in His Cause) and remained steadfast?

Sura: 3, Ayat: 142.

You shall certainly be tried and tested in your possessions and in your personal selves; and you shall certainly hear much that will grieve you, from those who received the Book before you and from those who worship many gods. But if you persevere patiently, and guard against evil, — then that will be a determining factor in all affairs.

Sura: 3, Ayat: 186.

It is He Who has made you (His) agents, inheritors of the earth: He has raised you in ranks, some above others: that He may try you in the gifts He has given you: For your Lord is quick in punishment: yet He is indeed Oft-Forgiving, Most Merciful.

Sura: 6, Ayat: 165.

We dispersed them through the earth in communities — some were righteous men, others were not — and tested them with blessings and misfortunes so that they might desist (from sin).

Sura: 7, Ayat: 168.

Did you imagine that you would be left alone before Allah has had time to

know those of you who have fought valiantly and served none but Him and His Apostle and the faithful? Allah is cognizant of all your actions.

Sura: 9, Ayat: 16.

Every soul shall have a taste of death: And We test you by evil and by good by way of trial. To Us must you return.

Sura: 21, Ayat: 35.

Do men think that they will be left alone on saying, 'We believe,' and that they will not be tested?

We did test those before them, and God will certainly know those who are true from those who are false.

Sura: 29, Ayat: 2-3.

Then there are among men such as say, 'We believe in God'; but when they suffer affliction in (the cause of) God, they treat men's oppression as if it were the Wrath of God! And if help comes (to them) from their Lord, they are sure to say, 'We have (always) been with you!" Does not God know best all that is in the hearts of all Creation?

And God most certainly knows those who believe, and as certainly those who are Hypocrites.

Sura: 29, Ayat: 10-11.

And We shall try you until We test those among you who strive their utmost and persevere in patience; and We shall try your reported (mettle).

Sura: 47, Ayat: 31.

We have tried them as We tried the owners of the orchard who had sworn that they would pluck its fruit next morning, without adding any reservations (such as: if it be God's will). A visitant from Allah came down upon it while they slept, and in the morning it was as black as midnight.

At daybreak they called out to one another, saying: 'Hurry to your orchard, if you would pick its fruit.' And off they went, whispering to one another: 'No beggar shall set foot in it today.'

Thus they went out, fixed in their resolve. But when they saw it they cried: 'We have been wrong, We are utterly ruined.'

The most upright among them said: 'Did I not bid you praise Allah?'

'Glory to our Lord,' they answered. 'We have assuredly done wrong.' And they began to blame one another.

'Woe to us!' they cried. 'We have been great transgressors. We hope our Lord will give us a better orchard in its place. To our Lord we return.'

Such was their punishment. But the punishment of the life to come is more terrible, if they but knew it.

Syra: 68, Ayat: 17–33.

In the name of Allah, The Compassionate, The Merciful

GREED FOR WEALTH

But those who before them, had homes (in Medina) and had adopted the Faith, show their affection to such as came to them for refuge, and entertain no desire in their hearts for things given to the (latter), but give them preference over themselves, even though poverty was their (own lot). And those saved from the covetousness of their own souls,—they are the ones that achieve prosperity.

Sura: 59, Ayat: 9.

So fear God as much as you can; listen (to Him) and obey; and spend in charity for the benefit of your own souls. And those saved from the covetousness of their own souls,—they are the ones that achieve prosperity.

Sura: 64, Ayat: 16.

Surely man is ungrateful to his Lord. To this he himself shall bear witness.

And truly on account of his love of wealth he is niggardly. Is he not aware that when those in the graves are raised and what is in the breasts is laid open, their Lord on that day will be Knowing?

Sura: 100, Ayat: 6—11.

Mutual rivalry for piling up (the good things of this world) diverts you (from the more serious things), until you visit the graves.

Sura: 102, Ayat: 1-2.

Woe to every backbiting slanderer who amasses wealth and counts it thinking his wealth will render him immortal!

By no means! They shall be flung to the Destroying Flame.

Would that you knew what the Destroying Flame is like!

It is Allah's own kindled fire, which will rise up to the hearts of men. It will close upon them from every side, in towering columns.

Sura: 104, Ayat: 1–9

In the name of Allah, The Compassionate, The Merciful

WEALTH AND CHILDREN

Those who disbelieve, neither their riches nor their children shall in the least save them from Allah. They shall become the fuel of Fire.

Sura: 3, Ayat: 10.

As for the unbelievers, neither their riches nor their children shall in the least protect them from Allah. They are the people of Fire, and there they shall remain forever.

Sura: 3, Ayat: 116.

O you that believe! Betray not the trust of God and the Apostle, nor misappropriate knowingly things entrusted to you.

And know you that your possessions and your progeny are but a trial; and that it is God with whom lies your highest reward.

Sura: 8, Ayat: 27-28.

Nothing prevents their offerings from being accepted except that they have denied Allah and His apostle. They pray half-heartedly and grudge their contributions.

Let neither their riches nor their children rouse your envy. Through these Allah seeks to punish them in this life, so that they shall be unbelievers.

Sura: 9, Ayat: 54-55.

This present life is only like water which We send down from the clouds so that the luxuriant herbage sustaining man and beast may grow; until when the earth puts on its lovely garment and becomes adorned, and its people think that they are its masters, down comes Our scourge upon it, by night or in broad day, laying it waste, as though it had not blossomed yesterday. Thus We make plain Our revelations to thoughtful men.

Sura: 10, Ayat: 24.

....Woe to the unbelievers, because of stern punishment. Those who love this life more than the life to come, debar others from the path of Allah and

seek to make it crooked are far astray.

Sura: 14, Ayat: 2-3.

Wealth and sons are allurements of the life of this world: But the things that endure, Good Deeds, are best in the sight of your Lord, as rewards, and best as (the foundation for) hopes.

Sura: 18, Ayat: 46.

When Our clear revelations are recited to them, the unbelievers say to the faithful: 'Which of the two parties has a better position or company?'

How many generations have We destroyed before them, far greater in riches and in splendour!

Say: 'The Merciful will bear long with those in error until they witness the fulfilment of His threats: be it a worldly scourge or the Hour of Doom. Then shall they know whose is the worse plight and whose the smaller following.'

Sura: 19, Ayat: 73—75.

Do they think that because We have granted them abundance of wealth and sons, We would hasten them on in every good? Nay, they do not understand.

Sura: 23, Ayat: 55-56.

The things you have been given are but the conveniences and the gaudy show of this present life. Better is Allah's reward and more lasting. Have you no sense?

Sura: 28, Ayat: 60.

Neither your riches nor your children shall bring you nearer to Us. But only those that have faith and do what is right—those shall be doubly rewarded for their deeds: they shall dwell in peace in the mansions (of Paradise). But those who strive to belittle Our revelations shall be brought for punishment.

Sura: 34, Ayat: 37-38.

Men, the promise of Allah is true. Let the life of this world not deceive you, nor let the Dissembler trick you about Allah. Satan is your enemy: therefore treat him as an enemy. He tempts his followers so that they may become the people of the Fire.

Sura: 35, Ayat: 5-6.

Know you (all), that the life of this world is but play and amusement, pomp and mutual boasting and multiplying, (in rivalry) among yourselves, riches and children. Here is a similitude: How rain and the growth which it brings forth, delight (the hearts of) of the tillers; soon it withers; you will see it grow

yellow; then it becomes dry and crumbles away. But in the Hereafter is a Penalty severe (for the devotees of wrong). And forgiveness from God and (His) Good Pleasure (for the devotees of God). And what is the life of this world, but goods and chattels of deception?

Sura: 57, Ayat: 20.

God has prepared for them a severe Penalty: evil indeed are their deeds.

They have made their oaths a screen (for their misdeeds): Thus they obstruct (men) from the Path of God: Therefore shall they have a humiliating Penalty.

Of no profit whatever to them, against God, will be their riches nor their sons: They will be companions of the Fire, to dwell therein forever!

Sura: 58, Ayat: 15–17.

On the Day of Resurrection neither your kinsfolk nor your children shall avail you. Allah will judge between you. He is cognizant of all your actions.

Sura: 60, Ayat: 3.

Believers, let neither your riches nor your children beguile you of Allah's remembrance. Those that do this shall have much to lose.

Sura: 63, Ayat: 9.

O you who believe! Truly, among your wives and your children are (some of them) enemies to yourselves: so beware of them! But if you forgive and overlook, and cover up (their faults), verily God is Oft-Forgiving, Most Merciful.

Sura: 64, Ayat: 14.

Your riches and your children may be but a trial: But in the presence of God, is the highest Reward.

So fear God as much as you can; Listen (to Him) and obey; and spend in charity for the benefit of your own souls. And those saved from the covetousness of their own souls,—they are the ones that achieve prosperity.

Sura: 64, Ayat: 15-16.

In the name of Allah, The Compassionate, The Merciful

DIVINE SUSTENANCE

....And for those who fear God, He (ever) prepares a way out.

And He provides for him from (sources) he never could imagine. And if anyone puts his trust in God, sufficient is (God) for him. For God will surely accomplish His purpose: Verily, for all things has God appointed a due proportion.

Sura: 65, Ayat: 2-3.

In the name of Allah, The Compassionate, The Merciful

GOD, THE BEST PROVIDER

Or is it that you ask them for some recompense? But the recompense of your Lord is best: He is the Best of those who give sustenance.

Sura: 23, Ayat: 72.

In the name of Allah, The Compassionate, The Merciful

DIFFERENT RANKS OF MANKIND

And in no wise covet those things in which God has bestowed His gifts more freely on some of you than on others: to men is allotted what they earn, and to women what they earn: But ask God of His bounty. For God has full knowledge of all things.

Sura: 4, Ayat: 32.

Men shall take full care of women with the bounties which God has bestowed more abundantly on the former than on the latter, and with what they may spend out of their possessions. ....

Sura: 4, Ayat: 34.

It is He who has made you (His) agents, inheritors of the earth: He has raised you in ranks, some above others: that He may try you in the gifts He has given you: For your Lord is quick in punishment: yet He is indeed Oft-Forgiving, Most Merciful.

Sura: 6, Ayat: 165.

Allah gives abundantly and sparingly to whom He pleases. Those who (are given abundance) rejoice in this life: but brief indeed is the comfort of this life compared to the life to come.

Sura: 13, Ayat: 26.

Allah has caused some of you to excel others in worldly possessions. Those who have been favoured do not give their wealth to those whom their right hands possess so as to be equal in that respect. Would they deny Allah's goodness?

Sura: 16, Ayat: 71.

Allah sets forth this parable. On the one hand, there is a helpless slave, the property of his master. On the other, a man on whom We have bestowed Our bounty, so that he gives of it both in private and in public. Are the two alike? (By no means;) Praise be to God. But most of them understand not.

Sura: 16, Ayat: 75.

He also sets forth the parable of two men. One of them is a dumb and helpless man, a burden on his master: wherever he sends him he returns with empty hands. Is he equal with one who enjoins justice and follows the right path?

Sura: 16, Ayat: 76.

See how We have bestowed more on some than on others; but verily the Hereafter is more in rank and gradation and more in excellence.

Sura: 17, Ayat: 21.

Do not strain your eyes towards the worldly benefits We have bestowed on some of them, for with these We seek only to test them. Your Lord's provision (to you) is better and more lasting.

Sura: 20, Ayat: 131.

Allah gives abundantly to whom He will, and sparingly to whom He pleases. He has knowledge of all things.

Sura: 29, Ayat: 62.

Do they not see that Allah gives abundantly to whom He will and sparingly to whom He pleases? Surely there are signs in this for true believers.

Sura: 30, Ayat: 37.

Say: 'Verily my Lord enlarges and restricts provision to whom He pleases, but most men understand not.'

Sura: 34, Ayat: 36.

Say: 'My Lord gives abundantly to whom He will, and sparingly to whom He pleases. Whatever you give in alms He will pay you back for it. He is the Most Munificent Giver.'

Sura: 34, Ayat: 39.

Do they not know that Allah gives abundantly to whom He will and sparingly to whom He pleases? Surely there are signs in this for true believers.

Sura: 39, Ayat: 52.

To Him belong the keys of the heavens and the earth: He enlarges and restricts sustenance to whom He will: for He knows full well all things.

Sura: 42, Ayat: 12.

Gracious is God to His servants: He gives sustenance to whom He pleases. And He has Power and can carry out His Will.

To any that desires the harvest of the Hereafter, We give increase in his harvest; and to any that desires the harvest of this world, We grant somewhat

thereof, but he has no share or lot in the Hereafter.

Sura: 42, Ayat: 19-20.

If God were to enlarge the provision for (all) His Servants, they would indeed transgress beyond all bounds through the earth; but He sends (it) down in due measure as He pleases. For He is with His Servants well-acquainted, Watchful.

Sura: 42, Ayat: 27.

Is it they who apportion your Lord's blessings? It is We who apportion to them their livelihoods in this world, exalting some in rank above others, so that the one may take the other into his service. Better is your Lord's mercy than all their hoarded treasures.

Sura: 43, Ayat: 32.

In the name of Allah, The Compassionate, The Merciful

MUSLIMS ARE BROTHERS

The Believers are but a single Brotherhood: so make peace and reconciliation between your two (contending) brothers; and fear God, that you may receive Mercy.

Sura: 49, Ayat: 10.

In the name of Allah, The Compassionate, The Merciful

GIVING A LONG ROPE TO INFIDELS

Let the unbelievers not think that We prolong their days for their good. We do so only that they may grow in wickedness. Theirs shall be a shameful punishment.

Sura: 3, Ayat: 178.

Do not be deceived by the activities of the unbelievers in this land. Their prosperity is brief. Hell shall be their home, a dismal resting-place.

Sura: 3, Ayat: 196-197.

Can he who was dead, to whom We gave life, and a Light whereby he can walk amongst men, be like him who is in the depths of darkness, from which he can never come out? Thus to those without Faith their own deeds seem pleasing.

Thus have We placed leaders in every town, its wicked men to plot and (and burrow) therein: But they only plot against their own souls, and they perceive it not.

Sura: 6, Ayat: 122-123.

Among those whom We created there are some who give true guidance and act justly. As for those that deny Our revelations, We will lead them step by step to ruin, whence they cannot tell; for though I bear with them, My strategem is sure.

Sura: 7, Ayat: 181—183.

Say: 'Whether you give willingly or with reluctance, your offerings shall not be accepted from you; for you are wicked men.'

Nothing prevents their offerings from being accepted except that they have denied Allah and His Apostle. They pray half-heartedly and grudge their contributions.

Let their riches nor their children rouse your envy. Through these Allah seeks to punish them in this life, so that they shall be unbelievers.

Sura: 9, Ayat: 53—55.

Had Allah hastened the punishment of men as they would (like Him to) hasten their reward, their fate would have certainly been decreed. Therefore We let those who deny the Last Judgement blunder about in sin.

Sura: 10, Ayat: 11.

Those that desire the life of this world with all its frippery shall be rewarded for their deeds in their own lifetime: they will not suffer any loss. These are the men who in the world to come will have nothing but the Fire. Vain is what they did in it and fruitless are their works.

Sura: 11, Ayat: 15-16.

Other apostles were mocked before you: but though I bore long with those who disbelieved. My scourge at length overtook them. And how (terrible) was My scourge!

Sura: 13, Ayat: 32.

If God were to punish men for their wrongdoing, He would not leave, on the (earth), a single living creature: But He gives them respite for a stated Term: When their Term expires, they would not be able to delay (the punishment) for a single hour, just as they would not be able to anticipate it (for a single hour).

Sura: 16, Ayat: 61.

When We resolve to annihilate a town, We first command those that live in luxury (to obey Us). But they transgress therein. Thus the sentence is justly pronounced against it and We utterly destroy it.

How many generations have We destroyed since Nuh's time! It is enough that your Lord knows and sees His servants' sins.

Sura: 17, Ayat: 16-17.

Say: 'If any men go astray (God) Most Gracious extends (the rope) to them, until, when they see the warning of God (being fulfilled)—either in punishment or in (the approach of) the Hour,—they will at length realise who is worst in position, and (who) weakest in forces!

Sura: 19, Ayat: 75.

Nay, We gave the good things of this life to these men and their fathers until the period grew long for them; see they not that We gradually reduce the land (in their control) from its outlying borders? Is it then, they who will win?

Sura: 21, Ayat: 44.

But if any reject Faith, let not his rejection grieve you: to Us is their Return, and We shall tell them the truth of their deeds: for God knows well all that is in (men's) hearts.

We grant them their pleasure for a little while. In the end shall We drive them to chastisement unrelenting.

Sura: 31, Ayat: 23-24.

So turn away from them for a while. And watch them and they shall see.

Do they wish to hasten Our punishment? When it descends upon their courtyards, evil will be the morning of those forewarned.

So turn away from then for a while. And watch them, and they shall see.

Sura: 37, Ayat: 174–179.

Therefore leave to Me those that deny this revelation. We will lead them step by step (to their ruin) in ways beyond their knowledge. I shall bear long with them: My stratagem is sure.

Sura: 68, Ayat: 44-45.

Leave to Me those that deny the truth, those that enjoy the comforts of this life; bear with them yet a little while. We have (in store for them) heavy fetters and a blazing fire, choking food and a harrowing torment.

Sura: 73, Ayat: 11–13.

They scheme a scheme, and I, too, scheme a scheme. Therefore bear with the unbelievers, and let them be alone for a while.

Sura: 86, Ayat: 15–17.

In the name of Allah, The Compassionate, The Merciful

RELATIVE COMPUTATION OF TIME

They ask you to hasten the punishment. God will not break His promise. Each day with your Lord is like a thousand years in your reckoning.

Sura: 22, Ayat: 47.

In the name of Allah, The Compassionate, The Merciful

NON-BELIEVER'S WEALTH

Say: 'Whether you give willingly or with reluctance, your offerings shall not be accepted from you; for you are wicked men.'

Nothing prevents their offerings from being accepted except that they have denied Allah and His Apostle. They pray half-heartedly and grudge their contributions.

Let neither their riches nor their children rouse your envy. Through these Allah seeks to punish them in this life, so that they shall be unbelievers.

Sura: 9, Ayat: 53—55.

In the name of Allah, The Compassionate, The Merciful

CORRECT ATTITUDE TOWARDS OTHERS' AFFLUENCE

Do not usurp one another's property by unjust means, nor bribe with it the judges in order that you may knowingly and wrongfully deprive others of a part of their possession.

Sura: 2, Ayat: 188.

Let those (disposing of an orphan's estate) have the same fear in their minds as they would have for their own if they had left a helpless family behind: Let them fear God, and speak words of appropriate (comfort).

Sura: 4, Ayat: 9.

Believers, do not devour your wealth among yourselves illegally, but rather trade with it by mutual consent.

You shall not kill one another. God has been to you Most Merciful!

Sura: 4, Ayat: 29.

And in no wise covet those things in which God has bestowed His gifts more freely on some of you than on others: to men is allotted what they earn, and to women what they earn: But ask God of His bounty. For God has full knowledge of all things.

Sura: 4, Ayat: 32.

We have given you the seven oft-repeated verses and the Glorious Qura'n Do not regard with envy the good things We have bestowed on certain groups of them, nor grieve on their account. Show kindness to the faithful. And say: 'I am the plain warner.'

Sura: 15, Ayat: 87—89.

Be neither miserly nor prodigal, for then you should either be reproached or be reduced to penury.

Your Lord gives abundantly to whom He will and sparingly to whom He pleases. He knows and observes His servants.

Sura: 17, Ayat: 29-30.

Do not strain your eyes towards the worldly benefits We have bestowed on some of them for with these We seek only to test them. Your Lord's provision is better and more lasting.

Sura: 20, Ayat: 131.

....His people said to him: 'Do not exult (in your riches); Allah does not love the exultant. But seek, by means of that which Allah has given you, to attain the abode of the Hereafter. Do not forget your share in this world. Be good to others as Allah has been good to you, and do not strive for evil in the land, for Allah does not love the evildoers.'

Sura: 28, Ayat: 76-77.

But he replied: 'These riches were given me on account of the knowledge I possess.'

Did he not know that Allah had destroyed before him from the generations men who were mightier and greater money-collectors than he? The wrongdoers shall not be questioned (immediately) about their sins.

Sura: 28, Ayat: 78.

And when he went out in all his finery among his people, those who loved this life said: 'Would that we had the like of Qarun's fortune! He is indeed a lucky man.'

Sura: 28, Ayat: 79.

But those to whom knowledge had been given said: 'Alas for you! Better is the reward of Allah for him who has faith and does good works; but none shall attain it save the patient.

Sura: 28, Ayat: 80.

We caused the earth to swallow him, together with his dwelling, so that he found none to protect him from Allah; nor was he one of those who defended themselves.

Sura: 28, Ayat: 81.

And those who on the day before had coveted his lot began to say: 'Behold! Allah gives abundantly to whom He will and sparingly to whom He pleases. Had he not shown us favour, He could have caused the earth to swallow us. Behold! The ungrateful shall never prosper.'

Sura: 28, Ayat: 82.

Allah gives abundantly to whom He will, and sparingly to whom He pleases. He has knowledge of all things.

Sura: 29, Ayat: 62.

ECONOMY

(16)

In the name of Allah, The Compassionate, The Merciful

IMMORAL MEANS OF LIVELIHOOD

Do not usurp one another's property by unjust means, nor bribe with it the judges in order that you may knowingly and wrongfully deprive others of a part of their possessions.

Sura: 2, Ayat: 188.

Believers, do not devour your wealth among yourselves illegally, but rather trade with it by mutual consent.

You shall not kill one another. Allah is Merciful, but he that does that through wickedness and injustice shall be burnt in fire. That is an easy thing for Allah.

Sura: 4, Ayat: 29-30.

Because of their iniquity We forbade the Jews good things which were formerly allowed them; because time after time they have debarred others from the path of Allah; because they practise usury—although they were forbidden it—and cheat others of their possessions. We have prepared a stern chastisement for those of them that disbelieve.

Sura: 4, Ayat: 160-161.

(They are fond of) listening to falsehood, of devouring anything forbidden. If they do come to you, either judge between them, or decline to interfere, they cannot hurt you in the least. If you judge, judge in equity between them. For God loves those who judge in equity.

Sura: 5, Ayat: 42.

When they come to you, they say: 'We believe': But in fact they enter with a mind against Faith, and they go out with the same. But God knows fully all that they hide.

Many of them, that you see, racing each other in sin and rancour, and their eating of things forbidden. Evil indeed are the things that they do.

Why do not the Rabbis and the doctors of law forbid them from their (habit of) uttering sinful words and eating things forbidden? Evil indeed are their

works.

Sura: 5, Ayat: 61–63.

Believers, many are the rabbis and the monks who defraud men of their possessions and debar people from the path of Allah. Those that hoard up gold and silver and do not spend it in Allah's cause—proclaim to them a woeful punishment.

Sura: 9, Ayat: 34.

In the name of Allah, The Compassionate, The Merciful

USURY

O believers, devour not usury, doubling its rate many times. Have fear of Allah, and you shall prosper. Guard yourselves against the Fire prepared for unbelievers.

Sura: 3, Ayat: 130—131.

That which you lay out for increase through the property of (other) people, will have no increase with God: But that which you lay out for charity, seeking the Countenance of God, (will increase): it is these who will get a recompense multiplied.

Sura: 30, Ayat: 39.

Those who devour usury shall rise up before Allah like men whom Satan has demented by his touch; for they claim that usury is like trading. But Allah has permitted trading and forbidden usury. He that receives an admonition from his Lord and mends his ways may keep what he has already earned; his fate is in the hands of Allah. But he that pays no heed shall be among the people of the Fire and shall remain in it forever.

Sura: 2, Ayat: 275.

Allah has laid His curse on usury and blessed almsgiving with increase. He bears no love for the ungrateful sinner.

Sura: 2, Ayat: 276.

O you who believe! Fear God, and give up what remains of your demand for usury, if you are indeed believers.

If you do it not, take notice of war from God and His Apostle: But if you turn back, you shall have your principal: Deal not unjustly, and you shall not be dealt with unjustly.

Sura: 2, Ayat: 278-279.

Because of their iniquity, We forbade the Jews good things which were formerly allowed them; because time after time they have debarred others from

the path of Allah; because they practise usury—although they were forbidden it—and cheat others of their possessions. We have prepared a stern chastisement for those of them that disbelieve.

Sura: 4, Ayat: 160-161.

In the name of Allah, The Compassionate, The Merciful

CORRECTNESS OF WEIGHTS AND MEASURES

....Give just weight and full measure.....

Sura: 6, Ayat: 151-152.

....A clear sign has come to you from your Lord. Give just weight and measure and do not defraud others of their possessions. Do not corrupt the land after it has been purged of evil. That is best for you, if you are true believers.

Sura: 7, Ayat: 85.

And to (the people of) Madain, We sent their brother Shu'ayb. He said: 'My people, serve Allah; you have no god but Him. Do not give short weight or measure. I see you are prosperous. And I fear for you the punishment of an all-compassing day.

'My people, give just weight and measure in all fairness. Do not defraud others of their possessions and do not corrupt the land with evil. What remains with Allah is better for you, if you are true believers. I am no guardian over you.'

Sura: 11, Ayat: 84—86.

Give full measure, when you measure, and weigh with even scales. That is fair, and better in the end.

Sura: 17, Ayat: 35.

Give just measure and defraud none. Weigh with even scales and do not cheat others of what is rightly theirs; nor corrupt the land with evil. Fear Him who created you and created those who have gone before you.

Sura: 26, Ayat: 181—184.

....He has set up the Balance (of Justice), in order that you may not transgress (due) balance. So establish weight with justice and fall not short in the balance.

Sura: 55, Ayat: 7—9.

Woe to those that deal in fraud, who, when others measure for them, exact in full, but when they measure or weigh for others, defraud them!

Do they not think that they will be raised to life upon a fateful day, the day when all mankind will stand before the Lord of the Worlds?

Sura: 83, Ayat: 1–6.

In the name of Allah, The Compassionate, The Merciful

BRIBERY IS FORBIDDEN

Do not usurp one another's property by unjust means, nor bribe with it the judges in order that you knowingly and wrongfully deprive others of a part of their possessions.

Sura: 2, Ayat: 188.

In the name of Allah, The Compassionate, The Merciful

ZAKAT (COMPULSORY AID FOR THE POOR)

Attend to your prayers and pay the alms-tax. Whatever good you do shall be rewarded by Allah. He is watching over all your actions.

Sura: 2, Ayat: 110.

Righteousness does not consist in whether you face towards the east or the west. The righteous man is he who believes in Allah and the Last Day, in the angels and the Book and the Prophets; who for the love of Allah gives his wealth to his kinsfolk, to the orphans, to the needy, to the wayfarers and to the beggars, and for the redemption of captives; who attends to his prayers and pays the alms-tax; who is true to his promises and steadfast in trial and adversity and in times of war. Such are the true believers; such are the God-fearing.

Sura: 2, Ayat: 177.

Those that have faith and do good works, attend to their prayers and pay the alms-tax, will be rewarded by their Lord and will have nothing to fear or to regret.

Sura: 2, Ayat: 277.

There are some among them who speak ill of you* concerning the distribution of alms. If a share is given them, they are contented: but if they receive nothing, they grow resentful.

Would that they were satisfied with what Allah and His Apostle have given them, and would say: 'Allah is All-sufficient for us. He will provide for us from His own abundance,. and so will His Apostle. To Allah, we will turn.'

Sura: 9, Ayat: 58-59.

Alms shall be only for the poor and the needy and for those employed to administer alms, and for those attracted to the faith, and for captives and debtors and for the cause of Allah and the wayfarer. That is a duty enjoined by Allah. He is Wise, Knowing.

Sura: 9, Ayat: 60.

***Muhammad**

The true believers both men and women, are friends to each other. They enjoin what is just and forbid what is evil; they attend to their prayers and pay the alms-tax and obey Allah and His Apostle. On these Allah will have mercy. He is Mighty, Wise.

Sura: 9, Ayat: 71.

And strive in His cause as you ought to strive, (with sincerity and under discipline). He has chosen you, and has imposed no difficulties on you in religion; it is the cult of your father Abraham. It is He Who has named you Muslims, both before and in this (Revelation); that the Apostle may be a witness for you, and you be witnesses for mankind! So establish regular Prayer, give regular Charity, and hold fast to God! He is your Protector — the best to protect and the Best to help!

Sura: 22, Ayat: 78.

Successful indeed are the believers,....who give alms.

Sura: 23, Ayat: 1—4.

Attend to your prayers, pay the alms-tax, and obey the Apostle, so that you may be shown mercy.

Sura: 24, Ayat: 56.

Ta sin. These are the verses of the Quran, the Book which indicates (right and wrong); a guidance and joyful news to true believers, who attend to their prayers and pay the alms-tax and firmly believe in the life to come.

Sura: 27, Ayat: 1—3.

That which you lay out for increase through the property of (other) people, will have no increase with God: but that which you lay out for charity seeking the Countenance of God, (will increase); it is these who will get a recompense multiplied.

Sura: 30, Ayat: 39.

These are the revelations of the Wise Book, a guidance and a blessing to the righteous, who attend to their prayers, pay the alms-tax, and firmly believe in the life to come. These are rightly guided by their Lord and will surely prosper.

Sura: 31, Ayat: 2—5.

....Attend to your prayers, pay the alms-tax, and give Allah a generous loan. Whatever good you do you shall surely find it with Allah, ennobled and richly rewarded by Him. Implore Allah to forgive you; He is Forgiving, Merciful.

Sura: 73, Ayat: 20.

And they have been commanded no more than this: to worship God, offering Him sincere devotion, being True (in faith); and to practise regular Charity; and that is the Religion Right and Straight.

Sura: 98, Ayat: 5.

In the name of Allah, The Compassionate, The Merciful

TAX ON AGRICULTURAL PRODUCT

O you who have attained to faith! Spend on others out of the good things which you may have acquired, and out of that which We bring forth for you from the earth; and choose not for your spending (on others) the bad things which you yourselves would not accept without averting your eyes in disdain. And know that God is Self-sufficient, ever to be praised.

Sura: 2, Ayat: 267.

It is He Who brings forth gardens (with) creepers and upright (plants), the palm and seed-produce with various fruits and the olive and pomegranates, similar (in kind) and different in variety. Eat of its fruits when it bears fruit and pay (unto the poor) what is due of them upon the harvest day. But do not be prodigal; Allah does not love the prodigal.

Sura: 6, Ayat: 141.

In the name of Allah, The Compassionate, The Merciful

CHARITY

This Book is not to be doubted. It is a guide for the righteous, who have faith in the unseen and are steadfast in prayer; who spend out of what We have given them.

Sura: 2, Ayat: 2-3.

Righteousness does not consist in whether you face towards the east or the west. The righteous man is he who believes in Allah and the Last Day, in the Angels and the Book and the Prophets; who for the love of Allah gives his wealth to his kinsfolk, to the orphans, to the needy, to the wayfarers and to the beggars, and for the redemption of captives; who attends to his prayers and pays the alms-tax; who is true to his promises and steadfast in trial and adversity and in times of war. Such are the true believers; such are the God-fearing.

Sura: 2, Ayat: 177.

And spend of your substance in the cause of God, and make not your own hands contribute to (your) destruction; but do good; for God loves those who do good.

Sura: 2, Ayat: 195.

They will ask you about alms-giving. Say: 'Whatever you bestow in charity must go to your parents and to your kinsfolk, to the orphan and to the poor man and to the wayfarer. Allah is aware of whatever good you do.'

Sura: 2, Ayat: 215.

....They ask you what they should spend in God's cause. Say: 'What you can spare.' Thus Allah makes plain to you His revelations, so that you may reflect upon this world and the Hereafter.

Sura: 2, Ayat: 219.

Who will grant Allah a generous loan? He will repay him many times over. It is Allah who enriches and makes poor. To Him you shall all return.

Sura: 2, Ayat: 245.

O believers, spend a part of what We have given you before that day arrives when there shall be neither trading nor friendship nor intercession. Truly, it is the unbelievers who are the wrongdoers.

Sura: 2, Ayat: 254.

They that give their wealth for the cause of Allah are like a grain of corn which brings forth seven ears, each bearing a hundred grains. Allah gives abundance to whom He will; He is Munificent and All-Knowing.

Sura: 2, Ayat: 261.

Those that spend their wealth for the cause of Allah and do not follow their spending with taunts and insults shall be rewarded by their Lord; they shall have nothing to fear or to regret.

Sura: 2, Ayat: 262.

O believers, do not mar your almsgiving with taunts and mischief-making, like him who spends his wealth for the sake of ostentation and believes neither in Allah nor in the Last Day. Such a man is like a smooth rock covered with earth; a shower falls upon it and leaves it hard and bare. They shall gain nothing from their works. Allah does not guide the unbelievers.

Sura: 2, Ayat: 264.

But those that give away their wealth from a desire to please Allah and to reassure their own souls are like a garden on a hill-side: if a shower falls upon it, it yields up twice its normal crop; and if no rain falls upon it, it is watered by the dew. Allah takes cognizance of all your actions.

Sura: 2, Ayat: 265.

O you who have attained to faith! Spend on others out of the good things which you may have acquired, and out of that which We bring forth for you from the earth; and choose not for your spending (on others) the bad things which you yourselves would not accept without averting your eyes in disdain. And know that God is Self-sufficient, ever to be praised.

Sura: 2, Ayat: 267.

Satan threatens you with poverty and orders you to commit what is indecent. But Allah promises you His forgiveness and His bounty. Allah is Munificent and All-knowing.

Sura: 2, Ayat: 268.

Whatever you spend and whatever vows you make are known to Allah. The evildoers shall have none to help them.

Sura: 2, Ayat: 270.

To be charitable in public is good, but to give alms to the poor in private is better and will atone for some of your sins. Allah has knowledge of all what you do.

Sura: 2, Ayat: 271.

It is not for you to guide them. Allah gives guidance to whom He will.

Whatever wealth you give shall rebound to your own advantage, provided that you give it for the love of Allah. And whatever wealth you give shall be paid back to you in full: you shall not be wronged.

Sura: 2, Ayat: 272.

(Charity) is for the poor who, being wholly preoccupied with the cause of Allah, cannot travel in the land (in quest of trading ventures.) The ignorant take them for men of wealth on account of their being too proud because they abstain (from begging). But you can recognize them by their – look they never importune men for alms. Whatever alms you give are known to Allah.

Sura: 2, Ayat: 273.

Those that give alms by day and night, in private and in public, shall be rewarded by their Lord. They have nothing to fear or to regret.

Sura: 2, Ayat: 274.

Allah has laid His curse on usury and blessed almsgiving with increase. He bears no love for the ungrateful sinner.

Sura: 2, Ayat: 276.

By no means shall you attain righteousness unless you give (freely) of that which you love; and whatever you give, of a truth God knows it well.

Sura: 3, Ayat: 92.

Be quick in the race for forgiveness from your Lord, and for a Garden whose width is that (of the whole) of the heavens and of the earth, prepared for the righteous — those who spend (freely), whether in prosperity, or in adversity; who restrain anger, and pardon (all) men; — for God loves those who do good.

Sura: 3, Ayat: 133-134.

Let not those who are niggardly in spending, from that which Allah granted them of His bounty, think that their avarice is good for them: it is nothing but evil. The riches they have piled up shall become their fetters on the Day of Resurrection. Allah is He Who will inherit the heavens and the earth. He is cognizant of what you do.

Sura: 3, Ayat: 180.

....Allah does not love arrogant and boastful men, who are themselves niggardly and enjoin others to be niggardly also; who conceal that which Allah of His bounty has bestowed upon them — We have prepared a shameful punishment for the unbelievers—and who spend their wealth for the sake of ostentation, believing neither in Allah nor in the Last Day. He that chooses the devil for his friend, an evil friend has he.

What harm could befall them if they believed in Allah and the Last Day and gave in alms of that which He has bestowed on them? Allah knows them all.

Sura: 4, Ayat: 36—39.

The true believers are those whose hearts are filled with awe at the mention of Allah, and whose faith grows stronger as they listen to His revelations. They are those who put their trust in their Lord, pray steadfastly, and spend of that which We have given them.

Sura: 8, Ayat: 2-3.

....All that you give for the cause of Allah shall be repaid you. You shall not be wronged.

Sura: 8, Ayat: 60.

Say: 'Spend (for the Cause) willingly or unwillingly: Not from you will it be accepted: for you are indeed a people rebellious and wicked.'

The only reason why their contributions are not accepted are: that they reject God and His Apostle; that they come to prayer without earnestness; and that they offer contributions unwillingly.

Sura: 9, Ayat: 53-54.

Some of the desert Arabs look upon their payments as a fine, and watch for disasters for you: on them be the disaster of Evil: For God is He that hears and knows (all things).

But some of the desert Arabs believe in God and the Last Day, and look on their payments as pious gifts bringing them nearer to God and to the prayers of the Apostle, Aye, indeed they bring them nearer (to Him): soon will God admit them to His Mercy: For God is Oft-Forgiving, Most Merciful.

Sura: 9, Ayat: 98-99.

Others there are who have confessed their sins; their good works had been intermixed with evil. Perchance Allah will turn to them in mercy. He is Forgiving, Merciful. Take alms from their wealth, so that they may thereby be cleansed and purified, and pray for them: for your prayers will give them comfort. Allah is Hearing, Knowing.

Do they not know that Allah accepts the repentance of His servants and takes their alms, and that Allah is The Forgiving One, The Merciful?

Sura: 9, Ayat: 102—104.

Each sum they give, be it small or large, and each journey they undertake, shall be noted down, so that Allah may reward them for their noblest deeds.

Sura: 9, Ayat: 121.

Those who for the sake of Allah endure with fortitude, attend to their prayers, and spend of what We have given them in private and in public; and who ward off evil with good; These shall have a blissful end.

Sura: 13, Ayat: 22.

Tell My servants, those who are true believers, to be steadfast in prayer and spend in charity in private and in public of what We have given them, before the coming of that day in which there is neither trading nor friendship.

Sura: 14, Ayat: 31.

Allah sets forth this parable. On the one hand, there is a helpless slave, the property of his master. On the other, a man on whom We have bestowed Our bounty, so that he gives of it both in private and in public. Are the two alike? Allah forbid! Most men have no knowledge.

Sura: 16, Ayat: 75.

Give to the near of kin their due, and also to the destitute and to the wayfarers. Do not squander (your substance) wastefully, for the wasteful are the devils' brothers: and the devil is ever ungrateful to his Lord. But if you turn away from them to seek your Lord's mercy, hoping to attain it then say kind words to them.

Sura: 17, Ayat: 26—28.

Be neither miserly nor prodigal, for then you should either be reproached or be reduced to penury.

Your Lord gives abundantly to whom He will and sparingly to whom He pleases. He knows and observes His servants.

Sura: 17, Ayat: 29-30.

....Give good news to the humble, whose hearts are filled with awe at the mention of their Lord: who endure their misfortunes with fortitude, attend to their prayers, and bestow in charity of that which We have given them.

Sura: 22, Ayat: 34-35.

Let not the honourable and rich among you swear not to give to their kindred, the poor, and those who have emigrated for the cause of Allah. Rather, let them pardon and forgive. Do you not wish Allah to forgive you? He is Forgiving, Merciful.

Sura: 24, Ayat: 22.

Say: 'My Lord gives abundantly to whom He will, and sparingly to whom He pleases. Whatever you give in alms He will pay you back for it. He is the Most Munificent Giver.'

Sura: 34, Ayat: 39

When it is recited to them, they say: 'We believe in it because it is the truth from Our Lord. We surrendered ourselves to Him before it came.'

Twice shall their reward be given them, because they have endured, repelling evil with good and giving in alms a part of that which We bestowed on them.

Sura: 28, Ayat: 53-54.

None believes in Our revelations save those who, when reminded of them, prostrate themselves in adoration and give glory to their Lord in all humility; who forsake their beds to pray to their Lord in fear and hope; who give in charity of that which We have bestowed on them.

Sura: 32, Ayat: 15-16.

Those who recite the Book of Allah and attend to their prayers and give alms in private and in public may hope for imperishable gain. Allah will give them their rewards and enrich them from His own abundance. He is Forgiving and Rewarding.

Sura: 35, Ayat: 29-30.

And when it is said to them: 'Give alms of that which Allah has given you.' The unbelievers say to the faithful: 'Are we to feed those whom Allah can feed if He chooses? Surely you are in undoubted error.'

Sura: 36, Ayat: 47.

That which you have been given is but the fleeting comfort of this life. Better and more enduring is that which Allah has for those who believe and put their trust in Him;....who bestow in alms a part of that which We have given them.....

Sura: 42, Ayat: 36—39.

The life of this world is but play and amusement: And if you believe and guard against evil, He will grant you your recompense, and will not ask you (to give up) your possessions.

Sura: 47, Ayat: 36.

If He demanded all and strongly pressed you, you would grow niggardly and this would show your ill feelings.

Sura: 47, Ayat: 37.

You are called upon to give in the cause of Allah. Some of you are niggardly; yet whoever is niggardly to this cause is niggardly to himself. Indeed, Allah is rich, but you are poor. If you give no heed, He will replace you by others. And these will not be like you.

Sura: 47, Ayat: 38.

The righteous shall dwell amidst gardens and fountains, and shall receive what their Lord will give them. For they were before doers of good. They used to sleep but little in the nighttime, praying at dawn for Allah's pardon, and in their wealth was a due share to the beggar and to him who is too proud to beg.

Sura: 51, Ayat: 15—19.

....For whoever of you believes and gives in alms shall be richly rewarded.

Sura: 57, Ayat: 7.

And why should you not give in the cause of Allah, when He alone will inherit the heavens and the earth? Those of you that gave of their wealth before the victory and took part in the fighting are not equal (to those who gave and fought thereafter). Their degree is greater. Yet Allah has promised you all a good reward; He has knowledge of all your actions.

Sura: 57, Ayat: 10.

Who is he that will loan to God a beautiful Loan? For (God) will increase it manifold to his credit, and he will have (besides) a liberal reward.

Sura: 57, Ayat: 11.

For those who give in Charity, men and women, and loan to God a Beautiful Loan, it shall be increased manifold (to their credit), and they shall have (besides) a liberal reward.

Sura: 57, Ayat: 18.

But those who before them, had homes (in Medina) and had adopted the Faith, — show their affection to such as came to them for refuge, and entertain no desire in their hearts for things given to the (latter), but give them preference over themselves, even though poverty was their (own lot). And those saved from the covetousness of their own souls,—they are the ones that achieve prosperity.

Sura: 59, Ayat: 9.

And spend something (in charity) out of the substance which We have bestowed on you, before Death should come to any of you and he should say, 'O my Lord! Why did you not give me respite for a little while? I should then have given (largely) in charity, and I should have been one of the doers of good'.

But to no soul will God grant respite when the time appointed (for it) has

come; and God is well acquainted with (all) that you do.

Sura: 63, Ayat: 10-11.

Your riches and your children may be but a trial: But in the Presence of God, is the highest Reward. So fear God as much as you can; listen (to Him) and obey; and spend in charity for the benefit of your own souls. And those saved from the covetousness of their own souls, they are the ones that achieve prosperity.

Sura: 64, Ayat: 15-16.

If you loan to God, a beautiful loan, He will ever increase it to your (credit), and He will grant you Forgiveness: For God is most Ready to appreciate (gratitude), Most Forbearing.

Sura: 64, Ayat: 17.

Indeed, man was created impatient. When evil befalls him he is despondent; but blessed with good fortune he grows niggardly.

Not so the worshippers who are steadfast in prayer; who set aside a due portion of their goods for the needy who asks, and him, who is prevented (for some reason from asking).

Sura: 70, Ayat: 19—25.

....Attend to your prayers, pay the alms-tax, and give Allah a generous loan. Whatever good you do you shall surely find it with Allah, ennobled and richly rewarded by Him. Implore Allah to forgive you; He is Forgiving, Merciful.

Sura: 73, Ayat: 20.

Your endeavours have different ends!

For him that gives (in charity) and guards himself (by obeying Allah) and believes in goodness, We shall smooth the path of salvation, but for him that neither gives nor seeks Allah's reward, and disbelieves in goodness We shall smooth the path of affliction. When he breathes his last, his riches will not avail him.

Sura: 92, Ayat: 4—11.

It is for Us to give guidance. Ours is (the dominion over) the life of this world and the life to come. I warn you, then, of the blazing fire, in which none shall burn save the hardened sinner, who denies the truth and gives no heed. But kept away from it will be the more righteous who gives in alms but not in return for any favour done to him, and who also does good only for the sake of the reward of God, Most High. Verily, he will be content.

Sura: 92, Ayat: 12—21.

In the name of Allah, The Compassionate, The Merciful

BENEFITS OF CHARITY

To be charitable in public is good, but to give alms to the poor in private is better and will atone for some of yours sins. Allah has knowledge of all what you do.

Sura: 2, Ayat: 271.

Others there are who have confessed their sins; their good works had been intermixed with evil. Perchance Allah will turn to them in mercy. He is Forgiving, Merciful. Take alms from their wealth, so that they may thereby be cleansed and purified, and pray for them: for your prayers will give them comfort. Allah is Hearing, Knowing.

Do they not know that Allah accepts the repentance of His servants and takes their alms, and that Allah is the Forgiving One, The Merciful?

Sura: 9, Ayat: 102–104.

If you loan to God a beautiful loan, He will ever increase it to your (credit), and He will grant you Forgiveness: For God is most Ready to appreciate (gratitude), Most Forbearing.

Sura: 64, Ayat: 17.

In the name of Allah, The Compassionate, The Merciful

RIDICULING CONTRIBUTIONS OF THE POOR

Those who slander such of the Believers as give themselves freely to (deeds of) charity, as well as such as can find nothing to give except the fruits of their labour, — and throw ridicule on them, — God will throw back their ridicule on them: And they shall have a grievious penalty.

Sura: 9, Ayat: 79.

In the name of Allah, The Compassionate, The Merciful

THE VOW

Whatever you spend and whatever vows you make are known to Allah. The evildoers shall have none to help them.

Sura: 2, Ayat: 270.

Some of them make a covenant with Allah (saying): 'If Allah is bountiful to us, we will give alms and live like righteous men.' But when Allah had bestowed His favours on them, they grew niggardly and, turning their backs, hurried away. He has caused hypocrisy to be in their hearts till the day they meet Him, because they have been untrue to the promise they made Him and because they have invented falsehoods.

Sura: 9, Ayat: 75—77.

Proclaim the pilgrimage to men. They will come to you on foot and on the backs of swift camels from every distant quarter; (they will come) to avail themselves of many a benefit and to pronounce on the appointed days the name of Allah over the cattle which He has given them. Eat of their flesh yourselves, and feed the poor and the unfortunate.

Then let the pilgrims accomplish their acts of cleansing, make their vows, and go round the Ancient House.

Sura: 22, Ayat: 27—29.

As to the righteous, they shall drink of a Cup (of Wine) mixed with Kafur, — A fountain where the Devotees of God do drink, making it flow in unstinted abundance. They perform (their) vows, and they fear a Day whose evil flies far and wide. And they feed, for the love of God, the indigent, the orphan, and the captive, — (Saying): 'We feed you for the sake of God alone; no reward do we desire from you, nor thanks. We only fear a Day of Distressful Wrath from the side of our Lord."

But God will deliver them from the evil of that Day, and will shed over them a Light of Beauty and a (blissful) Joy.

Sura: 76, Ayat: 5—11.

In the name of Allah, The Compassionate, The Merciful

THE NEEDY

Righteousness does not consist in whether you face towards the east or the west. The righteous man is he who believes in Allah and the Last Day, in the angels and the Book and the Prophets; who for the love of Allah gives his wealth to his kinsfolk, to the orphans, to the needy, to the wayfarers and to the beggars, and for the redemption of captives; who attends to his prayers and pays the alms-tax; who is true to his promises and steadfast in trial and adversity and in times of war. Such are the true believers; such are the God-fearing.

Sura: 2, Ayat: 177.

They will ask you about almsgiving. Say: 'Whatever you bestow in charity must go to your parents and to your kinsfolk, to the orphans and to the poor man and to the wayfarer. Allah is aware of whatever good you do.'

Sura: 2, Ayat: 215.

(Charity) is for the poor who, being wholly preoccupied with the cause of Allah, cannot travel in the land (in quest of trading venture). The ignorant take them for men of wealth on account of their being too proud because they abstain (from begging). But you can recognise them by their look — they never importune men for alms. Whatever alms you give are known to Allah.

Sura: 2, Ayat: 273.

If relatives, orphans, or needy men are present at the division of an inheritance give them, too, a share of it, and speak to them in kind words.

Sura: 4, Ayat: 8.

There are some among them who speak ill of you* concerning the distribution of alms. If a share is given them, they are contented: but if they receive nothing, they grow resentful.

Would that they were satisfied with what Allah and His Apostle have given them, and would say: 'Allah is All-sufficient for us. He will provide for us

***Muhammad**

from His own abundance, and so will His Apostle. To Allah, we will turn.'

Sura: 9, Ayat: 58-59.

Alms shall be only for the poor and the needy and for those employed to administer alms, and for those attracted to the faith, and for captives and debtors and for the cause of Allah and the wayfarer. That is a duty enjoined by Allah. He is Wise, Knowing.

Sura: 9, Ayat: 60.

Give to the near of kin their due, and also to the destitute and to the way-farers.....

Sura: 17, Ayat: 26.

Let not the honourable and rich among you swear not to give to their kindred, the poor, and those who have emigrated for the cause of Allah. Rather, let them pardon and forgive. Do you not wish Allah to forgive you? He is Forgiving, Merciful.

Sura: 24, Ayat: 22.

In the name of Allah, The Compassionate, The Merciful

HELPING PIOUS PEOPLE

And keep yourself content with those who pray to their Lord morning and evening, seeking His Face. And do not turn your eyes away from them in quest of the good things of this life nor obey him whose heart We have made heedless of Our remembrance; who follows his desires and whose case exceeds due bounds.

Sura: 18, Ayat: 28.

Allah will defend the true believers (against evil). Verily God does not love the treacherous and the thankless.

Sura: 22, Ayat: 38.

....But whoever helps Allah shall be helped by Him. Allah is truly Powerful and Mighty.

Sura: 22, Ayat: 39-40.

....Therefore give no help to the unbelievers.

Sura: 28, Ayat: 86.

In the name of Allah, The Compassionate, The Merciful

TRUST

....And if one of you deposits a thing on trust with another, let the trustee (faithfully) discharge his trust, and let him fear his Lord.....

Sura: 2, Ayat: 283.

God does command you to render back your Trusts to those to whom they are due; and when you judge between man and man, that you judge with justice: Verily how excellent is the teaching which He gives you! For God is He Who hears and sees all things.

Sura: 4, Ayat: 58.

O you that believe! Betray not the trust of God and the Apostle, nor misappropriate knowingly things entrusted to you. And know you that your possessions and your progeny are but a trial; and that it is God with whom lies your highest reward.

Sura: 8, Ayat: 27-28.

The Believers must (eventually) win through;....Those who faithfully observe their trusts and their covenants.

Sura: 23, Ayat: 1–8.

Truly man was created very impatient; fretful when evil touches him; and niggardly when good reaches him; not so those devoted to Prayers: Those who remain steadfast to their prayer;....and those who respect their trusts and covenants.

Sura: 70, Ayat: 19–32.

In the name of Allah, The Compassionate, The Merciful

BREACH OF TRUST

No prophet could (ever) be false to his trust. If any person is so false, he shall, on the Day of Judgement, restore what he misappropriated; then shall every soul receive its due, — whatever it earned, — and none shall be dealt with unjustly.

Sura: 3, Ayat: 161.

Contend not on behalf of such as betray their own souls; for God loves not one given to perfidy and crime; they may hide (their crimes) from men, but they cannot hide (them) from God, seeing that He is in their midst when they plot by night, in words that He cannot approve: and God does compass round all that they do.

Sura: 4, Ayat: 107-108.

But because of their breach of their Covenant, We cursed them, and made their hearts grow hard: They change the words from their (right) places and forget a good part of the Message that was sent them, nor will you cease to find them — barring a few — ever bent on (new) deceits: But forgive them, and overlook (their misdeeds): for God loves those who are kind.

Sura: 5, Ayat: 13.

O you that believe! Betray not the trust of God and the Apostle, nor misappropriate knowingly things entrusted to you. And know you that your possessions and your progeny are but a trial; and that it is God with Whom lies your highest reward.

Sura: 8, Ayat: 27-28.

If you fear treachery from any of your allies, you may throw back to them (their treaty) fairly. Allah does not love the treacherous.

Sura: 8, Ayat: 58.

'From this,' (said Joseph), '(my Lord) will know that I did not betray him

in his absence, and that Allah does not guide the work of the treacherous.

Sura: 12, Ayat: 52.

Allah will defend the true believers (against evil). Verily God does not love the treacherous and thankless.

Sura: 22, Ayat: 38.

In the name of Allah, The Compassionate, The Merciful

NIGGARDLINESS

Satan threatens you with poverty and orders you to commit what is indecent. But Allah promises you His forgiveness and His bounty. Allah is Munificent and All-knowing.

He gives wisdom to whom He will; and he that receives the gift of wisdom is rich indeed. Yet none except men of sense bear this in mind.

Sura: 2, Ayat: 268-269.

Let not those who are niggardly in spending from that which Allah granted them of His bounty think that their avarice is good for them: it is nothing but evil. The riches they have piled up shall become their fetters on the Day of Resurrection. Allah is He who will inherit the heavens and the earth. He is cognizant of what you do.

Sura: 3, Ayat: 180.

....Allah does not love arrogant and boastful men, who are themselves niggardly and enjoin others to be niggardly also; who conceal that which Allah of His bounty has bestowed upon them. We have prepared a shameful punishment for the unbelievers.

Sura: 4, Ayat: 36-37.

What harm could befall them if they believed in Allah and the Last Day and gave in alms of that which He has bestowed on them? Allah knows them all.

Sura: 4, Ayat: 39.

If a woman fears ill-treatment or desertion on the part of her husband, it shall be no offence for them to seek a mutual agreement, for agreement is best. Man is prone to avarice. But if you do what is right and guard yourselves against evil, know then that Allah is cognizant of all what you do.

Sura: 4, Ayat: 128.

Believers, many are the rabbis and the monks who defraud men of their possessions and debar people from the path of Allah. Those that hoard up

gold and silver and do not spend it in Allah's cause—proclaim to them a woeful punishment. (On that) day their treasures will be heated in the fire of Hell, and their foreheads, sides, and backs branded with them. They will be told: 'These are the riches which you hoarded. Taste then that which you were hoarding.

Sura: 9, Ayat: 34-35.

Some of them make a covenant with Allah (saying): 'If Allah is bountiful to us, we will give alms and live like righteous men.' But when Allah had bestowed His favours on them, they grew niggardly and, turning their backs, hurried away. He has caused hypocrisy to be in their hearts till the day they meet Him, because they have been untrue to the promise they made Him and because they have invented falsehoods.

Sura: 9, Ayat: 75—77.

Those who slander such of the Believers as give themselves freely to (deeds of) charity, as well as such as can find nothing to give except the fruits of their labour,—and throw ridicule on them,—God will throw back their ridicule on them: And they shall have a grievous penalty.

Sura: 9, Ayat: 79.

Be neither miserly nor prodigal, for then you should either be reproached or be reduced to penury.

Your Lord gives abundantly to whom He will and sparingly to whom He pleases. He knows and observes His servants.

Sura: 17, Ayat: 29-30.

Say: "If you had control of the Treasures of the Mercy of my Lord, Behold, you would keep them back, for fear of spending them: for man is (ever) niggardly!"

Sura: 17, Ayat: 100.

And when it is said to them: 'Give alms of that which Allah has given you,' the unbelievers say to the faithful. 'Are we to feed those whom Allah can feed if He chooses? Surely you are in undoubted error.'

Sura: 36, Ayat: 47.

The life of this world is but play and amusement: And if you believe and guard against evil, He will grant you your recompense, and will not ask you (to give up) your possessions.

If He were to ask you for all of them, and press you, you would covetously withhold, and He would bring out all your ill-feeling.

Behold, you are those invited to spend (of your substance) in the Way of God: But among you are some that are niggardly. But any who are niggardly

are so at the expense of their own souls. But God is free of all wants, and it is you that are needy. If you turn back (from the Path), He will substitute in your stead another people; then they would not be like you!

Sura: 47, Ayat: 36-37.

No misfortune can befall the earth, or your own persons, but is recorded in a book before We bring it into being. That is easy for Allah; so that you may not grieve for the good things you miss or be overjoyed at what you gain. Allah does not love the haughty, the vainglorious; nor those who, being niggardly themselves, enjoin others to be niggardly also. He that gives no heed (should know) that Allah is Self-sufficient and Worthy of praise.

Sura: 57, Ayat: 22-24.

Your riches and your children may be but a trial: Whereas with God there is a tremendous reward. So fear God as much as you can; listen (to Him) and obey; and spend in charity for the benefit of your own souls. And those saved from the covetousness of their own souls, — they are the ones that achieve prosperity.

Sura: 64, Ayat: 15-16.

By no means! For it would be the Fire of Hell! — Plucking out (his being) right to the skull! — Inviting (all) such as turn their backs and turn away their faces (from the Right), and collect (wealth) and hide it (from use). Truly man was created very impatient; — fretful when evil touches him; and niggardly when good reaches him.

Sura: 70, Ayat: 15—21.

But he who is a greedy miser and thinks himself self-sufficient, and gives the lie to the best, We will indeed make smooth for him the Path of Misery; nor will his wealth profit him when he falls headlong (into the Pit).

Sura: 92, Ayat: 8—11.

Woe to every backbiter, slanderer who amasses wealth and counts it thinking his wealth will render him immortal!

By no means! They shall be flung to the Destroying Flame.

Would that you knew what the Destroying Flame is like!

It is Allah's own kindled fire, which will rise up to the hearts of men. It will close upon them from every side, in towering columns.

Sura: 104, Ayat: 1—9.

In the name of Allah, The Compassionate, The Merciful

EXTRAVAGANCE

O Children of Adam! Wear your beautiful apparel at every time and place of prayer: eat and drink: but waste not by excess, for God loves not the waster.

Sura: 7, Ayat: 31.

Do not squander (your substance) wastefully, for the wasteful are the devils' brothers; and the devil is ever ungrateful to his Lord.

Sura: 17, Ayat: 26-27.

The servants of the Merciful are those....who when they spend are neither extravagant nor niggardly, but keep the golden mean.

Sura: 25, Ayat: 63–67.

In the name of Allah, The Compassionate, The Merciful

CORRECT SPENDING

Be neither miserly nor prodigal, for then you should either be reproached or be reduced to penury.

Your Lord gives abundantly to whom He will and sparingly to whom He pleases. He knows and observes His servants.

Sura: 17, Ayat: 29-30.

Those who when they spend are neither extravagant nor niggardly, but keep the golden mean.

Sura: 25, Ayat: 67.

In the name of Allah, The Compassionate, The Merciful

SAVING YOUR POSSESSIONS FROM THE IMMATURE

Do not give the feeble-minded the property with which Allah has entrusted you for their support; but maintain and clothe them with its proceeds, and give them good advice.

Sura: 4, Ayat: 5.

GRACEFUL LIVING

(17)

In the name of Allah, The Compassionate, The Merciful

RELATIONSHIP WITH PARENTS

When We made a covenant with the children of Israel: You serve none but Allah. Show kindness to your parents, to your kinsfolk, to the orphans, and to the destitute. Exhort men to righteousness. Attend to your prayers and pay the alms-tax. But you all turned your backs except a few, and gave no heed.

Sura: 2, Ayat: 83.

It is decreed that when death approaches, those of you that leave wealth shall bequeath it equitably to parents and kindred. This is a duty incumbent on the righteous.

Sura: 2, Ayat: 180.

They will ask you about alms-giving, Say: 'Whatever you bestow in charity must go to your parents and to your kinsfolk, to the orphan and to the poor man and to the wayfarer. Allah is aware of whatever good you do.'

Sura: 2, Ayat: 215.

Serve Allah and associate none with Him. Show kindness to your parents and your kindred, to the orphans and to the needy, to your near and distant neighbours, to your fellow-travellers, to the wayfarers, and to the slaves whom you own. Allah does not love arrogant and boastful men.

Sura: 4, Ayat: 36.

Say: 'Come, I will tell you what your Lord has made binding on you: ....that you shall show kindness to your parents: ....

Sura: 6, Ayat: 151.

Ibrahim prayed for his father only to fulfil a promise he had made him. But when he realized he was an enemy of Allah, he disowned him. Surely Ibrahim was a compassionate and tender-hearted man.

Sura: 9, Ayat: 114.

'Lord, make me and my descendants steadfast in prayer. Lord, accept my

prayer.

'Forgive me, our Lord, and forgive my parents and all the faithful on the Day of reckoning.'

Sura:14, Ayat: 40-41.

Serve no other gods besides Allah, lest you be despised, forsaken. Your Lord has enjoined you to worship none but Him, and show kindness to your parents. If either or both of them attain old age with you, show them no sign of impatience nor rebuke them; but speak to them kind words. Treat them with humility and tenderness and say: 'Lord, be merciful to them. They nursed me when I was an infant.'

Your Lord best knows what is in your hearts. If you are good, He will forgive those that turn to Him.

Sura: 17, Ayat: 23—25.

'O Yahya, hold fast to the Book,' We bestowed on him wisdom while yet a child and (gave him) pity (for others) and purity; and he grew up a righteous man; honouring his father and mother, and neither arrogant nor rebellious. Peace on him on the day he was born and the day he dies; and may peace be on him when he is raised to life.

Sura: 19, Ayat: 12—15.

She pointed to him. But they replied: 'How can we speak with a baby in the cradle? (Whereupon) he said: 'I am the servant of Allah. He has given me the Book and made me a prophet. He made me blessed wherever I go, and He has commanded me to be steadfast in prayer and to give alms to the poor as long as I shall live. He has made me kind to my mother and not insolent, miserable. So peace be on me on the day I was born, and on the day I die; and may peace be upon me on the day when I shall be raised to life.'

Sura: 19, Ayat: 29—33.

Sulayman smiled at her words, and said: 'Inspire me, Lord, to render thanks for the favours You have bestowed on me and on my parents, and to do good works that will please You. Include me, through Your mercy, among Your righteous servants.'

Sura: 27, Ayat: 19.

We have enjoined man to show kindness to his parents. But if they bid you to associate with Me what you know nothing of, do not obey them. To Me you will all return, and I shall declare to you all that you have done.

Sura: 29, Ayat: 8.

And We have enjoined on man (to be good) to his parents: in travail upon travail did his mother bear him, and in years twain was his weaning: (hear the

command), 'Show gratitude to Me and to your parents: to Me is (your final) Goal.

'But if they strive to make you join in worship with Me things of which you have no knowledge, obey them not; yet bear them company in this life with justice (and consideration), and follow the way of those who turn to Me (in love): In the End the return of you all is to Me, and I will tell you the truth (and meaning) of all that you did.'

Sura: 31, Ayat: 14-15.

We have enjoined man to show kindness to his parents. With much pain his mother bears him, and with much pain she brings him into the world. He is born and weaned in thirty months. When he grows to manhood and attains his fortieth year, let him say: Grant me, Lord, that I may give thanks for the favours You have bestowed on me and on my parents, and to do good works that will please You. Grant me good descendants. To You I turn and to You I surrender myself.'

Such are those from whom We will accept their noblest works and whose misdeeds We shall overlook. (We shall include them) among the people of Paradise: true is the promise that has been given them.

Sura: 46, Ayat: 15-16.

But (you find one) who says to his parents: 'Fie on you! Do you threaten me with a resurrection when entire generations have passed away before me?' But they pray for Allah's help and say: 'Woe to you! Have faith. the promise of Allah is true.' He replied: 'This is but a fable of the ancients.'

He shall justly deserve the fate of bygone nations of men and jinn: he shall assuredly be lost.

There are degrees for all, according to their deeds, so that Allah may duly requite them for their works.

Sura: 46, Ayat: 17—19.

Forgive me, Lord, and forgive my parents and every true believer who seeks refuge in my house. Forgive all the faithful, men and women, and hasten the destruction of the wrongdoers.'

Sura: 71, Ayat: 28.

In the name of Allah, The Compassionate, The Merciful

RELATIONSHIP WITH KITH AND KIN

When We made a covenant with the children of Israel: You serve none but Allah. Show kindness to your parents, to your kinsfolk, to the orphans, and to the destitute. Exhort men to righteousness. Attend to your prayers and pay the alms-tax. But you all turned your backs except a few, and gave no heed.

Sura: 2, Ayat: 83.

Righteousness does not consist in whether you face towards the east or the west. The righteous man is he who believes in Allah and the Last Day, in the angels and the Book and the prophets; who for the love of Allah gives his wealth to his kinsfolk, to the orphans, to the needy, to the wayfarers and to the beggars, and for the redemption of captives; who attends to his prayers and pays the alms-tax; who is true to his promises and steadfast in trial and adversity and in times of war. Such are the true believers; such are the God-fearing.

Sura: 2, Ayat: 177.

It is decreed that when death approaches, those of you that leave wealth shall bequeath it equitably to parents and kindred. This is a duty incumbent on the righteous.

Sura: 2, Ayat: 180.

They will ask you about alms-giving, Say: 'Whatever you bestow in charity must go to your parents and to your kinsfolk, to the orphan and to the poor man and to the wayfarer. Allah is aware of whatever good you do.'

Sura: 2, Ayat: 215.

Men, have fear of your Lord, who created you from a single soul. From that soul He created its mate, and through them He bestrewed the earth with countless men and women.

Fear Allah, in whose name you plead with one another, and honour the mothers who bore you. Allah is ever watching over you.

Sura: 4, Ayat: 1.

If relatives, orphans, or needy men are present at the division of an inheritance, give them, too, a share of it, and speak to them in kind words.

Sura: 4, Ayat: 8.

Serve Allah and associate none with Him. Show kindness to your parents and your kindred, to the orphans and to the needy, to your near and distant neighbours, to your fellow-travellers, to the wayfarers, and to the slaves whom you own. Allah does not love arrogant and boastful men.

Sura: 4, Ayat: 36.

O you who believe! Stand out firmly for justice, as witnesses to God, even as against yourselves, or your parents, or your kin, and whether it be (against) rich or poor: For God can best protect both. Follow not the lusts (of your hearts), lest you swerve, and if you distort (justice) or decline to do justice, verily God is well-acquainted with all that you do.

Sura: 4, Ayat: 135.

Say: 'Come, I will tell you what your Lord has made binding on you: ....Speak justly, even if it affects your own kinsmen..........

Sura: 6, Ayat: 151-152.

And know that out of all the booty that you may acquire (in war), a fifth share is assigned to God, — and to the Apostle, and to near relatives, orphans, the needy, and the wayfarer, — if you do believe in God and in the revelation We sent down to Our Servant on the Day of Testing (battle of Badr), – the Day of the meeting of the two forces. For God has power over all things.

Sura: 8, Ayat: 41.

Those that have embraced the faith and migrated from their homes and fought for the cause of Allah, and those that have sheltered them and helped them — they are the true believers. They shall receive mercy and a generous provision.

Those that have since embraced the faith and fled their homes and fought together with you — they too are of you. And according to the Book of Allah, those who are bound by ties of blood are nearest to one another. Allah has knowledge of all things.

Sura: 8, Ayat: 74-75.

It is not for the Prophet or the believers to beg forgiveness for polytheists, even though they be near of kin, after it has become manifest that they are the people of the Fire. Ibrahim prayed for his father only to fulfil a promise he had made with him. But when he realized he was an enemy of Allah, he disowned him. Surely Ibrahim was a compassionate and tender-hearted man.

Sura: 9, Ayat: 113-114.

Allah enjoins justice, kindness and charity to one's kindred, and forbids indecency, wickedness and oppression. He admonishes you so that you may take heed.

Sura: 16, Ayat: 90.

Give to the near of kin their due, and also to the destitute and to the wayfarers. Do not squander (your substance) wastefully.

Sura: 17, Ayat: 26.

Let not the honourable and rich among you swear not to give to their kindred, the poor, and those who have emigrated for the cause of Allah. Rather, let them pardon and forgive. Do you not wish Allah to forgive you? He is Forgiving, Merciful.

Sura: 24, Ayat: 22.

It shall be no offence for the blind, the lame, the sick and yourselves to eat at your table. Nor shall it be an offence for you to eat in your houses and in the houses of your fathers, your mothers, your brothers, your sisters, your paternal uncles, your paternal aunts, your maternal uncles, your maternal aunts or in houses with the keys of which you are entrusted, or in those of your friends. It shall be equally lawful whether you eat together or apart.

When you enter houses, salute one another with a salutation from Allah, blessed and kind. Thus Allah makes clear to you His revelations so that you may understand.

Sura: 24, Ayat: 61.

Admonish your nearest kinsfolk and show kindness to the believers who follow you. If they disobey you, say: 'I am not accountable for what you do.'

Sura: 26, Ayat: 214–216.

Give their due to the near of kin, to the needy, and to the wayfarers. That is best for those who seek the Countenance of Allah; such men will surely prosper.

Sura: 30, Ayat: 38.

The Prophet has a greater claim on the faithful than their own selves. His wives are their mothers.

Blood relations are closer to one another in the Book of Allah than to other believers or muhajirs*, although you are permitted to do your friends a kindness. This is decreed in Allah's Book.

Sura: 33, Ayat: 6.

***The emigrants to Madinah**

This is what Allah announces to true believers who do good works. Say: 'For this I demand of you no recompense except the love of those near of kin. He that does a good deed We add to its goodness for him. He is Forgiving and Bountiful in His rewards.'

Sura: 42, Ayat: 23.

You shall find no believers in Allah and the Last Day on friendly terms with those who oppose Allah and His Apostle, even though they be their fathers, their sons, their brothers, or their kindred. Allah has written the faith in their very hearts and strengthened them with a spirit of His own. He will admit them to gardens watered by running streams, where they shall dwell for ever. Allah is well pleased with them and they with Him. They are the party of Allah: and Allah's party shall surely triumph.

Sura: 58, Ayat: 22.

In the name of Allah, The Compassionate, The Merciful

BEHAVIOUR TOWARDS ORPHANS

When We made a covenant with the children of Israel: You serve none but Allah. Show kindness to your parents, to your kinsfolk, to the orphans, and to the destitute. Exhort men to righteousness. Attend to your prayers and pay the alms-tax. But you all turned your backs except a few, and gave no heed.

Sura: 2, Ayat: 83.

Righteousness does not consist in whether you face towards the east or the west. The righteous man is he who believes in Allah and the Last Day, in the angels and the Book and the prophets; who for the love of Allah gives his wealth to his kinsfolk, to the orphans, to the needy, to the wayfarers and to the beggars, and for the redemption of captives; who attends to his prayers and pays the alms-tax; who is true to his promises and steadfast in trial and adversity and in times of war. Such are the true believers; such are the God-fearing.

Sura: 2, Ayat: 177.

They will ask you about alms-giving, Say: 'Whatever you bestow in charity must go to your parents and to your kinsfolk, to the orphan and to the poor man and to the wayfarer. Allah is aware of whatever good you do.'

Sura: 2, Ayat: 215.

They question you concerning orphans. Say: 'To deal justly with them is best. If you mix their affairs with yours, remember they are your brothers. Allah knows the just from the unjust. If Allah wished, He could afflict you. He is Mighty and Wise.'

Sura: 2, Ayat: 220.

Give orphans the property which belongs to them. Do not exchange their valuables for worthless things or devour their possessions adding them to yours; for this would surely be a great sin.

Sura: 4, Ayat: 2.

If you fear that you cannot treat orphans with fairness, then you may

marry such women as seem good to you; two, three, or four of them. But if you fear that you cannot do justice, marry one only or those you possess. This will make it easier for you to avoid injustice.

Sura: 4, Ayat: 3.

Test the orphans until they reach the age of marriage; if then you find sound judgement in them, release their property to them; but consume it not wastefully, nor in haste against their growing up. If the guardian is well-off, let him claim no remuneration, but if he is poor, let him have for himself what is just and reasonable. When you release their property to them, call in some witnesses: But All-sufficient is God in taking account.

Sura: 4, Ayat: 6.

If relatives, orphans, or needy men are present at the division of an inheritance, give them, too, a share of it, and speak to them in kind words.

Sura: 4, Ayat: 8.

Let those (disposing of an orphan's estate) have the same fear in their minds as they would have for their own if they had left a helpless family behind: Let them fear God, and speak words of appropriate (comfort).

Sura :4, Ayat: 9.

Those that devour the property of orphans unjustly, swallow fire into their bellies; they shall burn in the flames of fire.

Sura: 4, Ayat: 10.

Serve Allah and associate none with Him. Show kindness to your parents and your kindred, to the orphans and to the needy, to your near and distant neighbours, to your fellow-travellers, to the wayfarers, and to the slaves whom you own. Allah does not love arrogant and boastful men.

Sura: 4, Ayat: 36.

They ask your instructions concerning the Women. Say: God does instruct you about them: And (remember) what has been rehearsed upon you in the Book, concerning the orphan women to whom you give not the portions prescribed, and yet whom you desire to marry, as also concerning the children who are weak and oppressed: That you stand firm for justice to orphans. There is not a good deed which you do, but God is well-acquainted therewith.

Sura: 4, Ayat: 127.

Do not touch the property of orphans, but strive to improve their lot until they reach maturity....

Sura: 6, Ayat: 152.

And know that out of all the booty that you may acquire (in war), a fifth share is assigned to God, — and to the Apostle, and to near relatives, orphans, the needy, and the wayfarer, — if you do believe in God and in the revelation We sent down to Our Servant on the Day of Testing (battle of Badr), – the Day of the meeting of the two forces. For God has power over all things.

Sura: 8, Ayat: 41.

Do not draw near the property of orphans except in a nice way, until they reach maturity. And keep your promise....

Sura: 17, Ayat: 34.

The spoils taken from the town-dwellers and assigned by Allah to His Apostle belong to Allah, the Apostle and his kinsfolk, the orphans, the poor and the wayfarers, so that they shall not become the property of the rich among you. Whatever the Apostle gives you, accept it; and whatever he forbids you, forbear from it. Have fear of Allah; He is stern in retribution.

Sura: 59, Ayat: 7.

And they feed, for the love of God, the indigent, the orphan, and the captive, (Saying), 'We feed you for the sake of God alone: No reward do we desire from you, nor thanks.

Sura: 76, Ayat: 8-9.

As for man, when his Lord tests him by exalting him and bestowing favours on him, he says: 'My Lord is bountiful to me'. But when He tests him by restricting his subsistence, he says: 'My Lord humiliates me.'

No! But you show no kindness to the orphan, nor do you urge one another to feed the poor. Greedily you lay your hands on the inheritance of the weak, and you love riches with all your hearts.

Sura: 89, Ayat: 15—20.

Have We not given him two eyes, a tongue, and two lips, and shown him the two highways (of good and evil). Yet he would not scale the height.

Would that you knew what the Height is! It is the freeing of a bondsman; the feeding, in the day of famine, of an orphaned relation or a needy man in distress; to be one of those who believe, enjoin patience and enjoin mercy.

Sura: 90, Ayat: 8—17.

Did He not find you wandering and guide you?

Did He not find you poor and enrich you?

Therefore do not oppress the orphan, nor drive away the beggar. But proclaim the bounty of your Lord.

Sura: 93, Ayat: 6—11.

Have you thought of him that denies the Last Judgement? It is he who turns away the orphan and does not urge others to feed the poor.

Sura: 107, Ayat: 1–3.

In the name of Allah, The Compassionate, The Merciful

BEHAVIOUR WITH SLAVES

Serve Allah and associate none with Him. Show kindness to your parents and your kindred, to the orphans and to the needy, to your near and distant neighbours, to your fellow-travellers, to the wayfarers, and to the slaves whom you own. Allah does not love arrogant and boastful men.

Sura: 4, Ayat: 36.

Marry those among you who are single, or the virtuous ones among your slaves, male or female: If they are in poverty, God will give them means out of His grace: For God encompasses all, and He knows all things.

Sura: 24, Ayat: 32.

Let those who cannot afford to marry live in continence until Allah enriches them of His bounty. As for those of your slaves who wish for a deed (of freedom), free them if you find in them any promise and bestow on them a part of the riches which Allah has given you.

You shall not force your slave-girls into prostitution in order that you may make money, if they wish to preserve their chastity. If any one compels them then surely after such compulsion, Allah will be Forgiving, Merciful (to them).

Sura: 24, Ayat: 33.

In the name of Allah, The Compassionate, The Merciful

BEHAVIOUR WITH NEIGHBOURS

Serve Allah and associate none with Him. Show kindness to your parents and your kindred, to the orphans and to the needy, to your near and distant neighbours, to your fellow-travellers, to the wayfarers, and to the slaves whom you own. Allah does not love arrogant and boastful men.

Sura: 4, Ayat: 36.

So woe to the worshippers who are neglectful of their Prayers, those who make a show (of piety), but refuse (to supply) (even) neighbourly needs.

Sura: 107, Ayat: 4—7.

In the name of Allah, The Compassionate, The Merciful

HELPING THE NEEDY

Give to the near of kin their due, and also to the destitute and to the wayfarers. Do not squander (your substance) wastefully, for the wasteful are the devils' brothers; and the devil is ever ungrateful to his Lord. But if you turn away from them (those in want) to seek your Lord's mercy, hoping to attain it, then say kind words to them.

Sura: 17, Ayat: 26—28.

In the name of Allah, The Compassionate, The Merciful

CONDUCT WITH DEBTORS

If the debtor is in a difficulty, grant him time till it is easy for him to repay. But if you remit it by way of charity, that is best for you if you only knew.

And fear the Day when you shall be brought back to God. Then shall every soul be paid what it earned, and none shall be dealt with unjustly.

Sura: 2, Ayat: 280-281.

In the name of Allah, The Compassionate, The Merciful

THE RIGHTS OF THE POOR

When We made a covenant with the children of Israel: You serve none but Allah. Show kindness to your parents, to your kinsfolk, to the orphans, and to the destitute. Exhort men to righteousness. Attend to your prayers and pay the alms-tax. But you all turned your backs except a few, and gave no heed.

Sura: 2, Ayat: 83.

Righteousness does not consist in whether you face towards the east or the west. The righteous man is he who believes in Allah and the Last Day, in the angels and the Book and the prophets; who for the love of Allah gives his wealth to his kinsfolk, to the orphans, to the needy, to the wayfarers and to the beggars, and for the redemption of captives; who attends to his prayers and pays the alms-tax; who is true to his promises and steadfast in trial and adversity and in times of war. Such are the true believers; such are the God-fearing.

Sura: 2, Ayat: 177

They will ask you about alms-giving, Say: 'Whatever you bestow in charity must go to your parents and to your kinsfolk, to the orphan and to the poor man and to the wayfarer. Allah is aware of whatever good you do.'

Sura: 2, Ayat: 215.

If relatives, orphans, or needy men are present at the division of an inheritance, give them, too, a share of it, and speak to them in kind words.

Sura: 4, Ayat: 8.

Serve Allah and associate none with Him. Show kindness to your parents and your kindred, to the orphans and to the needy, to your near and distant neighbours, to your fellow-travellers, to the wayfarers, and to the slaves whom you own. Allah does not love arrogant and boastful men.

Sura: 4, Ayat: 36.

And know that out of all the booty that you may acquire (in war), a fifth share is assigned to God, — and to the Apostle, and to near relatives, orphans,

the needy, and the wayfarer, — if you do believe in God and in the revelation We sent down to Our Servant on the Day of Testing (battle of Badr), – of the two forces. For God has power over all things.

Sura: 8, Ayat: 41.

Alms shall be only for the poor and the needy and for those employed to administer alms, and for those attracted to the faith, and for captives and debtors and for the cause of Allah and the wayfarer. That is a duty enjoined by Allah. He is Wise, Knowing.

Sura: 9, Ayat: 60.

Your Lord has enjoined you ....
Give to the near of kin their due, and also to the destitute and to the wayfarers....

Sura: 17, Ayat: 23—26.

Let not the honourable and rich among you swear not to give to their kindred, the poor, and those who have emigrated for the cause of Allah. Rather, let them pardon and forgive. Do you not wish Allah to forgive you? He is Forgiving, Merciful.

Sura: 24, Ayat: 22.

Give their due to the near of kin, to the needy, and to the wayfarers. That is best for those who seek the countenance of Allah; such men will surely prosper.

Sura: 30, Ayat: 38.

The spoils taken from the town-dwellers and assigned by Allah to His Apostle belong to Allah, the Apostle and his kinsfolk, the orphans, the poor and the wayfarers, so that they shall not become the property of the rich among you. Whatever the Apostle gives you, accept it; and whatever he forbids you, forbear from it. Have fear of Allah; He is stern in retribution.

Sura: 59, Ayat: 7.

(We shall say): 'Lay hold of him and bind him. Burn him in the blazing Fire, then fasten him with a chain seventy cubits long. For he did not believe in Allah, the Most High, nor did he urge the feeding of the poor. Today he shall have no friend, nor will he have any food except filth which only sinners eat.'

Sura: 69, Ayat: 30—37.

Each soul is held in pledge for what it earns, except those of the right hand. These will in their gardens ask the sinners: 'What has brought you into Hell?' They will reply: 'We, never prayed or fed the hungry. We engaged in vain dis-

putes and denied the Day of Reckoning till the inevitable (death) overtook us.'

Sura: 74, Ayat: 38—47.

They (the righteous) who keep their vows and dread the far-spread terrors of the Day (of Judgement), who, though they hold it dear, give sustenance to the poor man, the orphan, and the captive, (saying): 'We feed you for the love of God only; we seek of you neither recompense nor thanks: for we fear from Him a day of anguish and of woe.'

So Allah will deliver them from the evil of that day and make their faces shine with joy.

Sura: 76, Ayat: 7—11.

You show no kindness to the orphan, nor do you urge one another to feed the poor. Greedily you lay your hands on the inheritance of the weak, and you love riches with all your hearts.

Sura: 89, Ayat: 17—20.

Did He not find you an orphan and give you shelter?

Did He not find you wandering and guide you?

Did He not find you poor and enrich you?

Therefore do not oppress the orphan, nor drive away the beggar. But proclaim the bounty of your Lord.

Sura: 93, Ayat: 6—11.

Have you thought of him that denies the Last Judgement? It is he who turns away the orphan and does not urge others to feed the poor.

Sura: 107, Ayat: 1—3.

In the name of Allah, The Compassionate, The Merciful

TREATING A PRISONER

A prophet may not take captives until he has destroyed many disbelievers in his land. You seek the chance gain of this world, but Allah desires for you the world to come. And Allah is Mighty, Wise. Had there not been a previous sanction from Allah, you would have been sternly punished for what (ransom) you have taken.

Sura: 8, Ayat: 67-68.

O Prophet, say to those you have taken captive: 'If Allah finds goodness in your hearts, He will give you that which is better than what has been taken from you, and He will forgive you. Allah is Forgiving, Merciful.'

But if they seek to betray you, know that they had already betrayed Allah. Therefore, he has made you triumph over them. Allah is Wise and All-Knowing.

Sura: 8, Ayat: 70-71.

Therefore, when you meet the unbelievers (in the battlefield) strike off their heads and, when you have killed many of them, bind (your captives) firmly. Then grant them their freedom or take ransom from them, until war shall lay down its burdens.

Thus (shall you do), had Allah willed, He could Himself have punished them; but He has ordained it thus that He might test you, the one by the other.

As for those who are slain in the cause of Allah, He will not render their works vain....

Sura: 47, Ayat: 4—6.

They (the righteous) who keep their vows and dread the far-spread terrors of the Day (of Judgement), who, though they hold it dear, give sustenance to the poor man, the orphan, and the captive, (saying): 'We feed you for the love of God only; we seek of you neither recompense nor thanks: for we fear from Him a day of anguish and of woe.'

So Allah will deliver them from the evil of that day and make their faces shine with joy.

Sura: 76, Ayat: 7—11.

In the name of Allah, The Compassionate, The Merciful

TREATING A TRAVELLER

Serve Allah and associate none with Him. Show kindness to your parents and your kindred, to the orphans and to the needy, to your near and distant neighbours, to your fellow-travellers, to the wayfarers, and to the slaves whom you own. Allah does not love arrogant and boastful men.

Sura: 4, Ayat: 36.

Alms shall be only for the poor and the needy and for those employed to administer alms, and for those attracted to the faith, and for captives and debtors and for the cause of Allah and the wayfarers. That is a duty enjoined by Allah. He is Wise, Knowing.

Sura: 9, Ayat: 60

Your Lord has enjoined you....

Give to the near of kin their due, and also to the destitute and to the wayfarers. Do not squander (your substance) wastefully for the wasteful are the devils' brothers; and the devil is ever ungrateful to his Lord. But if you turn away from them (those in want) to seek your Lord's mercy, hoping to attain it, then say kind words to them.

Sura: 17, Ayat: 23–26.

Give their due to the near of kin, to the needy, and to the wayfarers. That is best for those who seek the countenance of Allah; such men will surely prosper.

Sura: 30, Ayat: 38.

In the name of Allah, The Compassionate, The Merciful

SERVING MEALS

They (the righteous) who keep their vows and dread the far-spread terrors of the Day (of Judgement), who, though they hold it dear, give sustenance to the poor man, the orphan, and the captive, (saying): 'We feed you for the love of God only; we seek of you neither recompense nor thanks:

Sura: 76, Ayat: 7–9.

You show no kindness to the orphan, nor do you urge one another to feed the poor. Greedily you lay your hands on the inheritance of the weak, and you love riches with all your hearts.

Sura: 89, Ayat: 17–20.

Have We not given him two eyes, a tongue, and two lips, and shown him the two highways (of good and evil)? Yet he would not scale the height.

Would that you knew what the Height is! It is the freeing of a bondsman; the feeding, in the day of famine, of an orphaned relation or a needy man in distress.

Sura: 90, Ayat: 8–16.

Have you thought of him that denies the Last Judgement? It is he who turns away the orphan and does not urge others to feed the poor.

Sura: 107, Ayat: 1–3.

SOCIAL LIFE

(18)

In the name of Allah, The Compassionate, The Merciful

SOCIAL ETIQUETTE

It is no fault in the blind nor in one born lame, nor in one afflicted with illness, nor in yourselves, that you should eat in your own houses, or those of your fathers, or your mothers, or your brothers, or your sisters, or your father's brothers or your father's sisters, or your mother's brothers, or your mother's sisters, or in houses of which the keys are in your possession, or in the house of a sincere friend of yours: there is no blame on you, whether you eat in company or separately. But if you enter houses, salute each other – a greeting of blessing and purity as from God. Thus does God make clear the Signs to you: that you may understand.

Sura: 24, Ayat: 61.

Believers, do not enter the houses of the Prophet for a meal without waiting for the proper time, unless you are given leave. But if you are invited, enter; and when you have eaten, disperse. Do not engage in familiar talk, for this would annoy the Prophet and he would be ashamed to bid you go; but of the truth Allah is not ashamed. If you ask his wives for anything, speak to them from behind a curtain. This is more chaste for your hearts and their hearts.

You must not annoy Allah's Apostle, nor shall you ever wed his wives after him; this would be a grave offence in the sight of Allah.

Sura: 33, Ayat: 53.

O you who believe! When you are told to make room in the assemblies, (spread out and) make room: (Ample) room will God provide for you. And when you are told to rise up, rise up: God will raise up, to (suitable) ranks (and degrees), those of you who believe and who have been granted (true) knowledge. And God is well-acquainted with all you do.

Sura: 58, Ayat: 11.

In the name of Allah, The Compassionate, The Merciful

RESPONSE TO GREETINGS

When a (courteous) greeting is offered you, meet it with a greeting still more courteous, or (at least) of equal courtesy. God takes careful account of all things.

Sura: 4, Ayat: 86.

....But if you enter houses, salute each other—a greeting of blessing and purity as from God. Thus does God make clear the Signs to you: that you may understand.

Sura: 24, Ayat: 61.

In the name of Allah, The Compassionate, The Merciful

PLEASING SPEECH

It was thanks to Allah's mercy that you dealt so leniently with them. Had you been cruel and hard-hearted, they would have surely deserted you. Therefore, pardon them and implore Allah to forgive them. Take counsel with them in the conduct of affairs; and when you are resolved, put your trust in Allah. Allah loves those that trust (in Him).

Sura: 3, Ayat: 159.

Tell My servants to be courteous in their speech. The devil would sow discord among them; he is the sworn enemy of man.

Sura: 17, Ayat: 53.

Therefore do not oppress the orphan, nor drive away the beggar. But proclaim the bounty of your Lord.

Sura: 93, Ayat: 9—11.

In the name of Allah, The Compassionate, The Merciful

WALKING AND SPEAKING SOFTLY

The true servants of the Merciful are those who walk humbly on the earth, and when the ignorant address them they say: 'Peace!'

Sura: 25, Ayat: 63.

Do not turn away from men with scorn, nor walk proudly on the earth: Allah does not love the arrogant and the vain-glorious. Rather let your gait be modest and your voice low: the harshest of voices is the braying of the asses.'

Sura: 31, Ayat: 18-19.

In the name of Allah, The Compassionate, The Merciful

"INSHA-ALLAH" (GOD WILLING)

Do not say of anything: 'I will do it tomorrow,' without adding: 'If Allah wills.' When you forget, remember your Lord and say: 'May Allah guide me ever closer (even) than this to the truth.'

Sura: 18, Ayat: 23-24.

MUTUAL RELATIONSHIPS

(19)

In the name of Allah, The Compassionate, The Merciful

UNITY

O you who believe! Fear God as He should be feared, and die not except in a state of Islam.

And hold fast, all together, by the Rope which God (stretches out for you), and be not divided among yourselves; and remember with gratitude God's favour on you; for you were enemies and He joined your hearts in love, so that By His Grace, you became brethren; and you were on the brink of the Pit of Fire, and He saved you from it. Thus does God make his Signs clear to you: That you may be guided.

Sura: 3, Ayat: 102-103.

Do not follow the example of those who became divided and opposed to one another after clear proofs had been given them. These shall be sternly punished on the day when some faces will be bright (with joy) and others blackened (with grief). To the black-faced sinners it will be said: 'Did you disbelieve after embracing the true faith? Taste then our scourge, for you were unbelievers! As for those whose faces will be bright, they shall abide forever in Allah's Mercy.

Sura: 3, Ayat: 105—107.

Say: 'He has power to let loose His scourge upon you from above your heads and from beneath your feet, and to divide you into discordant factions, causing the one to suffer at the hands of the other.'

See how We make plain Our revelations, that they may understand.

Sura: 6, Ayat: 65.

As for those who divide their religion and break up into sects, you have no part in them in the least: Their affair is with God: He will in the end tell them the truth of all that they did.

Sura: 6, Ayat: 159.

O believers, when you meet their army stand firm and pray fervently to Allah, so that you may triumph. Obey Allah and His Apostle and do not dispute with one another, lest you should lose courage and your resolve weaken.

Have patience: Allah is with those that are patient.

Sura: 8, Ayat: 45-46.

....He has made you strong with His help and rallied the faithful round you, making their hearts one. If you had given away all the riches of the earth, you could not have so united them; but Allah has united them. He is Mighty, Wise.

Sura: 8, Ayat: 62-63.

They sell Allah's revelations for a small price and debar others from His path. Evil is what they do. They honour with the believers neither treaties nor ties of kindred. Such are the transgressors.

If they repent and take to prayer and pay the alms-tax, they shall become your brothers in the faith. Thus We make plain Our revelations for men of understanding.

Sura: 9, Ayat: 9—11.

Turn to Allah and fear Him. Be steadfast in prayer and be not of those who associate others with Allah, those who split up their religion into sects, each exulting in its own beliefs.

Sura: 30, Ayat: 31-32.

The same religion has He established for you as that which He enjoined on Noah — that which We have sent by inspiration to you — And that which We enjoined on Abraham, Moses, and Jesus: Namely, that you should remain steadfast in Religion, and make no divisions therein: To those who worship other things than God, hard is the (way) to which you call them. God chooses to Himself those whom He pleases, and guides to Himself those who turn (to Him).

Sura: 42, Ayat: 13.

If two parties of believers take up arms against each other, make peace between them. If either of them commits aggression against the other, fight against the aggressors till they submit to Allah's judgement. When they submit, make peace between them in equity and justice; Allah loves the equitable.

The believers are brethren. Make peace among your brethren and fear Allah, so that you may be shown mercy.

Sura: 49, Ayat: 9-10.

In the name of Allah, The Compassionate, The Merciful

RULES FOR VISITING HOMES

They ask you concerning the New Moons. Say: They are but signs to mark fixed periods of time and for Pilgrimage. It is no virtue if you enter your houses from the back: It is virtue if you fear God. Enter houses through the proper doors: And fear God: That you may prosper.

Sura: 2, Ayat: 189.

Believers, do not enter the dwellings of other men until you have asked their owners' permission and wished them peace. That will be best for you. Perchance you will take heed.

If you find no one in them, do not go in till you are given leave. If you are refused admission, it is but right that you should go away. Allah has knowledge of all your actions.

It shall be no offence for you to seek shelter in uninhabited dwellings which can be of use to you. Allah knows what you hide and what you reveal.

Sura: 24, Ayat: 27–29.

It is no fault in the blind nor in one born lame, nor in one afflicted with illness, nor in yourselves, that you should eat in your own houses, or those of your fathers, or your mothers, or your brothers, or your sisters, or your father's brothers, or your father's sisters, or your mother's brothers, or your mother's sisters, or in houses of which the keys are in your possession, or in the house of a sincere friend of yours: there is no blame on you, whether you eat in company or separately. But if you enter houses, salute each other — a greeting of blessing and purity as from God. Thus does God make clear the Signs to you: that you may understand.

Sura: 24, Ayat: 61.

In the name of Allah, The Compassionate, The Merciful

LIVING TOGETHER

Men, have fear of your Lord, who created you from a single soul. From that soul He created its mate, and through them He bestrewed the earth with countless men and women.

Fear Allah, in whose name you plead with one another, and honour the mothers who bore you. Allah is ever watching over you.

Sura: 4, Ayat: 1.

Believers, do not devour your wealth among yourselves illegally, but rather trade with it by mutual consent.

You shall not kill one another. Allah is Merciful.

Sura: 4, Ayat: 29.

They ask you about the spoils of war, Say: 'The spoils belong to Allah and the Apostle. Therefore, have fear of Allah and end your disputes. Obey Allah and His Apostle, if you are true believers.'

Sura: 8, Ayat: 1.

Obey Allah and His Apostle and do not dispute with one another, lest you should lose courage and your resolve weaken. Have patience: Allah is with those that are patient.

Sura: 8, Ayat: 46

Those that have since embraced the faith and fled their homes and fought with you — they too are of you. And according to the Book of Allah, those who are bound by ties of blood are nearest to one another. Allah has knowledge of all things.

Sura: 8, Ayat: 75.

Be they men or women, the hypocrites are all alike. They enjoin what is evil, forbid what is just, and tighten their purse-strings. They forsook Allah, so Allah forsook them. Surely the hypocrites are evildoers.

Sura: 9, Ayat: 67.

The true believers, both men and women, are friends to each other. They enjoin what is just and forbid what is evil; they attend to their prayers and pay the alms-tax and obey Allah and His Apostle. On these Allah will have mercy. He is Mighty, Wise.

Sura: 9, Ayat: 71.

Believers, do not enter the dwellings of other men until you have asked their owners' permission and wished them peace. That will be best for you. Perchance you will take heed.

If you find no one in them, do not go in till you are given leave. If you are refused admission, it is but right that you should go away. Allah has knowledge of all your actions.

It shall be no offence for you to seek shelter in uninhabited dwellings which can be of use to you. Allah knows what you hide and what you reveal.

Sura: 24, Ayat: 27—29.

It is no fault in the blind nor in one born lame, nor in one afflicted with illness, nor in yourselves, that you should eat in your own houses, or those of your fathers, or your mothers, or your brothers, or your sisters, or your father's brothers, or your father's sisters, or your mother's brothers, or your mother's sisters, or in houses of which the keys are in your possession, or in the house of a sincere friend of yours: there is no blame on you, whether you eat in company or separately. But if you enter houses, salute each other — a greeting of blessing and purity as from God. Thus does God make clear the Signs to you: that you may understand.

Sura: 24, Ayat: 61.

And now, We have set you on the right path. Follow it and do not yield to the desires of ignorant men.

Sura: 45, Ayat: 18.

The wrongdoers are patrons to each other; but the righteous have Allah Himself for their patron.

These are clear proofs to men and a guidance and mercy for those who truly believe.

Sura: 45, Ayat: 19-20.

If two parties of believers take up arms against each other, make peace between them. If either of them commits aggression against the other, fight against the aggressors till they submit to Allah's judgement. When they submit, make peace between them in equity and justice; Allah loves the equitable.

Sura: 49, Ayat: 9.

The believers are brethren. Make peace among your brethren and fear Allah, so that you may be shown mercy.

Sura: 49, Ayat: 10.

Believers let no man mock another man, who may perhaps be better than himself. Let no woman mock another woman, who may perhaps be better than herself. Do not defame one another, nor call one another by nicknames. It is an evil thing to be called by a bad name after embracing the true faith. Those that do not repent are wrongdoers.

Sura: 49, Ayat: 11.

O you who believe! Avoid suspicion as much (as possible): for suspicion in some cases is a sin: and spy not on each other, nor speak ill of each other behind their backs. Would any of you like to eat the flesh of his dead brother? Nay, you would abhor it...But fear God: for God is Forgiving, Most Merciful.

Sura: 49, Ayat: 12.

O mankind! We created you from a single (pair) of a male and a female, and made you into nations and tribes, that you may know each other (not that you may despise each other). Verily the most honoured of you in the sight of God is (he who is) the most righteous of you. And God has full knowledge and is well acquainted (with all things).

Sura: 49, Ayat: 13.

....And those saved from the covetousness of their own Souls, — they are the ones that achieve prosperity.

And those who came after them say: 'Our Lord! forgive us, and our brethren who came before us into the Faith, and leave not, in our hearts, rancour (or sense of injury) against those who have believed. Our Lord!, You are indeed full of Kindness, Most Merciful.'

Sura: 59, Ayat: 9-10.

Woe, then, upon those praying ones whose hearts from their prayer are remote; those who want only to be seen and praised. But refuse (to supply) (even) neighbourly needs.

Sura: 107, Ayat: 4—7.

In the name of Allah, The Compassionate, The Merciful

SEEKING PEACE

In most of their secret talks there is no good: but if one exhorts to a deed of charity or justice or conciliation between men (secrecy is permissible): To him who does this, seeking the good pleasure of God, We shall soon give a reward of the highest (value).

Sura: 4, Ayat: 114.

If a woman fears ill-treatment or desertion on the part of her husband, it shall be no offence for them to seek a mutual agreement, for agreement is best. Man is prone to avarice. But if you do what is right and guard yourselves against evil, know then that Allah is cognizant of all what you do.

Sura: 4, Ayat: 128.

If two parties of believers take up arms against each other, make peace between them. If either of them commits aggression against the other, fight against the aggressors till they submit to Allah's judgement. When they submit, make peace between them in equity and justice; Allah loves the equitable.

The believers are brethren. Make peace among your brethren, and fear Allah, so that you may be shown mercy.

Sura: 49, Ayat: 9-10.

In the name of Allah, The Compassionate, The Merciful

HELPING THE HELPLESS

And why should you not fight for the cause of Allah and for the helpless old men, women, and children who say: 'Deliver us, Lord, from this city of wrongdoers; send forth to us a guardian from Your presence; send to us one that will help us'?

Sura: 4, Ayat: 75.

And keep your soul content with those who call on their Lord morning and evening, seeking His Face; and let not thine eyes pass beyond them, seeking the pomp and glitter of this Life; nor obey any whose heart We have permitted to neglect the remembrance of Us, one who follows his own desires, whose case has gone beyond all bounds.

Sura: 18, Ayat: 28.

In the name of Allah, The Compassionate, The Merciful

REBELLING AGAINST TRUTH

Say: The things that my Lord has indeed forbidden are: Shameful deeds, whether open or secret; sins and trespasses against truth or reason; assigning of partners to God, for which He has given no authority; and saying things about God of which you have no knowledge.

Sura: 7, Ayat: 33.

The unbelievers spend their wealth to hinder (men) from the path of God, and so will they continue to spend; but in the end they will have (only) regrets and sighs; at length they will be overcome: And the unbelievers will be gathered together to Hell: — In order that God may separate the impure from the pure, put the impure one on another, heap them together, and cast them into Hell. They will be the ones to have lost.

Sura: 8, Ayat: 36-37.

For the worst of beasts in the sight of God are those who reject Him: They will not believe. They are those with whom you did make a covenant, but they break their covenant every time, and they have not the fear (of God). If you gain the mastery over them in war, make of them a fearsome example for those who follow them, that they may remember. If you fear treachery from any group, throw back (their Covenant) to them, (so as to be) on equal terms: for God loves not the treacherous.

Sura: 8, Ayat: 55—58.

Those who annoy believing men and believing women undeservedly shall bear the guilt of slander and a gross sin.

Sura: 33, Ayat: 58.

Every soul will be (held) in pledge for its deeds, except the Companions of the Right Hand. (They will be) in Gardens (of Delight): they will question each other, and (ask of the Sinners): 'What led you into Hell-Fire?' They will say: 'We were not of those who prayed; nor were we of those who fed the indigent; but we used to talk vanities with vain talkers; and we used to deny the Day of Judgement, until there came to us (The Hour) that is certain.

Sura: 74, Ayat: 38—47.

EVIDENCE AND JUSTICE

(20)

In the name of Allah, The Compassionate, The Merciful

DUTY OF A WITNESS

....Who is more unjust than the man who hides a testimony which he has received from Allah? He is watching over all your actions.

Sura: 2, Ayat: 140.

....And get two witnesses, out of your own men, and if there are not two men, then a man and two women, such as you choose, for witnesses, so that if one of them errs, the other can remind her. The witnesses should not refuse when they are called on (for evidence)....and let neither scribe nor witness suffer harm. If you do (such harm) it would be wickedness in you. So fear God; for it is God that teaches you. And God is well acquainted with all things.

Sura: 2, Ayat: 282.

....Conceal not evidence; for whoever conceals it, — his heart is tainted with sin. And God knows all that you do.

Sura: 2, Ayat: 283.

Believers, conduct yourselves with justice and bear true witness before Allah, even though it be against yourselves, your parents, or your kinsfolk. Whether he be rich or poor, know that Allah has better right over both. So do not be led by passion, lest you should swerve from the truth. If you distort your testimony or decline to give it, know that Allah is cognizant of all that you do.

Sura: 4, Ayat: 135.

O you who believe! Stand out firmly for God, as witnesses to fair dealing and let not the hatred of others to you make you swerve to wrong and depart from justice. Be just: that is next to Piety: and fear God. For God is well-acquainted with all that you do.

Sura: 5, Ayat: 8.

Say: 'Come, I will tell you what your Lord has made binding on

you....Speak for justice, even if it affects your own kinsmen. Be true to the covenant of Allah. Thus He exhorts you, so that you may take heed.

Sura: 6, Ayat: 151-152.

(The true servants of the Merciful are those) who do not bear false witness and do not loose their dignity when listening to profane chatter.

Sura: 25, Ayat: 72.

Thus when they fulfil their waiting term appointed, either take them back on equitable terms; or part with them on equitable terms; and take for witness two persons from among you, endued with justice, and establish the evidence (as) before God. Such is the admonition given to him who believes in God and the Last Day. And for those who fear God, He (ever) prepares a way out.

Sura: 65, Ayat: 2.

Truly man was created very impatient; — fretful when evil touches him; — and niggardly when good reaches him; — Not so those devoted to Prayer; — ....and those who respect their trusts and covenants; and those who stand firm in their testimonies; and those who guard (the sacredness) of their worship; such will be the honoured ones in the Gardens (of Bliss).

Sura: 70, Ayat: 19—25.

In the name of Allah, The Compassionate, The Merciful

WRITTEN EVIDENCE

O you who believe! When you deal with each other in transactions involving future obligations in a fixed period of time, reduce them to writing. Let a scribe write down faithfully as between the parties: let not the scribe refuse to write: as God has taught him, so let him write. Let him who incurs the liability dictate, but let him fear His Lord God, and not diminish aught of what he owes. If the party liable is mentally deficient, or weak, or unable himself to dictate, let his guardian dictate faithfully. And get two witnesses, out of your own men, and if there are not two men, then a man and two women, such as you choose, for witnesses, so that if one of them errs, the other can remind her. The witnesses should not refuse when they are called on (for evidence). Disdain not to reduce to writing (your contract) for a future period, whether it be small or big: it is more just in the sight of God, more suitable as evidence, and more convenient to prevent doubts among yourselves. But if it be a transaction which you carry out on the spot among yourselves, there is no blame on you if you reduce it not to writing. But take witnesses whenever you make a commercial contract; and let neither scribe or witness suffer harm. If you do (such harm) it would be wickedness in you. So fear God; for it is God that teaches you. And God is well acquainted with all things.

Sura: 2, Ayat: 282.

If you are on a journey, and cannot find a scribe, a pledge with possession (may serve the purpose). And if one of you deposits a thing on trust with another, let the trustee (faithfully) discharge his trust, and let him fear his Lord. Conceal not evidence; for whoever conceals it — his heart is tainted with sin. And God knows all that you do.

Sura: 2, Ayat: 283.

In the name of Allah, The Compassionate, The Merciful

MORTGAGE WITH POSSESSION

If you are on a journey, and cannot find a scribe, a pledge with possession (may serve the purpose). And if one of you deposits a thing on trust with another, let the trustee (faithfully) discharge his trust, and let him fear his Lord. Conceal not evidence; for whoever conceals it — his heart is tainted with sin. And God knows all that you do.

Sura: 2, Ayat: 283.

In the name of Allah, The Compassionate, The Merciful

KEEPING PROMISES

Righteousness does not consist in whether you face towards the east or the west. The righteous man is he who believes in Allah and the Last Day, in the Angels and the Book and the prophets; who for the love of Allah gives his wealth to his kinsfolk, to the orphans, to the needy, to the wayfarers and to the beggars, and for the redemption of captives; who attends to his prayers and pays the alms-tax; who is true to his promises and steadfast in trial and adversity and in times of war. Such are the true believers; such are the God-fearing.

Sura: 2, Ayat: 177.

Indeed, those that keep faith and guard themselves against evil know that Allah loves the righteous.

Sura: 3, Ayat: 76.

Those that sell the covenant of Allah and their own oaths for a paltry price shall have no share in the world to come. Allah will neither speak to them, nor look at them, nor purify them on the Day of Resurrection. Theirs shall be a woeful punishment.

Sura: 3, Ayat: 77.

O you who believe! Fulfil (all) obligations. Lawful for you (for food) are all four-footed animals, but hunt of animals is forbidden while you are in the Sacred Precincts or in Pilgrim garb: For God does command according to His Will and Plan.

Sura: 5, Ayat: 1.

Say: 'Come, I will tell you what your Lord has made binding on you:....Be true to the covenant of Allah. Thus He exhorts you, so that you may take heed.

Sura: 6, Ayat: 151-152.

For the worst of beasts in the sight of God are those who reject Him: They will not believe. They are those with whom you did make a covenant, but they break their covenant every time, and they have not the fear (of God). If you

gain the mastery over them in war, make of them a fearsome example for those who follow them that they may remember. If you fear treachery from any group, throw back (their Covenant) to them (so as to be) on equal terms: For God loves not the treacherous.

Sura: 8, Ayat: 55—58.

A declaration of immunity by Allah and His Apostle to the idolaters with whom you have made agreements:

For four months you shall go unmolested in the land. But know that you shall not escape the judgement of Allah, and that Allah will humble the unbelievers.

Sura: 9, Ayat: 1-2.

A proclamation to the people by Allah and His Apostle on the day of the great pilgrimage:

(That) Allah and His Apostle are free from obligation to the idolaters. If you repent, it will be well with you; but if you give no heed, know that you shall not escape His judgement.

Proclaim a woeful punishment to the unbelievers, except those idolaters who have fully honoured their treaties with you and aided none against you. With these keep faith, until their treaties have run their term. Allah loves the righteous.

Sura: 9, Ayat: 3-4.

How can the idolaters have any treaty with Allah and His Apostle, save those with whom you have made treaties at the Sacred Mosque? So long as they keep faith with you, keep faith with them. Allah loves the righteous.

How (can you trust them)? If they prevail against you, they will respect neither agreements nor ties of kindred. They flatter you with their tongues, but their hearts refuse. Most of them are evildoers.

They sell Allah's revelations for a small price and debar others from His Path. Evil is what they do.

Sura: 9, Ayat: 7—9.

They honour with the believers neither treaties nor ties of kindred. Such are the transgressors.

If they repent and take to prayer and pay the alms-tax, they shall become your brothers in the faith. Thus We make plain Our revelations for men of understanding.

But if, after coming to terms with you, they break their oaths and revile your faith, make war on the leaders of unbelief-for no oaths are binding with them—so that they may desist.

Sura: 9, Ayat: 10—12.

Will you not fight against those who have broken their oaths and conspired

to banish the Apostle? They were the first to attack you. Do you fear them? Surely Allah is more deserving of your fear, if you are true believers.

Sura: 9, Ayat: 13.

Some of them make a covenant with Allah (saying): 'If Allah is bountiful to us, we will give alms and live like righteous men.' But when Allah had bestowed His favours on them, they grew niggardly and, turning their backs, hurried away. He has caused hypocrisy to be in their hearts till the day they meet Him, because they have been untrue to the promise they made Him and because they have invented falsehoods.

Sura: 9, Ayat: 75—77.

....Truly, none will take heed but the wise; those who keep faith with Allah and do not break their pledge; who join together what He has bidden to be united; who fear their Lord and dread the terrors of Reckoning-day.

Sura: 13, Ayat: 19—21.

As for those who break Allah's covenant after accepting it, who part what He has bidden to be united and commit evil in the land, a curse shall be laid on them, and they shall have an evil abode (in Hell).

Sura: 13, Ayat: 25.

Fulfil the Covenant of God when you have entered into it, and break not your oaths after you have confirmed them; indeed you have made God your surety; for God knows all that you do.

Sura: 16, Ayat: 91.

Do not barter away the covenant of Allah for a trifling price. His reward is better than all your gain, if you but knew it.

Sura: 16, Ayat: 95.

....And keep your promise. Surely it will be inquired into.

Sura: 17, Ayat: 34.

Successful indeed are the believers,....who are true to their trusts and pledges and those who strictly guard their prayers. These are the heirs who will inherit Paradise; they shall abide there for ever.

Sura: 23, Ayat: 1—11.

Before that, they swore to Allah never to turn their backs in flight. And an oath to Allah must surely be answered for.

Sura: 33, Ayat: 15.

Those that swear fealty to you swear fealty to Allah Himself. The Hand of

Allah is above their hands. He that breaks his oath breaks it at his own peril, but he that keeps his pledge to Allah shall be richly rewarded.

Sura: 48, Ayat: 10.

....And those who respect their trusts and covenants; and those who stand firm in their testimonies; and those who guard (the sacredness) of their worship; such will be the honoured ones in the Gardens (of Bliss).

Sura: 70, Ayat: 32-35.

In the name of Allah, The Compassionate, The Merciful

OATHS

And make not God's (name) an excuse in your oath against doing good, or acting rightly, or making peace between persons; for God is One who hears and knows all things.

Sura: 2, Ayat: 224.

God will not take you to task for oaths which you may have uttered without thought, but will take you to task (only) for what your hearts have conceived (in earnest): for God is much — forgiving, forbearing.

Sura: 2, Ayat: 225.

Allah will not take you to account for what is futile in your oaths. But He will take you to task for the oaths which you solemnly swear. The penalty for a broken oath is the feeding of ten needy men with such food as you normally offer to your own people; or the clothing of ten needy men; or the freeing of one slave. He that cannot afford any of these must fast three days. In this way you shall expiate your broken oaths. Therefore be true to that which you have sworn. Thus Allah makes plain to you His revelations, so that you may give thanks.

Sura: 5, Ayat: 89.

But if they violate their oaths after their covenant, and revile your Faith, fight you the chiefs of unbelief: for their oaths are nothing to them: that thus they may be restrained.

Sura: 9, Ayat: 12.

Fulfil the Covenant of God when you have entered into it, and break not your oaths after you have confirmed them; indeed you have made God your surety; for God knows all that you do.

Sura: 16, Ayat: 91.

And be not like a woman who breaks into untwisted strands the yarn which she has spun, after it has become strong. Nor take your oaths to practise de-

ception between yourselves, lest one party should be more numerous than another: for God will test you by this; and on the Day of Judgement He will certainly make clear to you (the truth of) that wherein you disagree.

Sura: 16, Ayat: 92.

And take not your oaths, to practise deception between yourselves, with the result that someone's foot may slip after it was firmly planted, and you may have to taste the evil (consequences) of having hindered (men) from the Path of God, and a mighty Wrath descend on you.

Sura: 16, Ayat: 94.

Do you see those that have befriended a people* who have incurred Allah's wrath? They belong neither to you nor to them. They knowingly swear to falsehoods. Allah has prepared for them a grievous scourge. Evil indeed is that which they have done.

They have made their oaths a screen (for their misdeeds): thus they obstruct (men) from the Path of God: Therefore shall they have a humiliating Penalty.

Neither their wealth nor their children shall in the least protect them from Allah. They are the people of the Fire, and there they shall abide for ever.

On the day when Allah restores them all to life, they will swear to Him as they now swear to you, thinking that their oaths will help them. Surely they are liars.

The Devil has gained possession of them and caused them to forget Allah's warning. They are the Devil's party; and the Devil's party shall assuredly be lost.

Sura: 58, Ayat: 14—19.

They have made their oaths a screen (for their misdeeds): thus they obstruct (men) from the path of God: Truly evil are their deeds.

Sura: 63, Ayat: 2.

God has already ordained for you, (O men), the dissolution of your oaths (in some cases): and God is your Protector, and He is Full of Knowledge and Wisdom.

Sura: 66, Ayat: 2.

***The Jews**

In the name of Allah, The Compassionate, The Merciful

RECOMMENDATIONS

Whoever recommends and helps a good cause becomes a partner therein: and whoever recommends and helps an evil cause, shares in its burden: and God has power over all things.

Sura: 4, Ayat: 85.

Plead not on behalf of such as betray their own souls; for God loves not one given to perfidy and crime; they may hide (their crimes) from men, but they cannot hide (them) from God, seeing that He is in their midst when they plot by night, in words that He cannot approve: and God does compass round all that they do. Ah! these are the sort of men on whose behalf you may plead in this world; but who will plead with God on their behalf on the Day of Judgement, or who will be their defender?

Sura: 4, Ayat: 107–109.

In the name of Allah, The Compassionate, The Merciful

JUSTICE

Thus have We made of you an Ummat justly balanced, that you might be witnesses over the nations and the Apostle a witness over yourselves....

Sura: 2, Ayat: 143.

God does command you to render back your Trusts to those to whom they are due; and when you judge between man and man, that you judge with justice: verily how excellent is the teaching which He gives you! For God is He Who hears and sees all things.

Sura: 4, Ayat: 58.

But no, by your Lord, they can have no (real) Faith, until they make you judge in all disputes between them, and find in their souls no resistance against your decisions, but accept them with the fullest conviction.

Sura: 4, Ayat: 65.

We have sent down to you the Book in truth, that you might judge between men, as guided by God: you shall not plead for traitors; but seek the forgiveness of God; for God is Oft-forgiving, Most Merciful.

Sura: 4, Ayat: 105-106.

O you who believe! Stand out firmly for justice, as witnesses to God, even as against yourselves, or your parents, or your kin, and whether it be (against) rich or poor: for God can best protect both. Follow not the lusts (of your hearts), lest you swerve, and if you distort (justice) or decline to do justice, verily God is well-acquainted with all that you do.

Sura: 4, Ayat: 135.

O you who believe! Stand out firmly for God, as witnesses to fair dealing, and let not the hatred of others to you make you swerve to wrong and depart from justice. Be Just: that is next to piety: and fear God. For God is well-acquainted with all that you do.

Sura: 5, Ayat: 8.

They are listeners to falsehoods and devourers of the unlawful. If they come to you, judge between them or turn away from them. If you avoid them they cannot harm you at all, but if you act as judge, judge between them with fairness. Allah loves those that deal justly.

Sura: 5, Ayat: 42.

....Have no fear of people; fear Me, and do not take a small price for my revelations. Unbelievers are those who do not judge in accordance with Allah's revelations.

Sura: 5, Ayat: 44.

Therefore let the followers of the Gospel judge in accordance with what Allah has revealed therein. Evildoers are those that do not base their judgements on Allah's revelations.

Sura: 5, Ayat: 47.

Say: 'Come, I will tell you what your Lord has made binding on you:....Speak for justice, even if it affects your own kinsmen. Be true to the covenant of Allah. Thus He exhorts you, so that you may take heed.

Sura: 6, Ayat: 151-152.

Say: 'My Lord has commanded justice; and that you set your whole selves (to Him) at every time and place of prayer, and call upon Him, making your devotion sincere as in His sight: such as He created you in the beginning, so shall you return.'

Sura: 7, Ayat: 29.

Say: The things that my Lord has indeed forbidden are: Shameful deeds, whether open or secret, sins and trespasses against truth or reason; assigning of partners to God, for which He has given no authority; and saying things about God of which you have no knowledge.

Sura: 7, Ayat: 33.

Allah enjoins justice, kindness and charity to one's kindred, and forbids indecency, wickedness and oppression. He admonishes you so that you may take heed.

Sura: 16, Ayat: 90.

(We said): 'Dawud, We have made you a vicegerent in the land. Rule with justice among men and do not yield to lust, lest it should turn you away from Allah's path. Those that stray from Allah's path shall be sternly punished, because they forget the Day of Reckoning.'

Sura: 38, Ayat: 26.

We sent aforetime our Apostles with Clear Signs and sent down with them

the Book and the Balance (of Right and Wrong), that men may stand forth in justice; and We sent down Iron which is mighty (material for war), as well as many benefits for mankind, that God may test who it is that will help, Unseen, Him and His Apostles: For God is Full of Strength, Exalted in Might (and able to enforce His Will).

Sura: 57, Ayat: 25.

Allah does not forbid you to be kind and equitable to those who have neither made war on your religion nor driven you from your homes. Allah loves the equitable. But He forbids you to make friends with those who have fought against you on account of your religion and driven you from your homes or abetted others to do so. Those who make friends with them are wrongdoers.

Sura: 60, Ayat: 8-9.

EDUCATION AND TRAINING

(21)

In the name of Allah, The Compassionate, The Merciful

EDUCATION AND CULTURE

....And God cares for all and He knows all things.

He grants wisdom to whom He pleases; and He to whom wisdom is granted receives indeed a benefit overflowing; but none will grasp the Message but men of understanding.

Sura: 2, Ayat: 268-269.

(Know that) Exalted be Allah, the King, the Truth.

Do not be quick with the Quran before its revelation is completed, but rather say: 'Lord, increase my knowledge'.

Sura: 20, Ayat: 114.

And such are the Parables We set forth for mankind, but only those understand them who have knowledge.

Sura: 29, Ayat: 43.

....From among His servants, it is the learned who fear Allah. Allah is Mighty and Forgiving.

Sura: 35, Ayat: 28.

(Do you deem yourself equal to) one who worships devoutly during the hours of the night prostrating himself or standing (in adoration), who takes heed of the Hereafter, and who places his hope in the Mercy of his Lord—? Say: 'Are those equal, those who know and those who do not know? It is those who are endued with understanding that receive admonition.

Sura: 39, Ayat: 9.

(God) Most Gracious! It is He Who has taught Quran. He has created man: He has taught him speech (and Intelligence).

Sura: 55, Ayat: 1—4.

O you who believe! When you are told to make room in the assemblies (spread out and) make room: (Ample) room will God provide for you. And

when you are told to rise up, rise up: God will raise up, to (suitable) ranks (and degrees), those of you who believe and who have been granted (true) Knowledge. And God is well-acquainted with all you do.

Sura: 58, Ayat: 11.

Nun. By the Pen and by the (Record) which (men) write, you are not, by the grace of your Lord, mad or possessed.

Sura: 68, Ayat: 1-2.

Proclaim! (or Read!) in the name of your Lord and Cherisher, Who created — created man, out of a (mere) clot of congealed blood: proclaim and your Lord is Most Bountiful, — He Who taught (man) the use of the Pen, — taught man that which he knew not.

Sura: 96, Ayat: 1—5.

In the name of Allah, The Compassionate, The Merciful

WISDOM

....Do not treat God's Signs as a jest, but solemnly rehearse God's favours on you, and the fact that He sent down to you the Book and Wisdom, for your instruction. And fear God, and know that God is well acquainted with all things.

Sura: 2, Ayat: 231.

....And God cares for all and He knows all things.
He grants wisdom to whom He pleases; and he to whom wisdom is granted receives indeed a benefit overflowing; but none will grasp the Message but men of understanding.

Sura: 2, Ayat: 268-269.

Allah has surely been gracious to the faithful in sending them an apostle from among themselves to declare to them His revelations, to purify them, and to instruct them in the Book and in wisdom, for before that they were in monstrous error.

Sura: 3, Ayat: 164.

But for the Grace of God to you and His Mercy, a party of them would certainly have plotted to lead you astray. But (in fact) they will only lead their own souls astray, and to you they can do no harm in the least. For God has sent down to you the Book and Wisdom and taught you what you knew not (before): and great is the Grace of God upon you.

Sura: 4, Ayat: 113.

Invite (all) to the Way of your Lord with wisdom and beautiful preaching; and argue with them in ways that are best and most gracious: for your Lord knows best, who have strayed from His Path, and who receive guidance.

Sura: 16, Ayat: 125.

And recite what is rehearsed to you in your Homes, of the Signs of God and

His Wisdom: For God understands the finest mysteries and is well-acquainted (with them).

Sura: 33, Ayat: 34.

In the name of Allah, The Compassionate, The Merciful

PURITY AND CLEANLINESS

They ask you about menstruation. Say: 'It is an indisposition. Keep aloof from women during their menstrual periods and do not touch them until they are clean again. Then have intercourse with them as Allah enjoined you. Allah loves those that turn to Him in repentance and purify themselves'.

Sura: 2, Ayat: 222.

Believers, do not approach your prayers when you are drunk, but wait till you can grasp the meaning of your words; nor when you are polluted — unless you are travelling the road — until you have washed yourselves. If you are ill or have relieved yourselves or had intercourse with women while travelling and can find no water, take some clean sand or earth and rub your faces and your hands with it. Allah is Pardoning, Forgiving.

Sura: 4, Ayat: 43.

O you who believe! When you prepare for prayer, wash your faces, and your hands (and arms) to the elbows; and pass your (wet) hands lightly over your head and (wash) your feet to the ankles. If you are in a state of ceremonial impurity, bathe your whole body. But if you are ill, or on a journey or one of you has relieved yourself or you have been in a contact with women, and you find no water, then take for yourselves clean sand or earth, and rub therewith your faces and hands. God does not wish to place you in a difficulty, but to make you clean, and to complete His favour to you, that you may be grateful.

Sura: 5, Ayat: 6.

Say: 'Not equal are things that are bad and things that are good, even though the abundance of the bad may dazzle you; so fear God, O you that understand; that (so) you may prosper.'

Sura: 5, Ayat: 100.

....It is more fitting that you should pray in a mosque founded on piety from the very first. There you shall find men who would keep pure. Allah loves those that purify themselves.

Sura: 9, Ayat: 107-108

....You shall admonish none but those who fear their Lord though they cannot see Him, and are steadfast in prayer. He that purifies himself has much to gain. To Allah shall all things return.

Sura: 35, Ayat: 18.

Happy shall be the man who purifies himself, who remembers the name of his Lord and prays to Him.

Sura: 87, Ayat: 14-15.

In the name of Allah, The Compassionate, The Merciful

PURE BETTER THAN THE IMPURE

Say: 'Not equal are things that are bad and things that are good, even though the abundance of the bad may dazzle you; so fear God, O you that understand; that (so) you may prosper.'

Sura: 5, Ayat: 100.

In the name of Allah, The Compassionate, The Merciful

FOOD

O you people! Eat of what is on earth, lawful and good; and do not follow the footsteps of the Evil One, for he is to you a sworn enemy.

Sura: 2, Ayat: 168.

O believers, eat of the wholesome things with which We have provided you and give thanks to Allah, if it is Him whom you worship.

Sura: 2, Ayat: 172.

He has only forbidden you dead meat, and blood, and the flesh of swine, and that on which any other name has been invoked besides that of God. But if one is forced by necessity, without wilful disobedience, nor transgressing due limits, — then is he guiltless. For God is Oft-Forgiving Most Merciful.

Sura: 2, Ayat: 173.

O you who believe! Fulfil (all) obligations. Lawful for you (for food) are all four-footed animals, with the exceptions named: but hunt of animals is forbidden while you are in the sacred Precincts or in pilgrim garb: for God does command according to His Will and Plan.

Sura: 5, Ayat: 1.

You are forbidden (to eat) that which dies of itself, blood, and the flesh of swine; also any flesh dedicated to any other than Allah. You are forbidden the flesh of strangled (animals) and of those beaten or gored to death; of those killed by a fall or mangled by beasts of prey, unless you find it still alive and slaughter it; also of animals sacrified on stones (to idols)

(You are forbidden) to seek division by the Arrows. That is a vicious practice.

The unbelievers have this day despaired of (vanquishing) your religion. Have no fear of them: fear Me.

This day I have perfected your religion for you and completed My favour to you. I have chosen Islam to be your faith.

But if any is constrained by hunger to eat of what is forbidden, not intend-

ing to commit sin, then surely Allah is Forgiving, Merciful.

Sura: 5, Ayat: 3.

They ask you what is lawful to them (as food). Say: Lawful for you are (all) things good and pure: and what you have taught your trained hunting animals (to catch) in the manner directed to you by God: Eat what they catch for you, but pronounce the name of God over it: and fear God; for God is swift in taking account.

Sura: 5, Ayat: 4.

This day are (all) things good and pure made lawful unto you. The food of the People of the Book is lawful upon you and yours is lawful upon them. ...

Sura: 5, Ayat: 5.

Believers, do not forbid the wholesome things which Allah has made lawful to you. Do not transgress; Allah does not love the transgressors.

Sura: 5, Ayat: 87.

Eat of the lawful and wholesome things which Allah has given you. Have fear of Allah, in Whom you believe.

Sura: 5, Ayat: 88.

No blame shall be attached to those that have embraced the faith and done good works in regard to any food they may have eaten, so long as they fear Allah and believe in Him and do good works; so long as they fear Allah and believe in Him; and again so long as they fear Allah and do good works. Allah loves the doers of good.

Sura: 5, Ayat: 93.

Lawful to you is the pursuit of water-game and its use for food, for the benefit of yourselves and those who travel; but forbidden is the pursuit of land-game; — in the Sacred Precincts or in pilgrim garb. And fear God, to Whom you shall be gathered back.

Sura: 5, Ayat: 96.

It was not God who instituted (superstitions like those of) a slit-ear, she-camel, or a she-camel let loose for free pasture, or idol sacrifices for twin-births in animals, or stallion-camels freed from work. It is blasphemers who invent a lie against God; but most of them lack wisdom.

Sura: 5, Ayat: 103.

Eat then of such as has been consecrated in the name of Allah, if you truly believe in His revelations.

Sura: 6, Ayat: 118.

And why should you not eat of that on which the name of Allah is mentioned when He has already made plain to you what is forbidden, except when you are constrained?

Many are those that are misled through ignorance by their fancies: but your Lord best knows the transgressors.

Sura: 6, Ayat: 119.

Do not eat of any flesh that has not been consecrated in the name of Allah; for that is sinful.

The devils will inspire their friends to argue with you. If you obey them, you shall indeed become polytheists.

Sura: 6, Ayat: 121.

And thus their associate-gods have induced many polytheists to kill their children so that they may ruin them and confuse them in their faith. But had Allah pleased, they would not have done so. Therefore, leave them to their false inventions.

They say: 'These cattle, and these crops are forbidden. None may eat of them save those whom we permit.' So they assert. And there are other cattle whose backs are forbidden, and others over which they do not pronounce the name of Allah, thus committing a sin against Him. Allah will punish them for their invented lies.

They also say: 'What is in the wombs of these cattle is lawful to our males but not to our wives.' But if it is still-born, they all partake of it. He will punish them for that which they attribute to Him. He is Wise, Knowing.

Lost are those that in their ignorance have wantonly slain their own children and made unlawful what Allah has given them, inventing falsehoods about Allah. They have gone astray and are not guided.

Sura: 6, Ayat: 137—140.

It is He who produces gardens, with trellises and without, and dates, and tilth with produce of all kinds, and olives and pomegranates, similar (in kind) and different (in variety): Eat of their fruit in their season, but render the dues that are proper on the day that the harvest is gathered: But waste not by excess: For God loves not the wasters.

Sura: 6, Ayat: 141.

And of the cattle, some are for carrying burdens and others for slaughter. Eat of that which Allah has given you and do not walk in the devil's footsteps; he is your sworn enemy.

Sura: 6, Ayat: 142.

Say: 'I find not in the Message received by me by inspiration any (meat) forbidden to be eaten by one who wishes to eat it, unless it be dead meat, or

blood poured forth, or the flesh of swine,—for it is an abomination or, what is impious (meat) on which a name has been invoked, other than God's. But (even so), if a person is forced by necessity, without wilful disobedience, nor transgressing due limits,—your Lord is Oft-Forgiving, Most Merciful.

Sura: 6, Ayat: 145.

O Children of Adam! Wear your beautiful apparel at every time and place of prayer: eat and drink: but waste not by excess, for God loves not the wasters.

Sura: 7, Ayat: 31.

Say: 'Who has forbidden you to wear the nice clothes or to eat the good things which Allah has bestowed upon His servants?

Say: 'These are for the faithful in the life of this world, (though shared by others); but they shall be theirs alone on the Day of Resurrection.'

Thus We make plain Our revelations to men of understanding.

Sura: 7, Ayat: 32.

It is not fitting for an Apostle that he should have prisoners of war until he has thoroughly subdued the land. You look for the temporal goods of this world; but God looks to the Hereafter: and God is Exalted in Might, Wise.

Had it not been for a previous ordainment from God, a severe penalty would have reached you for the (ransom) that you took.

But (now) enjoy what you took in war, lawful and good: but fear God: for God is Oft-Forgiving, Most Merciful.

Sura: 8, Ayat: 67—69.

Say: 'See you what things God has sent down to you for sustenance? Yet you hold forbidden some things thereof and (some things) lawful.' Say: 'Has God indeed permitted you, or do you invent (things) to attribute to God?'

And what think those who invent lies against God, of the Day of Judgement? Verily God is full of Bounty to mankind, but most of them are ungrateful.

Sura: 10, Ayat: 59-60.

Eat of the good and lawful things which Allah has bestowed on you and give thanks for His favours if you truly serve Him.

Sura: 16, Ayat: 114.

He has only forbidden you dead meat, and blood, and the flesh of swine, and any (food) over which the name of other than God has been invoked. But if one is forced by necessity, without wilful disobedience, nor transgressing due limits, — then God is Oft-Forgiving, Most Merciful.

Sura: 16, Ayat: 115.

But say not — for any false thing that your tongues may put forth, 'This is lawful, and this is forbidden', so as to ascribe false things to God. For those who ascribe false things to God, will never prosper. (In such falsehood) is but a paltry profit; but they will have a most grievous Penalty.

Sura: 16, Ayat: 116-117.

(Saying): 'Eat of the good things We have provided for your sustenance, but commit no excess therein, lest My Wrath should justly descend on you: and those on whom descends My Wrath do perish indeed!

But he that repents and believes in Me, does good works and follows the right path, shall be forgiven.

Sura: 20, Ayat: 81-82

Apostles! Eat of that which is wholesome and do good works: I have knowledge of all your actions.

Sura: 23, Ayat: 51.

O Prophet, why do you prohibit that which Allah has made lawful to you. Do you seek to please your wives?* Allah is Forgiving, Merciful.

Sura: 66, Ayat: 1.

***Reference here is either to the Prophet's promise not to eat honey or to his promise to separate from the Coptic Maria.**

In the name of Allah, The Compassionate, The Merciful

DRESS

It is now lawful for you to lie with your wives on the night of the fast; they are an apparel to you; as you are an apparel to them. ....

Sura: 2, Ayat: 187.

O You Children of Adam! We have bestowed raiment upon you to cover your shame, as well as to be an adornment to you. But the raiment of righteousness, — that is the best. Such are among the Signs of God, that they may receive admonition!

Sura: 7, Ayat: 26.

Children of Adam! Let the devil not deceive you, as he deceived your parents out of Paradise. He stripped them of their garments to reveal to them their nakedness. ....

Sura: 7, Ayat: 27.

O Children of Adam! Wear your beautiful apparel at every time and place of prayer: eat and drink: but waste not by excess, for God loves not the waster.

Sura: 7, Ayat: 31.

Say: 'Who has forbidden you to wear the nice clothes or to eat good things which Allah has bestowed upon His servants?

Say: 'These are for the faithful in the life of this world, (though shared by others); but they shall be theirs alone on the Day of Resurrection.'

Thus We make plain Our revelations to men of understanding.

Sura: 7, Ayat: 32.

In the name of Allah, The Compassionate, The Merciful

THE NATION ON THE MIDDLE PATH

....Say: To God belong both East and West: He guides whom He will to a Way that is straight.

Thus have We made of you an *Ummat* justly balanced, that you might be witnesses over the nations, and the apostle a witness over yourselves. ...

Sura: 2, Ayat: 142-143

....Do not treat God's Signs as a jest, but solemnly rehearse God's favours on you, and the fact that He sent down to you the Book and Wisdom, for your instruction. And fear God, and know that God is well acquainted with all things.

Sura: 2, Ayat: 231.

In the name of Allah, The Compassionate, The Merciful

MONASTICISM

Then, in their wake, We followed them up with (other of) Our Apostles: We sent after them Jesus the son of Mary, and bestowed on him the Gospel; and We ordained in the hearts of those who followed him, Compassion and Mercy. But the Monasticism which they invented for themselves, We did not prescribe for them: (We commanded) only the seeking for the good pleasure of God; but that they did not foster as they should have done. Yet We bestowed, on those among them who believed, their (due) reward, but many of them are rebellious transgressors.

Sura: 57, Ayat: 27.

PRAYERS

(22)

In the name of Allah, The Compassionate, The Merciful

WORSHIP OF GOD

(Say: 'Our life takes its) hue from God! And who could give a better hue (to life) than God, if we but truly worship Him?'

Sura: 2, Ayat: 138.

Remember Me, then, and I will remember you. Give thanks to Me and never deny Me.

Sura: 2, Ayat: 152.

When my servants question you about Me, tell them that I am near. I answer the prayer of the suppliant when he calls to Me; therefore, let them answer My call and put their trust in Me, that they may be rightly guided.

Sura: 2, Ayat: 186.

And when you have fulfilled your sacred duties (of pilgrimage), remember Allah as you remember your forefathers or with deeper reverence.

There are some who say: 'Lord, give us good in this world.' These shall have no share in the Hereafter. But there are others who say: 'Lord, give us what is good both in this world and in the next and keep us from the fire of Hell.' These shall have a share of what they have earned, swift is the reckoning of Allah.

Sura: 2, Ayat: 200—202.

Never did the Christ feel too proud to be God's servant, nor do the angels who are near unto Him. And those who feel too proud to serve Him and glory in their arrogance (should know that on Judgement Day) He will gather them all unto Himself:

Sura: 4, Ayat: 172.

Allah will reward those that have faith and do good works; He will enrich them from His own abundance. As for those who are scornful and proud, He will sternly punish them, and they shall find none besides Allah to protect or help them.

Sura: 4, Ayat: 173.

If a suggestion from Satan assail your (mind), seek refuge with God, for He hears and knows (all things).

Sura: 7, Ayat: 200.

And bethink yourself of your Sustainer humbly and with awe, and without raising your voice, at morning and at evening; and do not allow yourself to be heedless.

Sura: 7, Ayat: 205.

O believers, when you meet their army, stand firm and pray fervently to Allah, so that you may triumph.

Sura: 8, Ayat: 45.

Verily your Lord is God, Who created the heavens and the earth in Six Days, and is firmly established on the Throne (of authority), regulating and governing all things. No intercessor (can plead with Him) except after His leave (has been obtained); Him therefore serve you: will you not receive admonition?

Sura: 10, Ayat: 3.

Therefore stand firm (in the straight path) as you are commanded, you and those who with you turn (unto God); and transgress not (from the Path): for He sees well all that you do. And incline not to those who do wrong, or the Fire will seize you; and you have no protectors other than God, nor shall you be helped.

Sura: 11, Ayat: 112-113.

Allah alone has knowledge of what is unseen in the heavens and in the earth; to Him everything shall be referred. Serve Him, and put your trust in Him. Your Lord is watching over all your actions.

Sura: 11, Ayat: 123.

The unbelievers say: 'Why is not a Sign sent down to him from his Lord?' Say: 'Truly God leaves, to stray, whom He will; But He guides to Himself those who turn to Him in penitence. Those who believe, and whose hearts find satisfaction in the remembrance of God: for without doubt in the remembrance of God do hearts find satisfaction. For those who believe and work righteousness, is (every) blessedness, and a beautiful place of (final) return.

Sura: 13, Ayat: 27—29.

Those whom We have given the Book rejoice at what has been revealed unto you: but there are among the clans those who reject a part thereof. Say: 'I am commanded to worship God, and not to join partners with Him. Unto

him do I call, and unto Him is my return'.

Sura: 13, Ayat: 36.

We have given you the seven oft-repeated verses and the glorious Quran. Do not regard with envy the good things We have bestowed on certain groups of them, nor grieve on their account. Show kindness to the faithful. And say: 'I am the plain warner'.

Sura: 15, Ayat: 87—89

We do indeed know how your heart is distressed at what they say. But celebrate the praises of your Lord, and be of those who prostrate themselves in adoration. And serve your Lord until there come unto you the Hour that is Certain.

Sura: 15, Ayat: 97—99.

For, whatever good thing comes to you, comes from God; and whenever harm befalls you, it is unto Him that you cry for help. Yet as soon as He has removed the harm from you, some of you set up other gods besides Him giving no thanks for what We grant them.

Enjoy, then, your (brief) life: but in time you will come to know (the truth)!

Sura: 16, Ayat: 53—55.

Say: 'Praise be to God, Who begets no son, and has no partner in (His) dominion: nor (needs) He any to protect Him from humiliation: You magnify Him for His Greatness and Glory!'

Sura: 17, Ayat: 111.

He is the Lord of the heavens and the earth and all that is between them. Worship Him then and be patient in His service. Do you know any whose name is worthy to be mentioned side by side with His?

Sura: 19, Ayat: 65.

But when he came to the fire, a voice was heard: 'O Moses! 'Verily I am your Lord! Therefore (in My presence) put off your shoes: you are in the sacred valley Tuwa. I have chosen you: Listen to what shall be revealed. Verily, I am God: There is no god but I: So serve you Me (only), and establish regular prayer for celebrating My praise".

Sura: 20, Ayat: 11—14.

He said: 'Get you down, both of you,—all together, from the Garden, with enmity one to another: but if, as is sure, there comes to you Guidance from Me, whosoever follows My guidance, will not lose his way, nor fall into misery. But whosoever turns away from My Message, verily for him is a life narrowed down, and We shall raise him up blind on the Day of Judgment.'

Sura: 20, Ayat: 123-124.

Not an Apostle did We send before you without this revelation sent by Us to him: that there is no god but I; therefore worship and serve Me.

Sura: 21, Ayat: 25

Verily, this Brotherhood of yours is a single brotherhood, and I am your Lord and Cherisher: therefore serve Me (and no other).

Sura: 21, Ayat: 92.

And put your trust in Him Who lives and dies not; and celebrate His praise; and enough is He to be acquainted with the faults of His servants.

Sura: 25, Ayat: 58.

Yet when they (who are bent on denying the truth) are told, "Prostrate yourselves before the Most Gracious", they are wont to ask, 'And (who and) what is the Most Gracious? Are we to prostrate ourselves before whatever you bid us (to worship)?' – and so (your call) but increase their aversion.

Sura: 25, Ayat: 60.

Say (to the Rejecters): 'My Lord is not uneasy because of you if you call not on Him: But you have indeed rejected (Him), and soon will come the inevitable (punishment)!'

Sura: 25, Ayat: 77.

Put your trust in the Mighty One, the Merciful, who observes you when you stand upright and (sees) your movements among those who prostrate themselves. He hears all and knows all.

Sura: 26, Ayat: 217–220.

And (tell of) Ibrahim. He said to his people: 'Serve Allah and fear Him. That would be best for you, if you but knew it. You worship idols besides Allah and invent falsehoods. Those whom you serve besides Him can give you no provision. Therefore seek the bounty of Allah, and worship Him. Give thanks to him, for to Him you shall return.

Sura: 29, Ayat: 16-17.

Recite what is sent of the Book by revelation to you, and establish regular Prayer: for Prayer restrains from shameful and unjust deeds; and remembrance of God is the greatest (thing in life) without doubt. And God knows the (deeds) that you do.

Sura: 29, Ayat: 45.

O My servants who believe! Truly, spacious is My Earth: Therefore serve you Me – (and Me alone)!

Sura: 29, Ayat: 56.

O you who believe! Celebrate the praises of God, and do this often: And glorify Him morning and evening.

Sura: 33, Ayat: 41-42.

Verily it is We Who have revealed the Book to you in Truth: so serve God, offering Him sincere devotion. Is it not to God that sincere devotion is due? But those who take for protectors others than God (say): 'We only serve them in order that they may bring us nearer to God.' Truly God will judge between them in that wherein they differ. But God guides not such as are false and ungrateful.

Sura: 39, Ayat: 2-3.

Say: 'I am bidden to serve Allah and to worship none besides Him. I am bidden to be the first of those who shall submit to Him.'

Say: 'I fear, if I disobey my Lord, the torment of a fateful day.'

Say: 'It is Allah I serve in sincere devotion. As for yourselves, serve what you will besides Him.'

Say: 'They shall lose much, those who will forfeit their souls and all their kinsfolk on the Day of Resurrection. That will be the great loss indeed.

Sura: 39, Ayat: 11—15.

Nay, but worship God, and be of those who give thanks.

Sura: 39, Ayat: 66.

Pray, then, to Allah with sincere devotion, however much the unbelievers dislike it.

Sura: 40, Ayat: 14.

Therefore have patience; Allah's promise is true. Implore Him to forgive your sins, and celebrate His praise morning and evening.

Sura: 40, Ayat: 55.

He is the Living One; there is no god but Him. Pray to Him, then, and worship none besides Him. Praise be to Allah, Lord of the Worlds.

Sura: 40, Ayat: 65.

Say: 'I am forbidden to serve those whom you invoke besides Allah, now that clear proofs have been given me from my Lord. I am commanded to surrender myself to the Lord of the Worlds.

Sura: 40, Ayat: 66.

And if a malicious attempt is made by the devil to tempt you, seek refuge in Allah. He hears all and knows all.

Sura: 41, Ayat: 36.

We have truly sent you as a witness, as a bringer of Glad Tidings, and as a Warner: In order that you (O men) may believe in God and His Apostle, that you may assist and honour Him, and celebrate His praises morning and evening.

Sura: 48, Ayat: 8-9.

Bear, then, with patience, all that they say, and celebrate the praises of your Lord before the rising of the sun and before (its) setting. And during part of the night (also), celebrate His praises, and (so likewise) after the postures of adoration.

Sura: 50, Ayat: 39-40.

As to the Righteous, they will be in the midst of Gardens and Springs, taking joy in the things which their Lord gives them, because, before then, they lived a good life. They were in the habit of sleeping but little by night, and in the hours of early dawn, they (were found) praying for Forgiveness; and in their wealth and possessions (was remembered) the right of the (needy), him who asked, and him who (for some reason) was prevented (from asking).

Sura: 51, Ayat: 15−19.

We built the heaven with Our might, giving it a vast expanse, and stretched the earth beneath it. Gracious is He who spread it out. And all things We made in pairs, so that you may give thought.

Therefore seek Allah. I am warner to you from Him.

Sura: 51, Ayat: 47−50.

I only created mankind and the jinn that they might worship Me. I demand no livelihood of them, nor do I ask that they should feed Me.

Sura: 51, Ayat: 56-57.

Therefore await with patience the judgement of your Lord: We are watching over you. Glorify your Lord when you waken; in the night-time praise Him, and at the setting of the stars.

Sura: 52, Ayat: 48-49.

This is a warner like the warners of old. The coming (judgement) is near at hand; none but Allah can disclose its hour.

Do you marvel then at this revelation and laugh (lightheartedly) instead of weeping? Rather prostrate yourselves before Allah and worship Him.

Sura: 53, Ayat: 56−62.

Then celebrate with praises the name of your Lord, the Supreme!

Sura: 56, Ayat: 74.

Verily, this is the Very Truth and Certainty. So celebrate with praises the name of your Lord, the Supreme.

Sura: 56, Ayat: 95-96.

Is it not time that the hearts of all who have attained to faith should feel humble at the remembrance of God and of all the truth that has been bestowed (on them) from on high, lest they become like those who were granted revelation aforetime, and whose hearts have hardened with the passing of time so that many of them are (now) depraved?

Sura: 57, Ayat: 16.

O believers, when you are summoned to Friday prayers hasten to the remembrance of Allah and cease your trading. That would be best for you, if you but knew it. Then when the prayers are ended, disperse and go in quest of Allah's bounty. Remember Allah often, so that you may prosper.

Sura: 62, Ayat: 9-10.

O you who believe! Let not your riches or your children divert you from the remembrance of God. If any act thus, the loss is their own.

Sura: 63, Ayat: 9.

Said one of them, more just (than the rest): 'Did I not say to you, 'why not glorify (God)?' They said: 'Glory to our Lord! Verily we have been doing wrong!'

Sura: 68, Ayat: 28-29.

So glorify the name of your Lord Most High.

Sura: 69, Ayat: 52.

Say: 'I do no more than invoke my Lord, and I join not with Him any (false god).'

Sura: 72, Ayat: 20.

O you folded in garments! Stand (to prayer) by night, but not all night, half of it, or a little less, or a little more; and recite the Quran in slow, measured rhythmic tones. Soon shall We send down to you a weighty Message.

Sura: 73, Ayat: 1−5.

Truly the rising by night is most potent for governing (the soul), and most suitable for (framing) the Word (of Prayer and Praise). True, there is for you by day prolonged occupation with ordinary duties: But keep in remembrance the name of your Lord and devote yourself to Him whole-heartedly.

Sura: 73, Ayat: 6−8.

Your Lord knows that you* sometimes keep vigil nearly two-thirds of the night and sometimes half or one-third of it, and so does a party of those with you. Allah measures the night and the day. He knows that you cannot count it, and turns to you mercifully. Recite from the Quran as much as is easy (for you); He knows that among you there are sick men and others travelling the road in quest of Allah's bounty; and yet others fighting for His cause. Recite from it, then, as much as is easy (for you). Attend to your prayers, pay the alms-tax, and give Allah a generous loan. Whatever good you do you shall surely find it with Allah, ennobled and richly rewarded by Him. Implore Allah to forgive you; He is Forgiving, Merciful.

Sura: 73, Ayat: 20.

It is We Who have sent down the Quran to you by stages. Therefore be patient with constancy to the Command of your Lord, and hearken not to the sinner or the ingrate among them. And celebrate the name of your Lord morning and evening, and part of the night, prostrate yourself to Him; and glorify Him a long night through. As to these, they love the fleeting life, and put away behind them a Day (that will be) hard.

Sura: 76, Ayat: 23—27.

Glorify the name of your Guardian-Lord Most High, Who has created, and further, given order and proportion, Who has ordained laws. And granted guidance; and Who brings out the (green and luscious) pasture, and then does make it (but) swarthy stubble.

Sura: 87, Ayat: 1—5.

Therefore, when you are free (from your immediate task), still labour hard, and to your Lord turn (all) your attention.

Sura: 94, Ayat: 7-8.

Nay, pay you no heed to him, but prostrate yourself (before God) and draw close (to Him)!

Sura: 96, Ayat: 19.

So that the Quraysh might remain secure, secure in their winter and summer journeys. Let them, therefore, worship the Sustainer of this Temple, who has given them food against hunger, and made them safe from danger.

Sura: 106, Ayat: 1—4.

Celebrate the praise of your Lord and seek His pardon. He is ever disposed to Mercy.

Sura: 110, Ayat: 3.

***Muhammad**

Say: He is God, the One and only; God, the Eternal, Absolute; He begets not, nor is He begotten; and none is equal to (Him).

Sura: 112, Ayat: 1–4.

In the name of Allah, The Compassionate, The Merciful

CALL TO PRAYER

When you proclaim your call to prayer, they take it (but) as mockery and sport; that is because they are a people without understanding.

Sura: 5, Ayat: 58.

O believers, when you are summoned to Friday prayers hasten to the remembrance of Allah and cease your trading. That would be best for you, if you but knew it.

Sura: 62, Ayat: 9.

In the name of Allah, The Compassionate, The Merciful

ABLUTION

O you who have attained to faith! When you are about to pray, wash your face, and your hands and arms up to the elbows, and pass your (wet) hands lightly over your head, and (wash) your feet up to the ankles. And if you are in a state requiring total ablution, purify yourselves. But if you are ill, or are travelling, or have just satisfied a want of nature, or have cohabited with a woman, and can find no water — then take resort to pure dust, rub therewith lightly your face and your hands. God does not want to impose any hardship on you, but wants to make you pure, and to bestow upon you the full measure of His blessings, so that you might have cause to be grateful.

Sura: 5, Ayat: 6.

In the name of Allah, The Compassionate, The Merciful

PERFORMING ABLUTION WITHOUT WATER

O you who have attained to faith! Do not attempt to pray while you are in a state of drunkenness, (but wait) until you know what you are saying; nor yet (while you are) in a state requiring total ablution, until you have bathed — except if you are travelling (and are unable to do so). But if you are ill, or are travelling, or have just satisfied a want of nature, or have cohabited with a women, and can find no water — then take resort to pure dust, rub (there-with) lightly your face and your hands. Behold, God is indeed an absolver of sins, Much-forgiving.

Sura: 4, Ayat: 43.

O you who have attained to faith! When you are about to pray, wash your face, and your hands and arms up to the elbows, and pass your (wet) hands lightly over your head, and (wash) your feet up to the ankles. And if you are in a state requiring total ablution, purify yourselves. But if you are ill, or are travelling, or have just satisfied a want of nature, or have cohabited with a woman, and can find no water — then take resort to pure dust, rub therewith lightly your face and your hands. God does not want to impose any hardship on you, but wants to make you pure, and to bestow upon you the full measure of His blessings, so that you might have cause to be grateful.

Sura: 5, Ayat: 6.

In the name of Allah, The Compassionate, The Merciful

REGULAR PRAYER

Attend to your prayers, pay the alms-tax, and bow down with those who bow down.

Sura: 2, Ayat: 43

And seek aid in steadfast patience and prayer: and this, indeed, is a hard thing for all but the humble in spirit, who know with certainty that they shall meet their Sustainer and that unto Him they shall return.

Sura: 2, Ayat: 45-46.

And be steadfast in prayer and regular in charity: and whatever good you send forth for your souls before you, you shall find it with God: for God sees well all that you do.

Sura: 2, Ayat: 110.

O you who believe! seek help with patient perseverance and prayer: for God is with those who patiently persevere.

Sura: 2, Ayat: 153.

Righteousness does not consist in whether you face towards the east or the west. The righteous man is he who believes in Allah and the Last Day, in the Angels and the Book and the prophets; who for the love of Allah gives his wealth to his kinsfolk, to the orphans, to the needy, to the wayfarers and to the beggars, and for the redemption of captives; who attends to his prayers and pays the alms-tax; who is true to his promises and steadfast in trial and adversity and in times of war. Such are the true believers; such are the God-fearing.

Sura: 2, Ayat: 177.

Guard strictly your (habit of) prayers, especially the middle prayer; and stand before God in a devout (frame of mind).

Sura: 2, Ayat: 238.

When you are exposed to danger, pray on foot or while riding; and when

you are restored to safety remember Allah, as He has taught you what you did not know.

Sura: 2, Ayat: 239.

Those that have faith and do good works, attend to their prayers and pay the alms-tax, will be rewarded by their Lord and will have nothing to fear or regret.

Sura: 2, Ayat: 277.

O Mary! be obedient to your Lord; bow down and worship with the worshippers.

Sura: 3, Ayat: 43.

O you who have attained to faith! Do not attempt to pray while you are in a state of drunkenness, (but wait) until you know what you are saying; nor yet (while you are) in a state requiring total ablution, until you have bathed — except if you are travelling (and are unable to do). But if you are ill, or are travelling, or have just satisfied a want of nature, or have cohabited with a woman, and can find no water — then take resort to pure dust, rub (therewith) lightly over your face and your hands. Behold, God is indeed an absolver of sins, Much-forgiving.

Sura: 4, Ayat: 43.

It is no offence for you to shorten your prayers when travelling the road if you fear that the unbelievers may attack you. The unbelievers are your sworn enemies.

Sura: 4, Ayat: 101.

When you are with the faithful, conducting their prayers, let one party of them rise up with you, armed with their weapons. After making their prostrations, let them withdraw to the rear and then let another party who have not prayed come forward and pray with you and let these also be on their guard, armed with their weapons. It would much please the unbelievers if you neglected your arms and your baggage, so that they could swoop upon you with one assault. But it is no offence for you to lay aside your arms when overtaken by heavy rain or stricken with an illness, although you must be always on your guard. Allah has prepared a shameful punishment for the unbelievers.

When your prayers are ended, remember Allah standing, sitting, and lying down. Attend regularly to your prayers so long as you are safe: for prayer is a duty incumbent on the faithful, to be conducted at appointed hours.

Sura: 4, Ayat: 102-103.

....Say: 'God's guidance is the (only) guidance, and we have been directed

to submit ourselves to the Lord of the worlds; — to establish regular prayers and to fear God: For it is to Him that we shall be gathered together'.

Sura: 6, Ayat: 71-72.

And this is a Book which We have sent down, bringing blessings, and confirming (the revelations) which came before it: that you may warn the Mother of cities and all around her. Those who believe in the Hereafter believe in this (Book), and they are constant in guarding their Prayers.

Sura: 6, Ayat: 92.

Say: 'My prayers and my devotions, my life and my death, are all for Allah, Lord of the Creation: He has no partner. Thus I am commanded, being the first of the Muslims'.

Sura: 6, Ayat: 162.

O Children of Adam! Wear your beautiful apparel at every time and place of prayer: eat and drink: but waste not by excess, for God loves not the wasters.

Sura: 7, Ayat: 31.

As for those that strictly observe the Book and are steadfast in prayer, We do not waste the reward of the righteous.

Sura: 7, Ayat: 170.

Keep your Lord in mind within your own soul, humbly and with awe, and without raising your voice, at morn and at evening; and do not allow yourself to be heedless.

Sura: 7, Ayat: 205.

The true believers are those whose hearts are filled with awe at the mention of Allah, and whose faith grows stronger as they listen to His revelations. They are those who put their trust in their Lord, pray steadfastly, and spend of that which We have given them.

Sura: 8, Ayat: 2-3.

And establish regular prayers at the two ends of the day and at the approaches of the night: for those things that are good remove those that are evil: This is the word of remembrance to those who remember (their Lord):

Sura: 11, Ayat: 114.

Tell My servants, those who are true believers, to be steadfast in prayer and spend of what We have given them in private and in public, before the coming of that day in which there is neither trading nor friendship.

Sura: 14, Ayat: 31.

Keep your prayer at the decline of the sun till the darkness of the night and (keep) the recital of the Quran at dawn. Surely the recital of the Quran at dawn is witnessed. Pray during the latter part of the night, an additional duty (for which) your Lord may exalt you to a position of praise and glory.

Sura: 17, Ayat: 78-79.

Say: 'Call upon God, or call upon Rahman: By whatever name you call upon Him. (it is well): For to Him belong the Most Beautiful Names. Neither speak your Prayer aloud, nor speak it in a low tone, but seek a middle course between'.

Sura: 17, Ayat: 110.

'I am Allah. There is no god but Me. Serve Me, and recite your prayers in My remembrance.

Sura: 20, Ayat: 14.

Therefore be patient with what they say, and celebrate (constantly) the praises of your Lord, before the rising of the sun, and before its setting; You, celebrate them for part of the hours of the night, and at the sides of the day; that you might have (spiritual) joy.

Sura: 20, Ayat: 130.

Enjoin prayer on your people and be diligent in its observance. We ask you to provide no provision: We shall Ourself provide for you. Blessed shall be the end of the devout.

Sura: 20, Ayat: 132.

To every people did We appoint rites (of sacrifice), that they might celebrate the name of God over the sustenance He gave them from animals (fit for food). But your God is One God: Submit then your wills to Him (in Islam): and give the good news to those who humble themselves. To those whose hearts, when God is mentioned, are filled with fear, who show patient perseverance over their afflictions, keep up regular prayer, and spend (in charity) out of what We have bestowed upon them.

Sura: 22, Ayat: 34-35.

You that are true believers, kneel and prostrate yourselves. Worship your Lord and do good, so that you may triumph.

Sura: 22, Ayat: 77.

And strive in His cause as you ought to strive, (with sincerity and under discipline). He has chosen you, and has imposed no difficulties on you in religion; It is the cult of your father Abraham. It is He who has named you Muslims, both before and in this (Revelation); that the Apostle may be a witness for you

and you be witnesses for mankind! Give regular charity, and hold fast to God! He is your Protector — the best to protect and the best to help!

Sura: 22, Ayat: 78.

Successful indeed are the believers, who are humble in their prayers.

Sura: 23, Ayat: 1-2.

Successful indeed are believers,....who strictly guard their prayers.

Sura: 23, Ayat: 1 and 9.

Attend to your prayers, pay the alms-tax and obey the Apostle, so that you may be shown mercy.

Sura: 24, Ayat: 56.

The true servants of the Merciful are those who walk humbly on the earth; and when the ignorant address them they say: 'Peace!'; who pass the night standing and on their knees in adoration of their Lord.

Sura: 25, Ayat: 63-64.

Ta Sin. These are the verses of the Quran, the Book which indicates (right and wrong); a guidance and joyful news to true believers, who attend to their prayers and pay the alms-tax and firmly believe in the life to come.

Sura: 27, Ayat: 1—3.

Recite what is sent of the Book by revelation to you, and establish Regular Prayer: for Prayer restrains from shameful and unjust deeds; and remembrance of God is the greatest (thing in life) without doubt. And God knows the (deeds) that you do.

Sura: 29, Ayat: 45.

Therefore, glorify Allah when you reach evening and when you rise in the morning. Praise be to Him in the heavens and the earth, in the late afternoon and when the day begins to decline.

Sura: 30, Ayat: 17-18.

Alif lam mim. These are the revelations of the wise Book, a guidance and a blessing to the righteous, who attend to their prayers, pay the alms-tax, and firmly believe in the life to come. These are rightly guided by their Lord and will surely prosper.

Sura: 31, Ayat: 1—5.

'My son, (said Luqman) be steadfast in prayer, enjoin justice, and forbid evil. Endure with fortitude whatever befalls you. That is a duty incumbent on

all.

Sura: 31, Ayat: 17.

No (soul) shall bear another's burden. If a laden (soul) cries out for help, nothing of (its burden) will be carried even by a relative.

You shall admonish none but those who fear their Lord though they cannot see Him, and are steadfast in prayer. He that purifies himself has much to gain. To Allah shall all things return.

Sura: 35, Ayat: 18.

Those who recite the Book of Allah and attend to their prayers and give alms in private and in public may hope for imperishable gain. Allah will give them their rewards and enrich them from His own abundance. He is Forgiving, Rewarding.

Sura: 35, Ayat: 29-30.

Bear, then, with patience, all that they say, and celebrate the praises of your Lord, before the rising of the sun and before (its) setting, and during part of the night, (also,) celebrate His praises, and at every prayer's end.

Sura: 50, Ayat: 39-40.

Therefore await with patience the judgement of your Lord; We are watching over you. Glorify your Lord when you waken; in the night-time praise Him, and at the setting of the stars.

Sura: 52, Ayat: 48-49.

....Establish regular prayer; practise regular charity; and obey God and His Apostle. And God is well-acquainted with all that you do.

Sura: 58, Ayat: 13.

O believers, when you are summoned to Friday prayers hasten to the remembrance of Allah and cease your trading. That would be best, if you but knew it. Then when the prayers are ended, disperse and go in quest of Allah's bounty. Remember Allah often, so that you may prosper.

Sura: 62, Ayat: 9-10.

Truly man was created very impatient; fretful when evil touches him; and niggardly when good reaches him; not so those devoted to Prayer; those who remain steadfast to their prayer....and those who guard (the sacredness) of their worship. Such will be the honoured ones in the Gardens (of Bliss).

Sura: 70, Ayat: 19−35.

O you folded in garments! Stand (to prayer) by night, but not all night,—half of it,—or a little less, or a little more; and recite the Quran in

slow, measured rhythmic tones.

Sura: 73, Ayat: 1—4.

Truly the rising by night is most potent for governing (the soul) and most suitable for (framing) the Word (of Prayer and Praise). True, there is for you by day prolonged occupation with ordinary duties: But keep in remembrance the name of your Lord and devote yourself to Him wholeheartedly.

Sura: 73, Ayat: 6—8.

Your Lord knows that you* sometimes keep vigil nearly two-thirds of the night and sometimes half or one-third of it, and so does a party of those with you. Allah measures the night and the day. He knows that you cannot count it, and turns to you mercifully. Recite from the Quran as much as is easy (for you): He knows that among you there are sick men and others travelling the road in quest of Allah's bounty; and yet others fighting for His cause. Recite from it, then, as much as is easy (for you). Attend to your prayers, pay the alms-tax, and give Allah a generous loan. Whatever good you do you shall surely find it with Allah ennobled and richly rewarded by Him. Implore Allah to forgive you; He is Forgiving, Merciful.

Sura: 73, Ayat: 20.

Every soul will be (held) in pledge for its deeds. Except the Companions of the Right Hand. (They will be) in Gardens (of Delight): they will question each other, and (ask) of the Sinners: 'What led you into Hell-Fire?' They will say: 'We were not of those who prayed; nor were we of those who fed the indigent.'

Sura: 74, Ayat: 38—44.

And celebrate the name of your Lord morning and evening, and part of the night, prostrate yourself to Him; and glorify Him a long night through.

Sura: 76, Ayat: 25-26.

Happy shall be the man who purifies himself, who remembers the name of his Lord and prays to Him.

Sura: 87, Ayat: 14-15.

And they have been commanded no more than this: To worship God, offering Him sincere devotion, being True (in faith); to establish regular Prayer; and to practise regular Charity; and that is the Religion right and straight.

Sura: 98, Ayat: 5.

Woe, then, unto those praying ones whose hearts from their prayer are re-

---

***Muhammad**

mote — those who want only to be seen and praised, and, withal, deny all assistance (to their fellowmen)!

Sura: 107, Ayat: 4—7.

Pray to your Lord and sacrifice unto Him, He that hates you shall remain childless.

Sura: 108, Ayat: 2-3.

In the name of Allah, The Compassionate, The Merciful

FRIDAY PRAYERS

O believers, when you are summoned to Friday prayers hasten to the remembrance of Allah and cease your trading. That would be best for you, if you but knew it. Then when the prayers are ended, disperse and go in quest of Allah's bounty. Remember Allah often, so that you may prosper.

Sura: 62, Ayat: 9-10.

In the name of Allah, The Compassionate, The Merciful

BRIEF PRAYERS

It is no offence for you to shorten your prayers when travelling the road if you fear that the unbelievers may attack you. The unbelievers are your sworn enemies.

Sura: 4, Ayat: 101.

In the name of Allah, The Compassionate, The Merciful

"TAHAJJUD" I.E. PRAYERS IN THE LATTER PART OF NIGHT

Pray during the latter part of the night, an additional prayer (for which) your Lord may exalt you to a position of praise and glory.

Sura: 17, Ayat: 79.

O you folded in garments! Stand (to prayer) by night, but not all night,—half of it,—or a little less, or a little more; and recite the Quran in slow, measured rhythmic tones. Soon shall We send down to you a weighty Message. Truly the rising by night is most potent for governing (the soul) and most suitable for (framing) the word (of prayer and praise). True, there is for you by day prolonged occupation with ordinary duties: But keep in remembrance the name of your Lord and devote yourself to Him wholeheartedly.

Sura: 73, Ayat: 1—8.

Your Lord knows that you* sometime vigil nearly two-thirds of the night and sometimes half or one-third of it, and so does a party of those with you. Allah measures the night and the day. He knows that you cannot count it, and turns to you mercifully. Recite from the Quran as much as is easy (for you), He knows that among you there are sick men and others travelling the road in quest of Allah's bounty; and yet others fighting for His cause. Recite from it, then, as much as is easy (for you). Attend to your prayers, pay the alms-tax, and give Allah a generous loan. Whatever good you do you shall surely find it with Allah ennobled and richly rewarded by Him. Implore Allah to forgive you; He is Forgiving, Merciful.

Sura: 73, Ayat: 20.

And celebrate the name of your Lord morning and evening, and part of the night, prostrate yourself to Him; and glorify Him a long night through.

Sura: 76, Ayat: 25-26.

***Muhammad**

In the name of Allah, The Compassionate, The Merciful

CONFINEMENT IN MOSQUE FOR WORSHIP

And lo! We made the Temple a goal to which people might repair again and again, and a sanctuary: take, then, the place whereon Abraham once stood as your place of prayer.

And thus did We command Abraham and Ishmael: 'Purify My Temple for those who will walk around it, and those who will abide near it in meditation, and those who will bow down and prostrate themselves (in prayer)'.

Sura: 2, Ayat: 125.

....but do not associate (sexually) with your wives while you are in retreat in the mosques. Those are limits (set by) God: Approach not nigh thereto. Thus does God make clear His Signs to men: that they may learn self-restraint.

Sura: 2, Ayat: 187.

In the name of Allah, The Compassionate, The Merciful

FAST

O you who believe! Fasting is prescribed to you as it was prescribed to those before you, that you may (learn) self-restraint.

Sura: 2, Ayat: 183.

(Fasting) for a fixed number of days; but if any of you is ill, or on a journey, the prescribed number (should be made up) from days later. For those who can do it (with hardship), is a ransom, the feeding of one that is indigent (for one fast) but he that will give more, of his own free will, it is better for him. And it is better for you that you fast, if you only knew.

Sura: 2, Ayat: 184.

Ramadhan is the (month) in which was sent down the Quran, as a guide to mankind, also clear (Signs) for guidance and judgment (between right and wrong). So every one of you who is present (at his home) during that month should spend it in fasting, but if any one is ill, or on a journey, the prescribed period (should be made up) by days later. God intends every facility for you; He does not want to put you to difficulties, (He wants you) to complete the prescribed period, and to glorify Him in that He has guided you; and perchance you shall be grateful.

Sura: 2, Ayat: 185.

Permitted to you, on the night of the fasts, is the approach to your wives. They are your garments and you are their garments. God knows what you used to do secretly among yourselves; but He turned to you and forgave you; so now associate (sexually) with them, and seek what God has ordained for you, and eat and drink, until the white thread of dawn appear to you distinct from its black thread; then complete your fast till the night appear; but do not associate with your wives while you are in retreat in the mosques. Those are limits (set by) God: Approach not nigh thereto. Thus does God make clear His Signs to men: that they may learn self-restraint.

Sura: 2, Ayat: 187.

In the name of Allah, The Compassionate, The Merciful

HAJ AND UMRAH (PILGRIMAGE)

Safa and Marwa* are the Symbols of God. It shall be no offence for the pilgrim or the visitor to the Sacred House to walk around them. He that does good of his own accord shall be rewarded by Allah. Allah is Rewarding and Knowing.

Sura: 2, Ayat: 158.

They ask you concerning the New Moons. Say: They are but signs to mark fixed periods of time in (the affairs of) men, and for Pilgrimage....

Sura: 2, Ayat: 189.

And complete the Hajj or 'Umra in the service of God. But if you are prevented (from completing it), send an offering for sacrifice, such as you may find, and do not shave your heads until the offering reaches the place of sacrifice. And if any of you is ill, or has an ailment in his scalp, (necessitating shaving), (he should) in compensation either fast, or feed the poor, or offer sacrifice; and when you are in peaceful conditions (again), if any one wishes to continue the 'Umra on to the Hajj, he must make an offering, such as he can afford, but if he cannot afford it, he should fast three days during the Hajj and seven days on his return, making ten days in all. This is for those whose household is not in (the precincts of) the Sacred Mosque. And fear God, and know that God is strict in punishment.

Sura: 2, Ayat: 196.

For Hajj are the months well-known. If any one undertakes that duty therein, let there be no obscenity, nor wickedness, nor wrangling in the Hajj. And whatever good you do, (be sure) God knows it. And take a provision (with you) for the journey, but the best of provisions is piety. So fear Me, O you that are wise.

Sura: 2, Ayat: 197.

It is no crime in you if you seek the bounty of your Lord (during pilgrim-

---

***Two hills in Makkah**

age). Then when you pour down from (mount) 'Arafat, celebrate the praises of God at the Sacred Monument (Muzdalifa – a place between Arafat and Mina) and celebrate His praises as He has directed you, even though, before this, you went astray.

Sura: 2, Ayat: 198.

Then pass on at a quick pace from the place whence it is usual for the multitude so to do, and ask for God's forgiveness. for God is Oft-forgiving, Most Merciful.

Sura: 2, Ayat: 199.

So when you have accomplished your holy rites, celebrate the praises of God, as you used to celebrate the praises of your fathers, yea, with far more heart and soul. There are men who say: 'Our Lord! Give us (Your bounties) in this world!' But they will have no portion in the Hereafter.

Sura: 2, Ayat: 200.

And there are men who say 'Our Lord! Give us good in this world and good in the Hereafter, and defend us from the torment of the Fire!'

Sura: 2, Ayat: 201.

To these will be allotted what they have earned; and God is quick in account.

Sura: 2, Ayat: 202.

Celebrate the praises of God during the Appointed Days. But if any one hastens to leave in two days, there is no blame on him, and if any one stays on, there is no blame on him, if his aim is to do right. Then fear God, and know that you will surely be gathered unto Him.

Sura: 2, Ayat: 203.

The first House (of worship) appointed for men was that at Bakka (Makkah): full of blessing and guidance for all kinds of beings: In it are Signs Manifest; (for example), the Station of Abraham; whoever enters it attains security; pilgrimage thereto is a duty men owe to God,— those who can afford the journey; but if any deny faith, God stands not in need of any of His creatures.

Sura: 3, Ayat: 96-97.

O you who believe! Fulfil (all) obligations.

The lawful unto you (for food) are all four-footed animals, with the exceptions named: But hunt of animals is forbidden while you are in the Sacred Precincts or in pilgrim garb: For God does command according to His Will and Plan.

Sura: 5, Ayat: 1.

O you who believe! Violate not the sanctity of the Symbols of God, nor of the Sacred Months, nor of the animals brought for sacrifice, nor the garlands that mark out such animals, nor the people resorting to the Sacred House, seeking of the bounty and good pleasure of their Lord. But when you are clear of the Sacred Precincts and of pilgrim garb, you may hunt and let not the hatred of some people in (once) shutting you out of the Sacred Mosque lead you to transgression (and hostility on your part). Help you one another in righteousness and piety, but help you not one another in sin and rancour: Fear God: for God is strict in punishment.

Sura: 5, Ayat: 2.

O you who believe! God does but make a trial of you in a little matter of game well within reach of your hands and your lances, that He may test who fears Him unseen: Any who transgress thereafter, will have a grievous penalty.

Sura: 5, Ayat: 94.

Believers, kill no game whilst on pilgrimage. He that kills game by design, shall present, as an offering to the Ka'ba, the like of that which he has killed, to be determined by two just men among you; or (he shall), in expiation, (undertake) either the feeding of the poor or the equivalent of that in fasting, so that he may suffer the evil consequences of his deed. Allah has forgiven what is past, but if any one returns to sin He will avenge Himself on him: He is Mighty, capable of punishment.

Sura: 5, Ayat: 95.

Lawful to you is the game of the sea and its food, a good food for you and for the travellers. But you are forbidden the game of the land whilst you are on pilgrimage. Have fear of Allah, before whom you shall all be assembled.

Sura: 5, Ayat: 96.

Allah has made the Ka'ba the Sacred House, a foundation for people (in the affairs of religion); and (has made) the sacred month, and the sacrificial offerings and the victims with garlands, eternal values for mankind; so that you may know that Allah has knowledge of all that the heavens and the earth contain; that He has knowledge of all things.

Sura: 5, Ayat: 97.

And an announcement from God and His Apostle, to the people (assembled) on the day of the Great Pilgrimage, that God and His Apostle dissolve (treaty) obligations with the Pagans. If, then, you repent, it were best for you; but if you turn away, know you that you cannot frustrate God. And proclaim a grievous penalty to those who reject Faith.

Sura: 9, Ayat: 3.

When We assigned for Ibrahim the site of the Sacred Mosque, (We said): 'Worship none besides Me. Keep My House clean for those who walk around it and those who stand upright or kneel and prostrate themselves.

Proclaim the pilgrimage to men. They will come to you on foot and on the backs of swift camels from every distant quarter; (they will come) to avail themselves of many a benefit and to pronounce on the appointed days the name of Allah over the cattle which He has given them. Eat of their flesh yourselves, and feed the poor and the unfortunate.

Then let the pilgrims accomplish their acts of cleansing (their bodies) make their vows, and go round the Ancient House. Such (is Allah's commandment). He that reveres the sacred rites of Allah shall fare better in the sight of his Lord.

Sura: 22, Ayat: 26—30.

Allah has in all truth fulfilled His Apostle's vision. You shall certainly enter the Sacred Mosque in security if God wills, with hair cropped or shaven and without fear. He knew what you did not know; and what is more, He granted you a speedy victory.

Sura: 48, Ayat: 27.

In the name of Allah, The Compassionate, The Merciful

SACRIFICE

And complete the Hajj or 'umra in the service of God, but if you are prevented (from completing it), send an offering for sacrifice, such as you may find, and do not shave your heads until the offering reaches the place of sacrifice. And if any of you is ill, or has an ailment in his scalp, (necessitating shaving), (he should) in compensation either fast, or feed the poor, or offer sacrifice; and when you are in peaceful conditions (again), if anyone wishes to continue the 'umra on to the Hajj, he must make an offering, such as he can afford, but if he cannot afford it, he should fast three days during the Hajj and seven days on his return, making ten days in all. This is for those whose household is not in (the precincts of) the Sacred Mosque. And fear God, and know that God is strict in punishment.

Sura: 2, Ayat: 196.

Proclaim the pilgrimage to men. They will come to you on foot and on the backs of swift camels from every distant quarter; (they will come) to avail themselves of many a benefit and to pronounce on the appointed days the name of Allah over the cattle which He has given them. Eat of their flesh yourselves, and feed the poor and the unfortunate.

Sura: 22, Ayat: 27-28.

He that reveres Allah's rites, surely it is from the piety of the hearts. In them, you have benefits until an appointed time. Then their place of sacrifice is at the Ancient House (Ka'aba).

Sura: 22, Ayat: 32-33.

To every people did We appoint rites (of sacrifice), that they might celebrate the name of God over the sustenance He gave them from animals (fit for food). But your God is One God: hence, surrender yourselves unto Him: and give the good news to those who humble themselves.

Sura: 22, Ayat: 34.

And the camels We have made a part of Allah's rites. they are of much use

to you. Pronounce over them the name of Allah as they line up; and when they have fallen down on their sides, eat of their flesh and feed with it the contented and the beggar. Thus We have subjected them to you, so that you may give thanks.

Sura: 22, Ayat: 36.

Their flesh and blood does not reach Allah: it is your piety that reaches Him. Thus He has subjected them to you, so that you may glorify Him for guiding you.

And give good news to the righteous.

Sura: 22, Ayat: 37.

Pray to your Lord and sacrifice unto Him. He that hates you shall remain childless.

Sura: 108, Ayat: 2-3.

In the name of Allah, The Compassionate, The Merciful

RULES FOR THE KAABA AND MOSQUES

Hence, who could be more wicked than those who bar the mention of God's name from (any of) His houses of worship and strive for their ruin, (although) they have no right to enter them save in fear (of God)? For them, in this world, there is ignominy in store; and for them in the life to come, awesome suffering.

Sura: 2, Ayat: 114.

To Allah belongs the east and the west. Whichever way you turn, there is the face of Allah. He is Omnipresent and All-Knowing.

Sura: 2, Ayat: 115.

And Lo! We made the Temple a goal to which people might repair again and again, and a sanctuary: take, then, the place whereon Abraham once stood as your place of prayer.

And thus did We command Abraham and Ismael: 'Purify My Temple for those who will walk around it, and those who will abide near it in meditation, and those who will bow down and prostrate themselves (in prayer).'

And, lo, Abraham prayed: 'O my Sustainer! Make this a land secure, and grant its people fruitful sustenance—such of them as believe in God and the Last Day.'

(God) answered: 'And whoever shall deny the truth, him will I let enjoy himself for a short while—but in the end I shall drive him to suffering through fire: and how vile a journey's end!'

And when Abraham and Ismael were raising the foundations of the Temple, (they prayed:) 'O our Sustainer! Accept You this from us: for, verily, You alone are All-hearing, All knowing!

Sura: 2, Ayat: 125—127.

The Weak-minded among people will say, 'What has turned them away from the direction of prayer which they have hitherto observed?'

Say: 'God's is the east and the west: He guides whom He will on a straight way'.

And thus have We willed you to be a community of the middle way, so that

(with your lives) you might bear witness to the truth before all mankind, and that the Apostle might bear witness to it before you.

And it is only to the end that We might make a clear distinction between those who follow the Apostle and those who turn about on their heels that We have appointed (for this community) the direction of prayer which you (O Prophet) have formerly observed: for this was indeed a hard test for all but those whom God has guided aright. But God will surely not lose sight of your faith—for, behold, God is most compassionate towards man, a dispenser of grace.

Sura: 2, Ayat: 142-143.

We see the turning of your face (for guidance) to the heavens: now shall We turn you to a Qibla that shall please you. Turn then your face in the direction of the sacred Mosque: Wherever you are, turn your faces in that direction. The people of the Book know well that that is the truth from their Lord nor is God unmindful of what they do.

Sura: 2, Ayat: 144.

Even if you were to bring to the people of the Book all the Signs (together), they would not follow your Qibla; nor are you going to follow their Qibla nor indeed will they follow each other's Qibla. If you after the knowledge has reached you, were to follow their (vain) desires,— then were you indeed (clearly) in the wrong.

Sura: 2, Ayat: 145.

To each is a goal to which God turns him; then strive together (as in a race) towards all that is good. Wheresoever you are, God will bring you together. For God has power over all things.

Sura: 2, Ayat: 148.

From whencesoever you start forth, turn your face in the direction of the Sacred Mosque; that is indeed the truth from your Lord. And God is not unmindful of what you do.

Sura: 2, Ayat: 149.

So from whencesoever you start forth, turn your face in the direction of the Sacred Mosque; and wheresoever you are, turn your face thither: that there be no ground of dispute against you among the people, except those of them that are bent on wickedness; so fear them not, but fear Me; and that I may complete my favours on you, and you may (consent to) be guided.

Sura: 2, Ayat: 150.

Righteousness does not consist in whether you face towards the east or the west. The righteous man is he who believes in Allah and the Last Day, in the

Angels and the Book and the prophets; who for the love of Allah gives his wealth to his kinsfolk, to the orphans, to the needy, to the wayfarers and to the beggars, and for the redemption of captives; who attends to his prayers and pays the alms-tax; who is true to his promises and steadfast in trial and adversity and in times of war. Such are the true believers; such are the God-fearing.

Sura: 2, Ayat: 177

The first House (of worship) appointed for men was that at Bakka (Makkah): full of blessing and of guidance for all kinds of beings: In it are Signs manifest; (for example), the Station of Abraham; whoever enters it attains security; pilgrimage thereto is a duty men owe to God,—those who can afford the journey; but if any deny faith, God stands not in need of anything of His creatures.

Sura: 3, Ayat: 96-97.

O you who believe! Violate not the sanctity of the Symbols of God, nor of the Sacred Month, nor of the animals brought for sacrifice, nor the garlands that mark out such animals, nor the people resorting to the Sacred House, seeking of the bounty and good pleasure of their Lord. But when you are clear of the Sacred Precincts and of pilgrim garb, you may hunt and let not the hatred of some people in (once) shutting you out of the Sacred Mosque lead you to transgression (and hostility on your part), help you one another in righteousness and piety, but help you not one another in sin and rancour: Fear God: for God is strict in punishment.

Sura: 5, Ayat: 2.

Say: 'My Lord has commanded justice; and that you set your whole selves (to Him) at every time and place of prayer, and call upon Him, making your devotion sincere such as He created you in the beginning, so shall you return.'

Sura: 7, Ayat: 29.

But Allah was not to punish them whilst you were dwelling in their midst. Nor would He punish them if they sought forgiveness of Him.

And why should Allah not chastise them when they have debarred others from the Sacred Mosque, although they were not its guardians? Its only guardians are those that fear Allah, though most of them do not know it.

Sura: 8, Ayat: 33-34.

It is not for such as join gods with God, to visit or maintain the mosques of God while they (are) witness against their own souls to infidelity. The works of such bear no fruit: in Fire shall they dwell.

Sura: 9, Ayat: 17.

The mosques of God shall be visited and maintained by such as believe in

God and the Last Day, establish Regular prayers, and practise Regular charity, and fear none (at all) except God. It is they who are expected to be on true guidance.

Sura: 9, Ayat: 18.

Do you make the giving of drink to pilgrims, or the maintenance of the Sacred Mosque, equal to (the pious service of) those who believe in God and the Last Day, and strive with might and main in the cause of God? They are not comparable in the sight of God: and God guides not those who do wrong.

Sura: 9, Ayat: 19.

And there are those who built a mosque to cause harm and to spread unbelief and disunite the faithful, and to provide refuge for him* who had made war on Allah and His Apostle before. They swear that their intentions were good, but Allah bears witness that they are lying. You shall not set foot in it. It is more fitting that you should pray in a mosque founded on piety from the very first. There you shall find men who would keep pure. Allah loves those that purify themselves.

Who is a better man, he who founds his house on the fear of Allah and His good pleasure, or he who builds on the brink of a crumbling precipice, so that it will fall with him into the fire of Hell? Allah does not guide the wrongdoers.

The edifice which they have built shall ever inspire their hearts with doubt, until their hearts are cut in pieces. Allah is Knowing, Wise.

Sura: 9, Ayat: 107—110.

We inspired Moses and his brother with this Message: 'Provide dwellings for your People in Egypt, make your dwellings into places of worship, and establish regular prayers: and give Glad Tidings to those who believe!'

Sura: 10, Ayat: 87.

(Lit is such a Light) in houses, which God has permitted to be raised to honour; for the celebration, in them, of His name: in them is He glorified in the mornings and in the evenings, (again and again), by men whom neither traffic nor merchandise can divert from the Remembrance of God, nor from regular Prayer, nor from the practice of regular Charity: Their (only) fear is for the Day when hearts and eyes will be transformed (in a world wholly new),—that God may reward them according to the best of their deeds, and add even more for them out of His Grace: for God does provide for those whom He will, without measure.

Sura: 24, Ayat: 36—38.

***Abu 'Amir**

The places of worship are built for Allah's worship; invoke in them no other (god) besides Him.

Sura: 72, Ayat: 18.

In the name of Allah, The Compassionate, The Merciful

THE SACRED MOSQUE

And lo! We made the Temple a goal to which people might repair again and again, and a sanctuary: take, then, the place whereon Abraham once stood as your place of prayer.

And thus did We command Abraham and Ismael: 'Purify My Temple for those who will walk around it, and those who will abide near it in meditation, and those who will bow down and prostrate themselves (in prayer).'

Sura: 2, Ayat: 125.

We see the turning of your face (for guidance) to the heavens: now shall We turn you to a Qibla that shall please you. Turn then your face in the direction of the sacred Mosque: Wherever you are, turn your faces in that direction. The people of the Book know well that that is the truth from their Lord nor is God unmindful of what they do.

Sura: 2, Ayat: 144.

....So from whencesoever you start forth, turn your face in the direction of the Sacred Mosque; and wheresoever you are, turn your face thither: that there be no ground of dispute against you among the people, except those of them that are bent on wickedness; so fear them not, but fear Me; and that I may complete my favours on you, and you may (consent to) be guided.

Sura: 2, Ayat: 149-150.

Kill them wherever you find them. Drive them out of the places from which they drove you. Idolatry is worse than carnage. But do not fight them within the precincts of the Sacred Mosque unless they attack you there; if they attack you put them to the sword. Thus shall the unbelievers be rewarded: but if they desist, know that Allah is Forgiving and Merciful.

Sura: 2, Ayat: 191-192.

They ask you concerning fighting in the Prohibited Month. Say: 'Fighting therein is a grave (offence); but graver is it in the sight of God to prevent access to the path of God, to deny Him, to prevent access to the Sacred Mosque,

and drive out its members'. Tumult and oppression are worse than slaughter. Nor will they cease fighting you until they turn you back from your faith if they can....

Sura: 2, Ayat: 217.

The first House (of worship) appointed for men was that at Bakka (Makkah): full of blessing and of guidance for all kinds of beings.

Sura: 3, Ayat: 96.

In it are Signs manifest; (for example), the Station of Abraham; whoever enters it attains security; pilgrimage thereto is a duty men owe to God,—those who can afford the journey; but if any deny faith, God stands not in need of anything of His creatures.

Sura: 3, Ayat: 97.

Allah had made the Ka'aba the Sacred House, a foundation for people (in the affairs of religion); and (has made) the sacred month, and the sacrificial offerings and the victims with garlands, eternal values for mankind; so that you may know that Allah has knowledge of all that the heavens and the earth contain; that He has knowledge of all things.

Sura: 5, Ayat: 97.

But Allah was not to punish them whilst you were dwelling in their midst. Nor would He punish them if they sought forgiveness of Him.

And why should Allah not chastise them when they have debarred others from the Sacred Mosque, although they were not its guardians? Its only guardians are those that fear Allah, though most of them do not know it.

Sura: 8, Ayat: 33-34.

Do you make the giving of drink to pilgrims, or the maintenance of the Sacred Mosque, equal to (the pious service of) those who believe in God and the Last Day, and strive with might and main in the cause of God? They are not comparable in the sight of God: and God guides not those who do wrong.

Sura: 9, Ayat: 19.

O you who believe! Truly the Pagans are unclean; so let them not, after this year onwards approach the Sacred Mosque. And if you fear poverty, soon will God enrich you, if He wills, out of His bounty, For God is All-Knowing, All-Wise.

Sura: 9, Ayat: 28.

'Lord', I have settled some of my offspring in a barren valley near Your Sacred House, so that they may establish regular prayer. Put in the hearts of men kindness towards them, and provide them with the earth's fruits, so that

they may give thanks.

Sura: 14, Ayat: 37.

As to those who have rejected (God), and would keep back (men) from the Way of God, and from the Sacred Mosque, which we have made (open) to (all) men—equal is the dweller there and the visitor from the country—and any whose purpose therein is profanity or wrongdoing—them will We cause to taste of a most grievous Penalty.

Sura: 22, Ayat: 25.

When We assigned for Abraham the site of the Sacred Mosque, (We said): 'Worship none besides Me. Keep My House clean for those who walk around it and those who stand upright or kneel and prostrate themselves.

Sura: 22, Ayat: 26.

They say: 'If we accept the guidance with you, we shall be driven from our land. But have We not given them a sanctuary of safety to which fruits of every kind are brought as a provision from Ourself? Indeed, most of them do not know.

Sura: 28, Ayat: 57.

In the name of Allah, The Compassionate, The Merciful

IDOLATORS FORBIDDEN TO ENTER THE SACRED MOSQUE

O you who believe! Truly the Pagans are unclean; so let them not, after this year onward approach the Sacred Mosque. And if you fear poverty, soon will God enrich you, if He wills, out of His bounty, for God is All-Knowing, All-Wise.

Sura: 9, Ayat: 28.

(And) fight against those who—despite having been vouchsafed revelation (aforetime) — do not (truly) believe either in God or the Last Day, and do not consider forbidden that which God and His Apostle have forbidden, and do not follow the religion of truth (which God has enjoined upon them), till they (agree to) pay the exemption tax with a willing hand, after having been humbled (in war).

Sura: 9, Ayat: 29.

In the name of Allah, The Compassionate, The Merciful

PREVENTING PEOPLE FROM PRAYING

Hence, who could be more wicked than those who bar the mention of God's name from (any of) His houses of worship and strive for their ruin, (although) they have no right to enter them save in fear (of God)? For them, in this world, there is ignominy in store; and for them, in the life to come, awesome suffering.

Sura: 2, Ayat: 114.

They ask you concerning fighting in the Prohibited Month. Say: 'Fighting therein is a grave (offence); in the sight of God to prevent access to the Sacred Mosque, and drive out its members'. Tumult and oppression are worse than slaughter. Nor will they cease fighting you until they turn you back from your faith if they can. And if any of you turn back from their faith and die in unbelief, their works will bear no fruit in this life and in the Hereafter; they will be companions of the Fire and will abide therein.

Sura: 2, Ayat: 217.

As to those who have rejected (God), and would keep back (men) from the Way of God, and from the Sacred Mosque, which We have made (open) to (all) men—equal is the dweller there and the visitor from the country—and any whose purpose therein is profanity or wrongdoing—them will We cause to taste of a most grievous Penalty.

Sura: 22, Ayat: 25.

Have you ever considered him who tries to prevent a servant (of God) from praying? Have you considered whether he is on the right way, or is concerned with God-consciousness? Have you considered whether he may (not) be giving the lie to the truth and turning his back (upon it)? Does he, then, not know that God sees (all)?

Sura: 96, Ayat: 9—14.

In the name of Allah, The Compassionate, The Merciful

PRAYER

You alone we worship, and to You alone we look for help.

Sura: 1, Ayat: 4.

Guide us to the straight path, the Path of those upon whom You bestowed favours, not those who have invited Your wrath, nor those who have gone astray.

Sura: 1, Ayat: 5—7.

And when Abraham and Ismael were raising the foundations of the Temple (they prayed:) 'O our Sustainer! Accept You this from us: for, verily, You alone are All-hearing, All-knowing. 'O our Sustainer! Make us surrender ourselves unto You, and make out of our offspring a community that shall surrender itself unto You, and show us our ways of worship, and accept our repentance: for verily, You alone are the Acceptor of Repentance, the Dispenser of Grace'!

Sura: 2, Ayat: 127-128.

When My servants question you about Me, tell them I am near. I answer the prayer of the suppliant when he calls to Me; therefore, let them answer My call and put their trust in Me, that they may be rightly guided.

Sura: 2, Ayat: 186.

So when you have accomplished your holy rites, celebrate the praises of God, as you used to celebrate the praises of your fathers,—nay, with a yet keener remembrance. There are men who say: 'Our Lord! Give us (Your bounties) in this world." But they will have no portion in the Hereafter.

And there are men who say: 'Our Lord! Give us good in this world and good in the Hereafter, and defend us from the torment of the Fire.'

To these will be allotted what they have earned; and God is quick in account.

Sura: 2, Ayat: 200—202.

The Apostle believes in what has been revealed to him by his Lord, and so do the faithful. They all believe in Allah and His Angels, His Books, and His Apostles. We make no distinction (they say) between one and another of his Apostles. And they say: 'We hear and obey. Grant us your forgiveness, Lord; to You we shall all return.

Sura: 2, Ayat: 285.

Allah does not charge a soul with more than it can bear. It shall be requited for whatever good and whatever evil it has done. Lord, do not be angry with us if we forget or lapse into error. Lord, do not lay on us the burden you laid on those before us. Lord, do not charge us with more than we can bear. Pardon us, forgive us our sins, and have mercy upon us. You alone are our Protector. Give us victory over the unbelievers.

Sura: 2, Ayat: 286.

'Our Lord'! (they say), 'Let not our hearts deviate now after You have guided us, but grant us mercy from Thine own Presence; for You are the Grantor of bounties without measure'. 'Our Lord! You are He that will gather mankind together against a Day about which there is no doubt: for God never fails in His promise'.

Sura: 3, Ayat: 8-9.

Say: 'Shall I tell of better things than these, with which the righteous shall be rewarded by their Lord? Theirs shall be gardens watered by running streams, where they shall dwell forever; wives freed from impurity, and grace from Allah.' Allah is watching over His servants: those who say: 'Lord, we believe in you: forgive us our sins and keep us from the torment of Fire; who are steadfast, sincere, obedient, and charitable; and who implore forgiveness at break of day.

Sura: 3, Ayat: 15—17.

Say: 'O God! Lord of Power (and Rule), You give Power to whom You please, and you take away Power from whom You please: You endue with honour whom You please and You bring low whom You please: In Your hand is all good. Verily, over all things You have power.

Sura: 3, Ayat: 26.

All that they said was: 'Our Lord! forgive us our sins and anything We may have done that transgressed our duty: establish our feet firmly, and help us against those that resist Faith.'

Sura: 3, Ayat: 147.

Verily, in the creation of the heavens and the earth, and in the succession of night and day, there are indeed messages for all who are endowed with in-

sight, (and) who remember God when they stand, and when they sit, and when they lie down to sleep, and (thus) reflect on the creation of the heavens and the earth:

'O our Sustainer! You have not created (aught of) this without meaning and purpose. Limitless are You in Your glory! Keep us safe, then, from suffering through fire!

'O our Sustainer! Whomsoever You shall commit to the fire, him, verily, will You have brought to disgrace; and such evildoers will have none to succour them.

'O our Sustainer! Behold, we heard a voice call (us) unto faith, 'Believe in your Sustainer'!—and so we came to believe. 'O our Sustainer! Forgive us, then our sins and efface our bad deeds; and let us die the death of the truly virtuous!

'And, O our Sustainer, grant us that which You have promised us through Your Apostles, and disgrace us not on Resurrection Day! Verily, You never fail to fulfil Your promise!'

Sura: 3, Ayat: 190—194.

When they listen to that which was revealed to the Apostle, you will see their eyes fill with tears as they recognize its truth. They say: 'Lord, we believe. Count us among Your witnesses. Why should we not believe in Allah and in the truth that has come down to us? Why should we not hope for admission among the righteous?

Sura: 5, Ayat: 83-84.

Say: 'My Lord has commanded justice; and that you set your whole selves (to Him) at every time and place of prayer, and call upon Him, making your devotion sincere as in His sight: Such as He created you in the beginning, so shall you return.'

Sura: 7, Ayat: 29.

Pray to your Lord with humility and in secret. He does not love the transgressors.

Sura: 7, Ayat: 55.

Do not make mischief in the earth after it has been purged. Pray to Him with fear and hope; His mercy is within reach of the righteous.

Sura: 7, Ayat: 56.

The most beautiful names belong to God: So call on him by them; but shun such men as use profanity in His names: for what they do, they will soon be requited.

Sura: 7, Ayat: 180.

If a suggestion from Satan assail your (mind), seek refuge with God; for He hears and knows (all things).

Sura: 7, Ayat: 200.

And you (O reader!) Bring your Lord to remembrance in your (very) soul, with humility and in reverence, without loudness in words, in the mornings and evenings; and be not you of those who are unheedful.

Sura: 7, Ayat: 205.

It is not for the Prophet or the believers to beg forgiveness for polytheists, even though they be near of kin, after it has become manifest that they are the people of the Fire.

Sura: 9, Ayat: 113.

They said: 'In God do we put our trust. Our Lord! make us not a trial for those who practise oppression; 'and deliver us by Your Mercy from those who reject (You).'

Sura: 10, Ayat: 85-86.

He (Nuh) said: 'My Lord, I seek refuge with You from asking thee that of which I have no knowledge. If You do not pardon me and have mercy on me, I shall be among the losers.'

Sura: 11, Ayat: 47.

'O my Sustainer! You have indeed bestowed upon me something of power, and have imparted unto me some knowledge of the inner meaning of happenings. Originator of the heavens and the earth! You are Protector unto me in this world and in the life to come: let me die as one who has surrendered himself unto You, and make me one with the righteous!.'

Sura: 12, Ayat: 101.

'Lord, make me and my descendants steadfast in prayer. Lord accept my prayer.

'Forgive me, our Lord, and forgive my parents and all the faithful on the Day of Reckoning.'

Sura: 14, Ayat: 40-41.

Say: 'Lord, grant me a goodly entrance and a goodly exit, and sustain me with Your power.'

Sura: 17, Ayat: 80.

Behold, the youths betook themselves to the Cave: they said: 'Our Lord! bestow on us Mercy from Yourself, and dispose of our affair for us in the right

way!'

Sura: 18, Ayat: 10.

Said (Moses): 'O my Sustainer! Open up my heart (to Your light), and make my task easy for me, and loosen the knot from my tongue so that they might fully understand my speech.

Sura: 20, Ayat: 25–28.

(Know), then, (that) God is sublimely exalted, the Ultimate Sovereign, the Ultimate Truth: and (knowing this), do not approach the Quran in haste, ere it has been revealed unto you in full, but (always) say: 'O my Sustainer, cause me to grow in knowledge!'

Sura: 20, Ayat: 114.

....There is no god but You. Glory be to You!....

Sura: 21, Ayat: 87.

And (remember) Zakariyya, who invoked his Lord, saying: 'Lord, let me not remain childless, (though) of all heirs, You are the best.'

Sura: 21, Ayat: 89.

Say: 'O my Lord! Judge You in truth!' 'Our Lord Most Gracious is the One Whose assistance should be sought against the blasphemies you (non-believers) utter'!

Sura: 21, Ayat: 112.

'And say: 'O my Sustainer! Cause me to reach a destination blessed (by You)—for You are the best to show man how to reach his (true) destination!'

Sura: 23, Ayat: 29.

Say: 'Do not, O my sustainer, let me be one of those evildoing folk!'

Sura: 23, Ayat: 94.

And Say: 'Lord, I seek refuge in You from the promptings of the devils. Lord, I seek refuge in You from their presence.

Sura: 23, Ayat: 97-98.

Among My servants there were those who said: 'Lord, we believe in You. Forgive us and have mercy on us: You are the Best Who show mercy.'

Sura: 23, Ayat: 109.

Say: 'Lord, forgive and have mercy. You are the best of those that show mercy.'

Sura: 23, Ayat: 118.

The true servants of the Merciful are those who walk humbly on the earth, and when the ignorant address them they say: 'Peace!'; who pass the night standing and on their knees in adoration of their Lord; who say: 'Lord, ward off from us the punishment of Hell, for its punishment is everlasting: an evil dwelling and an evil resting-place.

Sura: 25, Ayat: 63—66.

And those who pray, 'Our Lord! grant to us wives and offspring who will be the comfort of our eyes, and give us (the grace) to lead the righteous.'

Sura: 25, Ayat: 74.

Say (to the unbelievers): 'Little cares my Lord for you if you do not invoke Him. Now that you have denied His revelations, His punishment is bound to overtake you.'

Sura: 25, Ayat: 77.

'Lord, bestow on me wisdom and let me join the righteous. Give me renown among posterity and place me amongst the heirs of the Blissful Garden. Forgive my father, for he has gone astray. Do not hold me to shame on the Day of Resurrection; the day when wealth and children will avail nothing and when none shall be saved except him who comes before his Lord with a pure heart.

Sura: 26, Ayat: 83—89.

Say: Praise be to God, and Peace on His servants whom He has chosen (For His Message). (Who) is better?—God or the false gods they associate (with Him).

Sura: 27, Ayat: 59.

Nay—who is it that responds to the distressed when he calls out to Him, and Who removes the ill (that caused the distress), and has made you inherit the earth?

Could there be any divine power besides God? How seldom do you keep this in mind!

Sura: 27, Ayat: 62.

He prayed: 'O my Lord! I have indeed wronged my soul! Do You then forgive me'! So (God) forgave him: for He is the Oft-Forgiving, Most Merciful.

Sura: 28, Ayat: 16.

He therefore got away therefrom, looking about, in a state of fear. He prayed: 'O my Lord! save me from people given to wrongdoing.'

Sura: 28, Ayat: 21.

....'O my Lord! Truly am I in (desperate) need of any good that You do send me'!

Sura: 28, Ayat: 24.

He said: 'O my Lord! Help You me against people who do mischief!'

Sura: 29, Ayat: 30.

Those who bear the Throne and those who stand around it give glory to their Lord and believe in Him. They implore forgiveness for the faithful (saying): 'Lord, You embrace all things in mercy and knowledge. Forgive those that repent and follow Your path. Shield them from the scourge of Hell. Admit them, Lord, to the gardens of Eden which You have promised them, together with all the righteous among their fathers, their wives, and their descendants. You are the Almighty, the Wise One.

Sura: 40, Ayat: 7-8.

Pray, then, to Allah with sincere devotion, however much the unbelievers dislike it.

Sura: 40, Ayat: 14.

And your Lord says: 'Call on Me; I will answer your (Prayer): But those who are too arrogant to serve Me will surely find themselves in Hell—in humiliation'!

Sura: 40, Ayat: 60.

He is the Living One; there is no god but Him. Pray to Him, then, and worship none besides Him. Praise be to Allah, Lord of the Worlds.

Sura: 40, Ayat: 65.

And if a malicious attempt is made by the devil to tempt you, seek refuge in Allah. He hears all and knows all.

Sura: 41, Ayat: 36.

He responds to the prayers of those who have faith and do good works, and gives them more of His bounty. But a woeful punishment awaits the unbelievers.

Sura: 42, Ayat: 26.

Now (among the best of the deeds which) We have enjoined upon man is goodness towards his parents. In pain did his mother bear him, and in pain did she give him birth; and her bearing him and his utter dependence on her took thirty months. And so, when he attains to full maturity and reaches forty years, he (that is righteous) prays: 'O my Sustainer! Inspire me so that I may forever be grateful for those blessings of Yours with which You have graced

me and my parents, and that I may do what is right (in a manner) that will meet with Your goodly acceptance; and grant me (with) righteousness in my offspring (as well). Verily unto You have I turned in repentance: for, verily, I am of those who have surrendered themselves unto You'.

Sura: 46, Ayat: 15.

Of Him seeks (its need) every creature in the heavens and on earth: Everyday in (new) Splendour does He (shine)!

Sura: 55, Ayat: 29.

But those who before them, had homes (in Medina) and had adopted the Faith, — show their affection to such as came to them for refuge, and entertain no desire in their hearts for things given to the (latter), but give them preference over themselves, even though poverty was their (own lot). And those saved from the covetousness of their own souls, – they are the ones that achieve prosperity.

And those who came after them say: "Our Lord! Forgive us, and our brethren who came before us into the Faith, and leave not, in our hearts, rancour (or sense of injury) against those who have believed. Our Lord! you are indeed Full of Kindness, Most Merciful."

Sura: 59, Ayat: 9-10.

....'Lord, in You we have put our trust; do not make us a trial for the unbelievers. Forgive us, our Lord; You are the Mighty, the Wise One.'

Sura: 60, Ayat: 4-5.

O believers, turn to Allah in true repentance. Your Lord may forgive you your sins and admit you to gardens watered by running streams, on a day when the Prophet and those who believe with him will suffer no disgrace at the hands of Allah. Their light will shine in front of them and on their right, and they will say: 'Lord, perfect our light for us and forgive us, You have power over all things.'

Sura: 66, Ayat: 8.

Forgive me, Lord, and forgive my parents and every true believer who seeks refuge in my house. Forgive all the faithful, men and women, and hasten the destruction of the wrongdoers.'

Sura: 71, Ayat: 28.

Celebrate the praise of your Lord and seek His pardon. He is ever disposed to mercy.

Sura: 110, Ayat: 3.

Say: I seek refuge with the Lord of the Dawn, from the mischief of created

things; from the mischief of Darkness as it overspreads; from the mischief of those who practise Secret Arts (witchcraft) and from the mischief of the envious one as he practises envy.

Sura: 113, Ayat: 1–5.

Say: I seek refuge with the Lord and Cherisher of Mankind, the King (or Ruler) of Mankind, the God (or Judge) of Mankind,—from the mischief of the Whisperer (of evil), elusive tempter who withdraws (after his whisper), – (The same) who whispers into the hearts of Mankind, – among Goblins and among Men.

Sura: 114, Ayat: 1–6.

FAMILY LAWS

(23)

In the name of Allah, The Compassionate, The Merciful

MARRIAGE

And do not marry women who ascribe divinity to aught besides God ere they attain to (true) belief: for any believing bondwoman (of God) is certainly better than a woman who ascribes divinity to aught besides God, even though she pleases you greatly. And do not give your women in marriage to men who ascribe divinity to aught besides God ere they attain to (true) belief: for any believing bondman (of God) is certainly better than a man who ascribes divinity to aught besides God, even though he pleases you greatly. (Such as) these invite unto the fire, whereas God invites unto paradise, and unto (the achievement of) forgiveness by His leave; and He makes clear His messages unto mankind, so that they might bear them in mind.

Sura: 2, Ayat: 221.

If a man divorces his wife, he cannot remarry her until she has wedded another man and been divorced by him; in which case it shall be no offence for either of them to return to the other, if they think that they can keep within the limits set by Allah.

Such are the bounds of Allah. He makes them plain to men of understanding.

Sura: 2, Ayat: 230.

If a man has divorced his wife and she has reached the end of her waiting period, do not prevent her from remarrying her (former) husband if they have come to an honourable agreement. This is enjoined on everyone of you who believes in Allah and the Last Day; it is more honourable for you and more chaste. Allah knows, but you do not.

Sura: 2, Ayat: 232.

And those of you who die and leave wives behind, such wives should keep in waiting for four months and ten days after their husbands' death.

When they have reached the end of their waiting period, it shall be no offence for you to let them do whatever they choose for themselves, provided

that it is lawful. Allah is cognizant of what you do.

Sura: 2, Ayat: 234.

It shall be no offence for you openly to propose marriage indirectly to such women or to cherish them in your hearts. Allah knows that you will remember them. Do not arrange to meet them in secret and, if you do, speak to them honourably. But you shall not tie the marriage-knot before the end of their waiting period. Know that Allah has knowledge of all your thoughts. Therefore take heed and bear in mind that Allah is Forgiving and Merciful.

Sura: 2, Ayat: 235.

If you fear that you cannot treat orphans with fairness, then you may marry such women as seem good to you: two, three, or four of them. But if you fear that you cannot do justice, marry one only or those you possess (slaves). This will make it easier for you to avoid injustice.

Sura: 4, Ayat: 3.

Henceforth, you shall not marry the women who were married to your fathers. That was an evil practice, indecent and abominable.

Sura: 4, Ayat: 22.

Forbidden to you are your mothers, your daughters, your sisters, your paternal and maternal aunts, the daughters of your brothers and sisters, your foster-mothers, your foster-sisters, the mothers of your wives, your step-daughters who are in your charge, born of the wives with whom you have consummated but it is no offence for you (to marry them) if you have not consummated your marriage with their mothers. (Forbidden to you also) are the wives of your own begotten sons and to take in marriage two sisters at one and the same time unless this had happened in the past. Allah is Forgiving and Merciful.

Sura: 4, Ayat: 23.

(Forbidden to you also) are married women, except those whom you own (slaves). Such is the decree of Allah. All women other than these are lawful to you, provided you seek them with your wealth, desiring chastity, not in fornication. Give them their dowry for the enjoyment you have had of them as a duty; but it shall be no offence for you to make any other agreement among yourselves after you have fulfilled your duty. Allah is Knowing, Wise.

Sura: 4, Ayat: 24.

If anyone of you cannot afford to marry free believing women, (let him marry) from among the owned (slaves) believing women. Allah best knows your faith: you are all alike (in terms of religion). Marry them with the permission of their masters and give them their dowry in all justice, provided

they are honourable and chaste and have not-entertained other men. If after marriage they commit adultery, they shall suffer half the penalty inflicted upon free adulteresses. Such is the law for those of you who fear to commit sin: but if you abstain, it will be better for you. Allah is Forgiving and Merciful.

Sura: 4, Ayat: 25.

They ask your instructions concerning the Women. Say: God does instruct you about them: And (remember) what has been rehearsed unto you in the Book, concerning the orphan girls to whom you give not the portions prescribed, and yet whom you desire to marry, as also concerning the children who are weak and oppressed: That you stand firm for justice to orphans. There is not a good deed which you do, but God is well-acquainted therewith.

Sura: 4, Ayat: 127.

This day are (all) things good and pure made lawful unto you. The food of the People of the Book is lawful unto you and yours is lawful unto them. (Lawful unto you in marriage) are (not only) chaste women who are believers, but chaste women among the People of the Book, revealed before your time,—when you give them their due dowers, and desire chastity, not lewdness, nor secret intrigues. If anyone rejects faith, fruitless is his work, and in the Hereafter he will be in the ranks of those who have lost (all spiritual good).

Sura: 5, Ayat: 5.

The adulterer may marry only an adulteress or an idolatress; and the adulteress may marry only an adulterer or an idolater. True believers are forbidden such (marriages).

Sura: 24, Ayat: 3.

Women impure are for men impure, and men impure for women impure and women of purity are for men of purity, and men of purity are for women of purity: These are not affected by what people say: For them there is forgiveness, and a provision honourable.

Sura: 24, Ayat: 26.

And (you ought to) marry the single from among you as well as such of your male and female slaves as are fit (for marriage).

If they (whom you intend to marry) are poor, (let this not deter you;) God will grant them sufficiency out of His bounty—for God is infinite (in His mercy), all-knowing. And as for those who are unable to marry, let them live in continence until God grants them sufficiency out of His bounty.

And if any of those whom you rightfully possess (slaves) desire (to obtain) a deed of freedom, write it out for them if you are aware of any good in them: and give them (their share) of the wealth of God which He has given you.

And do not, in order to gain some of the fleeting pleasures of this worldly life, coerce your (slave) maidens into whoredom if they happen to be desirous of marriage; and if anyone should coerce them, then, verily, after they have been compelled (to submit in their helplessness), God will be much-forgiving, a dispenser of grace!

Sura: 24, Ayat: 32-33.

The Prophet is closer to the Believers than their own selves, and his wives are their mothers....

Sura: 33, Ayat: 6.

And (remember) when you* said to the Man whom Allah as well as yourself have favoured: 'Keep your wife and have fear of Allah.' You sought to hide in your heart what Allah was to reveal. You were afraid of people, although it would have been more right to fear Allah. And when Zayed divorced his wife, We gave her to you in marriage, so that it should not be difficult for true believers to wed the wives of their adopted sons if they divorced them. Allah's will must needs be done.**

Sura: 33, Ayat: 37.

O'Prophet, We have made lawful to you the wives to whom you have granted dowries and those whom your right hand possesses (slaves) and whom Allah has given you as booty; the daughters of your paternal and maternal uncles and of your paternal and maternal aunts who migrated with you; and any other believing woman who gives herself to you and whom you wished to take in marriage. This is only for you and not any other believer.

We well know the duties We have imposed on the faithful concerning their wives and those whom your right hand possesses (slaves), so that there should be no difficulty for you. Allah is Forgiving and Merciful.

Sura: 33, Ayat: 50.

O you who believe! When there come to you believing women refugees, examine (and test) them: God knows best as to their Faith: if you ascertain that they are Believers, then send them not back to the Unbelievers. They are not lawful (wives) for the Unbelievers, nor are the (Unbelievers) lawful (husbands) for them. But pay the Unbelievers what they have spent (on their dowers). And there will be no blame on you if you marry them on payment of their dower to them. But hold not to the guardianship of Unbelieving women: ask for what you have spent on their dowers, and let the (Unbelievers) ask for what they have spent on their dowers, and let the (Unbelievers) ask for what

---

***Muhammad**

****Zayd, Muhammad's adopted son**

they have spent (on the dowers of women who come over to you). Such is the command of God: He judges (with justice) between you. And God is Full of Knowledge and Wisdom.

Sura: 60, Ayat: 10.

In the name of Allah, The Compassionate, The Merciful

RELATIONSHIP WITH WIFE

Permitted to you, on the night of the fasts, is the approach to your wives. They are your garments and you are their garments. God knows what you used to do secretly among yourselves; but He turned to you and forgave you; so now associate (sexually) with them, and seek what God has ordained for you, and eat and drink, until the white thread of dawn appear to you distinct from its black thread; then complete your fast till the night appear; but do not associate with your wives while you are in retreat in the mosques. Those are limits (set by) God: Approach not nigh thereto. Thus does God make clear His Signs to men: that they may learn self-restraint.

Sura: 2, Ayat: 187.

Your wives are as a tilth unto you; so approach your tilth when or how you will; but provide something for your souls beforehand; and fear God, and know that you are to meet Him (in the Hereafter), and give (these) good tidings to those who believe.

Sura: 2, Ayat: 223.

For those who take an oath for abstention from their wives, a waiting for four months is ordained; if then they return, God is Oft-Forgiving, Most Merciful. But if their intention is firm for divorce, God hears and knows all things.

Sura: 2, Ayat: 226-227.

...And women shall have rights similar to the rights against them, according to what is equitable; but men have a degree (of advantage) over them. And God is Exalted in Power, Wise.

Sura: 2, Ayat: 228.

When you have divorced your wives and they have reached the end of their waiting period, either retain them in honour or let them go with kindness. But you shall not retain them in order to harm them or to wrong them. Whoever

does this wrongs his own soul....

Sura: 2, Ayat: 231.

If a man has divorced his wife and she has reached the end of her waiting period, do not prevent her from remarrying her proposed husband (former or someone else) if they have come to an honourable agreement. This is enjoined on everyone of you who believes in Allah and the Last Day; it is more honourable for you and more chaste. Allah knows, but you do not.

Sura: 2, Ayat: 232.

And the mothers may nurse their children for two whole years, if they wish to complete the period of nursing; and it is incumbent upon him who has begotten the child to provide in a fair manner for their sustenance and clothing. No human being shall be burdened with more than he is well able to bear: neither shall a mother be made to suffer because of her child, nor, because of his child, he who has begotten it. And the same duty rests upon the (father's) heir.

And, if both (parents) decide, by mutual consent and counsel, upon separation (of mother and child), they will incur no sin (thereby)....

Sura: 2, Ayat: 233.

And those of you who die and leave wives behind, such wives should keep in waiting for four months and ten days after their husband's death.

When they have reached the end of their waiting period, it shall be no offence for you to let them do whatever they choose for themselves, provided that it is lawful. Allah is cognizant of what you do.

Sura: 2, Ayat: 234.

And if you divorce them before having touched them, but after having settled a dower upon them, then (give them) half of what you have settled — unless it be that they forego their claim or he in whose hand is the marriage-tie foregoes his claim (to half of the dower): and to forego what is due to you is more in accord with righteousness. And forget not (that you are to act with) grace towards one another: Verily, God sees all that you do.

Sura: 2, Ayat: 237.

Those of you who die and leave widows should bequeath for their widows a year's maintenance and residence; but if they leave (the residence), there is no blame on you for what they do with themselves, provided it is reasonable. And God is Exalted in Power, Wise. For divorced women maintenance (should be provided) on a reasonable (scale). This is a duty on the righteous.

Sura: 2, Ayat: 240-241.

O you who believe! You are forbidden to inherit women against their will.

Nor should you treat them with harshness, that you may take away part of the dower you have given them, — except where they have been guilty of open lewdness; on the contrary live with them on a footing of kindness and equity. If you take a dislike to them it may be that you dislike a thing, and God brings about through it a great deal of good

But if you decide to take one wife in place of another, even if you had given the latter a whole treasure for dower, take not the least bit of it back: Would you take it by slander and a manifest wrong?

And how could you take it when you have gone in unto each other, and they have taken from you a solemn covenant?

Sura: 4, Ayat: 19—21.

If anyone of you cannot afford to marry free believing women, (let him marry) from among the owned (slaves) believing women. Allah best knows your faith: you are all alike (in terms of religion). Marry them with the permission of their masters and give them their dowry in all justice, provided they are honourable and chaste and have not entertained other men. If after marriage they commit adultery, they shall suffer half the penalty inflicted upon free adulteresses. Such is the law for those of you who fear to commit sin: but if you abstain, it will be better for you. Allah is Forgiving, Merciful.

Sura: 4, Ayat: 25.

Men have authority over women because Allah has made the one superior to the other, and because they spend their wealth to maintain them. Good women are obedient. They guard their unseen (parts) because Allah has guarded them. As for those from whom you fear disobedience, admonish them and send them to beds apart and beat them. Then if they obey you, take no further action against them. Allah is High, Supreme.

If you fear a breach between a man and his wife, appoint an arbiter from his people and another from hers. If they wish to be reconciled, Allah will bring them together again. Allah is Knowing, Wise.

Sura: 4, Ayat: 34-35.

If a woman fears ill-treatment or desertion on the part of her husband, it shall be no offence for them to seek a mutual agreement, for agreement is best. Man is prone to avarice. But if you do what is right and guard yourselves against evil, know then that Allah is cognizant of all what you do.

Sura: 4, Ayat: 128.

In no way can you treat your wives in a just manner, even though you may wish to do that. Do not set yourself altogether against any of them, leaving her, as it were in suspense. If you do what is right and guard yourself against evil (you will find) Allah is Forgiving, Merciful. If they separate, Allah will

compensate each of them out of His own abundance: He is Munificent, Wise.

Sura: 4, Ayat: 129-130.

And among His Signs is this, that He created for you mates from among yourselves, that you may dwell in tranquillity with them, and He has put love and mercy between your (hearts): Verily in that are Signs for those who reflect.

Sura: 30, Ayat: 21.

Believers, if you marry believing women and divorce them before the marriage is consummated, you have no right to require them to observe a waiting period. Provide well for them and release them honourably.

Sura: 33, Ayat: 49.

O you who believe! Truly, among your wives and your children are (somethat are) enemies to yourselves: so beware of them! But if you forgive and overlook, and cover up (their faults), verily God is Oft-Forgiving, Most Merciful.

Sura: 64, Ayat: 14-15.

Thus when they fulfil their waiting term appointed, either take them back on equitable terms or part with them on equitable terms; and take for witness two persons from among you, endued with justice (as) before God. Such is the admonition given to him who believes in God and the Last Day. And for those who fear God, He (ever) prepares a way out.

And He provides for him from (sources) he never could imagine. And if anyone puts his trust in God, sufficient is (God) for him. For God will surely accomplish His purpose: Verily, for all things has God appointed a due portion.

Sura: 65, Ayat: 2-3.

Let the women live (in 'iddat) in the same style as you live, according to your means: annoy them not, so as to make their lives miserable. And if they carry (life in their wombs), then spend (your substance) on them until they deliver their burden: and if they suckle your (offspring), give them their recompense: And take mutual counsel together, according to what is just and reasonable. And if you find yourselves in difficulties, let another woman suckle (the child) on the (father's) behalf.

Let the man of means spend according to his means: and the man whose resources are restricted, let him spend according to what God has given him. God puts no burden on any person beyond what He has given him. After a difficulty, God will soon grant relief.

Sura: 65, Ayat: 6-7.

When the Prophet confided a secret to one of his wives; and when she disclosed it and Allah informed him of this, he made known one part of it and said nothing about the other. And when he had acquainted her with it, she said; 'Who told you this?' He replied: 'The Wise One, the All-Knowing, told me.'

Sura: 66, Ayat: 3.

In the name of Allah, The Compassionate, The Merciful

GOD'S PREFERENCE

Fighting is obligatory for you, much as you dislike it. But you may hate a thing although it is good for you, and love a thing although it is bad for you. Allah knows, but you do not.

Sura: 2, Ayat: 216.

...Treat them with kindness; for even if you do dislike them, it may well be that you may dislike a thing which Allah has meant for your own good.

Sura: 4, Ayat: 19.

In the name of Allah, The Compassionate, The Merciful

RIGHT OF WOMEN

Permitted to you, on the night of the fasts, is the approach to your wives. They are your garments and you are their garments....

Sura: 2, Ayat: 187.

Divorced women shall wait concerning themselves for three monthly periods. Nor is it lawful for them to hide what God has created in their wombs, if they have faith in God and the Last Day. And their husbands have the better right to take them back in that period, if they wish for reconciliation. And women shall have rights similar to the rights against them, according to what is equitable; but men have a degree (of advantage) over them. And God is Exalted in Power, Wise.

Sura: 2, Ayat: 228.

Those of you who die and leave widows should bequeath for their widows a year's maintenance and residence; but if they leave (the residence), there is no blame on you for what they do with themselves, provided it is reasonable. And God is Exalted in Power, Wise. For divorced women maintenance (should be provided) on a reasonable (scale). This is a duty on the righteous.

Sura: 2, Ayat: 240-41.

Give women their dowry as a free gift; but if they choose to make over to you a part of it, you may regard it as lawfully yours.

Sura: 4, Ayat: 4.

Men shall have a share in what their parents and kinsmen leave; and women shall have a share in what their parents and kinsmen leave; whether it be little or much, it is legally theirs.

Sura: 4, Ayat: 7.

O you who believe! You are forbidden to inherit women against their will. Nor should you treat them with harshness, that you may take away part of the dower you have given them, — except where they have been guilty of open

lewdness; on the contrary live with them on a footing of kindness and equity. If you take a dislike to them it may be that you dislike a thing, and God brings about through it a great deal of good.

But if you decide to take one wife in place of another, even if you had given the latter a whole treasure for dower, take not the least bit of it back: Would you take it by slander and a manifest wrong?

And how could you take it when you have gone in unto each other, and they have taken from you a solemn covenant?

Sura: 4, Ayat: 19—21.

Do not covet the favours by which Allah has exalted some of you above others. For men is a portion of what they earn, and for women is a portion of what they earn. Ask Allah for His grace. Allah has knowledge of all things.

Sura: 4, Ayat: 32.

Men have authority over women because Allah has made the one superior to the other, and because they spend their wealth to maintain them. Good women are obedient. They guard their unseen (parts) because Allah has guarded them. As for those from whom you fear disobedience admonish them and send them to beds apart and beat them. Then if they obey you, take no further action against them. Allah is High, Supreme.

Sura: 4, Ayat: 34.

If you fear a breach between a man and his wife, appoint an arbiter from his people and another from hers. If they wish to be reconciled, Allah will bring them together again. Allah is Knowing, Wise.

Sura: 4, Ayat: 35.

They ask your instructions concerning the Women. Say: God does instruct you about them: And (remember) what has been rehearsed unto you in the Book, concerning the orphan girls to whom you give not the portions prescribed, and yet whom you desire to marry, as also concerning the children who are weak and oppressed: That you stand firm for justice to orphans. There is not a good deed which you do, but God is well-acquainted therewith.

Sura: 4, Ayat: 127.

If a woman fears ill-treatment or desertion on the part of her husband, it shall be no offence for them to seek a mutual agreement, for agreement is best. Man is prone to avarice. But if you do what is right and guard yourselves against evil, know then that Allah is cognizant of all what you do.

Sura: 4, Ayat: 128.

In no way can you treat your wives in a just manner, even though you may wish to do that. Do not set yourself altogether against any of them, leaving

her, as it were, in suspense. If you do what is right and guard yourselves against evil (you will find) Allah is Forgiving, Merciful.

Sura: 4, Ayat: 129.

If they separate, Allah will compensate each of them out of His own abundance: He is Munificent, Wise.

Sura: 4, Ayat: 130.

Those who defame honourable but unaware believing women shall be cursed in this world and in the next. Theirs shall be a woeful punishment.

Sura: 24, Ayat: 23.

Believers, if you marry believing women and divorce them before the marriage is consummated, you have no right to require them to observe a waiting period. Provide well for them and release them honourably.

Sura: 33, Ayat: 49.

O Prophet! When believing women come to you to take the oath of fealty to you, that they will not associate in worship any other thing whatever with God, that they will not steal, that they will not commit adultery (or fornication), that they will not kill their children, that they will not utter slander, intentionally forging falsehood, and that they will not disobey you in any just matter, then do you receive their fealty, and pray to God for the forgiveness (of their sins): for God is Oft-Forgiving, Most Merciful.

Sura: 60, Ayat: 12.

Thus when they fulfil their waiting term appointed, either take them back on equitable terms or part with them on equitable terms; and take for witness two persons from among you, endued with justice, and establish the evidence (as) before God. Such is the admonition given to him who believes in God and the Last Day. And for those who fear God, He (ever) prepares a way out .

And He provides for him from (sources) he never could imagine. And if anyone puts his trust in God, sufficient is (God) for him. For God will surely accomplish His purpose: Verily, for all things has God appointed a due proportion.

Sura: 65, Ayat: 2-3.

Let the women live (in 'iddat) in the same style as you live, according to your means: annoy them not, so as to make their lives miserable. And if they carry (life in their wombs), then spend (your substance) on them until they deliver their burden: and if they suckle your (offspring), give them their recompense: And take mutual counsel together, according to what is just and reasonable. And if you find yourselves in difficulties, let another woman suckle (the child) on the (father's) behalf.

Let the man of means spend according to his means: and the man whose resources are restricted,let him spend according to what God has given him. God puts no burden on any person beyond what He has given him. After a difficulty, God will soon grant relief.

Sura: 65, Ayat: 6-7.

In the name of Allah, The Compassionate, The Merciful

EQUAL TREATMENT OF MAN AND WOMAN

Their Lord answers them, saying:

'I will deny no man or woman among you the reward of their labours. You are the offspring of one another.'...

Sura: 3, Ayat: 195.

In the name of Allah, The Compassionate, The Merciful

SUCKLING THE CHILD

"And the mothers may nurse their children for two whole years, if they wish to complete the period of nursing; and it is incumbent upon him who has begotten the child to provide in a fair manner for their sustenance and clothing. No human being shall be burdened with more than he is well able to bear: neither shall a mother be made to suffer because of her child, nor because of his child, he who has begotten it. And the same duty rests upon the (father's) heir.

And if both (parents) decide, by mutual consent and counsel, upon separation (of mother and child), they will incur no sin (thereby); and if you decide to entrust your children to foster-mothers, you will incur no sin provided you ensure, in a fair manner, the safety of the child which you are handing over. But remain conscious of God, and know that God sees all that you do.

Sura: 2, Ayat: 233.

"And (God says:) 'We have enjoined upon man goodness towards his parents: his mother bore him by bearing strain upon strain, and his utter dependence on her lasted two years: (hence, O man,) be grateful towards Me and towards your parents (and remember that) with Me is all journeys' end.

Sura: 31, Ayat: 14.

We have enjoined man to show kindness to his parents. With much pain his mother bears him, and with much pain she brings him into the world. He is born and weaned in thirty months. When he grows to manhood and attains his fortieth year, let him say: 'Grant me, Lord, that I may give thanks for the favours You have bestowed on me and on my parents, and to do good works that will please You. Grant me good descendants. To You I turn and to You I surrender myself.'

Sura: 46, Ayat: 15.

Let the women live (in 'iddat) in the same style as you live, according to your means: Annoy them not, so as to make their lives miserable. And if they carry (life in their wombs), then spend (your substance) on them until they de-

liver their burden: and if they suckle your (offspring), give them their recompense: And take mutual counsel together, according to what is just and reasonable. And if you find yourselves in difficulties, let another woman suckle (the child) on the father's behalf.

Let the man of means spend according to his means: and the man whose resources are restricted, let him spend according to what God has given him. God puts no burden on any person beyond what He has given him. After a difficulty, God will soon grant relief.

Sura: 65, Ayat: 6-7.

In the name of Allah, The Compassionate, The Merciful

DIVORCE

Those who take an oath that they will not approach their wives shall have four months of grace; and if they go back (on their oath) behold, God is much-forgiving, a dispenser of grace. But if they are resolved on divorce-behold, God is All-Hearing, All-Knowing.

Sura: 2, Ayat: 226-227.

Divorced women shall wait concerning themselves for three monthly periods. Nor is it lawful for them to hide what God has created in their wombs, if they have faith in God and the Last Day. And their husbands have the better right to take them back in that period, if they wish for reconciliation. And women shall have rights similar to the rights against them, according to what is equitable; but men have a degree (of advantage) over them. And God is Exalted in Power, Wise.

Sura: 2, Ayat: 228.

A divorce is only permissible twice: after that, the parties should either hold together on equitable terms, or separate with kindness. It is not lawful for you (men), to take back any of your gifts (from your wives), except when both parties fear that they would be unable to keep the limits ordained by God. If you (Judges) do indeed fear that they would be unable to keep the limits ordained by God, there is no blame on either of them if she gives something for her freedom. These are the limits ordained by God; so do not transgress them if any do transgress the limits ordained by God, such persons wrong (themselves as well as others).

Sura: 2, Ayat: 229.

So if a husband divorces his wife (irrevocably), he cannot, after that, remarry her until after she has married another husband and he has divorced her. In that case there is no blame on either of them if they re-unite, provided they feel that they can keep the limits ordained by God. Such are the limits ordained by God, which He makes plain to those who understand.

Sura: 2, Ayat: 230.

When you have divorced your wives and they have reached the end of their waiting period, either retain them in honour or let them go with kindness. But you shall not retain them in order to harm them or to wrong them. Whoever does this wrongs his own soul.

Do not make fun of Allah's revelations. Remember the favours He has bestowed upon you, and the Book and the wisdom which He has revealed for your instruction. Fear Allah and know that He has knowledge of all things.

Sura: 2, Ayat: 231.

If a man has divorced his wife and she has reached the end of her waiting period, do not prevent her from remarrying her proposed husband (former or someone else) if they have come to an honourable agreement. This is enjoined on everyone of you who believes in Allah and the Last Day; it is more honourable for you and more chaste. Allah knows, but you do not.

Sura: 2, Ayat: 232.

It shall be no offence for you to divorce your wives before the marriage is consummated or the dowry settled. Provide for them with fairness; the rich man according to his means, and the poor man according to his. This is binding on righteous men.

Sura: 2, Ayat: 236.

And if you divorce them before consummation, but after the fixation of a dower for them, then the half of the dower (is due to them), unless they remit it or (the man's half) is remitted by him in whose hands is the marriage tie; and the remission (of the man's half) is the nearest to righteousness. And do not forget liberality between yourselves. For God sees well all that you do.

Sura: 2, Ayat: 237.

For divorced women maintenance (should be provided) on a reasonable (scale). This is a duty on the righteous.

Sura: 2, Ayat: 241.

If you fear a breach between a man and his wife, appoint an arbiter from his people and another from hers. If they (man and wife) wish to be reconciled, Allah will bring them together again. Allah is Knowing, Wise.

Sura: 4, Ayat: 35.

If a woman fears ill-treatment or desertion on the part of her husband, it shall be no offence for them to seek a mutual agreement, for agreement is best. Man is prone to avarice. But if you do what is right and guard yourselves against evil, know then that Allah is cognizant of all what you do.

Sura: 4, Ayat: 128.

If they separate, Allah will compensate each of them out of His own abundance: He is Munificent, Wise.

Sura: 4, Ayat: 130.

Believers, if you marry believing women and divorce them before the marriage is consummated, you have no right to require them to observe a waiting period. Provide well for them and release them honourably.

Sura: 33, Ayat: 49.

Those of you who divorce their wives by zihar* should know that they are not their mothers. Their mothers are those only who gave birth to them. The words they utter are unjust and false: but Allah is Pardoning, Forgiving.

Those that divorce their wives by zihar and afterwards retract their words shall free a slave before they touch each other again. This you are enjoined to do: Allah is cognizant of all your actions. He that does not have (a slave) shall fast two successive months before they touch one another. If he cannot do this, he shall feed sixty of the poor....

Sura: 58, Ayat: 2–4.

O Prophet! When you do divorce women, divorce them at their prescribed periods (before beginning of menstrual periods), and count (accurately) their prescribed periods: and fear God your Lord: and turn them not out of their houses, nor shall they (themselves) leave, except in case they are guilty of some open lewdness, those are limits set by God: and any who transgresses the limits of God, does verily wrong his (own) soul: You know not if perhance God will bring about thereafter some new situation.

Sura: 65, Ayat: 1.

Thus when they fulfil their waiting term appointed, either take them back on equitable terms or part with them on equitable terms; and take for witness two persons from among you, endued with justice, and establish the evidence (as) before God. Such is the admonition given to him who believes in God and the Last Day. And for those who fear God, He (ever) prepares a way out.

And He provides for him from (sources) he never could imagine. And if anyone puts his trust in God, sufficient is (God) for him. For God will surely accomplish His purpose: Verily, for all things has God appointed a due proportion.

Sura: 65, Ayat: 2-3.

Let the women live (in 'iddat) in the same style as you live, according to your means: Annoy them not, so as to make their lives miserable. And if they carry (life in their wombs), then spend (your substance) on them until they

---

***Divorce by the formula: "Be to me as my mother's back"**

deliver their burden: and if they suckle your (offspring), give them their recompense: and take mutual counsel together, according to what is just and reasonable. And if you find yourselves in difficulties, let another woman suckle (the child) on the (father's) behalf.

Let the man of means spend according to his means: and the man whose resources are restricted, let him spend according to what God has given him. God puts no burden on any person beyond what He has given him. After a difficulty, God will soon grant relief.

Sura: 65, Ayat: 6-7.

In the name of Allah, The Compassionate, The Merciful

WIFE'S RIGHT TO CLAIM DIVORCE

A divorce is only permissible twice: after that, the parties should either hold together on equitable terms, or separate with kindness. It is not lawful for you (men), to take back any of your gifts (from your wives), except when both parties fear that they would be unable to keep the limits ordained by God. If you (Judges) do indeed fear that they would be unable to keep the limits ordained by God, there is no blame on either of them if she gives something for her freedom. These are the limits ordained by God; so do not transgress them if any do transgress the limits ordained by God, such persons wrong (themselves as well as others).

Sura: 2, Ayat: 229.

In the name of Allah, The Compassionate, The Merciful

DOWRY FOR THE WIFE

A divorce is only permissible twice: after that, the parties should either hold together on equitable terms, or separate with kindness. It is not lawful for you (men), to take back any of your gifts (from your wives), except when both parties fear that they would be unable to keep the limits ordained by God. If you (Judges) do indeed fear that they would be unable to keep the limits ordained by God, there is no blame on either of them if she gives something for her freedom. These are the limits ordained by God; so do not transgress them if any do transgress the limits ordained by God, such persons wrong (themselves as well as others).

Sura: 2, Ayat: 229.

And if you divorce them before consummation, but after the fixation of a dower for them, then the half of the dower (is due to them), unless they remit it or (the man's half) is remitted by him in whose hands is the marriage tie; and the remission (of man's half) is the nearest to righteousness. And do not forget liberality between yourselves. For God sees well all that you do.

Sura: 2, Ayat: 237.

Give women their dowry as a free gift; but if they choose to make over to you a part of it, you may regard it as lawfully yours.

Sura: 4, Ayat: 4.

O you who believe! You are forbidden to inherit women against their will. Nor should you treat them with harshness, that you may take away part of the dower you have given them, — except where they have been guilty of open lewdness; on the contrary live with them on a footing of kindness and equity. If you take a dislike to them it may be that you dislike a thing, and God brings about through it a great deal of good.

But if you decide to take one wife in place of another, even if you had given the latter a whole treasure for dower, take not the least bit of it back: Would you take it by slander and a manifest (wrong)? And how could you take it when you have gone in unto each other (had sexual intercourse) and they have

taken from you a solemn covenant?

Sura: 4, Ayat: 19—21.

(Except prohibition for marrying women already pronounced) Also (prohibited are) women already married, except those whom your right hand possess (slaves): Thus has God ordained (prohibitions) against you: except for these, all others are lawful, provided you seek (them in marriage) with gifts from your property, — desiring chastity, not lust. Seeing that you derive benefit from them, give them their dowers (at least) as prescribed; but if, after a dower is prescribed, you agree mutually (to vary it), there is no blame on you, and God is All-Knowing, All-Wise.

Sura: 4, Ayat: 24.

If anyone of you cannot afford to marry free believing women, (let him marry) from among the owned believing women (slaves). Allah best knows your faith: you are all alike (in terms of religion). Marry them with the permission of their masters and give them their dowry in all justice,...

Sura: 4, Ayat: 25.

Believers, if you marry believing women and divorce them before the marriage is consummated, you have no right to require them to observe a waiting period. Provide well for them and release them honourably.

Sura: 33, Ayat: 49.

O you who believe! When there come to you believing women refugees, examine (and test) them: God knows best as to their Faith: if you ascertain that they are Believers, then send them not back to the Unbelievers. They are not lawful (wives) for the Unbelievers, nor are the (unbelievers) lawful (husbands) for them. But pay the Unbelievers what they have spent (on their dower). And there will be no blame on you if you marry them on payment of their dower to them. But hold not to the guardianship of Unbelieving women: ask for what you have spent on their dowers, and let the (Unbelievers) ask for what they have spent (on the dowers of women who come over to you). Such is the command of God: He judges (with justice) between you. And God is Full of Knowledge and Wisdom.

And if any of your wives should go over to the Unbelievers, and you are thus afflicted in turn, then give unto those whose wives have gone away the equivalent of what they had spent (on their wives by way of dower), and remain conscious of God, in whom you believe!

Sura: 60, Ayat: 10-11.

In the name of Allah, The Compassionate, The Merciful

MENSTRUATION

They ask you about menstruation. Say: 'It is an indisposition. Keep aloof from women during their menstrual periods and do not touch them until they are clean again. Then have intercourse with them as Allah enjoined you. Allah loves those that turn to Him in repentance and purify themselves.'

Sura: 2, Ayat: 222.

In the name of Allah, The Compassionate, The Merciful

THE PERIOD OF WAITING

Divorced women must wait, keeping themselves from men, three menstrual courses. It is unlawful for them, if they believe in Allah and the Last Day, to hide what He has created in their wombs; in which case their husbands would do well to take them back, should they desire reconciliation....

Sura: 2, Ayat: 228.

If any of you die and leave widows behind, they shall wait concerning themselves four months and ten days: when they have fulfilled their term, there is no blame on you if they dispose of themselves in a just and reasonable manner. And God is well acquainted with what you do.

Sura: 2, Ayat: 234.

But you will incur no sin if you give a hint of (an intended) marriage-offer to (any of) these women, or if you conceive such an intention without making it obvious: (for) God knows that you intend to ask them in marriage. Do not, however, plight your troth with them in secret, but speak only in a decent manner; and do not proceed with tying the marriage-knot ere the ordained (term of waiting) has come to its end. And know that God knows what is in your minds, and therefore remain conscious of Him; and know, too, that God is Much-Forgiving, Forbearing.

Sura: 2, Ayat: 235.

Those of you who die and leave widows should bequeath for their widows a year's maintenance and residence; but if they leave (the residence), there is no blame on you for what they do with themselves, provided it is reasonable. And God is Exalted in Power, Wise.

For divorced women maintenance (should be provided) on a reasonable (scale). This is a duty on the righteous.

Sura: 2, Ayat: 240-241.

Believers, if you marry believing women and divorce them before the marriage is consummated, you have no right to require them to observe a waiting

period. Provide well for them and release them honourably.

Sura: 33, Ayat: 49.

O Prophet! When you do divorce women, divorce them at their prescribed periods (before beginning of menstrual periods), and count (accurately) their prescribed periods: and fear God your Lord: and turn them not out of their houses, nor shall they (themselves) leave, except in case they are guilty of some open lewdness, those are limits set by God: and any who transgresses the limits of God, does verily wrong his (own) soul: You know not if perchance God will bring about thereafter some new situation.

Sura: 65, Ayat: 1.

Thus when they fulfil their waiting term appointed, either take them back on equitable terms or part with them on equitable terms; and take for witness two persons from among you, endued with justice, and establish evidence (as) before God. Such is the admonition given to him who believes in God and the Last Day. And for those who fear God, He (ever) prepares a way out.

And He provides for him from (sources) he never could imagine. And if any one puts his trust in God, sufficient is (God) for him. For God will surely accomplish His purpose: Verily, for all things has God appointed a due proportion.

Sura: 65, Ayat: 2-3.

If you are in doubt concernig those of your wives who have ceased menstruating, know that their waiting period is three months. And let the same be the waiting period of those who have not yet menstruated. As for pregnant women, their term shall be the time they deliver their burden. Allah will ease hardship of the man who fears Him.

Sura: 65, Ayat: 4.

Let the women live (in 'iddat) in the same style as you live, according to your means: Annoy them not, so as to make their lives miserable. And if they carry (life in their wombs), then spend (your substance) on them until they deliver their burden: and if they suckle your (offspring), give them their recompense: and take mutual counsel together, according to what is just and reasonable. And if you find yourselves in difficulties, let another woman suckle (the child) on the (father's) behalf.

Let the man of means spend according to his means: and the man whose resources are restricted, let him spend according to what God has given him. God puts no burden on any person beyond what He has given him. After a difficulty, God will soon grant relief.

Sura: 65, Ayat: 6-7.

In the name of Allah, The Compassionate, The Merciful

"ZIHAR" (UNJUST AND FALSE DECLARATION OF RELATIONS)

God has not made for any man two hearts in his (one) body: nor has He made your wives whom you divorce by Zihar (as) your mothers: nor has He made your adopted sons your sons. Such is (only) your (manner of) speech by your mouths. But God tells (you) the Truth, and He shows the (right) Way.

Sura: 33, Ayat: 4.

Name your adopted sons after their fathers; that is more just in the sight of Allah. If you do not know their fathers, regard them as your brothers in the faith and as your cousins. Your (unintentional) mistakes shall be forgiven, but not your deliberate errors. Allah is Forgiving and Merciful.

Sura: 33, Ayat: 5.

Those that divorce their wives by zihar* should know that they are not their mothers. Their mothers are those only who gave birth to them. The words they utter are unjust and false: but Allah is Pardoning, Forgiving.

Sura: 58, Ayat: 2.

Those that divorce their wives by zihar and afterwards retract their words shall free a slave before they touch each other again. This you are enjoined to do: Allah is cognizant of all your actions. He that does not have (a slave) shall fast two successive months before they touch one another. If he cannot do this, he shall feed sixty of the poor. This is enjoined on you so that you may have faith in Allah and His Apostle. Such are the limits set by Allah. A grievous punishment awaits the unbelievers.

Sura: 58, Ayat: 3-4.

***Divorce by the formula: 'Be to me as my mother's back'**

INHERITANCE

(24)

In the name of Allah, The Compassionate, The Merciful

INHERITANCE

It is decreed that when death approaches, those of you that leave wealth shall bequeath (it) to parents and kindred. This is a duty incumbent on the righteous.

Sura: 2, Ayat: 180.

He that alters that (the will) after hearing it shall be accountable for his crime. Allah is Hearing and Knowing.

He that suspects an error or an injustice on the part of a testator and brings about a settlement among the parties incurs no guilt. Allah is Forgiving and Merciful.

Sura: 2, Ayat: 181-182.

Men shall have a share in what their parents and kinsmen leave; and women shall have a share in what their parents and kinsmen leave; whether it be little or much, it is legally theirs.

Sura: 4, Ayat: 7.

If relatives, orphans, or needy men are present at the division of an inheritance, give them, too, a share of it, and speak to them in kind words.

Sura: 4, Ayat: 8.

Let those (disposing of an estate) have the same fear in their minds as they would have for their own if they had left a helpless family behind: Let them fear God, and speak words of appropriate (comfort).

Those who unjustly eat up the property of orphans, eat up a Fire into their own bodies: they will soon be enduring a blazing Fire!

Sura: 4, Ayat: 9-10.

Allah has thus enjoined you concerning your children:

A male shalll inherit twice as much as a female. If there be more than two girls, they shall have two-thirds of the inheritance; but if there be one only, she shall inherit the half. Parents shall inherit a sixth each, if the deceased has

a child; but if he has no children and his parents be his heirs, his mother shall have a third. If he has brothers, his mother shall have a sixth after payment of any bequest he may have bequeathed, or debt.

You know not whether your parents or your children are more beneficial to you. But this is the law of Allah; He is Wise and All-Knowing.

Sura: 4, Ayat: 11.

You shall inherit the half of what your wives leave if they die childless. If they leave children, a quarter of what they leave shall be yours after payment of any bequest they may have bequeathed or debt.

Your wives shall inherit one quarter of what you leave if you die childless. If you leave children, they shall inherit one eighth, after payment of any bequest you may have bequeathed, or debt.

If a man or a woman leave neither children nor parents and have a brother or a sister, they shall each inherit one-sixth. If there be more, they shall equally share the third of the estate, after payment of any bequest that may have been bequeathed or debt without prejudice (to the rights of the heirs). This is a commandment from Allah. He is Gracious and All-Knowing.

Sura: 4, Ayat: 12.

Such are the bounds set by Allah. He that obeys Allah and His Apostle shall dwell forever in gardens watered by running streams. That is the supreme triumph.

Sura: 4, Ayat: 13.

But he that disobeys Allah and His Apostle and transgresses His bounds, shall be cast into fire and shall abide in it forever. A shameful punishment awaits him.

Sura: 4, Ayat: 14.

O you who believe! You are forbidden to inherit women against their will, Nor should you treat them with harshness, that you may take away part of the dower you have given them, — except where they have been guilty of open lewdness; on the contrary live with them on a footing of kindness and equity. If you take a dislike to them it may be that you dislike a thing, and God brings about through it a great deal of good.

Sura: 4, Ayat: 19.

And unto everyone have We appointed heirs to what he may leave behind: parents, and near kinsfolk, and those to whom you have pledged your troth: give them, therefore, their share. Behold, God is indeed a witness unto everything.

Sura: 4, Ayat: 33.

They ask you for a legal decision. Say: God directs (thus) about those who leave no descendants or ascendants as heirs. If it is a man that dies, leaving a sister but no child, she shall have the inheritance: If (such a deceased was) a woman, who left no child, her brother takes her inheritance: if there are two sisters, they shall have two-thirds of the inheritance (between them): if there are brothers and sisters, (they share), the male having twice the share of the females. Thus does God make clear to you (His law), lest you err. And God has knowledge of all things.

Sura: 4, Ayat: 176.

Those who believed, and adopted exile, and fought for the Faith, with their property and their persons in the cause of God, as well as those who gave (them) asylum and aid, — these are (all) friends and protectors, one of another. As to those who believed but came not into exile, you owe no duty of protection to them until they come into exile; but if they seek your aid in religion, it is your duty to help them, except against a people with whom you have a treaty of mutual alliance And (remember) God sees all that you do.

Sura: 8, Ayat: 72.

Those who believe, and adopt exile, and fight for the Faith, in the cause of God, as well as those who give (them) asylum and aid, — these are (all) in very truth the believers: For them is the forgiveness of sins and a provision most generous. And those who accept Faith subsequently, and adopt exile, and fight for the Faith in your company, — they are of you. But kindred by blood have prior rights against each other in the Book of God. Verily God is well acquainted with all things.

Sura: 8, Ayat: 74-75.

The Prophet is closer to the believers than their own selves, and his wives are their mothers. Blood-relations are closer to one another, in the Decree of God, than (the Brotherhood of) believers and muhajirs: Nevertheless do you what is just to your closest friends: such is the writing in the Decree (of God).

Sura: 33, Ayat: 6.

No! But you show no kindness to the orphan, nor do you urge one another to feed the poor. Greedily you lay your hands on the inheritance of the others and you love riches with all your hearts.

Sura: 89, Ayat: 17—20.

In the name of Allah, The Compassionate, The Merciful

ADOPTED CHILDREN

God has not made for any man two hearts in his (one) body: nor has He made your wives whom you divorce by Zihar as your mothers: nor has He made your adopted sons your sons. Such is (only) your (manner of) speech by your mouths. But God tells (you) the Truth, and He shows the (right) Way.

Sura: 33, Ayat: 4.

Name your adopted sons after their fathers; that is more just in the sight of Allah. If you do not know their fathers, regard them as your brothers in the faith and as your cousins. Your (unintentional) mistakes shall be forgiven, but not your deliberate errors. Allah is Forgiving and Merciful.

Sura: 33, Ayat: 5.

Behold! you did say to one who had received the grace of God and your favour: 'Retain you (in wedlock) your wife, and fear God.' But you did hide in your heart that which God was about to make manifest: you did fear the people, but it is more fitting that you should fear God. Then when Zaid had dissolved (his marriage) with her, with the necessary (formality), We joined her in marriage to you: in order that (in future) there may be no difficulty to the Believers in (the matter of) marriage with the wives of their adopted sons, when the latter have dissolved with the necessary (formality) (their marriage) with them. And God's command must be fulfilled.

Sura: 33, Ayat: 37.

In the name of Allah, The Compassionate, The Merciful

WILL

It is decreed that when death approaches, those of you that leave wealth shall bequeath it equitably to parents and kindred. This is a duty incumbent on the righteous.

Sura: 2, Ayat: 180.

He that alters that (the will) after hearing it shall be accountable for his crime. Allah is Hearing and Knowing.

Sura: 2, Ayat: 181.

He that suspects an error or an injustice on the part of a testator and brings about a settlement among the parties incurs no guilt. Allah is Forgiving and Merciful.

Sura: 2, Ayat: 182.

Those of you who die and leave widows should bequeath for their widows a year's maintenance and residence; but if they leave (the residence), there is no blame on you for what they do with themselves, provided it is reasonable. And God is Exalted in Power, Wise.

Sura: 2, Ayat: 240.

O you who believe! When death approaches any of you, (take) witnesses among yourselves when making bequests, — two just men of your own (brotherhood) or others from outside if you are journeying through the earth, and the chance of death befalls you (thus). If you doubt (their truth), detain them both after prayer, and let them both swear by God: 'We wish not in this for any worldly gain, even though the (beneficiary) be our near relation: we shall hide not the evidence before God: if we do, then behold! the sin be upon us!'

Sura: 5, Ayat: 106.

But if it gets known that these two were guilty of the sin (of perjury), let two others stand forth in their places, — nearest in kin from among those who

claim a lawful right: let them swear by God: "We affirm that our witness is truer than that of those two, and that we have not trespassed (beyond the truth): if we did, behold!, the wrong be upon us!"

Sura: 5, Ayat: 107.

That is most suitable: that they may give the evidence in its true nature and shape, or else they would fear that other oaths would be taken after their oaths. But fear God, and listen (to His counsel): for God guides not a rebellious people:

Sura: 5, Ayat: 108.

RULES TO GUARD RELATIONS BETWEEN MEN & WOMEN

(25)

In the name of Allah, The Compassionate, The Merciful

LOWER YOUR GAZE

Say to the believing men that they should lower their gaze and guard their modesty: that will make for greater purity for them: and God is well acquainted with all that they do.

Sura: 24, Ayat: 30.

And say to the believing women that they should lower their gaze and guard their modesty; that they should not display their beauty and ornaments except what (must ordinarily) appear thereof; that they should draw their veils over their bosoms and not display their beauty except to their husbands, their fathers, their husbands' fathers, their sons, their husbands' sons, or their sisters' sons, or their women, or the slaves whom their right hands possess, or male servants free of physical needs (sexual etc.), or small children who have no knowledge of sex; and that they should not strike their feet in order to draw attention to their hidden ornaments. And O you Believers! turn you all together towards God, that you may attain Bliss.

Sura: 24, Ayat: 31.

In the name of Allah, The Compassionate, The Merciful

RULES AGAINST SELF-DISPLAY

O you Children of Adam! We have bestowed raiment upon you to cover your private parts, as well as to be an adornment to you. But the garment of righteousness,—that is the best. Such are among the Signs of God, that they may receive admonition!

Sura: 7, Ayat: 26.

Say: Who has forbidden the beautiful (gifts) of God, for His servants, and the things, clean and pure (which He has provided) for sustenance? Say: They are, in the life of this world, for those who believe, (and) purely for them on the Day of Judgement. Thus do We explain the Signs in detail for those who understand.

Sura: 7, Ayat: 32.

O you who believe! Enter not houses other than your own, until you have asked permission and saluted those in them: that is best for you, in order that you may heed (what is seemly).

If you find no one in the house, enter not until permission is given to you: if you are asked to go back, go back: that makes for greater purity for yourselves: and God knows well all that you do.

It is no fault on your part to enter houses not used for living in, which serve some (other) use for you: and God has knowledge of what you reveal and what you conceal.

Sura: 24, Ayat: 27—30.

Say to the believing men that they should lower their gaze and guard their modesty: that will make for greater purity for them: and God is well acquainted with all that they do.

Sura: 24, Ayat: 30.

Say to the believing women that they should lower their gaze and guard their modesty; that they should not display their beauty and ornaments except

what (must ordinarily) appear thereof; that they should draw their veils over their bosoms and not display their beauty except to their husbands, their fathers, their husbands' fathers, their sons, their husbands' sons, their brothers or their brothers' sons, or their sisters' sons, or their women, or the slaves whom their right hands possess, or male servants free of physical needs (sexual etc.), or small children who have no knowledge of sex; and that they should not strike their feet in order to draw attention to their hidden ornaments. And O you Believers! turn you all together towards God, that you may attain Bliss.

Sura: 24, Ayat: 31.

O you who believe! 'Let those whom your right hands possess, and the (children) among you who have not come of age ask your permission (before they come to your presence), on three occasions: before morning prayer; the while you put off your clothes at noon; and after the late-night prayer: These are your three times of undress: outside those times it is not wrong for you or for them to move about attending to each other: Thus does God make clear the Signs to you: for God is full of knowledge and wisdom.

Sura: 24, Ayat: 58.

But when the children among you come of age, let them (also) ask for permission, as do those senior to them (in age): Thus does God make clear His Signs to you: for God is full of knowledge and wisdom.

Sura: 24, Ayat: 59.

Such elderly women as are past the prospect of marriage, there is no blame on them if they lay aside their (outer) garments, provided they make not a wanton display of their beauty: but it is best for them to be modest: and God is One Who sees and knows all things.

Sura: 24, Ayat: 60.

O Consorts of the Prophet! You are not like any of the (other) women: If you do fear (God), be not too complaisant of speech, lest one in whose heart is a disease should be moved with desire: but speak you a speech (that is) just.

Sura: 33, Ayat: 32.

And stay quietly in your houses, and make not a dazzling display, like that of the former Times of Ignorance; and establish regular Prayer, and give regular Charity; and obey God and His Apostle. And God only wishes to remove all abomination from you, you Members of the Family, and to make you pure and spotless. And recite what is rehearsed to you in your homes, of the Signs of God and His Wisdom: For God understands the finest mysteries and is well-acquainted (with them).

Sura: 33, Ayat: 33-34.

O you who have attained to faith! Do not enter the Prophet's dwellings unless you are given leave; (and when invited) to a meal, do not come (so early as) to wait for it to be readied: but whenever you are invited, enter (at the proper time); and when you have partaken of the meal, disperse without lingering for the sake of mere talk: that, behold, might give offence to the Prophet, and yet he might feel shy of (asking) you (to leave): but God is not shy of (teaching you) what is right.

And (as for the Prophet's wives,) whenever you ask them for anything that you need, ask them from behind a screen: this will but deepen the purity of your hearts and theirs. Moreover, it does not behove you to give offence to God's Prophet....

Sura: 33, Ayat: 53.

There is no blame (on these ladies if they appear) before their fathers or their sons, their brothers, or their brothers' sons, or their sisters' sons or their women, or the (slaves) whom their right hands possess. And, (ladies), fear God: for God is Witness to all things.

Sura: 33, Ayat: 55.

Prophet! Tell your wives and daughters, and the believing women, that they should cast their outer garments over their persons (when abroad): That is most convenient, that they should be known (as such) and not molested. And God is Oft-Forgiving, Most Merciful.

Sura: 33, Ayat: 59.

In the name of Allah, The Compassionate, The Merciful

WIVES OF THE PROPHET–MOTHERS OF BELIEVERS

The Prophet is closer to the Believers than their own selves, and his wives are their mothers. Blood-relations are closer to one another, in the Decree of God than (the brotherhood of) believers and muhajirs: Nevertheless do you what is just to your closest friends: such is the writing in the Decree (of God).

Sura: 33, Ayat: 6.

O Prophet, say to your wives: 'If you seek this life and all its finery, come, I will make provision for you and release you honourably. But if you seek Allah and His Apostle and the Hereafter, know that Allah has prepared a rich reward for those of you who do good works.'

Sura: 33, Ayat: 28-29.

Wives of the Prophet! Those of you who commit a proven sin shall be doubly punished. That is no difficult thing for Allah. But those of you who obey Allah and His Apostle and do good works shall be doubly rewarded; for them We have made a generous provision.

Sura: 33, Ayat: 30-31.

O Consorts of the Prophet! You are not like any of the (other) women: if you do fear (God), be not too complaisant of speech, lest one in whose heart is a disease should be moved with desire: but speak you a speech (that is) just.

Sura: 33, Ayat: 32.

And stay quietly in your houses, and make not a dazzling display, like that of the former Times of Ignorance; and establish regular Prayer, and give regular Charity; and obey God and His Apostle. And God only wishes to remove all abomination from you, you Members of the Family, and to make you pure and spotless. And recite what is rehearsed to you in your homes, of the Signs of God and His Wisdom: for God understands the finest mysteries and is well-acquainted (with them).

Sura: 33, Ayat: 33-34.

Prophet, We have made lawful to you the wives to whom you have paid their dowers and those whom your right hand possesses and whom Allah has given you as booty; the daughters of your paternal and maternal uncles and of your paternal and maternal aunts who migrated with you; and any other believing woman who gives herself to you and whom you wished to take in marriage. This is only for you and not any other believer.

We well know the duties We have imposed on the faithful concerning their wives and those whom your right hand possesses, so that there should be no difficulty for you. Allah is Forgiving and Merciful.

You may defer (the turn of) any of your wives you please and invite any of your wives you please. Nor is it unlawful for you to receive any of those whom you have temporarily set aside. That is more proper, so that they may be contented and not vexed, and may all be pleased with what you give them.

Allah knows what is in your hearts. He is All-knowing and Benignant.

No (other) women shall henceforth be lawful to you — nor are you (allowed) to supplant (any of) them by other wives, even though their beauty should please you greatly—: (none shall) be lawful to you) beyond those whom you (already) have come to possess. And God keeps watch over everything.

Sura: 33, Ayat: 50—52.

O you who have attained to faith! Do not enter the Prophet's dwellings unless you are given leave; (and when invited) to a meal, do not come (so early as) to wait for it to be readied: but whenever you are invited, enter (at the proper time); and when you have partaken of the meal, disperse without lingering for the sake of mere talk: that, behold, might give offence to the Prophet, and yet he might feel shy of (asking) you (to leave): but God is not shy of (teaching you) what is right.

And (as for the Prophet's wives,) whenever you ask them for anything that you need, ask them from behind a screen: this will but deepen the purity of your hearts and theirs. Moreover, it does not behove you to give offence to God's Prophet—just as it would not behove you ever to marry his widows after he has passed away: that, verily, would be enormity in the sight of God.

Whether you do anything openly or in secret, (remember that,) verily, God has full knowledge of everything.

Sura: 33, Ayat: 53-54.

There is no blame (on these ladies if they appear) before their fathers or their sons, their brothers, or their brothers' sons, or their sisters' sons or their women, or the (slaves) whom their right hands possess. And, (ladies), fear God; for God is Witness to all things.

Sura: 33, Ayat: 55.

O Prophet! Why do you, out of a desire to please (one or another of) your wives, impose (on yourself) a prohibition of something that God has made

lawful to you? But God is Much-Forgiving, a dispenser of grace.

Sura: 66, Ayat: 1.

When the Prophet confided a secret to one of his wives; and when she disclosed it and Allah informed him of this, he made known one part of it and said nothing about the other. And when he had acquainted her with it, she said: 'Who told you this?' He replied: 'The Wise One, The All-knowing, told me.'

If you two turn to Allah in repentance—for your hearts were inclined (to the prohibition)—you shall be pardoned; but if you back up each other against him, know that Allah is his Protector, and Gabriel, and the righteous amongst the faithful. The angels too are his helpers.

It may well be that, if he divorces you, his Lord will give him in your place better wives than yourselves, submissive to Allah and full of faith, devout, penitent, obedient, and given to fasting; both formerly married and virgins.

Sura: 66, Ayat: 3—5.

In the name of Allah, The Compassionate, The Merciful

INDECENCY

Say: "Come, I will rehearse what God has (really) prohibited you from": join not anything as equal with Him; be good to your parents; kill not your children on a plea of want;—We provide sustenance for you and for them;—come not nigh to shameful deeds, whether open or secret; take not life, which God has made sacred, except by way of justice and law: thus does He command you, that you may learn wisdom.

Sura: 6, Ayat: 151.

When they do aught that is shameful, they say: 'We found our fathers doing so', and "God commanded us thus": Say: "Nay, God never commands what is shameful: do you say of God what you know not?"

Sura; 7, Ayat: 28.

Say: The things that my Lord has indeed forbidden are: Shameful deeds, whether open or secret, sins and trespasses against truth or reason: assigning of partners to God, for which He has given no authority; and saying things about God of which you have no knowledge.

Sura: 7, Ayat: 33.

God commands justice, the doing of good, and liberality to kith and kin, and He forbids all shameful deeds, and injustice and rebellion: He instructs you that you may receive admonition.

Sura: 16, Ayat: 90.

Those who love (to see) scandal published or broadcast among the Believers, will have a grievous Penalty in this life and in the Hereafter: God knows, and you know not.

Sura: 24, Ayat: 19.

Whatever you are given (here) is (but) a convenience of this Life but that which is with God is better and more lasting: (It is) for those who believe and put their trust in their Lord; those who avoid the greater crimes and shameful deeds, and, when they are angry even then forgive.

Sura: 42, Ayat: 36-37.

ADULTERY AND SLANDER

(26)

In the name of Allah, The Compassionate, The Merciful

PUNISHMENT FOR ADULTERY

If any of your women commit fornication, call in four witnesses from among yourselves against them; if they testify to their guilt, confine them to their houses till death overtakes them or till Allah finds another way for them.

Sura: 4, Ayat: 15.

If two (men or man or woman) among you commit it punish them both. If they repent and mend their ways, leave them alone. Allah is Forgiving and Merciful.

Sura: 4, Ayat: 16.

O you who believe! You are forbidden to inherit women against their will. Nor should you treat them with harshness, that you may take away part of the dower you have given them, – except where they have been guilty of open lewdness; on the contrary live with them on a footing of kindness and equity. If you take a dislike to them it may be that you dislike a thing, and God brings about through it a great deal of good.

Sura: 4, Ayat: 19.

If anyone of you cannot afford to marry free believing women (let him marry) from among the owned (slave) believing women. Allah best knows your faith: you are all alike (in terms of religion). Marry them with the permission of their masters and give them their dowry in all justice, provided they are honourable and chaste and have not entertained other men. If after marriage they commit adultery, they shall suffer half the penalty inflicted upon free adulteresses. Such is the law for those of you who fear to commit sin: but if you abstain, it will be better for you. Allah is Forgiving, Merciful.

Sura: 4, Ayat: 25.

Say: "Come, I will rehearse what God has (really) prohibited you from":... come not nigh to shameful deeds, whether open or secret.

Sura: 6, Ayat: 151.

Your Lord has decreed.... nor come nigh to adultery: for it is a shameful (deed) and an evil, opening the road (to other evils).

Sura: 17, Ayat: 23−32.

The Believers must (eventually) win through,...who abstain from sex, except with those joined to them in the marriage bond, or (one's own slave girls) whom their right hands possess, for (in their case) they are free from blame, but those whose desires exceed those limits are transgressors.

Sura: 23, Ayat: 1....5−7.

This is a sura (chapter) which We have revealed and sanctioned, proclaiming in it clear revelations, so that you may take heed.

The adulterer and the adulteress shall each be given a hundred lashes. Let no pity for them detain you from obedience to Allah, if you truly believe in Allah and the Last Day; and let their punishment be witnessed by a number of believers.

Sura: 24, Ayat: 1-2.

The adulterer may marry only an adulteress or an idolatress; and the adulteress may marry only an adulterer or an idolater. True believers are forbidden such (marriages).

Sura: 24, Ayat: 3.

And those who launch a charge against chaste women, and produce not four witnesses (to support their allegations), −flog them with eighty stripes; and reject their evidence ever after: for such men are wicked transgressors; unless they repent thereafter and mend (their conduct); for God is Oft-Forgiving, Most Merciful.

Sura: 24, Ayt: 4-5.

Women impure are for men impure, and men impure are for women impure and women of purity are for men of purity, and men of purity are for women of purity: these are not affected by what people say: For them there is forgiveness, and a provision honourable.

Sura: 24, Ayat: 26.

And as for those who are unable to marry, let them live in continence until God grants them sufficiency out of His bounty.

And if any of those whom you rightfully possess desire (to obtain) a deed of freedom, write it out for them if you are aware of any good in them: and give them (their share) of the wealth of God which He has given you.

And do not, in order to gain some of the fleeting pleasures of this worldly life, coerce your (slave) maidens into whoredom if they happen to be desirous of marriage; and if anyone should coerce them, then, verily, after they have

been compelled (to submit in their helplessness), God will be much forgiving, a dispenser of grace!

Sura: 24, Ayat: 33.

And the servants of (God) most Gracious are those who walk on the earth in humility, and when the ignorant address them, they say, "peace!"; ... those who invoke not, with God, any other god, nor slay such life as God has made sacred, except for just cause, nor commit fornication; and any that does this (not only meets punishment (but) the Penalty on the Day of Judgment will be doubled to him, and he will dwell therein in ignominy, unless he repents, believes, and works righteous deeds, for God will change the evil of such persons into good, and God is Oft-Forgiving, Most Merciful.

Sura: 25, Ayat: 63...68–70.

Truly man was created very impatient fretful when evil touches him; and niggardly when good reaches him; not so those devoted to Prayer;... and those who guard their chastity, except with their wives and the (captives) whom their right hands possess, for (then) they are not to be blamed, but those who trespass beyond this are transgressors.

Sura: 70, Ayat: 19-22...29–31.

In the name of Allah, The Compassionate, The Merciful

PROHIBITION OF SODOMY

Say: "Come, I will rehearse what God has (really) prohibited you from":... come not nigh to shameful deeds, whether open or secret.

Sura: 6, Ayat: 151.

We also (sent) Lut: He said to his people: 'Do you commit lewdness such as no people in creation (ever) committed before you? "For you practise your lusts on men in preference to women: you are indeed a people transgressing beyond bounds.'

Sura: 7, Ayat: 80-81.

"Must you, of all people (lustfully) approach men, keeping yourselves aloof from all the (lawful) spouses whom your Sustainer has created for you? Nay, but you are people who transgress all bounds of what is right!"

Sura: 26, Ayat: 165-166.

(We also sent) Lut (as an apostle): behold He said to his people, "Do you do what is shameful though you see (its iniquity)? Would you really approach men in your lusts rather than women? Nay, you are a people (grossly) ignorant!

Sura: 27, Ayat: 54-55.

In the name of Allah, The Compassionate, The Merciful

SLANDER OF ADULTERY AND ITS PUNISHMENT

And those who launch a charge against chaste women, and produce not four witnesses (to support their allegations), — flog them with eighty stripes; and reject their evidence ever after; for such men are wicked transgressors; unless they repent thereafter and mend (their conduct); for God is Oft-Forgiving, Most Merciful.

Sura: 24, Ayat: 4-5.

And those who accuse their wives and have no witnesses except themselves, let each of them testify by swearing four times by Allah that his charge is true, calling down in the fifth time upon himself the curse of Allah if he is lying. But they shall spare her the punishment if she swears four times by Allah that his charge is false and calls down Allah's wrath upon herself if it be true.

Sura: 24, Ayat: 6—9.

Those who defame honourable but unaware (girls who have no knowledge of sex) believing women shall be cursed in this world and in the next. Theirs shall be a woeful punishment.

Sura: 24, Ayat: 23.

Women impure are for men impure, and men impure for women impure and women of purity are for men of purity, and men of purity are for women of purity: these are not affected by what people say: for them there is forgiveness, and a provision honourable.

Sura: 24, Ayat: 26.

In the name of Allah, The Compassionate, The Merciful

SLANDER OF ADULTERY AGAINST ONE'S WIFE

And those who accuse their wives and have no witnesses except themselves, let each of them testify by swearing four times by Allah that his charge is true, calling down in the fifth time upon himself the curse of Allah if he is lying. But they shall spare her the punishment if she swears four times by Allah that his charge is false and calls down Allah's wrath upon herself if it be true.

If it were not for Allah's grace and mercy on you and that He is Forgiving and Wise (He would immediately uncover your sins and hasten your punishment).

Sura: 24, Ayat: 6—10.

RETALIATION AND PUNISHMENTS

(27)

In the name of Allah, The Compassionate, The Merciful

LAWLESSNESS

And slay them wherever you catch them, and turn them out from where they have turned you out; for tumult and oppression are worse than slaughter; but fight them not at the Sacred Mosque, unless they (first) fight you there; but if they fight you, slay them. Such is the reward of those who suppress faith. But if they cease, God is Oft-Forgiving, Most Merciful.

Sura: 2, Ayat: 191-192.

And fight them on until there is no more tumult or oppression, and there prevail justice and faith in God; but if they cease, let there be no hostility except to those who practise oppression.

Sura: 2, Ayat: 193.

And fear tumult or oppression, which affects not in particular (only) those of you who have done wrong: and know that God is strict in punishment.

Sura: 8, Ayat: 25.

In the name of Allah, The Compassionate, The Merciful

PROHIBITION OF CREATING CHAOS

The punishment of those who wage war against God and His Apostle, and strive with might and main for mischief through the land is: execution, or crucifixion, or the cutting off of hands and feet from opposite sides, or exile from the land: that is their disgrace in this world, and a heavy punishment is theirs in the Hereafter; except for those who repent before they fall into your power: in that case, know that God is Oft-Forgiving, Most Merciful.

Sura: 5, Ayat: 33-34.

...But the revelation that comes to you from God increases in most of them their obstinate rebellion and blasphemy. Amongst them We have placed enmity and hatred till the Day of Judgment. Every time they kindle the fire of war, God does extinguish it; but they (ever) strive to do mischief on earth. And God loves not those who do mischief.

Sura: 5, Ayat: 64.

Do not make mischief in the earth after it has been purged. Pray to Him with fear and hope; His mercy is within the reach of the righteous.

Sura: 7, Ayat: 56.

And to Madian, We sent their brother Shu'aib. He said:.... Do not corrupt the land after it has been purged of evil. That is best for you, if you are true believers.

Do not sit in every road, threatening believers and debarring them from the path of Allah nor seek to make that path crooked. Remember how He multiplied you when you were few in number. Consider the fate of the evil-doers

'If there are some among you who believe in my message and others who disbelieve it, be patient until Allah shall judge between us. He is the best of judges.'

Sura: 7, Ayat: 85...86-87.

And fear tumult or oppression, which affects not in particular (only) those

of you who have done wrong: and know that God is strict in punishment.

Sura: 8, Ayat: 25.

When the magicians came, Musa said to them: 'Cast down what you may. And when they had thrown, he said: 'What you have brought is deception. Surely, God will render it vain. Allah does not bless the work of the evildoers. By His words He vindicates the truth, much as the guilty may dislike it.'

Sura: 10, Ayat: 80–82.

And unto (the people of) Madyan (We sent) their brother Shu'aib. He said: 'O my people! Worship God (alone): you have no deity other than Him; and do not give short measure and weight (in any of your dealings with men). Behold, I see you (now) in a happy state; but, verily, I dread lest suffering befall you on a Day that will encompass (you with doom)! Hence, O my people (always) give full measure and weight, with equity, and do not deprive people of what is rightfully theirs, and do not act wickedly on earth by spreading corruption. That which rests with God is best for you, if you but believe in (Him)! However, I am not your keeper.'

Sura: 11, Ayat: 84–86.

Why were there not, among the generations before you, persons possessed of balanced good sense, prohibiting (men) from mischief in the earth—except a few among them whom We saved (from harm)? But the wrongdoers pursued the enjoyment of the good things of life which were given them, and persisted in sin.

Sura: 11, Ayat: 116.

But those who break the Covenant of God, after having plighted their word thereto, and cut asunder those things which God has commanded to be joined, and work mischief in the land; — on them is the Curse; for them is the terribe Home!

Sura: 13, Ayat: 25.

Say to My servants that they should (only) say those things that are best: for Satan does sow dissensions among them: for Satan is to man an avowed enemy.

Sura: 17, Ayat: 53.

"Give just measure, and cause no loss (to others by fraud), and weigh with scales true and upright, and withhold not things justly due to men, nor do evil in the land, working mischief. And fear Him who created you and (Who created) the generations before (you)."

Sura: 26, Ayat: 181–184.

Qarun was doubtless, of the people of Moses; but he acted insolenty towards them: Such were the treasures We had bestowed on him, that their very keys would have been a burden to a body of strong men. Behold, his people said to him: 'Exult not, for God loves not those who exult (in riches).

"But seek, with the (wealth) which God has bestowed on you, the Home of the Hereafter, nor forget your portion in this world: but do you good, as God has been good to you, and seek not (occasion for) mischief in the land: for God loves not those who do mischief."

Sura: 28, Ayat: 76-77.

As for the abode of the Hereafter, we shall assign it to those who seek not to exalt in this world nor seek evil. The blessed end is for the righteous.

Sura: 28, Ayat: 83.

To the Madyan (people) (We sent) their brother Shu'aib. Then he said: 'O my people! Serve God, and fear the Last Day: nor commit evil on the earth, with intent to do mischief.

Sura: 29, Ayat: 36.

(Since they have become oblivious of God), corruption has appeared on land and in the sea as an outcome of what men's hands have wrought: and so He will let them taste (the evil of) some of their doings, so that they might return (to the right path).

Sura: 30, Ayat: 41.

In the name of Allah, The Compassionate, The Merciful

PILFERAGE AND ITS PUNISHMENT

As for the man or woman who is guilty of theft, cut off their hands to punish them for their crimes. That is the punishment enjoined by Allah. He is Mighty, Wise.

Sura: 5, Ayat: 38.

In the name of Allah, The Compassionate, The Merciful

ASSASSINATION

O believers, retaliation is decreed for you in bloodshed: a free man for a free man, a slave for a slave, and a female for a female. He who is pardoned by his aggrieved brother shall be prosecuted according to usage and shall pay him a liberal fine. This is an alleviation from your Lord and mercy. He that transgresses thereafter shall have stern punishment.

Sura: 2, Ayat: 178.

In retaliation you have a safeguard for your lives O men of understanding. So that you may guard yourselves against evil.

Sura: 2, Ayat: 179.

Believers, do not consume your wealth among yourselves illegally, but rather trade with it by mutual consent.

You shall not kill one another. Allah is Merciful, but he that does that through wickedness and injustice shall be burnt in fire. That is an easy thing for Allah.

Sura: 4, Ayat: 29-30.

It is unlawful for a believer to kill another believer except by mistake. He that kills a believer by mistake must free one believing slave and pay blood-money to the family of the victim, unless they choose to give it away in alms. If the victim be a believer from a hostile tribe, the penalty is the freeing of one believing slave. But if the victim be a member of an allied tribe, then blood-money must be paid to his family and a believing slave set free. If a man cannot afford to do this he must fast two consecutive months. Such is the penance imposed by Allah: He is Knowing, Wise.

Sura: 4, Ayat: 92.

He that kills a believer by design shall burn in Hell for ever. He shall incur the wrath of Allah, who will lay His curse on him and prepare for him a woeful scourge.

Sura: 4, Ayat: 93.

O believers, show discernment when you go out to fight for the cause of Allah, and do not say to those that offer you peace: 'You are not believers,' — seeking the fleeting gains of this world; for with Allah there are abundant gains....

Sura: 4, Ayat: 94.

That was why We laid down for the children of Israel that whoever killed a human being, except as a punishment for murder or for sedition in the earth, should be looked upon as though he had killed all mankind; and that whoever saved a human life should be regarded as though he had saved all mankind.

Our apostles brought them veritable proofs; yet even after that many of them committed great evils in the land.

Sura: 5, Ayat: 32.

Say: "Come, I will rehearse what God has (really) prohibited you from":.... Kill not your children on a plea of want; — We provide sustenance for you and for them;... take not life, which God has made sacred, except by way of justice and law:...

Sura: 6, Ayat: 151.

Your Lord has decreed.... Nor take life — which God has made sacred — except for just cause. And if anyone is slain wrongfully, We have given his heir authority (to demand Qisas — life for life or compensation or forgiveness depending on the heirs' wishes): but let him not exceed bounds in the matter of taking life; for he is helped (by the Law).

Sura: 17, Ayat: 23...33.

And the servants of (God) Most Gracious are those... who invoke not, with God, any other God, nor slay such life as God has made sacred, except for just cause, nor commit adultery; and any that does this (not only) meets punishment (but) the Penalty on the Day of Judgment will be doubled to him, and he will dwell therein in ignominy. Unless he repents, believes, and works righteous deeds, for God will change the evil of such persons into good, and God is Oft-Forgiving, Most Merciful.

Sura: 25, Ayat: 63... 68—70.

In the name of Allah, The Compassionate, The Merciful

RETALIATION AND REMISSION THROUGH BLOOD-WIT

O believers, retaliation is decreed for you in bloodshed: a free man for a free man, a slave for a slave, and a female for a female. He who is pardoned by his aggrieved brother shall be prosecuted according to usage and shall pay him a liberal fine. This is an alleviation from your Lord and mercy. He that transgresses thereafter shall have stern punishment.

Sura: 2, Ayat: 178.

In retaliation you have a safeguard for your lives O men of understanding. So that you may guard yourselves against evil.

Sura: 2, Ayat: 179.

A sacred month for a sacred month: sacred things too are subject to retaliation. If anyone attacks you, attack him as he attacked you. Have fear of Allah, and know that Allah is with the righteous.

Sura: 2, Ayat: 194.

We ordained therein for them: 'life for life, eye for eye, nose for nose, ear for ear, tooth for tooth, and wounds equal for equal.' But if anyone remits the retaliation by way of charity, it is an act of atonement for himself (for some of his past sins). And if any fail to judge by (the light of) what God has revealed, they are (no better than) wrongdoers.

Sura: 5, Ayat: 45.

Your Lord has decreed.... Nor take life — which God has made sacred — except for just cause. And if anyone is slain wrongfully, We have given his heir authority (to demand Qisas or to forgive): for he is helped (by the Law).

Sura: 17, Ayat: 23...33.

In the name of Allah, The Compassionate, The Merciful

MURDER

Believers, do not consume your wealth among yourselves illegally, but rather trade with it by mutual consent.

You shall not kill one another. Allah is Merciful, but he that does that through wickedness and injustice shall be burnt in fire. That is an easy thing for Allah.

Sura: 4, Ayat: 29-30.

Your Lord has decreed ... Nor take life — which God has made sacred — except for just cause. And if anyone is slain wrongfully, We have given his heir authority (to demand Qisas — life for life or compensation or forgiveness depending on the heirs' wishes): for he is helped (by the Law).

Sura: 17, Ayat: 23...33.

In the name of Allah, The Compassionate, The Merciful

INFANTICIDE

Even so, in the eyes of most of the Pagans, their Associate-gods made alluring the slaughter of their children, in order to lead them to their own destruction, and cause confusion in their religion. If God had willed, they would not have done so: but leave alone them and their inventions.

Sura: 6, Ayat: 137.

Lost, indeed, are they who, in their weak-minded ignorance, slay their children and declare as forbidden (food) that which God has provided for them as sustenance, falsely ascribing (such prohibitions) to God: they have gone astray and have not found the right path.

Sura: 6, Ayat: 140.

Say: "Come, I will rehearse what God has (really) prohibited you from":... Kill not your children on a plea of want; — We provide sustenance for you and for them;...

Sura: 6, Ayat: 151.

Your Lord has decreed... Kill not your children for fear of want: We shall provide sustenance for them as well as for you. Verily the killing of them is a great sin.

Sura: 17, Ayat: 23...31.

RISE AND FALL OF NATIONS

(28)

In the name of Allah, The Compassionate, The Merciful

CONDITIONS PREVAILING IN STATES

Yea unto God belong all things in the heavens and on earth, and enough is God to carry through all affairs.

If it were His Will, He could destroy you, O mankind, and create another race; for He has power this to do.

Sura: 4, Ayat: 132-133.

See they not how many of those before them We did destroy — Generations We had established on the earth, in strength such as We have not given to you — for whom We poured out rain from the skies in abundance, and gave (fertile) streams flowing beneath their (feet): yet for their sins We destroyed them, and raised in their wake fresh generations (to succeed them).

Sura: 6, Ayat: 6.

If the people of the towns had but believed and feared God, We should indeed have opened out to them (all kinds of) blessings from heaven and earth; but they rejected (the truth), and We brought them to book for their misdeeds.

Sura: 7, Ayat: 96.

Like Pharaoh's people and those that have gone before them, they disbelieved Allah's revelations. Therefore, Allah will smite them in their sinfulness. Mighty is Allah and stern His retribution.

This is because Allah does not withhold His favours from men until they change what is in their hearts. Allah is Hearing, Knowing.

Sura: 8, Ayat: 52-53.

Say: 'I have not the power to benefit or to harm myself except what Allah pleases. Unto every nation is a fixed term. When their term expires they cannot delay it for an hour, nor can they bring it before (its time).'

Sura: 10, Ayat: 49.

Why were there not, among the generations before you, persons possessed

of balanced good sense, prohibiting (men) from mischief in the earth — except a few among them whom We saved (from harm)? But the wrongdoers pursued the enjoyment of the good things of life which were given them, and persisted in sin.

Sura: 11, Ayat: 116.

Your Lord would not have ruined those towns, without just cause, had their inhabitants been righteous men.

Sura: 11, Ayat: 117.

...Verily never will God change the condition of a people until they change it themselves (with their own souls). But when (once) God wills a people's punishment, there can be no turning it back, nor will they find, besides Him, any to protect.

Sura: 13, Ayat: 11.

We sent not an apostle except (to teach) in the language of his (own) people, in order to make (things) clear to them. Now God leaves straying those whom He pleases and guides whom He pleases: And He is Exalted in Power, full of Wisdom.

We sent Moses with Our Signs (and the command). "Bring out your people from the depths of darkness into light, and teach them to remember the days of God*." Verily in this there are Signs for such as are firmly patient and constant, — grateful and appreciative.

Sura: 14, Ayat: 4-5.

Then the Blast overtook them with justice, and We made them as rubbish of dead leaves (floating on the stream of Time)! So away with the people who do wrong! Then We raised after them other generations. No people can hasten their terms, nor can they delay (it).

Sura: 23, Ayat: 41—43.

And how many populations We destroyed, which exulted in their life (of ease and plenty)! Now those habitations of theirs, after them, are deserted, all but a (miserable) few! And we are their heirs! Nor was your Lord the one to destroy a population until He had sent to its Centre an apostle, rehearsing to them our Signs; nor are We going to destroy a population except when its members practise iniquity.

Sura: 28, Ayat: 58-59.

Do they not travel through the earth, and see what was the End of those before them? They were superior to them in strength: they tilled the soil and

---

***Commemorative Days**

populated it in greater numbers than these have done, there came to them their apostles with Clear (Sign), (which they rejected, to their own destruction): it was not God who wronged them, but they wronged their own souls.

In the long run evil in the extreme will be the End of those who do evil; for that they rejected the Signs of God, and held them up to ridicule.

Sura: 30, Ayat: 9-10.

We did indeed aforetime give the Book to Moses: Be not then in doubt of its reaching (you): and We made it a guide to the Children of Israel. And We appointed, from among them, Leaders, giving guidance under Our command, so long as they persevered with patience and continued to have faith in Our signs.

Sura: 32, Ayat: 23-24.

Then give the glad tidings to the Believers, that they shall have from God a very great bounty. And obey not (the behests) of the unbelievers and the Hypocrites, and heed not their annoyances, but put your trust in God. For enough is God as a Dispenser of affairs.

Sura: 33, Ayat: 47-48.

Surely, the righteous have gardens of bliss with their Lord. Are We to deal with the true believers as We deal with the wrongdoers? What has come over you? How do you judge?

Sura: 68, Ayat: 34—36.

But what has befallen the unbelievers, that they scramble before you in multitudes from left and right?

Does every one of them seek to enter a garden of delight?

By no means. For We have created them out of something that they know.

I swear by the Lord of the East and the West that we have the power to destroy them and replace them by others better than them: nothing can hinder Us from so doing. So leave them to amuse themselves and blunder about in their folly until they face the day with which they are threatened; the day when they shall rush from their graves, like men rallying to a goal-post, with downcast eyes and countenances distorted with shame.

Such is the day with which they are threatened.

Sura: 70, Ayat: 36—44.

In the name of Allah, The Compassionate, The Merciful

NATIONS HAVE A FIXED TIME-LIMIT FOR THEIR EXISTENCE

And yet, they (who deny the truth) are wont to ask, "When is that promise (of resurrection and judgment) to be fulfilled? (Answer this, O you who believe in it,) if you are men of truth!" Say (O Prophet): "It is not within my power to avert harm from or bring benefit to, myself, except as God may please. For all people a term has been set: when the end of their term approaches, they can neither delay it by a single moment, nor hasten it".

Sura: 10, Ayat: 48-49.

Never have We destroyed a nation whose term of life was not ordained beforehand. No people can forestall their doom, nor can they retard it.

Sura: 15, Ayat: 4-5.

In the name of Allah, The Compassionate, The Merciful

MIGRATION

Those that have embraced the faith and those that have left their land and fought for the cause of Allah, may hope for Allah's mercy. Allah is Forgiving and Merciful.

Sura: 2, Ayat: 218.

Their Lord answers them, saying: 'I will deny no man or woman among you the reward of their labours. You are the offspring of one another.'

Those that fled their homes or were expelled from them, and those that suffered persecution and fought and died for My cause, shall be forgiven their sins and admitted to gardens watered by running streams, as a reward from Allah; it is Allah who holds the richest recompense.

Sura: 3, Ayat: 195.

They but wish that you should reject Faith, as they do, and thus be on the same footing (as they): But take not friends from their ranks until they flee from the domain of evil. But if they turn renegades, seize them and slay them wherever you find them; and (in any case) take no friends or helpers from their ranks; — except those who join a group between whom and you there is a treaty (of peace)....

Sura: 4, Ayat: 89-90.

Behold, those whom the angels gather in death while they are still sinning against themselves, (the angels) will ask, 'What was wrong with you?' They will answer: 'We were too weak and oppressed on earth.' (The Angels) will say: 'Was, then, God's earth not wide enough for you to forsake the domain of evil?'

For such, then, the goal is hell — and how evil a journey's end! But excepted shall be the truly helpless — be they men or women or children — who cannot bring forth any strength and have not been shown the right way: as for them, God may well efface their sin — for God is indeed an absolver of sins, much-forgiving.

Sura: 4, Ayat: 97—99.

He that flees his homeland for the cause of Allah shall find numerous places of refuge in the land and great abundance. He that leaves his dwelling to fight for Allah and His Apostle and is then overtaken by death, shall be rewarded by Allah. Allah is Forgiving, Merciful.

Sura: 4, Ayat: 100.

Those who believed, and adopted exile, and fought for the Faith, with their property and their persons, in the cause of God, as well as those who gave (them) asylum and aid, — these are (all) friends and protectors, one of another. As to those who believed but came not into exile, you owe no duty of protection to them until they come into exile; but if they seek your aid in religion, it is your duty to help them, except against a people with whom you have a treaty of mutual alliance. And (remember) God sees all that you do.

The Unbelievers are protectors, one of another; unless you do this, (protect each other), there would be tumult and oppression on earth, and great mischief.

Sura: 8, Ayat: 72-73.

Those who believe, and adopt exile, and fight for the Faith, in the cause of God, as well as those who give (them) asylum and aid, these are (all) in very truth the Believers: For them is the forgiveness of sins and a provision most generous.

And those who accept Faith subsequently, and adopt exile, and fight for the Faith in your company, — they are of you. But kindred by blood have prior rights against each other in the Book of God. Verily God is well-acquainted with all things.

Sura: 8, Ayat: 74-75.

Those that have embraced the faith and migrated from their homes and fought for Allah's cause with their wealth and their persons are held in higher regard by Allah. It is they who shall triumph. Their Lord has promised them joy and mercy, and gardens of eternal bliss where they shall dwell for ever. Allah's reward is great indeed.

Sura: 9, Ayat: 20—22.

To those who leave their homes in the cause of God, after suffering oppression, We will assuredly give a goodly home in this world; but truly the reward of the Hereafter will be greater. If they only realised (this)!

(They are) those who patiently persevere and put their trust on their Lord.

Sura: 16, Ayat: 41-42.

But verily your Lord, — To those who leave their homes after trials and persecutions, — and who thereafter strive and fight for the Faith and pa-

tiently persevere, — your Lord, after all this is Oft-Forgiving, Most Merciful.

Sura: 16, Ayat: 110.

Those who leave their homes in the cause of God, and are then slain or die, — on them will God bestow verily a goodly Provision; truly God is He Who bestows the best Provision.

Verily He will admit them to a place with which they shall be well pleased: For God is All-Knowing, Most Forbearing.

Sura: 22, Ayat: 58-59.

O My servants who believe! Truly, spacious is My earth: Therefore serve you Me — (and Me alone).

Sura: 29, Ayat: 56.

How many are the creatures that carry not their own sustenance? It is God Who feeds (both) them and you: (one should not stay back from migration on account of worldly riches) For He hears and knows (all things).

Sura: 29, Ayat: 60.

Say: 'My servants who believe, fear your Lord. Those who do good works in this life shall receive a good reward. Allah's earth is vast. Those that endure with fortitude shall be requited without measure.'

Sura: 39, Ayat: 10.

(Some part is due) to the indigent Muhajirs, those who were expelled from their homes and their property, while seeking Grace from God and (His) Good Pleasure, and aiding God and His Apostle: Such are indeed the sincere ones: — But those who before them, had homes (in Medina) and had adopted the Faith, — show their affection to such as came to them for refuge, and entertain no desire in their hearts for things given to the (latter), but give them preference over themselves, even though poverty was their (own lot). And those saved from the covetousness of their own souls, — they are the ones that achieve prosperity. And those who came after them say: 'Our Lord! Forgive us, and our brethren who came before us into the Faith, and leave not, in our hearts, rancour (or sense of injury) against those who have believed. Our Lord! You are indeed Full of Kindness, Most Merciful.'

Sura: 59, Ayat: 8—10.

O you who believe! When there come to you believing women refugees, examine (and test) them: God knows best as to their Faith: if you ascertain that they are Believers, then send them not back to the Unbelievers. They are not lawful (wives) for the Unbelievers, nor are the (Unbelievers) lawful (husbands) for them. But pay the Unbelievers what they have spent (on their dower). And there will be no blame on you if you marry them on payment of

their dower to them. But hold not to the guardianship of unbelieving women: ask for what you have spent on their dowers, and let the (Unbelievers) ask for what they have spent (on the dowers of women who come over to you). Such is the command of God: He judges (with justice) between you. And God is Full of Knowledge and Wisdom.

And if any of your wives deserts you to the Unbelievers, and you have an accession (by the coming over of a woman from the other side), then pay to those whose wives have deserted the equivalent of what they had spent (on their dower). And fear God, in Whom you believe.

Sura: 60, Ayat: 10-11.

In the name of Allah, The Compassionate, The Merciful

FRIENDLY ACCORD

Those who believed, and adopted exile, and fought for the Faith, with their property and their persons, in the cause of God, as well as those who gave (them) asylum and aid, — these are (all) friends and protectors, one of another. As to those who believed but came not into exile, you owe no duty of protection to them until they come into exile; but if they seek your aid in religion, it is your duty to help them, except against a people with whom you have a treaty of mutual alliance. And (remember) God sees all that you do.

Sura: 8, Ayat: 72.

JEHAD: STRIVING FOR THE HOLY CAUSE

(29)

In the name of Allah, The Compassionate, The Merciful

THE STRUGGLE

Do not say that those who are slain in the cause of Allah are dead; they are alive, although you are not aware of them.

Sura: 2, Ayat: 154.

Fight in the cause of God those who fight you, but do not transgress limits; for God loves not transgressors.

Sura: 2, Ayat: 190.

And slay them wherever you catch them, and turn them out from where they have turned you out; for tumult and oppression are worse than slaughter; but fight them not at the Sacred Mosque, unless they (first) fight you there; but if they fight you, slay them. Such is the reward of those who deny faith.

But if they cease, God is Oft-Forgiving, Most Merciful.

Sura: 2, Ayat: 191-192.

And fight them on until there is no more tumult or oppression, and there prevail justice and all worship God; but if they cease, let there be no hostility except to those who practise oppression.

Sura: 2, Ayat: 193.

Fighting is obligatory for you, much as you dislike it. But you may hate a thing although it is good for you, and love a thing although it is bad for you. Allah knows, but you do not.

They ask you about the sacred month. Say: 'To fight in this month is a grave offence; but to debar others from the path of Allah, to deny Him, and to expel His worshippers from the Holy Mosque, is far more grave in His sight. Tumult and oppression are worse than slaughter.'

They will not cease to fight against you until they force you to renounce your faith—if they are able. But whoever of you recants and dies an unbeliever, his works shall come to nothing in this world and in the world to come. Such men shall be the people of Hell, and there they shall abide forever.

Those that have embraced the faith and those that have left their land and fought for the cause of Allah, may hope for Allah's Mercy. Allah is Forgiving and Merciful.

Sura: 2, Ayat: 216–218.

Fight for the cause of Allah and bear in mind that He hears all and knows all.

Sura: 2, Ayat: 244.

So lose not heart, nor fall into despair: for you must gain mastery if you are true in Faith.

If a wound has touched you, be sure a similar wound has touched the others. Such days (of varying fortunes) We give to men and men by turns: that God may know those that believe, and choose from among you such as (with their lives) bear witness to the truth. And God loves not those that do wrong.

God's object also is to purge those that are true in faith and to deprive of blessing those that resist Faith.

Did you think that you would enter Heaven without God testing those of you who fought hard (in His Cause) and remained steadfast?

Sura: 3, Ayat: 139–142.

You used to wish for death before you met it, and now you have seen what it is like with your own eyes. Muhammad is no more than an apostle: other apostles have passed away before him. If he dies or be slain, will you recant? He that recants will do no harm to Allah. But Allah will reward the thankful.

No one dies unless Allah permits. The term of every life is fixed. And he that desires the reward of this world, We shall give him of it; and he that desires the reward of the life to come, We shall give him of it. And We will reward the thankful.

Sura: 3, Ayat: 143–145.

Many a prophet has fought side by side with many learned followers. They never lost heart on account of what befell them in the path of Allah: they neither weakened nor cringed abjectly. Allah loves the steadfast. Their only words were: 'Lord, forgive us our sins and our excesses; make us firm of foot and give us victory over the unbelievers.' Therefore, Allah gave them the reward of this life, and the glorious recompense of the life to come; Allah loves those who do good.

Sura: 3, Ayat: 146–148.

O you who have attained to faith! Be not like those who are bent on denying the truth and say of their brethren (who die) after having set out on a journey to faraway places or gone forth to war, "Had they but remained with us, they would not have died." or, "they would not have been slain" – for God will

cause such thoughts to become a source of bitter regret in their hearts, since it is God who grants life and deals death. And God sees all that you do.

Sura: 3, Ayat: 156.

And if indeed you are slain or die in God's cause, then surely forgiveness from God and His grace are better than all that one could amass (in this world): for, indeed, if you die or are slain, it will surely be unto God that you shall be gathered to-gether.

Sura: 3, Ayat: 157—158.

And do you, now that a calamity has befallen you after you had inflicted twice as much (on your foes), ask yourselves, "How has this come about?" Say: "It has come from your own selves.

Verily, God has the power to will anything: and all that befell you on the day when the two hosts met in battle happened by God's leave, so that He might mark out the (true) believers.

Sura: 3, Ayat: 165-166.

You must not think that those who were slain in the cause of Allah are dead. They are alive, and well provided for by their Lord; pleased with His gifts and rejoicing that those whom they left behind and who have not yet joined them have nothing to fear or to regret; they rejoice in Allah's grace and bounty. Allah will not deny the faithful their reward.

Sura: 3, Ayat: 169—171.

Of those who answered the call of God and the Apostle, even after, being wounded, those who do right and refrain from wrong have a great reward; men said to them: "A great army is gathering against you": and frightened them: but it (only) increased their Faith: they said: "For us God suffices, and He is the best Disposer of affairs." And they returned with Grace and Bounty from God: no harm ever touched them: for they followed the good pleasure of God: and God is the Lord of bounties unbounded. It is only the Evil One that suggests to you the fear of his votaries: be you not afraid of them, but fear Me, if you have Faith.

Sura: 3, Ayat: 172—175.

Their Lord answers them, saying: 'I will deny no man or woman among you the reward of their labours. You are the offspring of one another.'

Those that fled their homes or were expelled from them, and those that suffered persecution and fought and died for My cause, shall be forgiven their sins and admitted to gardens watered by running streams, as a reward from Allah; it is Allah who holds the richest recompense.

Sura: 3, Ayat: 195.

O believers, be patient and let your patience never be exhausted. Stand firm in your faith and fear Allah, so that you may triumph.

Sura: 3, Ayat: 200.

O you who believe! Take your precautions, and either go forth in parties or go forth all together. There are certainly among you men who would tarry behind: If a misfortune befalls you, they say: "God did favour us in that we were not present among them." But if good fortune comes to you from God, they would be sure to say — as if there had never been ties of affection between you and them — "Oh! I wish I had been with them; a fine thing should I then have made of it!"

Let those fight in the cause of God who sell the life of this world for the hereafter. To him who fights in the cause of God, — whether he is slain or gets victory — soon shall We give him a reward of great (value).

And why should you not fight in the cause of God and of those who, being weak, are ill-treated (and oppressed)? — Men, women, and children whose cry is: "Our Lord! Rescue us from this town, and raise for us from You one who will protect; and raise for us from You one who will help!"

Sura: 4, Ayat: 71—75.

The true believers fight for the cause of Allah, but the infidels fight for the devil. Fight then against the friends of the devil. The devil's cunning is weak indeed.

Sura: 4, Ayat: 76.

Have you not turned your vision to those who were told to hold back their hands (from fight) but establish regular prayers and spend in regular Charity? When (at length) the order for fighting was issued to them, Behold! a section of them feared men as — or even more than — they should have feared God: They said: "Our Lord! why have You ordered us to fight? Would You not grant us respite to our (natural) term, near (enough)? Say: 'Short is the enjoyment of this world: the Hereafter is the best for those who do right: Never will you be dealt with unjustly in the very least!

"Wherever you are, death will find you out, even if you are in towers built up strong and high?"....

Sura: 4, Ayat: 77-78.

Therefore fight for the cause of Allah. You are accountable for none but yourself. Rouse the faithful; perchance Allah will defeat the unbelievers. He is mightier and more capable of punishment than they.

Sura: 4, Ayat: 84.

Why should you be divided into two parties about the Hypocrites? God has upset them for their (evil) deeds. Would you guide those whom God has

thrown out of the Way? For those whom God has thrown out of the Way, never shall you find the Way.

They but wish that you should reject Faith, as they do, and thus be on the same footing (as they): But take not friends from their ranks until they flee in the way of God (From what is forbidden). But if they turn renegades, seize them and slay them wherever you find them; and (in any case) take no friends or helpers from their ranks; — Except those who join a group between whom and you there is a treaty (of peace), or those who approach you with hearts restraining them from fighting you as well as fighting their own people. If God had pleased, He could have given them power over you, and they would have fought you: Therefore if they withdraw from you but fight you not, and (instead) send you (guarantees of) peace, then God has opened no way for you (to war against them).

Others you will find that wish to gain your confidence as well as that of their people: Every time they are sent back to temptation, they succumb thereto: if they withdraw not from you nor give you (guarantees) of peace besides restraining their hands, seize them and slay them wherever you get them: in their case We have provided you with a clear argument against them.

Sura: 4, Ayat: 88—91.

(Hence), O you who have attained to faith, when you go forth (to war) in God's cause, investigate carefully, and do not — out of a desire for the fleeting gains of this worldly life—say unto anyone who offers you the greeting of peace, "You are not a believer": for with God there are gains abundant. You, too, were once in the same condition—but God has been gracious unto you. Use, therefore, your discernment: verily, God is always aware of what you do.

Sura: 4, Ayat: 94.

The believers who stay at home—apart from those that suffer from a grave impediment—are not equal to those who fight for the cause of Allah with their fortunes and their persons. Allah has given those that fight with fortunes and their persons a higher rank than those who stay at home. He has promised all a good reward; but far richer is the recompense of those who fight for Him: degrees of honour, forgiveness, and mercy. Allah is Forgiving, Merciful.

Sura: 4, Ayat: 95-96.

And slacken not in following up the enemy: if you are suffering hardships, they are suffering similar hardships; but you are hoping (to receive) from God, while they have none. And God is full of knowledge and wisdom.

Sura: 4, Ayat: 104.

O believers, when you encounter the infidels gathered (for battle) do not turn your backs to them in flight. If anyone on that day turns his back to them

in flight, except it be for tactical reasons, or to join another band, he shall incur the wrath of Allah and Hell shall be his home: an evil fate.

Sura: 8, Ayat: 15-16.

And fight them on until there is no more tumult or oppression, and there prevail justice and faith in God altogether and everywhere; but if they desist, verily God does see all that they do. If they refuse, be sure that God is your Protector—the Best to protect and the Best to help.

Sura: 8, Ayat: 39-40.

O you who believe! When you meet a force, be firm, and call God in remembrance much (and often); that you may prosper.

Sura: 8, Ayat: 45.

Verily, the vilest creatures in the sight of God are those who are bent on denying the truth and therefore do not believe.

As for those with whom you have made a covenant, and who thereupon break their covenant on every occasion, not being conscious of God—if you find them at war (with you), make of them a fearsome example for those who are their followers, so that they might take it to heart; or, if you have reason to fear treachery from people (with whom you have made a covenant, cast it back at them in an equitable manner: for, verily, God does not love the treacherous!

And let them not think – those who are bent on denying the truth – that they shall escape (God): behold, they can never frustrate (His purpose).

Sura: 8, Ayat: 55—59.

Muster against them all the men and cavalry at your disposal, so that you may strike a terror into (the hearts of) the enemies of Allah and your enemy and others besides them whom you do not know but Allah does. All that you give for the cause of Allah shall be repaid you. You shall not be wronged.

Sura: 8, Ayat: 60.

If they incline to peace, make peace with them, and put your trust in Allah. Surely He is the Hearing, the Knowing. Should they seek to deceive you, Allah is All-Sufficient for you. He has made you strong with His help and rallied the faithful round you.

Sura: 8, Ayat: 61-62.

Prophet, rouse the faithful to arms. If there are twenty patient and persevering men among you, you shall vanquish two hundred; and if there are a hundred, they shall rout a thousand unbelievers, for they are devoid of understanding.

Allah has now lightened your burden, for He knows that you are weak. If

there are a hundred patient and persevering men among you, they shall vanquish two hundred; and if there are a thousand, they shall, by Allah's will defeat two thousand. Allah is with those that are steadfast.

Sura: 8, Ayat: 65-66.

A declaration of immunity by Allah and His Apostle to the idolaters with whom you have made agreements:

For four months you shall go unmolested in the land. But know that you shall not escape the judgement of Allah, and that Allah will humble the unbelievers.

Sura: 9, Ayat: 1-2.

And an announcement from God and His Apostle, to the people (assembled) on the day of the Great Pilgrimage,—that God and His Apostle dissolve (treaty) obligations with the Pagans. If, then, you repent, it were best for you; but if you turn away, know you that you cannot frustrate God. And proclaim a grievous penalty to those who reject Faith.

(But the treaties are) not dissolved with those Pagans with whom you have entered into alliance and who have not subsequently failed you in aught, nor aided anyone against you. So fulfil your engagements with them to the end of their terms: for God loves the righteous.

Sura: 9, Ayat: 3-4.

When the sacred months are over, slay the idolaters wherever you find them. Arrest them, besiege them, and lie in ambush everywhere for them. If they repent and take to prayer and pay the alms-tax, let them go their way. Allah is Forgiving and Merciful.

Sura: 9, Ayat: 5.

If one amongst the Pagans ask you for asylum, grant it to him, so that he may hear the Word of God; and then escort him to where he can be secure. That is because they are men without knowledge.

Sura: 9, Ayat: 6.

How can the idolaters have any treaty with Allah and His Apostle, save those with whom you have made treaties at the Sacred Mosque? So long as they keep faith with you, keep faith with them. Allah loves the righteous.

How (can you trust them)? If they prevail against you, they will respect neither agreements nor ties of kindred. They flatter you with their tongues, but their hearts refuse. Most of them are evildoers.

Sura: 9, Ayat: 7-8.

God's messages have they bartered away for a trifling gain, and have thus turned away from His path: evil, behold, is all that they are wont to do, re-

specting no tie and no protective obligation with regard to a believer; and it is they, they who transgress the bounds of what is right!

Sura: 9, Ayat: 9-10.

But (even so), if they repent, establish regular prayers, and practise regular charity,—they are your brethren in Faith: (Thus) do We explain the Signs in detail, for those who understand.

Sura: 9, Ayat: 11.

But if, after coming to terms with you, they break their oaths and revile your faith, make war on the leaders of unbelief—for no oaths are binding with them—so that they may desist.

Will you not fight against those who have broken their oaths and conspired to banish the Apostle? They were the first to attack you. Do you fear them? Surely Allah is more deserving of your fear, if you are true believers.

Sura: 9, Ayat: 12-13.

Fight them, and God will punish them by your hands, cover them with shame, help you (to victory) over them, heal the breasts of Believers, and still the indignation of their hearts. For God will turn (in mercy) to whom He will; and God is All-Knowing, All-Wise.

Or think you that you shall be abandoned, as though God did not know those among you who strive with might and main, and take none for friends and protectors except God, His Apostle, and the (community of) believers? But God is well-acquainted with (all) that you do.

Sura: 9, Ayat: 14—16.

Those that have embraced the faith and migrated from their homes and fought for Allah's cause with their wealth and their persons are held in higher regard by Allah. It is they who shall triumph. Their Lord has promised them joy and mercy, and gardens of eternal bliss where they shall dwell for ever. Allah's reward is great indeed.

Sura: 9, Ayat: 20—22.

Say: If it be that your fathers, your sons, your brothers, your mates, or your kindred; the wealth that you have gained; the commerce in which you fear a decline: or the dwellings in which you delight—are dearer to you than God, or His Apostle, or the striving in His cause;—then wait until God brings about His Decision: and God guides not the rebellious.

Sura: 9, Ayat: 24.

Fight those who believe not in God nor the Last Day, nor hold that forbidden which has been forbidden by God and His Apostle, nor acknowledge the Religion of Truth (even if they are) of the People of the Book, until they pay

the Jizya (Compensatory law) with willing submission, and feel themselves subdued.

Sura: 9, Ayat: 29.

The number of months in the sight of God is twelve (in a year)—so ordained by Him the day He created the heavens and the earth; of them four are sacred: that is the ever true law. So wrong not yourselves therein, and fight the Pagans all together as they fight you all together. But know that God is with those who are conscious of Him.

Sura: 9, Ayat: 36.

O you who believe! What is the matter with you, that, when you are asked to go forth in the Cause of God, you cling heavily to the earth? Do you prefer the life of this world to the Hereafter? But little is the comfort of this life, as compared with the Hereafter.

Sura: 9, Ayat: 38.

Unless you go forth, He will punish you with a grievous penalty, and put others in your place; But Him you would not harm in the least. For God has power over all things.

Sura: 9, Ayat: 39.

Whether unarmed or well-equipped, march on and fight for the cause of Allah, with your wealth and your persons. This will be best for you, if you but knew it.

Sura: 9, Ayat: 41.

Those that believe in Allah and the Last Day will not beg you to exempt them from fighting with their wealth and their persons. Allah best knows the righteous. Only those seek exemption who disbelieve in Allah and the Last Day and whose hearts are in doubt, so that they are tossed in their doubts to and fro.

Sura: 9, Ayat: 44-45.

Say: 'Nothing will befall us except what Allah has ordained. He is our Guardian. In Allah, let the faithful put their trust.'

Sura: 9, Ayat: 51.

O Prophet! strive hard against the Unbelievers and the Hypocrites, and be firm against them. Their abode is Hell,—an evil refuge indeed.

Sura: 9, Ayat: 73.

Those who were left behind (in the Tabuk expedition) rejoiced in their inaction behind the back of the Apostle of God: they hated to strive and fight, with their goods and their persons, in the cause of God: they said, 'Go not

forth in the heat,' Say, 'The fire of Hell is hotter by far.' If only they could understand!

Sura: 9, Ayat: 81.

When a Sura comes down, enjoining them to believe in God and to strive and fight along with His Apostle, those with wealth and influence among them ask you for exemption, and say: 'Leave us (behind): we would be with those who sit (at home).'

They prefer to be with (the women), who remain behind (at home): their hearts are sealed and so they understand not.

But the Apostle, and those who believe with him, strive and fight with their wealth and their persons: for them are (all) good things: and it is they who will prosper.

God has prepared for them Gardens under which rivers flow, to dwell therein: that is the supreme felicity.

Sura: 9, Ayat: 86—89.

It shall be no offence for the disabled, the sick, and those lacking the means to spend, to stay behind, if they are true to Allah and His Apostle. The righteous shall not be blamed: Allah is Forgiving, Merciful.

Sura: 9, Ayat: 91.

Nor shall those (be blamed) who, when they came to you demanding conveyances (to the battle-front) and you said: 'I can find none to carry you.' went away in tears grieving that they could not find the means to spend.

But the blame is to be laid on those that seek exemption although they are men of wealth. They are content to remain with those who stay behind. Allah has set a seal upon their hearts; so they are devoid of understanding.

Sura: 9, Ayat: 92-93.

Allah has purchased of the faithful their lives and worldly goods in return for Paradise. They will fight for His cause, slay, and be slain. Such is the true pledge which He has made them in the Torah, the Gospel and the Quran. And who is more true to his promise than Allah? Rejoice then in the bargain you have made. That is the supreme triumph.

Sura: 9, Ayat: 111.

It was not fitting for the people of Medina and the Bedouin Arabs of the neighbourhood, to refuse to follow God's Apostle, nor to prefer their own lives to his: because nothing could they suffer or do, but was reckoned to their credit as a deed of righteousness,—whether they suffered thirst, or fatigue, or hunger, in the Cause of God, or trod paths to raise the ire of the Unbelievers, or received any injury whatever from an enemy: for God suffers not the reward to be lost of those who do good:—nor could they spend anything (for the

Cause)—small or great—nor cut across a valley, but the deed is inscribed to their credit; that God may requite their deed with the best (possible reward).

Sura: 9, Ayat: 120-121.

O believers, make war on the infidels who dwell around you. Let them find firmness in you. Know that Allah is with the righteous.

Sura: 9, Ayat: 123.

But verily your Lord,—to those who leave their homes after trials and persecutions,—and who thereafter strive and fight for the Faith and patiently persevere,—your Lord, after all this is Oft-Forgiving, Most Merciful.

Sura: 16, Ayat: 110.

To those against whom war is made, permission is given (to fight) because they are wronged; and verily, God is Most Powerful for their aid; (They are) those who have been expelled from their homes in defiance of right, (for no cause) except that they say, 'Our Lord is God'. Did not God check one set of people by means of another, there would surely have been pulled down monasteries, churches, synagogues, and mosques, in which the name of God is commemorated in abundant measure. God will certainly aid those who aid His (cause); for verily God is Full of Strength, Exalted in Might (Able to enforce His Will).

Sura: 22, Ayat: 39-40.

And strive in His cause as you ought to strive (with sincerity and under discipline). He has chosen you, and has imposed no difficulties on you in religion; it is the cult of your father Abraham. It is He Who has named you Muslims, both before and in this (Revelation); that the Apostle may be a witness for you, and you be witnesses for mankind! So establish regular Prayer, give regular Charity, and hold fast to God! He is your Protector — the best to protect and the best to help!

Sura: 22, Ayat: 78.

Whoever looks forward (with hope and awe) to meeting God (on Resurrection Day, let him be ready for it): for, behold, the end set by God (for everyone's life) is bound to come—and He alone is All-hearing, All-knowing! Hence whoever strives hard in (God's cause) does so only for his own good: for, verily, God does not stand in need of anything in all the worlds!

Sura: 29, Ayat: 5-6.

Say: 'Running away will not profit you if you are running away from death or slaughter; and even if (you do escape), no more than a brief (respite) will you be allowed to enjoy!'

Say: 'Who is it that can shield you from God if it be His wish to give you

Punishment or to give you Mercy?' Nor will they find for themselves, besides God, any protector or helper.

Sura: 33, Ayat: 16-17.

When the true believers saw the Confederates they said: 'This is what Allah and His Apostle have promised us: surely Their promise has come true.' And this only increased their faith and submission.

Sura: 33, Ayat: 22.

And those of the people of the Book who aided them — God did take them down from their strongholds and cast terror into their hearts, (so that) some you slew, and some you made prisoners.

And He made you heirs of their lands, their houses, and their goods, and of a land which you had never yet set foot (before), and God has power over all things.

Sura: 33, Ayat: 26-27.

Therefore, when you meet the Unbelievers (in fight), smite at their necks; at length, when you have thoroughly subdued them, bind a bond firmly (on them): thereafter (is the time for) either generosity or ransom: until the war lays down its burdens. Thus (are you commanded): but if it had been God's Will, He could certainly have exacted retribution from them (Himself); but (He lets you fight) in order to test you, some with others. But those who are slain in the way of God, He will never let their deeds be lost.

Soon will He guide them and improve their conditions, and admit them to the Garden which He has announced for them.

Sura: 47, Ayat: 4—6.

O you who have attained to faith! If you help (the cause of) God, He will help you, and will make firm your steps.

Sura: 47, Ayat: 7.

Now those who have attained to faith say, 'Would that a revelation (allowing us to fight) were bestowed from on high!'

But now that a revelation clear in and by itself, mentioning war, has been bestowed from on high, you can see those in whose hearts is disease looking at you, (O Muhammad,) with the look of one who is about to faint for fear of death! And yet, far better for them would be obedience (to God's call) and a word that could win (His) approval: for, since the matter has been resolved (by His revelation), it would be but for their own good to remain true to God.

Sura: 47, Ayat: 20-21.

And most certainly We shall try you all, so that We might mark out those of you who strive hard (in Our cause) and are patient in adversity: for We shall

put to a test (the truth of) all your assertions.

Sura: 47, Ayat: 31.

And so, (when you fight in a just cause,) do not lose heart and (never) beg for peace: for, seeing that God is with you, you are bound to rise high (in the end); and never will He let your (good) deeds go to waste.

Sura: 47, Ayat: 35.

Those who lagged behind (will say), when you (are free to) march and take booty (in war): 'Permit us to follow you.' They wish to change God's decree: Say: 'Not thus will you follow us: God has already declared (this) beforehand': then they will say, 'But you are jealous of us.' Nay, but little do they understand (such things).

Sura: 48, Ayat: 15.

It shall be no offence for the blind, the lame and the sick (to stay behind). He that obeys Allah and His Apostle shall be admitted to gardens watered by running streams; but he that turns away shall be sternly punished.

Sura: 48, Ayat: 17.

The true believers are those who have faith in Allah and His Apostle and never doubt; and who fight for His cause with their wealth and persons. Such are the truthful ones.

Sura: 49, Ayat: 15.

And what cause have you why you should not spend in the cause of God? — For to God belongs the heritage of the heavens and the earth. Not equal among you are those who spent (freely) and fought, before the Victory, (with those who did so later). Those are higher in rank than those who spent (freely) and fought afterwards. But to all has God promised a goodly (reward). And God is well acquainted with all that you do.

Sura: 57, Ayat: 10.

It is He Who got out the Unbelievers among the People of the Book from their homes at the first gathering (of the forces). Little did you think that they would get out: and they thought that their fortresses would defend them from God! But the (Wrath of) God came to them from quarters from which they little expected (it), and cast terror into their hearts, so that they destroyed their dwellings by their own hands and the hands of the Believers. Take warning, then, O you with eyes (to see)!

Sura: 59, Ayat: 2.

O you who believe! Take not My enemies and yours as friends (or protectors), — offering them (your) love, even though they have rejected the Truth

that has come to you, and have (on the contrary) driven out (the Prophet and yourselves (from your homes), (simply) because you believe in God your Lord! If you have come out to strive in My Way and to seek My Good Pleasure, (take them not as friends), holding secret converse of love (and friendship) with them: for I know full well all that you conceal and all that you reveal. And any of you that does this has strayed from the Straight Path.

Sura: 60, Ayat: 1.

Believers, why do you say what you never do? It is most odious in Allah's sight that you should say that which you do not do.

Allah loves those who fight for His cause in ranks as if they were a solid cemented edifice.

Sura: 61, Ayat: 2—4.

O believers! Shall I point out to you a bargain that will save you from a woeful scourge? Have faith in Allah and His Apostle and fight for His cause with your wealth and your persons. That would be best for you, if you but knew it.

Sura: 61, Ayat: 10-11.

Prophet, make war on the unbelievers and the hypocrites and deal sternly with them. Hell shall be their home, evil their fate.

Sura: 66, Ayat: 9.

In the name of Allah, The Compassionate, The Merciful

REWARD FOR THE STRUGGLE

It was not fitting for the people of Medina and the Bedouin Arabs of the neighbourhood, to refuse to follow Gods's Apostle, nor to prefer their own lives to his: because nothing could they suffer or do, but was reckoned to their credit as a deed of righteousness,—whether they suffered thirst, or fatigue, or hunger, in the Cause of God, or trod paths to raise the ire of the Unbelievers, or received any injury whatever from an enemy: for God suffers not the reward to be lost of those who do good; — nor could they spend anything (for the cause) — small or great — nor cut across a valley, but the deed is inscribed to their credit; that God may requite their deed with the best (possible reward).

Sura: 9, Ayat: 120-121.

In the name of Allah, The Compassionate, The Merciful

REFUSAL TO STRIVE FOR THE CAUSE OF ALLAH AND ITS PUNISHMENT

Those who were left behind (in the Tabuk expedition) rejoiced in their inaction behind the back of the Apostle of God: they hated to strive and fight, with their goods and their persons, in the Cause of God: they said, 'Go not forth in the heat.' Say, 'The fire of Hell is hotter by far.' If only they could understand!

Let them laugh a little: much will they weep: a recompense for the (evil) that they do.

If, then, God bring you back to any of them, and they ask your permission to come out (with you), say: 'Never shall you come out with me, nor fight an enemy with me: for you preferred to sit inactive on the first occasion: then sit you (now) with those who lag behind.'

Nor do you ever pray for any of them that dies, nor stand at his grave; for they rejected God and His Apostle, and died in a state of perverse rebellion.

Sura: 9, Ayat: 81–84.

In the name of Allah, The Compassionate, The Merciful

EXEMPTION FROM JOINING THE EXPEDITION

It shall be no offence for the disabled, the sick, and those lacking the means to spend, to stay behind, if they are true to Allah and His Apostle. The righteous shall not be blamed: Allah is Forgiving, Merciful.

Nor shall those (be blamed) who, when they came to you demanding conveyances (to the battle-front) and you said: 'I can find none to carry you.' went away in tears grieving that they could not find the means to spend.

But the blame is to be laid on those that seek exemption although they are men of wealth. They are content to remain with those who stay behind. Allah has set a seal upon their hearts; so they are devoid of understanding.

Sura: 9, Ayat: 91–93.

In the name of Allah, The Compassionate, The Merciful

POSSIBILITIES OF ACCIDENTAL DEATH DURING TRAVEL

O you who have attained to faith! Be not like those who are bent on denying the truth and say of their brethren (who die) after having set out on a journey to faraway places or gone forth to war, 'Had they but remained with us, they would not have died.' or, 'they would not have been slain' – for God will cause such thoughts to become a source of bitter regret in their hearts, since it is God who grants life and deals death. And God sees all that you do.

Sura: 3, Ayat: 156.

DEFENCE

(30)

In the name of Allah, The Compassionate, The Merciful

DEALING WITH TREACHEROUS PEOPLE

Verily, the vilest creatures in the sight of God are those who are bent on denying the truth and therefore do not believe.

As for those with whom you have made a covenant, and who thereupon break their covenant on every occasion, not being conscious of God — if you find them at war (with you), make of them a fearsome example for those who are their followers, so that they might take it to heart; or if you have reason to fear treachery from people (with whom you have made a covenant, cast it back at them in an equitable manner; for, verily, God does not love the treacherous!).

Sura: 8, Ayat: 55–58.

In the name of Allah, The Compassionate, The Merciful

INJUNCTIONS REGARDING WAR

Those who believe, fight in the cause of God, and those who reject Faith fight in the cause of Evil: so fight you against the friends of Satan: feeble indeed is the cunning of Satan.

Sura: 4, Ayat: 76.

When you (O Apostle) are with them, and stand to lead them in prayer, let one party of them stand up (in prayer) with you, taking their arms with them: when they finish their prostrations, let them take their position in the rear. And let the other party come up which has not yet prayed — and let them pray with you, taking all precautions, and bearing arms: the Unbelievers wish, if you were negligent of your arms and your baggage, to assault you in a single rush. But there is no blame on you if you put away your arms because of the inconvenience of rain or because you are ill; but take (every) precaution for yourselves. For the Unbelievers, God has prepared a humiliating punishment.

When you pass (congregation) prayers, celebrate God's praises, standing, sitting down, or lying down on your sides; but when you are free from danger, set up regular Prayers: for such prayers are enjoined on believers at stated times.

Sura: 4, Ayat: 102-103.

Verily, the vilest creatures in the sight of God are those who are bent on denying the truth and therefore do not believe.

As for those with whom you have made a covenant, and who thereupon break their covenant on every occasion, not being conscious of God — if you find them at war (with you), make of them a fearsome example for those who are their followers, so that they might take it to heart; or if you have reason to fear treachery from people (with whom you have made a covenant, cast it back at them in an equitable manner; for, verily, God does not love the treacherous!).

Sura: 8, Ayat: 55—58.

Muster against them all the men and cavalry at your disposal, so that you may strike terror into (the hearts of) the enemies of Allah and your enemy, and others besides them whom you do not know but Allah does. All that you give for the cause of Allah shall be repaid to you. You shall not be wronged.

Sura: 8, Ayat: 60.

If they incline to peace, make peace with them, and put your trust in Allah. Surely He is the Hearing, the Knowing. Should they seek to deceive you, Allah is All-sufficient for you. He has made you strong with His help and rallied the faithful round you, making their hearts one. If you had given away all the riches of the earth, you could not have so united them: but Allah has united them. He is Mighty, Wise.

O Prophet, Allah is your strength and the faithful who follow you.

Sura: 8, Ayat: 61—64.

Prophet, rouse the faithful to arms. If there are twenty steadfast men among you, you shall vanquish two hundred; and if there are a hundred, they shall rout a thousand unbelievers, for they are devoid of understanding.

Sura: 8, Ayat: 65.

Allah has now lightened your burden, for He knows that you are weak. If there are a hundred steadfast men among you, they shall vanquish two hundred; and if there are a thousand they shall, by Allah's will, defeat two thousand. Allah is with those that are steadfast.

Sura: 8, Ayat: 66.

It is not fitting for an Apostle that he should have prisoners of war until he has thoroughly subdued the land. You look for the temporal goods of this world; but God looks to the Hereafter: and God is exalted in might, Wise.

Had it not been for a previous ordainment from God, a severe penalty would have reached you for the (ransom) that you took.

But (now) enjoy what you took in war, lawful and good: but fear God: for God is Oft-Forgiving, Most Merciful.

Sura: 8, Ayat: 67—69.

O Prophet, say to those you have taken captive: 'If Allah finds goodness in your hearts, He will give you that which is better than what has been taken from you, and He will forgive you. Allah is Forgiving, Merciful.'

But if they seek to betray you, know that they had already betrayed Allah. Therefore, he has made you triumph over them. Allah is Wise and All-Knowing.

Sura: 8, Ayat: 70-71.

Those who believed, and adopted exile, and fought for the Faith, with their

property and their persons, in the cause of God, as well as those who gave (them) asylum and aid, — these are (all) friends and protectors, one of another. As to those who believed but came not into exile, you owe no duty of protection to them until they come into exile; but if they seek your aid in religion, it is your duty to help them, except against a people with whom you have a treaty of mutual alliance. And (remember) God sees all that you do.

The Unbelievers are protectors, one of another: unless you do this, (protect each other), there would be tumult and oppression on earth, and great mischief.

Sura: 8, Ayat: 72-73.

A declaration of immunity by Allah and His Apostle to the idolaters with whom you have made agreements:

For four months you shall go unmolested in the land. But know that you shall not escape the judgement of Allah, and that Allah will humble the unbelievers.

Sura: 9, Ayat: 1-2.

In the name of Allah, The Compassionate, The Merciful

PREPARATIONS FOR DEFENCE

Muster against them all the men and cavalry at your disposal, so that you may strike terror into (the hearts of) the enemies of Allah and your enemy, and others besides them whom you do not know but Allah does. All that you give for the cause of Allah shall be repaid to you. You shall not be wronged.

Sura: 8, Ayat: 60.

...And We sent down Iron, in which is (material for) mighty war, as well as many benefits for mankind, that God may test who it is that will help, unseen, Him and His Apostles: For God is Full of Strength, Exalted in Might (and able to enforce His Will).

Sura: 57, Ayat: 25.

In the name of Allah, The Compassionate, The Merciful

SACREDNESS OF FOUR MONTHS

Fight during the sacred months if you are attacked: for a violation of sanctity is (subject to the law of) just retribution. Thus, if anyone commits aggression against you, attack him just as he has attacked you — but remain conscious of God, and know that God is with those who are conscious of Him.

Sura: 2, Ayat: 194.

O you who believe! Violate not the sanctity of the Symbols of God, nor of the Sacred Month, nor of the animals brought for sacrifice, nor the garlands that mark out such animals, nor the people resorting to the Sacred House, seeking of the bounty of their Lord. But when you are clear of pilgrimage garb, you may hunt and let not the hatred of some people in (once) shutting you out of the Sacred Mosque lead you to transgression (and hostility on your part). Help you one another in righteousness and piety, but help you not one another in sin and rancour: fear God: for God is strict in Punishment.

Sura: 5, Ayat: 2.

The number of months in the sight of God is twelve (in a year) — so ordained by Him the day He created the heavens and the earth; of them four are sacred: that is the straight usage. So wrong not yourselves therein, and fight the Pagans all together as they fight you all together. But know that God is with those who restrain themselves.

Sura: 9, Ayat: 36.

The postponement of sacred months is a grossly impious practice, in which the unbelievers are misguided. They allow it one year and forbid it the next, so that they may make up for the months which Allah has sanctified, thus making lawful what Allah has forbidden. Their foul acts seem fair to them: Allah does not guide the unbelievers.

Sura: 9, Ayat: 37.

....Whoever honours the sacred rites of God, for him it is good in the sight of his Lord. Lawful to you (for food in Pilgrimage) are cattle, except those

mentioned to you (as exceptions): but shun the abomination of idols, and shun every word that is false,—

Being true in faith to God, and never assigning partners to Him: if anyone assigns partners to God, he is as if he had fallen from heaven and been snatched up by birds, or the wind had swooped (like a bird on its prey) and thrown him into a far-distant place.

Sura: 22, Ayat: 30-31.

In the name of Allah, The Compassionate, The Merciful

GAINS OF WAR

They ask you about the spoils. Say: 'The spoils belong to Allah and the Apostle. Therefore, have fear of Allah and end your disputes. Obey Allah and His Apostle, if you are true believers.

Sura: 8, Ayat: 1.

And know that to Allah, the Apostle, the Apostle's kinsfolk, the orphans, the needy, and the wayfarers, shall belong one fifth of whatever you take as spoils: if you truly believe in Allah and what We revealed to Our servant on the day of victory, the day when the two armies met. Allah has Power over all things.

Sura: 8, Ayat: 41.

It is not fitting for an Apostle that he should have prisoners of war until He has thoroughly subdued the land. You look for the temporal goods of this world; but God looks to the Hereafter: and God is Exalted in Might, Wise.

Had it not been for a previous ordainment from God, a severe penalty would have reached you for the (ransom) that you took.

But (now) enjoy what you took in war, lawful and good: but fear God: for God is Oft-Forgiving, Most Merciful.

Sura: 8, Ayat: 67—69.

And those of the people of the Book who aided them — God did take them down from their strongholds and cast terror into their hearts. (so that) Some you slew, and some you made prisoners.

And He made you heirs of their lands, their houses, and their goods, and of a land which you had never yet set foot (before). And God has Power over all things.

Sura: 33, Ayat: 26-27.

In the name of Allah, The Compassionate, The Merciful

CONQUERED PROPERTY AND TERRITORY, AND ITS USAGE

And those of the people of the Book who aided them — God did take them down from their strongholds and cast terror into their hearts. (so that) Some you slew, and some you made prisoners.

And He made you heirs of their lands, their houses, and their goods, and of a land which you had never yet set foot (before). And God has Power over all things.

Sura: 33, Ayat: 26-27.

Whether you cut down (O you Muslims!) the palm-trees, or you left them standing on their roots, it was by leave of God, and in order that He might cover with shame the rebellious transgressors.

What God has bestowed on His Apostle (and taken away) from them — for this you made no expedition with either cavalry or camelry: but God gives power to His Apostles over any He pleases: and God has Power over all things.

Sura: 59, Ayat: 5-6.

What God has bestowed on His Apostle (and taken away) from the people of the townships, — belongs to God, — to His Apostle and to kindred and orpans, the needy and the wayfarer; in order that it may not (merely) make a circuit between the wealthy among you. So take what the Apostle assigns to you, and deny yourselves that which he withholds from you. And fear God; for God is strict in Punishment.

Sura: 59, Ayat: 7.

(Some part is due) to the indigent Muhajirs, those who were expelled from their homes and their property, while seeking Grace from God and (His) Good Pleasure, and aiding God and His Apostle: such are indeed the sincere ones:—

But those who before them, had homes (in Medina) and had adopted the Faith, show their affection to such as came to them for refuge, and entertain

no desire in their hearts for things given to the (latter), but give them preference over themselves, even though poverty was their (own lot). And those saved from the covetousness of their own souls, — they are the ones that achieve prosperity.

And those who came after them say: 'Our Lord! Forgive us, and our brethren who came before us into the Faith, and leave not, in our hearts, rancour (or sense of injury) against those who have believed. Our Lord! You are indeed Full of Kindness, Most Merciful.'

Sura: 59, Ayat: 8–10.

In the name of Allah, The Compassionate, The Merciful

"JIZYAH"—TAX FOR PROTECTION OF NON-MUSLIMS

Fight those who believe not in God nor the Last Day, nor hold that forbidden which has been forbidden by God and His Apostle, nor acknowledge the Religion of Truth, (even if they are) of the People of the Book, until they pay the Jizyah (Compensatory Tax) with willing submission, and feel themselves subdued.

Sura: 9, Ayat: 29.

In the name of Allah, The Compassionate, The Merciful

PRAYERS ON ACHIEVING VICTORY

When comes the Help of God, and Victory, and you do see the People enter God's Religion in crowds, celebrate the Praises of your Lord, and pray for His Forgiveness: For He is ever an Accepter of repentance.

Sura: 110, Ayat: 1–3.

POLITICS

(31)

In the name of Allah, The Compassionate, The Merciful

SYSTEM OF GOVERNMENT

Their prophet said to them: 'Allah has raised Saul to be your king.' But they replied: 'Should he be given the king-ship, when we are more deserving of it than he? Besides, he is not rich at all.'
He said: 'Allah has chosen him to rule over you and made him grow in wisdom and stature. Allah gives His sovereignty to whom He will. He is Munificent and All-Knowing.'

Sura: 2, Ayat: 247.

The only true faith in Allah's sight is Islam. Those to whom the Book was given disagreed among themselves only after knowledge had been given them out of envy among themselves. He that denies Allah's revelations should know that He is swift in reckoning.

Sura: 3, Ayat: 19.

Have you not turned your vision to those who have been given a portion of the Book? They are invited to the Book of God, to settle their dispute, but a party of them turn back and decline (the arbitration).
This because they say: 'The Fire shall not touch us but for a few numbered days': For their false beliefs deceive them as to their own religion.

Sura: 3, Ayat: 23-24.

He that chooses a religion other than Islam, it will not be accepted from him, and in the world to come he will be one of the lost.

Sura: 3, Ayat: 85.

Who is it that listens to the (soul) distressed when it calls on Him, and who relieves its suffering, and makes you (mankind) inheritors of the earth? Could there be any divine power besides God? Little it is that you heed!

Sura: 27, Ayat: 62.

We sent aforetime Our Apostles with Clear Signs and sent down with them the Book and the Balance (of Right and Wrong), that men may stand forth in

justice; and We sent down Iron, in which is (material for) mighty war, as well as many benefits for mankind, that God may test who it is that will help, unseen Him and His Apostles: For God is Full of Strength, Exalted in Might (and able to enforce His Will).

Sura: 57, Ayat: 25.

In the name of Allah, The Compassionate, The Merciful

SOVEREIGNTY IS VESTED IN GOD

Do you not know that it is to Allah that the control over the heavens and the earth belongs, and that there is none besides Him to protect or help you?

Sura: 2, Ayat: 107.

Say: (O'Prophet) 'If you love Allah, follow me. Allah will love you and forgive your sins. Allah is Forgiving and Merciful.'

Sura: 3, Ayat: 31.

It is no concern of yours whether He will forgive or punish them. They are wrongdoers. His is all that the heavens and the earth contain. He pardons whom He will and punishes whom He pleases. Allah is Forgiving, Merciful.

Sura: 3, Ayat: 128-129.

To Allah belongs the kingdom of heavens and the earth. He has power over all things.

Sura: 3, Ayat: 189.

In blasphemy indeed are those that say that God is Christ the son of Mary. Say: "Who then has the least power against God, if His Will were to destroy Christ the son of Mary, his mother, and all—everyone that is on the earth? For to God belongs the dominion of the heavens and the earth, and all that is between. He creates what He pleases. For God has power over all things."

Sura: 5, Ayat: 17.

Do you not know that to Allah belongs the control of the heavens and the earth? He punishes whom He will and forgives whom He pleases. Allah has power over all things.

Sura: 5, Ayat: 40.

Say: 'For me, I (work) on a clear Sign from my Lord, but you reject Him. What you would see hastened, is not in my power. The Command rests with none but God: He declares the Truth, and He is the best of judges.'

Sura: 6, Ayat: 57.

"He reigns supreme over His servants. He sends forth guardians who watch over you and carry away your souls without fail when death overtakes you. Then are all men restored to Allah, their true Lord. His is the judgement, and most swift is His reckoning.

Sura: 6, Ayat: 61-62.

....Allah has knowledge of all things.

His is the sovereignty in the heavens and the earth; He ordains life and death. You have none besides Allah to protect or help you.

Sura: 9, Ayat: 115-116.

"All that you worship instead of God is nothing but (empty) names which you have invented — you and your fathers — (and) for which God has bestowed no warrant from on high. Judgement (as to what is right and what is wrong) rests with God alone — (and) He has ordained that you should worship nought but Him: this is the (one) ever-true faith; but most people know it not.

Sura: 12, Ayat: 40.

Further he (Jacob) said: My sons, do not enter from one gate. Enter from different doors. I cannot be of any help to you against Allah; judgement is His alone. In Him, I have put my trust. In Him alone let the trustful put their trust.'

Sura: 12, Ayat: 67.

Say: 'Praise be to Allah who has never begotten a son; who has no partner in His sovereignty; who needs none to defend Him from humiliation.' Proclaim his limitless greatness.

Sura: 17, Ayat: 111.

High above all is God, the King, the Truth! Be not in haste with the Quran before its revelation to you is completed, but say, 'O my Lord! advance me in knowledge.'

Sura: 20, Ayat: 114.

Say: "To whom belong the earth and all beings therein? (Say) if you know!"

They will say, "To God!" Say: 'Yet will you not receive admonition?"

Say: "Who is the Lord of the seven heavens, and the Lord of the Throne (of Glory) Supreme?"

They will say, "(They belong) to God." Say: "Will you not then be filled with awe?"

Say: "Who is it in whose hands is the governance of all things, — who protects (all), but against Him there is no protection? (Say) if you know."

They will say, "(It belongs) to God." Say: "Then how are you deluded?"
Sura: 23, Ayat: 84–89.

To Allah belongs the sovereignty in the heavens and the earth. To Him shall all things return.

Sura: 24, Ayat: 42.

The Lord of the heavens and the earth, Who has begotten no children and has no partner in His sovereignty; Who has created all things and ordained them in due proportion.

Sura: 25, Ayat: 2.

And He is God: there is no god but He. To Him be praise, at the first and at the last: For Him is the Command, and to Him shall you (all) be brought back.
Sura: 28, Ayat: 70.

And call not, besides God, on another god. there is no god but He. Everything (that exists) will perish except His Countenance (God Himself). To Him belongs the Command, and to Him will you (all) be brought back.
Sura: 28, Ayat: 88.

Glory be to Him who has control of all things, and to Him you will all be brought back.

Sura: 36, Ayat: 83.

Say: 'Lord, Creater of the heavens and the earth, who has knowledge of the visible and the invisible, You alone can judge the disputes of Your servants.'

Sura: 39, Ayat: 46.

And on whatever you may differ, (O believers,) the verdict thereon rests with God.
(Say, therefore:) 'Such is God, my Sustainer: in Him have I placed my trust, and unto Him do I always turn!"

Sura: 42, Ayat: 10.

To Allah belongs the sovereignty in the heavens and the earth. He creates what He will. He gives daughters to whom He will and sons to whom He pleases. To some He gives both sons and daughters, and to others He gives none at all. Mighty is Allah and All-Knowing.

Sura: 42, Ayat: 49-50.

It is He who is God in heaven and God on earth; He is the Wise One, the All-Knowing. Blessed be He to whom belongs the sovereignty in the heavens and

the earth and all that lies between them! With Him is the knowledge of the Hour of Doom. To Him you shall all return.

Sura: 43, Ayat: 84-85.

Say: 'It is Allah Who gives you life and later causes you to die. It is He Who will gather you all on the Day of Resurrection. Of this there is no doubt; yet most men do not understand it.'

Allah's is the sovereignty in the heavens and the earth. On the day when the Hour of Doom arrives, those who have denied His revelations will assuredly be lost.

Sura: 45, Ayat: 26-27.

Allah's is the sovereignty in the heavens and the earth. He pardons whom He will and punishes whom He pleases. Allah is Forgiving and Merciful.

Sura: 48, Ayat: 14.

His is the sovereignty in the heavens and earth. He ordains life and death and has power over all things.

Sura: 57, Ayat: 2.

All that is in heaven and earth glorifies Allah. His is the sovereignty, and His the praise. He has power over all things.

Sura: 64, Ayat: 1.

Blessed be He in Whose hands is all sovereignty: He has power over all things.

He created life and death that He might put you to the test and find out which of you acquitted himself best. He is The Mighty, The Forgiving One.

Sura: 67, Ayat: 1-2.

They ill-treated them for no other reason than that they believed in God, Exalted in Power, Worthy of all Praise! Him to Whom belongs the dominion of the heavens and the earth! And God is Witness to all things.

Sura: 85, Ayat: 4—9.

In the name of Allah, The Compassionate, The Merciful

MAN—VICEGERENT OF GOD ON EARTH

Behold, your Lord said to the angels: "I will create a vicegerent on earth." They said: 'Will you place therein one who will make mischief therein and shed blood? — While we do celebrate Your praises and glorify Your holy (name)?' He said: "I know what you know not.'

Sura: 2, Ayat: 30.

Say: "O God! Lord of Power (and Rule), You give Power (to rule etc.) to whom You please, and You strip off Power from whom You please: You endow with honour whom You please, and You bring low whom You please: In your hand is all Good. Verily, over all things You have power.

Sura: 3, Ayat: 26.

It is He Who has made you (His) agents (to rule etc.), inheritors of the earth: He has raised you in ranks, some above others: that He may try you in the gifts He has given you: For your Lord is quick in punishment: yet He is indeed Oft-Forgiving, Most Merciful.

Sura: 6, Ayat: 165.

Before this We wrote in the Psalms, after the Message (given to Moses): "My servants, the righteous, shall inherit (to rule etc.) the earth."

Verily in this (Quran) is a Message for people who would (truly) worship God.

Sura: 21, Ayat: 105-106.

He it is that has made you inheritors (to rule etc.) in the earth: If, then, any do reject (God), their rejection (works) against themselves: their rejection but adds to the odium for the Unbelievers in the sight of their Lord: Their rejection but adds to (their own) undoing.

Sura: 35, Ayat: 39.

(We said): "Dawud, We have made you a vicegerent in the land. Rule with justice among men and do not yield to lust, lest it should turn you away from

Allah's path. Those that stray from Allah's path shall be sternly punished, because they forget the Day of Reckoning.

Sura: 38: Ayat: 26.

In the name of Allah, The Compassionate, The Merciful

DIVINE PROMISE OF CONFERRING THE FAITHFUL WITH THE RULE OF THE EARTH

God has promised, to those among you who believe and work righteous deeds, that He will, of a surety, grant them in the land, inheritance (of power), as He granted it to those before them; that He will establish in authority their religion — the one which He has chosen for them; and that He will change (their state), after the fear in which they (lived), to one of security and peace: 'They will worship Me (alone and not associate aught with Me.' If any do reject Faith after this, they are rebellious and wicked.

Sura: 24, Ayat: 55.

In the name of Allah, The Compassionate, The Merciful

QUALITIES OF A RULER, AND OBEYING HIS RULE

Their prophet said to them: 'Allah has raised Saul to be your king.' But they replied: 'Should he be given the kingship, when we are more deserving of it than he? Besides, he is not rich at all.'

He said: 'Allah has chosen him to rule over you and made him grow in wisdom and in stature. Allah gives His sovereignty to whom He will. He is Munificent and All-Knowing.'

Sura: 2, Ayat: 247.

Say: 'O God! Lord of Power (and Rule), You give Power (to rule etc.) to whom you please, and You strip off Power from whom You please: You endow with honour whom You please, and You bring low whom You please: In Your hand is all Good. Verily, over all things You have power.

Sura: 3, Ayat: 26.

Are they seeking a religion other than Allah's, when every soul in heaven and earth has submitted to Him willingly or by compulsion? To Him they shall all return.

Say: "We believe in God, and in what has been revealed to us and what was revealed to Abraham, Isma'il: Isaac, Jacob, and the Tribes, and in (the Books) given to Moses, Jesus, and the Prophets, from their Lord: We make no distinction between one and another among them, and unto Him do we surrender ourselves."

He that chooses a religion other than Islam, it will not be accepted from Him, and in the world to come he will be one of the lost.

Sura: 3, Ayat: 83—85.

It was thanks to Allah's mercy that you dealt so leniently with them. Had you been cruel and hard-hearted they would have surely deserted you. Therefore, pardon them and implore Allah to forgive them. Take counsel with them in the conduct of affairs; and when you are resolved, put your trust in Allah. Allah loves those that trust (in Him).

Sura: 3, Ayat: 159.

O believers, obey Allah and the Apostle and those in authority among you. Should you disagree about anything refer it to Allah and the Apostle, if you truly believe in Allah and the Last Day. This will in the end be better and more just.

Sura: 4, Ayat: 59.

And keep your soul content (by keeping company) with those who call on their Lord morning and evening, seeking His Face; and let not thine eyes pass beyond them, seeking the pomp and glitter of this Life; nor obey any whose heart We have permitted to neglect the remembrance of Us, one who follows his own desires, whose case has gone beyond all bounds.

Sura: 18, Ayat: 28.

....Had Allah not repelled some men by the might of others, the monasteries and churches, the synagogues and mosques in which Allah's name is frequently remembered, would have been utterly destroyed. But whoever helps Allah shall be helped by Him. Allah is truly Powerful and Mighty He (will assuredly help) those who, if made masters in the lands, will attend to their prayers and pay the alms-tax, enjoin justice and forbid evil. Allah controls the destiny of all things.

Sura: 22, Ayat: 40-41.

God has promised, to those among you who believe and work righteous deeds, that He will of a surety, grant them in the land, inheritance (of power), as He granted it to those before them; that He will establish in authority their religion — the one which He has chosen for them; and that He will change (their state), after the fear in which they (lived), to one of security and peace: 'They will worship Me (alone) and not associate aught with Me.' If any do reject Faith after this, they are rebellious and wicked.

Sura: 24, Ayat: 55.

The believers are only those who have faith in Allah and His Apostle, and who, when gathered with him upon a grave occasion, do not depart till they have begged his leave. The men who ask your leave are those who truly believe in Allah and His Apostle. When they ask your leave to go away on some business of their own grant it to whomever you please and implore Allah to forgive them; Allah is Forgiving, Merciful.

Sura: 24, Ayat: 62.

She said: "Nobles, let me hear your counsel, for I make no decision except in your presence.'

They replied: 'We are possessors of strength and mighty prowess. It is for you to command, and we shall wait upon your pleasure.'

She said: 'When kings enter a city, they ruin it and humiliate its nobles.

These (men) will do the same.

Sura: 27, Ayat: 32–34.

(We said): 'Dawud, We have made you a vicegerent in the land. Rule with justice among men and do not yield to lust, lest it should turn you away from Allah's path. Those that stray from Allah's path shall be sternly punished, because they forget the Day of Reckoning.

Sura: 38, Ayat: 26.

In the name of Allah, The Compassionate, The Merciful

CONSULTATION

It was thanks to Allah's mercy that you dealt so leniently with them. Had you been cruel and hard-hearted, they would have surely deserted you. Therefore, pardon them and implore Allah to forgive them. Take counsel with them in the conduct of affairs; and when you are resolved, put your trust in Allah. Allah loves those that trust (in Him).

Sura: 3, Ayat: 159.

O believers, obey Allah and the Apostle and those in authority among you. Should you disagree about anything refer it to Allah and the Apostle, if you truly believe in Allah and the Last Day. This will in the end be better and more just.

Sura: 4, Ayat: 59.

Have you seen those who claim that they believe in what has been revealed to you and to other prophets before you? They (their real wish is to) seek the judgement from the powers of evil, although they have been bidden to deny him. The devil would lead them far astray.

Sura: 4, Ayat: 60.

And to you We have revealed the Book with the truth confirming what was revealed before it in the other Books, and standing as a guardian over it. Therefore give judgement among them in accordance with Allah's revelations and do not yield to their vain desires (swerving) from the truth that has been made known to you.

We have ordained a law and a path for each of you. Had Allah pleased, he could have made you single community: but that He might prove you by that which He has bestowed upon you. Vie with one another in good works, for to Allah you shall all return and He will show you the truth of the matters in which you dispute.

And pronounce judgement among them in accordance with Allah's revelations and do not be led by their vain desires, but beware of them lest they beguile you from any of that (teaching) which God has sent down to you. And

if they turn away, be assured that for some of their crimes it is God's purpose to punish them. And truly most men are rebellious.

Do they, perchance, desire (to be ruled by) the law of pagan ignorance? But for people who have inner certainty, who could be better law-giver than God?

Sura: 5, Ayat: 48–50.

They desire to extinguish the light of Allah with their mouths: but Allah seeks only to perfect His light, though the infidels abhor it.

It is He who has sent forth His Apostle with guidance and the true faith to make it prevail over all religions, however, much the polytheists may dislike it.

Sura: 9, Ayat: 32-33.

Had Allah not repelled some men by the might of others, the monasteries and churches, the synagogues and mosques in which Allah's name is frequently remembered, would have been utterly destroyed. But whoever helps Allah shall be helped by Him. Allah is truly Powerful and Mighty. (He will assuredly help) those who, if made masters in the lands, will attend to their prayers and pay the alms-tax, enjoin justice and forbid evil. Allah controls the destiny of all things.

Sura: 22, Ayat: 40-41.

That which you have been given is but the fleeting comfort of this life. Better and more enduring is that which Allah has for those who believe and put their trust in Him; who avoid gross sins and indecencies and, when angered, are willing to forgive; who obey their Lord, attend to their prayers, and conduct their affairs by mutual consent; who bestow in alms a part of that which We have given them.

Sura: 42, Ayat: 36–38.

In the name of Allah, The Compassionate, The Merciful

OPINION OF THE MAJORITY

Now if you pay heed unto the majority of those (common run) on earth, they will but lead you astray from the path of God: they follow but (other people's) conjectures, and they themselves do nothing but guess.

Sura: 6, Ayat: 116.

And thus We have revealed it, a (code of) judgements in the Arabic tongue. If you succumb to their vain desires after the knowledge you have been given, none shall save or protect you from Allah.

Sura: 13, Ayat: 37.

In the name of Allah, The Compassionate, The Merciful

FOLLOWING THE DIVINE LAWS

When it is said to them: "Follow what God has revealed:" they say: "Nay! we shall follow the ways of our fathers." What! even though their fathers were void of wisdom and guidance.

Sura: 2, Ayat: 170.

Have you seen those who claim that they believe in what has been revealed to you and to other prophets before you? They (their real wish is to) seek the judgement from the powers of evil, although they have been bidden to deny him. The devil would lead them far astray.

Sura: 4, Ayat: 60.

....Have no fear of people; fear Me, and do not take a small price for my revelations. Unbelievers are those who do not judge in accordance with God's revelations.

Sura: 5, Ayat: 44.

....The evildoers are those that do not judge in accordance with God's revelations.

Sura: 5, Ayat: 45.

....Evildoers are those that do not base their judgements on God's revelations.

Sura: 5, Ayat: 47.

And to you We have revealed the Book with the truth confirming that was revealed before it in the other Books, and standing as a guardian over it. Therefore give judgement among them in accordance with Allah's revelations and do not yield to their vain desires (swerving) from the truth that has been made known to you.

We have ordained a law and a path for each of you. Had Allah pleased, he could have made you single community: but that He might prove you by that which He has bestowed upon you. Vie with one another in good works, for to

Allah you shall all return and He will show you the truth of the matters in which you dispute.

Sura: 5,,Ayat: 48.

And pronounce judgement among them in accordance with Allah's revelations and do not be led by their vain desires, but beware of them lest they beguile you from any of that (teaching) which God has sent down to you. And if they turn away, be assured that for some of their crimes it is God's purpose to punish them. And truly most men are rebellious.

Sura: 5, Ayat: 49.

Do they, perchance, desire (to be ruled by) the law of pagan ignorance? But for people who have inner certainty, who could be better law-giver than God?

Sura: 5, Ayat: 50.

When it is said to them: "Come to what God has revealed; come to the Apostle": They say: "Enough for us are the ways we found our fathers following." What! even though their fathers were void of knowledge and guidance?

Sura: 5, Ayat: 104.

Say: "Bring forward your witnesses to prove that God did forbid so and so." If they bring such witnesses, do not bear witness with them: nor follow you the vain desires of such as treat our Signs as falsehoods, and such as believe not in the Hereafter: for they hold others as equal with their Guardian — Lord.

Sura: 6, Ayat: 150.

This path of Mine is straight. Follow it and do not follow other paths, for they will lead you away from Him. Thus Allah commands you, so that you may guard yourselves against evil.

Sura: 6, Ayat: 153.

Say: "O you men! Now truth has reached you from your Lord! Those who receive Guidance, do so for the good of their own souls; those who stray, do so to their own loss: and I am not responsible for your conduct.

Sura: 10, Ayat: 108.

Observe what is revealed to you, and have patience till Allah makes known his judgement. He is the best of judges.

Sura: 10, Ayat: 109.

He that reveres the sacred rites of Allah shall fare better in the sight of his Lord.

Sura: 22, Ayat: 30.

Such (is his state): and whoever holds in honour the Symbols of God (rites of pilgrimage), such (honour) should come truly from piety of heart.

Sura: 22, Ayat: 32.

In the name of Allah, The Compassionate, The Merciful

OBEYING GOD AND HIS PROPHET

The Apostle believes in what has been revealed to him by his Lord, and so do the faithful. They all believe in Allah and His Angels, His Books, and His Apostles. We make no distinction between one and another of His Apostles. They say: 'We hear and obey, Grant us your forgiveness, Lord; to You we shall all return.

Sura: 2, Ayat: 285.

Say: 'Obey Allah and the Apostle.' If they give no heed, then, truly, Allah does not love the unbelievers.

Sura: 3, Ayat: 32.

As for those who disbelieved, they shall be sternly punished in this world and in the world to come: there shall be none to help them.

Sura: 3, Ayat: 56.

As for those that have faith and do good works, they shall be given their reward in full. Allah does not love the evildoers.

Sura: 3, Ayat: 57.

....Say: "True guidance is the guidance of God: (fear you) lest a revelation be sent to someone (else) like unto that which was sent unto you? Or that those (receiving such revelation) should engage you in argument before your Lord?" Say: "All bounties are in the hand of God: He grants them to whom He pleases: and God cares for all, and He knows all things."

Sura: 3, Ayat: 73.

Say: "We believe in God, and in what has been revealed to us and what was revealed to Abraham, Isma'il: Isaac, Jacob and the Tribes, and in (the Books) given to Moses, Jesus and the Prophets, from their Lord: We make no distinction between one and another among them, and to God we surrender ourselves."

Sura: 3, Ayat: 84.

He that chooses a religion other than Islam, it will not be accepted from him, and in the world to come he will be one of the lost.

Sura: 3, Ayat: 85.

But how can you disbelieve when Allah's revelations are recited to you and His own Apostle is in your midst! He that holds fast to Allah shall be guided to the right path.

Sura: 3, Ayat: 100.

Believers, fear Allah as you rightly should, and do not die except as Muslims.

Sura: 3, Ayat: 102.

And hold fast, all together, by the Rope which God (stretches out for you) and be not divided among yourselves; and remember with gratitude God's favour on you: For you were enemies and He joined your hearts in love, so that by His Grace, you became brethren; and you were on the brink of the Pit of Fire, and He saved you from it. Thus does God make His Signs clear to you: That you may be guided.

Sura: 3, Ayat: 103.

Obey Allah and the Apostle that you may find mercy.

Sura: 3, Ayat: 132.

Such are the bounds set by Allah. He that obeys Allah and His Apostle shall dwell forever in gardens watered by running streams. That is the supreme triumph.

Sura: 4, Ayat: 13.

But he that disobeys Allah and His Apostle and transgresses His bounds, shall be cast into fire and shall abide in it forever. A shameful punishment awaits him.

Sura: 4, Ayat: 14.

O believers, obey Allah and the Apostle and those in authority among you. Should you disagree about anything refer it to Allah and the Apostle, if you truly believe in Allah and the Last Day. This is best and most suitable in the end.

Sura: 4, Ayat: 59.

Have you seen those who claim that they believe in what has been revealed to you and to other prophets before you? They (their real wish is to) seek the judgement from the powers of evil, although they have been bidden to deny

him. The devil would lead them far astray.

Sura: 4, Ayat: 60.

We sent not an Apostle, but to be obeyed, in accordance with the Will of God....

Sura: 4, Ayat: 64.

But no, by your Lord, they can have no (real) Faith, until they make you judge in all disputes between them, and find in their souls no resistance against your decisions, but accept them with the fullest conviction.

Sura: 4, Ayat: 65.

All who obey God and the Apostle are in the company of those on whom is the Grace of God, — of the Prophets (who teach), the Sincere (lovers of truth), the Witnesses (who testify), and the righteous (who do good): Ah! what a beautiful Fellowship! Such is the Bounty from God: and sufficient is it that God knows all.

Sura: 4, Ayat: 69-70.

He who obeys the Apostle, obeys God: but if any turn away, We have not sent you to be responsible for their actions.

Sura: 4, Ayat: 80.

There is no virtue in much of their secret talks: only in him who enjoins charity, kindness, and peace among men. He that does this to please Allah shall be richly rewarded.

He that disobeys the Apostle after guidance has been made clear to him and follows a path other than that of the faithful, shall be given what he has chosen. We will cast him into Hell: a dismal end.

Sura: 4, Ayat: 114-115.

And who has a nobler religion than the man who surrenders himself to Allah, does what is right, and follows the faith of Ibrahim the upright, whom Allah Himself chose to be His friend?

Sura: 4, Ayat: 125.

....We have enjoined those to whom the Book was given before you and (enjoin) you to fear Allah. If you deny Him, know that to Allah belongs all that the heavens and the earth contain. He is Self-Sufficient and Praiseworthy.

Sura: 4, Ayat: 131.

O believers, have faith in Allah and His Apostle, in the Book He has revealed to His Apostle, and in the Book He formerly revealed. He that denies Allah, His Angels, His Scriptures, His Apostles and the Last Day, has strayed

far from the truth.

Sura: 4, Ayat: 136.

To those who believe in God and His Apostles and make no distinction between any of the Apostles, We shall soon give their (due) rewards. For God is Oft-Forgiving, Most Merciful.

Sura: 4, Ayat: 152.

O mankind! the Apostle has come to you in truth from God: believe in him: It is best for you. But if you reject Faith, to God belong all things in the heavens and on earth: and God is All-Knowing, All-Wise.

Sura: 4, Ayat: 170.

O mankind! Verily there has come to you a convincing proof from your Lord: For We have sent unto you a light (that is) manifest.

Sura: 4, Ayat: 174.

Those that believe in Allah and hold fast to Him shall be admitted to His mercy and His grace. He will guide them to Him along a straight path.

Sura: 4, Ayat: 175.

And (always) remember the blessings which God has bestowed upon you, and the solemn pledge by which He bound you to Himself when you said, "We have heard, and we pay heed." Hence, remain conscious of God: verily, God has full knowledge of what is in the hearts (of men).

Sura: 5, Ayat: 7.

Let the People of the Gospel judge by what God has revealed therein. If any do fail to judge by (the light of) what God has revealed, they are (no better than) those who rebel.

Sura: 5, Ayat: 47.

Obey God, and obey the Apostle, and beware (of evil): if you do turn back, know you that it is our Apostle's duty to proclaim (the Message) in the clearest manner.

Sura: 5, Ayat: 92.

....Say: 'The guidance of God is the only guidance. We are commanded to surrender ourselves to the Lord of the Creation and to pray, and fear Him. Before Him you shall be assembled.

Sura: 6, Ayat: 71-72.

Follow what you are taught by inspiration from your Lord: There is no god but He:....

Sura: 6, Ayat: 106.

This path of Mine is straight. Follow it and do not follow other paths, for they will lead you away from Him. Thus Allah commands you, so that you may guard yourselves against evil.

Sura: 6, Ayat: 153.

Observe that which is brought down to you from your Lord and do not follow other masters besides Him. But you seldom take warning.

Sura: 7, Ayat: 3.

Children of Adam, when Apostles of your own come to proclaim to you My revelations, those that take warning and mend their ways will have nothing to fear or to regret, but those that deny and scorn Our revelations shall be the people of the Fire, and there they shall remain for ever.

Sura: 7, Ayat: 35-36.

But those who believe and work righteousness, — no burden do We place on a soul, but that which it can bear, – They will be companions of the Garden, therein to dwell (for ever).

Sura: 7, Ayat: 42.

And to Madian, We sent their brother Shu'ayb. He said: 'Serve Allah, my people, for you have no god but Him. A clear sign has come to you from your Lord. Give just weight and measure and do not defraud others of their possessions. Do not corrupt the land after it has been purged of evil. That is best for you, if you are true believers.

Do not sit in every road, threatening believers and debarring them from the path of Allah, nor seek to make that path crooked. Remember how He multiplied you when you were few in number. Consider the fate of the evildoers.

'If there are some among you who believe in my message and others who disbelieve it, be patient until Allah shall judge between us. He is the best of judges.'

Sura: 7, Ayat: 85—87.

....and to those that shall follow the Apostle — the Unlettered Prophet — whom they shall find mentioned in the Torah and the Gospel. He will enjoin righteousness upon them and forbid them to do evil. He will make good things lawful to them and prohibit all that is foul. He will relieve them of their burdens and of the shackles that weigh upon them. Those that believe in him and honour him, those that aid him and follow the light sent down with him, shall surely succeed.'

Sura: 7, Ayat: 157.

Say: 'People, I am sent forth to you all by Allah. His is the sovereignty in

the heavens and the earth. There is no god but Him. He ordains life and death. Therefore, have faith in Allah and His Apostle, the Unlettered Prophet, who believes in Allah and His Word. Follow him so that you may be rightly guided.'

Sura: 7, Ayat: 158.

They ask you concerning (things taken as) spoils of war. Say: '(Such) spoils are at the disposal of God and the Apostle: so fear God, and keep straight the relations between yourselves: Obey God and His Apostle, if you do believe.'

Sura: 8, Ayat: 1.

O you who believe! Obey God and His Apostle, and turn not away from him when you hear (him speak). Nor be like those who say, "We hear," but listen not: For the worst of beasts in the sight of God are the deaf and the dumb, those who understand not.

If God had found in them any good, He would indeed have made them listen: (As it is), even if He had made them listen, they would but have turned back and declined (faith).

Sura: 8, Ayat: 20—23.

O believers, obey Allah and the Apostle when he calls you to that which gives you life. Know that God intervenes between man and (the desires of) his heart, and that in His presence you shall all be gathered.

Sura: 8, Ayat: 24.

O you who believe! Betray not the trust of God and the Apostle, nor misappropriate knowingly things entrusted to you. And know you that your possessions and your progeny are but a trial; and that it is God with whom lies your highest reward.

Sura: 8, Ayat: 27-28.

And obey God and His Apostle; and fall into no disputes, lest you lose heart and your power depart; and be patient and persevering: For God is with those who patiently persevere:

Sura: 8, Ayat: 46.

It is He Who has sent His Apostle with Guidance and the Religion of Truth, to prevail it over all religions, even though the Pagans may detest (it).

Sura: 9, Ayat: 33.

And among them are men who slander you in the matter of (the distribution of) the alms: if they are given part thereof, they are pleased, but if not, behold! they are indignant!

If only they had been content with what God and His Apostle gave them,

and had said, "Sufficient unto us is God! and His Apostle will soon give us of His bounty: To God do we turn our hopes!" (That would have been the right course).

Sura: 9, Ayat: 58-59.

They swear in the name of Allah in order to please you. But it is more fitting that they should please Allah and His Apostle, if they are true believers.

Sura: 9, Ayat: 62.

Are they not aware that the man who defies Allah and His Apostle shall abide for ever in the fire of Hell? That surely is the supreme humiliation.

Sura: 9, Ayat: 63.

The Believers, men and women, are protectors, one of another: they enjoin what is just, and forbid what is evil: they observe regular prayers, practice regular charity, and obey God and His Apostle. On them will God pour His mercy: for God is Exalted in power, Wise.

Sura: 9, Ayat: 71.

....(I was bidden): 'Set your face steadfastly towards religion and do not be a polytheist.

Sura: 10, Ayat: 105.

Say: 'Men! The truth has come to you from your Lord. He that follows the right path follows it to his own advantage and he that goes astray does so at his own peril and I am not responsible for your conduct.'

Sura: 10, Ayat: 108.

Observe what is revealed to you, and have patience till Allah makes known his judgement. He is the best of judges.

Sura: 10, Ayat: 109.

....Follow then the right path as you are bidden together with those who have repented with you, and do not transgress. He is aware of what you do.

Sura: 11, Ayat: 112.

But when true believers are called to Allah and His Apostle that he may pass judgement upon them, their only reply is: 'We hear and Obey.' Such men shall surely prosper.

Those who obey Allah and His Apostles, those that revere Allah and fear Him, shall surely triumph.

Sura: 24, Ayat: 51-52.

Say: 'Obey God, and obey the Apostle: but if you turn away, he is only re-

sponsible for the duty placed on him and you for that placed on you. If you obey him, you shall be on right guidance. The Apostle's duty is only to preach the clear (Message).

Sura: 24, Ayat: 54.

Attend to your prayers, pay the alms-tax, and obey the Apostle, so that you may be shown mercy.

Sura: 24, Ayat: 56.

Only those are Believers, who believe in God and His Apostle: when they are with him on a matter requiring collective action, they do not depart until they have asked for his leave; those who ask for your leave are those who believe in God and His Apostle; so when they ask for your leave, for some business of theirs, give leave to those of them whom you will, and ask God for their forgiveness: For God is Oft-Forgiving, Most Merciful.

Sura: 24, Ayat: 62.

Deem not the summons of the Apostle among yourselves like the summons of one of you to another: God does know those of you who slip away under shelter of some excuse: then let those beware who would go against the Apostle's order, lest some trial befall them, or grievous Penalty be inflicted on them.

Sura: 24, Ayat: 63.

Those who, when they are admonished with the Signs of their Lord, droop not down at them as if they were deaf and blind.

Sura: 25, Ayat: 73.

Obey what is revealed to you from your Lord, for Allah is cognizant of all your actions; and put your trust in Him: for none is as worthy of trust as God.

Sura: 33, Ayat: 2-3.

You have indeed in the Apostle of God a beautiful pattern (of conduct) for anyone whose hope is in God and the Final Day, and who remembers unceasingly the praise of God.

Sura: 33, Ayat: 21.

It is not fitting for a believer, man or woman, when a matter has been decided by God and His Apostle, to have any choice about their decision: if anyone disobeys God and His Apostle, he is indeed on a clearly wrong path.

Sura: 33, Ayat: 36.

Believers, do not behave like those who slandered Musa. Allah cleared him of their calumny and he was exalted in Allah's sight.

Believers, fear Allah and speak the truth. He will bless your works and forgive you your sins. He who obeys Allah and His Apostle, has already attained the highest Achievement.

Sura: 33, Ayat: 69—71.

Those who give no heed to the one (Allah's summoner) who invites (us) to God shall not be beyond reach on earth, nor shall anyone protect them besides Him. They are in gross error.

Sura: 46, Ayat: 32.

How (will it be) when the angels carry away their souls and strike them on their heads and backs?

That is because they follow what has incurred the wrath of Allah and abhor what pleases Him, and so He has caused all their (good) deeds to come to nought.

Sura: 47, Ayat: 27-28.

Believers, obey Allah and His Apostle and let not your (good) deeds come to nought!

Sura: 47, Ayat: 33.

We have sent you* forth as a witness and as a bearer of good news and warnings, so that you may have faith in Allah and His Apostle and that you may assist Him, honour Him, and praise Him, morning and evening.

Sura: 48, Ayat: 8-9.

Those that swear fealty to you swear fealty to Allah Himself. The Hand of Allah is above their hands. He that breaks his oath breaks it at his own peril, but he that keeps his pledge to Allah shall be richly rewarded.

Sura: 48, Ayat: 10.

No blame is there on the blind, nor is there blame on the lame, nor on one ill (if he joins not the war): But he that obeys God and His Apostle,—(God) will admit him to Gardens beneath which rivers flow; and he who turns back, (God) will punish him with a grievous Penalty.

Sura: 48, Ayat: 17.

It is He that has sent forth His Apostle with guidance and the true faith, so that he make it prevail over all religions. Allah is the All-Sufficient Witness.

Sura: 48, Ayat: 28.

Believers do not put yourself forward in the presence of Allah and His Apostle. Have fear of Allah: He hears all and knows all.

Sura: 49, Ayat: 1.

***Muhammad**

The Arabs of the desert say, "We believe." Say, "You have no faith; but you (only) say, "We have submitted our wills to God," for not yet has Faith entered your hearts. But if you obey God and His Apostle, He will not belittle aught of your deeds: for God is Oft-Forgiving, Most Merciful."

Sura: 49, Ayat: 14.

The true believers are those who have faith in Allah and His Apostle and never doubt, and who fight for His cause with their wealth and persons. Such are the truthful ones.

Sura: 49, Ayat: 15.

Why should you not believe in God? — And the Apostle invites you to believe in your Lord, and has indeed taken your Covenant, if you are men of faith.

Sura: 57, Ayat: 8.

For, they who attained to faith in God and His Apostle — it is they, they who uphold the truth, and they who bear witness (thereto) before God: They shall have their reward and their light, but those who reject God and deny our Signs, — they are the Companions of Hell-Fire.

Sura: 57, Ayat: 19.

We sent aforetime our Apostles with Clear Signs and sent down with them the Book and the Balance (of Right and Wrong), that men may stand forth in justice; and We sent down Iron, in which is (material for) Mighty war, as well as many benefits for mankind, that God may test who it is that will help, unseen, Him and His Apostles: For God is Full of Strength, Exalted in Might (and able to enforce His Will).

Sura: 57, Ayat: 25.

O you that believe! Fear God, and believe in his Apostle, and He will bestow on you a double portion of His Mercy: He will provide for you a Light by which you shall walk (straight in your path), and He will forgive you (your past sins): For God is Oft-Forgiving, Most Merciful.

Sura: 57, Ayat: 28.

Do you, perchance, fear lest (you may be sinning if) you cannot offer up anything in charity on the occasion of your consultation (with the Apostle)? But if you fail to do it (for lack of opportunity), and God turns unto you in His mercy, remain but constant in prayer and render the purifying dues, and (thus) pay heed unto God and His Apostle: for God is fully aware

of all that you do.

Sura: 58, Ayat: 13.

It is He who has sent His Apostle with guidance and the Faith in Truth, so that He make it prevail over all religions, much as the Pagans may dislike it.

Sura: 61, Ayat: 9.

O you who believe! Be you helpers of God: As said Jesus the son of Mary to the Disciples, "Who will be my helpers to (the work of) God?" Said the Disciples, "We are God's helpers!"....

Sura: 61, Ayat: 14.

Believe, therefore, in God and His Apostle, and in the Light which We have sent down. And God is well acquainted with all that you do.

The Day that He assembles you (all) for a Day of Assembly,—that will be a day of mutual loss and gain (among you). And those who believe in God and work righteousness,—He will remove from them their bad deeds, and He will admit them to gardens beneath which rivers flow, to dwell therein for ever: that will be the Supreme Achievement.

Sura: 64, Ayat: 8-9.

So obey God, and obey His Apostle: but if you turn away, the duty of Our Apostle is but to proclaim (the Message) clearly and openly.

Sura: 64, Ayat: 12.

When we heard His guidance we believed in Him: he that believes in his Lord shall never be wronged or harmed.

Sura: 72, Ayat: 13.

We have sent to you, (O men!) an Apostle, to be a witness concerning you, even as We sent an Apostle to Pharaoh. But Pharaoh disobeyed the Apostle; so We seized him with a heavy punishment. Then how shall you, if you deny (God), guard yourselves against a Day that will make children grey-headed? Whereon the sky will be cleft asunder? His Promise needs must be accomplished.

Verily this is an Admonition: Therefore, whosoever will, let him take a (straight) path to his Lord!

Sura: 73, Ayat: 15—19.

This is an admonition: Whosoever will, let him take a (straight) Path to his Lord.

But you will not, except as God wills; For God is full of Knowledge and Wisdom.

Sura: 76, Ayat: 29-30.

In the name of Allah, The Compassionate, The Merciful

MAKING DECISIONS IN ACCORDANCE WITH THE QURAN

We have revealed to you the Book with the truth, so that you may judge among men by that which Allah has shown you. You shall not plead for those who betray their trust. Implore Allah's forgiveness: He is Forgiving, Merciful.

Sura: 4, Ayat: 105-106.

In the name of Allah, The Compassionate, The Merciful

THE FINALITY OF THE WORD OF GOD AND HIS APOSTLE

Have you not turned your vision to those who have been given a portion of the Book? They are invited to the Book of God, to settle their dispute, but a party of them turn back and decline (the arbitration).

Sura: 3, Ayat: 23.

Say: "We believe in God, and in what has been revealed to us and what was revealed to Abraham, Isma'il: Isaac, Jacob, and the Tribes, and in (the Books) given to Moses, Jesus, and the Prophets, from their Lord: We make no distinction between one and another among them, and to God do we surrender ourselves."

He that chooses a religion other than Islam, it will not be accepted from Him, and in the world to come he will be one of the lost.

Sura: 3, Ayat: 84-85.

O believers, obey Allah and the Apostle and those in authority among you. Should you disagree about anything refer it to Allah and the Apostle, if you truly believe in Allah and the Last Day. This is best and most suitable for final determination.

Sura: 4, Ayat: 59.

Have you seen those who claim that they believe in what has been revealed to you and to other prophets before you? They (their real wish is) seek the judgement from the powers of evil, although they have been bidden to deny him. The devil would lead them far astray.

Sura: 4, Ayat: 60.

But no, by your Lord, they can have no (real) Faith, until they make you judge in all disputes between them, and find in their souls no resistance against your decisions, but accept them with the fullest conviction.

Sura: 4, Ayat: 65.

We have revealed to you the Book with the truth so that you may judge among men by that which Allah has shown you. You shall not plead for those who betray their trust. Implore Allah's Forgiveness: He is Forgiving, Merciful.

Sura: 4, Ayat: 105-106.

They are listeners to falsehoods and devourers of the unlawful. If they come to you, judge between them or turn away from them. If you avoid them they cannot harm you at all, but if you act as judge, judge between them with fairness. Allah loves those that deal justly.

Sura: 5, Ayat: 42.

We have revealed the Torah having guidance and light. By it, the prophets who surrendered themselves to Allah judged the Jews, and so did the rabbis and the divines, by what they were required to guard of Allah's books, and to what they are witnesses.

Have no fear of people; fear Me, and do not take a small price for my revelations. Unbelievers are those who do not judge in accordance with God's revelations.

(In the Torah) We decreed for them a life for a life, an eye for an eye, a nose for a nose, an ear for an ear, a tooth for a tooth, and wounds equal for equal. But if a man charitably forbears from retaliation, his remission shall atone for him. The evildoers are those that do not judge in accordance with God's revelations.

Sura: 5, Ayat: 44-45.

After those prophets We sent forth Isa, the son of Mariam, confirming the Torah already revealed, and gave him the Gospel, in which there is guidance and light, corroborating that which was revealed before it in the Torah, a guide and an admonition to the righteous. Therefore let the followers of the Gospel judge in accordance with what Allah has revealed therein. Evildoers are those that do not base their judgements on Allah's revelations.

Sura: 5, Ayat: 46-47.

And to you We have revealed the Book with the truth confirming what was revealed before it in the other Books, and standing as a guardian over it. Therefore give judgement among them in accordance with Allah's revelations and do not yield to their vain desires (swerving) from the truth that has been made known to you.

We have ordained a law and a path for each of you. Had Allah pleased, He could have made you single community: but that He might prove you by that which He has bestowed upon you. Vie with one another in good works, for to Allah you shall all return and He will show you the truth of the matters in which you dispute.

And pronounce judgement among them in accordance with Allah's revelations and do not be led by their vain desires, but beware of them lest they beguile you from any of that (teaching) which God has sent down to you. And if they turn away, be assured that for some of their crimes it is God's purpose to punish them. And truly most men are rebellious.

Do they, perchance, desire (to be ruled by) the law of pagan ignorance? But for people who have inner certainty, who could be better law-giver than God?

Sura: 5, Ayat: 48–50.

Your Guardian-Lord is God, Who created the heavens and the earth in six Days, and is firmly established on the Throne (of authority): He draws the night as a veil over the day, each seeking the other in rapid succession: He created the sun, the moon, and the stars, (all) governed by laws under His Command. His is the creation, His the Command. Blessed be God, the Lord of the Worlds!

Sura: 7, Ayat: 54.

And when they are called to Allah and His Apostle that he may judge between them, a party of them turn away. Had justice been on their side, they would have come to him in all obedience.

Is there a disease in their hearts, or are they in doubt? Do they fear that Allah and His Apostle may deny them justice? Surely these are wrongdoers.

But when true believers are called to Allah and His Apostle that He may pass judgement upon them, their only reply is: 'We hear and obey'. Such men shall surely prosper.

Those who obey Allah and His Apostle, those that revere Allah and fear Him, shall surely triumph.

Sura: 24, Ayat: 48–52.

It is not fitting for a believer, man or woman, when a matter has been decided by God and His Apostle, to have any choice about their decisions: If anyone disobeys God and His Apostle, he is indeed on a clearly wrong path.

Sura: 33, Ayat: 36.

(We said): 'Dawud, We have made you a vicegerent in the land. Rule with justice among men and do not yield to lust, lest it should turn you away from Allah's path. Those that stray from Allah's path shall be sternly punished, because they forget the Day of Reckoning.

Sura: 38, Ayat: 26.

Whatever it be wherein you differ, the decision thereof is with God: Such is God my Lord: In Him I trust, and to Him I turn.

Sura: 42, Ayat: 10.

EXPLANATION OF ISLAMIC TERMS:

Translation of certain Arabic words into English

The late Dr. Ismail Raji al-Faruqi in his book "Towards Islamic English" writes:

> "Many Arabic words are simply not translatable into English. Many are rendered into English with difficulty."

Some of such words are:

As-Salah often translated as "prayer." Prayer actually more closely corresponds to "Dua." Salah is the act of worship performed five times daily according to prescribed ways.

Ibadah often translated as "worship" actually means to worship Allah and out of love for Him to obey Him in what He has ordered and to follow the example of His Prophet Muhammad (peace be upon him).

Iman often translated as "faith" etc. actually means the conviction or certainty that Allah is indeed the One and Only God and that Muhammad is His last prophet and commitment to obey their commands.

Zakah often translated "Alms Tax," "charity" etc. actually means obligatory sharing of wealth with the poor and the community in order to purify the rest. This is to say the right of Allah in the fortune of His servants, which right is assigned to specific categories of the needy.

Sabr often translated as "patience" etc. actually means to remain firm and steadfast against ordeals and calamities.

Qadar often translated as "fate" actually means Allah's assignment of ends to all process of life and existence.

Shirk often translated as "association of some being with Allah" actually includes all means, things and concepts, etc.

Kafir often translated as "disbeliever" etc. actually means one who solemnly says that Allah is not God or is not the subject of His attributes. It also means that who disavows the bounties of God, the ungrateful.

Zulm often translated as "transgression" etc. actually means the act or action of committing injustice.

Fitnah often translated as "mischief" or "tumult" etc. actually means misguidance, dissuasion etc. from the path laid by Allah.

Fasad often translated as "dispute" etc. actually means all of the following: disruption — imbalance — disharmony — corruption - danger — drought.

Ihsan often translated as "doing a favor" etc. actually means the perfect fulfillment of the commandments of Allah in whatever one is doing in relation to others or to himself.

Jihad often translated as "holy war" etc. actually means self exertion in the cause of Allah including against baser self or others and including peaceful and violent means.

Von Canon Library
168827
REMOTE BP 109 .M64 1991 / Commandments by God in the Qu